"Horror Plum'd":

An International
Stephen King
Bibliography and Guide

1960-2000

By
Michael R. Collings

"Horror Plum'd":

An International
Stephen King
Bibliography and Guide

1960-2000

By
Michael R. Collings

Overlook Connection Press
Biblio Series
2002

"Horror Plum'd":
An International
Stephen King
Bibliography and Guide
©2002 by Michael R. Collings

"Introduction: Light Behind a Shadow Trapped within the Words"
by Michael R. Collings ©2002

Published by
Overlook Connection Press
P.O. Box 526 Woodstock GA 30188
Phone: 770-926-1762 Fax: 770-516-1469
http://www.overlookconnection.com
E-mail: overlookcn@aol.com

Hardcover: 1-892950-45-6

Casebound Hardcover: 1-892950-30-8

Trade Paperback: 1-892950-31-6

All rights reserved. No part of this book may be reproduced or transmitted in any form or by any means, electronic or mechanical, without the written permission of the Publisher, The Overlook Connection Press.

Book Design & Typesetting:
David G. Barnett/Fat Cat Design

DEDICATIONS:

Stephen—for the Stories

Dave—for the Opportunity

Judi—for Patience
beyond all mortal limits

On th'other side *Satan* allarm'd
Collecting all his might dilated stood,
Like *Teneriff* or *Atlas* unremov'd:
His stature reacht the Skie, and on his Crest
Sat horror Plum'd....

John Milton, *Paradise Lost* (1667)
Book 4, 985-990

CONTENTS

Introduction:
Light Behind the Shadow Trapped Within the
    Words   9

Bibliography

A. Books: Novels, Short-Fiction Collections,
    Non-Fiction, etc. Including Reprints and
    Multi-media Adaptations of Book Titles
                                                            21

B. Short Fiction: Including Published Excerpts
    From Longer Works; Screenplays pub-
    lished in anthologies, etc.   421

C. Short Nonfiction   585

D. Poetry   517

E. Audio and/or Video Adaptations of
    Original King Materials   521

Index   529

Introduction:

Light Behind the Shadow Trapped Within Words

by

Michael R. Collings[1]

PLOT SUMMARY:
A handful of people sit clustered in a battered building at the center of a small town. Inside, they have found safety...or at least the illusion of safety. Outside crouch darkness, and fear, and death. The meager daylight is dying. With the night will come the monster. The people huddle close for warmth, for comfort. They know that by the time the sun dawns again some, or most—or all—of them will be dead.

A plot outline for a Stephen King story? A thumbnail synopsis of *The Mist*, perhaps? Or *'Salem's Lot*? An initial script-concept for *Storm of the Century*? These would be good guesses. They seem logical. To a degree even possible, if not probable. But *The Mist* was not the story I had in mind as I typed that summary, nor *'Salem's Lot*, nor *Storm of the Century*, nor indeed any of the scores of tales King has contributed to our general store of literature. No, the tale I had in mind was written down quite a bit before Stephen King assumed the public mantle—willingly or not—of undisputed King of Terror. In fact, in written form it predates his stories by more than a thousand years; in oral form, it was even then already centuries old, passed down from poet to poet, from bard to bard, from generation to generation.

That tale is *Beowulf*, the oldest and greatest of the surviving early Germanic epics and the first undeniable masterpiece in the English literary tradition. In its inimitable way, using conventions of poetry and storytelling that still compel readers after more than a thousand years (witness the unanticipated critical and public responses to Seamus Heaney's recent translation) *Beowulf* recounts the story of an isolated community confronted by external horror and terror beyond its darkest imaginings. The building in which they meet is the great golden-walled Mead-Hall of Heorot. The people themselves are the strong-thewed warriors of a proud Germanic king, Hrothgar. The monster they await in fearful dread is *Grendel*, the creature that has visited the Mead-Hall often before, in the depths of night, and each time he has left behind a grisly trail of blood and pain and death.

But it is intriguing as well as instructive to note how completely the authors of these stories—the anonymous eighth-century *Beowulf*-poet and the twentieth-century Stephen King—represent parallel departures from a similar, almost identical, perspective. Both focus on a small group of potential victims, a nexus of a culture that defines essential traits in the individual and the in the society. They both depict communities isolated by external, physical darkness and by an even more destructive internal darkness. The groups are forced to come together for communal strength and protection—but in spite of everything they can do, their gathering proves inefficacious. Inevitably, they must confront the darkness, and their fear, and the on-coming specter of death.

There are significant differences, to be sure. In *Beowulf*, we quickly discover that the poet has found a Hero, a single warrior endowed with sufficient courage and power to confront and ultimately to combat the monster. The monster has devoured thirty of King Hrothgar's retainers; the hero Beowulf, symmetrically enough, is endowed with the strength of thirty men. In the fury of single battle with Grendel, he rips the monster's arm from its body and nails the bloody trophy on the wall over the entry to Heorot—an episode recounted in loving detail, with a careful eye to developing sensationalism, horror, and gore.

In *The Mist*, to take but one example from King's canon, events do not proceed quite as smoothly. There is no Hero. In a technologically oriented world such as ours, which (it firmly believes) has outdistanced such primitive traits as superstition and fear of the supernatural, individual heroism is generally not encouraged; nor does King insult his reader's intelligence by importing a Hero—not even from the distant, almost mythic shores of Geatland (modern-day Sweden). There are individual battles fought against the monsters that inhabit the mist, certainly, and occasionally the humans prevail; but in King's complex vision there is, and finally there can be, no simple, straight-line, heroic ending. His characters are systematically stripped of everything that the technological world has offered them, until all that remains is the raw courage of a few to face the darkness directly and by doing so to attempt to discover the extent of the mist…and of the monsters it encompasses.

Then the next wave of monsters strikes, in *Beowulf* as well as in *The Mist*. Even Beowulf, the impervious hero, ultimately suffers defeat in battle against the Firedrake. All that he has accomplished—the deaths of Grendel and Grendel's mother, the restoration of peace and harmony to Hrothgar's kingdom, the subsequent consolidation of Beowulf's own nation, his fifty years of faultless rule as King[2]—all of this is denied as his body burns and the forces of darkness gather once again to devour and destroy. In *The Mist*, King has condensed the narrative time frame from fifty years to hours and days, but the effect is the same. Humanity may raise mighty buildings, and construct complex moral and civil codes, and create a veneer of civility—thicker in some spots than in others, but a veneer nonetheless—but against the naked face of darkness, most of that counts for nothing.

King's story confronts humans—us—with monsters; the *Beowulf*-Poet does precisely the same thing. Perhaps we would do well to remember that the latter story was transcribed into the single existing tenth-century manuscript, not out of any long-ago sense that it was an irretrievable masterpiece of literature to be preserved for future ages, but because it was a rollicking good monster-story (along with the other monster-stories contained in the same manuscript). Its author—and, apparently, its audience—*believed* in such things. As one modern scholar has written:

> It seems inconceivable that the poet of *Beowulf* should have intended to sublimate his evil dragon into draconity, making what has reality in the Bible into something abstract or symbolic, something acceptable to a twentieth-century audience willing to swallow monsters only as myths or symbols. Moreover, however we ourselves may wish to read *Beowulf*, of one thing we can be pretty sure on the evidence of the manuscript: the Anglo-Saxons read the poem as an account of Beowulf the monster-slayer, and preserved it with other accounts of monsters.
>
> ... Most of us now think tales of monsters a low order of literature, unless redeemed in the handling. The poet of *Beowulf* handles his story with literary artistry; he has made the story rich with spirituality. That has led some modern critics to look away from the reality of the monsters, to make them *be* wholly the powers of darkness towards which they tend...[3]

The implications of the stories and of this comment are consistent with a pervasive theme in Western literature, captured by both the *Beowulf*-poet and Stephen King: 'Here there be tygers' ... *here*, in the darkness of the human soul, and *here*, in the darkness of the worlds we imagine.

Let's try another Story.

Plot Summary:
A frightened man confronts a midnight apparition, a specter that by all reason and logic should not, cannot exist, but does. He speaks to it, he conjures it to speak to him, and it reveals tales of darkness and fear and death. It grants him visions of murder, blood, revenge, and—again—death.

MICHAEL R. COLLINGS

Does this describe *The Dark Half?* Or a segment of *It?* Perhaps. Certainly the synopsis could apply equally to either of King's novels. But again, neither of those was the story I had in mind. Instead, I was thinking of *Hamlet.* There, three times in the course of what is almost universally hailed as the greatest tragedy in English literature (some would broaden that to include Western literature), we find of all things ... a ghost. A specter. A haunted shade whispering deliciously of murders past and murders yet to come.

By all surviving accounts, the audiences of Shakespeare's day must have loved the play. They flocked to the Globe Theater to watch it, standing for the full four hours of its performance (unlike modern audiences, they were not subjected to editors and rewriters who, knowing more about dramaturgy than the Bard himself, hack at the play to make it fit externally imposed time constraints). They might have stood in the rain to see it. They might have paid as much as the equivalent of a week's wages for the privilege.

Why? Did they come to admire a well-publicized, once-in-a-lifetime live performance of the greatest play by the greatest English playwright?

Hardly.

F. E. Halliday begins his cogent study, *Shakespeare and His Critics,* by noting that at the time of Shakespeare's death, there were no popular newspapers to herald the tragic tidings from shore to shore; and even if there had been, "it is more than probable that the death in the provinces of a retired actor and writer of plays which could scarcely be considered as serious literature would have passed unnoticed."[4] In fact no one, not even Shakespeare's highly respected (and highly egotistical) fellow playwright and former fellow-actor, Ben Jonson, so much as refers to Shakespeare's death until literally years later[5]. And it would be a century or so after that before scholars and critics would initiate the systematic efforts in Bardolatry that would see his plays elevated to the heights they still maintain today.

No, the Elizabethan playgoers went to see a *drama*, and, not coincidentally, to see as much as possible of blood and fear, revenge and death, madness, mayhem, ... and ghosts!

Samuel Johnson, writing over a century after Shakespeare's death about another of Shakespeare's wildly popular theatrical successes, *Titus Andronicus,* urged that the play not be considered part of the Master's canon: "The barbarity of the spectacles, and the general massacre, which are here exhibited, can scarcely be conceived tolerable to any audience; yet we are told by [Ben] Jonson, that they were not only borne, but praised. That Shakespeare wrote any part ... I see no reason for believing."[6] In spite of now being frequently excoriated as among Shakespeare's least effective plays, however, *Titus Andronicus* was unusually and undeniably popular in its time. G. B. Harrison notes in his edition of the plays that it remained in the stage repertory for two full decades after it first appeared. Based on tales preserved for over a thousand years in classical myth, and specifically in Seneca's Latin revenge tragedies (one of the demonstrably popular genres of the Elizabethan period), the story was inherently sensational and horrific, excessive and extreme even for the Elizabethans, full of graphic representations of blood and death. Many of the more objectionable episodes in the play may have been eliminated by scholars and critics as interpolations penned by Shakespeare's contemporaries, but even in his acknowledged masterworks, such as *Hamlet, Othello, Macbeth, King Lear,* Shakespeare never spares his audience's sensibilities.

Mainstream critics today generally agree that, even if by Shakespeare, *Titus Andronicus* fails miserably; if it were produced for a modern audience, it would probably be laughed off the stage as simply too much, too over-the-top, too sensational for the sheer reveling in sensation. Shakespeare's audience, however—not being 'modern' playgoers and lacking the requisite foreknowledge that they were in the presence of a work by one of the premier dramatists of Western culture—found nothing absurd in the presentation of horrors that included, among other bloody episodes, the on-stage severing of Titus Andronicus' hand, after which the character coolly puns on multiple meanings of 'giving one's hand' as a symbol of loyalty. One of my undergraduate Shakespeare professors, in fact, lectured at length on that scene, noting that the actor portraying Titus Andronicus would often wear a bladder of pig's blood beneath his arm and, at the climactic moment, spray blood onto the footlings surrounding the stage (shades of *Carrie*—either the novel, the film, or the Broadway/London musical).

Whether by dramatizing ghostly visitations that lead to revenge and bloody death, or more directly by the on-stage removal of body parts, Shakespeare shows himself well acquainted with the age-old techniques of fear, terror, and horror—including what King has described in his own words as the 'gross out.'

This is not to argue simplistically that Stephen King is a twentieth-century Shakespeare (although a strong case for a related contention has been made by Professor Carroll Terrell in his *Stephen King: Man and Artist*). It is to suggest, instead, that Shakespeare—and the *Beowulf*-poet, for that matter—could be considered, in essentials, early Stephen Kings; that is, they were writers who recognized the pulse of their audiences, who gave them what they wanted to see, who acknowledged and exorcised the ageless human preoccupation with fear and terror, and did so through stories so strong and compelling that they survive to this day.

May we look at one final Story?

Plot Summary:

A lone, dark figure—human-like in form, perhaps, but clearly more than human—contemplates a naively innocent world and plots its destruction. He/It has contended once before for human souls, and will do so again, even knowing that the struggle will be futile, that to persist will only bring pain and torment. He/It is insatiable..., hungry..., starving..., desperate for revenge, for blood and discord and death.

The Stand? The Eyes of the Dragon? The Dark Tower? Needful Things?

MICHAEL R. COLLINGS

Desperation? Possibly, but again, no. This passage summarizes a key moment in a universally acknowledged masterpiece; a work revered and imitated for over three centuries; a poem that elevated English language and literature to a level sufficient to challenge the two greatest writers in the Western tradition, the Latin poet Virgil, and Homer himself; a panorama of cosmic battles and hand-to-hand encounters between good and evil, between the Light and the Dark; and an unsurpassed treatment of monsters, demons, devils, and Death itself.

It is John Milton's *Paradise Lost,* the defining epic of a period and a people.

Of course, Stephen King is no John Milton. While King has written a number of poems, some remarkably effective within the range they attempt, he has demonstrated no interest in composing a long narrative in verse, celebrating twentieth-century America in elevated language and consciously poetical diction. Even if he in fact cultivated such an interest, contemporary literary taste would make it impossible for him to reach more than a handful of readers.

Instead, King has chosen to parallel, not to imitate. His long narratives—if not celebrations then certainly analyses, anatomies, and critiques of twentieth-century American society—are in prose, a stripped-down, almost colloquial prose that is as appropriate to King's purposes and talents as Milton's blank verse was to his. In some instances, King's 'epics' seem complete within a single volume, as in *IT, The Talisman, Needful Things, Storm of the Century,* or *Desperation.* In others, most noticeably and most intriguingly in the on-going Dark Tower series, *The Stand, The Eyes of the Dragon, Insomnia, Hearts in Atlantis* and *Black House* (co-written by Peter Straub), his narratives intertwine with the complexity and subtlety of a Renaissance Romance-Epic, suggesting layers of connections that he has not yet made fully apparent. Yet in spite of these substantial differences, and regardless of their form, their length, or their genre, his 'epics' tackle the same perennial themes as Milton's: life and death, sin and salvation, despair and redemption. More than once he has granted us explicit engagements with a Paradise Lost, and haunting visions of a possible Paradise Regained.

The point of this long disquisition on literary history and heritage is not to argue that King 'deserves' to be treated on the same level as the *Beowulf*-poet, Shakespeare, or Milton, and to harangue more conservative mainstream scholars and critics for not doing so; but rather to demonstrate that his distinguished predecessors attempted to communicate in their own ways, according to their own times and traditions, similar fundamental themes and concerns—that they, and King, are Storytellers serving essential and enduring purposes.

This may seem a large assertion when applied, as I have done, to a mere 'horror' writer, one whose own evaluations of his writings run along the lines of a "Big Mac with fries." Yet, I would suggest, King's work does deserve to be taken seriously, if on no other basis than that he sees it as part of a literary tradition.

To give but one example:

On the surface, *Desperation* seems a run-of-the-mill horror novel, a story of murder and decay and dismemberment, of disembodied monsters and mind-controlled zombies. This sense was unfortunately heightened, perhaps, by the publishing strategy that linked it indelibly with *The Regulators*—which is a distinctly different kind of book, more consciously surrealistic, more elusively symbolic than *Desperation*. Whether for that reason or for others (including the appearances of the richly mythic *Rose Madder*, the innovative six-part serial novel, *The Green Mile*, and the long-awaited *Dark Tower IV: Wizard and Glass* all in the short period of 1995-1997), *Desperation* has received relatively little critical attention.

Yet in its own way, *Desperation* is a highly literary novel, one intimately in touch with the heritage and tradition I have attempted to delineate here. It is an allusive novel in the best sense; rather than quoting or paraphrasing superficially from the 'great works' of the past, it integrates them into its own texture.

It echoes *Beowulf* at precisely the moment in its own narrative when a graphic, stomach-wrenching reference to a warrior ripping living arm off of a monstrous enemy is appropriate (p. 481).

It misquotes *Hamlet*—"Alas poor Urine...I knew him well" (p. 642)—at a structurally parallel moment, as the speaker, Johnny Marinville, literally and figuratively prepares himself to leap into an open grave and embrace death.

It paraphrases *Paradise Lost* as it invites us into the mind of an imprisoned Immortal that prides itself on its intransigence, on its perverse belief that it is better to reign in Hell than to serve in Heaven—or, as Tak/Audrey puts it, "Sweet to rule, even in the desert" (p. 455).[7] And, like the poem, the novel takes as an essential starting point the critical importance of human choice in obeying or disobeying the desires of a cruel—but ultimately just—God.

It is Storytelling at the deepest, most important levels of the mind and soul.

From this assertion, it requires only a small step to understand the rationale behind the present volume. *"Horror Plum'd": An International Stephen King Bibliography and Guide* attempts more than a simple enumeration of editions and issues. On a more fundamental level, it assumes that the almost unbelievable quantities of novels, stories, articles, poems, films, teleplays, etc., that it tallies are themselves evidence that Stephen King's particular brand of Storytelling and the vision it entails have touched and continue to touch multitudes. This is not the place to argue in depth the philosophical, moral, or literary values of Science Fiction, Fantasy, and Horror—such issues have been dealt with in innumerable books and articles—but the social and cultural implications of an author whose writings number in the tens of millions, if not hundreds of millions of copies world-wide seem inescapable. Whether 'literary' or not, whether commercial 'hack-work' or not, Stephen King's fertile and prolific imagination; his unspoken and spoken assumptions about humanity, community, and society; his inimitable ability to transform abstract threats into palpable monsters and succeed in communicating on both levels; his deftness at exploring the general within the specific; his deep and abiding concern for children, for family, for the abused and displaced at multiple levels, for society itself, for the eternal conflict between the

Light and the Dark—all of these and more are being exported in extraordinary numbers throughout the world, being discovered by and in turn influencing generations of readers.

Horror Plum'd attempts to document the extent of that influence.

This work has been in progress for over a decade and a half. Its earliest manifestation appeared as a brief bibliography in *The Many Facets of Stephen King* (1985), written with the undeviating encouragement of the late Ted Dikty, founder of Starmont House, and subsequently expanded into *The Annotated Guide to Stephen King: A Primary and Secondary Bibliography of the Works of America's Premier Horror Writer* (1986) at his request. Shortly before Ted's death, he arranged for my Stephen King studies to be transferred to Rob Reginald's Borgo Press, where, again, Rob supported continuing research that resulted a decade later in a re-formatted and much expanded bibliography, *The Work of Stephen King: An Annotated Bibliography and Guide* (1996). The present volume represents the final evolution of that initial bibliography.

Even at that, however, *Horror Plum'd* does not—indeed *cannot*—attempt a comprehensive collection of *all* King-related materials; by now, there is simply too much available to compress into a single volume. For that reason, this book focuses attention on primary works only: King's novels and book-length collection of fiction and non-fiction; his short stories, poetry, reviews, and short non-fiction; his poetry and published screenplays. Given his prolific writing, his avowed and obvious dedication to writing, his quarter of a century as a major figure in defining and in part determining the directions of American culture, and his enormous popularity world-wide, the seemingly straight-forward task of compiling lists of his publications—and their transformations into various audio-visual formats—is intimidating enough.

At the same time, however, the exponential increase in studies of King's output has itself reached the stage of a cultural phenomenon. Several years have already passed since one of my colleagues expressed incredulity at my claim for almost 3,000 entries in an earlier King bibliography, many of them secondary. "For a *living* author?" he asked, arching one brow to emphasize his utter astonishment. Yet by now, that number has easily doubled. Writing *about* Stephen King has become as fascinating and involving a project as attempting to *read* everything by him. To accommodate the sheer quantity of materials, I have decided to include only selected articles and reviews as addenda to individual entries in *Horror Plum'd*. A second volume, tentatively titled *About Stephen King: An International Bibliography of Scholarship, Criticism, and Reviews* to accompany and complete this one, is in progress for The Overlook Connection Press.

In addition to my specific indebtedness to Ted and Rob, thanks are due to a number of others as well: to John M. Steadman, who instructed me in the art and the delight of literary study and bibliography; to Roger Schlobin, who gave me my first chance at writing a book-length publication, and then invited me to write another; to George Beahm, whose series of King studies have provided me with constant reservoirs of information and—to the generous extent that he opened them to my participation—opportunities to solidify my own understanding of King's novels and stories; to Dave Hinchberger, who is actually willing to publish this behemoth and who, along with Dave Barnett, has helped transform workaday bibliographies into works of art.

I also owe an enormous debt to known and unknown King enthusiasts who have diligently searched out Things-King for their books, articles, letters, newsletters, E-mails, and websites, particularly: Neil Barron, Eddy C. Bertin, Charles Brown, Benoît Domis, Daniel Conrad, Tom Egeland, Charles Fried, Arnar Freyr Gudmundsson, Lars Jedinski, Hans-Ake Lilja, Anthony Magistrale, Michael Yu. McAlcin, Hughes Morin, Kevin Quigley, Karsten Runge, Stephen Spignesi, and Bev Vincent. Thanks to all—and apologies to any I have inadvertently omitted.

Notes to: Introduction: Light Behind the Shadow Trapped Within the Words

[1] Portions of this essay have appeared as "Introduction: The Persistence of Darkness—Shadows Behind the Life Behind the Story" in *The Stephen King Story: A Literary Profile*, by George Beahm (Kansas City: Andrews & McMeel, October 1991), pp. 1-6; and "Stephen King, *Beowulf*, and the Necessary Landscapes of Darkness," the foreword to *Stephen King from A to Z: An Encyclopedia of His Life and Work*, by George Beahm (Kansas City MO: Andrews & McMeel, 1998). The title quotes the concluding line of my poem "*Blothisojan," first published in *Studia Mystica* (Sacramento State University) Vol. 7, No. 4 (Winter 1984): 26.

[2] Not intended literally, of course, given the radically limited life expectancy in eighth-century England; rather, the neatly rounded number simply implies an extremely long time, almost an infinity of good rule.

[3] Stanley, E. G. "*Beowulf*" in *Beowulf: Basic Readings*. Edited by Peter S. Baker. New York: Garland, 1995, p. 6.

[4] New York: Schocken Books, 1963.

[5] In like vein, John Milton's first published poem, "On Shakespeare," one of several tributes to Shakespeare comissioned for the Second Folio of 1632, eulogizes the power of Shakespeare's poetry but does not so much as mention his plays.

[6] Halliday, p. 142.

[7] *Desperation* echoes, in addition, an intriguing assortment of Seventeenth-Century writers, among them Sir Thomas Browne, with his adamant assertion that the existence of evil—in his case, witches—both necessitated and proved the existence of God (p. 519); Richard Crashaw's baroque inversions of sensual imagery in eyes that are mouths and mouths that are eyes (p. 663), and George Herbert's quiet assurances that all it takes is God's quiet voice whispering "Child" to make us, even against our conscious wills, choose to listen (p. 507)

"Horror Plum'd":

An International
Stephen King
Bibliography and Guide

_1960-2000_

Section A.

Books:

Novels, Short-Fiction Collections, Non-Fiction, etc.

Including Reprints and Multi-media Adaptations of Book Titles:

Audiocassettes
Audio CDs
Computer Games
Films
Stage Plays
TelePlays and MiniSeries
Videocassettes

NOTE: Titles are repeated in sub-entries only when they differ from the English-language titles; i.e., *Carrie* is assumed as title unless an international edition has published the book under a different title. Unless otherwise indicated by a foreign-language entry or the notation "Title unknown," all books are entered under the original English title.

CARRIE. London, England: New English Library. Paperback '80s edition.

A1.
CARRIE
(1974)

A1. *Carrie*. Garden City NY: Doubleday, 1974, 199 pp., 21 cm., $5.95, hardcover. 1st edition of 30,000 copies. ISBN 0-385-08695-4.

PLOT SUMMARY: *Carrie* details the story of Carrie White, a naive young girl whose first bitter experiences in high school parallel her first awareness of mature sexuality and the onset of frightening psycho-kinetic powers. An outsider by temperament and upbringing, Carrie attempts to fit in with others her own age and to overcome her mother's repressed, obsessively theological rigidity. Befriended by several students and teachers, Carrie moves closer to acceptance until a series of disastrous events at the high school prom results in her death and the devastation of the small town of Chamberlain.

REPRINTS AND ADAPTATIONS:
b. London, England: New English Library, May 1974, 240 pp., hardcover.
c. Garden City NY: Doubleday, [n.d.], hardcover. Science Fiction Book Club edition.
d. Burnsville MN: Econo-Clad/Sagebrush, [1974?], 245 pp., $14.55, library binding. #1003136.
e. Barcelona, Spain: Pomaire, [1974], 327 pp., 275 pta., 22 cm., paperback. Spanish translation by Gregorio Vlastelica. ISBN 84-286-0439-8.
f. New York: Signet/New American Library, April 1975, 245 pp., $1.75, mass-market paperback. Reference #451-E6410-175. ISBN 0-451-15744-3. 64th printing by 1994.
g. London, England: New English Library, July 1975, 192 pp., paperback.
h. Utrecht/De Bilt, Belgium: De Fontein, FONTEIN PAPERBACKS, 1975, 205 pp., trade paperback. Dutch translation by Ingrid Nijkerk. ISBN 90-261-0108-2. * 3rd printing, 1986, ISBN 90-245-1652-8.
i. As: *E sa pedras choveram do céu* ['It rains stones from the sky' (?)]. Mem Martins, Portugal: Európa-América, SÉCULO XX #134, 1975, 206 pp., 21 cm. Portuguese translation by Fernanda Pinto Rodrigues.
j. Barcelona, Spain: Pomaire, January 1975, 328 pp., 375 pta., 22 cm., hardcover. ISBN 84-286-0440-1. Spanish translation by Gregorio Vlastelica.

k. Barcelona, Spain and Buenos Aires, Argentina: Círculo de Lectores, [1975], 213 pp., 20 cm. Spanish translation by Gregorio Vlastelica. 1st printing. ISBN 84-226-0631-3. * Reprint, 1977, 205 pta., 21 cm., paperback. * Reprint, February 1978, 295 pta.
l. As: [Title Unknown]. Tokyo, Japan: Schinchosya, 1975. Japanese translation by Nagai Jun.
m. Paris, France: Gallimard, 1976, 226 pp., 29 F, 22 cm., paperback. French translation by Henri Robillot. ISBN 2-07-029430-7.
n. Barcelona, Spain: Pomaire, BOLSILLO #8, 1976, 232 pp., 125 pta., 18 cm., paperback. Spanish translation by Gregorio Vlastelica. ISBN 84-286-0101-1. * Reprint, 1977. * Reprint, October 1978. * Reprint, 1980.
o. London, England: New English Library, 1977, 189 pp., paperback.
p. Buenos Aires, Argentina: Javier Vergara, 1977, 327 pp., 20 cm. Spanish translation.
q. Milan, Italy: Sonzogno, NARRATIVA SONZOGNO, 1977, 176 pp. Italian translation by Brunella Gasperini.
r. Munich, West Germany: Franz Schneekluth, 1977, 235 pp., 20.00 DM, hardcover (?). German translation by Elisabeth Epple. ISBN 3-7951-0358-4.
s. Munich, West Germany: Wilhelm Heyne, TASCHENBUCH #5374, 1977, paperback. German translation by Elisabeth Epple. "Deutsche Erstausgabe" ["German first edition"]. * Reprint, January 1993. ISBN 3-404-28111-X.
t. Paris, France: J'ai-Lu/Épouvante, 1980. French translation.
u. Barcelona, Spain: Pomaire, NOVELA, 1980, 240 pp., 400 pta., 21 cm., paperback. Spanish translation by Gregorio Vlastelica. ISBN 84-286-0605-6. 2nd printing, September 1981.
v. Stockholm, Sweden: Askild and Kärnekull, 1980, 228 pp. Swedish translation by G. A. Ericsson. ISBN 91-7008-816-0.
w. In: *The Shining, 'Salem's Lot, Night Shift, Carrie*. London, England: Octopus Books, 1981, hardcover. Omnibus edition. See also A13.
x. As: *Carrie; El Umbral de la Noche* [*Carrie*; *Night Shift* as 'The threshold of the night']. Barcelona, Spain: Mundo Actual de Ediciones, NARRADORES DE ÉXITO, April 1982, 568 pp., 825 pta., 21 cm., hardcover. Spanish translation by Gregorio Vlastelica and Eduardo Goligorsky. ISBN 84-7475-190-5.
y. Utrecht, Belgium: Luitingh/Veen, 1983, 205 pp., trade paperback. Dutch translation by Ingrid Nijkerk. ISBN 90-204-0940-9. * 3rd printing, 1986.
z. Sao Paulo, Brazil: Abril Cultural, GRANDES SUCCESSOS, 1983, 183 pp., 20 cm. Portuguese translation by Erika R. Engert Rizzo.
aa. Bergisch Gladbach, West Germany: Bastei-Lübbe, #28111, 1983, 284 pp., 19.80 DM, paperback. German translation by Elisabeth Epple. Includes interview with King and excerpts from other novels. ISBN 3-404-28111-X.
bb. In: *The Shining, 'Salem's Lot, Carrie*. London, England: Octopus Books, Heinemann, July 1983, 747 pp., hardcover.
cc. Milan, Italy: Bompiani, I GRANDI TASCIBILI #28, February 1984, 176 pp., paperback. Italian translation by Brunella Gasperini. ISBN 88-452-1000-6. * 4th edition, January 1987.

dd. Barcelona, Spain: Plaza & Janés, GRAN PARADA, March 1984, 256 pp., 750 pta., 22 cm., paperback. Spanish translation Gregorio Vlastelica. ISBN 84-01-36054-4.
ee. Oslo, Norway: Hjemmets, CASINO GRØSSER, 1984, 239 pp. Norwegian translation by Ernst Poleszynski. ISBN 82-7315-250-2.
ff. Esplugas de Llobregat, Barcelona, Spain: Plaza & Janés, 1985, 288 pp., 18 cm., paperback. Spanish translation Gregorio Vlastelica. ISBN 84-01-49065-0. * 2nd printing, JET #65, December 1985. * 9th printing, May 1992, ISBN 84-01-49888-0.
gg. Bergisch-Gladbach, West Germany: Bastei-Lübbe ALGEMEINE REIHE #13121, 1 November 1987, 236 pp., 6.80 DM, 18 cm., paperback. German translation by Elisabeth Epple; edited by Brunhilde Janáen, with abridged interview with King. ISBN 3-404-13121-5. * 13th printing, 1991.
hh. Sao Paulo, Brazil: Nova Cultural, SUPER SUCCESSOS, 1987, 183 pp., 19 cm. Portuguese translation by Erika R. Engert Rizzo.
ii. Helsinki, Finland: Tammi, 1987, 205 pp. Finnish translation by Tuula Saarikoski. ISBN 951-30-6513-8.
jj. Stockholm, Sweden: Legenda, 1987, 228 pp., 19 cm. Swedish translation by G. A. Ericsson. 2nd edition. ISBN 91-582-0698-1.
kk. Barcelona, Spain: Laertes, L'ARCÀ #39, September 1988, 188 pp., 962 pta., 20 cm., paperback. Spanish translation by Andrew Langdon-Davies. ISBN 84-7584-085-X.
ll. Esplugues de Llobregat, Barcelona, Spain: Plaza & Janés Editores, JET #102/8, BIBLIOTECA DE STEPHEN KING #8, 1988, 282 pp., 18 cm., paperback. Spanish translation by Gregorio Vlastilica. ISBN 84-01-49888-0. * Reprint, 1989.
mm. As: *Keri: roman* ['Carrie: Novel']. Belgrade, Yugoslavia: Beogradski izdavacki-graficki zavod, BIBLIOTEKA HITAC, 1988, 227 pp., 21 cm. Slovakian translation by Nina 'Zivancevic. ISBN 86-13-00302-8.
nn. Stockholm, Sweden: Legenda, 1989, 228 pp., 22 cm., hardcover. Swedish translation by G. A. Ericsson. 5th printing. ISBN 91-582-0768-6.
oo. Kornwesterheim, Austria: Europäische Bildungsgemeinschaft; Gütersloh, Austria: Bertelsmann Lesering; Vienna, Austria: Buchgemeinschaft Donauland; Zug, Switzerland: Buch-und-Schallplattenfreunde, [1989], 235 pp. Book Club edition.
pp. New York: Doubleday, 1990, hardcover. Issued in conjunction with publication of uncut version of *The Stand*.
qq. Utrecht, Belgium: Luitingh-Sijthoff, 1990, 205 pp., hardcover. Dutch translation by Ingrid Nijkerk. 7th printing. ISBN 90-245-1696-X.
rr. Copenhagen, Denmark: Artia, 1990, 206 pp., 98 KR, 20 cm., paperback. Danish translation by Mogens Wenzel Andreasen. ISBN 87-89294-35-1.
ss. Warsaw, Poland: Iskry, 1990, 188 pp., 21 cm. Polish translation by Danuta Górska. ISBN 8320712963.
tt. Mem Martins, Portugal: Európa-América, LIVROS DE BOLSO, SÉRIE PÊNDULO

Carrie. Garden City, NY: Doubleday, 1974. Hardcover.

#45, 1990, 206 pp., 18 cm., paperback. Portuguese translation by Fernanda Pinto Rodrigues. ISBN 972-1-03101-1.
uu. London, England: New English Library, May 1991, £3.99, 222 pp., paperback. Reissue. ISBN 0-450-02517-9.
vv. New York: Plume/New American Library, October 1991, xvii + 152 pp., $12.95, 24 cm., trade paperback. "Collector's Edition," with new introduction by Tabitha King; color reproduction of original hardcover dust-jacket by Neil Stuart. ISBN 0-452-26719-6.
ww. Munich, Germany: Bastei-Lübbe, 28 February 1992, 285 pp., 29.80 DM, hardcover. German translation by Wolfgang Neuhaus. ISBN 3-7857-0627-8.
xx. New York: Penguin/Signet, July 1992, 213 pp., $5.99, mass-market paperback. Reissue, 67th printing. ISBN 0-451-15744-3.
yy. As: *The Shining/Carrie/Misery*. London, England: Chancellor Press, September 1992, 686 pp., £6.99, hardcover. ISBN 1-85152-247-6.
zz. Munich, Germany: Bastei-Lübbe, 1992, 300 pp., 9.80 DM, paperback. German translation by Wolfgang Neuhaus. ISBN 3-404-13121-5. Reprinted 1995.
aaa. [Oslo, Norway]: Hjemmets, 1992, 201 pp., Norwegian translation by Ernst W. Poleszynski. ISBN 82-590-1071-2.
bbb. New York: Doubleday, October 1993, 199 pp., $25.00, hardcover. Cover art by Thomas Holdorf. Reissue of 1st edition. ISBN 0-385-08695-4.
ccc. As: *Carrie/Tommyknockers*. London, England: Hodder & Stoughton, July 1994, 791 pp., £6.99, hardcover. Omnibus volume. ISBN 0-340-62335-7.
ddd. New York: Signet, December 1994, 245 pp., $7.99, mass-market paperback. Reissue edition. ISBN 0-451-15744-3.
eee. Skokie IL: Distribooks Intl., 1994. ISBN 3404131215.
fff. Thorndike, Maine: G. K. Hall, G. K. HALL LARGE PRINT, 1994, 270 pp., 25 cm., hardcover. Large-print edition. ISBN 0-8161-5687-5.
ggg. Paris, France: France Loisirs, 1994, 278 pp., 78 F, hardcover. French translation by Henri Robillot. ISBN 2-7242-8043-1.
hhh. As: *Carrie: Roman*. Paris, France: Michel Albin, 1994, 278 pp., 98 F, 24 cm., paperback. French translation by Henri Robillot. ISBN 2-226-06980-1.
iii. As: *Carrie: Roman*. [Paris, France]: le Grand livre du mois, 1994, 278 pp., 98 F, hardcover. French translation by Henri Robillot. Book Club edition.
jjj. Amsterdam, Netherlands: Poema Pocket, 1994, 205 pp., paperback. Dutch translation by Ingrid Nijkerk. 9th printing. ISBN 90-245-1409-6.
kkk. Barcelona, Spain: Plaza & Janés, JET #102, BIBLIOTECA DE STEPHEN KING #8, January 1995, 288 pp., 254 pta., 18 cm., paperback. Spanish translation Gregorio Vlastelica. ISBN 84-01-00865-4. * Reprint, 1998, ISBN 84-01-49966-6.
lll. Barcelona, Spain: Orbis, BIBLIOTECA GRANDES ÉXITOS, NOVELAS DE CINE #15, September 1995, 286 pp., 22 cm. Spanish translation by Gregorio Vlastelica. ISBN 84-402-1820-6.
mmm. As: *Carrie: Roman*. [Paris, France]: le Grand livre du mois, 1995, 280 pp., 98 F, hardcover. French translation by Henri Robillot. Book Club edition. ISBN 2-7028-0477-2.

nnn. [Oslo, Norway]: Hjemmets, EGMONT SPENNING #49, 1995, 200 pp. Norwegian translation by Ernst W. Poleszynski. ISBN 82-04-03982-4.
ooo. Oslo, Norway: Egmont Bøker Fredhøi, 1996, 201 pp., 179.00, [*innbundet*]. Norwegian translation by Ernst W. Poleszynski. ISBN 82-590-1660-5.
ppp. Warsaw, Poland: Prima, 1996, 237 pp., 21 cm., paperback. Polish translation by Danuta Górska. ISBN 8371520255.
qqq. Tallinn, Estonia: Katariina, 1997, 219 pp., 16 cm., paperback. Estonian translation by Peeter Villmann. ISBN 9985842316.
rrr. Milan, Italy: Bompiani, 1997. Italian translation.
sss. Warsaw, Poland: Prima, BESTSELLERY ŒWIATOWEJ PROZY, 1998, 221 pp., 18 cm., paperback. Polish translation by Danuta Górska. ISBN 8371521073.
ttt. Barcelona, Spain: La Magrana, L'ESPARVER #145, 1999, 224 pp., 20 cm. Spanish translation by Andrew Langdon-Davies. 1st edition. ISBN 84-8264-193-X.
uuu. New York: Pocket, October 1999, 256 pp., $7.99, mass-market paperback. ISBN 0-671-03972-5.
vvv. Milan, Italy: R. L. Libri, SUPERPOCKET #91, October 1999, 174 pp., 18 cm., paperback. Italian translation by Brunella Gasperini. ISBN 88-462-0106-X.
www. Amsterdam, Netherlands: Poema Pocket, 1999, 253 pp., paperback. Dutch translation by Ingrid Nijkerk. 13th edition. ISBN 90-245-3595-6.
xxx. As *Carrie:* Cologne, Germany: Lingen. German translation.
yyy. As: [Title unknown]. Moscow, Russia: AST. Russian translation.
zzz. As: [Title unknown]. Moscow, Russia: Cadman. Russian translation.
aaaa. As: *A Boszorkánylány*. Hungary. Hungarian translation.
bbbb. As: *Carrie*. Hungary. Hungarian translation.
cccc. As: *Kapy*. Greece. Greek translation.
dddd. Paris, France: J'ai Lu, #835, 2000, mass-market paperback.. French translation by Henri Robillot. ISBN 2-290-30251-1.

eeee. As FILM: United Artists, 1976. Produced by Paul Monash. Directed by Brian De Palma. Screenplay by Lawrence D. Cohen. 97 minutes. Rating: R. CAST: Sissy Spacek, Piper Laurie, Amy Irving, William Katz, Nancy Allen, John Travolta.

NOTE: In March, 1999, a film sequel appeared: *The Rage: Carrie 2*. Directed by Katt Shea. CAST: Amy Irving, Emily Bergl, Jason London, Dylan Bruno, Rachel Blanchard, Zachery Ty Bryan.

SELECTED FILM REVIEWS AND ARTICLES:
Babington, Bruce. "Twice a Victim: *Carrie* Meets the BFI" [British Film Institute]. *Screen* Vol. 23 (September/October 1982).
Bathrick, S. K. *Jump Cut* 14 (1977): 9.
Bowers, S. *Film Information* Vol. 7, No. 12 (December 1976): 3.
Childs, Mike, and Alan Jones. "De Palma Has the Power." *Cinefantastique* Vol. 6, No. 1 (Summer 1977): 4.

Citron, M. *Jump Cut* 14 (1977): 10.
Coleman, J. *New Statesman* [England] Vol. 93, No. 2391 (14 January 1977): 63.
Combs, R. BFI: *Monthly Film Bulletin* [England] 44:516 (January 1977): 3.
Crist, Judith. The *Saturday Review* Vol. 4, No. 6 (11 December 1976): 78.
Ebert, Roger. *Roger Ebert's Movie Home Companion*, 1988 Edition. Kansas City MO: Andrews, McMeel & Parker, 1987. 98.
Film & BroadCasting Review Vol. 41, No. 23 (15 December 1976): 132.
Film Bulletin Vol. 45 (1976): 43.
Goldstein. P. *Creem* Vol. 8, No. 10 (March 1977): 56.
Greenspun, Roger. "Carrie and Sally and Leatherface Among the Film Buffs." *Film Comment* Vol. 13, No. 1 (January/February 1977): 16.
Hollywood Reporter (1 November 1976): 4.
Independent Film Journal Vol. 78 (26 November 1976).
Jameson, Richard T. *Film Comment* Vol. 16, No. 2 (March/April 1980): 13.
Kael, Pauline. *The New Yorker* Vol. 52, No. 39 (15 November 1976): 177. Reprinted: *5001 Nights at the Movies: A Guide from A to Z*. New York: Holt, Rinehart & Winston, 1982, hardcover. 95.
Kelley, B. *Cinefantastique* Vol. 5, No. 3 (1976): 20.
Larsen, John. "*Carrie*: For Less than the Price of a Double Latte." 28 October 1998. Online at: http://lightviews.com/carrie.htm
Leake, Simon. Editorial Reviews. *Amazon.com*
Lorenz, Janet. "*Carrie*." *Magill's Survey of Cinema*, 2nd Series, Vol. 1. Edited by Frank N. Magill. Englewood Cliffs, NJ: Salem Press, 1981, hardcover. 408-411.
Los Angeles Times 17 November 1976: IV, 23.
Mack. *Variety* Vol. 284, No. 13 (3 November 1976): 27.
Maslin, J. *Newsweek* Vol. 88, No. 21 (22 November 1976): 113.
Matusa, P. *Film Quarterly* Vol. 31, No. 1 (Fall 1977): 31.
Miller, E. *Seventeen* Vol. 36, No. 2 (1977): 61.
Minton, L. *McCall's* Vol. 104, No. 5 (February 1977): 78.
Motion Picture Herald Product Digest (24 November 1976): 50.
Nash, Robert Jay, and Stanley Ralph Moss. "*Carrie*." *The Motion Picture Guide, 1927-1983*, Vol. II. Chicago: Cinebooks, 1985, hardcover. 364.
New York Times 17 September 1976): II, 6.
New York Times 5 December 1976): II, 13.
New York Times 12 December 1976): II, 13.
Pirie, David. *Movie* [England] Vol. 25 (Winter 1977-1978): 20.
Playboy Vol. 24, No. 2 (February 1977): 26.
Rainer, P. *Mademoiselle* Vol. 83, No. 2 (February 1977): 173.
Ripp, J. *Parents* Vol. 52, No. 1 (January 1977): 16.

Michael R. Collings

Carrie. New York: NAL, 1975.
Mass-market paperback front cover.

HORROR PLUM'D

Rosen, D. *Cinefantastique* Vol. 8, No. 1 (1977): 37.
Sarris, A. *The Village Voice* Vol. 21, No. 48 (29 November 1976): 53.
Schenker, S. *Take One* [Canada] Vol. 5, No. 6 (January 1977): 37.
Schickel, R. *Variety* Vol. 284, No. 13 (3 November 1976): 27.
Schow, David J. "Return of the Curse of the Son of Mr. King: Book Two." *Whispers* No. 17/18 (August 1982): 49-56.
Sight and Sound [England] Vol. 46, No. 2 (Spring 1977): 132.
Stainer, K. *Mother Jones* Vol. 2, No. 1 (January 1977): 59.
Stein, R. *Audience* 100 (19 January 1977): 3.
Stoop, N. M. *After Dark* Vol. 9, No. 9 (January 1977): 89.
Swires, S. *Films in Review* Vol. 8, No. 1 (January 1977): 59.
Time Vol. 108, No. 19 (8 November 1976): 110.
Timpone, Anthony. "Amy Irving's DePalma Days." *Fangoria* Vol. 52 (1986): 46-47.
Turan, K. *The Progressive* Vol. 41, No. 1 (January 1977): 47.
The Village Voice 6 December 1976: 59-60.
Vertlieb, S. *Black Oracle* Vol. 10 (Spring 1977): 31.

ffff. As MUSICAL ADAPTATION: *Carrie*. Produced by Friedrich Kurz and the Royal Shakespeare Company association with White Cap Productions. Book by Lawrence D. Cohen; music by Michael Gore; lyrics by Dean Pitchford. Directed by Terry Hands; choreographed by Debbie Allen. English opening, Stratford-Upon-Avon, 18 February 1988. American opening, Virginia Theater, New York City, 12 May 1988; closed 15 May 1988. CAST: Barbara Wood [London], Betty Buckley [NY], Linzi Hateley, Charlotte D'Amboise, Paul Gygnell, Gene Anthony Ray, Darlene Love, Sally Anne Triplett

SELECTED REVIEWS AND ARTICLES:
"Annie It Ain't." *USA Today* 22 February 1988.
Barnes, Clive. "Musical *Carrie* Soars on Blood, Guts, and Gore." *New York Post* 13 May 1988.
Barnes, Clive. *New York Post* 29 December 1988.
"*Carrie* Proves Costly Failure." *New York Post* 17 May 1988.
"*Carrie* to be Musical." *Castle Rock: The Stephen King Newsletter* Vol. 2, No. 4 (April 1986): 6.
"*Carrie* to Open at Virginia Theater." *Castle Rock: The Stephen King Newsletter* Vol. 4, No. 3 (March 1988).
Cziraky, Dan. "Buckets of Talent Wasted in *Carrie*." *Castle Rock: The Stephen King Newsletter* Vol. 4, No. 8 (August 1988): 6, 10.
Ebron, Betty Lou. "Apple Sauce." *New York Daily News* (March 1988).
Foster, Tim. "*Carrie* as a Musical." *Castle Rock: The Stephen King Newsletter* Vol. 4, No. 2 (February 1988).
Goden, Craig. "Black and White and Read All Over—*Carrie* on Broadway." *Castle Rock: The Stephen King Newsletter* Vol. 4, No. 7 (July 1988).

Henry, William A. "The Biggest All-Time Flop Ever—*Carrie*'s $7 Million Close Shows Why Musicals Are Like Dinosaurs." *Time* (30 May 1988).

Henry, William A. "Getting All Fired Up Over Nothing." *Time* Vol. 131 (23 May 1988): 65.

Holden, Stephen. *New York Times* 8 May 1988: II, 5.

Kroll, Jack. "Shakespeare to Stephen King: The Sins of Carrie." *Newsweek* (23 May 1988).

"Name Game." *USA Today* 22 March 1988.

Maychick, Diana. "Warming Up for *Carrie*." *New York Post* 12 May 1988.

Mills, Richard. "Musical *Carrie* Is a Strange Spectacle." *Castle Rock: The Stephen King Newsletter* Vol. 4, No. 4 (April 1988).

Munster, Bill. "You Read the Book, Saw the Movie, But What About the Show." *Castle Rock: The Stephen King Newsletter* Vol. 4, No. 7 (July 1988): 6, 7.

O'Haire, Patricia. "Stage Fright." *New York Daily News* 8 May 1988.

Osborne, Brian. "More Carrie-ing On." *Castle Rock: The Stephen King Newsletter* Vol. 4, Nos. 5/6 (May-June 1988): 1, 7.

Rich, Frank. *New York Times* 13 May 1988: III, 3.

Roura, Phil, and Tom Poster. "Buckley Comes on in *Carrie*." *New York Daily News* 29 March 1988.

Sauvage, Leo. *The New Leader* Vol. 71 (27 June 1988): 23.

Scapperotti, Dan R. "Stephen King Musical Lays Eggs on Broadway." *Cinefantastique* Vol. 19 (1989). Reprinted: *The Stephen King Companion*. Edited by George Beahm. Kansas City MO: Andrews & McMeel, September 1989. 174-175.

Snyder, Heidi. "*Carrie*." 9 January 2000. At: http://meowser.com

Spignesi, Stephen. "'*Carrie*: The Musical'—The Biggest Flop in Broadway History." *The Complete Stephen King Encyclopedia*. Ann Arbor MI: Popular Culture, Ink, May 1991. 556-558. Includes a "diary" of related events from November 1985 through 29 December 1988.

"Stephen King's Carrie Coming to Broadway." *Science Fiction Chronicle* Vol. 7, No. 4 (January 1986): 6.

New York Daily News 3 January 1988.

New York Daily News 13 May 1988.

New York Times (November 1985). Article announcing the Royal Shakespeare Company plans for production.

New York Times 17 May 1988: III, 15. Review.

Newsweek (23 May 1988). Review, with photographs.

"What a Carrie On." *Castle Rock: The Stephen King Newsletter* Vol. 4, Nos. 5/6 (May/June 1988).

Williams, Jeannie. "Sneaks." *USA Today* 5 May 1988.

gggg. As video-cassette: Carrie. CBS/Fox Video, 1984. Beta, VHS, Laser, CED. 97 minutes.

    SELECTED VIDEO REVIEWS AND ARTICLES:
    Arkush, A. *American Film* Vol. 9, No. 10 (September 1984): 66.
    Barker, Clive. *American Film* Vol. 12, No. 10 (September 1987): 63.
    Farber, J. *Video Review* Vol. 8, No. 8 (November 1987): 131.
    Hoberman, J. *The Village Voice* Vol. 31, No. 26 (1 July 1986): 57.
    Sarris, A., and T. Allen. *The Village Voice* Vol. 32, No. 31 (4 August 1987): 47.
    Sikov, E. *Premiere* Vol. 3 (November 1987): 94.

COMMENTS: Told equally as narration and as pseudo-documentation, *Carrie* was King's fifth manuscript but first published novel. Originally intended as short story, in part to demonstrate that King could write about a female protagonist, it quickly outgrew that form and was submitted as a novel to Bill Thompson at Doubleday.

SELECTED ARTICLES, RESPONSES, AND REVIEWS:
Alexander, Alex E. "Stephen King's *Carrie*: A Universal Fairy Tale." *Journal of Popular Culture* (Fall 1979): 282-288. Reprinted: *Contemporary Literary Criticism*, Vol. 26. Detroit MI: Gale Research, 1983, pp. 234-236.
Bright, David. "Hampden Teacher Hits Jackpot with New Book." *Bangor Daily News* [ME] 25 May 1973.
Booklist Vol. 70 (1 July 1974): 1180.
Bryant, Edward. *Locus* Vol. 27, No. 5, #370 (November 1991).
Callendar, Newgate (pseud.). "Criminals at Large." *The New York Times Book Review* 26 May 1974: 17.
Clinch, Monty. "Carrie's Mom and Danny's Dad.," *Ms London* [England] (9 April 1979): 10.
Coccia, Dario. "*Carrie* di Stephen King." *It: La Revista Horror del Cyberspazio*. Available online at: http://www.fabula.it/IT/classici_0.html
Egan, James. "Apocalypticism in the Fiction of Stephen King." *Extrapolation* Vol. 25, No. 3 (Fall 1984): 214-227.
Egan, James. "Technohorror: The Dystopian Vision of Stephen King." *Extrapolation* Vol. 29, No. 2 (Summer 1988): 140-152.
Ehlers, Leigh A. "*Carrie*: Book and Film." *Ideas of Order in Literature and Film*. Edited by Peter Ruppert and others. Tallahassee FL: University Presses of Florida, 1980. 39-50. Reprinted as: "*Carrie*: Book and Film." *Literature Film Quarterly* (Spring 1981): 32-39.
Gordon, J. S. *New York Times Book Review* 11 September 1977: 3.
Hall, Elizabeth. Review. *Psychology Today* Vol. 9 (September 1975): 76. Reprinted: *Contemporary Literary Criticism*, Vol. 12, Young Adult Literature. Edited by Dedria Bryfonski. Detroit MI: Gale Research, 1980,

hardback.o.308.309.
Hatlen, Burton. "Alumnus Publishes Symbolic Novel, Shows Promise." *The Maine Campus* [University of Maine, Orono] 12 April 1974.
Kirkus Reviews Vol. 42 (1 February 1974): 137.
Kirkus Reviews Vol. 42 (1 March 1974): 257.
Library Journal Vol. 99 (15 February 1974): 584.
Library Journal Vol. 99 (15 April 1974): 1150.
Library Journal Vol. 99 (15 May 1974): 1453.
Library Journal Vol. 99 (15 December 1974): 3249.
Neilson, Keith. "*Carrie*." *Survey of Modern Fantasy Literature*, Vol. 5. Edited by Frank N. Magill. Englewood Cliffs, NJ: Salem Press, 1983. 197-202.
Publishers Weekly Vol. 205 (25 February 1974).
Thompson, Bill. "A Girl Named Carrie: Introduction." *Kingdom of Fear: The World of Stephen King*. Edited by Tim Underwood and Chuck Miller. Columbia PA: Underwood-Miller, 1986, hardcover. 29-34, cloth. [See I13].
Washington Post Book World 26 May 1974: 4.
Washington Post Book World 15 June 1975: 4.
Wilson Library Journal Vol. 48 (June 1974): 802.
Wilson, Philip. "Before the Brand Name." *Castle Rock: The Stephen King Newsletter* Vol. 4, Nos. 5-6 (May-June 1988): 4.
Yarbro, Chelsea Quinn. "Cinderella's Revenge: Twists on Fairy Tale and Mythic Themes in the Work of Stephen King." *Fear Itself: The Horror Fiction of Stephen King*. Edited by Tim Underwood and Chuck Miller. San Francisco CA: Underwood-Miller, 1982. 45-55.

Horror Plum'd

'SALEM'S LOT. Garden City, NY: Doubleday, 1975. Hardcover.

A2.
'SALEM'S LOT
(1975)

A2. *'SALEM'S LOT.* Garden City NY: Doubleday, 1975, 439 pp., 22 cm., $8.95, hardcover. Cover art by Thomas Holdorf. Horror novel. * 18th printing, October 1993, $25.00. ISBN 0-385-00751-5. * 20th printing, August 1998.

PLOT SUMMARY: Ben Mears returns to his hometown of Jerusalem's Lot to confront specters of his own past; he also uncovers the town's secret—that a vampire inhabits the sinister old Marsten House. Mear's struggles for personal integrity and survival parallel the town's as vampires systematically take over 'Salem's Lot.

REPRINTS AND ADAPTATIONS:
b. Garden City NY: Doubleday, 1975, 439 pp., hardcover. * 16th printing by September 1989.
c. Garden City NY: Doubleday, [n.d.], 405 pp., hardcover. Science Fiction Book Club edition.
d. Burnsville MN: Econo-Clad/Sagebrush, 432 pp., $15.15, library binding. #1005016.
e. As: *Bezeten Stad* ['Possessed city']. Laren, Netherlands: Luitingh, 1975. Dutch translation by W. van Mancius.
f. New York: Signet/New American Library, August 1976, 428 pp., $1.95, mass-market paperback. Front cover with embossed figure and a single drop of red blood; no title or author's name on cover of first printing. ISBN 0-451-16588-8. * 55th printing, ISBN 0-451-16808-9. * 60th printing, July 1992, $5.99.
g. As: *La Hora del Vampiro* ['Hour of the vampire']. Barcelona, Spain, and Buenos Aires, Argentina: Pomaire, 1976, 589 pp., 500 pta., 20 cm. Spanish translation by Marta I. Guastavino. ISBN 84-286-0114-3. * Reprint, 1977.
h. London, England: New English Library, February 1977, 440 pp., paperback.
i. As: *Salem.* [Paris, France]: Alta, 1977, 408 pp., 42 F., paperback. French translation by Christiane Thiollier and Joan Bernard.
j. As: *La Hora del Vampiro* ['The hour of the vampire']. Barcelona, Spain: Círculo de Lectores, 1977, 477 pp., 350 pta., 20 cm. Spanish translation by Marta I. Guastavino. ISBN 84-226-0865-0.

Michael R. Collings

k. As: *Bezeten Stad* ['Possessed city']. Utrecht, Belgium: Luitingh/Veen, 1978, 445 pp., f 34.90, trade paperback. Dutch translation by W. van Mancius. ISBN 90-245-0471-6. * 6th printing, 1986.

l. As: *Hora del Vampiro* ['Hour of the vampire']. Barcelona, Spain, and Buenos Aires, Argentina: Pomaire, COLLECIÓN DE BOLSILLA #28, 1978, 555 pp., 18 cm., paperback. Spanish translation by Marta I. Guastavino. ISBN 84-286-0286-7.

m. As: *Brennen Muß Salem—Salem's Lot* ['Salem must burn']. Vienna, Austria, and Hamburg, Germany: Paul Zsolnay, April 1979, 437 pp., 35.00 DM, paperback. Abridged German translation by Ilse Winger and Christoph Wagner. ISBN 3-552-03108-1.

n. As: *Salem*. Paris, France: Presses pocket, 1979, 387 pp., paperback. French translation by Chrisatiane Thiollier and Joan Bernard. ISBN 2-266-00782-3.

o. As: *Notti di Salem* ['Night of Salem']. Milan, Italy: Sonzogno, NARRATIVA SONZOGNO, July 1980, 448 pp. Italian translation by Carlo Brera.

p. As: *Bezeten Stad* ['Possessed city']. Utrecht, Belgium: Skarabee, 1980 (?), trade paperback. Dutch translation.

q. In: *The Shining, 'Salem's Lot, Night Shift, Carrie*. London, England: Octopus Books, 1981. Omnibus edition. See A13.

r. As: *Brennen Muß Salem* ['Salem must Burn']. Munich, Germany: Deutscher Taschenbuchverlag, DTV PHANTASTICA #1877, 1981, 374 pp., 12.80 DM, trade paperback. Abridged German translation by Ilse Winger and Christoph Wagner. ISBN 3-423-01877-1.

s. As: *Korku a∂*. [Istanbul, Turkey]: Alt´yn Kitaplar Yay´ynevi, 1982. Turkish translation by Öz Dokuman.

t. In: *The Shining, 'Salem's Lot, Carrie. London, England:* Octopus Books, Heinemann, July 1983, 747 pp., hardcover. Omnibus edition. See A13.

u. As: *Brennen Muß Salem* ['Salem must burn']. Kornwesterheim, Austria: Europäische Bildungsgemeinschaft; Gütersloh, Austria: Bertelsmann Lesering; Vienna, Austria: Buchgemeinschaft Donauland; Zug, Switzerland: Buch-und-Schallplattenfreunde, February 1985, 447 pp., paperback. German translation by 'Iris' [error for Ilse] Winger and Christoph Wagner. Book Club editions.

v. As: *Staden som Försvann* ['City that disappeared']. Stockholm, Sweden: Legenda, 1985, 476 pp., 129 MK, 24 cm., hardcover. Swedish translation by Lennart Olafsson. ISBN 91-582-0621-3. * 2nd printing, 1987.

w. As: *Brennen Muß Salem* ['Salem must burn']. Munich, Germany: Wilhelm Heyne, ALLGEMEINE REIHE TB #6478, 1985, 374 pp., 9.80 DM, 18 cm., paperback. German translation by Ilse Winger and Christoph Wagner. ISBN 3-453-02053-7. * 16th printing, 1992. * 27th printing, 1995. * 30th printing, 1996.

x. As: *El Misterio de Salem's Lot* ['The mystery of Salem's Lot']. Esplugues de Llobregat, Barcelona, Spain: Plaza & Janés, ÉXITOS, November 1985, 400 pp., 21 cm., paperback. Spanish translation by Marta I. Guastavino. ISBN 84-01-32136-0. * 2nd printing, 1986, 22 cm., ISBN 84-01-32136-0.

y. As: *Brennen Muß Salem* ['Salem must burn']. Gütersloh, Austria:

HORROR PLUM'D

Bertelsmann Lesering, 1986. German translation by Iris [error for 'Ilse'] Winger and Christoph Wagner. Book club edition.

z. As: *La Hora del Vampiro* ['The hour of the vampire']. Buenos Aires, Argentina: Eméce, 1986, 397 pp., 20 cm., paperback. Spanish translation. ISBN 950-04-0543-1. * Reprint, 1988. * Reprint, 1989. * Reprint, 1992. * Reprint, 1994, GRANDES NOVELISTAS.

aa. As: *Le notti di Salem* ['The night of Salem']. Milan, Italy: Bompiani, I GRANDI TASCABILI #64, April 1987, paperback. Italian translation by Carlo Brera. ISBN 88-452-0229-1. * 6th edition, 1991.

bb. London, England: New English Library, October 1987, 439 pp., £3.50, paperback. ISBN 0-450-03106-3. * 17th printing, May 1991, £4.99.

cc. As: *A hora do vampiro* ['The hour of the vampire']. Sao Paulo, Brazil: Nova Cultural, SUPER SUCESSOS, 1988, 550 pp., 20 cm. Portuguese translation by Luzia Machado da Costa.

dd. As: *Salem.* Paris, France: Presses Pocket, 1988, 387 pp., 26 F, paperback. French translation by Christiane Thiollier and Joan Bernard. ISBN 2-266-02175-3. * Reprint, 1989, ISBN 2-266-02961-4.

ee. As: *El Misterio de Salem's Lot* ['The mystery of Salem's Lot']. Esplugues de Llobregat, Barcelona, Spain: Plaza & Janés JET 102, BIBLIOTECA DE STEPHEN KING #6, 1988, 524 pp., 18 cm., paperback. Spanish translation by Marta I. Guastavino. ISBN 84-01-49886-4. * 5th printing, 1990, ISBN 84-01-49886-4. * 10th printing, 1993, ISBN 84-01-49989-5.

ff. As: *Shining/Salem/Danse Macabre.* Paris, France: J.-C. Lattès, 1989, 1181 pp., 150 F, paperback. French translations by Joan Bernard, Christiane Thiollier, Lorris Murail and Natalie Zimmermann.

gg. As: *Staden som Försvann* ['City that disappeared']. Stockholm, Sweden: Legenda, 1989, 476 pp., 22 cm., hardcover. Swedish translation by Lennart Olafsson. 6th edition. ISBN 91-582-1002-4.

hh. New York: Doubleday, May 1990, 451 pp., $21.95, hardcover. Special reissue to coincide with publication of the uncut version of *The Stand.* ISBN 0-385-00751-5.

ii. As: *Painajainen.* Helsinki, Finland: Tammi, 1990, 476 pp. Finnish translation by Heikki Karjalainen. ISBN 951-30-9382-4.

jj. As: *Brennen Muß Salem* ['Salem must burn']. Stuttgart and Munich, Germany: Deutsche Bücherbund, [1990], 430 pp., hardcover. German translation by Ilse Winger and Christoph Wagner. Book Club edition.

kk. As: *Brennen Muß Salem* ['Salem must burn']. Munich, Germany: Wilhelm Heyne, HEYNE TOP TEN, 1990, 374 pp., 8.00 DM, paperback. German translation by Ilse Winger and Christoph Wagner. ISBN 3-453-05050-9.

ll. As: *Bezeten Stad* ['Possessed city']. Amsterdam, Netherlands: Luitingh-Sijthoff, 1990, 440 pp. Dutch translation by W. van Mancius. 9th printing. ISBN 90-245-1048-1. * 12th printing, 1993.

mm. As: *Staden som Försvann* ['City that disappeared']. Stockholm, Sweden: Legenda, POCKET, 1990, 476 pp., 18 cm., paperback. Swedish translation by Lennart Olafsson. 3rd paperback edition. ISBN 91-582-1856-4.

nn. New York, Plume/New American Library, October 1991, 381 pp., $14.95, trade paperback. "Collector's Edition." Includes a color reproduction of the original hardcover art by Neil Stuart. Introduction by Clive Barker. ISBN 0-452-26721-8.

oo. As: *Hora del Vampiro* ['The hour of the vampire']. Buenos Aires, Argentina: Emecé, GRANDES NOVELISTAS, 1991, 396 pp., 20 cm. Spanish translation. ISBN 950-04-0543-1.

pp. As: *Bezeten Stad* ['Possessed city']. Utrecht, Belgium: Luitingh-Sijthoff, 1991, 440 pp., hardcover. Dutch translation by W. van Mancius. 10th printing. ISBN 90-245-1708-7.

qq. As: *A hora do vampiro* ['The hour/time of the vampire']. Sao Paulo, Brazil: Nova Cultural, 1991, 550 pp., 19 cm., paperback. Portuguese translation by Luzia Machado da Costa.

rr. As: *De dødes* ['The dead']. Copenhagen, Denmark: Artia, 1991, 465 pp., 298 KR, paperback. Danish translation by Mogens Wenzel Andreasen. ISBN 87-89294-62-9.

ss. As: *Miasteczko Salem* ['Small-town Salem']. Warsaw, Poland: "Amber," 1991, 413 pp., 21 cm. Polish translation by Arkadiusz Nakoniecznik. ISBN 83-8507-983-1.

tt. As: *Brennen Muß Salem* ['Salem must burn']. Vienna, Austria: Paul Zsolnay, 1992, 437 pp., 19.80 DM, hardcover. German translation by Ilse Winger and Christoph Wagner. ISBN 3-552-04407-8.

uu. As: *De dødes* ['The dead']. Copenhagen, Denmark: Artia, EN ARTIA PAPER-BACK, 1993, 516 pp., 88 KR, paperback. Danish translation by Mogens Wenzel Andreasen. ISBN 87-89918-22-3.

vv. As: *De dødes* ['The dead']. 2 vols. [Valby], Denmark: Paperback Bogklubben Wangel, 1993, 465 pp., 32,85 KR, paperback. Danish translation by Mogens Wenzel Andreasen. ISBN 87-7803-407-8, 87-7803-408-6.

ww. Thorndike ME: G. K. Hall, LARGE PRINT CORE COLLECTION, [before 1994], hardcover. Large print edition.

xx. As: *Salem*. Paris, France: France Loisirs, 1994, 409 pp., 96 F, hardcover. French translation by Christiane Thiollier and Joan Bernard. ISBN 2-7242-7846-1.

yy. As: *Salem*. [Paris, France]: J.-C. Lattés, 1994, 408 pp., 129 F, paperback. French translation by Christiane Thiollier and Joan Bernard. ISBN 2-7096-1442-1.

zz. As: *Bezeten Stad* ['Possessed city']. Amsterdam, Netherlands: Poema Pocket, 1994, 478 pp., paperback. Dutch translation by W. van Mancius. 13th printing. ISBN 90-245-1160-7.

aaa. As: *Brennen Muß Salem* ['Salem must burn']. Vienna, Austria: Paul Zsolnay, 1995, 479 pp., hardcover. German translation by Peter Robert. ISBN 3-552-04702-6.

bbb. As: *El Misterio de Salem's Lot* ['The mystery of Salem's Lot']. Barcelona, Spain: Orbis, NOVELAS DE CINE, 1995, 524 pp., 21 cm. Spanish translation by Marta I. Guastavino. ISBN 84-402-1866-4.

HORROR PLUM'D

ccc. As: *Brennen Muß Salem* ['Salem must burn']. Rheda-Wiedenbrück, Germany: Bertelsmann-Club; Vienna, Austria: Buchgemeinschaft Donauland Kremayr und Scheriau, [1996], 479 pp., hardcover. German translation by Peter Robert. Book Club edition.

ddd. Excerpted in: *Blood Thirst: 100 Years of Vampire Fiction*. Edited by Leonard Wolf. New York: Oxford University Press, October 1997, 379 pp., $25.00, hardcover. 51-66. ISBN 0-19-511593-7.

eee. As: *Le notti di Salem* ['The night of Salem']. Milan, Bompiani: 1997. Italian translation.

fff. As: *Brennen Muß Salem* ['Salem must burn']. Munich, Germany: Wilhelm Heyne, ALLGEMEINE REIHE #10356, 1997, 573 pp., 14.90 dm, paperback. New unabridged German translation by Peter Robert. ISBN 3-453-12527-4.

ggg. As: *El Misterio de Salem's Lot* ['The mystery of Salem's Lot']. Barcelona, Spain: Plaza & Janés, JET 102, BIBLIOTECA DE STEPHEN KING #6, 1997, 509 pp., 18 cm., paperback. Spanish translation by Marta I. Guastavino. ISBN 84-01-47456-6.

hhh. As: *Miasteczko Salem* ['Small-town Salem']. Warsaw, Poland: Prószyñski i S-ka SA, 23 November 1998, 472 pp., 19 cm., paperback. Polish translation by Arkadiusz Nakoniecznik. ISBN 83-7180-915-8.

iii. As: *El Misterio de Salem's Lot* ['The mystery of Salem's Lot']. Barcelona, Spain: Plaza & Janés, 1998, 395 pp., 22 cm.. Spanish translation by Marta I. Guastavino. 1st edition in this format. ISBN 84-01-32424-6.

jjj. As: Salems Lot. Greek translation.

kkk. As: [Title unknown]. 2 vols. Japanese translation.

lll. As: [Title unknown]. Russia: Cadman. Russian translation.

mmm. As: *Borzalmak Varosa*. Budapest, Hungary: Európa. Hungarian translation.

nnn. As TELEVISION MINI-SERIES: As teleplay: *Salem's Lot*. Warner Brothers, CBS. 17 and 24 November 1979. Produced by Richard Kobritz. Directed by Tobe Hooper; teleplay by Paul Monash. 210 minutes. CAST: David Soul, James Mason, Lance Kerwin, Bonnie Bedelia, Lew Ayres, Reggie Nalder, Ed Flanders.

ooo. As VIDEOCASSETTE: *Salem's Lot*. Warner Brothers, 1979. 157 minutes. Edited videocassette version of television mini-series. An unauthorized sequel to the telefilm—named *Return to Salem's Lot* but with few recognizable connections to King narrative—also appeared on videocassette

> SELECTED FILM REVIEWS AND ARTICLES:
> Casey, Susan. "On the Set of '*Salem's Lot*.'" *Fangoria* Vol. 4 (1980): 38-41, 45. Preview of the television mini-series, based on comments by cast members, producer, director, set designer, and others. Includes stills from the film.
> *Fangoria* Vol. 38. Includes *Salem's Lot* pullout poster.
> Kelley, Bill. "'*Salem's Lot*: Filming Horror for Television." *Cinefantastique* Vol. 9, No. 2 (Winter 1979).

43

Leishman, Katie. "When Is Television Too Scary for Children." *TV Guide* (10 January 1981): 5-8.
Schow, David J. "Return of the Curse of the Son of Mr. King: Book Two." *Whispers* No. 17/18 (August 1982): 49-56.
Spignesi, Stephen. "A Stop at the Marsten House: An Interview with Tobe Hooper." *The Shape Under the Sheet: The Complete Stephen King Encyclopedia.* Ann Arbor MI: Popular Culture, Ink, May 1991. 561-566.

ppp. As VIDEOCASSETTE: *Salem's Lot.* Warner Brothers, 1979. 157 minutes. Edited videocassette version of television mini-series. An unauthorized sequel to the telefilm—named *Return to Salem's Lot* but with few recognizable connections to King narrative—also appeared on videocassette

COMMENTS: One of King's favorites among his own novels, '*Salem's Lot* embodies an intense, imaginative treatment of the vampire motif translated into uniquely American idioms. The novel demonstrates how readily vampires might survive in contemporary American society, and in doing so uses the monster as a base metaphor for a perceptive study of fear, individual and communal isolation, and social fragmentation. Some particularly gruesome passages were edited from King's original manuscript (see Beahm's *The Stephen King Companion* for details), but the novel does justice to the tradition defined by Stoker's *Dracula* and has in fact gained recognition as the finest treatment of the vampire mythos since Stoker's definitive version.

SELECTED ARTICLES, RESPONSES, AND REVIEWS:

Bobbie, Walter. *Best Sellers* Vol. 35 (January 1976): 304. Reprinted in: *Contemporary Literary Criticism*, Vol. 12, Young Adult Literature. Edited by Dedria Bryfonski. Detroit MI: Gale Research Co., 1980, hardcover. 309.
Booklist Vol. 72 (1 January 1976): 613.
Egan, James. "Technohorror: The Dystopian Vision of Stephen King." *Extrapolation* 29:2 (Summer 1988): 140-152.
Hatlen, Burton. "'*Salem's Lot* Critiques American Civilization." *The Maine Campus* [University of Maine, Orono] 12 December 1975.
Hicks, James E. "Stephen King's Creation of Horror in '*Salem's Lot*: A Prolegomenon Towards a New Hermeneutic of the Gothic Novel." *The Gothic World of Stephen King: Landscape of Nightmares.* Edited by Gary Hoppenstand and Ray B. Browne. Bowling Green OH: Bowling Green State University Popular Press, December 1987. 75-83.
Kirkus Reviews (15 August 1975): 935. Excerpted: *Contemporary Literary Criticism*, Vol. 12, Young Adult Literature. Edited by Dedria Bryfonski. Detroit MI: Gale Research, 1980. 309.
Munster, Bill. "Why and How to Teach Stephen King." *Castle Rock: The Stephen King Newsletter* Vol. 2, No. 8 (August 1986): 1, 4.
Pharr, Mary. " Vampiric Appetite in *I Am Legend*, '*Salem's Lot*, and *The Hunger. The Blood is the Life: Vampires in Literature.* Edited by Leonard G. Heldreth

and Mary Pharr. Bowling Green OH: Bowling Green University Popular Press, 1999, hardcover and trade paper simultaneously. 93-103.

Publishers Weekly (11 August 1975): 109.

Publishers Weekly (7 June 1976): 73.

Ryan, Alan. "The Marsten House in '*Salem's Lot*.'" *Fear Itself: The Horror Fiction of Stephen King*. Edited by Tim Underwood and Chuck Miller. San Francisco CA: Underwood-Miller, 1982. 169-180.

Sarrantonio, Al. "Stephen King: '*Salem's Lot*.'" *Horror: 100 Best Books*. Edited by Stephen Jones and Kim Newman. London, England: Xanadu, 1988. 161-162.

School Library Journal Vol. 22 (December 1975): 70.

Voice of Youth Advocates Vol. 6 (December 1983): 267.

Village Voice Literary Supplement (November 1985): 27.

Watson, Christine. "Salem's Lot." *Survey of Modern Fantasy Literature*, Vol. 3. Edited by Frank N. Magill. Englewood Cliffs NJ: Salem Press, 1983. 1350-1354.

THE SHINING. Garden City, NY: Doubleday, 1977. Hardcover.

A3.
THE SHINING
(1977)

A3. THE SHINING. Garden City NY: Doubleday, 1977, 447 pp., $8.95, hardcover. Horror novel. * 14th printing, May 1990, 450 pp., $21.95. ISBN 0-385-12167-9. * 17th printing, October 1993, $25.00.

PLOT SUMMARY: Jack Torrence, his wife Wendy, and his young son Danny winter in an isolated hotel in the Colorado Rockies. As the season progresses, Jack descends further into madness as an evil in the Overlook Hotel works to possess him and through him Danny's extraordinary gift, the "Shine."

REPRINTS AND ADAPTATIONS:
b. London, England: New English Library, September 1977, 447 pp., hardcover. ISBN 0-450-03220-5.
c. As: *Insólito esplendor* ['Unusual splendor']. Barcelona, Spain: Círculo de Lectores, 1977, 514 pp., 395 pta., 20 cm. Spanish translation by Marta I. Guastavino. ISBN 84-226-0938-X.
d. London, England: New English Library, April 1978, 416 pp., paperback.
e. London, England: New English Library, April 1979, 320 pp., paperback.
f. New York: Signet/New American Library, January 1978, 447 pp., $2.50, mass-market paperback. Silver Mylar cover on first edition; modified or new covers for later printings. ISBN 0-451-07872-1.
g. New York: Signet/New American Library, January 1978, 447 pp., paperback. Movie tie-in edition, with new cover.
h. Garden City NY: Doubleday, [n.d.], 447 pp., hardcover. Science Fiction Book Club edition.
i. Burnsville MN: Econo-Clad/Sagebrush, 447 pp., $15.15, library binding. #1006667.
j. As: *Het Tweede Gezicht* ['The second sight/face']. Baarn, Netherlands: De Fontein, 1978, 339 pp., f 29.50, trade paperback. Dutch translation by Johan Cornelisz. ISBN 90-261-2089-3.
k. Utrecht, Belgium. Book Club Edition.
l. Milan, Italy: Bompiani, TASCABILI BOMPIANI #226 ['Bompiani pockets'], 1978,

430 pp., mass-market paperback. Italian translation by Adriana Dell'Orto. * Reprint, 9 March 1981, ISBN 88-452-0755-2. * Reprint, February 1987.

m. As: *Insólito Esplendor* ['Unusual splendor']. Barcelona, Spain, and Buenos Aires, Argentina: Pomaire, 1978, 599 pp., 20 cm. Spanish translation by Marta I. Guastavino. * Reprint, 1980, ISBN 84-286-0588-2. * Reprint, 1981, ISBN 84-286-0588-2.

n. As: *L'Enfant Lumiére* ['The child light']. Paris, France: Williams-Alta, 1979, 429 pp., 43.50 F, paperback. French translation by Joan Bernard.

o. As: *L'Enfant Lumiére* ['The child light']. [Bagneux, France]: [le Livre de Paris], 1979, 429 pp., hardcover. French translation by Joan Bernard.

p. As: *Insólito Esplendor* ['Unusual splendor']. Barcelona, Spain: Círculo de Lectores, 1979. Spanish translation.

q. As: *Drengen der Skinnede* ['Boy of the shining']. Copenhagen, Denmark: Borgen/Narayana, 1980, 436 pp., 98 KR, paperback. Danish translation by Niels Søndergaard. ISBN 87-418-2903-4.

r. As: *L'Enfant Lumiére* ['The child light']. Paris, France: France Loisirs, 1980, 429 pp., 46 F, hardcover. French translation by Joan Bernard. ISBN 2-7242-0809-9.

s. Bergisch Gladbach, West Germany: Bastei-Lübbe, TB 28100, 1980, 400 pp., paperback. German translation by Harro Christensen. Reprinted 1982. ISBN 3-404-28100-4.

t. As: *Varsel* ['Premonition/foreshadowing']. Stockholm, Sweden: Askild and Kärnekull, 1980, 458 pp. Swedish translation by G. A. Ericsson. * Reprint, 1981. * Reprint, 1983.

u. As: *You guang* [or *Yu kuang*]. Taipei, Taiwan: Hao Shi Nian, 1980. Chinese translation by Wang An-chen.

v. As: *Shining: L'Enfant Lumière* ['Shining: the child light']. Paris, France: J'ai-Lu, #1197, 1981, 571 pp., 10,51 F, mass-market paperback. French translation by Joan Bernard. ISBN 2-277-21197-4. * Reprint, 1992.

w. As: *Vidovitost*. Zagreb, Yugoslavia/Croatia, 1981. Serbo-Croatian translation.

x. As: *Ondskapens Hotell*. ['Hotel of evil']. Norway: Fredhøis, FREDHØIS BEST-SELGERE, 1981, 379 pp. Norwegian translation by Øyvind Viestad. ISBN 82-04-01011-7.

y. As: *El Resplandor* ['The brightness/gleam']. Barcelona, Spain: Pomaire, 1981. Spanish translation. ISBN 84-286-0588-2.

z. In: *The Shining, 'Salem's Lot, Night Shift, Carrie*. London, England: Octopus Books, 1981, hardcover. Omnibus edition; see A13.

aa. As: *El Resplandor* ['The brightness/gleam']. Esplugas de Llobregat, Barcelona, Spain: Plaza & Janés, JET #9, January 1982, 509 pp., 325 pta., 18 cm. mass market-paperback. Spanish translation by Marta I. Guastavino. ISBN 84-01-49008-1. * Reprint, 1986, JET #8, ISBN 84-01-49008-1. * 3rd printing, 1986. * Reprint, 1987, ISBN 84-01-49008-1

bb. In: *The Shining, 'Salem's Lot, Carrie*. London, England: Octopus Books, Heinemann, July 1983, 747 pp., hardcover.

cc. As: *De Shining*. Utrecht and Antwerp, Belgium, Netherlands:

Skarabee/Bruna, 1983, 339 pp., f 11.90. Dutch translation by Johan Cornelisz. Movie tie-in edition with new cover art. ISBN 90-6071-250-1. * 2nd printing, 1987.

dd. As: *De Shining*. Utrecht, Belgium, Netherlands: Veen, 1983. Revised Dutch translation.

ee. As: *O iluminado* ['The illuminated']. Sao Paulo, Brazil: Abril Cultural, GRANDES SUCCESSOS—SERIE ORO, 1984, 445 pp., 20 cm. Portuguese translation by Betty Ramos Albuquerque.

ff. As: *O iluminado* ['The illuminated']. Sao Paulo, Brazil: Record, [1984?], 395 pp., 21 cm. Portuguese translation by Betty Ramos Alguquerque.

gg. As: *Shining: L'Enfant Lumière* ['Shining: the child light']. Paris, France: J'ai-Lu, March 1984, 575 pp., paperback. French translation by Joan Bernard.

hh. As: *El Resplandor* ['The brightness/gleam']. Esplugas de Llobregat, Barcelona, Spain: Plaza & Janés, 1984, 503 pp., 19 cm. Spanish translation by Marta I. Guastavino. ISBN 84-01-37175-9.

ii. As: *Hohto* ['Gloss']. Helsinki/Porvoo, Finland: Wsoy, 1985, 512 pp. Finnish translation by Pentti Isomursu. ISBN 951-0-12904-6. * 2nd printing: BEST SELLER, 1991 ISBN 951-0-16862-9. * 5th printing, 1993.

jj. As: *Shining*. Bergisch Gladbach, West Germany: Bastei-Lübbe, TB 13008, 1985, 493 pp., 7.80 DM, paperback. German translation by Harro Christensen. ISBN 3-404-13008-1.

kk. As: *Shining*. Kornwesterheim, Austria: Europäische Bildungsgemeinschaft; Gütersloh, Austria: Bertelsmann Club; Vienna, Austria: Buchgemeinschaft Donauland; Zug, Switzerland: Buch-und-Schallplattenfreunde, [November 1985], 477 pp., paperback. German translation by Harro Christensen. Book Club editions

ll. As: *A Ragyogas: regeny* ['The shining: novel']. Zageb, Yuygoslavia: Forum/Európa, 1986, 471 pp., 20 cm., paperback. Hungarian translation by Prekop Gabriella. ISBN 86-323-0014-8.

mm. As: *A Ragyogas: regeny* ['The shining: novel']. Budapest, Hungary: Arkadia, 1986, 471 pp., 20 cm., paperback. Hungarian translation by Prekop Gabriella. ISBN 963-307-042-2. Also ISBN 963-07-3761-2.

nn. As: *Shyainingu*. 2 vols. Tokyo, Japan: Bungei Shunju, 1986. Japanese translation by Fukamachi Mariko.

oo. London, England: New English Library, October 1987, 416 pp., £2.95, paperback. ISBN 0-450-04018-6.

pp. As: *Die Shining*. Utrecht, Belgium: Luitingh-Sijthoff, February 1987, 339 pp., paperback. Dutch translation by Johan Cornelisz. 2nd printing. ISBN 90-245-1851-2. * 4th printing, 1990.

qq. As: *Shining*. Bergisch Gladbach, West Germany: Gustav Lübbe, 27 February 1987, 400 pp., hardcover. German translation by Harro Christensen. ISBN 3-7857-0461-5.

rr. As: *O iluminado* ['The illuminated']. Sao Paulo, Brazil: Nova Cultural, BEST SELLERS, 1987, 445 pp., 19 cm. Portuguese translation by Betty Ramos Albuquerque.

ss. As: *Shining*. Paris, France: J'ai-Lu/Épouvante, 1988. French translation.
tt. As: *Shining*. Stuttgart and Munich, Germany: Deutscher Bücherbund, 1988, 455 pp. German translation by Harro Christensen. Book Club edition.
uu. As: *Shining: A Casa do Horror* ['Shining: in the house of horror' (?)]. [Lisbon, Portugal]: Círculo de Leitores, 1988, 457 pp., 21 cm. Portuguese translation by M. Filomena Duarte.
vv. As: *El Resplandor* ['The brightness/gleam']. Esplugas de Llobregat, Barcelona, Spain: Plaza & Janés, JET 102/2, BIBLIOTECA DE STEPHEN KING #2, 1988, 505 pp., 18 cm., paperback. Spanish translation by Marta I. Guastavino. ISBN 84-01-49882-1. * Reprint, 1989.
ww. As: *L'Enfant Lumiére* ['The child light']. [Paris, France]: Editions de la Seine, 1989, 429 pp., 66 F, hardcover. French translation by Joan Bernard. ISBN 2-73-820158-X.
xx. As: *Shining/Salem/Danse Macabre*. Paris, France: J.-C. Lattès, 1989, 1181 pp., 150 F, paperback. French translations by Joan Bernard, Christiane Thiollier, Lorris Murail and Natalie Zimmermann.
yy. As: *A Luz* ['The light']. 2 vols. Mem Martins: Europa-América, LIVROS DE BOLSO, SÉRIE PÊNDULO #39-40, 1989, 18 cm., paperback. Portuguese translation by Lúcia Teles. ISBN 972-1-02691-3, 972-1-02738-3.
zz. Milan, Italy: Bompiani, I GRANDI TASCABILI #132, March 1990, paperback. Italian translation by Adriana Dell'Orto. ISBN 88-452-1559-8.
aaa. New York: Doubleday, 1990, 447 pp., hardcover. Issued in conjunction with the publication of the uncut version of *The Stand*.
bbb. As: *Ondskapens Hotell*. ['Hotel of evil']. Oslo, Norway: Fredhois, 1990, 379 pp. Norwegian translation by Øyvind Viestad. ISBN 82-04-02420-7.
ccc. As: *Jasnocs* ['Brightness']. Warsaw, Poland: Iskry, 1990, 358 pp., 21 cm. Polish translation by Zofia Zinserling. ISBN 83-2071-340-4.
ddd. As: *Varsel* ['Premonition/foreshadowing']. [Stockholm, Sweden]: Månpocket, 1990, 458 pp., 18 cm., paperback. Swedish translation by G. A. Ericsson. ISBN 91-7642-579-7.
eee. New York: Plume, October 1991, 416 pp., $14.95, trade paperback. "Special King Collector's Edition." Introduction by Ken Follett. ISBN 0-450-26722-6.
fff. As: *Ondskabens hotel* ['Malicious/vicious hotel'] Valby, Denmark: Borgen/Narayana, BORGEN PAPERBACK, 1991, 436 pp., 98 KR, paperback. Danish translation by Niels Søndergaard. 2nd edition, 2nd printing. ISBN 87-418-8820-0.
ggg. As: *Varsel* ['Premonition/foreshadowing']. [Stockholm, Sweden]: Legenda, POCKET, 1991, 458 pp., 18 cm., paperback. Swedish translation by G. A. Ericsson. 2nd printing. ISBN 91-582-1902-1; 91-582-0304-4.
hhh. New York: Signet, July 1992, 416 pp., $5.99, mass-market paperback. 52nd printing ISBN 0-451-26722-5.
iii. As: *The Shining/Carrie/Misery*: London, England: Chancellor Press, September 1992, 686 pp., £6.99, paperback. Omnibus edition. ISBN 1-85152-247-6.

jjj. As: *Shining: L'Enfant Lumiére* ['Shining: the child light']. [Paris, France]: J.-C. Lattès, 1992, 429 pp. 119 F, paperback. French translation by Joan Bernard. ISBN 2-7096-1201-1.

kkk. As: *Shining: als Buch und Film ein Welterfolg* ['Shining: as book and film a world-success']. Bergisch Gladbach, West Germany: Bastei-Lübbe, ALLGEMEINE REIHE #13008, 1992, 619 pp., 12.80 DM, paperback. German translation by Harro Christensen. ISBN 3-404-13008-1. * Reprint, 1992, ISBN 3-404-25210-1.

lll. Thorndike ME: G. K. Hall, LARGE PRINT CORE COLLECTION, [before 1994]. Large print edition.

mmm. As: *Shining: als Buch und Film ein Welterfolg* ['Shining: as book and film a world-success']. Bergisch Gladbach, West Germany: Bastei-Lübbe, 1 March 1993, paperback (*kartoniert*). German translation. ISBN 3-404-28100-4. "Deutsche Erstausgabe"

nnn. As: *Surmahotell.* 2 vols. Tallinn, Estonia: Katherina/Pakett/ Ühiselu, 1994, 323+339 pp., 17 cm., paperback. Estonian translation by Matti Piirimaa.

ooo. As: *Shining: L'Enfant Lumiére* ['Shining: the child light']. Paris, France: France Loisirs, 1994, 432 pp., 95 F, hardcover. French translation by Joan Bernard. ISBN 2-7242-7847-X.

ppp. As: *De Shining.* Amsterdam, Netherlands: Poema Pocket, 1994, 416 pp., paperback. Dutch translation by Johan Cornelisz. 7th printing. ISBN 90-245-1223-9.

qqq. Bergisch Gladbach, West Germany: Bastei-Lübbe, ALLGEMEINE REIHE #13008, 1995, 619 pp., 12.90 DM, paperback German translation by Harro Christensen. 33rd edition. ISBN 3-404-13008-1.

rrr. As: *Shining: Roman.* [Paris, France]: le Grand livre du mois, 1996, 429 pp., 120 F, hardcover. French translation by Joan Bernard. Book Club edition.

sss. As: *Nattens hus* ['Night's house']. [Oslo], Norway: Hjemmets, STEPHEN KINGS URVALGTE, [1996], 431 pp., hardcover. Norwegian translation by Ernst W. Poleszynski. ISBN 82-590-1656-7. Book Club edition.

ttt. As: *El Resplandor* ['The brightness/gleam']. Barcelona, Spain: Plaza & Janés, JET 102/2, BIBLIOTECA DE STEPHEN KING #2, 1996, 503 pp., 18 cm., paperback. Spanish translation by Marta I. Guastavino. ISBN 84-01-49985-2. * Reprint, 1998, ISBN 84-01-49985-2.

uuu. As: *El Resplandor* ['The brightness/gleam']. [Barcelona], Spain: Orbis, [1996], 505 pp., 22 cm. ISBN 84-402-2061-8.

vvv. New York: Signet, May 1997, 464 pp., $7.99, mass-market paperback. 59th printing. Movie tie-in edition. ISBN 0-451-19388-1.

www. As: *El Resplandor* ['The brightness/gleam']. Barcelona, Spain: Plaza & Janés, JET 102/2, BIBLIOTECA DE STEPHEN KING #2, 1997, 651 pp., 18 cm., paperback. Spanish translation by Marta I. Guastavino. ISBN 84-01-47452-3. * Reprint, 1998, ISBN 84-01-49985-2.

xxx. As: *Lœnienie* ['Shining']. Warsaw, Poland: Prószyñski i S-ka SA, POZA SERIA, 21 October 1998, 488 pp., 19 cm., paperback. Polish translation by Zofia Zinserling. ISBN 83-7180-207-2.

yyy. As: *Ondskabens hotel* ['Malicious/vicious hotel']. Copenhagen, Denmark: Peter Asschenfeldts 1999, 436 pp., 168 KR, hardcover. Danish translation by Niels Søndergaard. ISBN 87-7880-436-1. Book Club edition.

zzz. As: *Shining*. Germany: Bechtermünz. German translation.

aaaa. As: [Title unknown]. Tel Aviv, Israel: Modin. Hebrew translation.

bbbb. As: [Title unknown].Moscow, Russia: AST. Russian translation.

cccc. As: [Title unknown]. Greece: Antaeia & Tpomoe. Greek translation.

dddd. As AUDIOTAPE: *The Shining*. Victoria, Australia: Louise Braille Productions, 1988.

eeee. As FILM: *The Shining*. Warner Brothers/Hawks Films, 1980. Produced and directed by Stanley Kubrick. Screenplay by Stanley Kubrick and Diane Johnson. 145 minutes. Rating: R. CAST: Jack Nicholson, Shelley Duvall, Danny Lloyd, Scatman Crothers, Barry Nelson.

COMMENTS: Critics generally consider Kubrick's adaptation a brilliant film when taken on its own, but flawed when considered against King's narrative. The film undeniably shifts emphasis from an overtly, externally haunted "Bad Place" to a study of internal madness—incorporating at the same time a savage indictment of alcoholism.

SELECTED FILM REVIEWS AND ARTICLES:

Alberton, Jim, and Peter S. Perakos. "*The Shining*." *Cinefantastique* Vol. 7, Nos. 3/4 (1978).

Allen, T. *The Village Voice* Vol. 25, No. 22 (2 June 1980): 41.

Anderson, P. *Films in Review* Vol. 16, No. 4 (August/September 1980): 438.

Asahina, Robert. "Summer Doldrums." *New Leader* Vol. 63, No. 13 (14 June 1980): 19-20.

Audio *Video Review Digest* Vol. 2, No. 1 (May 1990): 180.

Blake, R. A. *America* Vol. 142, No. 23 (14 June 1980): 504.

Blakemore, Bill. "Kubrick's 'Shining' Secret." *The Washington Post* 12 July 1987.

Blue, Tyson. "'The Shining' Comes to Local Theater." *Courier Herald* [Dublin GA] 6 July 1980.

Brodsky, Allen. "Reflection and Desire: *The Shining*." *Cinemacabre* (Summer 1984). 9-page article.

Bromell, Henry. "The Dimming of Stanley Kubrick." *The Atlantic* Vol. 246, No. 2 (August 1980): 80-83.

Brown, Garrett. "The Steadicam and *The Shining*." *American Cinematographer* (August 1980): 786.

Christensen, Dan. "Stephen King: Living in 'Constant Deadly Terror.'" *Bloody Best of Fangoria* (1982): 30-33. King's reactions to Kubrick's filming of *The Shining*.

Caldwell, Larry W., and Samuel J. Umland. "'Come and Play With Us': The Play Metaphor in Kubrick's *The Shining*." *Literature/Film*

Quarterly Vol. 14, No. 2 (1986): 106-111.

Ciment, Michel. *Kubrick*. Translated by Gilbert Adair New York: Holt, Rinehart & Winston, 1983, hardcover.

Coleman, J. *New Statesman* [England] Vol. 100, No. 2584 (3 October 1980): 30.

Combs, R. *Monthly Film Bulletin* [England] Vol. 47, No. 562 (November 1980): 222.

Cook, D. A. *Literature Film Quarterly* Vol. 12, No. 1 (January 1984): 2+.

Crist, Judith. "This Week's Movies." *TV Guide* (30 April-6 May 1983): A5-A6.

Denby, D. *New York Magazine* Vol. 13, No. 23 (9 June 1980): 60.

Edwards, Phil. "The Shining." *Starburst* [England] (1980): 24-27.

Fangoria No. 7 (1980?). Cover article.

Fangoria No. 33 (1993). Pullout poster.

Film [England] Vol. 91 (November 1980): 12.

Film BroadCasting Review Vol. 45, No. 12 (15 June 1980): 70.

Film Comment Vol. 16, No. 4 (July/August 1980): 28.

Flatley, G. *Cosmopolitan* Vol. 189, No. 2 (August 1980): 18.

Geduld, Harry. M. "Mazes and Murders." *The Humanist* Vol. 40, No. 5 (September/October 1980): 49-50.

Hala, James. "Kubrick's *The Shining*: The Specters and the Critics." *The Shining Reader*. Edited by Anthony Magistrale. Mercer Island WA: Starmont House, 1989, hardcover. 203-216.

Harvey, S. *Saturday Review* Vol. 7, No. 11 (July 1980): 64.

Hatch, R. *The Nation* Vol. 230, No. 23 (14 June 1980): 732.

Hofsess, John. "Kubrick: Critics Be Damned." *Soho News* [NY] 28 May 1980.

Hofsess, John. "The Shining Example of Kubrick." *Los Angeles Times* "Calendar" 1 June 1980: 1.

Hogan, D. J. *Cinefantastique* Vol. 10, No. 2 (Fall 1980): 38.

Hoile, C. Literature *Film Quarterly* Vol. 12, No. 1 (January 1984): 5+.

Jameson, Richard T. "Kubrick's *Shining*." *Film Comment* Vol. 16, No. 4 (July/August 1980): 28-32.

Jenkins, Greg. *Stanley Kubrick and the Art of Adaptation: Three Novels, Three Films.* Jefferson NC and London, England: McFarland, 1997. viii+173. ISBN 0786402814.

Kael, Pauline. *The New Yorker* Vol. 56, No. 16 (9 June 1980): 130-147.

Kael, Pauline. *5001 Nights at the Movies: A Guide from A to Z.* New York: Holt, Rinehart and Winston, 1982, hardcover. 528.

Kauffmann, Stanley. "The Dulling." *New Republic* Vol. 182, No. 24 (14 June 1980): 26-27.

Keeler, Greg. "*The Shining*: Ted Kramer Has a Nightmare." *Journal of Popular Film and Television* (Winter 1981): 2-8.

Kennedy, Harlan. "Kubrick Goes Gothic." *American Film* Vol. 5, No. 8 (June 1980): 49+ [4-page article].

Kroll, Jack. "Stanley Kubrick's Horror Show." *Newsweek* Vol. 95, No. 21 (26 May 1980): 96-99.

Leibowitz, F., and L. Jeffress. *Film Quarterly* Vol. 34, No. 3 (Spring 1981): 45.

Library Journal 114 (15 October 1989): 46.

Lightman, Herb. "Photographing Stanley Kubrick's *The Shining*: An Interview with John Alcott." *American Cinematographer* (August 1980): 760.

Macklin, Anthony F. "Understanding Kubrick: *The Shining*." *Journal of Popular Film and Television* Vol. 9, No. 2 (Summer 1981): 93-95.

Madigan, Mark. "'Orders From the House': Kubrick's *The Shining* and Kafka's 'The Metamorphosis.'" *The Shining Reader*. Edited by Anthony Magistrale. Mercer Island WA: Starmont House, 1989, hardcover. 193-202.

Magistrale, Anthony, ed. *The Shining Reader*. Mercer Island WA: Starmont House, 1989, cloth.

Malpezzi, Frances M., and William M. Clements. "The Shining." *Magill's Survey of Cinema*, 2nd Series, Vol. 5. Edited by Frank N. Magill. Englewood Cliffs, NJ: Salem Press, 1981: 2175-2178.

Mayersberg, Paul. "Overlook Hotel." *Sight and Sound* [England] Vol. 50, No. 1 (Winter 1980/1981): 54-55.

Miller, E. *Seventeen* Vol. 39, No. 8 (August 1980): 81.

Minton, L. *McCall's* Vol. 107, No. 11 (August 1980): 136.

Molina, Vincente. "An Interview with Stanley Kubrick." *Cahiers du Cinema* No. 319 (1981): 5-11.

Monthly Film Bulletin Vol. 47, No. 562 (November 1980): 228.

Munroe, D. *Film Bulletin* Vol. 49, No. 3 (May/June 1980).

Nash, Jay Robert, and Stanley Ralph Ross. "The Shining." *The Motion Picture Guide, 1927-1983*, Vol. VII. Chicago: Cinebooks, 1987, hardcover. 2886.

Nelson, Thomas Allen. "*The Shining*: Remembrance of Things Forgotten." *Kubrick: Inside a Film Artist's Maze*. Bloomington, IN: Indiana University Press, 1982, paper. 197-231.

Norton, M. J. *Creem* Vol. 12, No. 4 (September 1980): 47.

Otis, G. *Cinefantastique* Vol. 10, No. 3 (Winter 1980): 16.

Pearce, Howard D. "*The Shining* as Lichtung: Kubrick's Film, Heidegger's Clearing." *Forms of the Fantastic: Selected Essays from the Third International Conference on the Fantastic in Literature and Film*. Edited by Jan Nolanson and Howard Pearce. Westport, CT: Greenwood Press, 1986, hardcover. 49-57.

Powell, D. *Punch* [England] Vol. 279, No. 7301 (8 October 1980): 611.

Rainer, P. *Mademoiselle* Vol. 86, No. 8 (August 1980): 64.

Rothenbuecher, B. *Christian Century* Vol. 97, No. 2 (30 July-6 August 1980): 771.

Sarris, A. *The Village Voice* Vol. 25, No. 45 (5 November 1980): 49.

Sarris, A., and T. Allen. *The Village Voice* Vol. 28, No. 19 (10 May 1983): 59.
Schickel, Richard. "Red Herrings and Refusals." *Time* Vol. 115, No. 22 (2 June 1980): 69.
Schiff, S. *Glamour* Vol. 78, No. 8 (August 1980): 40.
Schow, David J. "Return of the Curse of the Son of Mr. King: Book Two." *Whispers* No. 17/18 (August 1982): 49-56.
Simon, J. *National Review* Vol. 32, No. 13 (27 June 1980): 795.
Smith, James. "Kubrick's or King's—Whose Shining Is It?" *The Shining Reader*. Edited by Anthony Magistrale. Mercer Island WA: Starmont House, 1989, hardcover. 181-192.
Snyder, S. *Film Criticism* Vol. 7 (Fall 1982): 4.
Stoop, N. M. *After Dark* Vol. 1, No. 4 (August 1980): 25.
Schillaci, P. *Mass Media* Vol. 17, No. 4 (14 July 1980): 7.
Titterington, P. L. "Kubrick and *The Shining*." *Sight and Sound* [England] Vol. 50, No. 2 (Spring 1981): 117-121.
Variety Vol. 299, No. 4 (28 May 1980): 14.
Video Choice 2 (October 1989): 2.
Wells, J. *Films in Review* Vol. 16, No. 4 (August/September 1980): 438.
Westerbeck, Collin. L., Jr. "The Waning of Stanley Kubrick." *Commonweal* Vol. 107, No. 14 (1 August 1980): 438-440.
Williamson, B. *Playboy* Vol. 27, No. 9 (September 1980): 28.
Wilson, William. "Riding the Crest of the Horror Craze." *New York Times Magazine* (11 May 1980): 42+.
Wynorski, Jim. "A New Definition for Ultimate Horror: *The Shining*." *Fangoria* (August 1980).

eeee. As FILM: *The Shining*. England: Warner Brothers, 1980. 120 minutes. 2 film reels, 16 mm.; only this shorter version is available in 16 mm. film.

ffff. As TELEPLAY/MINISERIES: *The Shining*. ABC, 1997. Produced by Mark Carliner. Directed by Mick Garris. Teleplay by Stephen King. On location at the Stanley Hotel, Estes Park CO. Aired 27 April, 28 April, 1 May 1997. Six hours. CAST: Steven Weber, Rebecca De mornay, Courtland Mead.
SELECTED FILM REVIEWS AND ARTICLES:
Schwed, Mark. "*The Shining*—It Lives Again." *TV Guide* Vol. 45, No. 17, Issue 2300 (26 April –2 May 1997): 18-22.

hhhh. As VIDEOCASSETTE: *The Shining*. Warner Brothers/Hawk Films. VHS, Beta. 143 minutes. Rated R. * SELECTED REVIEWS AND ARTICLES: * Sarris, A., and T. Allen. *The Village Voice* Vol. 32, No. 30 (28 July 1987): 49. * Thomson, D. *American Film* Vol. 11, No. 1 (October 1985): 76.

iiii. As VIDEOCASSETTE: *The Shining*. 1997. Swedish and English. VHS. 2 cassettes; 4 hours, 15 minutes.

jjjj. As VIDEODISC: *The Shining.* Burbank CA: Warner Brothers, 1980. 144 minutes. 2 videodiscs; extended play format.

COMMENTS: A superlative study of hauntings and madness, *The Shining* reflects the influence of Shirley Jackson's *The Haunting of Hill House* and stands as one of King's most consciously literary works and among those most accessible to classroom discussion; in addition, it is frequently included in "Best-of-King" lists and more scholarly lists of King's works that may achieve enduring status in literary canons. Originally structured as a five-act tragedy [see "Before the Play" B69], the novel was heavily revised to remove many overt signals of that structure. The Overlook Hotel is a compelling setting for interaction among several of King's strongest characters, including Dick Hallorann, who would reappear later in *IT*.

SELECTED ARTICLES, RESPONSES, AND REVIEWS:
Best Sellers (January 1976): 304.
Best Sellers (May 1977): 39.
Booklist (1 March 1977): 992.
Best of the Times [*New York Times*] Vol. 3 (August 1980): 387.
BooksWest Vol. 1, No. 1 (October 1977): 21.
Cohen, Alan. "The Collapse of Family and Language in Stephen King's *The Shining.*" *The Shining Reader.* Edited by Anthony Magistrale. Mercer Island WA: Starmont House, 1991. 47-60.
Dickerson, Mary Jane. "The 'Masked Author Strikes Again': Writing and Dying in Stephen King's *The Shining.*" *The Shining Reader.* Edited by Anthony Magistrale. Mercer Island WA: Starmont House, 1991. 11-22.
Eller, Jackie. "Wendy Torrance, One of King's Women: A Typology of King's Female Characters." *The Shining Reader.* Edited by Anthony Magistrale. Mercer Island WA: Starmont House, 1991. 33-46.
English Journal Vol. 68 (January 1979): 58.
Ferreira, Patricia. "Jack's Nightmare at the Overlook: The American Dream Inverted." *The Shining Reader.* Edited by Anthony Magistrale. Mercer Island WA: Starmont House, 1991. 23-32.
Hala, James. "Kubrick's *The Shining*: The Specters and the Critics." *The Shining Reader.* Edited by Anthony Magistrale. Mercer Island WA: Starmont House, 1991. 203-216.
Hatlen, Burton. "Good and Evil in Stephen King's *The Shining.*" *The Shining Reader.* Edited by Anthony Magistrale. Mercer Island WA: Starmont House, 1991. 81-104.
Hatlen, Burton. "Steve King's Third Novel Shines on." *The Maine Campus* [University of Maine, Orono] 1 April 1977.
Harris, Ian. "Two Versions of *The Shining.*" *Castle Rock: The Stephen King Newsletter* Vol. 3, No. 1 (December 1986-January 1987): 14-15.
Horner, Avril, and Sue Zlosnik. *Comic Gothic.* Salford, England: University of Salford, European Studies Research Institute, WORKING PAPERS IN LITERARY

AND CULTURAL STUDIES #32, 1998, 41 pp. ISBN 1901471802. Includes discussion King, George du Maurier, John Updike, and Bram Stoker.

Hyles, Vernon. "The Dark Side of Childhood: The 500 Hats of Bartholomew Cubbins and *The Shining.*" *The Shining Reader.* Edited by Anthony Magistrale. Mercer Island WA: Starmont House, 1991. 169-178.

Kent, Brian. "Canaries in a Gilded Cage: Mental and Marital Decline in *McTeague* and *The Shining.*" *The Shining Reader.* Edited by Anthony Magistrale. Mercer Island WA: Starmont House, 1991. 139-154.

Kirkus Reviews (1 December 1976): 1277.

Kliatt Paperback Book Guide Vol. 12 (Spring, 1978): 8.

Lehman-Haupt, Christopher. *New York Times* 24 June 1980: C9.

Lingeman, Richard R. "Something Nasty in the Tub." *New York Times* [Daily] 1 March 1977: 35.

Library Journal (1 February 1977): 404.

Madigan, Mark. "'Orders From the House': Kubrick's *The Shining* and Kafka's 'The Metamorphosis.'" *The Shining Reader.* Edited by Anthony Magistrale. Mercer Island WA: Starmont House, 1991. 193-202.

Magistrale, Tony. "Shakespeare in 58 Chapters: *The Shining* as Classical Tragedy." *The Shining Reader.* Edited by Anthony Magistrale. Mercer Island WA: Starmont House, 1991. 155-168.

Magistrale, Tony, ed. *The Shining Reader.* Mercer Island WA: Starmont House, 1991.

Meyers, Julia. "*The Shining.*" *Masterplots II: American Fiction Series, Vol. 4.* Edited by Frank N. Magill. Englewood Cliffs NJ: Salem Press, 1986, hardcover. 1407-1410.

Mustazza, Leonard. "The Red Death's Sway: Setting and Character in Poe's 'The Mask of the Red Death' and King's *The Shining.*" *The Shining Reader.* Edited by Anthony Magistrale. Mercer Island WA: Starmont House, 1991. 105-120.

Neilson, Keith. "*The Shining.*" *Survey of Modern Fantasy Literature*, Vol. 3. Edited by Frank N. Magill. Englewood Cliffs NJ: Salem Press, 1983. 1402-1406.

Patten, Frederick. *Delap's Fantasy and Science Fiction Review* (April 1977): 6. Excerpted: *Contemporary Literary Criticism, Vol. 12, Young Adult Literature.* Edited by Dedria Bryfonski. Detroit MI: Gale Research Co., 1980, hardcover. 310.

Publishers Weekly (6 December 1976): 52.

Publishers Weekly (14 November 1977): 64.

Reesman, Jeanne Campbell. "Stephen King and the Tradition of American Naturalism in *The Shining.*" *The Shining Reader.* Edited by Anthony Magistrale. Mercer Island WA: Starmont House, 1991. 121-138.

San Francisco Chronicle 27 March 1977: 34.

School Library Journal (December 1975): 70.

Smith, James. "Kubrick's or King's—Whose Shining Is It?" *The Shining Reader.* Edited by Anthony Magistrale. Mercer Island WA: Starmont House, 1991. 181-192.

Stanton, Michael N. "Once, Out of Nature: The Topiary." *The Shining Reader*. Edited by Anthony Magistrale. Mercer Island WA: Starmont House, 1991. 3-10.

Straub, Peter. "Stephen King: *The Shining*." *Horror: 100 Best Books*. Edited by Stephen Jones and Kim Newman. London, England: Xanadu, 1988. 171-172.

Sullivan, Jack. "Ten Ways to Write a Gothic." *New York Times Book Review* (20 February 1977): 8. Reprinted: *Contemporary Literary Criticism,* Vol. 12, Young Adult Literature. Edited by Dedria Bryfonski. Detroit MI: Gale Research, 1980, hardcover. 309-310.

Voice of Youth Advocates Vol. 6 (December 1983): 267.

Washington Post Book World [Washington DC] Vol. 16 (7 December 1986): 7.

Weller, Greg. "The Redrum of Time: A Meditation on Francisco Goya's 'Saturn Devouring His Children' and Stephen King's *The Shining*." *The Shining Reader*. Edited by Anthony Magistrale. Mercer Island WA: Starmont House, 1991. 61-78.

West Coast Review of Books (May 1977): 26.

Wiater, Stanley. "King's *Shining*—Very Bright." *The Valley Advocate* [Hatfield MA] 25 June 1980.

Wilson Library Bulletin (April 1977): 674.

Young, Elizabeth J. *New Statesman & Society* Vol. 3 (7 December 1990): 34.

El Resplandor. Barcelona, Spain: Plaza & Janés, 1982.
Mass-market paperback.

Rage. New York, NY: Signet/New American Library, 1977. Mass-market paperback.

A4.
RAGE
AS RICHARD BACHMAN
(1977)

A4. *RAGE*, by 'Richard Bachman.' New York: Signet/New American Library, 1977, 211 pp., $1.50, mass-market paperback. 451-W7645.

PLOT SUMMARY: High-school student Charlie Dekker shoots a teacher and holds his class hostage. As the students confront their insecurities and fears, they generate cutting indictments of American educational systems, of the American family, and of each other.

REPRINTS AND ADAPTATIONS:
b. London, England: New English Library, January 1983, 224 pp., paperback.
c. In: *The Bachman Books: Four Early Novels by Stephen King*. New York: New American Library, October 1985, hardcover. 1-131. See A30.
d. As *Razernij* ['Rage'] in: *4 X Stephen King*. Utrecht, Belgium: Luitingh, 1986, trade paperback. Dutch translation by Margot Bakker.
e. As: *Raseri* ['Rage']. Stockholm, Sweden: Legenda, 1987, 183 pp., 22 cm, hardcover and paperback. Swedish translation by Karl G. Fredriksson and Lilian Fredriksson. ISBN 91-582-1117-9; 91-582-1447-X.
f. As: *Raseri* ['Rage']. Höganäs, Sweden: Bra Böcker, 1987, 183 pp. Swedish translation.
g. As: *Rabia* ['Rage']. Barcelona, Spain: Martínez Roca, 1987, 203 pp., 22 cm., paperback. Spanish translation by Hernán Sabaté. ISBN 84-270-1150-4.
h. As: *Razernij* ['Rage'], by Stephen King. Utrecht, Belgium, Netherlands: Luitingh, 1988, 155 pp. Dutch translation by Margot Bakker. 90-245-1524-6. * Reprint, 1991, 403 pp. ISBN 90-245-1999-3.
i. As: *Amok* ['Crazy']. Munich, Germany: Wilhelm Heyne, TASCHENBUCH #7695, 1988, 220 pp., 7.80 DM, paperback. German translation by Joachim Honnef. * 17th edition, 1995. ISBN 3-453-02554-7.
j. As: *Raseri* ['Rage']. Stockholm, Sweden: Legenda, 1988, 183 pp., hardcover. Swedish translation by Karl G. Fredriksson and Lilian Fredriksson. ISBN 91-582-1302-3.

k. As: ['High school panic']. Tokyo, Japan: Fososha, 1988. Japanese translation by Hidano Yuko.
l. As: *Mareritt in rom 16* ['Nightmare in room 16']. Oslo, Norway: Egmont Bøker Fredhøi, 1989, 205 pp. Norwegian translation by Thomas Bjørnseth. ISBN 82-04-02263-8.
m. As: *Ossessione* ['Obsession']. Milan, Italy: Bompiani, I GRANDI TASCABILI BOMPIANI #140, 1991, 231 pp., 21 cm., paperback. Italian translation by Tullio Dobner. 3rd edition.
n. As: *Raivo/Pitkä marssi* ['Rage/Long walk']. Helsinki, Finland: Tammi, 1992, 446 pp., 23 cm. Finnish translation by Leevi Lehto. * 2nd printing, 1992. ISBN 951-30-9901-6.
o. Paris, France: J'ai Lu, #3439, 1993, 249 pp., 25 F, mass-market paperback. French translation by Évelyne Châtelain. ISBN 2-277-23439-7.
p. As: *Amok* ['Crazy']. Munich, Germany: Wilhelm Heyne Verlag, ALLGEMEINE REIHE #8933—AMERIKANISCHE BESTSELLER-AUTOREN 1993, 219 pp., 10.00 DM, paperback. ISBN 3-453-07371-1.
q. Paris, France: France Loisirs, 1994, 71 F, hardcover. French translation by Évelyne Châtelain. ISBN 2-7242-8196-9.
r. As: *Richard Bachman Todesmarch/Amok; Zwei Romane in einem Band* ['Richard Bachman—Deathmarch/Crazy: two novels in one volume']. Munich, Germany: Wilhelm Heyne, ALLGEMEINE REIHE #9468, April 1995, 315+219 pp., 14.00 DM, paperback. German translation by Nora Jensen. ISBN 3-453-082494-X.
s. As: *Rabia* ['Rage']. Barcelona, Spain: Planeta, 1995. Spanish translation. ISBN 84-27-01150-4.
t. As: *Mareritt in rom 16* ['Nightmare in room 16']. Oslo, Norway: Egmont Bøker Fredhøi, 1997, 205 pp., 595.00K, paperback [*heftet*]. Norwegian translation by Thomas Bjønrseth. ISBN 82-04-04971-4.
u. As: *Rabia* ['Rage']. Barcelona, Spain: Plaza & Janés, JET 102/18, BIBLIOTECA DE STEPHEN KING #18, 1997, 274 pp., 18 cm., paperback. Spanish translation by Hernán Sabaté. ISBN 84-01-47468-X.
v. As: *Rabia* ['Rage']. Barcelona, Spain: Martínez Roca, [1998], 203 pp., 23 cm. Spanish translation by Hernán Sabaté. ISBN 84-270-2413-4.
w. As: [Title unknown]. Moscow, Russia: Cadman. Russian translation
x. As: [Title unknown]. Moscow, Russia: AST. Russian translation.
y. As: *Rage*. Paris, France: J'ai Lu #3439, 2000, mass-market paperback. French Translation by Evelyne Châtelain. ISBN 2-290-30670-3.

z. AS STAGE PLAY: *Rage*. Blackburn Theater, Gloucester MA. 30 March 1989. Stageplay by Robert B. Parker and Joan Parker. Pearl Productions
    SELECTED REVIEWS AND ARTICLES:
    Hartigan, Patti. "The Play's the Thing for the Parker Family." *Castle Rock: The Stephen King Newsletter* Vol. 5, No. 6 (June 1989): 1, 12.
    "World Premiere of 'Rage' Hits Community March 30: Robert B.

Parker Sets Stage for Stephen King Novel." *PR Newswire* (8 March 1989).

COMMENTS: King's first novel published under the 'Richard Bachman' penname, *Rage* was begun while he was in high school and completed during his first year at the University of Maine, Orono. It is at times a moving and emotionally strong novel, but is generally considered by critics as among his lesser works.

Following an incident in 1998, in which a copy of *Rage* was found in the locker of a student involved in an *Rage*-like shooting, King withdrew the novel from print.

SELECTED ARTICLES, RESPONSES, AND REVIEWS:
Booklist Vol. 74 (15 October 1977): 353.
Brown. Stephen P. "The Life and Death of Richard Bachman: Stephen King's Doppelgänger." *Kingdom of Fear: The World of Stephen King*. Edited by Tim Underwood and Chuck Miller. San Francisco CA: Underwood-Miller, 1986. 109-126.
D'Ammassa, Don. "Three by Bachman." *Discovering Stephen King*. Edited by Darrell Schweitzer. Mercer Island WA: Starmont House, STARMONT STUDIES IN LITERARY CRITICISM #8, 1985.
Hatlen, Burton. "Stephen King and the American Dream: Alienation, Competition, and Community in *Rage* and *The Long Walk*." *Reign of Fear: Fiction and Film of Stephen King*. Edited by Don Herron. Los Angeles CA: Underwood-Miller, 1989. 19-50.
Kesseli, Douglas. "Kentucky Hostage Crisis Sounded Familiar to King." *Bangor Daily News* [ME] 20 September 1989. As microfiche: *NewsBank: Literature* 16 (November 1989): Fiche 112, F11. As microfiche: *NewsBank: Names in the News* Vol. 11 (October 1989): Fiche 290, F6.
Lowell, Dave. "King Play Is Raging Success." *Castle Rock: The Stephen King Newsletter* Vol. 5, No. 5 (May 1989): 4. Review of stage adaptation.
Porteau, Chris. "The Individual and Society: Narrative Structure and Thematic Unity in *Rage*." *Journal of Popular Culture* Vol. 27, No. 1 (Summer 1993): 171-177.
Publishers Weekly Vol. 212 (12 July 1977): 69.
Wilson Library Bulletin Vol. 52 (February 1978): 467.

The Stand. Garden City, NY: Doubleday, 1978. Hardcover.

A5.
THE STAND
EXPURGATED EDITION
(1978)

A5. *THE STAND.* Garden City NY: Doubleday, 1978, 823 pp., $12.95, hardcover. ISBN 0-382-12168-7. [See also A40]

PLOT SUMMARY: In a world devastated and nearly depopulated by a technologically designed plague, the Superflu, survivors struggle to restore order, purpose, and civilization to their ravaged world, as well as to understand the implications of mystical dreams that threaten to the vestiges of humanity into two opposing camps—one representing goodness and life, the other dedicated to evil and death. As characters work to restore their lives, they must choose to follow Abigail Freemantle or to throw their lot with an archetypal "Dark Man," Randall Flagg (see "The Dark Man" [D2], *The Eyes of the Dragon* [A24], The Dark Tower novels [A17, A34, A43, A61, and additional novels], *Insomnia* [A48], and *Hearts in Atlantis* [A65]).

REPRINTS AND ADAPTATIONS:
b. London, England: New English Library, March 1979, 840 pp., hardcover.
c. New York: Signet/New American Library, January 1980, 817 pp., paperback. 36th printing by September 1989.
d. London, England: New English Library, February 1980, 736 pp., paperback.
e. Garden City NY: Doubleday, [n.d.], 823 pp., hardcover. Science Fiction Book Club edition.
f. As: *Le Fléau* ['The plague/calamity']. Paris, France: Éditions Alta, 1981, 458 pp., 61,68 F, paperback. French translation by Richard Matas.
g. As: *L'Ombra dello Scorpione* ['The shadow of the scorpion']. Milan, Italy: Sonzogno, I ROMANZI, October 1983, 928 pp. Italian translation by Adriana Dell'Orto and Bruno Amato.
h. As: *De Beproeving* ['The test/ordeal']. Utrecht, Belgium: Luitingh/ Veen, 1984, 520 pp., trade paperback. Slightly abridged Dutch translation by Annelies van Dijck. ISBN 90-204-0961-1. 4th printing, 1986.
i. As: *L'Ombra dello Scorpione* ['The shadow of the scorpion']. Milan, Italy: Bompiani, I GRANDI TASCABILI #43, May 1985, 688 pp. Italian translation by Adriana Dell'Orto and B. Amato. Reprinted 1997.

j. As: *Das Letzte Gefecht* ['The last battle']. Bergisch Gladbach, West Germany: Bastei-Lübbe TB 28186, 1985, 864 pp., 24.80 DM, paperback. German translation by Harro Christensen. ISBN 3-404-28126-8.

k. As: *De Beproeving* ['The test/ordeal']. Utrecht, Belgium: Luitingh-Sijthoff, 1986, 520 pp. Slightly abridged Dutch translation by Annelies van Dijck. 3rd printing. ISBN 90-245-1542-4. 5th printing, 1990.

l. As: *Das Letzte Gefecht* ['The last battle']. Bergisch Gladbach, West Germany: Bastei-Lübbe Verlag, GEBUNDENE AUSGABE ['bound edition'], 1986, 763 pp., 38.00 DM., hardcover (?). German translation by Harro Christensen. 3rd edition 1987. ISBN 3-7857-0426-7.

m. As: *La Danza de la Muerte* ['The dance of death']. Esplugues de Llobregat, Barcelona, Spain: Plaza & Janés, ÉXITOS, 1986, 616 pp., 22 cm., paperback. Spanish translation by Eduardo Goligorsky. ISBN 84-01-32168-9; 84-286-0557-2. * 2nd printing, 1986, ISBN 84-01-32168-9. * 3rd printing, 1987.

n. London, England: New English Library, October 1987, 734 pp., £3.95, paperback. ISBN 0-450-04552-8.

o. As: *La Danza de la Muerte* ['The dance of death']. Buenos Aires, Argentina: Emecé, GRANDES NOVELISTAS, 1987, 632 pp., 20 cm. Spanish translation by Eduardo Goligorsky. ISBN 950-04-0666-7. * Reprint 1990. * Reprint, 1991. * Reprint, 1992. * Reprint, 1993.

p. As: *Le Fléau* ['The plague/calamity']. Paris, France: J'ai Lu, ÉPOUVANTE #2326, 1988, 571 pp., 30 F, mass-market paperback. French translation by Richard Matas. ISBN 2-277-22326-3.

q. As: *Pestens Tid* ['Time of pestilence/plagues']. Stockholm, Sweden: Legenda, 1988, 833 pp., 22 cm, hardcover. Swedish translation by Lennart Olaffson. ISBN 91-582-0921-2.

r. As: *Pestens Tid* ['Time of pestilence/plagues']. Höganäs, Sweden: Bra Böcker, 1988, 737 pp., hardcover. Swedish translation by Lennart Olaffson. No ISBN assigned.

s. As: *Das Letzte Gefecht: eine Vision von Untergang and Wiedergeburt der Menschheit* ['The last battle: a vision of the destruction and restoration of mankind']. Bergisch Gladbach, West Germany: Bastei-Lübbe Verlag, TB #13213, 1989, 1017 pp., 14.80 DM, paperback. German translation by Harro Christensen. ISBN 3-404-13213-0.

t. As: *Das Letzte Gefecht* ['The last battle']. Gütersloh, Austria: Bertelsmann Lesering, [1989], 762 pp., paperback. German translation by Harro Christensen. Book Club edition.

u. As: *Slutspil: Dødens skygge.* ['End-game/play: death's shadow'—Book One: Captain Trips]. [Copenhagen], Denmark: Bogfabrikken, 1989, 215 pp. Danish translation by Mogens Wenzel Andreasen. ISBN 87-72971037.

v. As: *Slutspil: Grænslandet* ['End-game/play: borderland'—Book Two: On the Border]. [Copenhagen], Denmark: Bogfabrikken, 1989, 290 pp. Danish translation by Mogens Wenzel Andreasen. ISBN 87-72971045.

w. As: *Slutspil: Den rensende ild* ['End-game/play: the cleansing fire'—Book Three: The Stand]. [Copenhagen], Denmark: Bogfabrikken, 1989, 167 pp.

Danish translation by Mogens Wenzel Andreasen. ISBN 87-72971053..

x. As: *Das Letzte Gefecht* ['The last battle']. Stuttgart and Munich, Germany: Deutscher Bücherbund, [1989], 762 pp. German translation by Harro Christensen. Book Club edition.

y. As: *La Danza de la Muerte* ['The dance of death']. Esplugues de Llobregat, Barcelona, Spain: Plaza & Janés, JET #102/11, BIBLIOTECA DE STEPHEN KING #11, 1989, 860 pp., 844 pta, 18 cm., paperback. Spanish translation by Eduardo Goligorsky. 1st edition in this format. ISBN 84-01-49891-0.

z. New York: Doubleday, 1990, 823 pp., hardcover. Issued in conjunction with the publication of the uncut version of *The Stand*.

aa. As: *La Danza de la Muerte* ['The dance of death']. Barcelona, Spain: Círculo de Lectores, 1990, 794 pp., 1769 pta., 23 cm., hardcover. Spanish translation by Eduardo Goligorsky. ISBN 84-226-3241-1.

bb. As: *L'Ombra dello Scorpione* ['The shadow of the scorpion']. Milan, Italy: Sonzogno, I ROMANZI, June 1991. Italian translation by Adriana Dell'Orto and Bruno Amato. Revised and expanded edition. ISBN 88-454-0400-5.

cc. As: *L'Ombra dello Scorpione* ['The shadow of the scorpion']. Milan, Italy: Bompiani, I GRANDI TASCABILI #43, October 1992, paperback. Italian translation by Adriana Dell'Orto and Bruno Amato. Revised and expanded edition.

dd. As: *The Stand*. Bergisch Gladbach, West Germany: Bastei-Lübbe, 1 November 1999, paperback (*kartoniert*). German translation. ISBN 3-404-25524-0.

ee. As AUDIOCASSETTE: *The Stand*. Newport Beach CA: Books on Tape, #2163-A and 2163-B, 1987; 33 tapes in 2 boxed parts; unabridged, 49_ hours. Read by Grover Gardner. ISBN 3353843-003, 3357414-001
    SELECTED REVIEWS:
    Audio Video Review Digest, 1989 Cumulation. Edited by Susan L.
        Stetler. Detroit MI: Gale Research, 1990. 619.
    Hiett, John. *Library Journal* Vol. 114 (15 March 1989): 100.

ff. As AUDIOCASSETTE: *The Stand*. Victoria, Australia: Louise Braille Productions, 1988.
    SELECTED REVIEWS:
    Library Journal Vol. 114 (14 March 1989): 100. (?)

gg. As AUDIOCASSETTE: *The Stand*. [Vancouver, British Columbia]: Library Services Branch, Province of British Columbia, 1993. 24 cassettes; 30 hours, 40 minutes.

hh. As TELEPLAY: *Stephen King's The Stand*. ABC miniseries. May 8-9, 11-12, 1994. Greengrass and Laurel/Spelling. Executive producers: Richard P. Rubinstein and Stephen King. Associate producer: Michael Gornick.

Directed by Mick Garris; teleplay by Stephen King. CAST: Gary Sinise, Adam Storke, Rob Lowe, Molly Ringwald, Corin Nemec, Jamey Sheridan, Miguel Ferrer, Laura San Giacomo, Ruby Dee, Bill Fagerbakke, Ray Walston, Ed Harris, Ossie Davis, Matt Frewer, Kareem Abdul-Jabbar, Kathy Bates.

Promotional brochure includes "The Making of The Stand" and a short interview with King; some copies also include a four-color card from ABC signed by director Garris

Part I, Episode 1: "The Plague." Sunday, May 8, 9:00-11:00 PM; 89 minutes.

Part I, Episode 2: "The Dreams." Monday, May 9, 9:00-11:00 PM; 89 minutes.

Part II, Episode 3: "The Betrayal." Wednesday, May 11, 9:00-11:00 PM; 89 minutes.

Part II, Episode 4: "The Stand." Thursday, May 12, 9:00-11:00 PM; 93 minutes.

SELECTED FILM REVIEWS AND ARTICLES:

Everett, Tod. "The Stand." *Variety* Vol. 355, No. 1 (2 May 1994): 42.

Giles, Jeff. "The Stand." *Newsweek* Vol. 123, No. 19 (9 May 1994): 70.

Jarvis, Jeff. "The Couch Critic: Stephen King's The Stand." *TV Guide* Vol. 42, No. 19 #2145 (7 May 1994): 7.

Leonard, John. *New York* Vol. 27, No. 19 (9 May 1994): 84.

O'Connor, John J. "Stephen King's The Stand." *The New York Times* Vol. 143 (6 May 1994): B12 (N), D17 (L).

Wood, Gary. "The Stand: The Filming of King's Masterpiece Has Been a Movie Deal More Than Ten Years in the Making." *Cinefantastique* Vol. 21, No. 4 (February 1991): 28-29.

Zoglin, Richard. *Time* Vol. 143, No. 19 (9 May 1994): 83.

ii. As VIDEOCASSETTE: *Stephen King's The Stand.* Republic Pictures; Greengrass Productions, 1994. Four cassettes. Also available in LASERDISC box set, which includes "The Making of The Stand."

COMMENTS: 175,000 mass-market paperback copies sold in 1979; the book ranked 6th on the *Publishers Weekly* annual paperback bestsellers list for that year. Thirteen hardcover printings had appeared by September, 1989. King subsequently published an uncut, slightly updated version of the novel [see A40].

Complex intertwining of characters and plots gives the novel a surprising depth, while King's skill at characterization and his shift from science-fictional disaster motifs into quasi-religious apocalyptic fantasy elevates the novel above usual run-of-the-mill, end-of-the-world novels and—in hindsight—set the standard for this particular cross-genre. *The Stand* frequently ranks with general readers and fans as a favorite among King's novels; with its complicated tone, its minute realism of presentation, and its vastness of scope, the novel is also among his most successful, especially within the classroom.

SELECTED ARTICLES, RESPONSES, AND REVIEWS:
Analog Science Fiction/Science Fact Vol. 100 (August 1980): 163.
Arrington, Carl Wayne. "Stephen King: The Making of 'The Stand.'" *TV Guide* Vol. 42, No. 19, #2145 (7 May 1994): 11-13. Interview-article in conjunction with the television mini-series.
Booklist Vol. 75 (1 December 1978): 601.
The Catalyst [Salt Lake City UT] (1988).
Chanen, Audrey Wolff. "American Holocaust Novels (John Hersey, Leon Uris, Flannery O'Connor, Stephen King)." Unpublished Ph.D. Dissertation, University of Iowa, 1987, 172 pp.
Cheever, Leonard. "Apocalypse and the Popular Imagination: Stephen King's *The Stand*." *RE: Artes Liberales* Vol. 8 (Fall 1981).
Collings, Michael R. "*The Stand*: Science Fiction into Fantasy." *Discovering Stephen King*. Edited by Darrell Schweitzer. Mercer Island WA: Starmont House, STARMONT STUDIES IN LITERARY CRITICISM #8, 1985. 83-90.
Collins, Anne. "No Sympathy for the Devil." *Maclean's Magazine* Vol. 91 (18 December 1978): 51. Excerpted: *Contemporary Literature Criticism*, Vol. 12, Young Adult Literature. Edited by Dedria Bryfonski. Detroit MI: Gale Research Co., 1980, hardcover. 311.
Conaty, Barbara. *Library Journal* Vol. 103 (15 November 1978): 2351.
Cousins, Diane. "Reader's Pick: *The Stand*." *Castle Rock: The Stephen King Newsletter* Vol. 1, No. 11 (November 1985): 1, 2.
Egan, James. "Apocalypticism in the Fiction of Stephen King." *Extrapolation* [Kent State University] Vol. 25 (Fall 1984): 214-227.
Egan, James. "Technohorror: The Dystopian Vision of Stephen King." *Extrapolation* [Kent State University] Vol. 29, No. 2 (Summer 1988): 140-152.
Furgeson, Mary. "*The Stand*." *Survey of Modern Fantasy Literature*, Vol. IV. Edited by Frank Magill. Englewood Cliffs NJ: Salem Press, 1983, hardcover. 1801-1806.
Gustainis, J. Justin. *Best Sellers* Vol. 38 (March 1979): 378. Excerpted: *Contemporary Literary Criticism*, Vol. 12, Young Adult Literature. Edited by Dedria Bryfonski. Detroit MI: Gale Research Co., 1980, hardcover. 311.
Hatlen, Burton. "The Destruction and Re-Creation of the Human Community in Stephen King's *The Stand*." *Footsteps* Vol. 5 (April 1985): 56-60.
Hatlen, Burton. "Steve King's *The Stand*." *Kennebec* (April 1979).
Indick, Ben P. "Stephen King as an Epic Writer." *Discovering Modern Horror Fiction*, Vol. I. Edited by Darrell Schweitzer. Mercer Island WA: Starmont House, STARMONT STUDIES IN LITERARY CRITICISM #4, July 1985. 56-67.
Jarvis, Jeff. "The Couch Critic: *Stephen King's The Stand*." *TV Guide* Vol. 42, No. 19, #2145 (7 May 1994): 7. Review of television mini-series.
Kirkus Reviews Vol. 46 (1 September 1978): 965-966. Excerpted: *Contemporary Literary Criticism*, Vol. 12, Young Adult Literature. Edited by Dedria Bryfonski. Detroit MI: Gale Research Co., 1980, hardcover. 309.
Laidlaw, Bill. *Nyctalops* Vol. 2, No. 7 (1978): 34. Excerpted: *Contemporary*

Literary Criticism, Vol. 12, Young Adult Literature. Edited by Dedria Bryfonski. Detroit MI: Gale Research Co., 1980, hardcover. 311.
Levin, Martin. "Genre Items." *New York Times Book Review* (4 February 1979): 15.
Los Angeles Times Book Review (18 December 1978): 51.
Magistrale, Tony. "Free Will and Sexual Choice in *The Stand*." *Extrapolation* [Kent State University] Vol. 34, No. 1 (Spring 1993): 30-38.
McDonald, J. V. *America* Vol. 140 (17 February 1979): 117.
McLellan, Joseph. "Vision of Holocaust." *Washington Post* [Washington DC] 30 August 1979.
Meyers, Julia. *"The Stand."* *Masterplots II: American Fiction Series,* Vol. 4. Edited by Frank N. Magill. Englewood Cliffs NJ: Salem Press, 1986, hardcover. 1532-1535.
Murphy, Mary. "Rob Lowe Saves Himself—And the World." *TV Guide* Vol. 42, No. 19, #2145 (7 May 1994): 15-17. In conjunction with the television mini-series.
New Yorker 54 (15 January 1979): 109.
Osbourne, Linda B. "The Supernatural Con Man vs. the Hymn-Singing Mother." *Washington Post* [Washington DC] 23 November 1978.
Publishers Weekly Vol. 214 (25 September 1978): 127.
Publishers Weekly (12 November 1979): 56.
Rathburn, Fran Miller. "Anatomy of a Best Seller: Form, Style, and Symbol in Stephen King's *The Stand*." Unpublished M.A. Thesis, Stephen F. Austin State University, 1981, 191 pp.
Roraback, Dick. "Gift of Sight: Visions from a Nether World." *Los Angeles Times Book Review* (26 August 1979).
Schwed, Mark. "Playing the Devil's Advocate." *TV Guide* Vol. 42, No. 19, #2145 (7 May 1994): 17 [sidebar]. In conjunction with the television mini-series.
Shiner, Lewis. "A Collision of Good and Evil." *Dallas Morning News* [TX] 28 November 1978.
Spignesi, Stephen J. *"The Stand."* *The Shape Under the Sheet: The Complete Stephen King Encyclopedia.* Ann Arbor MI: Popular Culture, Ink., May 1991, hardcover. 204-225.

Horror Plum'd

MICHAEL R. COLLINGS

NIGHT SHIFT. Garden City, NY: Doubleday, 1978. Hardcover.

A6.
NIGHT SHIFT
(1978)

A6. *NIGHT SHIFT.* Garden City NY: Doubleday & Co., 1978, xxii+336 pp., $8.95, hardcover. Short-fiction collection. ISBN 0-385-12991-2. * 11th hardcover printing by September, 1989. * 13th printing, May 1990. * Reprint, October 1993, $30.00.

CONTENTS: "Introduction," by John D. MacDonald; "Foreword," by King (see C55); "Jerusalem's Lot" (1978; see B38); "Graveyard Shift" (1970; see B12); "Night Surf" (1969; see B8); "I Am the Doorway" (1971; see B14); "The Mangler" (1972; see B18); "The Boogeyman" (1973; see B19); "Gray Matter" (1973; see B21); "Battleground" (1972; see B17); "Trucks" (1973; see B20); "Sometimes They Come Back" (1974; see B23); "Strawberry Spring" (original version 1968; see B7); "The Ledge" (1976; see B28); "The Lawnmower Man" (1975; see B24); "Quitters, Inc." (1978; see B40); "I Know What You Need" (1976; see B29); "Children of the Corn" (1977; see B31); "The Last Rung on the Ladder" (1978; see B39); "The Man Who Loved Flowers" (1977; see B34); "One For the Road" (1977; see B32); "The Woman in the Room" (1978; see B41).

REPRINTS AND ADAPTATIONS:
b. Garden City NY: Doubleday, [n.d.], 336 pp., hardcover. Science Fiction Book Club edition.
c. Burnsville MN: Econo-Clad/Sagebrush, 326 pp., $14.55, library binding. #1008044.
d. London, England: New English Library, 1978, xxiii+336 pp., hardcover.
e. As: *Una Splendida Festa di Morte* ['A splendid feast of death']. Milan, Italy: Sonzogno, NARRATIVA SONZOGNO, 1978, 432 pp. Italian translation by Adriana Dell'Orto.
f. New York: Signet/New American Library, February 1979, 327 pp., paperback. ISBN 0-451-17011-3. * 44th printing by September, 1989. * Reprint, December 1994, $7.99.
g. London, England: New English Library, 1979, 316 pp., paperback.
h. As: *El Umbral de la Noche* ['The threshold of the night']. Barcelona, Spain:

Pomaire, 1979, 426 pp., 432 pta., 20 cm., paperback. 20 stories from *Night Shift*, plus King's "Preface" and introduction by John D. MacDonald. Spanish translation by Eduardo Goligorsky. ISBN 84-286-0357-X/0356-1.

CONTENTS: "Introducción," de John MacDonald; "Prefacio"; "Los misterios del gusano" ['The mystery of the worm'; "Jerusalem's Lot"] ; "El último turno" ['The last turn/shift'; "Graveyard Shift"]; "Marejada nocturna" ['Heavy sea of night'; "Night Surf"]; "Soy la puerta" ['I am the door']; La trituradora" ['The crusher/grinder'; "The Mangler"]; "El coco" ["The Boogeyman"]; "Materia gris" ["Gray Matter"]; "Campo de batalla" ['battlefield'; "Battleground"]; "Camiones" ["Trucks"]; "A veces vuelven" ['Sometimes they return'; "Sometimes They Come Back"]; "La primavera de fresa" ["Strawberry Spring"]; "La Cornisa" ['The cornice'; "The Ledge"]; "El hombre de la cortadora de césped" ["The Lawnmower Man"]; "Basta, S.A." ['That's enough, limited'; "Quitters, Inc."]; "Sé lo que necesitas" ["I Know What You Need"]; "Los niños del maiz" ["Children of the Corn"]; "El último peldaño de la escalera" ["The Last Rung on the Ladder"]; "El hombre que amaba las flores" ["The Man Who Loved Flowers"]; "Un trago de despedida" ['The farewell-mouthful': "One for the Road"]; "La mujer de la habitación" ["The Woman in the Room"].

i. As: *Danse Macabre: Nouvelles* [Danse macabre: short stories']. [Paris, France]: Alta, 1980, 349 pp., 42,05 F, paperback. French translations by Lorris Murail and Natalie Zimmermann.

j. In: *The Shining, 'Salem's Lot, Night Shift, Carrie*. London, England: Octopus Books, 1981, hardcover. Omnibus edition. [see A13].

k. As: *A volte ritornano* ['The turn re-turned' (?)]. Milan, Italy: Sonzogno, NARRATIVA SONZOGNO, January 1981. Italian translation by Hilia Brinis.

CONTENTS: Prefazione ["Preface"] pp. 9-22; "Jerusalem's Lot" pp. 23-59; "Secondo turno di notte" ["Graveyard Shift"] pp. 60-78; "Risacca notturne" ["Night Shift"] pp. 79-88; "Io sono la porte" ['I am the Door"] pp. 89-103; "Il compressore" ["The Mangler"] pp. 104-125; "Il baubau" ["The Boogeyman"] pp. 126-138; "Materia grigia" ["Gray Matter"] pp. 139-151; "Campo di Battaglia" ["Battleground"] pp. 152-162; "Camion" ["Trucks"] pp. 163-180; "A volte ritornano" ["Night Shift"] pp. 181-211; "Primavera da fragole" ["Strawberry Spring"] pp. 212-222; "Il cornicione" ["The Ledge"] pp. 223-241; "La falciatrice" ["The Lawnmower Man"] pp. 242-252; "Quitters, Inc." pp. 253-274; "So di che cosa hai bisogno" ["I Know What You Need"] pp. 275-299; "Il figli del grano" ["The Children of the Corn"] pp. 300-330; "L'ultimo piolo" ["The Last Rung on the Latter"] pp. 331-343; "L'uomo che amava I fiori" ["The Man Who Loved Flowers"] pp. 344-349; "Il bicchiere della staffa" ["One for the Road"] pp. 350-366; "La donna nella stanza" ["The Woman in the Room"] pp. 367+.

l. As: *Sombras da noite* ['Shadows of night']. Rio de Janeiro, Brazil: Francisco Alves, MESTRES DO HORROR E DA FANTASIA, 1982, 380 pp., 21 cm.

Portuguese translation by Luis Horatia da Matta. * 2nd printing, 1987. * 3rd printing, 1991.
m. New York: Signet, March 1984, 327 pp., $3.50, mass-market paperback. 28th printing; movie tie-in edition with *Children of the Corn*. ISBN 0-451-12656-4.
n. As: *Nachtschicht* ['Night-shift']. Bergisch Gladbach, West Germany: Bastei-Lübbe, 1984, 414 pp., 19.80 DM, paperback. ISBN 3-404-28114-4.
o. As: *Nattmennesker* ['Night-men']. Oslo, Norway: Hjemmets, CASINO GRØSSER, 1984, 319 pp. Norwegian translation by Thor Dag Halvorsen. ISBN 82-7315-302-9.
p. As: *De Satanskinderen en andere Verholen* ['Satan's children and other stories']. Utrecht, Belgium: Luitingh/Veen, 1985, 248 pp., trade paperback. Abridged. Dutch translation by F. J. Bruning. ISBN 90-204-0997-2. * 3rd printing, 1986, ISBN 90-245-1541-6.

   CONTENTS: "De Satanskinderen" ['Satan's children'; "Children of the Corn"]; "Ratten" ['Rats'; "Graveyard Shift"]; "De Boeman" ['The Boogeyman"]; "Doodtij" ['Dead tide'; "Night Surf"]; "De Rozige Lente" ['The rose spring'; "Strawberry Spring"]; "De Richel" ['The Ledge"]; "De Patiente van Kamer 312" ['The patient in room 312'; "The Woman in the Room"]; "Een Afzakkertje" ['One for the road"]; "Twee maal twee is vier" ["Grey Matter']; "Soms keren ze terug" ['Two times they come back'; "Sometimes They Come Back"]; "De Mangel" ["The Mangler"]; "Ik Ben de Toegang" ["I Am the Doorway"]; "Pastorale" ['Pastoral'; "The Lawnmower Man"]; "Afspraak met Norman" ['Rendezvous with Norman'; "The Man Who Loved Flowers"].
q. As: *It Weet Wat Je Wilt* ['I know what you want']. Utrecht, Belgium: Luitingh/Veen, Autumn 1985, 320 pp., trade paperback. Abridged Dutch translations by F. J. Brunning and Pauline Moody. ISBN 90-245-1398-7. * 2nd printing, 1986.

   CONTENTS: Seven stories from *Night Shift* and *Different Seasons*, including: "Stop ermee B. V." ["Quitters' Inc."]; "Jerusalem's Lot"; "Trucks"; "Ik weet wat je wilt" ["I Know What You Want"]; "De laatste laddersport" ["The Last Rung on the Ladder"]; "De ademhalingsmethode" ["The Breathing Method"].
r. As: *Dödsbädden* ['Death-bed']. [Stockholm, Sweden]: B. Wahlström, 1985, 409 pp., hardcover. Swedish translation. ISBN 91-32-31231-8.
s. As: *El Umbral de la Noche* ['The threshold of the night']. Esplugues de Llobregat, Barcelona, Spain: Plaza & Janés, JET #102—BIBLIOTECA DE AUTOR DE: STEPHEN KING #3, 1985, 519 pp., paper. Spanish translation by Eduardo Goligorsky and Gregorio Vlastelica. 1st edition. ISBN 84-01-49883-X. * 2nd printing 1986, 406 pp., 18 cm., paperback, ISBN 84-01-49883-X. * 3rd printing, 1987, ISBN 84-01-49883-X. * 7th printing, 1989, ISBN 84-01-49883-X.
t. As: *Yhu mi tien te hai tzu*. Taipei, Taiwan: Huang kuan chu pan she, 1985. Chinese translation by Chang Ting and Yin Chin-sheng.

Michael R. Collings

u. As: *Katzenauge* ['Cat's Eye']. Bergish Gladbach, West Germany: Bastei-Lübbe TB #13088, 1986, 236 pp., paperback. German translations by Karin Balfer, Harro Christensen, Barbara Heidkamp, Ingrid Herrmann, Wolfgang Holbein, Michael Kubiak, Sabine Kuhn, Ulrike A. Pollay, Bernd Seligman, Stefan Sturm. ISBN 3-404-13088-X. * 9th printing, 1 January 1990. * 12th printing, 1992. * 18th printing, 1995. * 19th printing, 1996.

CONTENTS: "Geschichten aus den Dunkel—Über des Phänomen des Schriftstellers, Drehbuchautors und Film Regisseurs Stephen King" ['Stories from the dark—concerning the phenomenon of writers, screen-writers and directors for Stephen King's films'], by Willy Loderhose; "Katzenauge: Wie es zu der Verfilmung kam" ['Cat's Eye: how it came to be filmed"], by Willy Loderhose; "Quitters Inc."; "Der Mauervorsprung" ['The Ledge"]; "Trucks: Bemerkungen vor Filmung" ['Trucks: comments about the filming'], by Willy Loderhose; "Trucks"; "Kinder des Zorns: Bemerkungen zur Entstehung des Films" ['Children of Wrath: comments on the film"], by Willy Loderhose; "Kinder des Mais" ["Children of the Corn"]

v. As: *A volte ritornano* ['The turn re-turned' (?)]. Milan, Italy: Bompiani, I Grandi Tascabili #56, October 1986. Italian translation by Hilia Brinis. ISBN 88-452-0169-4.

w. As: *Trucks*. Bergisch Gladbach, West Germany: Bastei-Lübbe Verlag, #13043, 1986, 185 pp., 6.80 DM, paperback. Abridged German translations by Karin Balfer, Harro Christensen, Barbara Heidkamp, Ingrid Herrmann, Wolfgang Hohlbein, Michael Kubiak, Sabine Kuhn, Ulrike A. Pollay, Bernd Seligman, Stefan Sturm. * Reprinted August 1990. * 12th printing, 1992. * 18th printing, 1995. ISBN 3-404-13043-X.

CONTENTS: "Geschichten aus den Dunkel—Über des Phänomen des Schriftstellers, Drehbuchautors und Film Regisseurs Stephen King" ['Stories from the dark—concerning the phenomenon of writers, screen-writers and directors for Stephen King's films'], by Willy Loderhose; "Trucks," "Kinder des Zorns" ['Children of the Corn'], "Der Mauervorsprung" ['The Ledge'], and "Quitters, Inc."

x. As: [Title unknown]. Tokyo, Japan: Sankei Shuppan, 1986. Japanese translation.

y. London, England: New English Library, October 1987, 409 pp., £3.50, paperback. ISBN 0-450-04268-5. * Reprint, May 1991. Movie tie-in edition with *Graveyard Shift*. * 23rd printing, August 1992, £4.99.

z. As: *De Laatste Laddersport* ['The last ladder-rung']. Utrecht, Belgium: Luitingh, 1987, 173 pp. Abridged Dutch translation by F. J. Bruning. ISBN 90-245-1783-4.

aa. As: *Trucks*. Utrecht, Belgium: Luitingh, 1987, 188 pp. Abridged Dutch translation by F. J. Bruning. ISBN 90-245-1773-7.

bb. As: *Dödsbädden* ['Death-beds']. [Falun], Sweden: B. Wahlström, 1987, 410 pp., 18 cm., paperback. Swedish translation by Ansis Grinbergs. 3rd edition. ISBN 91-32-42672-0.

cc. As: *Nachtschicht: Meistererzählungen. Horror bis zum Morgengrauen* ['Night-shift: master stories. Horror until morning light']. Bergisch Gladbach, West Germany: Gustav Lübbe, 21 August 1987, 416 pp., hardcover. German translation. ISBN 3-7857-0467-4.
dd. As: *Tomorokoshi batake no kodomotachi* [or *Shinya kinmu*]. Tokyo, Japan: Sankei Shuppan, 1987. Japanese translation by Takabatake Fumio.
ee. As: [Title unknown]. Rio de Janeiro, Argentina: Francisco Alves, 1987. Portuguese translation.
ff. As: *Nachtschicht* ['Night-shift']. Bergisch Gladbach, West Germany: Bastei-Lübbe, 1988, 340 pp., 9.80 DM, paperback. German translation by Barbara Heidkamp and others. * 8th printing, 1992. ISBN 3-404-13160-6. * Reprint, 1 March 1993, 'Deutsche Erstausgabe'; ISBN 3-404-28114-4
gg. As: *De Satanskinderen en andere Verholen* ['Satan's children and other stories']. Utrecht, Belgium: Luitingh-Sijthoff, 1988, 365 pp. Dutch translation by F. J. Bruning. 5th printing. ISBN 90-245-1794-X. * 6th printing, 1990,
hh. As: *Dödsbädden* ['Death-beds']. [Stockholm, Sweden]: B. Wahlström, 1989, 410 pp., 22 cm., hardcover. Swedish translation by Ansis Grinbergs. 2nd edition. ISBN 91-32-31453-1.
ii. As: *El Umbral de la Noche* ['The threshold of the night']. Esplugues de Llobregat, Barcelona, Spain: Plaza & Janés Editores, JET #102—BIBLIOTECA DE AUTOR DE: STEPHEN KING #3, 1989, 414 pp., trade paperback. Spanish translation by Gregorio Vlastilica and Eduardo Goligorsky. ISBN 84-01-49102-9. * 2nd printing, May 1992.
jj. As: *Yön Äänet* ['Night silence']. Helsinki, Finland: Viihdeviikarit, 1989, 285 pp., 18 cm. Finnish translation by Reijo Kalvas. ISBN 951-611-270-6. * 3rd printing, 1992.
kk. New York: Doubleday, 1990, 336 pp., hardcover. Issued in conjunction with the publication of the uncut version of *The Stand*.
ll. As: *Nachtschicht* ['Night-shift']. Kornwesterheim, Austria: Europäische Bildungsgemeinschaft; Gütersloh, Austria: Bertelsmann Lesering; Zug, Switzerland: Buch-und-Schallplattenfreunde, [1990], 414 pp. German translation. Book Club edition.
mm. As: *Natholdet* ['Night-team'—*Night Shift*, part 1]. Copenhagen, Denmark: Artia, 1990, 242 pp., 18 cm., 128 KR, paperback. Danish translation by Mogens Wenzel Andreasen. ISBN 87-89294-23-8.
nn. As: *Væddemålet* ['The bet' (?)—*Night Shift*, part 2]. Copenhagen, Denmark: Artia, 1990, 204 pp., 18 cm., 128 KR, paperback. Danish translation by Mogens Wenzel Andreasen. ISBN 87-89294-25-4.
oo. As: *Turno da noite* ['Night shift/turn']. Venda Nova, Portugal: Bertrand, 1990, 506 pp., 24 cm. Portuguese translation by Maria Meonor Macedo. ISBN 972-25-0498-3.
pp. London, England: New English Library, September 1991, 336 pp., £14.99, hardcover. ISBN 0-450-03692-8.
qq. As: *Nachtschicht: Meistererzählungen* ['Night-shift: master-stories']. Stuttgart and Munich, Germany: Deutsche Bücherbund, [1991], 410 pp.

German translation by Karin Balfer. Book Club edition.
rr. As: *Natholdet* ['Night-team']. Copenhagen, Denmark: Artia, 1992, 442 pp., 88 KR, paperback. Danish translation by Mogens Wenzel Andreasen. Complete text in one volume. ISBN 87-89918-04-5.
ss. New York: Doubleday, October 1993, 441 pp., $25.00, hardcover. Cover art by Thomas Holdorf. ISBN 0-385-12991-2.
tt. As: *Danse Macabre*. Paris, France: J C Lattés, SUSPENSE & CIE, 1993, 349 pp., paperback. French translations by Lorris Murail and Natalie Zimmermann. ISBN 2-7096-1331-X.
uu. As: *Danse Macabre*. Paris, France: France Loisirs, 1994, 407 pp., 88 F, hardcover. French translations by Lorris Murail and Natalie Zimmermann. ISBN 2-7242-7840-2.
vv. As: *Nocna zmiana* ['Night shift']. Warsaw, Poland: "Prima," BESTSELLERY LITERATURY ŒWIATOWEJ, 1994, 382 pp., 20 cm. Polish translation by Michal Wroczyñski. ISBN 83-8585-540-8.
ww. As: *Nachtschicht* ['Night-shift']. Bergisch Gladbach, West Germany: Bastei-Lübbe, 1995, 447 pp., 9.90 DM, paperback. German translation by Barbara Heidkamp and others. 15th printing. ISBN 3-404-13160-6.
xx. As: *Nattmennesker* ['Night-men']. Oslo, Norway: Hjemmets bokforlag, 1996, 319 pp., 179.00, hardcover [*innforbundet*]. Norwegian translation by Thor Dag Halvorsen. ISBN 82-590-1654-0.
  CONTENTS: "Jerusalems Lot"; "Hundevakt" ["Graveyard Shift"]; "Mørke bølger" ["Night Surf"]; "Jeg er et redskap" ["I am the Doorway"]; "Vaskeriet" ["The Mangler"]; "Busemannen" ["The Boogeyman"]; "Slagmark" ["Battleground"]; "Trucks"; "Mareitt fra fortiden" ["Sometimes They Come Back"]; "Jordbaervår" ["Strawberry Summer"]; "Gesimsen Plenklipp" ["The Lawnmower Man"]; "Jeg vet hva du trenger" ["I Know What You Need"]; "Maisbarna" ["Children of the Corn"]; "Det siste trinnet på stigen" ["The Last Rung on the Ladder"]; "Mannen som elsket blomster" ["The Man Who Loved Flowers"]; "Skål for vinteren" ["One for the Road"]; "Kvinnen i sykevaerlset" ["Gray Matter"]; "Quitters, Inc."
yy. As: *El Umbral de la Noche* ['The threshold of the night']. Esplugues de Llobregat, Barcelona, Spain: Plaza & Janés Editores, JET 102—BIBLIOTECA DE AUTOR DE: STEPHEN KING #3, 1995, 416 pp., 18 cm., paperback. Spanish translation by Gregorio Vlastilica and Eduardo Goligorsky. 2nd edition; 11th printing. ISBN 84-01-49986-0.
zz. As: *Trucks*. Bergisch Gladbach, West Germany: Bastei-Lübbe Verlag, #13088, 1996, 236 pp., 9.90 DM, paperback. Abridged German translations by Karin Balfer, Harro Christensen, Barbara Heidkamp, Ingrid Herrmann, Wolfgang Hohlbein, Michael Kubiak, Sabine Kuhn, Ulrike A. Pollay, Bernd Seligman, Stefan Sturm. ISBN 3-404-13088-X.
aaa. As: *Satanskinderen*. Amsterdam, Netherlands: Poema Pocket, 1996, 365 pp., paperback. Dutch translation by F. J. Bruning. 8th printing. ISBN 90-245-2676-0.

bbb. As: *Nattmennesker* ['Night-men']. Oslo, Norway: Hjemmets, STEPHEN KINGS UTVALGTE, 1996, 319 pp., hardcover. Norwegian translation by Thor Dag Halvorsen. ISBN 82-590-1654

ccc. As: *A volte ritornano* ['The turn re-turned' (?)]. Milan, Italy: R. L. Libri, SUPER POCKET #5, February 1997, paperback. Italian translation by Hilia Brinis. ISBN 88-462-0004-7.

ddd. Excerpted as: *L'homme qu'il vous faut: et autres nouvelles* ['The man that you want: and other stories'—*Danse Macabre/Night Shift*, vol. 3]. Paris, France: J'ai Lu, #233, 1998, 90 pp., 10 F, mass-market paperback. French translations by Lorris Murail and Natalie Zimmermann. ISBN 2-277-30233-3.

eee. Excerpted as: *Les enfants du maïs: et autres nouvelles* ['Children of the corn: and other stories'—*Danse Macabre/Night Shift* 4]. Paris, France: J'ai Lu, #249, 1998, 93 pp., 10 F, mass-market paperback. French translations by Lorris Murail and Natalie Zimmermann. ISBN 2-277-30249-X.

fff. New York: Signet, February 1999, 326 pp., $7.99, mass-market paperback. 66th printing. ISBN 0-451-17011-3.

ggg. As: [Title unknown]. Greece: Ataeia & Tpomoe. Greek translation.

hhh. As AUDIOCASSETTE: *Night Shift*. New York: Warner Audio, 1986. Directed by Stuart Leigh. Read by Colin Fox. 6 cassettes. Abridged as: *Stories from Night Shift*, New York: Sound Editions/Random House, 1988. 2 cassettes; 130 minutes. Read by Colin Fox.
CONTENTS: "Strawberry Spring," "The Boogeyman," "Graveyard Shift," "The Man Who Loved Flowers," "One for the Road," "The Last Rung on the Ladder," "I Know What You Need," "Jerusalem's Lot," "I Am the Doorway."
SELECTED AUDIOCASSETTE REVIEWS:
Publishers Weekly Vol. 231 (3 July 1987): 38.
School Library Journal Vol. 32 (August 1986): 24.

iii. As AUDIOCASSETTE: *Night Shift, Vol. 1*. New York: BDD [Bantam Doubleday Dell] Audio, 1994. Read by John Glover. 4 cassettes.
CONTENTS: "The Bogeyman," "I Know What You Need," "Strawberry Spring," "The Woman in the Room," "Battleground."

jjj. As AUDIOCASSETTE: *Graveyard Shift and Other Stories from Night Shift* [*Night Shift*. Vol. 2]. New York.: BDD [Bantam Dell Doubleday] Audio, July 1994. 3 cassettes; 205 minutes. ISBN 0-553-47245-3.

kkk. As AUDIOCASSETTE: *The Lawnmower Man and Other Stories from Night Shift*. Read by John Glover. ASIN 0-553-47661-0.

lll. As AUDIOCASSETTE: *Gray Matter and Other Stories*. 1993. ASIN 0-553-47183-X.

mmm. As AUDIOCASSETTE: *Stephen King: Nachtschicht*. Bergisch Gladbach: Lübbe Audio, 14 October 1996. 3 cassettes, 256 minutes, boxed set. 29.90 DM. Read by Joachim Kerzel. ISBN 3-7857-1000-3. Ranked #2 on the Lübbe Audio charts.

nnn. As AUDIOCASSETTE: *Stephen King Collection: Stories from Night Shift*. New York: Bantam, 2000. Read by John Glover.
   CONTENTS: "Gray Matter," "The Boogeyman," "I Know What You Need," "Strawberry Spring," "The Woman in the Room," "Battleground," "The Graveyard Shift," "The Man Who Loved Flowers," "The Last Rung on the Ladder," "Night Surf," "Jerusdalem's Lot," "The Lawnmower Man," "The Mangler," "Quitters, Inc. ," "The Ledge," "Sometimes They Come Back."
ooo. As AUDIO CD: *Stephen King: Trucks—Der Rasenmähermann* ['Trucks—The lawnmower-man']. Bergisch Gladbach, West Germany: Audio Lübbe, 9 April 1999. 1 CD, 3 hours, 23 minutes. Read by Joachim Kerzel; music by Michael Marianetti. ISBN 3-7857-1045-3.
ppp. Excerpted as FILM: *Cat's Eye*. MGM/United Artists, April 1985. Executive producer, Dino de Laurentiis. Directed by Martha J. Schumacher. Directed by Lewis Teague. Screenplay by Stephen King. 94 minutes. Rating: PG-13.
qqq. As VIDEOCASSETTE: Beta/VHS. 94 minutes.
   CAST: Drew Barrymore, James Woods, Alan King, Kenneth McMillan, Robert Hays, Candy Clark, James Naughton.
   EPISODES: "Quitter's Inc." [38 minutes; see B40]; "The Ledge" [26 minutes; see B28]; "The General" [30 minutes; original to the film].
   SELECTED FILM REVIEWS AND ARTICLES:
   Adams, Jim. "'Cat's Eye' Only 'Mildly Interesting.'" *Union Leader* [Manchester NH] 19 April 1985. As microfiche: *Newsbank: Film and Television* Vol. 11 (May 1985): Fiche 109, E8.
   Ansen, Davie. "Cat Calls and Wolf Whistles." *Newsweek* Vol. 105, No. 18 (6 May 1985): 73. Excerpted: *Contemporary Literary Criticism*, Vol. 37. Edited by Daniel G. Marowski. Detroit MI: Gale Research, 1986, hardcover. 206.
   Baron, David. "King's Latest Chiller Not Up to His Scary Standards." *Times Picayune* [New Orleans LA] 18 April 1985. As microfiche: *Newsbank: Film and Television* Vol. 11 (May 1985): Fiche 109, E3.
   Briggs, Joe Bob [pseud. for John Bloom]. "Big Steve Is the Cat's Pajamas." *USA Today* 8 May 1985.
   Canby, Vincent. "'Cat's Eye' Is a Stylish, Clever Thriller." *Sacramento Bee* [CA] 15 April 1985. As microfiche: *Newsbank: Film and Television* Vol. 11 (May 1985): Fiche 109, D6-D7.
   "Cat's Eye." *Take One* (October 1985).
   "Cat's Eye Reviews." *Castle Rock: The Stephen King Newsletter* Vol. 1, No. 6 (June 1985): 5.
   Cosford, Bill. "Three Thrillers for Feline Fans." *Miami Herald* [FL] 17 April 1985. As microfiche: *Newsbank: Film and Television* 11 (May 1985): Fiche 109, D13.
   Edelstein, D. *The Village Voice* Vol. 30, No. 17 (23 April 1985): 57.
   Elliot, David. "The Gleam in 'Cat's Eye' Doesn't Hide Blind Spots." *San Diego Union* [CA] 23 April 1985. As microfiche: *Newsbank:*

Film and Television Vol. 11 (May 1985): Fiche 109, D8.

Fangoria No. 43 (March 1985).

Fiely, Dennis. "New King a 'Cat' Above." *Columbus Dispatch* [OH] 15 April 1985. As microfiche: *Newsbank: Film and Television* Vol. 11 (May 1985): Fiche 109, F1.

French, Lawrence. "Cat's Eye." *Cinefantastique* Vol. 15, No. 4 (October 1985): 36.

"From King, Shivers and Laughs." *Philadelphia Inquirer* [PA] 13 April 1985. As microfiche: *Newsbank: Film and Television* Vol. 11 (April 1985): Fiche 98, B1.

Hewitt, Tim. "*Cat's Eye*: Horror Master Stephen King Blends Stories from *Night Shift* with a Dash of Macabre Humor." *Cinefantastique* Vol. 15, No. 2 (May 1985): 9-11.

Hewitt, Tim. "Stephen King's Cat's Eye." *Cinefantastique* Vol. 15, No. 4 (October 1985): 34-39.

Horsting, Jessie. "A Director's Eye View of Stephen King's *Cat's Eye*." *Fantastic Films* (June 1985): 20-21, 42.

Hunter, Stephen. "'Cat's Eye' Raises Questions King Won't Answer." *Sun* [Baltimore MD] 15 April 1985. As microfiche: *Newsbank: Film and Television* Vol. 11 (April 1985): Fiche 98, A13.

Johnson, Malcolm. "Fearless Feline Ties Together Fun Tales of 'Cat's Eye.'" *Hartford Courant* [CT] 17 April 1985. As microfiche: *Newsbank: Film and Television* Vol. 11 (May 1985): Fiche 109, D11.

Johnson, Paul. "'Cat's Eye' Relies on Ironic Twist." *Arkansas Gazette* [Little Rock AR] 26 April 1985. As microfiche: *Newsbank: Film and Television* Vol. 11 (May 1985): Fiche 109, D3.

Kelley, Bill. "Cat's Eye." *Cinefantastique* Vol. 14, No. 3 (July 1985): 52.

Leydon, Joe. "More Fun Than Fright in King's 'Cat's Eye.'" *Houston Post* [TX] 16 April 1985. As microfiche: *Newsbank: Film and Television* Vol. 11 (May 1985): Fiche 109, F3.

Loderhose, Willy. "Geschichten aus dem Dunkel: Über des Phänomen des Schriftstellers, Drehbuchautors und Filmregisserus Stephen King" ['Tales from the dark: Concerning the phenomenon of writers, screenwriters, and film directors for Stephen King films']. *Katzenauge* ['Cat's Eye']. Bergisch Gladbach, West Germany: Bastei-Lübbe, 1986.

Loderhose, Willy. "Katzenauge: Wie es zu der Verfilmung Kam" [Cat's Eye: How it came to be filmed']. *Katzenauge* ['Cat's Eye']. Bergisch Gladbach, West Germany: Bastei-Lübbe, 1986.

Loderhose, Willy. "Trucks: Bermerkungen zur Verfilmung" ['Trucks: Comments on the filming']. *Katzenauge* ['Cat's Eye']. Bergisch Gladbach, West Germany: Bastei-Lübbe, 1986.

Lovell, Glen. "Scares to Give You Pause in 'Cat's Eye.'" *San Jose*

Mercury News [CA] 13 April 1985. As microfiche: *Newsbank: Film and Television* Vol. 11 (May 1985): Fiche 109, D10.

Lucas, W. D., and W. Miedema. *Classical Images* Vol. 126 (December 1985): 19.

Lyman, Rick. "'Cat's Eye' Winningly Macabre Horror Trio." *The Oregonian* [Portland OR] 17 April 1985. As microfiche: *Newsbank: Film and Television* Vol. 11 (May 1985): Fiche 109, F2.

Matheny. Dave. "King Writes Screenplay and Produces a Hit in 'Cat's Eye.'" *Minneapolis Star and Tribune* [MN] 19 April 1985. As microfiche: *Newsbank: Film and Television* Vol. 11 (May 1985): Fiche 109, E6.

McLeod, Michael. "'Cat's Eye' Works as Comedy, Horror." *Cincinnati Enquirer* [OH] 15 April 1985. As microfiche: *Newsbank: Film and Television* Vol. 11 (May 1985): Fiche 109, E13.

Minton, L. *McCalls* Vol. 112, No. 10 (July 1985): 50.

Morrison, Bill. "Stephen King Leaves Out Terror, Makes 'Cat's Eye' Seem Like TV Movie." *News and Observer* [Raleigh NC] 25 April 1985. As microfiche: *Newsbank: Film and Television* Vol. 11 (May 1985): Fiche 109, E11.

Moynihan, Martin. "King's Pen Crackles to Life in 'Cat's Eye.'" *Times Union* [Albany NY] 18 April 1985. As microfiche: *Newsbank: Film and Television* Vol. 11 (May 1985): Fiche 109, E9.

Mueller, Roxanne T. "Violent Steve King Beats a Dead Horse." *Cleveland Plain Dealer* [OH] 16 April 1985. As microfiche: *Newsbank: Film and Television* Vol. 11 (May 1985): Fiche 109, E14.

Newman, K. *Monthly Film Bulletin* Vol. 52, No. 618 (July 1985): 211.

O'Connor, Bill. "'Cat's Eye' Should've Been TV Show." *Akron Beacon Journal* [OH] 19 April 1985. As microfiche: *Newsbank: Film and Television* Vol. 11 (May 1985): Fiche 109, E12.

Patton, Charlie. "Stephen King Film Anthology Shows Whimsy of Horror Master." *Florida Times-Union* [Jacksonville FL] 25 April 1985. As microfiche: *Newsbank: Film and Television* Vol. 11 (May 1985): Fiche 109, D12.

People Weekly (6 May 1985). Review with photographs.

Rainer, Paul. "'Cat's Eye': The Latest Model Stephen King." *Los Angeles Herald Examiner* [CA] 12 April 1985. As microfiche: *Newsbank: Film and Television* Vol. 11 (May 1985): Fiche 109, D4.

Rhetts, JoAnn. "'Cat's Eye': The Latest Film from Stephen King's Work." *Charlotte Observer* [NC] 17 April 1985. As microfiche: *Newsbank: Film and Television* Vol. 11 (May 1985): Fiche 109, E10.

Ricky, Carrie. "Tabby with ESP Is the Real Star." *Boston Herald* [MA] 12 April 1985. As microfiche: *Newsbank: Film and Television* Vol. 11 (April 1985): Fiche 98, A14.

Roddick, N. *Cinema Papers* No. 54 (November 1985): 74.

Rose, Rita. "King Trilogy Is Stomach-Turner." *Indianapolis Star* [IN] 16 April 1985. As microfiche: *Newsbank: Film and Television* Vol. 11 (May 1985): Fiche 109, E1.

Salamon, Julie. *Wall Street Journal* (April 25, 1985): 34.

Shorey, Kenneth. "'Cat's Eye.'" *Birmingham News* [AL] 18 April 1985. As microfiche: *Newsbank: Film and Television* Vol. 11 (May 1985): Fiche 109, D2.

Siskel, Gene. "King's 'Cat's Eye' Trio Dogged by Limp Pause." *Chicago Tribune* [IL] 15 April 1985. As microfiche: *Newsbank: Film and Television* Vol. 11 (May 1985): Fiche 109, D14.

Spignesi, Stephen J. "Dog (and Cat) Days: An Interview With Lewis Teague." *The Shape Under the Sheet: The Complete Stephen King Encyclopedia*. Ann Arbor MI: Popular Culture, Ink, May 1991, hardcover. 572-574.

Stack, Peter. "'Cat's Eye': Three Tales from Stephen King." *San Francisco Chronicle* [CA] 15 April 1985. As microfiche: *Newsbank: Film and Television* Vol. 11 (May 1985): Fiche 109, D9.

"Stephen King's Cat's Eye." *Des Moines Register* [IA] 18 April 1985. As microfiche: *Newsbank: Film and Television* Vol. 11 (May 1985): Fiche 109, E2.

"Stephen King's Latest Effort Isn't a Classic, But Holds Its Own With Some Suspense, Humor." *Grand Rapids Press* [MI] 16 April 1985. As microfiche: *Newsbank: Film and Television* Vol. 11 (May 1985): Fiche 109, E4.

Strauss, Bob. "Stephen King's Cat's Eye." *Monsterland* (June 1985): 55-57, 66. Interview-article with Candy Clark, Drew Barrymore's mother in "The General."

Thomas, Kevin. "A Sly Trio of Vignettes from a 'Cat's Eye' View." *Los Angeles Times* [CA] 12 April 1985. As microfiche: *Newsbank: Film and Television* Vol. 11 (May 1985): Fiche 109, D5.

Trussell, Robert C. "Film Is Entertaining, But Barely Scratches Surface." *Kansas City Star* [MO] 15 April 1985. As microfiche: *Newsbank: Film and Television* Vol. 11 (May 1985): Fiche 109, E7.

Variety Vol. 318, No. 12 (17 April 1985): 10.

Vincent, Mal. "'Cat's Eye' Has Been Declawed." *Virginian-Pilot* [Norfolk VA] 17 April 1985. As microfiche: *Newsbank: Film and Television* Vol. 11 (May 1985): Fiche 109, F4.

Wilson, Gahan. "TZ Screen." *Twilight Zone Magazine* Vol. 5, No. 4 (October 1985): 96-98.

Wood, Gary. "Animal Lovers vs. Pets Run Amuk." *Cinefantastique* Vol. 21, No. 4 (February 1991): 42.

"Writer King Is the Attraction of His Homogenized Movies." *Atlanta Journal-Constitution* [GA] 21 April 1985. As microfiche: *Newsbank: Film and Television* Vol. 11 (May 1985): Fiche 112.

rrr. Excerpted as VIDEOCASSETTE: *Night Shift Collection*. Granite Entertainment Group, Canoga Park CA. Includes film versions of *The Boogeyman* and *The Woman in the Room*.
    SELECTED FILM REVIEWS AND ARTICLES:
    Fangoria No. 52 (1986).
    sss. Excerpted as VIDEOCASSETTE: *Stephen King's Nightshift Collection*. Karl James Associates. Directed by John Woodward and Jack Garrett. 1989. 45 minutes. No rating.
    EPISODES: "Disciples of the Crow" (1983); "The Night Waiter" (1987—student film).

SELECTED ARTICLES, RESPONSES, AND REVIEWS:
Booklist Vol. 74 (15 March 1978): 1165.
Crider, Bill. *Best Sellers* 38 (April 1978): 6-7. Excerpted: *Contemporary Literary Criticism*, Vol. 12, Young Adult Literature. Edited by Dedria Bryfonski. Detroit MI: Gale Research Co., 1980, hardcover. 310-311.
Kirkus Reviews Vol. 45 (1 December 1977): 1285.
Kliatt's Paperback Book Guide Vol. 13 (Spring 1979): 27.
Los Angeles Times "Books" (23 April 1978): 13.
Lyles, W. H. *Library Journal* Vol. 103 (February 1978): 385. Excerpted: *Contemporary Literary Criticism,* Vol. 12, Young Adult Literature. Edited by Dedria Bryfonski. Detroit MI: Gale Research Co., 1980, hardcover. 31+.
Magistrale, Tony. "Stephen King's Vietnam Allegory: An Interpretation of 'Children of the Corn.'" *Cuyahoga Review* Vol. 2, No. 1 (Spring/Summer 1984): 61-66. Reprinted: *Footsteps* Vol. 5 (April 1985): 61-65.
Mewshaw, Michael. "Novels and Stories." *New York Times Book Review* 26 March 1978: 13, 23. Excerpted: *Contemporary Literary Criticism,* Vol. 12, Young Adult Literature. Edited by Dedria Bryfonski. Detroit MI: Gale Research Co., 1980, hardcover. 310.
Neilson, Keith. "Night Shift." *Survey of Modern Fantasy Literature*, Vol. 3. Edited by Frank N. Magill. Englewood Cliffs, NJ: Salem Press, 1983, hardcover. 116-120.
Nolan, William F. "The Good Fabric: Of Night Shifts and Skeleton Crews." *Kingdom of Fear: The World of Stephen King*. Edited by Tim Underwood and Chuck Miller. Columbia PA: Underwood-Miller, 1986. 99-106.
Publishers Weekly Vol. 212 (28 November 1977): 46.
Voice of Youth Advocates Vol. 6 (December 1983): 266.
West Coast Review of Books Vol. 4 (May 1978): 33.

Horror Plum'd

THE DEAD ZONE. New York, NY: Viking, 1979. Hardcover.

A7.
THE DEAD ZONE
(1979)

A7. *THE DEAD ZONE.* New York: Viking Press, 30 August 1979, 426 pp., 25 cm., $11.95, hardcover. 1st edition of about 50,000 copies. ISBN 0-670-26077-0. * Reissued, July 1987.

PLOT SUMMARY: Johnny Smith emerges from an extended accident-induced coma able to see the future. Distanced from his normal world by his gift and by its increasingly enervating effects on him, he attempts to use his visions wisely. When he foresees a cataclysmic disaster, however, he must choose between murdering a single individual or allowing a world to suffer under the threat of destruction.

REPRINTS AND ADAPTATIONS:
b. New York: Viking, [n.d.], 372 pp., hardcover. Science Fiction Book Club edition.
c. London, England: Macdonald and Jane's, RAVEN, 1979, 426 pp., hardcover.
d. New York: Signet/New American Library, August 1980, 403 pp., paper. ISBN 0-451-15575-0. * 30th printing by September, 1989. * 50th printing, January 1999.
e. London, England: Futura, August 1980, 467 pp., paperback. ISBN 0-7088-1874-9.
f. As: *Dodelijk Dilemma* ['Deadly dilemma']. Utrecht, Belgium: Luitingh/Veen, 1980, 408 pp., f 24.50, trade paperback. Lightly abridged Dutch translation by Margot Bakker. ISBN 90-204-0275-7. * 8th printing, 1986.
g. As: *Das Attentat* ['The assault/attempted murder']. Munich, West Germany: Moewig, PLAYBOY-ROMAN, 1980, 416 pp., 7.80 dm, paperback. Radically abridged German translation by Alfred Dunkel. ISBN 3-8118-6110-7.
h. As: *Morke Krefter* ['Dark forces']. Oslo, Norway: Hjemmets Bokklubb, 1980, 336 pp. Norwegian translation by Axel S. Seeberg. ISBN 82-7001-671-3.
i. As: *La Zona Muerta* ['The dead zone']. Barcelona, Spain: Pomaire, 1980,

491 pp., 750 pta., 21 cm. Spanish translation by Edouardo Goligorsky. ISBN 84-286-0591-2. * Reprint, 1981.

j. As: *La Zona Morta* ['The dead zone']. Milan, Italy: Sperling & Kupfer, PANDORA #112, September 1981, 464 pp. Italian translation by A[ndrea] Terzi. 88-200-0175-6.

k. As: *A zona da morte* ['The zone of death']. Lisbon, Portugal: Livros do Brasio, VIDA E AVENTURA #34, 1981, 427 pp., 22 cm. Portuguese translation by Virgínia Motta.

l. As: *La Zone Muerta* ['The dead zone']. Barcelona, Spain: Mundo Actual de Ediciones, 1981, 481 pp., 20 cm. Spanish translation by Eduardo Goligorsky. ISBN 84-7454-142-5.

m. As: *Zona Morta* ['Zone of death']. Rio de Janeiro, Brazil: Record, [1982?], 397 pp., 21 cm. Portuguese translation by Luzia Machado da Costa.

n. As: *La Zona Muerta* ['The dead zone']. Panama: Printer Internacional de Panamá, 1982. Spanish translation.

o. As: [Title unknown]. Bogota, Colombia: Circulo de Lectores, 1982. Spanish translation.

p. New York: Signet, 1983, paperback. Movie tie-in edition. ISBN 0-451-12666-1.

q. Anstey, Leicestershire, England: Thorpe, CHARNWOOD LIBRARY SERIES, Ulversoft Large Print Books, December 1983, 656 pp., hardcover. Large print edition.

r. As: *L'Accident* ['The accident']. Paris: Jean-Claude Lattés, 1983, 375 pp., 23 cm., paperback. French translation by Richard Matas.

s. As: *Död Zon* ['Dead zone']. Stockholm, Sweden: Askild and Kørnekull, 1983, 508 pp., paperback. Swedish translation by Jimmy Hofsö. ISBN 91-582-0314-1. * Reprinted 1984.

t. As: *Dodelijk Dilemma* ['Deadly dilemma']. Utrecht, Belgium: Skarabee, 1984, 408 pp., trade paperback. Dutch translation by Margot Bakker. 5th printing. ISBN 90-6071-292-7.

u. As: *Dead Zone*. Paris, France: Librairie générale française, LE LIVRE DE POCHE #7488, 1984, 477 pp. French translation. ISBN 2-253-03526-2.

v. As: *The Dead Zone: Buch zum Film* ['Book to film']. Rastatt, West Germany: Arthur Moewig, TB 2277, 1984, 416 pp., 7.80 DM, paperback. Radically abridged German translation by Alfred Dunkel. As "Buch zum Film." ISBN 3-8118-2277-2.

w. As: *La Zona Muerta* ['The dead zone']. Esplugues de Llobregat, Barcelona, Spain: Plaza & Janés, JET #68, July 1985, 456 pp., 18 cm., paperback. Spanish translation by Eduardo Goligorsky. ISBN 81-04-49068-5. * Reprint, 1986, ISBN 81-04-49068-5. * Reprint 1989, BIBLIOTECA DE STEPHEN KING, Vol. 5.

x. As: *La Zona Muerta* ['The dead zone']. Buenos Aires, Argentina: Emecé, GRANDES NOVELISTAS, 1985, 491 pp., 20 cm., paperback. Spanish translation by Eduardo Goligorsky. ISBN 950-04-0461-3. * Reprint, 1988. * Reprint, 1990. * Reprint, 1996.

HORROR PLUM'D

y. As: *Zona Morta* ['Zone of death']. Sao Paulo, Brazil: Circulo de Livro, [1985], 391 pp., 22 cm. Portuguese translation by Luzia Machado da Costa.

z. As: *Zona Morta* ['Zone of death']. Sao Paulo, Brazil: Abril Cultural, BEST SELLERS, 1985, 389 pp., 19 cm. Portuguese translation by Luzia Machado da Costa.

aa. As: *Morke Krefter* ['Dark forces']. Oslo, Norway: Hjemmets Bokklubb, 1985, 335 pp. Norwegian translation by Axel S. Seeberg. ISBN 82-7315-377-0.

bb. As: *Zona Muerta* ['Dead zone']. Ciudad de Mexico: Edivisión Compaña Editorial, 14 March 1986, 452 pp., trade paperback. Spanish translation by Eduardo Goligarsky. 15,000 copies. ISBN 968-13-1556-1.

cc. London, England: Futura, July 1986, 467 pp., £2.95, paperback. ISBN 0-7088-1874-9.

dd. As: *Dodelijk Dilemma* ['Deadly dilemma']. Utrecht, Belgium [later Amsterdam, Netherlands]: Luitingh-Sijthoff, 1986, 408 pp. Dutch translation by Margot Bakker. 7th printing. ISBN 90-245-1991-8. * 11th printing, 1991. * 13th printing, 1994.

ee. As: *La Zona Morta* ['The dead zone']. Milan, Italy: Arnoldo Mondadori, OSCAR #1929, January 1987, 464 pp. Italian translation by A[ndrea] Terzi. ISBN 88-04-29726-3.

ff. As: *Dead Zone: Das Attentat* ['Dead Zone: the assault/attempted murder']. Munich, Germany: Wilhelm Heyne, TB #6953, 1987, 558 pp., 9.80 DM, 18 cm., paperback. Unabridged German translation by Joachim Körber, based on the abridged translation by Alfred Dunkel. ISBN 3-453-00704-2. * 4th printing, 1988. * 10th printing, 1990. * 11th printing, 1991. * 15th printing, 1992. * 21st printing, 1993. * 24th printing, 1994. * 27th printing, 1995.

gg. As: *Mertvaia Zona*. Moscow, Russia: Molodaia Gvardiia, 1987. Russian translation by N. Paltseva.

hh. As: *La Zona Muerta* ['The dead zone']. Esplugues de Llobregat, Barcelona, Spain: Plaza & Janés, JET 102/5, 1987, 450 pp., 18 cm., paperback. Spanish translation by Eduardo Goligorsky. ISBN 84-01-49885-6. * Reprint, 1990, BIBLIOTECA DE STEPHEN KING #5. * Reprint, 1996. * Reprint, 1998, ISBN 84-01-49988-7.

ii. Tokyo, Japan: Shinchoshya, 1987, paperback. 2 vols. Japanese translation by Yoshino Mieko.

jj. As: *Den døde zone* ['The dead zone']. Copenhagen, Denmark: Artia, 1988, 433 pp., 21 cm., 198 KR, paperback. Danish translation by Mogens Wenzel Andreasen. ISBN 87-89294-00-9. * Reprint, 1989.

kk. As: *Das Attentat* ['The assault/attempted murder']. Kornwesterheim, Austria: Europäische Bildungsgemeinschaft; Gütersloh, Austria: Bertelsmann Lesering; Zug, Switzerland: Buch-und-Schallplattenfreunde, [1988], 475 pp. German translation by Joachim Körber. Book Club edition.

ll. Stuttgart/Hamburg, Munich, Germany: Deutscher Bücherbund, 1988. German translation by Joachim Körber. Book Club edition.

mm. As: *La Zona Morta* ['The dead zone']. Milan, Italy: Arnoldo Mondadori,

89

Michael R. Collings

BESTSELLERS OSCAR #135, September 1989. Italian translation by A[ndrea] Terzi. ISBN 88-04-32941-6.

nn. As: *Död Zon* ['Dead zone']. [Stockholm, Sweden]: Legenda, POCKET, 1988, 508 pp., paperback. Swedish translation by Jimmy Hofsö. ISBN 91-582-0554-3.

oo. As: *Kosketus* ['Touch']. Helsinki, Finland: Tammi, 1989, 463 pp., 23 cm. Finnish translation by Heikki Karjalainen. ISBN 951-30-7036-0.

pp. As: *Dead Zone: L'accident.* [Paris, France]: de la Seine, SUCCÈS DU LIVRE, 1989, 375 pp., 66 F, hardcover. French translation by Richard Matas. ISBN 2-7382-0159-8.

qq. As: *Morke Krefter* ['Dark forces']. Oslo, Norway: Damm, DAMMS BESTE #6, 1989, 336 pp. Norwegian translation by Axel S. Seeberg. ISBN 82-517-7118-8.

rr. As: *Död Zon* ['Dead zone']. Stockholm, Sweden: Legenda, 1990, 508 pp., 22 cm., *kartonn*. Swedish translation by Jimmy Hofsö. 7th printing. ISBN 91-582-0605-1.

ss. As: *Den døde zone* ['The dead zone']. [Copenhagen], Denmark: Bogsamleren, 1991, 319 pp. Danish translation by Mogens Wenzel Andreasen. ISBN 87-75313251.

tt. As: *Den døde zone* ['The dead zone']. Copenhagen, Denmark: Hørst, HORST PAPERBACK, 1992, 431 pp., 98 KR, paperback. Danish translation by Mogens Wenzel Andreasen. ISBN 87-14-19169-5. * 2nd printing, 1993.

uu. As: *Den døde zone* ['The dead zone']. Copenhagen, Denmark: Wangel, WANGEL POCKET, 1992, 319 pp., 31,95 KR, paperback. Danish translation by Mogens Wenzel Andreasen. ISBN 87-7443-691-0.

vv. As: *Dead Zone: L'accident.* [Lyon, France]: Profrance-Maxi livres, 1992, 375 pp., 52 F, paperback. French translation by Richard Matas. ISBN 2-87628-467-7.

ww. As: [Title unknown]: South Korea, 1992, 345 pp.[313 pp.?], 23 cm. Korean translation. ISBN 89-85315-08-0.

xx. As: *La Zona Muerta* ['The dead zone']. Barcelona, Spain: Plaza & Janés, ÉXITOS, 1992, 450 pp., 22 cm.. Spanish translation by Eduardo Goligorsky. ISBN 84-01-32420-3.

yy. Thorndike ME: G. K. Hall, LARGE PRINT CORE COLLECTION, 1993, 626 pp., 24 cm., hardcover [?]. ISBN 0-8161-5668-9. Large print edition.

zz. London, England: Warner UK, March 1993, 467 pp., £5.99, paperback. Cover art by Christopher Brown. 2nd printing. ISBN 0-7517-0432-7.

aaa. As: *Dead Zone: L'accident.* [Paris, France]: J C Lattès, SUSPENSE & CIE, 1993, 375 pp., 119 F, paperback. ISBN 2-7096-1250-X.

bbb. As: *Strefa smierc* ['Death-zone']. Gdańsk, Poland: Phantom Press International, KONESER, 1993, 472 pp., 20 cm. Polish translation by Krzysztof Sokolowski. ISBN 83-7075-528-3.

ccc. As: *La Zona Muerta* ['The dead zone']. Barcelona, Spain: RBA, GRANDES ÉXITOS #23, 1993, 450 pp., 22 cm. Spanish translation by Eduardo Goligorsky. ISBN 84-473-0197-4.

ddd. New York: Easton Press, MASTERPIECES OF SCIENCE FICTION, January 1994, 426 pp., [no price listed], hardcover. Introduction by James Gunn; Art by Jill Bauman. By subscription only; approximately 3,000 copies.
eee. As: *La Zona Morta* ['The dead zone']. Milan, Italy: Sperling Paperback, SUPERBESTSELLER #322, January 1994, paperback. Italian translation by A[ndrea] Terzi. 88-7824-376-0.
fff. New York, Plume/New American Library, October 1994, xx+399 pp., $14.95, 24 cm., trade paperback. Introduction by Anne Rivers Siddons. "Collector's Edition" with color reproduction of original hardcover art. ISBN 0-452-27329-3.
ggg. New York: New American Library, December 1994, 416 pp., $7.99, mass-market paperback. Reissue edition. ISBN 0-451-15575-0.
hhh. As: *L'accident.* Paris, France: France Loisirs, 1994, 376 pp., 94 F, 25 cm., paperback. French translation by Richard Matas. ISBN 2-7242-7843-7.
iii. As: *La Zona Muerta* ['The dead zone']. Barcelona, Spain: RBA, GRANDES ÉXITOS #23, 1994, 457 pp., 21 cm. Spanish translation. ISBN 84-473-0197-4.
jjj. As: *Morke Krefter* ['Dark forces']. Oslo, Norway: Hjemmets EGMONT SPENNING #48, 1995, 335 pp. Norwegian translation by Axel S. Seeberg. ISBN 82-04-03981-6.
kkk. As: *Dodelijk Dilemma* ['Deadly dilemma']. Amsterdam, Netherlands: Poema Pocket, 1996, 455 pp., trade paperback. Dutch translation by Margot Bakker. 14th printing. ISBN 90-245-2686-8.
lll. As: *Morke Krefter* ['Dark forces']. Oslo, Norway: Egmont Hjemmets Bokforlag, 1996, 336 pp., 179.00, hardcover [*innbundet*]. Norwegian translation. ISBN 82-59-01653-2.
mmm. As: *Strefa smierc*['Death-zone']. Warsaw, Poland, "Prima," 1998, 429 pp., 21 cm. Polish translation by Krzysztof Sokolowski. ISBN 83-7186-020-X.
nnn. As: *La Zona Muerta* ['The dead zone']. Esplugues de Llobregat, Barcelona, Spain: Plaza & Janés, JET 102, BIBLIOTECA DE STEPHEN KING #5, 1998, 450 pp., 18 cm., paperback. Spanish translation by Eduardo Goligorsky. ISBN 84-01-49988-7. * Reprint, 1999, ISBN 84-01-49988-7.
ooo. As: *Strefa smierc* ['Death-zone']. Warsaw, Poland, "Prima," BESTSELLERY ŒWIATOWEJ PROZY, 1999, 429 pp., 18 cm., paperback. Polish translation by Krzysztof Sokolowski. ISBN 83-7186-097-8.
ppp. As: *A Holtxáv.* Budapest, Hungary: Európa. Hungarian translation.
qqq. As: *A Holtxáv.* Hungary: Magvetö. Hungarian translation.
rrr. As: [Title unknown]. Russia: Cadman. Russian translation.

sss. As FILM: *Dead Zone.* Paramount Pictures/Dino de Laurentiis, October 1983. Produced by Debra Hill. Directed by David Cronenberg. Screenplay by Jeffrey Boam. Rating: R.
   CAST: Christopher Walken, Brooke Adams, Tom Skerrit, Herbert Lom, Anthony Zerbe, Colleen Dewhurst, Martin Sheen.
   COMMENTS: As adapted for film by Cronenberg, the novel provided the

Zona Muerta. Barcelona, Spain: Pomaire, 1980. Hardcover.

basis for what is considered by critics and fans alike one of the handful of unusually sensitive and intelligent film versions of King's works; it frequently appears in lists of the best King adaptations and remains a strong film in its own right, entirely consistent with the atmosphere and vision of King's print original.

SELECTED ARTICLES, RESPONSES, AND REVIEWS:

Ansen, D. *Newsweek* Vol. 102, No. 19 (7 November 1983): 128.

Ayscough, S. *Cinema Canada* Vol. 102 (December 1983): 18.

Christian Science Monitor 10 November 1983: 36.

Chute, D. *Rolling Stone* 391 (17 March 1983): 36.

Ebert, Roger. *Roger Ebert's Movie Home Companion, 1988 Edition.* Kansas City MO: Andrews, McMeel & Parker, 1987. 142.

Fangoria No. 29 (1983). An article on the set of *Dead Zone*.

Fangoria No. 30 (?).

Fangoria No. 31 (?).

Handling, Piers, ed. *The Shape of Rage: The Films of David Cronenberg.* Toronto: General Publishing Company, 1983; New York: Zoetrope, 1983.

Hoberman, J. *The Village Voice* Vol. 28, No. 45 (8 November 1983): 46.

Hogan, David J. "King and Cronenberg: It's the Best of Both Worlds." *Cinefantastique* Vol. 14, No. 2 (December 1983/January 1984): 51+.

Hubin, Allen J., ed. Novel indexed *in 1981-1985 Supplement to Crime Fiction 1749-1980.* New York: Garland, 1988, hardcover. 68.

Jenkins, S. *Monthly Film Bulletin* Vol. 51, No. 604 (May 1984): 147.

Lucas, Tim. "*Dead Zone*: David Cronenberg to Direct Stephen King's Chilling ESP Saga for Dino DeLaurentiis." *Cinefantastique* Vol. 13, No. 3 (November/December 1982).

Lucas, Tim. "David Cronenberg Shuns the Auteur Route To Adapt Stephen King's ESP Novel to the Screen." *Cinefantastique* Vol. 13, No. 5 (June/July 1983): 17.

Lucas, Tim. "David Cronenberg's *The Dead Zone*: Horror Film Auteur David Cronenberg Takes a Brief Hiatus in Stephen King Territory." *Cinefantastique* Vol. 14, No. 2 (December 1983-January 1984): 24-31, 60-61.

Nash, Robert Jay, and Stanley Ralph Ross. "*The Dead Zone.*" *The Motion Picture Guide, 1927-1983*, Vol. II. Chicago: Cinebooks, 1985. 594-595.

Powell, D. *Punch* Vol. 286, No. 7484 (9 May 1984): 67.

Sarris, A. *The Village Voice* Vol. 28, No. 45 (8 November 1983): 43.

Stric, P. *Sight and Sound* Vol. 53, No. 2 (Spring 1984): 150.

Tuchman, Michael. "From Niagara-on-the-Lake, Ontario." *Film Comment* Vol. 19, No. 3 (May-June 1983). Interview with Cronenberg on the filming.

Variety Vol. 312, No. 11 (12 October 1983): 20.

Vernier, James. "On the Set of Dead Zone." *Twilight Zone Magazine* (December 1983): 55.
Vernier, James. "A Talk With David Cronenberg." *Twilight Zone Magazine* (December 1983): 56-58.
Vernier, James. "Zeroing in on the *Dead Zone*." *Twilight Zone Magazine* (December 1983): 52-54.
Wheen, F. *New Statesman* Vol. 107, No. 2773 (11 May 1984): 30.
Williamson, B. *Playboy* Vol. 31, No. 1 (January 1984): 50.

ttt. As VIDEOCASSETTE: *Dead Zone*. Paramount Pictures, 1983. Beta, VHS, Laser, CED. 103 minutes.

COMMENTS: Ranked #6, *Publishers Weekly* annual hardcover Bestsellers list, 1979.

One of King's most restrained novels, and often considered one of the finest among his earlier works, *The Dead Zone* anatomizes a common man in extraordinary circumstances, a literal 'John Smith' struggling to survive a conflict with uncommon and unwanted abilities. The novel's considerable strengths include compassionate characterization, intricate and effective use of symbol and image, and an understated sense of horror nestled almost invisibly within the ordinary.

SELECTED ARTICLES, RESPONSES, AND REVIEWS:
Best of the Times [*New York Times*] Vol. 2 (August 1979): 391.
Best Sellers Vol. 39 (October 1979): 238.
Brown, Charles N. "On Books: The Best of 1979." *Isaac Asimov's Science Fiction Magazine* Vol. 27 (May 1980): 17.
Booklist Vol. 76 (1 September 1979): 24.
Card, Orson Scott. "Books." *Eternity SF* No. 1 (1979): 13-19.
Easton, Tom. *Analog Science Fiction/Science Fact* Vol. 101, No. 4 (30 March 1981): 164-165. Excerpted: *Contemporary Literary Criticism*, Vol. 26. Edited by Jean C. Stine. Detroit MI: Gale Research Co., 1983, hardcover. 238.
Gault, John. "Not Quite Fright." *Maclean's Magazine* Vol. 93 (24 September 1979): 56. Excerpted: *Contemporary Literary Criticism*, Vol. 26. Edited by Jean C. Stine. Detroit MI: Gale Research Co., 1983, hardcover. 234.
Graham, Mark. "Moral Dilemma in Latest Novel by Stephen King." *Rocky Mountain News* [Denver CO] 9 September 1979: 36.
Kirkus Reviews Vol. 47 (15 June 1979): 705.
Lehman-Haupt, Christopher. New York *Times* 17 August 1979: C23.
Library Journal Vol. 104 (July 1979): 1485.
Los Angeles Times Book Review 26 August 1979: 1.
Murphy, Patrick D. "The Realities of Unreal Worlds: King's *The Dead Zone*, Schmidt's *Kensho*, and Lem's *Solaris*." *Spectrum of the Fantastic: Selected Essays from the Sixth International Conference on the Fantastic in the Arts*. Edited by Donald Palumbo. CONTRIBUTIONS TO THE STUDY OF SCIENCE

FICTION AND FANTASY, #31. Series editor, Marshal Tymn. Westport CT: Greenwood Press, 1988, hardcover. 175-183.

Neilson, Keith. "The Dead Zone." *Magill's Literary Annual 1980*, Vol. 1. Edited by Frank N. Magill. Englewood Cliffs, NJ: Salem Press, 1980, hardcover. 205-209.

Ott, Bill. *Booklist* Vol. 78, No. 21 (July 1982): 1394. Excerpted: *Contemporary Literary Criticism*, Vol. 26. Edited by Jean C. Stine. Detroit MI: Gale Research Co., 1983, hardcover. 240.

Publishers Weekly Vol. 215 (11 June 1979): 97.

Publishers Weekly Vol. 217 (13 June 1980): 72.

Watson, Christine. "The Dead Zone." *Survey of Modern Fantasy Literature*, Vol. 1. Edited by Frank N. Magill. Englewood Cliffs, NJ: Salem Press, 1983, hardcover. 350-354.

Wilson Library Bulletin Vol. 54 (January 1980): 323.

THE LONG WALK. New York, NY: Signet/New American Library, 1979. Mass-market paperback.

A8.
THE LONG WALK
AS RICHARD BACHMAN
(1979)

A8. *THE LONG WALK*, by 'Richard Bachman.' New York: Signet/New American Library, July 1979, 244 pp., $1.95, mass-market paperback. ISBN 0-451-13539-3.

PLOT SUMMARY: Ray Garraty and ninety-nine other young men compete in a non-stop walk from Maine to Boston. Their goal: to walk as long as possible without stopping; walkers who drop out are killed. The reward: *anything* the survivor wants. The walkers' physical and mental tortures provide the structure for this taut, often psychologically grueling novel.

REPRINTS AND ADAPTATIONS:
b. As: *La lunga marcia* ['The long march'], by Richard Bachman. Milan, Italy: Arnoldo Mondadori, URANIA #1001, July 1985. Italian translation by Beata Della Frattina.
c. *The Bachman Books: Four Early Novels by Stephen King*. New York: New American Library, October 1985, hardcover. 133-322. [see A30]
d. As: *De Marathon* ['The marathon'] in: *4 X Stephen King*. Utrecht, Belgium: Luitingh, 1986, paperback. Dutch translation by Mariella de Kuyper-Snel.
e. As: *La Larga Marcha* ['The long march'], by Stephen King, "escribiendo como Richard Bachman." Barcelona, Spain: Martínez Roca, GRAN SUPERFICCIÓN 1986, 286 pp., 22 cm., trade paperback. Spanish translation by Hernán Sabaté; cover art by Geest and Hoverstad. ISBN 84-270-1023-0.
COMMENTS: The term *march* in the Spanish title (which includes explicit military connotations), coupled with futuristic, equally militaristic cover art by Geest and Hoverstad, suggests a very different sort of novel than King's English title conveys.
f. As: *La Lunga Marcia: L'Uomo in Fuga* ['The long march: the man in flight']. Milan, Italy: Mondadori, 1986, 412 pp. Italian translation by M. Tropea. Dual volume with *The Long Walk* and *The Running Man*.
g. As: *La Larga Marcha* ['The long march'], Barcelona, Spain: Círculo de Lectores, 1987, 279 pp., 22 cm. Spanish translation by Hernán Sabaté. ISBN 84-226-2274-2.

LA LARGA MARCHA. Barcelona, Spain: Martínez Roca, 1986.
Trade Paperback

h. As: *Maratonmarschen* ['Marathon-march']. Stockholm, Sweden: Legenda, 1987, 275 pp., 22 cm., hardcover. Swedish translation by Karl G. Fredriksson and Lilian Fredriksson. * 2nd printing, 1988. 91-582-1119-5.
i. As: *Todesmarch* ['Death-march']. Munich, Germany: Wilhelm Heyne, ALLGEMEINE REIHE #6848, 1987, 315 pp., 6.80 DM, paperback. German translation by Nora Jensen. ISBN 3-453-00239-3. * 5th printing, 1988. * 10th printing, 1991. * 18th printing, 1993. * 24th printing, 1996.
j. As: *De Marathon*, by Stephen King. Utrecht, Belgium: Luitingh, 1988, 263 pp., Dutch translation by Mariella de Kuyper-Snel. ISBN 90-245-1534-3.
k. As: *La lunga marcia* ['The long march']. Milan, Italy: Arnoldo Mondadori, BESTSELLERS OSCAR #152, November 1989. Italian translation by Beata Della Frattina. ISBN 88-04-32674-3.
l. As: *March ou crève* ['March or die(?)]. Paris: France: Albin Michel, 1989, 320 pp. French translation by France-Marie Watkins. ISBN 2-226-03870-1.
m. As: *Maratonmarschen* ['Marathon-march']. [Stockholm, Sweden]: Legenda, POCKET, 1989, 275 pp., 18 cm., paperback. Swedish translation by Karl G. Fredriksson and Lilian Fredriksson. 1st-3rd pocket editions. ISBN 91-582-1449-6.
n. Tokyo, Japan: Fusosha, 1989. Japanese translation by Numajiri Motoko.
o. As: *Raivo/Pitkä marssi* ['Rage/Long walk']. Helsinki, Finland: Tammi, 1992, 446 pp., 23 cm. Finnish translation by Leevi Lehto. * 2nd printing, 1992, ISBN 951-30-9901-6.
p. As: *Marche ou crève* ['March or die(?)]. Paris, France: J'ai Lu, #3203, 1992, 345 pp., 33 F, paperback. French translation by France-Marie Watkins. ISBN 2-277-23203-3. * Reprint, 2000.
q. As: *Marche ou crève* ['March or die(?)]. Paris, France: France Loisirs, 1994, 321 pp., 76 F, hardcover. French translation by France-Marie Watkins. ISBN 2-7242-8193-4.
r. As: *Wielki marsz* ['Long march']. Poznañ, Poland: CIA-Books/SVARO, 1992, 267 pp., 20 cm. Polish translation by Romana Kolarzowa. ISBN 83-8510-032-6.
s. As: [Title unknown]. South Korea, 1994, 424 pp., 23 cm. Korean translation. ISBN 89-7717-009-5.
t. As: *Richard Bachman Todesmarch/Amok; Zwei Romane in einem Band* 'Richard Bachman—Deathmarch/Rage; Two Novels in one Volume']. Munich, Germany: Wilhelm Heyne, ALLGEMEINE REIHE #9468, April 1995, 315+219 pp., 14.00 DM, paperback. German translation by Nora Jensen. ISBN 3-453-082494-X.
u. As: *Dødsspille* ['Deaths-play']. Oslo, Norway: Egmont Bøker Fredhøi, 1997, 318 pp., 595.00, paperback [*heftet*]. Norwegian translation. ISBN 82-04-04969-2.
v. As: *La lunga marcia* ['The long march']. Milan, Italy: Sperling & Kupfer, NARRATIVA [#260], August 1998. Italian translation by Beata Della Frattina. ISBN 88-200-2634-1.
w. As: *La larga marcha* ['The long march']. Barcelona, Spain: Plaza & Janés,

JET 102/19, BIBLIOTECA DE STEPHEN KING #19, 1998, 349 pp., 18 cm., paperback. Spanish translation by Hernán Sabaté. ISBN 84-01-47469-8.
x. As: *Todesmarch* ['Death-march']. Munich, Germany: Pavilion, PAVILION TASCHENBUCH #2, 1999, 315 pp., 8.00 DM, paperback. German translation by Nora Jensen. ISBN 3-453-16422-9.
y. As: [Title unknown]. Russia: Cadman. Russian translation.
z. As: [Title unknown]. Greek translation.
aa. New York: Penguin, April 1999, &7.99, paperback. ISBN 0-451-19671-6.
bb. As: *Marche ou crève* ['March or die(?)']. Paris, France: Albin Michel, 1999. French translation by France-Marie Watkins. ISBN 2-226-10688-X.

COMMENTS: The second 'Bachman' novel, *The Long Walk* was written while King was still in college; from his own accounts, the novel emerged essentially as originally published. It presents the incremental horror of the walkers as they move through a landscape simultaneously physical and symbolic, real and illusory, naturalistic and surrealistic, present and near-future. This foray into marginal science-fiction critiques—albeit obliquely—contemporary American society while overtly acknowledging the young King's debt to Shirley Jackson and others. As with the other 'Bachman' novels, elements of horror are consciously muted, with individuals, personalities, and social pressures emerging more clearly.

SELECTED ARTICLES, RESPONSES, AND REVIEWS:
Brown. Stephen P. "The Life and Death of Richard Bachman: Stephen King's Doppelgänger." *Kingdom of Fear: The World of Stephen King*. Edited by Tim Underwood and Chuck Miller. San Francisco CA: Underwood-Miller, 1986.109-126.
D'Ammassa, Don. "Three by Bachman." *Discovering Stephen King*. Edited by Darrell Schweitzer. Mercer Island WA: Starmont House, STARMONT STUDIES IN LITERARY CRITICISM #8, 1985. 123-130.
Gallagher, Steve. "Standing by Jericho." *Science Fiction Review* Vol. 12, No. 1 (February 1983): 35-36. Excerpted: *Contemporary Literary Criticism*, Vol. 37. Edited by Daniel G. Marowski. Detroit MI: Gale Research Co., 1986, hardcover. 201.
Hatlen, Burton. "Stephen King and the American Dream: Alienation, Competition, and Community in *Rage* and *The Long Walk*." *Reign of Fear: Fiction and Film of Stephen King*. Edited by Don Herron. Los Angeles CA: Underwood-Miller, 1988, hardcover. 19-50.

HORROR PLUM'D

FIRESTARTER. New York, NY: Viking, 1980. Hardcover

A9.
FIRESTARTER
(1980)

A9. *FIRESTARTER.* Huntington Woods MI: Phantasia Press, 1980, 428 pp., hardcover. Limited edition of 725 copies, with dust jacket and slipcase. Horror novel. * Asbestos-bound lettered state, A-Z.

PLOT SUMMARY: Born of parents who had participated in a scientific experiment, Charlie McGee is gifted/cursed with pyrokinesis, the ability to start fires. Fleeing from the government agency that killed her mother, hounded her father, and wants to control her, she magnifies her power beyond the limits even the Shop directors can imagine.

REPRINTS AND ADAPTATIONS:
b. New York: Viking, 29 September 1980, 428 pp., hardcover. 1st trade edition. ISBN 0-670-31541-9.
c. London, England: Macdonald Futura, October 1980, 428 pp., hardcover.
d. New York: Viking, [n.d.], 371 pp., hardcover. Science Fiction Book Club edition.
e. Burnsville MN: Econo-Clad/Sagebrush, 401 pp., $15.15, library binding. #1026137.
f. As: *Jan shao ti ning shih* [or *Ran shao di ning shi*]. Taipei, Taiwan: Huang kuan chu pan she, 1980. Chinese translation by Mao Chi-cheuan..
g. New York: Signet/New American Library, August 1981, 403 pp., paperback. ISBN 0-451-16780-5. * 9th printing, May 1984, ISBN 0-451-13234-3. * 21st printing, September 1989. * 35th printing, July 1992. * Reissue, December 1994.
h. London, England: Macdonald Futura, August 1981, 512 pp., paperback.
i. As: *Eldfödd* ['Fire-born']. Stockholm, Sweden: Askild and Kørnekull, 1981, 439 pp. Swedish translation by Jimmy Hofsö. Reprinted 1983
j. As: *Ogen van Vuur* ['Eyes of fire']. Utrecht, Belgium: Luitingh/Veen, 1981, 413 pp., trade paperback. Dutch translation by Margot Bakker. 1st Dutch edition. ISBN 90-204-0280-3. * 6th printing, 1984, ISBN 90-204-0995-6. * 7th–8th printings, 1986, ISBN 90-245-1582-3. * 9th printing, 1988, movie tie-in edition. * 11th printing, 1991. * 12th printing, 1993.

MICHAEL R. COLLINGS

k. As: *Ildbarnet* ['Child of fire']. Oslo, Norway, 1981, 440 pp. Norwegian translation by Jan Nergaard. Reprinted 1982, ISBN 82-7001-862-7.
l. As: *Ildbarnet* ['Child of fire']. Oslo, Norway: Hjemmets Bokforlag, 1981, 440 pp. Norwegian translation by Jan Nergaard, ISBN 82-7001-862-7. Book Club edition.
m. As: *Ojos de Fuego* ['Eyes of fire']. Barcelona, Spain: Pomaire, 1981, 463 pp., 20 cm. Spanish translation by Eduardo Goligorsky. ISBN 84-286-0626-9. * Reprint 1981, ISBN 84-286-0626-9.
n. As: *Firestarter.* Anstey, Leicestershire, England: Charnwood Library Services/Ulversoft Large Print Books, December 1982, 633 pp., hardcover. Large print edition. ISBN 0-7089-8086-4
o. As: *Tulisilmä* ['Fire-eye']. Helsinki, Finland: Tammi, 1982, 372 pp., 19 cm. Finnish translation by Aarne T. K. Lahtinen. 2nd printing 1991, ISBN 951-30-9786-2. * 3rd printing, 1991.
p. .As: *Feuerkind* ['Fire-child']. Bergish Gladbach, West Germany: Bastei-Lübbe, TB 28103, 1982, 393 pp., 19.80 DM, paperback. German translation by Harro Christensen. * 29th printing, 1994, TB 13001, 478 pp., ISBN 3404130014.
q. As: *L'Incendiària* ['Fire-starter']. Milan, Italy: Sperling & Kupfer, PANDORA #146, 1982, 408 pp., hardcover. Italian translation by Maria Grazia Prestini. ISBN 88-200-0338-4.
r. As: *Faia Sutata.* Tokyo, Japan: Shinchoshya, 1982. Japanese translation by Fukamachi Mariko.
s. As: *Ojos de Fuego* ['Eyes of fire']. Panama: Printer Internacional de Panamá, 1982. Spanish translation.
t. As: *Ojos de Fuego* ['Eyes of fire']. Barcelona, Spain: Mundo Actual de Ediciones, NARRADORES DE ÉXITO, 1982, 417 pp., 21 cm. Spanish translation. ISBN 84-7454-198-0.
u. As: *Feuerkind* ['Fire-child']. Gütersloh, Austria: Bertelsmann Lesering, 1983. German translation by Harro Christensen
v. As: *A Incendiaria* ['The fire-starter']. Rio de Janeiro, Brazil: Record, [1983?], 410 pp., 22 cm. Portuguese translation by Luiza Ribeiro.
w. New York: Signet, 1984, paperback. Movie tie-in edition. ISBN 0-451-13234-3.
x. As: *Charlie.* Paris: Albin Michel, 1984, 435 pp., 79 F, paperback. French translation by F. M. Lennox. ISBN 2-226-02156-6.
y. As: *Feuerkind* ['Fire-child']. Stuttgart, West Germany: Europäische Bildungsgemeinschaft; Gütersloh, Austria: Bertelsmann Club; Vienna, Austria: Buchgemeinschaft Donauland; Zug, Switzerland: Buch-und-Schallplattenfreunde, [1984], 413 pp. German translation by Harro Christensen. Book Club editions.
z. As: *Feuerkind: Das Buch zum Film 'Feuerteufel'* ['Fire-Child: The book for the film 'Fire-devil'"], Bergisch Gladbach, Germany: Bastei-Lübbe, TB 13001, 1984, 478 pp., 6.80 DM, paperback. German translation by Harro Christensen. ISBN 3-404-13001-4. * 23rd printing, 1992. * 31st printing, 1996.

aa. As: *Ojos de Fuego* ['Eyes of fire']. Buenos Aires, Argentina: Emecé, 1985, 463 pp., 20 cm. Spanish translation by Eduardo Goligorsky. ISBN 950-04-0501-6. * Reprint, 1986. * Reprint, 1989. * Reprint, 1991.
bb. As: [Title unknown]. Mexico: Edivision, 1985. Spanish translation.
cc. As: *Ildbarnet* ['Child of fire:]. Oslo, Norway: Hjemmets Bokklubb, 1985, 440 pp. Norwegian translation by Jan Nergaard. ISBN 82-7315-361-4.
dd. As: *A incendiária* ['The fire-starter']. Lisbon, Portugal: Livros do Brazil, VIDA E AVENTURA #39, 1985, 413 pp., 22 cm. Portuguese translation by Iva Delgado.
ee. As: *Ojos de Fuego* ['Eyes of fire']. Esplugues de Llobregat, Barcelona, Spain: Plaza & Janés, 1985, 432 pp., 18 cm., paperback. Spanish translation by Eduardo Goligorsky. ISBN 84-01-49067-7. * Reprint, 1987, ISBN 84-01-49067-7. Reprint, 1989, ISBN 84-01-49067-7.
ff. London, England: Futura, July 1986, 510 pp., £2.95, paperback. ISBN 0-7088-2101-4. * 14th printing, May 1991.
gg. As: *Charlie*. Paris: J'ai-Lu, ÉPOUVANTE #2089, October 1986, 466 pp., 26 F, paperback. French translation by F. M. Lennox. ISBN 2-277-22089-2.
hh. As: *L'Incendiària* ['Fire-starter']. Milan, Italy: Milan, Italy: Arnoldo Mondadori, OSCAR #1968, 8 July 1987. Italian translation by Maria Grazia Prestini. ISBN 88-04-30275-5.
ii. As: *A Incendiaria* ['The fire-starter']. Rio de Janeiro, Brazil: Circulo de Livre, [1987], 433 pp., 22 cm. Portuguese translation by Luiza Ribeiro.
jj. As: *Ojos de Fuego* ['Eyes of fire']. Esplugues de Llobregat, Barcelona, Spain: Plaza & Janés, JET 102/4, 1985, 428 pp., 18 cm., paperback. Spanish translation by Eduardo Goligorsky. ISBN 84-01-49884-8.
kk. As: *Eldfödd* ['Fire-born']. Stockholm, Sweden: Legenda, 1987, 439 pp., 22 cm., hardcover. Swedish translation by Jimmy Hofsö. 5th edition. ISBN 91-582-0501-2.
ll. As: *L'Incendiària* ['Fire-starter']. Milan, Italy: Arnoldo Mondadori, BESTSELLERS OSCAR #102, April 1988. Italian translation by Maria Grazia Prestini. ISBN 88-04-31685-3.
mm. As: *Brandstifter* ['Fire-starter']. Copenhagen, Denmark: Artia, 1988, 433 pp. Danish translation by Mogens Wenzel Andreasen. ISBN 87-89294-02-5.
nn. As: *Feuerkind/Cujo* ['fire-child/Cujo']. Munich, Germany: Gustav Lübbe Verlag, 14 March 1990, 703 pp., 38,00 dm, hardcover. German translation by Harro Christensen. Omnibus edition of *Firestarter* and *Cujo*. * 2nd printing, 1992, ISBN 3-7857-0573-5.
oo. As: *El Ojos de Fuego* ['Eyes of fire']. Esplugues de Llobregat, Barcelona, Spain: Plaza & Janés, JET #102, BIBLIOTECA DE AUTOR DE: STEPHEN KING #4, 1993, 428 pp., 18 cm. paper. Spanish translation by Eduardo Goligorsky. ISBN 84-01-49984-8.
pp. As: *Eldfödd* ['Fire-born']. Stockholm, Sweden: Bonnier, 1990, 439 pp., 22 cm., hardcover. Swedish translation by Jimmy Hofsö. 5th edition. ISBN 91-0-050526-9.

qq. As: *Feuerkind* ['Fire-child']. Stuttgart and Munich: Deutsche Bücherbund, [1990], 436 pp.. German translation by Harro Christensen. Book Club edition.

rr. As: *Brandstifter* ['Fire-starter']. Copenhagen, Denmark: Hørst, HØRST PAPERBACK, 1991, 433 pp., 98 KR, paperback. Danish translation by Mogens Wenzel Andreasen. ISBN 87-14-19138-5.

ss. As: *Charlie*. Paris, France: Albin Michel, 1992. French translation by F. M. Lennox. ISBN 2-226-12509-4.

tt. As: [Title Unknown]. Gdańsk, Poland: Phantom Press International, HORROR, 1992, 446 pp., 20 cm. Polish translation by Krzysztof Sokolowski. ISBN 83-7075-063-X.

uu. As: [Title unknown]. South Korea, 1992, 353 + 340 pp., 23 cm. Korean translation. ISBN 89-7547-005-9, 89-7547-004-0, 89-7547-006-7.

vv. London, England: Warner UK, March 1993, 510 pp., £5.99, paperback. ISBN 0-7515-0439-4.

ww. As: *El Ojos de Fuego* ['Eyes of fire']. Esplugues de Llobregat, Barcelona, Spain: Plaza & Janés, JET #102, BIBLIOTECA DE AUTOR DE: STEPHEN KING #4, 1993, 523 pp., 18 cm. paper. Spanish translation by Eduardo Goligorsky. ISBN 84-01-49987-9.

xx. As: *L'Incendiària* ['Fire-starter']. Milan, Italy: Sperling Paperback, SUPERBESTSELLER #353, May 1994, paperback. Italian translation by Maria Grazia Prestini. ISBN 88-7824-418-X.

yy. New York, Plume/New American Library, October 1994, 382 pp., $14.95, trade paperback. "Collector's Edition." Introduction by John Grisham. Includes a color reproduction of the original hardcover art by Geoff Grove. ISBN 0-452-27330-7.

zz. As: *Charlie*. Paris, France: France Loisirs, 1994, 436 pp., 98 F, hardcover. French translation by F. M. Lennox. ISBN 2-7242-7837-2.

aaa. As: *Charlie*. [Paris], France: le Grand livre du mois, 1995, 435 pp., 120 F, hardcover. French translation by F. M. Lennox. Book Club edition.

bbb. As: *Ojos de Fuego* ['Eyes of fire']. [Barcelona, Spain]: [Plaza & Janés], EDICIÓN ESPECIA PARA PRYCA, 1995, 523 pp., 18 cm. paper. Spanish translation by Eduardo Goligorsky. ISBN 84-01-00875-1.

ccc. As: *Ojos de fuego* ['Eyes of fire']. Barcelona, Spain: Orbis, NOVELAS DE CINE, 1995, 428 pp., 22 cm. Spanish translation by Eduardo Goligorsky. ISBN 84-01-1859-1.

ddd. As [Title unknown]. Hebrew translation, 1996, 354 pp.

eee. As: *A Tüzgyújtó* ['The fire-spark']. Budapest, Hungary: Európa, 1996, 494 pp., 20 cm. Hungarian translation by Boris János.

fff. As: *Ildbarnet* ['Child of fire:]. Oslo, Norway: Hjemmets Bokforlag, EGMONT SPENNING #50, 1995, 440 pp. Norwegian translation by Jan Nergaard. ISBN 82-04-03983-2.

ggg. As: *Ogen van Vuur* ['Eyes of fire']. Amsterdam, Netherlands: Poema Pocket, 1996, 427 pp., paperback. Dutch translation by Margot Bakker. 1st Dutch edition. ISBN 90-204-0280-3.

Horror Plum'd

hhh. As: *Ildbarnet* ['Child of fire:]. Oslo, Norway: Hjemmets Bokforlag, 1996, 440 pp., paperback. Norwegian translation by Jan Nergaard. 13th printing. ISBN 90-245-2666-3.

iii. As: *Ojos de Fuego* ['Eyes of fire']. Barcelona, Spain: Plaza & Janés, 1999, 582 pp., 19 cm.. Spanish translation by Eduardo Goligorsky. ISBN 84-01-24274-6.

jjj. As: [Title unknown]. 2 vols. Japanese translation.

kkk. As: [Title unknown]. Moscow, Russia: Cadman. Russian translation.

lll. As: [Title unknown]. Hungary: Maecenas. Hungarian translation.

mmm. As FILM: *Firestarter.* Universal Pictures, Dino de Laurentiis, October 1984. Produced by Frank Capra, Jr. Directed by Mark Lester. Screenplay by Stanley Mann. 115 minutes. Rated: R.
CAST: David Keith, Drew Barrymore, Freddie Jones, Heather Locklear, Martin Sheen, George C. Scott, Art Carney, Louise Fletcher.
NOTE: The film version is paradoxically a strictly—almost literally—faithful but ultimately static adaptation, which retains the dialogue-framework of King's novel but loses its dynamism.
SELECTED FILM REVIEWS AND ARTICLES:
Adler, Andrew. "'Firestarter' Opens at Several Theaters." *Courier-Journal* [Louisville KY] 12 May 1984. As microfiche: *Newsbank: Film and Television* Vol. 10 (June 1984): Fiche 109, E9.
American Film Vol. 9, No. 7 (May 1984): 69.
Blue, Tyson. "'Firestarter' Is Latest Movie from Novel by Stephen King." *Courier Herald* [Dublin GA] 9 June 1984.
Boyum, J. G. *Glamour* Vol. 82, No. 7 (July 1984): 107.
Briggs, Joe Bob [pseud. for John Bloom]. "Burned-up NOW Bimbos Can't Hold a Candle to Firestarter." *Joe Bob Goes to the Drive-In.* New York: Delacorte Press, 1987, paperback. Reprinted As: "A Review of Firestarter." *The Stephen King Companion*, by George Beahm. Kansas City MO: Andrews and McMeel, September 1989, paperback. 222-223.
Buckley, M. *Films in Review* Vol. 35, No. 7 (August/September 1984): 434.
Butler, Richard. "Actors Glow in Stephen King's Thriller 'Firestarter.'" *Kansas City Star* [MO] 13 May 1984.. As microfiche: *Newsbank: Film and Television* Vol. 10 (June 1984): Fiche 109, F1.
Cain, Scott. "Slapdash 'Firestarter' Burns Out in Spite of Its Powerful Potential." *Atlanta Journal-Constitution* [GA] 14 May 1984. As microfiche: *Newsbank: Film and Television* Vol. 10 (June 1984): Fiche 109, E6.
Canby, Vincent. "King's Latest Is a Hot Item." *San Diego Union* [CA] 12 May 1984. As microfiche: *Newsbank: Film and Television* Vol. 10 (June 1984): Fiche 109, D13.

Christian Science Monitor. "Arts & Leisure" (24 May 1984): 24.

Cosford, Bill. "'Firestarter' Provides Thrills Without Chills." *Miami Herald* [FL] 12 May 1984. As microfiche: *Newsbank: Film and Television* Vol. 10 (June 1984): Fiche 109, E3.

Curtright, Bob. "'Firestarter' a Mere Comedy of Terrors." *Wichita Eagle* [KS] 15 May 1984. As microfiche: *Newsbank: Film and Television* Vol. 10 (June 1984): Fiche 109, E8.

Dimeo, Steve. *Cinefantastique* Vol. 14, No. 4/5 (September 1984): 109.

Douglas, John A. "Sci-fi Movie with the Right Combustion." *Grand Rapids Press* [MI] 15 May 1984. As microfiche: *Newsbank: Film and Television* Vol. 10 (June 1984): Fiche 109, E14.

Douglas, John A. "Firestarter." *Cinefantastique* Vol. 15, No. 1 (January 1985): 48.

Edelstein, D. *The Village Voice* Vol. 29, No. 21 (22 May 1984): 61.

"Firestarter." *Magill's Cinema Annual, 1985: A Survey of 1984 Films.* Edited by Frank N. Magill. Englewood Cliffs, NJ: Salem Press, 1985, hardcover. 519.

"'Firestarter' Burns Out in Corniness." *Tallahassee Democrat* [FL] 17 May 1984. As microfiche: *Newsbank: Film and Television* Vol. 10 (June 1984): Fiche 109, E5.

Flatley, G. *Cosmopolitan* Vol. 197, No. 1 (July 1984): 26.

French, Thomas. "Stephen King's 'Firestarter' Fails to Kindle Interest." *St. Petersburg Times* [FL] 12 May 1984. As microfiche: *Newsbank: Film and Television* Vol. 10 (June 1984): Fiche 109, E4.

Haun, Harry. "'Firestarter' Flames in Cliches." *Daily News* [NY] 13 May 1984. As microfiche: *Newsbank: Film and Television* Vol. 10 (June 1984): Fiche 109, F2.

Healy, Michael. "'Firestarter' Belongs on Burned-out Ash Heap." *Denver Post* [CO] 12 May 1984. As microfiche: *Newsbank: Film and Television* Vol. 10 (June 1984): Fiche 109, E2.

Hogan, David J. "Firestarter: ET's Drew Barrymore Gets Scary as the Title Character in Stephen King's Bestseller." *Cinefantastique* Vol. 14, No. 3 (May 1984): 28-30.

Hogan, David J. "Firestarter." *Cinefantastique* Vol. 14, Nos. 4/5 (September 1984): 16-25.

Hunter, Stephen. "The Movie 'Firestarter' Is an Incendiary Bomb." *Sun* [Baltimore MD] 14 May 1984. As microfiche: *Newsbank: Film and Television* Vol. 10 (June 1984): Fiche 109, E10-E11.

Jenkins, S. *Monthly Film Bulletin* Vol. 51, No. 606 (July 1984): 202.

Kass, Carole. "'Firestarter' Surges, Wanes." *Richmond Times-Dispatch* [VA] 12 May 1984. As microfiche: *Newsbank: Film and Television* Vol. 10 (June 1984): Fiche 109, F7.

King, Stephen. "King on Firestarter: Who's to Blame?" *Cinefantastique* Vol. 21, No. 4 (February 1991): 35.

Leydon, Joe. "Actors Save Movie from Crash, Burn." *Houston Post*

[TX] 14 May 1984. As microfiche: *Newsbank: Film and Television* Vol. 10 (June 1984): Fiche 109, F4.

Lovell, Glen. "'Firestarter' a Burned Out Idea." *San Jose Mercury* [CA] 16 May 1984. As microfiche: *Newsbank: Film and Television* Vol. 10 (June 1984): Fiche 109, E1.

Martin, Robert H. [Bob]. "Mark Lester Directs Firestarter." *Fangoria* 36 (1984): 12-15.

Martin, Robert H. [Bob]. "On the Set of Firestarter: Exclusive Scoop! It's Not a Horror Picture." *Fangoria* 35 (1984): 56-59.

McLeod, Michael. "'Firestarter' Kindles Real Emotion." *Cincinnati Enquirer* [OH] 14 May 1984. As microfiche: *Newsbank: Film and Television* Vol. 10 (June 1984): Fiche 109, F4.

Miller, E. *Seventeen* Vol. 43, No. 7 (July 1984): 71.

Mills, Bart. "David Keith: On Fire Over Stephen King." *Los Angeles Times* [CA] Vol. 102 (20 November 1983): C39.

Mills, Bart. "'Firestarter' in Thriller Tradition." *Boston Herald* [MA] 13 May 1984. As microfiche: *Newsbank: Film and Television* Vol. 10 (June 1984): Fiche 109, E12.

Minton, L. *McCalls* Vol. 111, No. 11 (August 1984): 28.

The Movie Magazine (Spring 1984). A two-page article with color photographs.

Munster, Bill. "Footsteps in the Dark." *Footsteps IV* (Summer 1984): 76-79.

Novak, Ralph. "Firestarter." *People* (28 May 1984): 12.

O'Connor, Bill. "'Firestarter' Top-Heavy with Special Effects." *Akron Beacon Journal* [OH] 17 May 1984. As microfiche: *Newsbank: Film and Television* Vol. 10 (June 1984): Fiche 109, F3.

Powell, D. *Punch* [England] Vol. 287, No. 7493 (11 July 1984): 43.

Rose, Rita. "Drew 'Sizzling' in New Film." *Indianapolis Star* [IN] 12 May 1984. As microfiche: *Newsbank: Film and Television* Vol. 10 (June 1984): Fiche 109, E7.

Scapperotti, Dan. "Gary Zeller." *Cinefantastique* Vol. 14, Nos. 4/5 (September 1984): 22.

"Script Puts Damper on 'Firestarter.'" *Detroit Free Press* 13 May 1984. As microfiche: *Newsbank: Film and Television* Vol. 10 (June 1984): Fiche 109, E13.

Stack, Peter. "Hollywood Grinds Out Yet Another Stephen King Horror." *San Francisco Chronicle* [CA] 12 May 1984. As microfiche: *Newsbank: Film and Television* Vol. 10 (June 1984): Fiche 109, D14.

Thomas, Kevin. "'Firestarter': Hot on a Child's Trail." *Los Angeles Times* [CA] 11 May 1984. As microfiche: *Newsbank: Film and Television* Vol. 10 (June 1984): Fiche 109, D12.

Variety Vol. 315, No. 2 (9 May 1984): 10.

Vincent, Mal. "Will Someone Please Douse 'Firestarter,' the Latest

Stephen King Non-Thriller?" *Virginian-Pilot* [Norfolk VA] 16 May 1984. As microfiche: *Newsbank: Film and Television* 10 (June 1984): Fiche 109, F6.

Williamson, B. *Playboy* Vol. 31, No. 8 (August 1984): 25.

Wood, Gary. "*Firestarter*: Director Mark Lester Takes off the Gloves to Respond to King's Knock That This Adaptation Is 'The Worst of the Bunch.'" *Cinefantastique* Vol. 21, No. 4 (February 1991): 34.

nnnn. As VIDEOCASSETTE: Universal Pictures, 1984. Beta, VHS, CED. 115 minutes.

oooo. As LASER DISC: Universal Studios Home Video. $34.98.

COMMENTS: 285,000 copies sold in 1980; ranked #4 on the *Publishers Weekly* annual hardcover Bestsellers List

By restricting himself to a science-fictional rationale for horror, King develops *Firestarter* more directly as narrative than he will in some later novels. The story is unencumbered by multiple subplots, satisfyingly creating its momentum through characterization and visualization.

SELECTED ARTICLES, RESPONSES, AND REVIEWS:

Barkham, John. "A Story Fired with Imagination, Protest." *Philadelphia Inquirer* [PA] 31 August 1980).

Best of the Times [*New York Times*] Vol. 3 (November 1980): 541.

Best Sellers Vol. 40 (November 1980): 273.

Brosnahan, John. "Firestarter." *Booklist* Vol. 76 (15 June 1980): 1464. Excerpted: *Contemporary Literary Criticism*, Vol. 26. Edited by Jean C. Stine. Detroit MI: Gale Research Co., 1983, hardcover. 237.

Budrys, Algis. "King's *Firestarter*: It's Hot Stuff, All Right." *Chicago Sun-Times* [IL] 21 September 1980.

Clark, Jeff. *Library Journal* Vol. 105 (August 1980): 1660.

Demarest, Michael. "Hot Moppet." *Time* Vol. 116 (15 September 1980): K12, K18.

Egan, James. "Technohorror: The Dystopian Vision of Stephen King." *Extrapolation* Vol. 29, No. 2 (Summer 1988): 140-152.

Graham, Mark. "New King Novel Will Frighten You." *Rocky Mountain News* [Denver CO] 14 September 1980): 31.

Granger, Bill. "Stephen King Strikes Again." *Chicago Tribune Book World* [IL] 24 August 1980.

Kirkus Reviews Vol. 48, No. 14 (15 July 1980): 930. Excerpted: *Contemporary Literary Criticism*, Vol. 26. Edited by Jean C. Stine. Detroit MI: Gale Research Co., 1983. 237.

Lehmann-Haupt, Christopher. *New York Times* 8 September 1980: III, 15.

Los Angeles Times Book Review 28 September 1980: 4.

Neilson, Keith. "Firestarter." *Survey of Modern Fantasy Literature*, Vol. 2. Edited

by Frank N. Magill. Englewood Cliffs, NJ: Salem Press, 1983, hardcover. 553-556.
New Republic Vol. 184 (21 February 1981): 38.
Prescott, P. S. "Hot Tot." *Newsweek* Vol. 96 (6 October 1980): 96.
Publishers Weekly Vol. 218 (25 July 1980): 147.
Publishers Weekly Vol. 219 (12 June 1981): 53.
San Francisco Chronicle [CA] 25 August 1980: 45.
School Library Journal Vol. 27 (November 1980): 93.
Stuewe, Paul. "American Thrillers: *Firestarter*, Brass Diamonds, Brain 2000." *Quill and Quire* Vol. 46 (October 1980): 40-41. Excerpted: *Contemporary Literary Criticism*, Vol. 26. Edited by Jean C. Stine. Detroit MI: Gale Research Co., 1983, hardcover. 237.
Voice of Youth Advocates Vol. 3 (February 1981): 31.
Voice of Youth Advocates Vol. 6 (December 1983): 266.
Wall Street Journal 4 September 1980: 26.
Washington Post Book World 26 August 1980: 1.
Wilson Library Journal Vol. 55 (February 1981): 456.
Winter, Douglas E. "Shadowings: *Firestarter* by Stephen King." *Fantasy Newsletter* (November 1980).

Michael R. Collings

ROADWORK. New York, NY: Signet/New American Library, 1981. Mass-market paperback.

A10.
ROADWORK
AS RICHARD BACHMAN
(1981)

A10. *ROADWORK: A NOVEL OF THE FIRST ENERGY CRISIS*, by 'Richard Bachman.' New York: Signet/New American Library, April (?) 1981, 247 pp., mass-market paperback. ISBN 451-E9668. Suspense novel

PLOT SUMMARY: When the city decides to construct a freeway through George Dawes's home, he fights back, in the process losing his wife, his job, his sense of self, and finally his life.

REPRINTS AND ADAPTATIONS:
b. London, England: New English Library, June 1983, 282 pp., paperback.
c. In: *The Bachman Books: Four Early Novels by Stephen King*. New York: New American Library, October 1985. 323-530. [See A30].
d. As: *Werk in Uitvoering* ['Work to carry out'], in: *4 X Stephen King*, by Stephen King. Utrecht, Belgium: Luitingh, 1986, paper. Dutch translation by Hugo Kuipers.
e. As: *Sprengstoff* ['Explosive"], by Richard Bachman. Munich, Germany: Wilhelm Heyne TB 6762, 1986, 343 pp., 7.80 DM, paperback. German translation by Nora Jensen. ISBN 3-453-02375-7. * 5th printing, 1988. * 8th printing, 1990. * 17th printing, 1994. * 19th printing, 1996.
f. As: *Carretera Maldita* ['Damned/cursed road'], by Stephen King, ['escribiendo como Richard Bachman']. Barcelona, Spain: Ediciones Martínez Roca, GRANSUPERTERROR, March 1987, 256 pp., 1827 pta., 22 cm., trade paperback. Spanish translation by Joseph M. Apfelbäume; cover art by Olivé Milá. ISBN 84-270-1096-6.
g. As: *Chantier* ['Worksite']. Paris, France: Albin Michel, 1987, 348 pp., 85 F, paperback. French translation by Frank Straschitz. Le Grand livre du Mois, 1988. ISBN 2-226-03018-2.
h. As: *Uscito per l'inferno* ['Emergency exit to hell']. Milan, Italy: Sonzogno, 1987. Italian translation by Tullio Dobner.
i. As: *Werk in Uitvoering* ['Work to carry out']. Utrecht, Belgium: Luitingh, 1988, 271 pp. Dutch translation by Hugo Kuipers. ISBN 90-245-1544-0.

j. As: *Vägbygge* ['Road-construction']. Höganäs, Sweden: Legenda/ Bra Spänning, 1988, 305 pp., 22 cm., hardcover. Swedish translation by Jimmy Hofsö. ISBN 91-582-1157-8.

k. As: *Vägbygge* ['Road-construction']. Stockholm, Sweden: Legenda, 1989, 305 pp., 22 cm., hardcover. Swedish translation by Jimmy Hofsö. ISBN 91-582-1493-3.

l. Tokyo, Japan: Fusosha, 1989. Japanese translation by Murio Shuzo.

m. As: *Werk in Uitvoering* ['Work to carry out']. Utrecht, Belgium: Luitingh, 1991, 459 pp. Dutch translation by Hugo Kuipers. ISBN 90-245-1508-4.

n. As: *Fluch/Menschenjagd/Sprengstoff: Drei Romane in einem Band* ['Curse/Man-hunt/Explosive: Three novels in one volume']. Munich, Germany: Wilhelm Heyne, #9116, September 1994, 346 pp., 15.00 DM, paperback. German translation by Nora Jensen. * 3rd printing, 1995, ISBN 3-453-07567-6.

o. As: *Carretera Maldita* ['Damned/cursed road'].Barcelona, Spain: Plaza & Janés, July 1997, 368 pp., 668 pta., 19 cm., paperback. 1st edition in this format. Spanish translation by Joseph M. Apfelbáume. ISBN 84-01-62048-1.

p. As: *Besettelse* ['Possessions (?)]. Oslo, Norway: Egmont Bøker Fredhøi, 1997, 297 pp., 595.00, paperback [*heftet*]. Norwegian translation. ISBN 82-04-04969-7.

q. As: *Carretera Maldita* ['Damned/cursed road'].Barcelona, Spain: Plaza & Janés, JET #102, BIBLIOTECA DE STEPHEN KING #22, June 1998, 368 pp., 938 pta., 18 cm., paperback. Spanish translation by Joseph M. Apfelbáume. ISBN 84-01-47472-8.

r. New York: Signet, June 1999, 307 pp., $7.99, mass-market paperback. With introduction by King. ISBN 0-451-19787-9.

s. As: *Chantier* ['Worksite']. Paris, France: J'ai Lu, #2974, 2000, paperback. French translation by Frank Straschitz. ISBN: 2-290-30669-X.

COMMENTS: The third 'Richard Bachman' novel, this meticulously realistic study of psychological fragmentation under stress demonstrates King's unique narrative touch without importing extraneous supernatural horror; its horrors are the mundane horrors of cancer, isolation, and modern bureaucratic impersonality. Based upon and written during the oil crisis of 1974, it none the less retains its topicality and interest after over a quarter of a century.

SELECTED ARTICLES, RESPONSES, AND REVIEWS:
Brown. Stephen P. "The Life and Death of Richard Bachman: Stephen King's Doppelgänger." *Kingdom of Fear: The World of Stephen King*. Edited by Tim Underwood and Chuck Miller. San Francisco CA: Underwood-Miller, 1986. 109-126.

Horror Plum'd

Michael R. Collings

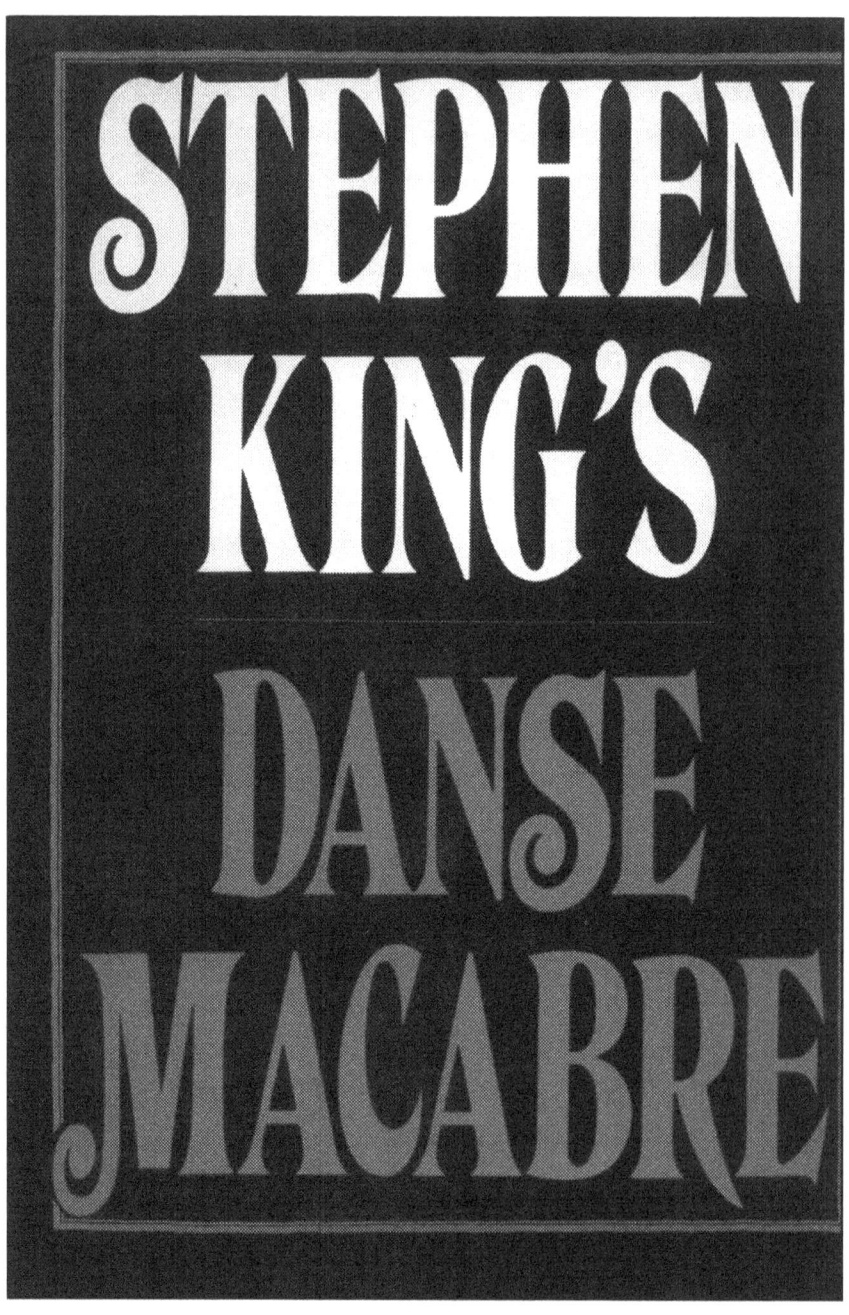

Stephen King's Danse Macabre. New York, NY: Everest House, 1981. Hardcover.

A11.
DANSE MACABRE
(1981)

A11. *STEPHEN KING'S DANSE MACABRE*. New York: Everest House, July (?) 1981, 400 pp., hardcover. Nonfiction. ISBN not listed. * LIMITED EDITION; lettered state. * LIMITED EDITION—numbered state, plain tissue dust jacket and slipcase, 250 copies. * LIMITED EDITION—publisher's state, limited to 35 copies not originally for sale. No dust jacket or slipcase.

CONTENTS: Forenote; "I. October 4, 1957, and an Invitation to Dance"; "II. Tales of the Hook"; "III. Tales of the Tarot"; "IV. An Annoying Autobiographical Pause"; "V. Radio and the Set of Reality"; "VI. The Modern American Horror Movie—Text and Subtext"; "VII. The Horror Movie as Junk Food"; "VIII. The Glass Teat, or, This Monster Was Brought to You by Gainsburgers"; "IX. Horror Fiction"; "X. The Last Waltz—Horror and Morality, Horror and Magic"; "Afterword," by King; "Appendix 1. The Films"; "Appendix 2. The Books"; Index.

REPRINTS AND ADAPTATIONS:
b. New York: Book of the Month Club, [n.d.], hardcover.
c. London, England: Macdonald Futura, July 1981, 448 pp., hardcover. ISBN 0-354-04647-0; 0-354-04646-2.
d. London, England: Futura, July 1981, 480 pp., paperback.
e. New York: Berkley, May 1982, xiv+400 pp., trade paperback.
f. New York: Berkley, December 1983, 437 pp., mass-market paperback. 20th printing by September 1989.
g. As: *Danse Macabre*. Paris, France: J'ai-Lu, #1355, 1982, 413 pp., 16 F, paperback. French translation by Lorris Murail and Natalie Zimmermann. ISBN 2-277-21355-1. * Reprint, 1997.
h. New York: Berkley, April 1985, 437 pp., $4.50, mass-market paperback. ISBN 0-425-07984-8.
i. As: *Danse Macabre*. Italy: Theoria, 1985, 176 pp. Italian translation by E. Turchetti.
j. London,: Futura, July 1986, 479 pp., £2.95, paperback. Reissue. ISBN 0-7088-2181-2. * 10th printing, May 1991, £4.99.

STEPHEN KING'S DANSE MACABRE. New York, NY: Berkley, 1983. Mass-market paperback.

k. As: *Danse Macabre*. Amsterdam, Netherlands: Loeb, 1986, viii+397 pp., paperback. Dutch translation by Mariella de Kuyper. ISBN 90-6213-844-6. 2nd printing, 1988.
l. As: *Danse Macabre: Die Welt des Horrors in Literatur und Film* ['Danse Macabre: The world of horror in literature and film']. Munich, Germany: Wilhelm Heyne, SACHBUCH 2, 1988, 543 pp., 12.80 DM, paperback. German translation by Joachim Körber, following the expanded, corrected U.S. edition of 1982. ISBN 3-453-02971-2. * 4th printing, 1992.
m. As: *Danca Macabra*. Rio de Janeiro, Brazil: Francisco Alves, MESTRES DO HORROR E DA FANTASIA, 1989, 471 pp., 21 cm., paperback. Portuguese translation by Maria Claudia Santos Lopes. ISBN 85-265-0197-6.
n. As: *Shining/Salem/Danse Macabre*. Paris, France: J.-C. Lattès, 1989, 1181 pp., 150 F, paperback. French translations by Joan Bernard, Christiane Thiollier, Lorris Murail and Natalie Zimmermann.
o. Amsterdam, Netherlands: Loeb, 1989, viii+397 pp., paperback. Dutch translation by Mariella Snel. 3rd printing. ISBN 90-6213-844-6.
p. As: *Dödsdansen* ['Death's dance']. [Höganäs, Sweden]: Wiken, 1991, 510 pp., 23 cm., hardcover. Swedish translation by Börje Crona. ISBN 91-7024-811-7.
q. Baam, Netherlands: In den Toren, TOREN POCKETS, 1992, viii+397 pp., paperback. Dutch translation by Mariella de Kuyper. ISBN 90-6074-764-X.
r. London, England: Warner, 1993, 479 pp., ISBN 0-7515-0437-8.
s. As: *Anatomie l'horreur* [Anatomy of horror']. Monaco [Paris, France]: Éditions du Rocher, 1995, 313 pp., 119 F, paperback. ISBN 2-268-01993-4.
t. As: *Pages noires—Anatomie l'horreur 2* ['Black pages: Anatomy of horror, 2']. Monaco [Paris, France]: Éditions du Rocher, SUSPENSE, 1996, 286 pp., 119 F, 24 cm., paperback. French translation by Jean-Daniel Brèque. Notes by Jean-Pierre Croquet. ISBN 2-268-02079-7.
u. New York: Berkley, 1997. ISBN 0-451-0433-8.
v. As: *Anatomie l'horreur* [Anatomy of horror']. 2 vols. Edited by Jean-Pierre Croquet. Paris, France: J'ai Lu #4410-4411, 1997, 378+378 pp., 36 F, 18 cm., paperback. French translation by Jean Daniel Brèque. ISBN 2-290-04410-5, 2-290-04411-3.

COMMENTS: *Danse Macabre* reads as much like a novel as it does literary-, film-, or cultural-criticism, since King blends his personal vision and colloquial style in analyzing dark fantasy from 1953 (Jack Arnold's *It Came From Outer Space*) through 1978 (John Carpenter's *Halloween* and David Lynch's *Eraserhead*). King discusses major films; television series such as *Thriller*, *Outer Limits*, and *Twilight Zone*; and fiction, with particular attention to Peter Straub's *Ghost Story*, Anne Rivers Siddons's *The House Next Door*, Shirley Jackson's *The Haunting of Hill House*, Ira Levin's *Rosemary's Baby*, Jack Finney's *The Invasion of the Body Snatchers*, Ray Bradbury's *Something Wicked This Way Comes*, Richard Matheson's *The Shrinking Man*, and works by Ramsey Campbell and James Herbert. King connects the imagined worlds of dark fantasy to external reality, then concludes by defending the magic underlying both fantasy and imagination. As criticism, *Danse Macabre* is valuable and entertaining; as a reflection of King's beliefs, it brilliantly illuminates his own writing.

SELECTED ARTICLES, RESPONSES, AND REVIEWS:

Adams, Michael. "*Danse Macabre.*" *Magill's Literary Annual, Book of 1981*, Vol. 1. Edited by Frank N. Magill. Englewood Cliffs, NJ: Salem Press, 1982. 171-174.

Best of the Times [*New York Times*] Vol. 4 (July 1981): 296.

Book World Vol. 11 (12 April 1981): 4.

Book World Vol. 12 (6 June 1982): 12.

Booklist Vol. 77 (15 January 1981): 651.

Choice Vol. 19 (September 1981): 80.

Egan, James. "Technohorror: The Dystopian Vision of Stephen King." *Extrapolation* Vol. 29, No. 2 (Summer 1988): 140-152.

English Journal Vol. 76 (March 1987): 72.

Graham, Mark. "A Dance into Horror with Stephen King." *Rocky Mountain News* [Denver CO].

Hemesath, J. B. *Library Journal* Vol. 106 (1 April 1981): 797.

Kendrick, Walter. "Stephen King Gets Eminent." *The Village Voice* Vol., No. 18 (29 April-5 May 1981): 45. Excerpted: *Contemporary Literary Criticism*, Vol. 37. Edited by Daniel G. Marowski. Detroit MI: Gale Research Co., 1986. 197-198.

Kirkus Reviews Vol. 49 (1 March 1981): 332.

Klavan, Andrew. *Saturday Review* Vol. 8 (April 1981): 80.

Kliatt Paperback Book Guide Vol. 16 (Fall 1982): 24.

Lehmann-Haupt, Christopher. "Books of the Times." *The New York Times* 14 April 1981: C11. Late edition.

Morrison, Michael. "Carrie on Screaming." *Times Educational Supplement* (21 August 1981): 18. Excerpted: *Contemporary Literary Criticism*, Vol. 37. Edited by Daniel G. Markowski. Detroit MI: Gale Research Co., 1986. 199-200.

New York Times Book Review Vol. 87 (May 23, 1982): 39.

Publishers Weekly Vol. 219 (27 February 1981): 144.

Quill & Quire Vol. 47 (July 1981): 66.

Rockett, W. H. "The Door Ajar: Structure and Convention in Horror Films That Would Terrify." *Journal of Popular Film and Television* (Fall 1981): 130-136.

School Library Journal Vol. 28 (September 1981): 147.

Science Fiction Review No. 10 (August 1981): 26.

Slung, Michelle. "Scare Tactics." *New York Times Book Review* Vol. 86 (10 May 1981): VII 15, 27. Excerpted: *Contemporary Literary Criticism*, Vol. 37. Edited by Daniel G. Marowski. Detroit MI: Gale Research Co., 1986. 198-199.

Top of the News Vol. 39 (Fall 1982): 98.

Voice of Youth Advocates Vol. 6 (December 1983): 266.

Wiater, Stanley. "Stephen King's *Danse Macabre*." *The Valley Advocate* [Hatfield, MA] 27 May 1981.

Wilson Library Bulletin Vol. 55 (June 1981): 775.

MICHAEL R. COLLINGS

Cujo. New York, NY: Viking Press, 1981. Hardcover.

A12.
CUJO
(1981)

A12. *CUJO.* New York: New York: Viking Press, 8 September 1981, 319 pp., $13.95, 24 cm., hardcover. Horror novel. ISBN 0-670-45193-2.

PLOT SUMMARY: The internal disintegration of a marriage parallels the external separation of a husband from his family. When the family car breaks down, Donna Trenton and her son Tad threatened by a rabid St. Bernard, Cujo. The Trentons remain in the car for several days; when help finally arrives, it is too late.

REPRINTS AND ADAPTATIONS:
b. New York: Mysterious Press, 1981, 319 pp., hardcover. LETTERED STATE (limited to 26 copies), not for sale when originally published. LIMITED EDITION, signed, numbered, Mylar cover and slipcase, 750 copies.
c. As: *K'uang ch'huan k'u ch'iu.* Taipei, Taiwan: Crown Publishers, 1981. Chinese translation by Ch'en min-ts'ui.
d. London, England: Macdonald, February 1982, 320 pp., hardcover.
e. New York: Signet/New American Library, August 1982, 305 pp., mass-market paperback. ISBN 0-451-16135-1. 28th printing by 1994.
f. London, England: Futura, August 1982, 352 pp., paperback.
g. New York: Viking [n.d.], 309 pp., hardcover. Science Fiction Book Club edition.
h. Barcelona, Spain: Grijalba Mondadori, BESTSELLER ORO, 10 November 1982, 414 pp., 19 cm., paperback. Spanish translation by María Antonia Menini. 84-253-1442-9.
i. Barcelona, Spain: Grijalba Mondadori, BESTSELLER ORO, 10 November 1982, 414 pp., 20 cm. Spanish translation by María Antonia Menini. 84-253-1443-7.
j. As: *Cujo: Roman.* Paris, France: Albin Michel, SPÉCIAL SUSPENSE, 1982, 360 pp., 59 F, paperback. French translation by Natalie Zimmermann. ISBN 2-226-01487-X.
k. As: *Cujo: Roman.* Paris France: France Loisirs, 1982, 351 pp., 47 F, hardcover. French translation by Natalie Zimmermann. ISBN 2-7242-1499-5.
l. As: *Cujo: Roman.* [Paris, France]: [le Grand livre du mois], 1982, 351 pp.,

59 F., hardcover. French translation by Natalie Zimmermann. Book Club edition.
m. As: [Title unknown]. South Korea, 1982, 326 pp., 22 cm. Korean translation.
n. Stockholm, Sweden: Askild and Kørnekull, 1982, 342 pp. Swedish translation by Jimmy Hofsö. ISBN 91-582-0408-3. * Reprint, 1984.
o. Utrecht, Belgium: Luitingh/Veen, 1982, 288 pp., f 24.50, trade paperback. Dutch translation by Margot Bakker. ISBN 90-204-1019-9.
p. Miguel Hidalgo, México: Editorial Grijalbo, BESTSELLERS ORO, February 1983, 416 pp., paperback. Spanish translation by María Antonia Menini. 1st edition of 5,000 copies.
q. Anstey, Leicestershire, England: Thorpe, CHARNWOOD LIBRARY SERVICES/Ulversoft Large Print Books, June 1983, 476 pp., hardcover. Large print edition. ISBN 0-7089-8123-2.
r. Milan, Italy: Sperling & Kupfer, PANDORA #191, September 1983. Italian translation by Tullio Dobner. ISBN 88-200-0338-4.
s. New York: Signet, 1983, paperback. Movie tie-in edition. ISBN 0-451-12650-5.
t. Paris, France: J'ai-Lu, EPOUVANTE, #1590, 1983, 379 pp., mass-market paperback. French translation by Natalie Zimmermann. ISBN 2-277-21590-2. * Reprint, 1984. * Reprint, 1992. * Reprint, 1997.
u. Bergisch Gladbach, West Germany: Bastei-Lübbe, PAPERBACK 2109, 1983, 315 pp., 19.80 DM, paperback. German translation by Harro Christensen. ISBN 0-404-28109-8.
v. Milan, Italy: Mondadori, 1983, 376 pp. Italian translation by T. Dobner. * Reprint, 1986.
w. Tokyo, Japan: Shinchoshya, 1983. Japanese translation.
x. As: *Faresonen* ['Danger-son']. Oslo, Norway: Hjemmets bokforlag, 1983, 343 pp. Norwegian translation by Jan Nergaard. ISBN 82-7001-966-6.
y. Barcelona, Spain: Círculo de Lectores, 1983. Spanish translation.
z. Panama: Printer Internacional de Panamá, 1983. Spanish translation.
aa. As: *Cão raivoso* ["Rabid/enraged dog']. Rio de Janeiro, Brazil: Record, [1984?], 332 pp., 21 cm. Portuguese translation by Luis Corcao. 2nd printing, 1985.
bb. As: *Cujo: Spændingsroman* ['Cujo: suspense novel'] Valby, Denmark: Borgen/Narayana Press, 1984, 317 pp., 23 cm., 198 KR, paperback. Danish translation by Niels Søndergaard. ISBN 87-418-7105-7.
dd. Barcelona, Spain: Grijalba Mondadori, BOLSILLO, 1985, 413 pp., 18 cm., paperback. Spanish translation by María Antonia Menini. 3rd printing; 1st pocket edition. ISBN 84-253-1700-2. * Reprint, 1987.
ee. Stockholm, Sweden: Legenda, 1985, 342 pp., paperback. Swedish translation by Jimmy Hofsö.
ff. Milan, Italy: Arnoldo Mondadori, OSCAR #1906, 25 August 1986. Italian translation by Tullio Dobner.
gg. As: *Cujo: ein unheimlicher Thriller* ['Cujo: a sinister/uncanny thriller']. Bergisch Gladbach, West Germany: Bastei-Lübbe TB 13035, 1986, 351 pp.,

6.80 DM, paperback,. German translation by Harro Christensen. * 19th printing, 1992. * 26th printing, 1996. ISBN 3-404-13035-9.
hh. Kornwesterheim, Austria: Europäische Bildungsgemeinschaft; Gütersloh, Austria: Bertelsmann Lesering; Zug, Switzerland: Buch-und-Schallplattenfreunde, [August 1986], 383 pp., paperback. German translation by Harro Christensen. Book Club editions.
ii. Utrecht, Belgium: Luitingh, [1986], 288 pp. Dutch translation by Margot Bakker. 5th printing. ISBN 90-245-1501-7. * 9th printing, 1991.
jj. Barcelona, Spain: Grijalbo, LITERATURA CONTEMPORÁNEA, 1986, 419 pp., 21 cm., hardcover. Spanish translation by Mariá Antonia Menini. 2nd edition. ISBN 84-253-1819-X. * Reprint, 1989.
kk. London, England: Futura, October 1987, 345 pp., £3.50, paperback. ISBN 0-7088-2171-5. * 10th printing, May 1991.
ll. As: *Kudzo*. Gornji Milanovac, Croatia: Decje novine, 1987, 299 pp., 24 cm. Croatian translation by Svetlana Bezdanov. ISBN 86-367-0048-5.
mm. Helsinki, Finland: Book Studio, 1987, 374 pp. Finnish translation by Reijo Kalvas. ISBN 951-611-486-5; ISBN 951-611-494-6. * Reprint, 1992.
nn. Ljubljana, Slovenia: Mladinska knjiga, ZBIRKA ZENIT, 1988, 298 pp., 21 cm. Slovenian translation by Jure Potokar. ISBN 86-11-01065-5.
oo. Stockholm, Sweden: Legenda, 1988, 342 pp., 19 cm., hardcover and paperback. Swedish translation by Jimmy Hofsö. ISBN 91-582-047205, 91-582-0604-3.
pp. As: *Feuerkind/Cujo*. Munich, Germany: Gustav Lübbe, 14 March 1990, 38,00 DM, hardcover. German translation.. ISBN 3-7857-0573-5. Omnibus edition of *Firestarter* and *Cujo*.
qq. As: *Faresonen* ['Danger-son']. Oslo, Norway: Hjemmets bokforlag, 1990, 343 pp. Norwegian translation by Jan Nergaard. ISBN 82-590-0644-8.
rr. As: *Dræberhunden Cujo* ['Killer-dog']. Valby, Denmark: Borgen/ Narayana Press, 1991, 317 pp., 88 KR, paperback. Danish translation by Niels Søndergaard. ISBN 87-418-6291-0. * 2nd printing, 1992.
ss. Milan, Italy: Sperling Paperback, SUPERBESTSELLER #220, July 1992, paperback. Italian translation by Tullio Dobner. ISBN 88-7824-235-7.
tt. London, England: Warner Books, 1992, 345 pp. ISBN 0-7515-0440-8.
uu. As: [Title unknown]. South Korea, 1992, 444 pp., 23 cm. Korean translation.
vv. Munich, Germany: Bastei-Lübbe, 1 March 1993, paperback. German translation. ISBN 3-404-28109-8. "Deutsche Erstausgabe" ['German first edition'].
ww. Barcelona, Spain: Grijalba Mondadori, LA PUERTA OSCURA, April 1992, 416 pp., 2788 pta., 18 cm., trade paperback. Spanish translation by María Antonia Menini. ISBN 84-253-2417-3. * 8th edition 1992, LA PUERTA OSCURA, ISBN 84-253-2417-3.
xx. Stuttgart and Munich, Germany: Deutscher Bücherbund, [1992], 315 pp. German translation by Harro Christensen. Book Club edition.
yy. Thorndike ME: G. K. Hall, LARGE PRINT CORE COLLECTION, [1993], 474 pp., 25 cm., hardcover [?]. Large print edition. ISBN 0-8161-5667-0.
zz. Cologne, Germany: Lingen, [1993], 389 pp. German translation by Harro

MICHAEL R. COLLINGS

Cujo. Barcelona, Spain: Grijalba Mondadori, 1982. Paperback.

Christensen. Special edition.

aaa. As: *Faresonen* ['Danger-son']. Oslo, Norway: Egmont Bøker Fredhøi, EGMONT SPENNING #24, 1993, 342 pp., 495.00, paperback [*heftet*]. Norwegian translation. ISBN 82-04-03023-1.

bbb. Barcelona, Spain: RBA Collecionables, GRANDES ÉXITOS #35, 1993, 416 pp., 966 pta., 22 cm, trade paperback. Spanish translation by María Antonia Menini. ISBN 84-473-0241-5. * Reprint, 1998.

ccc. New York, Plume/New American Library, October 1994, xvii + 277 pp., $14.95, 24 cm., trade paperback. Introduction by Dan Simmons. "Collector's Edition" with color reproduction of original hardcover art by Geoff Grove. ISBN 0-452-27328-5.

ddd. New York: New American Library, December 1994, $7.99, mass-market paperback. Reissue edition. ISBN 0-451-16135-1.

eee. Paris, France: France Loisirs, 1994, 352 pp., 92 F, hardcover. French translation by Natalie Zimmermann. ISBN 2-7242-7836-4.

fff. Amsterdam, Netherlands: Poema Pocket, 1994, 319 pp., paperback. Dutch translation by Margot Bakker. 11th printing. ISBN 90-245-1087-2.

ggg. Warsaw, Poland: "Prima," BESTSELLERY LITERATURY ŒWIATOWEJ, 1994, 301 pp., 20 cm. Polish translation by Jacek Manicki. ISBN 83-8585-539-4.

hhh. Barcelona, Spain: Grijalbo, LIBRO DE MANO #12, 1995, 393 pp., 21 cm, trade paperback. Spanish translation by María Antonia Menini. ISBN 84-253-2805-5.

iii. As: *Faresonen* ['Danger-son']. Oslo, Norway: Egmont Hjemmets Bokforlag, 1996, 343 pp., 179.00, hardcover [*innbundet*]. Norwegian translation by Jan Nergaard. ISBN 82-59-01658-3. Book Club edition.

jjj. Barcelona, Spain: RBA Collecionables, GRANDES ÉXITOS #66, 1996, 416 pp., 578 pta., 21 cm., mass-market paperback. Spanish translation by María Antonia Menini. ISBN 84-473-1024-8. * Reprint, 1998, ISBN 84-473-1356-5.

kkk. Barcelona, Spain: Mondadori, MITOS BOLSILLO, [1999], 393 pp., 18 cm., paperback. Spanish translation by María Antonia Menini. 1st printing in this format. ISBN 84-397-0315-5.

lll. As FILM: *Cujo*. Warner Communications, Sunni Classic Pictures, Taft Entertainment Co., 1983. Produced by Daniel H. Blatt and Robert Singer. Directed by Lewis Teague. Screenplay by Don Carlos Dunaway and Lauren Currier [Barbara Turner]. 93 minutes. Rating: R.
CAST: Dee Wallace, Daniel Hugh-Kelly, Christopher Stone, Ed Lauter, Danny Pintauro.
   SELECTED ARTICLES, RESPONSES, AND REVIEWS:
   Blue, Tyson. "King's Novel Cujo Is a Motion Picture Delight." *Courier Herald* [Dublin GA] 13 August 1983.
   Coleman, J. *New Statesman* [England] Vol. 106, No. 2748 (18 November 1983): 28.
   Counts, Kyle. "King's Shaggy Dog Thriller Only Succeeds at the Shock Level." *Cinefantastique* Vol. 14, No. 2 (December 1983-January

1984): 50.

Everett, David. "*Cujo*: Lewis Teague, The Alligator Director, Talks About Bringing Stephen King's Rabid Saint Bernard to the Screen." *Fangoria* (October 1983).

"Fantasy Films '83: The Year of Living Langorously." *Twilight Zone Magazine* Vol. 3, No. 6 (January/February 1984): 49.

Horsting, Jessie. "*Cujo*: Director Lewis Teague Reveals the Difficulties of Adapting the Best-Selling Novel for the Screen." *Fantastic Films* No. 36 (November 1983).

Horsting, Jessie. "*Cujo*: The Movie." *Fantastic Films* No. 36 (November 1983).

Jenkins, S. *Monthly Film Bulletin* Vol. 50, No. 598 (November 1983): 301.

Jenkins, S. *Sight and Sound* Vol. 52, No. 1 (Winter 1983/1984): 4.

Minton, L. *McCall's* Vol. 111, No. 2 (November 1983): 82.

Nash, Jay Robert, and Stanley Ralph Ross. "Cujo." *The Motion Picture Guide, 1927-1983*, Vol. II. Chicago: Cinebooks, 1985, hardcover. 535.

Powell, D. *Punch* Vol. 285, No. 7461 (23 November 1983): 73.

San Francisco Chronicle [CA] 15 August 1983: 40.

Sight and Sound Vol. 52, No. 1 (Winter 1983/1984): 76.

Spignesi, Stephen J. "Dog (and Cat) Days: An Interview With Lewis Teague." *The Shape Under the Sheet: The Complete Stephen King Encyclopedia*. Ann Arbor MI: Popular Culture, Ink, May 1991, hardcover. 572-574.

Stein, F. *The Village Voice* Vol. 28, No. 34 (23 August 1983): 49.

Time Vol. 122, No. 11 (12 September 1983): 70.

Variety Vol. 312, No. 3 (17 August 1983): 23.

Wood, Gary. "Animal Lovers vs. Pets Run Amuk." *Cinefantastique* Vol. 21, No. 4 (February 1991): 42.

mmm. As VIDEOCASSETTE: Warner Communications, Taft Entertainment, 1983. Beta, VHS, CED. 120 minutes

COMMENTS: 350,000 copies sold in 1981; the novel ranked #3 on the *Publishers Weekly* annual hardcover Bestsellers List, 1981.

Closer to mainstream fiction than many of King's earlier works, *Cujo* may originally have been intended as a 'Richard Bachman' novel. In the second draft, King incorporated references to Frank Dodd and the Castle Rock mystique, as well as the supernatural elements of the monster in the closet, in order to bring the novel closer to the atmosphere and tone of those already published under his name. The novel essentially demonstrates the incremental horrors of daily life as love is betrayed and trust leads to death.

SELECTED ARTICLES, RESPONSES, AND REVIEWS:

Bishop, Michael. "Mad Dogs...and Englishmen." *Washington Post Book World* 11 (23 August 1981): 1-2.

Bishop, Michael. "The Saint Bernard That Becomes an Engine of Madness and Death." *SF Chronicle* "Review" (20 September 1981): 3. Excerpted: *Contemporary Literary Criticism*, Vol. 26. Edited by Jean C. Stine. Detroit MI: Gale Research Co., 1983, hardcover. 238-239.

Booklist Vol. 77 (15 May 1981): 1213.

Broderick, Dorothy M. *Voice of Youth Advocates* Vol. 4, No. 4 (October 1981): 34.

Budrys, Algis. "A Doggy New Novel from Stephen King." *Chicago Sun-Times* [IL] 6 September 1981.

Chute, David. "King Gives Second-Best Horror Effort in *Cujo*." *Los Angeles Herald Examiner* 9 September 1981.

Davis, L. J. "A Shabby Dog Story from Stephen King." *Chicago Tribune Book World* (16 August 1981).

English Journal Vol. 72 (January 1983): 79.

Graham, Mark. "Mouth Foaming for Good Scare?" *Rocky Mountain News* [Denver CO] 6 September 1981: 32.

Green, Michael. *Saturday Review* Vol. 8 (September 1981): 59.

Hall, Melissa Mia. "Stephen King Thinks It's Fun to 'Get the Reader.'" *Fort Worth Star-Telegram* [TX] 23 August 1981).

Hatlen, Burton. "The Mad Dog and Maine." *Shadowings*. Edited by Douglas E. Winter. Mercer Island WA: Starmont House, 1983. 33-38.

Kirkus Reviews Vol. 49 (1 July 1981): 825.

Kirkus Reviews Vol. 49 (15 July 1981): 878.

Lehmann-Haupt, Christopher. "Books of the Times." *The New York Times* 14 August 1981: C21. Late edition.

Pascal, Sylvia. *School Library Journal* Vol. 28, No. 2 (October 1981): 162.

Publishers Weekly Vol. 220, No. 3 (17 July 1981): 80.

Publishers Weekly Vol. 221 (11 June 1982): 61.

San Francisco Chronicle 21 August 1981: 59.

Science Fiction Review Vol. 11 (May 1982): 47.

Starship Vol. 18 (Summer 1981): 5.

Strouse, Jean. "Beware of the Dog." *Newsweek* 98 (31 August 1981): 64.

Stump, Debra. "A Matter of Choice: King's *Cujo* and Malamud's *The Natural*." *Discovering Stephen King*. Edited by Darrell Schweitzer. STARMONT STUDIES IN LITERARY CRITICISM, #8. Mercer Island WA: Starmont House, 1985. 131-140.

Thompson, Thomas. "King's Latest a Shaggy Rabid Dog Story." *Los Angeles Times Book Review* 6 September 1981: 5. Reprinted As: "*Cujo*: Tale About a Mad Dog Ought to be Put to Sleep." *Baltimore News American* [MD] 6 September 1981.

Winter, Douglas E. "King's *Cujo*: 'Nope, Nothing Wrong Here'." *Fantasy Newsletter* (November 1981): 9-11.

Yamamoto, Judith. *Library Journal* Vol. 106 (July 1981): 1442.

MICHAEL R. COLLINGS

A13.
THE SHINING, 'SALEM'S LOT, NIGHT SHIFT, CARRIE
(1981 – Omnibus)

A13. *The Shining, 'Salem's Lot, Night Shift, Carrie*. London, England: Octopus Books, September 1981, 991 pp., hardcover. Omnibus collection

CONTENTS: *The Shining* (1977, see A3); *'Salem's Lot* (1975, see A2); *Night Shift* (1978, see A6); *Carrie* (1974, see A1).

REPRINTS AND ADAPTATIONS:
b. As: *The Shining, 'Salem's Lot, Carrie*. London, England: Octopus Books, Heinemann, July 1983, 747 pp., hardcover. *Night Shift* not included.
c. Peerage Books, 1986, 1991 pp., hardcover. Restores the original text of the 1981 version; issued in one slipcase with the omnibus editions, *Isaac Asimov* and *Robert Ludlum*.

MICHAEL R. COLLINGS

THE RUNNING MAN. London: New English Library, 1983. Mass-market paperback.

A14.
THE RUNNING MAN
AS RICHARD BACHMAN
(1982)

A14. THE RUNNING MAN, by 'Richard Bachman.' New York: Signet/New American Library, May 1982, 219 pp., mass-market paperback. 451-AE1508. Science-fiction novel.

PLOT SUMMARY: Unemployed and desperate in the business-controlled America of 2025, Ben Richards becomes a contestant on the TV program, *The Running Man*, hoping to earn enough money to rescue his wife and daughter from poverty; ironically, they are killed by thieves looking for the money the network advances them. Richards eludes capture long enough to return to network headquarters and extract his vengeance.

REPRINTS AND ADAPTATIONS.:
b. As: *El Fugitivo* ['The fugitive']. Buenos Aires, Argentina: Círculo de Lectores, [1982?], 232 pp., 19 cm. Spanish translation. ISBN 950-19-0319-2.
c. London, England: New English Library, December 1983, 219 pp., paperback.
d. As: *L'uomo in Fugi* ['The man in flight']. Milan, Italy: Arnoldo Mondadori, URANIA #962, 22 January 1984. Italian translation by Delio Zinoni.
e. In: *The Bachman Books: Four Early Novels by Stephen King*. New York: New American Library, October 1985, hardcover. 531-692. [See A30].
f. As: *Vlucht Naar de Top* ['Flight to the top'], in: *4 X Stephen King*. Utrecht, Belgium: Luitingh, 1986, pp., paperback. Dutch translation by Frank de Groot.
g. As: *Menschenjagd* ['Manhunt'], by Richard Bachman. Munich, Germany: Wilhelm Heyne TB 6687, 1986, 253 pp., 6.80 DM, paperback. German translation by Nora Jensen. Cover includes the note that "Bachman est King." ISBN 0-453-02291-2. * 4th printing, 1987. * 7th printing, film tie-in, 1988. * 11th printing, 1989. * 14th printing, 1991. * 21st printing, 1993* 25th printing, 1995.
h. As: *Den Flyende Mannen* ['The fleeing man'], by "Stephen King alias Richard Bachman." Stockholm, Sweden: Legenda, 1986, 226 pp. Swedish

translation by Jimmy Hofsö. * 2nd printing, 1988, ISBN 91-582-1155-1. * Reprint, 1989, ISBN 91-582-1495-X.
i. As: *El Fugitivo* ['The fugitive']. Barcelona, Spain: Ediciones Martínez Roca, 1986, 258 pp., 22 cm., hardcover. Spanish translation by Hernán Sabaté.
j. As: *El Fugitivo* ['The fugitive']. Barcelona, Spain: Martínez Roca, GRANSUPERFICCION, 1986, 258 pp., 22 cm., paperback. Spanish translation by Hernán Sabaté. ISBN 84-2709-1021-1. * Reprint, 1987, ISBN 84-270-1031-1.
k. As: *El Fugitivo* ['The fugitive']. Barcelona, Spain: Círculo de Lectores, 1986, 212 pp., 22 cm. Spanish translation by Hernán Sabaté. ISBN 84-226-2188-6.
l. As: *Batorurunna* Tokyo, Japan: Fusosha, 1987. Japanese translation by Sakai Akinobu.
m. London, England: New English Library, September 1988, 219 pp., £2.99, paperback. "Stephen King writing as Richard Bachman." ISBN 0-450-05642-2.
n. New York: Signet/New American Library, 1988, 219 pp., movie tie-in edition. * 7th printing by September, 1989.
o. As: *Vlucht Naar de Top* ['Flight to the top'], by Stephen King. Utrecht, Belgium: Luitingh, 1988, 199 pp. Dutch translation by Frank de Groot. ISBN 90-245-1554-8.
p. Paris, France: Albin Michel, 1988, 258 pp., 79 F, paperback. French translation by Frank Straschitz. ISBN 2-226-03381-5.
q. [Paris, France]: [le Grand livre du mois], 1988, 258 pp., 79 F, hardcover. French translation by Frank Straschitz. Book Club edition.
r. Paris, France: France Loisirs, 1988, 258 pp., 60 F, hardcover. French translation by Frank Straschitz. ISBN 2-7242-4221-1.
s. As: *L'uomo in fuga* ['The man in flight']. Milan, Italy: Arnoldo Mondadori, OSCAR #2099, February 1989. Italian translation by Delio Zinoni. ISBN 88-04-31992-5.
t. Paris, France: J'ai Lu, SUSPENSE #2694, 1989, 249 pp., 21 F., paperback. French translation by Frank Straschitz. ISBN 2-277-22694-7.
u. As: [Title unknown]. Mexico: Ediciones Roca, 1989. Spanish translation.
v. As: *Den Flyende Mannen* ['The fleeing man'], by "Stephen King alias Richard Bachman." Stockholm, Sweden: Legenda, 1990, 226 pp., 18 cm., paperback. Swedish translation by Jimmy Hofsö. ISBN 91-582-1629-4.
w. As: *L'uomo in fuga* ['The man in flight']. Milan, Italy: Arnoldo Mondadori, BESTSELLERS OSCAR #227, 26 July 1991. Italian translation by Delio Zinoni. ISBN 88-04-35410-0.
x. As: *Uciekinier* ['Refugee' (?)]. Poznañ, Poland: CIA-Books/ SVARO, 1992, 282 pp., 18 cm., paperback. Polish translation by Robert P. Lipski. ISBN 83-8510-038-5.
y. As: *Den løbende mand* ['The Running Man']. Copenhagen, Denmark: Bogsamleren, 1993, 237 pp., 75,00 KR, hardcover. Danish translation by

Mogens Wenzel Andreasen. ISBN 87-7531-408-8.
z. Paris, France: France Loisirs, 1994, 259 pp., 76 F, hardcover. French translation by Frank Straschitz. ISBN 2-7242-8197-7.
aa. As: *Fluch/Menschenjagd/Sprengstoff: Drei Romane in einem Band* ['Curse/Manhunt/Explosive: Three Novels in one Volume']. Munich, Germany: Wilhelm Heyne, #9116, September 1994, 346 pp., 15.00 DM, paperback. German translation by Nora Jensen. * 3rd printing, 1995, ISBN 3-453-07567-6.
bb. As: *Den løbende mand* ['The running man']. Copenhagen, Denmark: Paperback Bogklubben, 1996, 237 pp., 39,50 KR, paperback. Danish translation by Mogens Wenzel Andreasen. ISBN 87-7803-522-8.
cc. As: *L'uomo in fuga* ['The man in flight']. Milan, Italy: Sperling & Kupfer, NARRATIVA [#238], September 1997. Italian translation by Tullio Dobner. ISBN 88-200-2250-8.
dd. As: *Flykt for livet* ['Flight for life']. Oslo, Norway: Egmont Bøker Fredhøi, 1997, 253 pp., 595.00, paperback [*heftet*]. Norwegian translation. ISBN 82-04-04970-6.
ee. As: *El Fugitivo* ['The fugitive']. Barcelona, Spain: Plaza & Janés, JET 102/BIBLIOTECA DE STEPHEN KING #17, 1997, 298 pp., 18 cm. Spanish translation by Hernán Sabaté. ISBN 84-01-47467-1.
ff. New York: Signet, August 1999, 317 pp., $7.99, mass-market paperback. ISBN 0-451-1979-6.
gg. As: [Title unknown]. Greek translation.
hh. As: [Title unknown]. Moscow, Russia: Cadman. Russian translation.
ii. As: [Title unknown]. Helsinki, Finland. Finnish translation. Omnibus edition with *Roadwork*.

jj. As FILM: *The Running Man*. Tri-Star/Taft Entertainment 13 November 1988. Executive producers, Keith Barish, Rob Cohen. Produced by Tim Zinneman, George Linder. Directed by Paul Michael Glasser. Screenplay by Steven E. de Souza. 101 minutes. Rating: R. CAST: Arnold Schwarzenegger, Maria Conchita Alonso, Yaphet Kotto, Jim Brown, Richard Dawson.
 SELECTED ARTICLES, RESPONSES, AND REVIEWS:
 Blue, Tyson. "'Running Man': Fun for Arnie." *Castle Rock: The Stephen King Newsletter* Vol. 4, No. 2 (February 1988): 5.
 Collings, Michael R. "*The Running Man* and Stephen King: Not a Bad Film." *Castle Rock: The Stephen King Newsletter* Vol. 4, No. 2 (February 1988): 1, 4.
 Fangoria No. 69 (December 1987). Four-page article with photographs.
 Harris, Ian. "Arnold Who?" *Castle Rock: The Stephen King Newsletter* Vol. 2, No. 6 (June 1986): 2.
 McGuigan, C., and J. Huck. *Newsweek* Vol. 110, No. 23 (7 December 1987): 84.
 Magid, R. *American Cinematographer* Vol. 68, No. 12 (December 1987): 70.

"More Comments on *The Running Man*." *Castle Rock: The Stephen King Newsletter* Vol. 4, No. 2 (February 1988): 4-5. Reader-response reviews to the film.

Scapperotti, D. *Cinefantastique* Vol. 17, No. 5 (September 1987): 17.

Schweitzer, Darrell. "*The Running Man* and Stephen King: *The Running Man* Is Fundamentally Dishonest." *Castle Rock: The Stephen King Newsletter* Vol. 4, No. 2 (February 1988): 1, 4.

Starlog (December 1987).

kk. As VIDEOCASSETTE: *The Running Man*. Taft, 1989. VHS. Rated: R.

COMMENTS: The fourth 'Bachman' novel, *The Running Man* was written in a weekend while King was a student at the University of Maine, Orono, and subsequently published almost unrevised. The novel has a distinctive science-fictional basis, allowing King to explore extrapolative satire based on the media, television game shows, and American culture in general. Along with *Roadwork*, the novel prefigures with almost clinical sharpness his subsequent interest in largely non-horror treatments of social and political themes, particularly during the 1990's.

SELECTED ARTICLES, RESPONSES, AND REVIEWS:

Brown. Stephen P. "The Life and Death of Richard Bachman: Stephen King's Doppelgänger." *Kingdom of Fear: The World of Stephen King*. Edited by Tim Underwood and Chuck Miller. San Francisco CA: Underwood-Miller, 1986. 109-126.

Donovan, Diane C. *Voice of Youth Advocates* Vol. 6, No. 1 (April 1983): 44. [No reference to King as author]. Excerpted: *Contemporary Literary Criticism*, Vol. 37. Edited by Daniel G. Marowski. Detroit MI: Gale Research, 1986. 201.

D'Ammassa, Don. "Three by Bachman." *Discovering Stephen King*. Edited by Darrell Schweitzer. STARMONT STUDIES IN LITERARY CRITICISM, #8. Mercer Island WA: Starmont House, 1985. 123-130.

HORROR PLUM'D

CREEPSHOW. New York, NY: Plume/New American Library, 1982. Over-sized trade paperback.

A15. *Creepshow* (1982)

A15. *Stephen King's Creepshow: A George A. Romero Film.* Artwork by Berni Wrightson. New York: Plume/New American Library, July 1982, [64] pp., oversized trade paperback. Comic-book collection of horror short stories.

CONTENTS: "Father's Day" (1982; see B65); "The Lonesome Death of Jordy Verrill" (as "Weeds," 1976; see B66 and B27); "The Crate" (1979; see B43); "Something to Tide You Over" (1982; see B67); "They're Creeping Up on You" (1982; see B68).

REPRINTS AND ADAPTATIONS:
b. Garden City NY: Plume/New American Library, [n.d.], 64 pp., paper. Science Fiction Book Club edition.
c. Garden City NY: Mystery Guild Book Club, [n.d.], paper.
d. Amsterdam, Netherlands: W. L. Beck, 1983, [64] pp., f 25,-, hardcover. Dutch translation by professional translation studio. Printed in Spain. ISBN 90-6756-201-7.
e. Paris, France: L'Echo des Savanes/Albin Michel, Spécial USA, 1983, 64 pp., 45 F, hardcover. French translation by Janine Bharucha. ISBN 2-226-01754-2.
f. Barcelona, Spain: IHASA, [1983], [64] pp., 29 cm. Spanish translation. ISBN 84-499-9376-8.
g. Barcelona, Spain: Toutain and Alvagraf, 1984, 68 pp., 28 cm. Spanish translation.
h. Bergish Gladbach, West Germany: Bastei-Lübbe TB 71202, 1989, [64] pp., 12.80 DM, paperback. German translation. ISBN 3-404-71202-1.
COMMENTS: A comic-book adaptation of the King-Romero film, *Creepshow*, the book was published in softcover format, with frames suggesting E. C. Comics originals. "The Crate" and "The Lonesome Death of Jordy Verrill" (as "Weeds") had appeared previously; the remaining tales are original to the film and the collection. The book deletes the film's framing tale.

i. AS FILM: *CREEPSHOW*: Warner Brothers, Laurel Films, United Film Distribution, October 1982. Produced by Richard Rubinstein. Directed by George A. Romero. Screenplay by Stephen King. 120 minutes. Rating: R.
CAST: Viveca Lindfors, Carrie Nye, Ed Harris, Stephen King, Leslie Nelson, Ted Danson, Gaylen Ross, Hal Holbrook, Adrienne Barbeau, Fritz Weaver, E. G. Marshall, Joe King.
EPISODES: "Prologue"; "Father's Day" [17 minutes]; "The Lonesome Death of Jordy Verrill" [14 minutes]; "Something to Tide You Over" [25 minutes]; "The Crate" [37 minutes]; "They're Creeping Up On You" [14 minutes]; "Epilogue."

SELECTED FILM REVIEWS AND ARTICLES.:

American Film Vol. 7, No. 9 (July/August 1982): 79.

"Are These The Scariest Men in America." *Cinefantastique* Vol. 13, No. 1 (September/October 1982).

Blue, Tyson *Courier Herald* [Dublin GA] 6 November 1982.

Chute, D. *Film Comment* Vol. 18, No. 5 (September/October 1982): 13+.

"'*Creepshow*' Horrifies Viewers by Playing on Human Phobias." *Arkansas Gazette* [Little Rock AR] 5 December 1982. As microfiche: *Newsbank: Film and Television* Vol. 9 (January 1983): Fiche 60, G7.

"'*Creepshow*' Isn't Just Another Slice-and-Dice Horror Movie." *Concord Monitor* [NH] 2 December 1982. As microfiche: *Newsbank: Film and Television* Vol. 9 (January 1983): Fiche 60, G9.

"'*Creepshow*': It's Awful Times Two." *Bulletin & Advertiser* [Honolulu HI] 15 November 1982. As microfiche: *Newsbank: Film and Television* Vol. 9 (January 1983): Fiche 60, G8.

Ebert, Roger. *Roger Ebert's Movie Home Companion, 1988 Edition.* Kansas City MO: Andrews, McMeel & Parker, 1987, pp. 126.

Everitt, David. "Of Roaches and Snakes." *Fangoria* No. 20 (1982): 13-16.

Everman, Welch D. "TZ Video." *Twilight Zone Magazine* (February 1986): 88-91.

Famous Monsters Film Fantasy Yearbook, 1983. [4-page article].

"Front Row Seats at the *Creepshow*." *Twilight Zone Magazine* (May 1982).

Fangoria 37 ( ). Article and pull-out poster.

Fangoria 45 ( ). King portrayed in a pull-out poster.

Gagne, Paul R. *Cinefantastique* Vol. 12, No. 1 (February 1982): 6.

Gagne, Paul R. "*Creepshow*: Five Jolting Tales of Horror! from Stephen King and George Romero." *Cinefantastique* Vol. 12, Nos. 2/3 (April 1982): 16+.

Gagne, Paul R. "*Creepshow*: It's an $8 Million Comic Book, from George Romero and Friends." *Cinefantastique* Vol. 13, No. 1

(September-October 1982): 17-35.

Gagne, Paul R. *Cinefantastique* Vol. 13, Nos. 2/3 (November-December 1982): 10+.

Gagne, Paul R. *The Zombies That Ate Pittsburgh: The Films of George A. Romero*. New York: Dodd, Mead, 1987, 236 pp., paperback.

Gilbert, R. *New York Magazine* Vol. 15, No. 37 (20 September 1982): 36.

Hansen, Ron. "*Creepshow*: The Dawn of a Living Horror Comedy." *Esquire* (January 1982): 72-73, 76. Excerpted: *Contemporary Literary Criticism*, Vol. 26. Edited by Jean C. Stine. Detroit MI: Gale Research, 1983, hardcover. 239-240.

Hoberman, J. *The Village Voice* Vol. 27, No. 47 (23 November 1982): 62.

Hogan, David J. "*Creepshow*: Romero, King Bring Back the Gory Glory Days of E.C. Comics." *Cinefantastique* Vol. 13, No. 4 (April-May 1983).

"Horrors! Romero and King Tap the Funny Bone in '*Creepshow*.'" *Des Moines Register* [IA] 18 November 1985. As microfiche: *Newsbank: Film and Television* Vol. 9 (February 1983): Fiche 73, B5.

Lundegaard, Bob. "Have No Fear, '*Creepshow*' Is Hardly Crawling with Horror." *Minneapolis Star and Tribune* [MN] 19 November 1985. As microfiche: *Newsbank: Film and Television* Vol. 9 (February 1983): Fiche 73, B6.

Mahar, Ted. "Horror Anthology '*Creepshow*' Creeps on Much Too Long." *The Oregonian* [Portland OR] 20 November 1982. As microfiche: *Newsbank: Film and Television* Vol. 9 (January 1983): Fiche 60, G10.

Martin, Robert H. [Bob]. "TZ Screen Preview: *Creepshow*." *Twilight Zone Magazine* (September 1982).

Martin, Robert H. [Bob]. "A Casual Chat with Mr. George A. Romaro." *Fangoria* (October 1982). On *Creepshow*, with stills from the film.

Martin, Robert H. [Bob]. "On (and Off) the Set of *Creepshow*: Tom Savini at Work; Stephen King at Home." *Fangoria* 20 (1982): 40-43. King's work with *Creepshow* and plans for other projects.

McDonnell, David, and John Sayers. "*Creepshow*: The First Look Inside George Romero's New Bestiary." *Mediascene Prevue* (May 1982): 61-63.

Milne, T. *Monthly Film Bulletin* [England] Vol. 49, No. 586 (November 1982): 260.

Mitchell, Blake, and Jim Ferguson. "Director George Romero Talks About *Creepshow*." *Fantastic Films* No. 32 (February 1983).

Naha, Ed. "Fritz Weaver and *Creepshow*." *Fangoria* (May 1982): 43.

Naha, Ed. "Front Row Seats at the *Creepshow*." *Twilight Zone Magazine* (May 1982): 46-50.

Nash, Jay Robert, and Stanley Ralph Ross. "*Creepshow.*" *The Motion Picture Guide, 1927-1983*, Vol. II. Chicago: Cinebooks, 1985, hardcover. 512.

Rambeau, Catharine. "Zombies Carry Director into Limelight." *Detroit Free Press* [MI] 11 August 1985. As microfiche: *Newsbank: Film and Television* Vol. 12 (September 1985): Fiche 31, E2-E3.

"Reel Comic Book." *Arizona Republic* [Phoenix AZ] 29 November 1982. As microfiche: *Newsbank: Film and Television* Vol. 9 (January 1983): Fiche 60, G6.

San Francisco Chronicle "Reviews" [CA] 19 December 1982: 6.

Sragow, Michael. "Stephen King's *Creepshow*: The Aesthetics of Gross-Out." *Rolling Stone* 383 (25 November 1982): 48, 54. Excerpted: *Contemporary Literary Criticism*, Vol. 26. Edited by Jean C. Stine. Detroit MI: Gale Research, 1983, hardcover. 243-244.

Stein, J. "*Creepshow.*" *Fantastic Films* (November 1982).

Taggart, Patrick. "'*Creepshow*'—Director Aims for More Visibility." *American-Statesman* [Austin TX] 21 November 1982. As microfiche: *Newsbank: Film and Television* Vol. 9 (January 1983): Fiche 60, G11.

Variety Vol. 307, No. 4 (26 May 1982): 17.

Voice of Youth Advocates Vol. 6 (December 1983): 266.

Wiater, Stanley. "Stephen King and George Romero: Collaboration in Terror." *Bloody Best of Fangoria* (1982): 28-29. On *Creepshow* and *Children of the Corn*, with backgrounds for both films.

Williamson, B. *Playboy* Vol. 29, No. 11 (November 1982): 42.

Winter, Douglas E. "I Want My Cake!: Thoughts on *Creepshow* and E.C. Comics." *Fantasy Newsletter* (February 1983). Revised: *Shadowings*. Edited by Douglas E. Winter. Mercer Island WA: Starmont House, 1983, hardcover. 135-138.

j. As: VIDEOCASSETTE: *Creepshow*. Warner Home Video, 1982, $14.95. VHS, Beta, CED. 120 minutes. Rated R. ASIN 6305335745
SELECTED VIDEOCASSETTE REVIEWS AND ARTICLES:
Dauphin, E. *Creem* Vol. 14, No. 11 (April 1983): 47.
Hogan, D. J. "My Dribble Cup Runneth Over." *Cinefantastique* Vol. 13, No. 4 (April/May 1983): 56.
Minton, L. *McCall's* Vol. 110, No. 5 (February 1983): 128.
Sight and Sound Vol. 52, No. 1 (Winter 1982/1983): 76.

k. As DVD: Warner Home Video, 26 October 1999, $19.98, 120 minutes. Rated: R. ASIN 0790744295. With theatrical trailers.

SELECTED ARTICLES, RESPONSES, AND REVIEWS:
Ansen, David. "The Roaches Did It." *Newsweek* Vol. 100, No. 21 (22 November

1982): 118A. Movie review. Excerpted: *Contemporary Literary Criticism*, Vol. 26. Edited by Jean C. Stine. Detroit MI: Gale Research Co., 1983. 243.

Corliss, Richard. "Jolly Contempt." *Time* Vol. 120, No. 21 (22 November 1982): 108-110. Excerpted: *Contemporary Literary Criticism*, Vol. 26. Edited by Jean C. Stine. Detroit MI: Gale Research, 1983. 243.

Los Angeles Times Book Review 29 August 1982: 6.

Science Fiction Review Vol. 12 (November 1983): 47.

Village Voice Literary Supplement (September 1982): 6.

Winter, Douglas E. "Collecting King." *Twilight Zone Magazine* Vol. 5, No. 6 (February 1986): 32-33, 97.

MICHAEL R. COLLINGS

DIFFERENT SEASONS. New York, NY: Viking Press, 1982. Hardcover.

A16.
DIFFERENT SEASONS
(1982)

A16. DIFFERENT SEASONS. New York: Viking Press, 27 August 1982, 527 pp., $16.95. hardcover. Novella collection. ISBN 0-670-27266-3.

CONTENTS (all original): "Hope Springs Eternal: Rita Hayworth and Shawshank Redemption" [see B61]; "Summer of Corruption: Apt Pupil" [see B62]; "Fall from Innocence: The Body" [see B63]; "A Winter's Tale: The Breathing Method" [see B64]; "Afterword," by King [see C96].

REPRINTS AND ADAPTATIONS [SEE ALSO ENTRIES UNDER INDIVIDUAL SHORT-FICTION TITLES]:

b. London, England: Macdonald, October 1982, 468 pp., hardcover.
c. As: *Szu chi*. Taipei, Taiwan: Huang kuan chu pan she, 1982. Chinese translation by Shih Chi-ching and Chao Yung-fen.
d. As *Szu chi*. Taipei, Taiwan: Huan guan, 1982. Chinese translation by Shi Jiging and Zhao Yongfen.
e. New York: Signet/New American Library, August 1983, 507 pp., mass-market paperback. ISBN 0-451-16753-8. Reissue October 1986, 507 pp., $4.50, mass-market paperback. Movie tic-in edition with *Stand by Me;* new cover, includes blurb: "*Stand by Me*—now a smash movie based on *The Body*, a novella in DIFFERENT SEASONS." 13th printing. ISBN 0-451-14764-2. * Reissue, New York: Penguin/Signet, July 1992, $5.99, mass-market paperback. ISBN 0-451-14764-2. * Reprint as *Stephen King: The Shawshank Redemption—Different Seasons*, 1994, movie tie-in with *The Shawshank Redemption*.
f. London, England: Futura, September 1983, 560 pp., paperback.
g. Thorndike, ME: Thorndike Press, 1983. Large-print edition.
h. Excerpted as: *Sommardåd—två berättelser* ['Summer's day: two stories']. Stockholm, Sweden: Askild and Kørnekull, 1983, 305 pp. Swedish translation by Martin Edlund.
i. Excerpted as: *El Cuerpo: Verano de Corrupción* ['The Body: Summer of corruption'—"Rita Hayworth…" and "Apt Pupil"]. Barcelona, Spain and

Buenos Aires, Argentina: Grijalbo, BESTSELLER ORO, 1983, 356 pp., 21 cm., paperback. Spanish translation by José Manuel Pérez and Ángela Pérez. ISBN 84-253-1481-X [Spain], 950-28-0019-2 [Argentina]. * 2nd edition, EDIBOLSILLO, 1986, 18 cm., paperback, ISBN 84-253-1855-6. * Reprint, 1989.

j. Excerpted as: *El cuerpo* ['The body'; with *El método de respiración,* 'The Breathing Method']. Barcelona, Spain, and Buenos Aires, Argentina: Grijalbo, BESTSELLER ORO, 1983, 296 pp., 19/20 cm., paperback. Spanish translation by José Manuel Peréz and Angela Peréz. ISBN 84-253-1484-4 [Spain], 950-28-0028-1 [Brazil]. * 2nd printing, 1983, BESTSELLER ORO. * 3rd printing, 1987.

k. As: *Sommardåd—två berättelser* ['Summer's day: two stories']. Stockholm, Sweden: Askild & Kärnekull, 1983, 305 pp., hardcover. Swedish translation by Mårten Edlund. ISBN 91-582-0254-4.

l. As: *4 Seizoenen* [4 seasons']. Utrecht, Belgium: Veen, 1984. Dutch translation by Pauline Moody.
CONTENTS: "De Ontsnapping" ['The escape']; "De Leerling" ['The pupil]; "Het Lijk" ['The body']; "De Ademhalungsmethode" ['The breathing-method'].

m. As: *Frühling, Sommer, Herbst und Tod: vier Kurzromane* ['Spring, summer, autumn, and death: four short-novels']. Leipzig, East Germany. German translation by Harro Christensen.

n. As: *Frühling, Sommer, Herbst und Tod: vier Kurzromane* ['Spring, summer, autumn, and death: four short-novels']. Bergish Gladbach, West Germany: Bastei-Lübbe TB 28120, 1984, 550 pp., 19.80 DM, paperback. German translation by Harro Christensen. ISBN 3-404-21820-9.

o. Excerpted as: *Winterverk: Tva Berättelser* ['Winter-work: two stories']. Stockholm, Sweden: Askild and Kärnekull, 1984, 252 pp., 22 cm., hardcover. Swedish translation by Jimmy Hofsö. ISBN 91-582-0257-9.

p. Excerpted as: *De Leerling* ['The pupil']. Utrecht, Belgium: Veen, 1984, 271 pp., trade paperback. Dutch translation by Pauline Moody. ISBN 90-204-3741-0. 2nd printing, 1988.
CONTENTS: "De Leerling" ['The pupil'] and "De Ontnapping" ['The escape' "Rita Hayworth and Shawshank Redemption"].

q. Excerpted as: *Verano de Corrupción: El Cuerpo* ['Summer of corruption: the body']. Barcelona, Spain: Mundo Actual de Ediciones, 1984, 530 pp., 22 cm. Spanish translation by José Manuel Pérez and Ángela Pérez. ISBN 84-7454-276-6. Book Club edition.

r. Excerpted as: *It Weet Wat Je Wilt* ['I know what you want']. Utrecht, Belgium: Luitingh/Veen, Autumn 1985, 320 pp., trade paperback. Dutch translations by F. J. Brunning and Pauline Moody. * 2nd printing by 1986.
CONTENTS: Seven stories from *Night Shift* and *Different Seasons,* including "De Laaste Laddersport" ['The Last Ladder Game'="The Last Rung on the Ladder"]; "Ik Weet Wat Je Wilt" ['I Know What You Want'="I Know What You Need"]; "Stop Ermee, B.V." ['Stop It, Inc.'="Quitters,

Inc."]; "Jerusalem's Lot"; "Trucks"; "Het Lijk" ['The Corpse'="The Body"]; "De Ademhalingsmethode" ["The Breathing Method"].

s. London, England: Futura, July 1986, 560 pp., £2.95, paperback. ISBN 0-7088-2360-2. * Reprint, May 1991.

t. As: *Différentes Saisons*. Paris, France: Albin Michel, 1986, 529 pp., 98 F, hardcover. French translation by Pierre Alien. ISBN 2-226-02671-1.

u. As: *Différentes Saisons*. [Paris, France]: [le Grand livre du mois], 1986, 529 pp., 98 F, hardcover. French translation by Pierre Alien. Book Club edition.

v. As: *Différentes Saisons*. Paris, France: France Loisirs, 1986, 529 pp., 78 F, hardcover. French translation by Pierre Alien. ISBN 2-7242-3219-4. * Reprint, 1994; ISBN 2-7242-7841-0.

w. Excerpted as: *El Cuerpo* ['The body']. Barcelona, Spain: Grijalbo, EDIBOLSILLO, 1986, 296 pp., 19 cm., paperback. Spanish translation by J. N. Peréz and Angela Peréz. 2nd edition; 1st pocket edition. ISBN 84-253-1886-6.

x. As: *Stagioni Diverse* ['Different seasons']. Milano: Sperling & Kupfer PANDORA #335, March 1987, 588 pp. Italian translation by Bruno Amato, Paola Formenti, and M. B. Piccioli. 88-200-0665-0.

y. Excerpted as: *Jahreszeiten: Herbst und Winter* ['The seasons: fall and winter']. Bergisch Gladbach: Bastei-Lübbe, TB 13114, 1987, 331 pp., paperback. German translation by Harro Christensen.
CONTENTS: "Herbstsonate: Die Leiche" ['Autumn sonata: The Body'] and "Ein Winter Märchen: Atemtechnik" ['A winter's tale: The Breathing Method']; "Nachwort" ['Afterword'].

z. Excerpted as: *De Leerling* ['The pupil']. Utrecht, Belgium: Luitingh, 1987, 271 pp. Dutch translation by Pauline Moody. ISBN 90-245-1832-6.

aa. Tokyo, Japan, Shonchoshya, 1987. 2 vols. Japanese translation by Yamada Junko.

bb. As: *Quatro Estacoes* ['Four seasons']. 4 vols. Rio de Janeiro, Brazil: Francisco Alves, MESTRES DO HORROR E DA FANTASIA, 1988, 22 cm. Vol. 1, Primavera eterna; Vol. 2, Verao da corrupcao; Vol. 3, Outono da inocencia; Vol. 4, Inverno no clube. Portuguese translation by Andrea Oliviera da Costa. ISBN 85-265-0145-3.

cc. As: *Différentes Saisons*. Paris, France: J'ai Lu, ÉPOUVANTE #2434, 1988, 634 pp., 36 F, 17 cm., paperback. French translation by Pierre Alien. ISBN 2-277-22434-0. Reprint 1990.

dd. Excerpted as: *Jahreszeiten: Frühling & Sommer* ['The seasons: spring and summer']. Bergish Gladbach: Bastei-Lübbe Verlag, TB 13115, 1988, pp., paperback. German translation by Harro Christensen.

ee. As: *Stagioni diverse* ['Different seasons']. Milan, Italy: Sperling Paperback, SUPERBESTSELLER #44, July 1989, paperback. Italian translation by Bruno Amato and Paola Formenti. ISBN 88-7824-048-6.

ff. As: *4 Seizoenen* ['4 seasons']. Utrecht, Belgium, Netherlands: Luitingh-Sijthoff, 1989, 473 pp. Dutch translation by Pauline Moody. ISBN 90-245-1599-8. 2nd printing 1989.

gg. As: *Frühling, Sommer, Herbst und Tod: vier Kurzromane* ['Spring, summer, autumn, and death']. Gütersloh, Austria: Bertelsmann-Club; Kornwesterheim, Germany: EBG; Gütersloh, Austria: Deutsche Buch-Gemeinschaft Koch; Vienna, Austria: Buchgemeinschaft Donauland und Scheriau; Vienna, Austria: Deutsche Buch-Gemeinschaft Koch; Zug, Switzerland: Buch- und Schallplattenfreunde, [1990], 550 pp. German translation by Harro Christensen. Book Club editions.

hh. As: *Liget i skoven* ['. Copenhagen, Denmark: Vega, 1990, 262 pp., 21 cm., 298 KR, paperback. Danish translation of "The Body" and "The Breathing Method" by Bjarne Skovlund. ISBN 87-88133-95-8.

ii. As: *Rita Hayworth i Shawshank fængslet*. Copenhagen, Denmark: Vega/DBK, 1990, 360 pp., 21 cm., 298 KR, paperback. Danish translation of "Rita Hayworth..." and "Apt Pupil" by Bjarne Skovlund. ISBN 87-588-0457-9.

jj. Excerpted as: *Winterverk: Tva Berättelser* ['Winter-work: two stories']. Stockholm, Sweden: Legenda, 1990, 250 pp., 22 cm., hardcover. Swedish translation by Jimmy Hofsö. ISBN 91-582-1372-4.

kk. As: *Die Ontsnapping—De Leerling* ['The escape—the pupil']. Utrecht, Belgium: Luitingh-Sijthoff, 1991, 395 pp. Dutch translation by Pauline Moody. 1st printing. ISBN 90-245-1518-1.

ll. As: *Liget i skoven.* Copenhagen [Ruds-Vedby], Denmark: Vega, VEGA PAPERBACK, 1991, 262 pp., 21 cm., 98 KR, paperback. Danish translation of "The Body" and "The Breathing Method" by Bjarne Skovlund. ISBN 87-89677-81-1.

mm. As: *Rita Hayworth i Shawshank fængslet—Mønstereleven.* Copenhagen [Ruds-Vedby], Denmark: Vega, VEGA PAPERBACK, 1991, 360 pp., 98 KR, paperback. Danish translation of "Rita Hayworth..." and "Apt Pupil" by Bjarne Skovlund. ISBN 87-89677-83-8.

nn. As: *The Body.* Copenhagen, Denmark: Buldendal, 1991, 232 pp., 94 KR, paperback. 1st Danish edition. Danish translation by Jørgen Riber Christensen. ISBN 87-00-03443-6.

oo. Excerpted as: *Sommardåd—två berättelser.* [Stockholm, Sweden]: Legend, POCKET, 1991, 18 cm., paperback. Swedish translation by Mårten Edlund. 5th pocket edition. ISBN 91-582-1895-5.

pp. Excerpted as: *Winterverk: Tva Berättelser* ['Winter-work: two stories']. [Stockholm, Sweden]: Legenda, POCKET, 1991, 250 pp., 18 cm., paperback. Swedish translation by Jimmy Hofsö. ISBN 91-582-1893-9.

qq. As: *Frühling, Sommer, Herbst und Tod: vier Kurzromane* ['Spring, summer, autumn, and death']. Munich, Germany: Wilhelm Heyne, ALLGEMEINE REIHE #8403, May 1992, 620 pp., 14.80 DM, paperback. German translation by Harro Christensen. ISBN 3-453-05618-3. * 5th printing, 1993. * 8th printing, 1994. 14th printing, 1995

rr. As: *Kauhun Vuodenajat* ['Terror seasons' (?)]. Finland: Book Studio, 1992, 319 pp., 18 cm. Finnish translation by Tapio Tamminen. ISBN 951-611-462-8; 951-611-463-6.

ss. As: *Kauhun Vuodenajat 2* ['Terror seasons' (?)]. Finland: Book Studio,

1992, 287 pp., 19 cm. Finnish translation by Tapio Tamminen. ISBN 951-611-522-5; 951-611-536-5.
tt. London, England: Warner UK, March 1993, 560 pp., £5.99, paperback. Cover art by Christopher Brown. 2nd printing. ISBN 0-7515-0433-5.
uu. As: *Las cuatro estaciones* ['The four seasons']. Barcelona, Spain: Grijalbo Mondadori, BESTSELLER ORO, September 1993, 480 pp., 2404 pta., 24 cm., paperback. Spanish translation by J. M. Álvares and Angela Pérez. 1st Spanish edition. ISBN 84-253-2562-5. * Trade paperback, ISBN 84-253-2330-4.
vv. As: [Title unknown]. South Korea, 1993, 289+342+298 pp., 23 cm. Korean translation.
ww. As: [Title unknown—*Stand by Me*]. South Korea, 1993, 607 pp., 23 cm. Korean translation.
xx. As: *The Shawshank Redemption* [cover] and *Different Seasons featuring The Shawshank Redemption* [spine]: London, England: Warner UK, February 1995, 560 pp., £5.99, paperback. ISBN 0-7515-1462-4.
yy. As: *Stephen King #03-3 Vol. Boxed Set*. New York: Signet, mass-market paperback. ISBN 0-451-93138-6. Boxed set with *Different Seasons, Skeleton Crew,* and *Nightmares and Dreamscapes.*
zz. As: *En verden udenfor* ['A world outside']. Ruds-Vedby, Denmark: Tellerup, VEGA PAPERBACK, 1995, 360 pp., 98 KR, paperback. Danish translations of "Rita Hayworth…" and "Apt Pupil" by Bjarne Skovlund. ISBN 87-89677-31-5.
aaa. As: *Rita Hayworth—avain pakoon* ['Rita Hayworth—escape key']. Helsinki, Finland: Book Studio, 1995, 319 pp., 19 cm. Finnish translation by Tapio Tamminen. Includes "Etevä oppilas" ['Apt Pupil'—pp. 108-319]. ISBN 951-611-720-1.
bbb. As: *Les évadés…*['The escapees']. Paris, France: Albin Michel, 1995, 529 pp., 130 F, paperback. French translations by Pierre Alien. ISBN 2-226-07778-2.
ccc. As: *Les évadés…*['The escapees']. [Paris, France]: [le Grande livre du mois], 1995, 529 pp., 130 F, hardcover. French translations by Pierre Alien. Book Club edition.
ddd. As: *Die Verurteilten: Frühling, Sommer, Herbst und Tod: vier Kurzromane* ['Spring, summer, autumn, and death']. Munich, Germany: Wilhelm Heyne, HEYNE-BÜCHER #1, ALLGEMEINE REIHE #9628, 1995, 620 pp., 15.00 DM, paperback. German translation by Harro Christensen. * 5th printing, 1995. ISBN 3-453-09057-8.
eee. As: *4 seizonen* ['4 seasons']. Amsterdam, Netherlands: Poema Pocket, 1995, 621 pp. Dutch translation by Pauline Moody. ISBN 90-245-2298-6.
fff. As: *Las cuatro estaciones* ['The four seasons']. 2 vols. Barcelona, Spain: Grijalbo, LIBRO DE MANO #71/1-71/2, [1997], 21 cm. Spanish translation by J. M. Álvares and Angela Pérez. ISBN: Vol. 1, 84-253-2972-8,
ggg. New York: Penguin/Signet, November 1998, 508 pp., $7.99, mass-market paperback. Movie tie-in with *Apt Pupil*. ISBN 0-451-19712-7.

hhh. As: *Mallioppilas* ['Model-pupil'—"Apt Pupil"—*Different Seasons*]. Helsinki, Finland: Book Studio. 1998. Finnish translation.

iii. As: *Un élève doué: différentes saisons* ['A bright pupil'—different seasons']. Paris, France: Albin Michel, 1998, 529 pp., 130 F, paperback. French translations by Pierre Alien. ISBN 2-226-07778-2.

jjj. As: *Skazani na Shawshank: cztery pory rouk* ['Prisoner at Shawshank:. Warsaw, Poland: "Prima," 1998, 511 pp., 21 cm. Polish translation by Zbigniew A. Królicki. ISBN 83-7186-022-6.

kkk. As: *Skazani na Shawshank: cztery pory rouk* ['Prisoner at Shawshank']. Warsaw, Poland: "Prima," BESTSELLERY ŒWIATOWEJ PROZY, 1998, 511 pp., 18 cm., paperback. Polish translation by Zbigniew A. Królicki. 2nd printing. ISBN 83-7186-025-0.

lll. As: *Apt Pupil* [cover]: London, England: Warner UK, April 1999, 560 pp., £6.99, 18 cm., paperback. Movie tie-in edition. ISBN 0-75150256707.

mmm. As: *Primavera y Verano* ['Spring and summer']. Barcelona, Spain: Mondadori, MITOS BOLSILLO, 1999, 392 pp., 18 cm., paperback. Spanish translation by José María Álvares-Flores and Angela Pérez. ISBN 84-397-0398-8.

nnn. As: *Las cuatro estaciones: Otoño-Invierno* ['The four seasons: autumn-winter']. Barcelona, Spain: Grijalbo Mondadori, LIBRO DE MANO #71-1, 1999, 296 pp., 1250 pta., paperback. Spanish translation by José María Álvares-Flores and Angela Pérez . ISBN 84-253-2972-8.

ooo. As: *Las cuatro estaciones: Primavera-Verano* ['The four seasons: spring-summer']. Barcelona, Spain: Grijalbo Mondadori, LIBRO DE MANO #71-2, 1999, 360 pp., 1250 pta., paperback. Spanish translation by José María Álvares-Flores and Angela Pérez . ISBN 84-253-2988-4.

ppp. As: *Quatro Estações* ['Four seasons']. Rio de Janeiro, Brazil: Francisco Alves, 19—. Portuguese translation.

qqq. As [Title unknown] ["Apt Pupil"]. Greek translation.
rrr. As [Title unknown] ["The Body"]. Greek translation.
sss. As [Title unknown] ["The Breathing Method"]. Greek translation
ttt. As [Title unknown] ["The Shawshank Redemption"]. Greek translation.
uuu. As: [Title unknown]. Bulgarian translation.

vvv. As AUDIOCASSETTE: *Different Seasons.* New York: Penguin Audiobooks, November 1999. 0-147-71352-8.

www. As AUDIOCASSETTE: See also entries under individual stories.

xxx. As FILM: See entries under titles of individual stories.

COMMENTS: The volume sold 270,264 copies in 1982, and ranked seventh on the *Publishers Weekly* annual hardcover Bestsellers List for 1982, an unusual feat for a collection of short fiction.

SELECTED ARTICLES, RESPONSES, AND REVIEWS:

Atchity, Kenneth. "Stephen King: Making Burgers with the Best." *Los Angeles Times Book Review* 29 August 1982: 7. Excerpted: *Contemporary Literary Criticism* Vol. 26. Edited by Jean C. Stine. Detroit MI: Gale Research, 1983. 241.

Bertin, Eddy C. "Stephen King in the Lowlands: An Annotated Bibliography of His Works as Published in the Netherlands (Holland and Belgium)." *Castle Rock: The Stephen King Newsletter* Vol. 1, No. 11 (November 1985): 7-8.

Bertin, Eddy C. "Additions to 'Stephen King in the Lowlands.'" Letter in an unknown publication.

Best Sellers Vol. 42 (October 1982): 259.

Budrys, Algis. *The Magazine of Fantasy & Science Fiction* Vol. 64 (February 1983): 61.

Cheuse, Alan. "Horror Writer's Holiday." *New York Times Book Review* 29 August 1982: VII 10. Excerpted: *Contemporary Literary Criticism*, Vol. 26. Edited by Jean C. Stine. Detroit MI: Gale Research Co., 1983, hardcover. 242.

English Journal Vol. 72 (December 1983): 69.

Gifford, Thomas. "Stephen King's Quartet." *Washington Post Book World* Vol. 12 (22 August 1982): 1-2. Excerpted: *Contemporary Literary Criticism*, Vol. 26. Edited by Jean C. Stine. Detroit MI: Gale Research Co., 1983. 240-241.

Graham, Mark. "Stephen King Shows Another Grisly Side." *Rocky Mountain News* [Denver CO] 19 September 1982: 22N.

Grant, Charles L., and others. "Different Writers on *Different Seasons*." *Fantasy Newsletter* (February 1983).

Gray, Paul. "Master of Postliterate Prose." *Time* Vol. 120 (20 August 1982): 87. Excerpted: *Contemporary Literary Criticism*, Vol. 26. Edited by Jean C. Stine. Detroit MI: Gale Research Co., 1983. 242-243.

Hard, Anette. "King: Novellas from a Consummate Story Teller." *Houston Chronicle* [TX] 12 September 1982.

Heldreth, Leonard. "Viewing 'The Body': King's Portrait of the Artist as Survivor." *The Gothic World of Stephen King: Landscape of Nightmares*. Edited by Gary Hoppenstand and Ray B. Browne. Bowling Green OH: Bowling Green State University Popular Press, December 1987. 64-74.

Kirkus Reviews Vol. 50, No. 12 (15 June 1982): 693. Excerpted: *Contemporary Literary Criticism*, Vol. 26. Edited by Jean C. Stine. Detroit MI: Gale Research Co., 1983, hardcover. 240.

Lehmann-Haupt, Christopher. "Books of the Times." *New York Times* [Daily] Vol. 131 (11 August 1982): III, 22.

McCoy, W. Keith. *Library Journal* Vol. 107 (August 1982): 1481.

Neilson, Keith. "Different Seasons." *Magill's Literary Annual, Book of 1983*, Vol. 1. Edited by Frank Magill. Englewood Cliffs, NJ: Salem Press, 1984. 189-193.

Publishers Weekly (18 June 1982): 64.

Publishers Weekly Vol. 223 (24 June 1983): 56.

Reed, Glenn. "Different Seasons." *Science Fiction & Fantasy Book Review* (January/February 1983): 29-30.

Science Fiction Review Vol. 12 (February 1983): 28.

Seelye, John. "Wizard of Ooze with Four Novellas Makes Poe a Piker." *Chicago Tribune Bookworld* 22 August 1983.

Voice of Youth Advocates Vol. 5 (December 1982): 33.

Waters, Kate. *School Library Journal* Vol. 29 (November 1982): 106.

Wilson Library Bulletin Vol. 57 (December 1982): 336.

Winter, Douglas E., ed. *Shadowings: The Reader's Guide to Horror Fiction, 1981-1982.* STARMONT STUDIES IN LITERARY CRITICISM, #1. Mercer Island WA: Starmont House, 1983. 38-43.

Horror Plum'd

THE DARK TOWER: THE GUNSLINGER. New York, NY: Prime/New American Library, 1988. Trade paperback.

A17.
THE DARK TOWER:
THE GUNSLINGER
(1982)

A17. THE DARK TOWER: THE GUNSLINGER. West Kingston RI: Donald M. Grant Publisher, August (?) 1982, 224 pp., hardcover. Illustrations by Michael Whelan. Limited edition; lettered state and publisher's state. Fantasy novel. * LIMITED EDITION, numbered and signed by author and artist, 500 slipcased copies. * 1ST TRADE EDITION, $20.00, 10,000 copies. * 2ND TRADE EDITION, March 1984, $20.00, hardcover. 10,000 copies. ISBN 0-937986-50-X. * 3rd printing, 1998, 15,000 copies, in boxed set with DTII and DTIII.

CONTENTS: "The Gunslinger" (1978; see B36); "The Way Station" (1980; see B44); "The Oracle and the Mountain" (1981; see B51); "The Slow Mutants" (1981; see B53); "The Gunslinger and the Dark Man" (1981; see B57); Afterword, by King (see C124).

REPRINTS AND ADAPTATIONS:
b. New York: Plume/New American Library, September 1988, 224 p, $10.95, trade paperback. Illustrations by Michael Whelan. ISBN 0-452-26134-1. Reprinted: November 1997. ISBN 0-452-27960-7.
c. London, England: Sphere, September 1988, 224 pp., £6.99, trade paperback. ISBN 0-7474-0099-7.
d. As: *De Donkere Toren: 1. De Scherpschutter* ['The dark tower: 1. The sharpshooter']. Utrecht, Belgium: Luitingh-Sijthoff, 1988, 206 pp. Dutch translation by Hugo Timmerman. 1st Dutch edition. ISBN 90-245-1664-1. * 4th printing, 1991.
e. As: *Schwarz* ['Black']. Munich, Germany: Wilhelm Heyne, HEYNE-JUMBO-BÄNDE #41, 1989 [1988?], 236 pp., paperback. 1st German edition. German translation by Joachim Körber. ISBN 3-453-02912-7.
f. London, England: Sphere Overseas, June 1989, 240 pp., £3.50, paperback. Cover art by Michael Whelan. ISBN 0-7474-0100-4. Open market edition not distributed in the UK.
g. New York: Signet/New American Library, July 1989, 315 pp., 4.95, mass-market paperback. No illustrations. ISBN 0-451-16052-5. Reissue

December 1994. Reprint November, 1998, 315 pp., $7.99, mass-market paperback. * 35th printing, ISBN 0-451-16052-5.

h. As: *L'ultimo cavaliere* ['The last knight']. Milan, Italy: Sperling & Kupfer, PANDORA [#470], October 1989, hardcover. Italian translation by Tullio Dobner. ISBN 88-200-0951-X.

i. London, England: Sphere, December 1989, 249 pp., £3.50, paperback. ISBN 0-7474-0100-4.

j. As: *Schwarz* ['Black']. Gütersloh, Austria: Bertelsmann Lesering, 1989, 238 pp., hardcover. German translation by Joachim Körber. Book Club edition.

k. As: *La hierba del diablo: La torre oscura 1* ['The herb of the devil: the dark tower 1']. Barcelona, Spain: Ediciones B, ÉXITOS INTERNACIONAL, 1989, 226 pp., 24 cm. Spanish translation by Jorge Luis Mustieles. ISBN 84-406-0746-6. * Reprint, 1994. * Reprint, 1998, ISBN 84-406-0746-6.

l. As: *Revolvermannen* ['Gunmen']. Stockholm, Sweden: Legenda, 1989, 236 pp., 23 cm., hardcover. Swedish translation by Lennart Olofsson. ISBN 91-582-1509-3.

m. As: *Le pistolero* ['The gunman']. Paris, France: J'ai Lu, SCIENCE FICTION #2950, 1991, 254 pp., 22 F, paperback. French translation by Gérard Lebec. ISBN 2-277-22950-4.

n. As: *Det svarta tornet: Revolvermannen* ['The tower of blackness: gunmen']. Stockholm, Sweden: Natur och Kultur, 1990, 236 pp., 22 cm., hardcover. Swedish translation by Lennart Olofsson. ISBN 91-582-1698-7.

o. As: *Revolvermanden: Det mørke tårn 1* ['Gunmen: the dark tower']. Copenhagen, Denmark: Artia, 1991, 223 pp., 178 KR, paperback. Danish translation by Mogens Wenzel Andreasen. ISBN 87-89294-40-8.

p. As Boxed edition: *The Dark Tower: The Gunslinger, The Drawing of the Three, The Waste Lands.* New York: Plume, October 1992, trade paperback. ISBN 0-451-15346-8.

q. As: *Musta torni* ['Black tower']. Helsinki, Finland: Book Studio, 1992, 229 pp., 18 cm. Finnish translation by Kari Salminen. ISBN 951-611-534-9; 951-611-537-3; ISBN 951-611-534-9.

r. As: *La hierba del diablo: La torre oscura 1* ['The herb of the devil: the dark tower 1']. Barcelona, Spain: Ediciones B, VIB 13/1, 1992, 226 pp., 18 cm., paperback. Spanish translation by Jorge Luis Mustieles. ISBN 84-406-3011-5. * Reprint, 1992 (imp. 1994), 333 pp., 18 cm., ISBN 84-406-3011-5.

s. As: *Mracna kula: Revolvera_.* Belgrade, Yugoslavia: Goran Skrobonja, 1992, 165 pp., 21 cm. Slovak translation by Goran Skrobonja.

t. As: *Le pistolero.* Paris, France: Éditions de la Seine, 1993, 254 pp., 59 F, hardcover. French translation by Gérard Lebec. ISBN 2-7382-0658-1

u. As: *L'ultimo Cavaliere* ['The last knight']. Milan, Italy: Sperling Paperback, SUPERBESTSELLER #378, November 1994, paperback. Italian translation by Tullio Dobner. ISBN 88-7824-457-0.

v. As Boxed edition: *The Dark Tower: The Gunslinger, The Drawing of the Three, The Waste Lands.* New York: New American Library, September 1997, $23.97, mass-market paperback. ISBN 0-451-93554-3.

w. As: *La tour sombre* ['The dark tower']. Paris, France: France Loisirs, 1994, 1169 pp., 118 F, hardcover. French translations by Gérard Lebec, Jean-Daniel Brèque and Christiane Poulain. ISBN 2-7242-8191-8. Omnibus with *Le pistolero, Les troi cartes* and *Terres perdues.*
x. As: *Det svarta tornet: Revolvermannen* ['The tower of blackness: gunmen']. Stockholm, Sweden: Natur och Kultur, NOK POCKET, 1994, 235 pp., paperback. Swedish translation by Lennart Olofsson. ISBN 91-27-03919-6.
y. As: *Schwarz: Der Dunkle Turm 1* ['Black: the dark tower 1']. Munich, Germany: Wilhelm Heyne TB 10428, November 1997, 14.90 DM, paperback. German translation. ISBN 3-453-12384-0.
z. London, England: New English Library, December 1997, 212 pp., £6.99, paperback. Cover art by Bob Warner. ISBN 0-340-70750-X.
aa. As: *L'ultimo Cavaliere* ['The last knight']. Milan, Italy: Sperling & Kupfer, 1997. Italian translation.
bb. As: *De Donkere Toren: 1. De Scherpschutter* ['The dark tower: 1. The sharpshooter']. Amsterdam, Netherlands: Poema Pocket, 1997, 206 pp., paperback. Dutch translation by Hugo Timmerman. 8th printing. ISBN 90-245-2688-4.
cc. As: *Musta torni 1-3.* ['Black tower 1-3']. Helsinki, Finland: Book Studio, 1998, 654 pp. Finnish translation . ISBN 951-611-901-8.
dd. As: *Le pistolero.* Paris, France: Éditions 84, 1998, 235 pp., 70 F, 24 cm., paperback. French translation by Gérard Lebec. ISBN 2-277-25032-5.
ee. As: *Schwarz* ['Black']. Rheda-Wiedenbrück, Germany: Bertelsman-Club; Zug, Switzerland: Bertelsmann-Medien; Vienna, Austria: Buchgemeinschaft Donauland Kremayr und Scheriau, and others, [1998], 191 pp., hardcover. German translation by Joachim Körber. Book Club edition.
ff. As: *Revolvermanden: Det mørke tårn 1* ['Gunmen: the dark tower 1']. Copenhagen, Denmark: Vinten, VINTENS PAPERBACKS/VINTENS FANTASY, 1998, 219 pp., 78 KR, paperback. Danish translation by Mogens Wenzel Andreasen. ISBN 87-612-0166-9.
gg. As: *De Scherpschutter: De Donkere Toren 1* ['The sharpshooter']. Amsterdam, Netherlands: Luitingh-Sijthoff, 1998, 191 pp. Dutch translation by Hugo Timmerman. 10th printing. ISBN 90-245-1296-4.
hh. As: *The Dark Tower.* West Kingston RI: Donald M. Grant, February 1999, $117.00, boxed set containing *The Gunslinger*, 3rd printing; *The Drawing of the Three,* 2nd edition; and *The Waste Lands.* ISBN 1-880418-40-1.
ii. As: *La Tour sombre: Le pistolero—Les troi cartes—Terres perdues* ['The dark tower: the gunslinger—the three cards—the wasted lands]. France, 19—, 992 pp. French translation.
jj. As: [title unknown]. Japanese translation.
kk. As: [Title unknown].Moscow, Russia: AST, 19—. Russian translation.
ll. As: [title unknown]. Russia: Cadman, 19—. Russian translation. Omnibus with Dark Tower 2

mm. AS AUDIOCASSETTE: *The Dark Tower: The Gunslinger.* New Audio Library,

July 1988. Read by Stephen King. 4 cassettes; 6 hours, 18 minutes. Unabridged. * LIMITED EDITION, $100, numbered edition of 800 sets signed by King.
SELECTED ARTICLES, RESPONSES, AND REVIEWS:
Blue, Tyson. "Dark Tower Tape Reviewed." *Castle Rock: The Stephen King Newsletter* Vol. 4, No. 8 (August 1988): 5.

nn. As AUDIOCASSETTE: New York: Penguin Audiobooks, May 1998, $29.95, unabridged. Read by Frank Muller. 4 cassettesISBN 0-140-86716-3.

COMMENTS: One of King's most controversial and sought-after texts, because of its very limited initial print run, *The Dark Tower* collects five stories originally appearing in *The Magazine of Fantasy & Science Fiction*. Here King demonstrably transcends 'mere' horror to suggest instead the opening books of a Epic-quest, in the strict literary sense of the term. The narratives are more static than usual for King, and the characters less rounded—as befits the more elevated, distanced genre. Yet the narrative is compelling, particularly as an introduction to an epic quest.

The cycle continues in *The Drawing of the Three* [see also A34], *The Waste Lands* [see also A43], *Wizard and Glass* [see A61], and at least two novels beyond, while at the same time making important connections with *The Stand* [A5, A40], *Eyes of the Dragon* [see A24] , *Insomnia* [A48], *Hearts in Atlantis* [A65], and other novels. It remains to be seen whether King will complete the cycle as an essentially self-contained narrative, with only minor references to the other novels; or whether he will enlarge the vision of the Tower to suggest the kind of nexus of worlds defined in *The Talisman,* and thereby unify a significant portion of his novels, stories, and poems into a single fictive-universe. The scope of the installments to date, and the complexity of their inter-connections with earlier and subsequent manifestations of the Dark Man, indeed suggest the latter.

SELECTED ARTICLES, RESPONSES, AND REVIEWS:
American Fantasy Vol. 1, No. 2 (May 1982). On the release of the *Dark Tower.*
Beaulieu, Janet C. "King Excels in Quest for Dark Tower." *Bangor Daily News* [ME] 10 January 1989. As microfiche: *NewsBank: Literature* 16 (February 1989): Fiche 19: B6-B7. Reprinted: *Castle Rock: The Stephen King Newsletter* Vol. 5, No. 3 (March 1989): 1, 6.
Beaulieu, Janet C. "Gunslinger Stalks Darkness in Human Spirit." *Castle Rock: The Stephen King Newsletter* Vol. 5, No. 3 (March 1989): 1, 3.
Bertin, Eddy C. "DT Books Make Dutch Appearance." *Castle Rock: The Stephen King Newsletter* Vol. 5, No. 12 (December 1989).
Blue, Tyson. "Mass Market Edition of Gunslinger Released." *Castle Rock: The Stephen King Newsletter* Vol. 4, No. 10 (October 1988): 5.
Booklist Vol. 84 (July 1988): 1755.
Donovan, Mark. *People Weekly* Vol. 30 (7 March 1988): 38.
Easton, Tom. *Analog Science Fiction/Science Fact* Vol. 109 (June 1989): 185.

Egan, James. "*The Dark Tower*: Stephen King's Gothic Western." *The Gothic World of Stephen King: Landscape of Nightmares*. Edited by Gary Hoppenstand and Ray B. Browne. Bowling Green OH: Bowling Green State University Popular Press, December 1987. 95-106.
Emergency Librarian Vol. 16 (March 1989): 47.
Fuller, Richard. *New York Times Book Review* 8 January 1989: 22-23.
Graham, Mark. "*Dark Tower* Shows King in Different Light." *Rocky Mountain News* [Denver CO] 1 August 1982.
Guardian Weekly Vol. 137 (1 November 1987): 27.
Kirkus Reviews Vol. 56 (15 July 1988): 1019.
Mehegan, S. L. "*The Dark Tower: The Gunslinger.*" *Castle Rock: The Stephen King Newsletter* Vol. 2, No. 5 (May 1986): 3.
Publishers Weekly Vol. 234 (29 July 1988): 227.
San Francisco Chronicle "Reviews" (15 August 1982): 10.
Science Fiction Chronicle Vol. 10 (December 1988): 45.
West Coast Review of Books Vol. 13, No. 3 (1987): 60.
Winders, Glenda. "King Takes a Browning Poem, and Sets 'Gunfighter' in Future." *San Diego Union* [CA] 4 December 1988. As microfiche: *NewsBank: Literature* Vol. 16 (January 1989): Fiche 6, G13.
Woods, Larry D. *Science Fiction & Fantasy Book Review* (January/February 1983): 28-29.

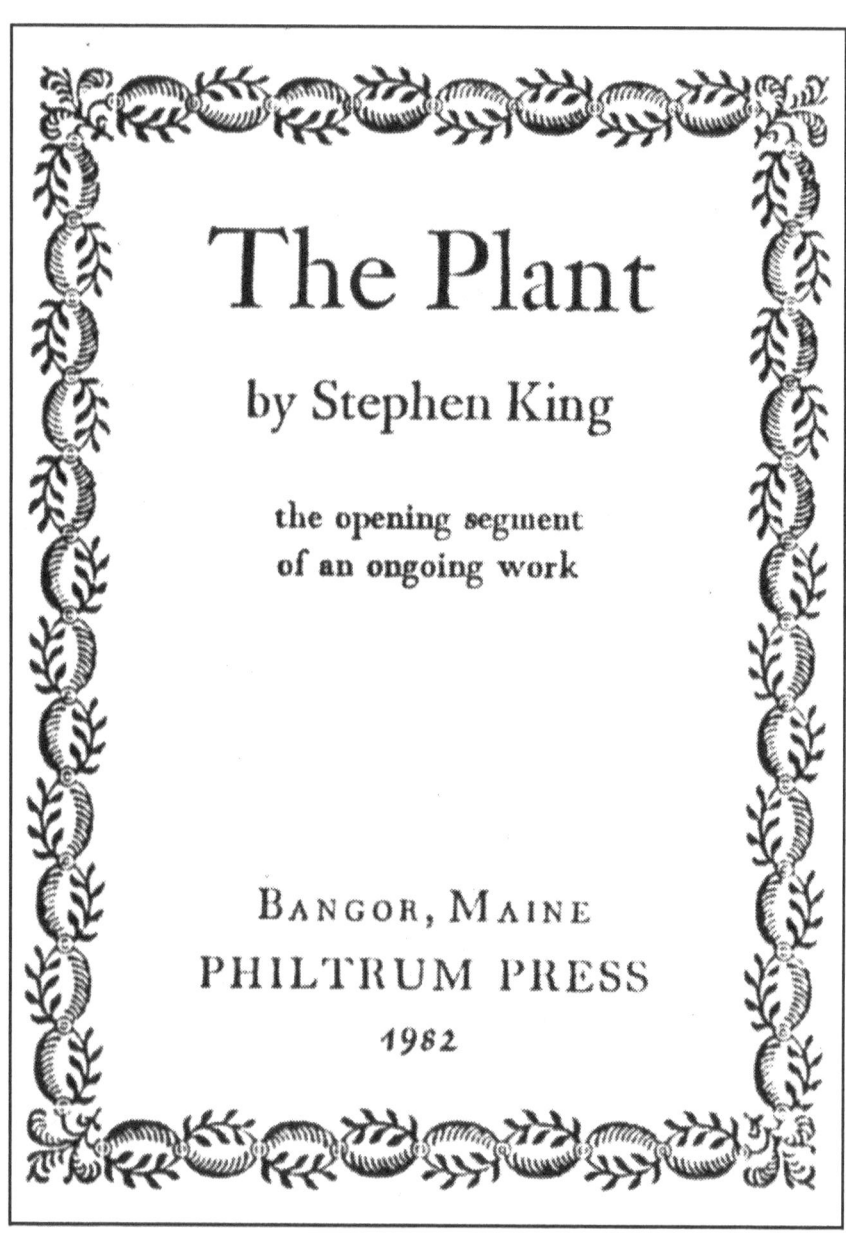

THE PLANT. Online issue.

A18.
THE PLANT
(1982)

A18. THE PLANT. Bangor ME: Philtrum Press, December (?) 1982, 32 pp., paperback. Limited to 226 copies, all signed by King, 26 copies lettered from A-Z, the rest numbered from 1. Horror fiction.

COMMENTS: The first installment of a novel-in-progress, privately published by King and sent as Christmas greetings. See the sequels A23, A31; and the completion of Book One, Parts I-VI, as an internet publication [A70].

SELECTED ARTICLES, RESPONSES, AND REVIEWS:
Blue, Tyson. "The Plant: The Unseen King." *Castle Rock: The Stephen King Newsletter* Vol. 2, No. 6 (June 1986): 1, 3.

MICHAEL R. COLLINGS

CHRISTINE. New York, NY: Viking, 1983. Hardcover.

A19.
CHRISTINE
(1983)

A19. *CHRISTINE: A NOVEL.* West Kingston RI: Donald M. Grant, Publisher, 1983, 544 pp., hardcover. Horror novel. * LIMITED EDITION, letter state; not originally for sale. * LIMITED, LETTERED A-Z, with dust-jackets and slipcases; 26 copies signed by author and artist. * LIMITED EDITION, numbered, with dust jackets and slipcases; 1000 copies, $65, signed by the author and artist.

PLOT SUMMARY: When Arnie Cunningham buys a dilapidated old car—Christine—his life abruptly changes…at first, definitely for the better. But gradually the car intrudes into his life and the lives of those around him, with deadly results. Both haunted and haunting, Christine seeks to possess Arnie at all costs.

REPRINTS AND ADAPTATIONS:
b. New York: Viking, 29 April 1983, viii+526 pp., 24 cm., hardcover. ISBN 0-670-22026-4. * Reprinted, December 1984, ISBN 0-670-36045-5
c. London, England: Hodder and Stoughton, May 1983, 482 pp., hardcover.
d. Barcelona, Spain: Plaza & Janés Editores, GRAN PARADA, October 1983, 416 pp., 802 pta., 21 cm., trade paperback. Spanish translation by Adolfo Martín. ISBN 84-01-36045-5. * Reprint, 1983, ISBN 84-01-36045-5.
e. New York: Signet, December 1983, 503 pp., $3.99, mass-market paperback. ISBN 0-451-16044-4. * Reprinted as movie tie-in edition, 1983, ISBN 0-451-12838-9.
f. New York: Viking, [n.d.], 471 pp., hardcover. Science Fiction Book Club edition.
g. Garden City NY: Mystery Guild Book Club, [n.d.], cloth.
h. New York: Signet/New American Library, December 1983, 505 pp., mass-market paperback. * 21st printing by 1994.
i. Rio de Janeiro, Brazil: Francisco Alves, MESTRES DO HORROR E DA FANTASIA, 1983, 547 pp., 21 cm. Portuguese translation by Luisa Ibanez. * 2nd edition, 1983.
j. Bergish Gladbach, West Germany: Bastei-Lübbe TB 28118, 1983, 496 pp., paperback. German translation by Harro Christensen.

k. Utrecht, Belgium: Luitingh/Veen, 1983, 446 pp., trade paperback. Slightly abridged Dutch translation by Margot Bakker. ISBN 90-204-1031-8. * 3rd printing, 1986.
l. As: *Ko-li-ssu-ting*. Taipei, Taiwan: Huang guan chu pan she, 1983. Chinese translation by Chung Yen-Iun.
m. Istanbul, Turkey: Alt´yn Kitaplar, 1983. Turkish translation by Gülten Severen.
n. As: *Christine, la machina infernale* ['Christine, the hellish machine']. Milan, Italy: Sperling & Kupfer, PANDORA #209, February 1984, 634 pp. Italian translation by Tullio Dobner. ISBN 88-200-0372-4.
o. Buenos Aires, Argentina: Emecé, 1984, 415 pp., 20 cm. Spanish translation by César Aira. ISBN 950-04-0320-X. * Reprint, 1992. * Reprint, 1994, GRANDES NOVELISTAS.
p. Gütersloh, Austria: Bertelsmann Lesering, 1984. German translation.
q. As: *Christine: Tappaja-Auto* ['Christine: killer-car']. Helsinki, Finland: Suuri Suomalainen Kirjakerho, 1984, 413 pp. Finnish translation by Pentti Isomursu. ISBN 951-643-219-0.
r. México: Edivisión, 1984, pp., paperback. Spanish translation.
s. Panama: Printer Internacional de Panamá, July 1984, 528 pp., $7.00, hardcover. Spanish translation by Adolfo Martín. ISBN 84-8386-346-4.
t. Paris, France: Albin Michel, 1984, 351 pp., 75 F, paperback. French translation by Marie Milpois. ISBN 2-226-01943-X.
u. As: *Christine: Roman*. [Paris, France]: [le Grand livre du mois], 1984, 351 pp., 75 F, hardcover. French translation by Marie Milpois. ISBN 2-226-01943-X.
v. London, England: New English Library, March 1984, 608 pp., paperback.
w. Stuttgart, Germany: Europäische Bildungsgemeinschaft; Gütersloh, Austria: Bertelsmann Club; Vienna, Austria: Buchgemeinschaft Donauland; Zug, Switzerland: Buch-und-Schallplattenfreunde, April 1985, 607 pp., paperback. German translation by Bato Bauman. Book Club editions.
x. Paris: J'ai-Lu, ÉPOUVANTE #1866, 1985, 381 pp., 22 F, paperback. French translation by Marie Milpois. ISBN 2-277-21866-9.
y. Paris, France: France Loisirs, 1985, 351 pp., 60 F. French translation. ISBN 2-7242-2210-5.
z. Höganäs, Sweden: Bra Spänning, 1985, 336 pp. Swedish translation by Jimmy Hofsö. ISBN not assigned.
aa. Sao Paulo, Brazil: Nova Cultural, BEST SELLERS, 1986, 552 pp., 19 cm. Portuguese translation by Luisa Ibanez.
bb. Stockholm, Sweden: Legenda, 1986, 679 pp., hardcover. Swedish translation by Jimmy Hofsö.
cc. Bergisch Gladbach, Germany: Bastei-Lübbe TB 13054, 1986, 620 pp., 9.80 DM, paperback. German translation by Harro Christensen. ISBN 3-404-13054-5.
dd. Stockholm, Sweden: Legenda, 1987, 679 pp., 19 cm., pocket paperback. Swedish translation by Jimmy Hofsö. ISBN 91-582-1039-3.

ee. London, England: New English Library, October 1987, 597 pp., £3.50, paperback. Reissue. ISBN 0-450-05674-0.
ff. As: [Title unknown]. Tokyo, Japan: Shinchosya, 1987. 2 vols. Japanese translation.
gg. As: *Christine, la macchina infernale* ['Christine, the hellish machine']. Milan, Italy: Arnoldo Mondadori, OSCAR #2003, February 1988. Italian translation by Tullio Dobner. ISBN 88-04-30745-5.
hh. As: *Christine, la macchina infernale* ['Christine, the hellish machine']. Milan, Italy: Arnoldo Mondadori, BESTSELLERS OSCAR #107, October 1988. Italian translation by Tullio Dobner. ISBN 88-04-31933-X.
ii. Copenhagen, Denmark: Artia, 1989, 533 pp., 22 cm., 228 KR, paperback. Danish translation by Mogens Wenzel Andreasen. ISBN 87-89284-01-7.
jj. As: *Christine: Roman*. [Paris, France]: de la Seine, SUCCÈS DU LIVRE, 1989, 351 pp., 59 F, hardcover. French translation by Marie Milpois. ISBN 2-7382-0221-7.
kk. Esplugues de Llobregat, Barcelona, Spain: Plaza & Janés, JET #102, BIBLIOTECA DE STEPHEN KING #9, 1988, 582 pp., 18 cm., paperback. Spanish translation by Adolfo Martín. 1st edition in this collection, ISBN 84-01-49889-9. * 3rd printing, 1989, ISBN 84-01-49889-9. * Reprint, May 1992, ISBN 84-01-49889-9. * Reprint, May 1995, ISBN 84-01-49967-4. * Reprint, 1998, ISBN 84-01-49967-4.
ll. New York: New American Library, November 1990, $7.99, mass-market paperback. Reissue edition. ISBN 0-451-16044-4.
mm. As: *Christine: Tappaja-Auto* ['Christine: killer-car']. Helsinki, Finland: Tammi, 1984, 582 pp. Finnish translation by Pentti Isomursu. * 2nd printing, 1990. ISBN 951-30-9439-1. * 4th printing, 1994. ISBN 951-31-0306-4.
nn. Utrecht, Belgium: Luitingh-Sijthoff, 1990, 446 pp., hardcover. Dutch translation by Margot Bakker. ISBN 90-245-1795-8. * 6th printing, 1990, ISBN 90-245-1592-0.
oo. As: [Title unknown]. South Korea, 1990, 636 pp., 23 cm. Korean translation.
pp. Oslo, Norway: Damm, 1990, 277/277-530 pp. Norwegian translation by Ernst W. Polcszynski. 2 vols. ISBN 82-517-7131-5, 82-517-7132-3.
qq. [Stockholm, Sweden]: Legenda, 1990, 679 pp., 22 cm.. Swedish translation by Jimmy Hofsö. 5th *kartonnerade* edition. ISBN 91-582-0927-1.
rr. London, England: Hodder & Stoughton, May 1991, 482 pp., £15.99, hardcover. Cover art by Gerald Grace. Reissue; 5th printing.
ss. Copenhagen, Denmark: Hørst, HØRST PAPERBACK, 1991, 533 pp., 98 KR, paperback. Danish translation by Mogens Wenzel Andreasen. ISBN 87-14-19139-3.
tt. Munich, Germany: Wilhelm Heyne, HEYNE-BÜCHER #1; ALLGEMEINE REIHE #8325, 1991, 651 pp., 12.80 dm, paperback. German translation by Bodo Baumann. ISBN 3-453-05254-4. * 6th printing, 1992. * 10th printing, 1993. * 13th, printing 1994. * 16th printing, 1995.
uu. Barcelona, Spain: Plaza & Janés, JET #102—BIBLIOTECA DE STEPHEN KING #9, May 1992, 592 pp., 750 pta., paperback. Spanish translation by Adolfo

Martín. ISBN 84-01-49889-9. * Reprint, May 1995, ISBN 84-01-49967-4.
vv. New York: Penguin/Signet, July 1992, 503 pp., $5.99, paperback. Reissue edition, 33rd printing. ISBN 0-451-12838-9.
ww. Warsaw, Poland: "Amber," 1992, 207+382 pp., 21 cm. Polish translation by Arkadiuscz Nakoniecznik. 2 vols. ISBN 83-7082-018-2.
xx. Oslo, Norway: Egmont Bøker Fredhøi, 1993, 270 pp., 405.00, [heftet]. Norwegian Translation. Volume 1: ISBN 82-04-03006-1, Vol. 2: ISBN 82-04-03008-8.
yy. [Oslo, Norway]: Hjemmets bokforlag, EGMONT SPENNING #7-8, 1993, 270+252 pp., 49.50 NKR + 49.50 NKR, hardcover. 2 vols. Norwegian translation by Ernst W. Poleszynski.. ISBN 82-04-03006-1, 82-04-03008-8.
zz. Paris, France: France Loisirs, 1994, 351 pp., 92 F, paperback. French translation by Marie Milpois. ISBN 2-7242-7838-0.
aaa. As: *Christine, la machina infernale* ['Christine, the hellish machine']. Milan, Italy: Sperling Paperback, SUPERBESTSELLER #393, January 1995, paperback. Italian translation by Tullio Dobner. ISBN 88-7824-514-3.
bbb. As: *Christine: Roman.* [Paris, France]: [le Grand livre du mois], 1995, 351 pp., 120 F, hardcover. French translation by Marie Milpois. Book Club edition.
ccc. Amsterdam, Netherlands: Poema Pocket, 1995, 479 pp., paperback. Dutch translation by Margot Bakker and Christine Brackmann. 9th edition. ISBN 90-245-2311-7.
ddd. Oslo, Norway: Hjemmets, STEPHEN KINGS UTVALGTE, 1996, 525 pp., 179.00, hardcover [*Innbundet*]. Norwegian translation by Ernst W. Poleszynski. 2nd edition. ISBN 82-59-01659-1.
eee. [Barcelona], Spain: Orbis, 1997, 582 pp., 22 cm. Spanish translation by Adolfo Martín. ISBN 84-402-2062-6.
fff. Oxford, England, and Melbourne, Australia: Compass Press, Australian Large Print Audio and Video, 1997, 745 pp., 24 cm. Simultaneous large-print editions.
ggg. Warsaw, Poland: Proszynski i S-ka SA, POSA, 21 October 1998, 596 pp., 19 cm., paperback. Polish translation by Arkadiuscz Nakoniecznik. ISBN 83-7180-907-7.
hhh. Rio de Janeiro, Brazil: Objetiva, 1998, 321 pp., 23 cm., paperback. Portuguese translation by Louisa Ibañez. ISBN 85-730-2188-8.
iii. As: [Title unknown]. Russia: Cadman, 19—. Russian translation.
jjj. As: *Christine.* Rio de Janeiro, Brazil: Francisco Alves, 19—. Portuguese translation
kkk. As: *Christine.* Hungary: Árkádía, 19—. Hungarian translation.
lll. As: *Christine.* Budapest, Hungary: Európa, 19—. Hungarian translation.
mmm. As: *Kristin.* Greek translation.

nnn. As FILM: *Christine.* Columbia Pictures, Polar Film Corporation, December 1983. Produced by Richard Kobritz. Directed by John Carpenter. Screenplay by Bill Phillips. 110 minutes. Rating: R.

HORROR PLUM'D

CAST: Keith Gordon, John Stockwell, Alexandra Paul, Robert Prosky, Harry Dean Stanton.

SELECTED ARTICLES, RESPONSES, AND FILM REVIEWS:

Anderson, P. *Films in Review* Vol. 35, No. 2 (February 1984): 109.

Ansen, D. *Newsweek* Vol. 105, No. 25 (19 December 1983): 66.

Blue, Tyson. "Fury is Furious." *Courier Herald* [Dublin GA] 21 January 1984.

Corliss, Richard. *Time* Vol. 122, No. 26 (19 December 1983): 74.

Ebert, Roger. *Roger Ebert's Movie Home Companion, 1988 Edition.* Kansas City MO: Andrews, McMeel & Parker, 1987, hardcover. 104.

Harper, L. Christine. "Christine." *Mile High Futures* (22 January 1984): 22.

Hogan, David J. "Carpenter Borrowed King's Car, But Doesn't Know How to Drive." *Cinefantastique* Vol. 14, No. 3 (May 1984): 56.

Johnson, Kim. "*Christine*: Stephen King and John Carpenter Take a Joy Ride into Terror." *Mediascene Prevue* (1983): 24-26.

Kelley, Bill. "Effects Man Roy Arbogast Was in Charge of the Film's Amazing Automotive Star." *Cinefantastique* Vol. 14, No. 3 (May 1984).

Kelley, Bill. "John Carpenter's Christine: Bringing Stephen King's Best Seller to the Screen." *Cinefantastique* Vol. 13-14, Nos. 6, 1 (August/ September 1983): 8.

Kilbourne, Dan. "Christine." *Magill's Cinema Annual 1984.* Edited by Frank N. Magill. Englewood Cliffs, NJ: Salem Press, 1984.

Lofficier, Randy. "Stephen King Talks About *Christine.*" *Twilight Zone Magazine* Vol. 3, No. 6 (February 1984): 73-74.

Martin, Robert H. [Bob]. "Keith Gordon and *Christine.*" *Fangoria* 32 (1983): 19-22.

Martin, Robert H. [Bob]. "Richard Kobritz and *Christine.*" *Fangoria* 32 (1983): 14-17.

Nash, Robert Jay, and Stanley Ralph Ross. "Christine." *The Motion Picture Guide, 1927-1983*, Vol. II. Chicago: Cinebooks, 1985, hardcover. 422.

People Weekly (9 January 1984). On Keith Gordon and review of film.

Radburn, Barry. "Stephen King and John Carpenter: Cruisin' with Christine." *Footsteps* Vol. V (April 1985): 47-49.

San Francisco Chronicle [CA] 10 December 1983: 34.

Stein, E. *The Village Voice* Vol. 268, No. 51 (20 December 1983): 82.

Variety Vol. 313, No. 6 (7 December 1983): 14.

Vernier, James. "Christine." *Twilight Zone Magazine* (February 1984): 69-74.

ooo. AS VIDEOCASSETTE: *Christine.* Columbia Pictures, 1983. Beta, VHS, Laser, CED. 110 minutes.

Michael R. Collings

COMMENTS: The book sold 303,589 hardcover copies in 1983, and ranked #5 on the *Bowkers Annual* hardcover fiction bestsellers list for 1983. King was also represented on the list by *Pet Sematary*, the first time since 1972 that an author had had two books on the list simultaneously—the distinction merely set the stage, however, for King's record-shattering accumulation of simultaneous bestsellers, frequently reaching three, often four, and occasionally even an astounding five titles.

Christine responds directly to America's love-affair with machines, especially with the automobile, as epitomized by a 1958 Plymouth Fury with a definite mind of her own. Interwoven beneath the surface of horror motifs, however, are serious considerations of equally important concerns over youth, maturity, responsibility; over the role of parents (which is, in the words of Arnie Cunningham, to kill their children) and the consequences when adults abdicate the concomitant responsibilities; over disturbing and sometimes fatal deficiencies in the American school system; and the perennial frustrations of being young in late-twentieth-century American society. One of the earliest of King's few first-person novel-length narratives (and even that distinction is interrupted by a long passage in the third-person), *Christine* evokes the difficulties of growing up, a recurrent pattern that stands out as central in his novels as early as *Carrie* and *Rage,* that culminates as a primary theme in the masterful *It,* and, though leavened by increasingly dominating concerns for adults and their places in society, nevertheless persists at least through *Hearts in Atlantis.*

SELECTED ARTICLES, RESPONSES, AND REVIEWS:

Aig, M. R. "Buying a Used Car From Stephen King." *St. Louis Globe-Democrat* [MO] (30 April-1 May 1983). As microfiche: *NewsBank: Literature* Vol. 9 (June 1983): Fiche 97, D12.

Aig, M. R. "A Neurotic Car?" *Minneapolis Tribune* 1 May 1983). As microfiche: *NewsBank: Literature* Vol. 9 (June 1983): Fiche 97, D10.

Anders, Smiley. "Youthful Exuberance in King's Horror Tale." *Morning Advocate* [Baton Rouge LA] 15 May 1983. As microfiche: *NewsBank: Literature* Vol. 9 (June 1983): Fiche 97, D8.

Anker, Roger. "An Artist's Profile: Stephen Gervais." *Fantasy Review* No. 84 (October 1985): 8-11. Includes photographs of Gervais's illustrations for the limited edition of *Christine.*

Barry, Dave. "Christine Is Demon for Punishment." *Philadelphia Inquirer* [PA] 27 March 1983.

Bean, Covey. "Even King Fans Won't Buy This," *Daily Oklahoman* [Oklahoma City OK] 3 July 1983. As microfiche: *NewsBank: Literature* Vol. 10 (August 1983): Fiche 11, B11.

Best Sellers Vol. 43 (July 1983): 123.

Boesch, Barry. "King Tale More Than Boy-Meets-Car Story," *Dallas Morning News* [TX] 3 July 1983. As microfiche: *NewsBank: Literature* Vol. 10 (August 1983): Fiche 11, B12.

Booklist Vol. 79 (1 February 1983): 697.

Books and Bookmen (July 1983): 32.
Chandler, Randy. "Horror Master Tells Motor-Vating Tale." *Atlanta Journal-Constitution* [GA] 17 April 1983.
Chelton, Mary K. *Voice of Youth Advocates* Vol. 6 (August 1983): 146.
Egan, James. "Technohorror: The Dystopian Vision of Stephen King." *Extrapolation* Vol. 29, No. 2 (Summer 1988): 140-152, esp. pp. 144.
English Journal Vol. 73 (December 1984): 66.
Gorner, Peter. "King Drives at Horror with Less-Than-Usual Fury." *Chicago Tribune* 6 April 1983.
Graham, Mark. "Stephen King Causes a 'Fury' of a Monster, 1958 Vintage." *Rocky Mountain News* [Denver CO] 8 May 1983).
Henderson, Randi. "A Boy, a Car, and a Horror." *Sun* [Baltimore MD] 1 May 1983. As microfiche: *NewsBank: Literature* Vol. 9 (June 1983): Fiche 97, D9.
"King Tries to Make Novel Wheel Scary." *Houston Post* [TX] 15 May 1983. As microfiche: *NewsBank: Literature* Vol. 9 (June 1983): Fiche 97, E1.
Kirkus Reviews Vol. 51 (1 February 1983: 138.
Kliatt Paperback Book Guide Vol. 18 (Spring 1984): 19.
Lamott, Anne. "A Boy, a Girl, and Christine." *San Francisco Chronicle* 7 April 1983: 55. As microfiche: *NewsBank: Literature* Vol. 9 (May 1983): Fiche 87, B14.
Landgarter, Steven. "Christine." *Tulsa World* [OK] 22 May 1983. As microfiche: *NewsBank: Literature* Vol. 9 (June 1983): Fiche 97, D14.
Lehmann-Haupt, Christopher. "Books of the Times" *The New York Times Daily* Vol. 132 (12 April 1983): III, 15.
Lewis, Don. "The Horror King Rules the Road." *Milwaukee Journal* 24 April 1983). As microfiche: *NewsBank: Literature* Vol. 9 (May 1983): Fiche 87, C4.
Lyons, Gene. "King of High-School Horror." *Newsweek* Vol. 101 (2 May 1983): 76.
The Magazine of Fantasy & Science Fiction Vol. 65 (August 1983): 15.
Pautz, Peter J. *Science Fiction & Fantasy Book Review* [Science Fiction Research Association] No. 16 (July-August 1983): 35.
Pendergast, Lolo. "'Christine' is Wild, Wonderful Adventure and Subsequent Love Affair With the Car." *Clarion-Ledger* [Jackson MS] 24 April 1983). As microfiche: *NewsBank: Literature* Vol. 9 (May 1983): Fiche 87, C1-C2.
Potter, Chuck. "Killer Car's Not So Silly As It Sounds." *Wichita Eagle* [KS] 24 April 1983). As microfiche: *NewsBank: Literature* Vol. 9 (June 1983): Fiche 97, D7.
Publishers Weekly Vol. 223 (25 February 1983): 80. Excerpted: *Contemporary Literary Criticism*, Vol. 26. Edited by Jean C. Stine. Detroit MI: Gale Research Co., 1983, hardcover. 244.
Publishers Weekly Vol. 224 (7 October 1983): 93.
Riggenbach, Jeff. "Suspense Accelerates in King's Christine." *San Jose Mercury News* [CA] 1 May 1983). As microfiche: *NewsBank: Literature* Vol. 9 (June 1983): Fiche 97, D6.

Schleier, Curt. "King Covers Terror-tory in Story of Murderous Car." *Kansas City Star* [MO] 22 May 1983. As microfiche: *NewsBank: Literature* Vol. 9 (June 1983): Fiche 97, D11.

Science Fiction Review No. 12 (November 1983): 39.

See, Carolyn. "A Bumper Crop of Horror." *Los Angeles Times Book Review* 8 May 1983: 3. As microfiche: *NewsBank: Literature* Vol. 9 (June 1983): Fiche 97, D4-D5.

Shea, Jeremy C. "Scary Ride in a Spooky Car." *St. Louis Post-Dispatch* [MO] 8 May 1983. As microfiche: *NewsBank: Literature* Vol. 9 (June 1983): Fiche 97, D13.

Shestak, George. "Tale to Please King Fans, Auto Buffs." *Omaha World-Herald* [NB] 17 April 1983. As microfiche: *NewsBank: Literature* Vol. 9 (May 1983): Fiche 87, C3.

Silva, Mary. *Horn Book Magazine* Vol. 59 (August 1983): 479.

Stasio, Marilyn. "High Suspense." *Penthouse* (July 1983): 56.

Steuwe, Paul. *Quill and Quire* (June 1983): 37.

Van Rjndt, Phillipe. "The Other Woman Was a Car." *New York Times Book Review* Vol. 88 (3 April 1983): 12. Late edition.

Walther, Jim. "Novel Lulls Readers into Trap." *Montgomery Advertiser* [AL] 8 May 1983. As microfiche: *NewsBank: Literature* Vol. 9 (June 1983): Fiche 97, D3.

Ward, Frank. *Library Journal* Vol. 108 (1 March 1983): 517.

Washington Post Book World 23 March 1983: 1.

West Coast Review of Books Vol. 9 (May 1983): 36.

Winter, Douglas E. "Stephen King's Christine: Where Innocence Peels Away Like Burnt Rubber and Death Rides Shotgun." *Fantasy Newsletter* (February 1983).

Horror Plum'd

CYCLE OF THE WEREWOLF. New York, NY: Plume/new American Library, 1985. Trade paperback.

A21.
CYCLE OF THE WEREWOLF
(1983)

A21. *CYCLE OF THE WEREWOLF*. Westland, MI: The Land of Enchantment, Christopher Zavisa, 1983, 114 pp., hardcover. Artwork by Berni Wrightson. A limited edition consisting of eight presentation copies. * COLLECTOR'S STATE, 100 copies, dust jacket and slipcase, with artwork by Wrightson tipped in. * DELUXE LIMITED, 250 copies, numbered 100-350, with portfolio of Wrightson's artwork signed by Wrightson and King. * DELUXE LIMITED without the portfolio. * LIMITED TRADE EDITION of 7,500 copies. [See also A29] Horror novella.

PLOT SUMMARY: Young Marty Coslaw becomes convinced that a werewolf haunts the small town of Tarker's Mills. Confined to a wheelchair, Marty nevertheless involves his sister and his uncle in the struggle to identify and defeat the werewolf.

REPRINTS AND ADAPTATIONS:
b. As: *El ciclo del hombre lobo* ['Cycle of the man-wolf']. Buenos Aires, Argentina: Planeta, 1983, 156 pp., 21 cm. Spanish translation by Joaquín María Adsuar Ortega. ISBN 950-37-0330-1.
c. New York: Plume/New American Library, April 1985, 128 pp., $8.95, trade paperback. ISBN 0-451-82111-4. * Reprinted October, 1985. * Reprinted, December 1989, $15.95, trade paperback. ISBN 0-451-82219-6.
d. London/Sevenoaks England: New English Library, October 1985, 128 pp., paperback.
e. Incorporated into: *Silver Bullet*. New York: Plume/New American Library, October 1985, pp. 17-138, trade paperback. [See A29]
f. As: *Das Jahr des Werwolfs* ['The year of the werewolf']. Bergish Gladbach, West Germany: Bastei-Lübbe TB 28135, 1985, 191 pp., 16.80 DM, paperback. German translation by Harro Christensen. Includes "Von *Carrie* bis *Christine*—Stephen King, der Meister des Makabren," by Douglas E. Winter; translated by Helmut W. Pesch. ISBN 3-404-28135-7.

g. As: *Unico indizzio: la luna piena* ['Unique sign: the full moon']. Milan, Italy: Longanesi, LA GAJA SCIENZA, February 1986. Italian translation by Carlo Brera. ISBN 88-304-0624-4.
h. As: *L'Année du Loup-Garou* ['The year of the werewolf']. Paris: Albin Michel, 1986, 126 pp., 75 F, hardcover. French translation by François Lasquin. ISBN 2-226-02127-2.
i. As: *El ciclo del hombre lobo* ['Cycle of the man-wolf']. Barcelona, Spain: Planeta, CONTEMPORÁNEA #66, January 1986, 160 pp., 21 cm., paperback. 1st edition. Spanish translation by Joaquín María Adsuar Ortega. ISBN 84-320-5845-9. * Reprint, September 1990, ISBN 84-320-3806-7.
j. As: *Peur bleue* ['Blue funk']. Paris, France: J'ai Lu, ÉPOUVANTE #1999, 1986, 227 pp., 19 F. ISBN 2-277-21999-1.
k. As: *Unico Indizio: La Luna Piena* ['Unique sign: the full moon']. Italy: Longanesi, 1986, 144 pp. Italian translation by C. Brera.
l. As: *Silver Bullet: Het Uur van de Weerwolf* ['Silver bullet: the hour of the Werewolf']. Utrecht, Belgium: Luitingh, 1986, 127 pp. Dutch translation by Margot Bakker. ISBN 90-245-1061-9. * 2nd printing, 1990, ISBN 90-245-1666-8.
m. As: *Varulvens År* ['Werewolf's year']. Stockholm, Sweden: B. Wahlström, [1986], 127 pp., 24 cm., hardcover. Swedish translation by Britt-Marie Thieme. ISBN 91-32-31333-0.
n. As: *A hora do lobisomem* ['The hour/time of the wolf-man']. Porto Alegre, Brazil: L & PM Editores, 1987, 128 pp., 21 cm. Portuguese translation by Jimmy Joe.
o. As: *Varulvens År* ['Werewolf's year']. Oslo, Norway: Fredhøi, 1987, 127 pp. Norwegian translation by Benedicta Stubrud. ISBN 82-04-01786-3.
p. As: *Varulvens År* ['Werewolf's year']. Copenhagen, Denmark: Artia, 1988, 127 pp. 128 KR, hardcover. Danish translation by Mogens Wenzel Andreasen. ISBN 87-981865-7-4.
q. As: *Das Jahr des Werwolfs* ['The year of the werewolf']. Bergisch Gladbach, West Germany: Bastei-Lübbe TB 25007, 1988, 200 pp., paperback. German translation by Harro Christensen. Issued without the translation of Winter's article. ISBN 3-404-25007-9.
r. As: *Ihmissuden vuosi* ['Man-wolf year']. Helsinki, Finland: Book Studio, 1990, 126 pp. Finnish translation by Annika Eräpuro. ISBN 951-611-332-X.
s. As: [Title unknown.] South Korea, 1992, 179 pp., 23 cm. Korean translation. ISBN 89-7559-001-1
t. As: *El Ciclo del Hombre Lobo* ['Cycle of the man-wolf']. Barcelona, Spain: Planeta, PLANETA BOLSILLO #23, October 1993, 160 pp., 769 pta., 19 cm., paperback. Spanish translation by Joaquín María Adsuar Ortega. ISBN 84-08-01032-8.
u. As: *Peur bleue* ['Blue funk']. Paris, France: France Loisirs, 1994, 299 pp., 76 F, hardcover. French translations by Michel Darroux, Bernadette Emerich and François Lasquin. ISBN 2-7242-8194.
v. As: *Silver Bullet: Het Uur van de Weerwolf* ['Silver bullet: the hour of the

werewolf']. Amsterdam, Netherlands: Piramide, 1995, 127 pp. Dutch translation by Margot Bakker. ISBN 90-254-0955-5.

w. As: *L'Année du Loup-Garou* ['The year of the werewolf']. [Paris]: [le Grand livre du mois], 1996, 126 pp., 98 F, 29 cm. French translation by François Lasquin. ISBN 2-226-02127-2.

x. As: *El Ciclo del Hombre Lobo* ['Cycle of the man-wolf']. Barcelona, Spain: Planeta, BOOKET #181, November 1997, 160 pp., 913 pta., 18 cm., paperback. Spanish translation by Joaquín María Adsuar Ortega. ISBN 84-08-02321-7.

y. As: *Silver Bullet*. Amsterdam, Netherlands, 1999, 127 pp. Dutch translation by Margot Bakker. 4th printing. ISBN 90-245-3530-1.

z. As FILM and VIDEOCASSETTE: see *Silver Bullet* [A29]

COMMENTS: Conceived initially as a calendar with vignettes for each month, *Cycle of the Werewolf* evolved into King's first extended treatment of the werewolf as monster and as literary symbol. The vignettes expanded to become the skeleton of a novel-length story, further enfleshed by King's screenplay for *Silver Bullet* (1985; see A29).

SELECTED ARTICLES, RESPONSES, AND REVIEWS:
Blue, Tyson. "Prolific Author Produces a 'Werewolf'." *Courier Herald* [Dublin GA].
Book Report Vol. 6 (September 1987): 30. Review of *El Ciclo Del Hombre Lobo*.
Chow, Dan. *Locus* Vol. 17, No. 1, #276 (January 1984).
Klein, Jeanne. "King Recycles a Chilling Tale." *Seattle Post-Intelligencer* [WA] 6 May 1985: B-12.
Larson, Randall. "Cycle of the Werewolf and the Moral Tradition of Horror." *Discovering Stephen King*. Edited by Darrell Schweitzer. Starmont Studies in Literary Criticism, No. 8. Mercer Island WA: Starmont House, 1985. 102-108.
Munster, Bill. "50% of the Cycle: Berni Wrightson." *Footsteps* Vol. VI (December 1985): 47-54.
San Francisco Chronicle "Reviews" 9 June 1985: 5.
Science Fiction Chronicle Vol. 7 (January 1986): 34.
Science Fiction Review No. 14 (November 1985): 5.
Science Fiction Review No. 15 (February 1986): 26.
Sherman, David. "Nightmare Library." *Fangoria* No. 35 (1984): 37.
Stamm, Michael E. "Not for the Average King Fan." *Fantasy Review* No. 65 (March 1984): 32. Excerpted: *Contemporary Literary Criticism*, Vol. 37. Edited by Daniel G. Marowski. Detroit MI: Gale Research Co., 1986, hardcover. 17-198.
Voice of Youth Advocates Vol. 8 (August 1985): 185.
West Coast Review of Books Vol. 11 (May 1986): 46.

PET SEMATARY. Garden City, NY: Doubleday & Co., 1983. Hardcover.

A22.
PET SEMATARY
(1983)

A22. *PET SEMATARY.* Garden City NY: Doubleday & Co., 14 November 1983, 373 pp., $15.95, hardcover. Horror novel. ISBN 0-385-18244-9. * 14th printing, October 1993.

PLOT SUMMARY: Louis Creed and his family move to a small town in Maine. At the back of their property lies a children's "Pet Sematary"; further back, however, hidden in the depths of the forest, however, lies another, older, darker cemetery—one with the power to restore the dead to life. Louis first buries his daughter's cat, Church, in the Indian cemetery; and even though Church returns fundamentally changed and frequently frightening, Louis repeats his actions when his young son Gage is accidentally killed.

REPRINTS AND ADAPTATIONS:
b. London, England: Hodder & Stoughton, February 1984, 368 pp., hardcover. 0-340-34148-3.
c. New York: Signet/New American Library, November 1984, 413 pp., $4.50, mass-market paperback. ISBN 0-451-13237-8. * 24th printing, May 1989, $4.95. Movie tie-in edition. ISBN 0-451-16207-2. * 25th printing, September 1989.
d. Bath, England: Chivers Press, November 1984, 648 pp., hardcover. Large print edition.
e. Garden City NY: Doubleday, [June 1984.], 374 pp., hardcover. Science Fiction Book Club edition #14803.
f. Garden City NY: Mystery Guild Book Club, [n.d.]., hardcover.
g. Boston MA: G. K. Hall, 1984, hardcover. Large-print edition.
h. Boston MA: G. K. Hall, 1984, trade paperback. Large-print edition.
i. As: *Cementario de Animales* ['Cemetery of the animals']. Buenos Aires, Argentina: Emecé, GRANDES NOVELISTAS, 1984, 343 pp., 20 cm. Spanish translation. ISBN 950-04-0352-8. * Reprint, 1986. * Reprint, 1989. * Reprint, 1990* Reprint, 1993. * Reprint, 1994, GRANDES NOVELISTAS.
j. As: *Cementario de Animales* ['Cemetery of the animals']. Barcelona, Spain:

Plaza & Janés, November 1984, 304 pp., 22 cm., paperback. Spanish translation by Anna María de las Fuente. ISBN 84-01-32109-3.
k. Scarborough, Ontario, Canada: NAL of Canada, 1984.
l. London/Sevenoaks, England: New English Library, 1984, 423 pp., paperback.
m. As: *O cemiterio* ['The cemetery']. Rio de Janeiro, Brazil: Francisco Alves, MESTRES DO HORROR E DA FANTASIA, 1984, 394 pp., 22 cm. Portuguese translation by Mario Molina. 2nd printing 1985. * 4th printing, 1987, 21 cm., paperback. ISBN 85-265-0047-3. * 5th printing, 1989, 21 cm., paperback. ISBN 85-265-0047-3.
n. As: *Cementario de Animales* ['Cemetery of the animals']. Valencia, Spain: Círculo de Lectores, 1984, 304 pp., paperback. Spanish translation by Anna María de las Fuente.
o. As: *Cementario de Animales* ['Cemetery of the animals']. Buenos Aires, Argentina: Emece, 1984, 343 pp. Translated by César Aira. Spanish translation. Reprint 1992, GRANDES NOVELISTAS, 19 cm. ISBN 950-04-0352-8.
p. As: *Dodenwake* ['Deathwatch']. Utrecht, Belgium: Luitingh/Veen, 1984, 367 pp., trade paperback. Dutch translation by Margot Bakker. ISBN 90-204-1043-1.
q. As: *Jurtikyrkogården* ['Ominous church-garden/yard']. [Höganäs, Sweden]: Bra Spänning, 1984, 493 pp. Swedish translation by Lennart Olafsson.
r. As: *Chung wu feng chang*. Taipei, Taiwan: Huang kuan chu pan she, 1984. Chinese translation by Chao Erh-hsin.
s. As: *Semetario de Mascotas* ['Cemetery (misspelled) of mascots']. México: Edivisión, 1985, 395 pp. Spanish translation by Angelika Scherp.
t. London, England: New English Library, February 1985, 432 pp., paperback.
u. As: *Pet Sematary*. Milan, Italy: Sperling & Kupfer, PANDORA #266, April 1985. Italian translation by Hilia Brinis. ISBN 88-200-0460-7.
v. As: *Friedhof der Kuscheltiere—Pet Sematary* ['Cemetery of the snuggly-animals']. Hamburg, West Germany: Hoffman and Campe Verlag, 1985, 379 pp., 38.00 DM, hardcover. German translation by Christel Wiemkin. ISBN 3-455-03736-4. * 3rd printing, 1986. * 4th printing, 1987. * 5th printing, 1988. * 6th printing, 1993.
w. Excerpted as: "Friedhof der Kuscheltiere." *Der Stern* No. 19-No. 33 (1985). In 15 parts.
x. As: *Simetière* ['Cemetery' (misspelled)]. Paris: Albin Michel, 1985, 480 pp. French translation.
y. As: *De levende døde* ['The living dead']. Oslo, Norway: Hjemmets, 1985, 240 pp. Norwegian translation by Torfinn Haukås. ISBN 82-590-0095-4.
z. As: *Cementario de Animales* ['Cemetery of the animals']. Barcelona, Valencia, Spain: Círculo de Lectores, 1985, 360 pp., 778 pta., 21 cm., hardcover. Spanish translation by Anna María de las Fuente. ISBN 84-226-1868-0. * 3rd printing, January 1996.
aa. As: [Title unknown]. Mexico: Diana, 1985. Spanish translation.
bb. Boston: G. K. Hall & Co., October 1986, x+634 pp., $17.95, hardcover.

HORROR PLUM'D

Large print edition. ISBN 0-8161-3691-2.
cc. As: *O cemiterio* ['The cemetery']. Rio de Janeiro, Brazil: Rio Grafica, 1986, 388 pp., 19 cm. Portuguese translation by Mario Molina.
dd. As: *Uinu, uinu, lemmikkini.* Helsinki, Finland: Tammi, 1986, 476 pp., 23 cm. Finnish translation by Pirkko Talvio-Jaatinen. ISBN 951-30-6161-2. * 7th printing, 1992.
ee. As: *Simetière* ['Cemetery' (misspelled)]. Paris, France: France Loisirs, 1986, 474 pp., 70 F, hardcover. French translation by François Lasquin. ISBN 2-7242-2991-6.
ff. As: *Simetière* ['Cemetery' (misspelled)]. [Paris, France]: [le Grand livre du mois], 1986, 475 pp., 89 F. hardcover. French translation by François Lasquin. Book Club edition.
gg. As: *Bet-k'varot.* Tel Aviv, Israel: Modin, 1986, 319 pp. Hebrew translation by Nurit Perez.
hh. As: *Dodenwake* ['Deathwatch']. Utrecht, Belgium: Luitingh, 1986, 368 pp. Dutch translation by Margot Bakker. 4th printing. ISBN 90-245-1662-5. * 8th printing, 1991.
ii. As: *Jurtikyrkogården* ['Ominous church-garden/yard']. Stockholm, Sweden: Legenda, 1986, 493 pp., 21 cm. Swedish translation by Lennart Olaffson. 3rd-6th *kartonniert* edition. ISBN 91-582-0737-6.
jj. London, England: New English Library, October 1987, 424 pp., £3.50, paperback. ISBN 0-450-05769-0. * 16th printing, October 1989, movie tie-in edition. * 23rd printing, 1992, £4.99.
kk. As: *Simetière* ['Cemetery' (misspelled)]. Paris, France: J'ai Lu, ÉPOUVANTE #2266, 1987, 569 pp., paperback. French translation. ISBN 2-277-22266-6.
ll. As: *Cementario de Animales* ['Cemetery of the animals']. Esplugues de Llobregat, Barcelona, Spain: Plaza & Janés, ÉXITOS, 1987, 304 pp., 22 cm., hardcover. Spanish translation by Anna María de las Fuente. 2nd edition. ISBN 84-01-32109-3.
mm. As: *Cementario de Animales* ['Cemetery of the animals']. Esplugues de Llobregat, Barcelona, Spain: Plaza & Janés, JET #102/1, 1987, 409 pp., 18 cm., paperback. Spanish translation by Anna María de las Fuente. 2nd edition, 1st printing thus. ISBN 84-01-49881-3. * 11th-13th printings, 1993, BIBLIOTECA DE STEPHEN KING #1, ISBN 84-01-49984-4. * Reprint, October 1996, 480 pp., 18 cm. ISBN 84-01-49984-4.
nn. As: *Cementario de Animales* ['Cemetery of the animals']. Barcelona, Spain: Plaza & Janés, JET #102—BIBLIOTECA DE STEPHEN KING #1, May 1992, 416 pp., 728 pta., 18 cm., paperback. 10th edition. Spanish translation by Ana Mariá de la Fuente. ISBN 84-01-49881-3.
oo. As: *Friedhof der Kuscheltiere* ['Cemetery of the snuggly-animals']. Kornwesterheim, Austria: Europäische Bildungsgemeinschaft; Gütersloh, Austria: Bertelsmann Club; Vienna, Austria: Buchgemeinschaft Donauland; Zug, Switzerland: Buch-und-Schallplattenfreunde, [April 1987], 379 pp., paperback. German translations by Christel Wiemkin. Book Club editions.
pp. As: *Friedhof der Kuscheltiere* ['Cemetery of the snuggly-animals'].

Gütersloh, Austria: Bertelsmann Lesering, 1987, pp. German translation by Christel Wiemkin.

qq. As: *Simetière* ['Cemetery' (misspelled)]. Paris, France: J'ai-Lu/Epouvante, 1987, 572 pp., paperback. French translation by François Lasquin.

rr. As: *Dyrekirkegården* ['Animal-churchyard/cemetery']. Copenhagen [Valby], Denmark: Gode Böger, 1987, 298 pp. Danish translation by Elsebeth Eskestad. ISBN 87-74435949.

ss. As: *Friedhof der Kuscheltiere* ['Cemetery of the snuggly-animals']. Munich, Germany: Wilhelm Heyne, TB 7627, 1988, 459 pp., 9.80 DM, 18 cm., paperback. Unabridged German translation by Christel Wiemkin. ISBN 3-453-00786-7. * 10th printing, 1989. * 14th-16th printing, 1990. * 21st printing, 1991. * 26th printing, 1992. * 30th printing, 1993. * 34th printing, 1994.

tt. As: *Friedhof der Kuscheltiere* ['Cemetery of the snuggly-animals']. Stuttgart: Deutscher Bücherbund, [1988], 379 pp. German translation by Christel Wiemkin. Book Club edition.

uu. As: *Pet Sematary*. Milan, Italy: Sperling Paperback, SUPERBESTSELLER #32, March 1989, paperback. Italian translation by Hilia Brinis. ISBN 88-7824-030-3.

vv. As: *Macje pokopalisce*. Ljubljana, Slovenia: Drzavna zaloba Slovenije, 1989, 331 pp., 20 cm. Slovenian translation by Andrej Blatnikj. ISBN 86-341-0313-7.

ww. As: *De levende døde* ['The living dead']. Oslo, Norway: Damm, DAMMS BESTE #3, 1989, 240 pp. Norwegian translation by Torfinn Haukås. ISBN 82-517-7039-4.

xx. As: *Samitério das mascotes* ['Cemetery of mascots' (misspelled)]. Lisbon, Portugal: Círculo de Leitores, 1989, 404 pp., 21 cm. Portuguese translation by Maria Emília Ferros Moura.

yy. As: *Cementario de Animales* ['Cemetery of animals']. Esplugues de Llobregat, Barcelona, Spain: Plaza & Janés Editores, BIBLIOTECA DE STEPHEN KING, Vol. 1. 1989, 304 pp., paperback. Spanish translation.

zz. Tokyo, Japan: Bungeishunju, 1989. 2 vols. Japanese translation by Fukamachi Mariko.

aaa. As: *Cementario de Animales* ['Cemetery of animals']. Barcelona, Spain: Plaza & Janés, ÉXITOS, February 1990, 304 pp., 1038 pta., paperback. 3rd edition. Spanish translation by Ana Mariá de la Fuente. ISBN 84-01-32109-3. Trade paperback: 2650 pta, ISBN 84-01-32425-4.

bbb. As: *Simetière* ['Cemetery' (misspelled)]. Paris, France: Albin Michel, 1990, 474 pp., 120 F. paperback. French translation by François Lasquin. ISBN 2-226-02482-4.

ccc. As: *Simetière* ['Cemetery' (misspelled)]. [Paris, France]: Editions de la Seine, 1991, 474 pp., 84 F, hardcover. French translation by François Lasquin. ISBN 2-7382-0442-2.

ddd. As: *Friedhof der Kuscheltiere* ['Cemetery of the snuggly-animals']. Munich, Germany: Wilhelm Heyne, #8499, 1992, 459 pp., 15.00 DM, paperback. German translation by Christel Wiemkin. ISBN 3-453-06326-0. New edition.

eee. As: *Smêtarz dla Zwierzakó* ['Cemetery of little animals']. Bydgoszcz, Warsaw, Poland: "Somix," "AS-Editor," 1992, 368 pp., 21 cm. Polish translation by Michal Wroczyñski.
fff. As: *Cemeteri d'animals* ['Cemetery of animals']. Barcelona, Spain: Columna, April 1994, 336 pp., 3173 pta. Spanish translation by Lluis Miquel Bennàsser. ISBN 84-7809-586-1.
ggg. As: *Cementiri d'animals* ['Cemetery of animals']. Barcelona, Spain: Enciclopèdia Catalana, BEST SELLER #6, April 1994, 348 pp., 3173 pta., 24 cm., paperback. New edition. Spanish translation by Lluís Miguel Bennàsser. ISBN 84-7739-625-6.
hhh. As: *Simetière* ['Cemetery' (misspelled)]. Paris, France: France Loisirs, 1994, 475 pp., 96 F. hardcover. French translation by François Lasquin. ISBN 2-7242-7848-8.
iii. As: [Title unknown]. South Korea, 1994, 466 pp., 23 cm. Korean translation. ISBN 89-85934-91-07.
jjj. As: *Dodenwake* ['Deathwatch']. Amsterdam, Netherlands: Poema Pocket, 1994, 368 pp., paperback. Dutch translation by Margot Bakker. 10h printing. ISBN 90-245-1156-9.
kkk. As: *De levende døde* ['The living dead']. Oslo, Norway: Hjemmets bokforlag, EGMONT SPENNING #28, 1994, 240 pp. Norwegian translation by Torfinn Haukås. ISBN 82-04-03386-9.
lll. As: *Cementario de Animales* ['Cemetery of the animals']. [Buenos Aires]: Emece, TOP EMECÉ #12, 1994, 441 pp., 18 cm., paperback. Spanish translation by César Aira. ISBN 950-04-1390-6.
mmm. As: *Cementario de Animales* ['Cemetery of the animals']. Barcelona, Spain: Plaza & Janés, JET, June 1995, 409 pp., 18 cm., paperback. Spanish translation by Ana Mariá de la Fuente. ISBN 84-01-62022-8.
nnn. As: *Simetière* ['Cemetery' (misspelled)]. [Paris, France]: [le Grand livre du mois], 1995, 475 pp., 120 F, hardcover. French translation by François Lasquin. Book Club edition.
ooo. As: *Friedhof der Kuscheltiere—Pet Sematary* ['Cemetery of the snuggly-animals']. Munich, Germany: Wilhelm Heyne, 1996, 459 pp. German translation. 38th printing. ISBN 3-453-06326-0.
ppp. As: *De levende døde* ['The living dead']. Oslo, Norway: Egmont Bøker Fredhøi, 1996, 240 pp., [*innbundet*]. Norwegian translation. ISBN 82-59-01652-4.
qqq. As: *De levende døde* ['The living dead']. Oslo, Norway: Hjemmets, STEPHEN KINGS UTVALGTE, 1996, 240 pp. Norwegian translation by Torfinn Haukås. ISBN 82-590-1652-4.
rrr. As: *Cementario de Animales* ['Cemetery of the animals']. Barcelona, Spain: Plaza & Janés, 1996, 424 pp., 23 cm. Spanish translation by Ana Mariá de la Fuente. 2nd printing in this collection. ISBN 84-01-32425-4.
sss. As: *Dyrekirkegården* ['Animal-churchyard/cemetery']. Copenhagen, Denmark: Vinten, VINTENS PAPERBACKS, 1997, 298 pp., 78 KR, paperback. Danish translation by Elsebeth Eskestad. ISBN 87-612-0150-2.

ttt. Oxford, England, and Melbourne, Australia: Compass/Isis; Tullamarine, Victoria: Australian Large Print Audio and Video, 1997, 583 pp., 24 cm. Simultaneous large-print editions.
uuu. As: *O cemitério* ['The cemetery']. Rio de Janeiro, Brazil: Objetiva, 1998, 243 pp., 21 cm., paperback. Portuguese translation by Mário Molina. ISBN 85-730-2187-X.
vvv. Thorndike ME: G. K. Hall, Large Print Core Collection, [before 1994], , hardcover and paperback [?]. Large Print edition.
www. As: *Álla Emetö*. Budapest, Hungary: Európa, 19—. Hungarian translation.
xxx. As: [Title unknown]. Rio de Janeiro, Brazil: Francisco Alves, 19—. Portuguese translation.
yyy. As: [Title unknown]. Russian translation. Omnibus with *The Eyes of the Dragon*.

zzz. As AUDIOCASSETTE: *Pet Semetary*. London: BBC, distributed by Simon & Schuster Audioworks, 1988. 2-cassette dramatization.
aaaa. As: AUDIOCASSETTE; *Pet Semetary (BBC Radio Presents)*. New York: Simon & Schuster Audio, February 2001, $23.50. Abridged. ISBN 0-743-51844-6.

bbbb. As FILM: Paramount Pictures, 14 April 1989. Produced by Richard Rubinstein. Directed by Mary Lambert. Screenplay by Stephen King. Filmed entirely in the Ellsworth/Bangor area of Maine. 95 minutes. Rated: R.
CAST: Dale Midkiff, Fred Gwynne, Denise Crosby, Blaze Berhahl, Miko Hughes, Brad Greenquist, Susan J. Blommaert, Michael Lombard; with cameo role by King.
NOTE: According to Gary Wood, the project was rejected by Universal, United Artists, and twice by Paramount, but *Pet Sematary* became the "most profitable Stephen King adaptation to [that] date," earning Paramount "over $26 million in domestic theatrical film rentals alone in 1989."
SELECTED FILM REVIEWS AND RESPONSES:
Armstrong, David. "King's 'Pet Sematary'—Stylish But a Bit of a Stiff." *San Francisco Examiner* 21 April 1989). As microfiche: *Newsbank: Film and Television* Vol. 16 (May 1989): Fiche 55, E1.
Burke-Block, Candace. "Master of Ghouls Fears Loss of a Child." *Washington [DC] Times* 9 May 1989). As microfiche: *Newsbank: Film and Television* 16 (May 1989): Fiche 65, A13.
Canby, Vincent. *New York Times* 22 April 1989: A16.
Carr, Jay. "'Pet Sematary' Doesn't Live Up to Previous King Film Adaptations." *Denver Post* [CO] 23 April 1989. As microfiche: *Newsbank: Film and Television* 16 (May 1989): Fiche 55, E2.
Chicago Tribune 24 April 1989: V, 2.
Cinefantastique Vol. 19 (March 1989): 4.
Collings, Michael R. "Resting in Pieces: *Pet Sematary* Offers Grounds for Intense Horror Scenes." *The Blood Review: The Journal of Horror Criticism* Vol. 1, No. 1 (October 1989): 46-49.

Courier-News [NJ] 22 April 1989.

Degan, Anne. "*Pet Sematary*: Moviemaking Next Door Can Really Change Scenes." *Maine Sunday Telegram* [Portland ME] 2 October 1988: 10E-11E, 13E. As microfiche: *Newsbank: Film and Television* Vol. 15 (October 1988): Fiche 159, D8-D10.

Draheim, Tom. "*Pet Sematary* Doesn't Draw Raves in Boston." *Boston Globe* 21 April 1989: 46. Reprinted: *Castle Rock: The Stephen King Newsletter* Vol. 5, No. 6 (June 1989): 1, 12.

Edelstein, David. "Grave Doings." *New York Post* 22 April 1989. As microfiche: *Newsbank: Film and Television* Vol. 16 (May 1989): Fiche 55, E9-E10.

Fangoria No. 80 (1988). One-page article.

Fangoria No. 81 (1988). Four-page article with photographs.

Freedman, Richard. "'Pet Sematary' Unearths Deadly Secrets in Stephen King's Fast-Paced Shocker." *Star-Ledger* [Newark NJ] 22 April 1989. As microfiche: *Newsbank: Film and Television* Vol. 16 (May 1989): Fiche 55, E8.

Gadberry, Greg. "'Pet Sematary' Continued King Tradition." *Maine Sunday Telegram* [Portland ME] 2 October 1988: 11E.

Gadberry, Greg. "Two Maine Actresses Put Their Scare into 'Pet Sematary.'"*Maine Sunday Telegram* [Portland ME] 16 April 1989. As microfiche: *Newsbank: Film and Television* Vol. 16 (May 1989): Fiche 55, D13.

Garner, Jack. "It's a Grave New World in King's Disturbingly Real 'Pet Sematary.'"*Detroit News* [MI] 24 April 1989. As microfiche: *Newsbank: Film and Television* Vol. 16 (May 1989): Fiche 55, E7.

Gruezone No. 8 (July 1989). Cover article.

Johnson, Malcolm. "'Pet Sematary' Unable to Resurrect King's Terror." *Hartford Courant* [CT] 22 April 1989. As microfiche: *Newsbank: Film and Television* Vol. 16 (May 1989): Fiche 55, E3-E4.

"King's 'Pet Sematary': A Grave Mistake." *Washington [DC] Times* 24 April 1989. As microfiche: *Newsbank: Film and Television* Vol. 16 (May 1989): Fiche 55, E12-E13.

Klein, Andy. "The Horrors of 'Pet Sematary.'" *Los Angeles Examiner* [CA] 24 April 1989. As microfiche: *Newsbank: Film and Television* Vol. 16 (May 1989): Fiche 55, D14.

Los Angeles Times [CA] 24 April 1989: VI, 5.

Martin, Robert H. [Bob]. "George Romero on *Day of the Dead* and *Pet Sematary*." *Fangoria* No. 48 (October 1985): 43-47.

McGarrigle, Dale. "Audience at 'Pet Sematary' Debut Praises Film's Faithfulness to Book." *Bangor Daily News* [ME] 11 April 1989. As microfiche: *Newsbank: Film and Television* Vol. 16 (May 1989): Fiche 55, D12.

McKibben, Robert. "On Location: Maine's Not Profiting from Hollywood as Much as It Might." *Maine Times* [Topsham ME] 23

September 1988. As microfiche: *Newsbank: Film and Television* Vol. 15 (October 1988): Fiche 159, D11-D13.

Mulay, James. "Pet Sematary." *The Motion Picture Guide, 1990 Annual.* Evanston, IL: Cinebooks, 1990, hardcover. 175-176.

People Weekly Vol. 31 (15 May 1989): 13.

"'Pet Sematary' Is Strong Shocker, One of Best from Stephen King." *Seattle Times* [WA] 21 April 1989. As microfiche: *Newsbank: Film and Television* Vol. 16 (May 1989): Fiche 55, E11.

Rambeau, Catharine. "Zombies Carry Director into Limelight." *Detroit Free Press* [MI] 11 August 1985. As microfiche: *Newsbank: Film and Television* Vol. 12 (September 1985): Fiche 31, E2-E3.

Roeper, Richard. "'Pet Sematary' Should Have Been Interred, Not Released." *Chicago Sun Times* [IL] 25 April 1989. As microfiche: *Newsbank: Film and Television* Vol. 16 (May 1989): Fiche 55, E5.

Rosenthal, Donna. "In 'Pet Sematary,' Stephen King Replays the Horror on Film." *Daily News* [NY] 17 April 1989. As microfiche: *Newsbank: Film and Television* Vol. 16 (May 1989): Fiche 53, A14-A15.

Schaefer, Stephen. "King Digs Horror in 'Pet Sematary.'" *Boston Herald* [MA] 16 April 1989. As Microfiche: *Newsbank: Film and Television* Vol. 16 (June 1989): Fiche 65, A10-A12. Also as microfiche: *NewsBank: Names in the News* Vol. 11 (May 1989): Fiche 134, C1-C3.

"SK Brings Hollywood to Maine." *Maine* (September/October 1989). Cover article.

Spruce, Christopher. "Do You Know Where Your Kid Is Tonight?" *Castle Rock: The Stephen King Newsletter* Vol. 5, No. 5. (May 1989): 1, 12.

Us Vol. 3 (29 May 1989): 62.

Variety Vol. 135 (26 April 1989): 26.

Verniere, James. "'Pet Sematary' Dogged by Copycat Horror Plot." *Boston Herald* [MA] 21 April 1989. As microfiche: *Newsbank: Film and Television* Vol. 16 (May 1989): Fiche 55, E6.

Washington Post [DC] 22 April 1989: C1.

Welsh, James M. "Pet Sematary." *Magill's Cinema Annual, 1990: A Survey of the films of 1989.* Edited by Frank N. Magill. Englewood Cliffs, NJ: Salem Press, 1990. 271-274.

"What the Newspaper Critics Said...." *The Blood Review: The Journal of Horror Criticism* Vol. 1, No. 1 (October 1989): 49.

Wood, Gary. "Stephen King Strikes Back!" *Cinefantastique* Vol. 20, No. 3 (January 1990).

Wood, Gary. "*Pet Sematary*: More Creative Control over His Own Screenplay Translated into One of the Author's Biggest Success Stories at the Movies." *Cinefantastique* Vol. 21, No. 4 (February 1991): 39.

cccc. As VIDEOCASSETTE: Paramount, 1989. VHS #1949. 103 minutes. Rated: R. ISBN 0-7921-1074-9.
SELECTED FILM REVIEWS AND ARTICLES:
McCullaugh, Jim. "Horror Video: September Is Horror Month." *Billboard Magazine* Vol. 101, No. 38 (23 September 1989): 54.
dddd. As VIDEOCASSETTE: *Stephen King's Friedhof der Kuscheltiere.* Frankfurt am Main, Germany: CIC-Video, HOLLYWOOD-COLLECTION, 1992. 98 minutes.

COMMENTS: The book sold 657,741 hardcover copies in 1983, King's highest year-end sales to that date, and was ranked #3 on the *Bowkers Annual* hardcover fiction bestsellers list for 1983. Appearing with *Christine*, *Pet Semetary* marked the first time since 1972 that an author had had two books on the list simultaneously. Over 750,000 hardcover copies had been sold in 11 hardcover printings by September, 1989. The novel appeared for more than thirty weeks on the *New York Times* bestsellers list.

King himself has noted that this novel is darker than most of his others, exploring deeper and darker motives. Based loosely on W. W. Jacob's classic story, "The Monkey's Paw," *Pet Sematary* directly confronts the reality of death and its role in human life. Each major character must discover what death truly signifies, why it is important, how it must be reconciled with life. The novel methodically recreates an unendurable tension as it moves toward what still stands as arguably King's most chilling final sentence.

King did not originally intend the novel for publication; contractual disputes with Doubleday forced him to release the manuscript, but he refused to promote the book actively.

SELECTED ARTICLES, RESPONSES, AND REVIEWS:
Analog Science Fiction/Science Fact Vol. 104 (September 1984): 169.
Anders, Smiley. "Scaring Readers Silly." *Morning Advocate* [Baton Rouge LA] 6 November 1983. As microfiche: *NewsBank: Literature* Vol. 10 (December 1983): Fiche 44, E9.
Best Sellers Vol. 43 (January 1984): 360.
Bleiler, Richard. "Burial Grounds Disturb Family." *Columbus Evening Dispatch* [OH] 20 November 1983. As microfiche: *NewsBank: Literature* Vol. 10 (December 1983): Fiche 44, E13.
Blue, Tyson. "King Deals Directly with Death." *Courier Herald* [Dublin GA] 12 November 1983.
Booklist Vol. 80 (15 September 1983): 114.
Chelton, Mary K. *Voice of Youth Advocates* Vol. 7 (April 1984): 32.
Clark, Roxanne. "'Pet Sematary' a Top King Novel, But Don't Read It Before Bed!" *Indianapolis Star* [IN] 20 November 1983. As microfiche: *NewsBank: Literature* Vol. 10 (December 1983): Fiche 44, E8.
Dickerson, James. "King's Book of Pet Horrors." *Commercial Appeal* [Memphis TN] 18 December 1983. As microfiche: *NewsBank: Literature* Vol. 10 (January 1984): Fiche 51, E7.

Michael R. Collings

The Ecphorizer [Sunnyvale CA] (December 1984). Relationship of *Pet Sematary* to King's body of work.
English Journal Vol. 73 (December 1984): 66.
Garner, Jack. "America's Boogeyman Is Raising Hair Again, Including His Own." *Rochester Democrat and Chronicle* [NY] 30 October 1983. As microfiche: *NewsBank: Literature* Vol. 10 (December 1983): Fiche 44, E11-E12.
Gottlieb, Anne. "Something Lurks in Ludlow." *The New York Times Book Review* Vol. 88 (6 November 1983): VII 15. Excerpted: *Contemporary Literary Criticism*, Vol. 37. Edited by Daniel G. Marowski. Detroit MI: Gale Research, 1986. 203.
Graham, Mark. "Macabre Master." *Rocky Mountain News* [Denver CO] 4 December 1983: 38M.
Henderson, Randi. "More of the Same Sort of Spooky Shenanigans." *Sun* [Baltimore MD] 6 November 1983. As microfiche: *NewsBank: Literature* Vol. 10 (December 1983): Fiche 44, E9.
Herron, Don, ed. *Reign of Fear*. Los Angeles CA: Underwood-Miller, June 1988.
"Horror King Stumbles Again." *Chicago Tribune* [IL] 10 November 1983. As microfiche: *NewsBank: Literature* Vol. 10 (December 1983): Fiche 44, E7.
Kirkus Reviews Vol. 51 (1 September 1983): 968.
Lehmann-Haupt, Christopher. "Books of the Times." *New York Times* Vol. 133 (21 October 1983): III, 31.
Lewis, Don. "A Few Stones Unturned in King's 'Pet Sematary'!" *Milwaukee Journal* [WI] 6 November 1983. As microfiche: *NewsBank: Literature* Vol. 10 (December 1983): Fiche 44, E14.
Libertore, Karen. "Gruesome and Gross." *San Francisco Examiner* [CA] 6 November 1983. As microfiche: *NewsBank: Literature* 10 (December 1983): Fiche 44, E6
Magistrale, Tony. "Stephen King's Pet Sematary: Hawthorne's Woods Revisited." *The Gothic World of Stephen King: Landscape of Nightmares*. Edited by Gary Hoppenstand and Ray B. Browne. Bowling Green OH: Bowling Green State University Popular Press, December 1987. 126-134.
Maychick, Diana. "Unearthing the Origins of Stephen King's 'Pet Sematary.'" *New York Post* 16 April 1989. As microfiche: *NewsBank: Names in the News* Vol. 11 (May 1989): Fiche 134, C4-C5. As microfiche: *Newsbank: Film and Television* Vol. 16 (May 1989): Fiche 53, 2-B3.
Miller, Ronnie. "'Pet Sematary' Is King's Latest Journey into Horror." *Oregon Statesman* [Salem OR] 11 December 1983. As microfiche: *NewsBank: Literature* Vol. 10 (January 1984): Fiche 51, E6.
Pharr, Mary Ferguson. "A Dream of New Life: Stephen King's Pet Sematary as a Variant of Frankenstein." *The Gothic World of Stephen King: Landscape of Nightmares*. Edited by Gary Hoppenstand and Ray B. Browne. Bowling Green OH: Bowling Green State University Popular Press, December 1987. 115-125.
Publishers Weekly Vol. 224 (23 September 1983): 61.

Publishers Weekly Vol. 226 (28 September 1984): 111.

Rosenbaum, Mary Helene. "Pet Sematary." *Christian Century* Vol. 101 (21-28 March 1984): 316.

Sales, Grover. "King Rules over Scare-Fiction." *Los Angeles Times Book Review* [CA] 20 November 1983: 17. As microfiche: *NewsBank: Literature* Vol. 10 (December 1983): Fiche 44, E5.

San Francisco Chronicle "Reviews" [CA] 6 November 1983: 7.

Schaefer, Stephen. "Stephen King Philosophizes From the Grave." *Record* [Hackensack NJ] 21 April 1989. As microfiche: *NewsBank: Names in the News* Vol. 11 (July 1989): Fiche 203, C13-C14.

Schleier, Curt. "'Sematary' Frightening Even to King of Horror." *Kansas City Star* [MO] 18 December 1983. As microfiche: *NewsBank: Literature* Vol. 10 (January 1984): Fiche 51, E5.

School Library Journal Vol. 30 (August 1984): 38.

Schroeder, Natalie. "'Oz the Gweat and Tewwible' and 'The Other Side': The Theme of Death in Pet Sematary and Jutterbug Perfume." *The Gothic World of Stephen King: Landscape of Nightmares*. Edited by Gary Hoppenstand and Ray B. Browne. Bowling Green OH: Bowling Green State University Popular Press, December 1987. 135-141.

Science Fiction Review Vol. 13 (February 1984): 42.

Slifkin, Irv. "Occupation: Offending." *Philadelphia Inquirer* [PA] 12 October 1989. As microfiche: *NewsBank: Names in the News* Vol. 11 (November 1989): Fiche 315, D10-D11.

Stamm, Michael R. "Pet Sematary: Opposing Views...Flawed, Unsatisfying." *Fantasy Review* No. 64 (January 1984): 49.

Stamm, Michael R. *Science Fiction & Fantasy Book Review* No. 20 (December 1983): 35-36. Excerpted: *Contemporary Literary Criticism*, Vol. 37. Edited by Daniel G. Marowski. Detroit MI: Gale Research, 1986. 204.

"Stephen King on Pet Sematary." *The Blood Review: The Journal of Horror Criticism* Vol. , No. 1 (October 1989): 49.

Stuewe, Paul. *Quill and Quire* Vol. 50 (Fall 1984): 41.

Top of the News Vol. 42 (Fall 1985): 96.

Ward, Frank. *Library Journal* Vol. 108 (15 October 1983): 1973.

Washington Post Book World [DC] 2 October 1983: 6.

Wilson School Journal Vol. 202 (28 October 1983): 28.

Winter, Douglas E. *Washington Post Book World* [DC] 13 November 1983): 1. Excerpted: *Contemporary Literary Criticism*, Vol. 37. Edited by Daniel G. Marowski. Detroit MI: Gale Research, 1986. 203-204.

Zizek, Slavoj. *Looking Awry: An Introduction to Jacques Lacan Through Popular Culture*. Cambridge, MA: MIT Press, 1991, hardcover. 23-26.

THE PLANT

by Stephen King

part two of a novel in progress

PHILTRUM PRESS

Bangor, Maine 2000

THE PLANT: PART 2. Chapbook.

A23.
THE PLANT: PART 2
(1983)

A23. *THE PLANT [PART 2].* Bangor ME: Philtrum Press, December (?) 1983, 36 pp., chapbook. Limited edition consisting of 26 lettered copies signed by King plus 200 numbered copies. Horror fiction pamphlet.

COMMENTS: The second installment of a novel-in-progress, privately published by King and sent as Christmas greetings. See also the other two parts A18, A31, and the completion of Book One, Parts I-VI, as an internet publication [A71].

SELECTED ARTICLES, RESPONSES, AND REVIEWS:
Blue, Tyson. "The Plant: The Unseen King." *Castle Rock: The Stephen King Newsletter* Vol. 2, No. 6 (June 1986): 1,3.

THE EYES OF THE DRAGON. New York, NY: Viking, 1987. Hardcover.

A24.
THE EYES OF THE DRAGON
(1984)

A24. *THE EYES OF THE DRAGON.* Bangor ME: Philtrum Press, 1984, 314 pp., hardcover. Illustrations by Kenneth R. Linkhäuser [Linkhaus]. No ISBN assigned. Red- and black-lettered states, 26 copies each, A-Z. Fantasy novel, children's novel. * LIMITED EDITION: 1250 copies, numbered in red (1-250) or black (1-1000) ink, with slipcase, $120.00.

DEDICATION: "This story is for my great friend Ben Straub, and for my daughter, Naomi King."

PLOT SUMMARY: In the kingdom of Delain, the death of the reigning king brings unusual disorder and disruption, orchestrated by the mysterious and malevolent Flagg. The usurping younger brother, Thomas, falls under Flagg's spell; only the true king, Peter, who has been falsely imprisoned for his father's murder, can restore peace and order to the realm.

REPRINTS AND ADAPTATIONS:
b. New York: Viking, 2 February 1987, 326 pp., $18.95, hardcover. Illustrations by David Palladini. ISBN 0-670-81458-X.
    COMMENTS: First printing: 1,000,000 copies; sold 525,000 copies by the end of 1987; ranked #10 on the annual fiction hardcover bestsellers list.
c. London, England: Macdonald, April 1987, 336 pp., £10.95, hardcover. Illustrations by David Palladini. ISBN 0-356-14224-8.
d. As: *Los Ojos de Dragon* ['The eyes of the dragon']. Buenos Aires, Argentina: Emece, 1987, 463 pp. Spanish translation by Rosa S. Corgatelli.
e. As: *Ogen van de Draak* ['Eyes of the Dragon']. Utrecht, Belgium: Luitingh-Sijthoff, 1987, 311 pp. Dutch translation by Margot Bakker. ISBN 90-245-1642-0.
f. As: *Long zhi mian.* Taipei, Taiwan: Huang Guan, 1987. Chinese translation by Jiang Guan Yu.

g. As: *Wangja ui Pimil.* Seoul-si, South Korea: Munhak Saenhwalsa, 1987, 23 cm. 2 vols. Korean translation by Sol Yong-hwan omgim.
h. As: *Dragens øjne* ['Dragon's eyes']. [Ruds-Vedby, Denmark]: Tellerup Christensen Grafik, 1989, 427 pp., 21 cm., 248 KR, paperback. Danish translation by Bjarne Skovlund. ISBN 87-588-0385-8.
i. As: *Die Augen des Drachen* ['The eyes of the dragon']. Munich, Germany: Wilhelm Heyne, TB 6824, 1987, 381 pp., 9.80 DM, paperpack. German translation by Joachim Körber. ISBN 3-453-02435-4. * 4th printing, 1988. * 9th printing, 1991. * 18th printing, 1993. * 20th printing, 1994. * 23rd printing, 1995.
j. As: *Die Augen des Drachen* ['The eyes of the dragon']. Linkenheim, Germany: Phantasia, 1987, [15] pp., 78.00 dm, portfolio of 13 illustrations by Johan Peterka. Limited edition of 100 numbered copies, I-XX not offered for sale. ISBN 3-924959-09-9.
k. As: [Title unknown]. Taipei, Taiwan: Huang guan, 1987. Chinese translation.
l. New York: Signet/New American Library, January 1988, 380 pp., $4.50 mass-market paperback. Illustrations by David Palladini. ISBN 0-451-16658-2. * 7th printing, by September 1989. * Reprint, December 1994, $7.99.
m. London, England: Futura, January 1988, 427 pp., £3.50, paperback. ISBN 0-7088-3574-0.
n. Bath, England: Windsor Selection Series/Chivers Press, May 1988, 443 pp., £9.99, hardcover. Large print edition. ISBN 0-86220-237-X.
o. As: *Gli Occhí del Drago* ['The eyes of the dragon']. Milan, Italy: Sperling & Kupfer, PANDORA [#412], November 1988. Italian translation by Tullio Dobner. ISBN 88-200-0819-X.
p. Boston MA: G. K. Hall & Co., 1988, 443 pp., 25 cm. hardcover. Large print edition.
q. Book-of-the-Month Club selection.
r. London, England: Futura, 1988, 427 pp., paperback.
s. As: *Los ojos del dragón* ['The eyes of the dragon']. Buenos Aires, Argentina: Emecé, GRANDES NOVELISTAS, 1988, 316 pp., 21 cm. Spanish translation. ISBN 950-04-0745-0.
t. As: *Die Augen des Drachen* ['The eyes of the dragon']. Gütersloh, Austria: Bertelsmann Lesering; Kornwesterheim, Germany: EBG; Vienna, Austria: Buchgemeinschaft Donauland; Zug, Switzerland: Buch- und Schallplattenfreunde; Berlin, Darmstadt, and Vienna: Deutsche Buch-Gemeinschaft, GEBUNDENE AUSGABE, [1988], 319 pp. German translation by Joachim Körber. Book Club edition.
u. As: *Os Olhos do Dragão* ['The eyes of the dragon']. Rio de Janeiro, Brazil: Francisco Alves, MESTRES DO HORROR E DA FANTASIA, 1988, 301 pp., 21 cm., paperback. Portuguese translation by Joao Guilherme Linke. ISBN 85-265-0129-1.
v. As: *Los Ojos del Dragon* ['The eyes of the dragon']. Esplugues de Llobregat,

Barcelona, Spain: Plaza & Janés, ÉXITOS, 1988, 272 pp., 22 cm. Spanish translation by Jorge Miguel Lech. ISBN 84-01-32235-9. * Reprint, 1989.

w. As: *Los Ojos del Dragón* ['The eyes of the dragon']. Barcelona, Spain: Círculo de Lectores, 1988, 325 pp., 21 cm., hardcover. Spanish translation by Jorge Miguel Lech. ISBN 84-226-2663-2. * Reprint, 1989, ISBN 84-226-2663-2.

x. As: *Drakens Ögen* ['Dragon's eyes']. Höganäs and Stockholm, Sweden: Legenda/Bra Böcker, 1988, 352 pp., 22 cm., hardcover. Swedish translation by Karl G. Fredriksson and Lilian Fredriksson. 91-582-1182-9.

y. As: *Die Augen des Drachen* ['The eyes of the dragon']. Stuttgart/Hamburg/Munich, Germany: Deutscher Bücherband, [1989], 365 pp. German translation by Joachim Körber. Book Club editions.

z. As: *Drakens Ögen* ['Dragon's eyes']. Stockholm, Sweden: Legenda, 1989, 352 pp., 22 cm., [*kartonn.*]. Swedish translation by Karl G. Fredriksson and Lilian Fredriksson. 91-582-1517-4.

aa. As: *Ogen van de Draak* ['Eyes of the dragon']. Utrecht, Belgium: Luitingh-Sijthoff, 1990, 311 pp. Dutch translation by Margot Bakker. 2nd printing. ISBN 90-245-1799-0

bb. London, England: Warner Books, 1992, 427 pp. ISBN 0-7515-0457-2.

cc. As: *Oczy smoka* ['Dragon eyes']. Warsaw, Poland, "Amber," FANTASY, 1992, 349 pp., 20 cm. Polish translation by Sylwia Twardo. ISBN 83-8542-306-0.

dd. As: *Los Ojos del Dragon* ['The eyes of the dragon']. Barcelona, Spain: Plaza & Janés, JET 102/12, BIBLIOTECA DE STEPHEN KING #12, 1992, 381 pp., 18 cm., paperback. Spanish translation by Jorge Miguel Lech. ISBN 84-01-49102-9.

ee. As: *Gli Occhí del Drago* ['The eyes of the dragon']. Milan, Italy: Sperling Paperback, SUPERBESTSELLER #191, March 1993, paperback. Italian translation by Tullio Dobner. ISBN 88-7824-309-4.

ff. As: *Los ojos del dragón* ['The eyes of the dragon']. Buenos Aires, Argentina: Emecé, GRANDES NOVELISTAS, 1993, 314 pp., 22 cm. Spanish translation.

gg. As: *Lohikäärmeen silmät* ['Dragon's eyes']. Helsinki, Finland: Book Studio, 1993, 324 pp., 19 cm. Finnish translation by Tapio Tamminen. ISBN 951-611-595-0; * Reprint, 1993, 324 pp., 18 cm., ISBN 951-611-546-2.

hh. As: *Les yeux du dragon* ['The eyes of the dragon']. Paris, France: Albin Michel, 1995, 382 pp., 150 F, hardcover. French translation by Evelyne Châtelain. ISBN 2-226-07143-1.

ii. As: *Ogen van de Draak* ['The eyes of the dragon']. Amsterdam, Netherlands, and others: Piramide, 1995, 311 pp. Dutch translation by Margot Bakker. 5th printing. ISBN 90-254-1362-5. * 6th printing, 1987, ISBN 90-245-2715-5.

jj. As: *Los Ojos del Dragon* ['The eyes of the dragon']. Barcelona, Spain: Plaza & Janés, JET 102/12, BIBLIOTECA DE STEPHEN KING #12, 1996, 394 pp., 18 cm., paperback. Spanish translation by Jorge Miguel Lech. ISBN 84-01-47462-0.

LOS OJOS DEL DRAGÓN. Buenos Aires, Argentina: Emece, 1987. Paperback.

kk. As: *Dragens øjne* ['Dragon's eyes']. Ruds-Vedby, Denmark: Tellerup, 1997, 327 pp., 21 cm., 148 KR, paperback. Danish translation by Bjarne Skovlund. ISBN 87-588-0679-2.
ll. As: *Les yeux du dragon* ['The eyes of the dragon']. Paris, France: France Loisirs, 1996, 382 pp., 150 F, hardcover. French translation by Evelyne Châtelain. ISBN 2-7242-9663-X.
mm. As: *Les yeux du dragon* ['The eyes of the dragon']. Paris, France: Pocket Junior, 1997, 382 pp., 44 F, paperback. French translation by Evelyne Châtelain. ISBN 2-226-07551-9.
nn. As: *Les yeux du dragon* ['The eyes of the dragon']. Paris, France: Pocket, COLLECTION TERREUR #9170, 1998, 295 pp., 35 F, paperback. French translation by Evelyne Châtelain. ISBN 2-226-07550-0.
oo. As: *Ogen van de Draak* ['The eyes of the dragon']. Amsterdam, Netherlands: Poema Pocket, 1998, 311 pp., paperback. Dutch translation by Margot Bakker. 7th printing. ISBN 90-245-2150-0.
pp. As: *A Sárkány Szeme* ['Dragon's eyes']. Hungary: King Könyvek, 19—. Hungarian translation.
qq. As: *A Szem* ['The eyes']. Budapest, Hungary: Európa, 19—. Hungarian translation.
rr. As: *A Mágus*. Hungarian translation.
ss. As [Title unknown]. Israel: Modan, 19—. Hebrew translation.
tt. As: [Title unknown]. Moscow, Russia: Cadman, 19—. Russian translation.
uu. As: *Draci Oci* ['Dragon's eyes']. Czechoslovakia: Laser. Czech translation.

COMMENTS: An engaging children's fantasy (that also touches adult readers) as it relates the fairy-tale story of the kingdom of Delain, the novel first appeared in a limited edition from King's Philtrum press; its re-appearance as a hardcover trade edition from Viking included textual changes and new artwork. *The Eyes of the Dragon* frequently provides a non-threatening approach to King's fictions, since it retains his expected narrative vigor, his deft characterizations, and his epic/mythic vision while avoiding overt horror. With its implicit and explicit connections between Randall Flagg and other 'RF'/'dark men', the novel is particularly intriguing when read in conjunction with *The Stand,* the Dark Tower novels, *Insomnia, Hearts in Atlantis, Black House* and other related stories.

SELECTED ARTICLES, RESPONSES, AND REVIEWS:
Alpert, Michael. "Designing The Eyes of the Dragon." *Castle Rock: The Stephen King Newsletter* Vol. 1, No. 8 (August 1985): 1, 4, 6.
Atlanta Journal-Constitution [GA] 1 February 1987.
Belden, Elizabeth A., and Judith M. Beckman. *English Journal* Vol. 78 (April 1989): 89
Blue, Tyson. "Editing Eyes: An Interview with Deborah Brodie." *Castle Rock: The Stephen King Newsletter* Vol. 3, No. 3 (March 1987): 5, 8.
Blue, Tyson. "King's New Novel a Captivating Fantasy." *Macon Telegraph & News* [Macon GA] 18 January 1987.

Blue, Tyson. "Review: *The Eyes of the Dragon*." *Castle Rock: The Stephen King Newsletter* Vol. 3, No. 2 (February 1987): 4-5.
Book Report Vol. 6 (September 1987): 39.
Booklist Vol. 83 (1 November 1986): 370.
Booklist Vol. 85 (15 November 1988): 568.
Carlton, Michael. "Stephen King Delivers a Fantasy for Adolescents." *Denver Post* [CO] 15 February 1987. As microfiche: *NewsBank: Literature* Vol. 13 (March 1987): Fiche 75, C11.
Cassada, Jackie. *Library Journal* Vol. 111 (December 1986): 141.
Chalker, Jack L. "On Specialty Presses: The State of the Art." *Fantasy Review* No. 85 (November 1985): 11-12, 40. Disparaging assessment of Philtrum press and the production of *The Eyes of the Dragon*.
Chandler, Randy. "King's 'Eyes of the Dragon' a Grim Fairy Tale." *Atlanta Journal-Constitution* [GA] 1 February 1987. As microfiche: *NewsBank: Literature* Vol. 13 (March 1987): Fiche 75, C12.
Chow, Dan. *Locus* Vol. 20, No. 1, #312 (January 1987).
Clayton, Walnum. "The 'Eyes' Have It." *Fantasy Review* (May 1986): 40.
Collier, Cynthia. "'Eyes of the Dragon' an Alluring Fairy Tale." *San Diego Union* [CA] 22 February 1987. As microfiche: *NewsBank: Literature* Vol. 13 (March 1987): Fiche 75, C8.
Collins, Robert A. "The Editor's Notebook: Read the Letters First, Friends." *Fantasy Review* (May 1986): 4.
de Camp, L. Sprague. "The Glass-Eyed Dragon." *Reign of Fear: Fiction and Film of Stephen King*. Edited by Don Herron. Los Angeles CA: Underwood-Miller, June 1988. 63-68.
de Lint, Charles. "Privately Printed Fantasy King's Best." *Fantasy Review* No. 81 (July 1985): 19.
Dockery, Bill. "King's 'Dragon' Has Fluff, Puff, but Not a Lot of Fire." *Knoxville News Sentinel* [TN] 8 February 1987. As microfiche: *NewsBank: Literature* Vol. 13 (March 1987): Fiche 75, D3.
Donovan, Mark. Review in "Picks & Pans." *People Weekly* (13 April 1987).
Dugherty Marianne. "Stephen King's 'Dragon' an Imaginative Fairy Tale." *Pittsburgh Press* [PA] 15 February 1987. As microfiche: *NewsBank: Literature* Vol. 13 (March 1987): Fiche 75, D1.
Fantasy Review No. 9 (July 1986): 28.
Freeman, Mark. "The Eyes of the Dragon: New King, Old King." *Castle Rock: The Stephen King Newsletter* Vol. 3, No. 6 (June 1987): 5.
Graham, Mark. "Stephen King's Fairy Tale Come True." *Rocky Mountain News* [Denver CO] 7 February 1987: 33-M.
Gustavons-Larsen, Anita. "Stephen King's 'Dragon' to Charm Young Readers." *St. Paul Pioneer Press-Dispatch* [MN] 7 February 1987. As microfiche: *NewsBank: Literature* Vol. 13 (March 1987): Fiche 75, C14.
Kenny, Kevin. *Voice of Youth Advocates* (August/September 1987): 121.
Kirkus Reviews Vol. 54 (1 November 1986): 1606.
Lawhorn, Jonelle. "King's Regal Fairy Tale." *Boston Herald* [MA] 8 February

1987. As microfiche: *NewsBank: Literature* Vol. 13 (March 1987): Fiche 75, C13.
Leonard, Stephanie. "And Now, the Publisher's Apprentice." *Fantasy Review* 91 (May 1986): 40.
Lewis, Don. "Stephen King Puts the Horror on Hold." *Milwaukee Journal* [WI] 15 February 1987. As microfiche: *NewsBank: Literature* Vol. 13 (March 1987): Fiche 75, D4.
Liberatore, Karen. "The Triumph of Good in a Fairy Tale by King." *San Francisco Examiner* [CA] 25 January 1987. As microfiche: *NewsBank: Literature* Vol. 13 (March 1987): Fiche 75, C9-C10.
Macleans Vol. 100 (20 July 1987): 51.
Miller, G. Wayne. "A Pretty Fair Fantasy from King of Horror." *Journal* [Providence RI] 8 February 1987. As microfiche: *NewsBank: Literature* Vol. 13 (March 1987): Fiche 75, D2.
Penny, Karl. *School Library Journal* (June/July 1987): 116.
Publishers Weekly Vol. 230 (5 December 1986): 63.
School Library Journal Vol. 33 (February 1987): 99.
School Library Journal Vol. 33 (June 1987): 116.
Schweitzer, Darrell. "Book Review: The Eyes of the Dragon." *Castle Rock: The Stephen King Newsletter* Vol. 3, No. 9 (September 1987): 5.
Science Fiction Chronicle Vol. 8 (May 1987): 46.
Taub, K. Deborah. "Science Fiction and Fantasy: Two Outdo King's Try." *Washington Times* [DC] 30 March 1987. As microfiche: *NewsBank: Literature* Vol. 13 (April 1987): Fiche 86, A7-A8.
Time Vol. 129 (23 February 1987): 79.
Tritel, Barbara. "What the Wicked Magician Did." *The New York Times Book Review* Vol. 92 (22 February 1987): VII, 12.
Turner, Billy. "Stephen King: Horror Master Changes Style." *Clarion-Ledger* [Jackson MS] 6 March 1987. As microfiche: *NewsBank: Literature* Vol. 13 (April 1987): Fiche 86, A6.
Underwood, Tim, and Chuck Miller, eds. *Kingdom of Fear: The World of Stephen King*. Columbia PA: Underwood-Miller, April 1986.
Village Voice Vol. 32 (3 March 1987): 46.
Voice of Youth Advocates Vol. 10 (August 1987): 121.
Washington Post Book World Vol. 17 (6 December 1987): 19.
Washington Post Book World Vol. 17 (15 February 1987): 8.
West Coast Review of Books Vol. 12, No. 5 (1987): 26.
Wilson School Journal Vol. 209 (3 February 1987): 30.

MICHAEL R. COLLINGS

THE TALISMAN. New York, NY: Viking, 1984. Hardcover.

A26.
THE TALISMAN
with Peter Straub
(1984)

A26. *The Talisman*, by Stephen King and Peter Straub. New York: Viking, G. P. Putnam's Sons, 8 November 1984, x+646 pp., $18.95, hardcover. Fantasy novel. ISBN 0-670-69199-2.

PLOT SUMMARY: Young Jack Sawyer must travel westward—through the heartland of America as well as through its analogue in the Territories—in order to discover the Talisman that will save his mother's life. Alone and without any apparent external supports, Jack confronts physical and psychological horrors, ranging from cancer to nuclear devastation to systematic child abuse, and their parallels in both landscapes as he moves from the objective world of America to the fantastical one of the Territories; he overcomes each obstacle, matures as an individual, and along the way alters the lives of those he contacts as well as his own.

REPRINTS AND ADAPTATIONS:
b. West Kingston RI: Donald M. Grant, 1984, 2 volumes; hardcover, limited slipcased edition, 70 presentation copies; signed by Stephen King, Straub, and the illustrators. Signature page reads: "This presentation copy #[ ] of 70 copies of this special illustrated first edition of The Talisman is signed by the participants in this edition and is not for sale."
c. London, England: Viking Penguin UK, October 1984, 646 pp., £9.95, hardcover. Appeared simultaneously with the American edition although scheduled to appear earlier. ISBN 0-670-69199-2.
d. As: *El Talisman*. Barcelona, Spain: Planeta, CONTEMPORÁNEA, 1984, 572 pp., 21 cm. Spanish translation by Pilar Giralt Gorina. ISBN 950-37-0339-5.
e. West Kingston RI: Donald M. Grant, February 1985, 2 vols., 464 pp.+336 pp. ARTIST'S PRESENTATION STATE: 70 numbered copies, signed by both authors and all artists, slipcased; not for sale. * ARTIST'S PRESENTATION STATE: slipcased, signed by both authors and all artists, lettered. * DELUXE LIMITED EDITION: February 1985, 2 vols., 464 pp.+336 pp., $120.00, hardcover; signed by King and Straub, numbered, limited, slipcased edition,

1200 copies. Ten full-color illustrations. ISBN 0-937986-65-8. * TRADE EDITION: February 1985, 464 pp.+336 pp., $65.00, hardcover; slipcased trade edition. ISBN 0-937986-66-6.
f. New York: Berkley Books, March 1985, 770 pp., $4.95, mass-market paperback. ISBN 0-42-08181-8.
g. London: Penguin Books, August 1985, 784 p., paperback.
h. As: *De Talisman.* Utrecht, Belgium: Luitingh-Sijthoff/Veen, 1985, 470 pp., trade paperback. Substantially abridged Dutch translation by Margot Bakker, with around 100 pages deleted from descriptions. ISBN 90-204-0861-5. * 3rd printing 1986, 420 pp., ISBN 90-245-1811-3. * 6th printing 1990, 468 pp., ISBN 90-245-1811-3.
i. As: *The Talisman.* Israel, 1985, 606 pp., hardcover.
j. As: *O talisma.* Rio de Janeiro, Brazil: Francisco Alves, MESTRES DO HORROR E DA FANTASIA, 1985, 815 pp., 21 cm. Portuguese translation by Mario Molina.
k. As: *Mo Fu.* Taipei, Taiwan: Huang kuan chu pan she, 1985, 495 pp. Chinese translation by Mao Chi-cheuen.
l. As: *Der Talisman.* Hamburg, West Germany: Hoffman & Campe, 1986, 713 pp., 39.80 DM, hardcover. German translation by Christel Wiemkin. ISBN 3-455-03737-2.
m. As: *Il Talismano.* Milan, Italy: Sperling & Kupfer, PANDORA #295, February 1986, 635 pp., 20 cm. Italian translation by Tullio Dobner. ISBN 88-200-0522-0.
n. As: *Il Talismano.* Milan, Italy: CDE, 1986, 705 pp., 22 cm. Italian translation by Tullio Dobner.
o. As: *Le Talisman.* Paris, France: Editions Albin Michel #7075, 1986, 1084 pp., paperback. French translation by Beatrice Gartenberg and Isabelle Delord. ISBN 88-200-0522-0.
p. As: *Le Talisman des Territoires* ['The Talisman of the Territories']. Paris, France: Éditions Robert Laffont, BEST SELLERS, APRIL 1986, 649 pp., 120.00 FF, hardcover. French translation by Béatrice Gartenberg and Isabelle Delord. ISBN 2-221-04819-9.
q. As: *Le Talisman des Territoires.* [Paris, France]: le Grand livre du mois, 1986, 645 pp., 120 F. French translation. Book Club edition.
r. As: *Talismanen.* Stockholm, Sweden: Legenda/Norstedt, 1986, 798 pp., 202:00 SEK (Swedish Kronor), 23 cm., hardcover. Swedish translation by Lennart Olofsson. ISBN 91-582-0715-5.
s. As: *Talismanen.* Höganäs, Sweden: Bro Böcker, 1986, 798 pp., hardcover. Swedish translation by Lennart Olofsson. Book Club Edition.
t. As: *Ty´lsy´m: Roman.* Istanbul, Turkey: Inky´âp Kitabevi, [1986?]. Turkish translation by Belky´s Çorakçy´.
u. As: *Le Talisman.* Paris, France: Livre de Poche [LGF] SCIENCE-FICTION #7075, April 1987, 1085 pp., 48.00 FF, paperback. French translation by Béatrice Gartenberg and Isabelle Delord. ISBN 2-253-04181-5.
v. As: *Der Talisman.* Stuttgart, Germany: Deutscher Bücherbund, [1987], 713 pp. German translation by Cristel Wiemkin. Book Club Edition.

w. As: *Der Talisman*. Götersloh, Austria: Bertelsmann Lesering, 1987. German translation by Cristel Wiemken.
x. As: *Talismanen*. Stockholm, Sweden: Legenda/Norstedt, 1987, 798 pp., 112:00 SEK (Swedish Kronor), hardcover without dust jacket. Swedish translation by Lennart Olaffson. ISBN 91-582-1135-7. * 2nd printing, 1988.
y. As: *Talismanen*. Stockholm, Sweden: Legenda/Norstedt, 1987, 798 pp., 56:50 SEK (Swedish Kronor), paperback. Swedish translation by Lennart Olaffson. ISBN 91-582-1244-2.
z. As: *Talismanen*. Höganäs, Sweden: Bro Böcker, 1987, 798 pp. Book Club Edition. Swedish translation by Lennart Olofsson.
aa. As: *The Talisman*. 2 volumes. Tokyo, Japan: Shinchoshya, 1987, 578 pp. (Vol. I), 566 pp. (Vol.2), 1280 Y, paperback. ISBN 4-10-219308-1 (Vol. 1); 4-10-219309-X (Vol. 2). Japanese translation by Yano Kozaburo.
bb. As: *O talisma*. Mem Martins: Europa América, SÉCULO XX #283/287, 1987, 388+ pp., 21 cm. Portuguese translation by Clarisse Tavares. 2 vols.
cc. As: *El Talismán*. Barcelona, Spain: Planeta, CONTEMPORÁNEA #91, January 1988, 569 pp., 21 cm., trade paperback. Spanish translation by Pilar Giralt Gorina. ISBN 84-320-3823-7. * 2nd printing, March 1988. ISBN 84-320-3823-7.
dd. As: *Der Talisman*. München, West Germany: Wilhelm Heyne Verlag, HEYNE ALLGEMEINE REIHE TB-07662, 1988, 713 pp., DM 16,90, hardcover. German translation by Cristel Wiemken. ISBN 3-453-02523-7. * 5th printing, 1989. * 7th printing, 1991. * 11th-13th printings, 1993. * 16th printing, 1994. * 18th printing, 1995.
ee. As: *Der Talisman*. Gütersloh, Austria: Bertelsmann Lesering; Kornwesterheim, Germany: EBG; Vienna, Austria: Buchgemeinschaft donauland; Zug, Switzerland: Buch- und Schallplattenfreunde; Berlin, Darmstadt, and Vienna: Deutsche Buch-Gemeinschaft, [1988], 713 pp. German translation by Cristel Wiemkin. Book Club Edition.
ff. As: *Il Talismano*. Milan, Italy: Sperling Paperback, SUPERBESTSELLER [#8], April 1988, 655 pp., L 15.000, 20 cm., paperback. Italian translation by Tullio Dobner. ISBN 88-7824-008-7. * 12th printing 1995.
gg. As: *Talisman*. Gornji Milanovac [Croatia?]: Decje novine, 1989, 716 pp., 21 cm. Translation by Svetlana Bezdanov-Gostimir and Ranko Nedeljkovic. ISBN 86-367-0175-9.
hh. New York: Berkeley, January 1991, $7.99, mass-market paperback reissue. ISBN 0-425-10533-4.
ii. As: *Talismaani*. Hyvinkaa, Finland: Book Studio/Hangon Kirjapaino Oy, 1991, 859 pp., paperback. Finnish translation by Kari Salminen. ISBN 951-611-418-0 (sid), 951-611-427-X (nid).
jj. As: *El Talismán*. Barcelona, Spain: Editorial Planeta, BOLSILLO #11, August 1992, 572 pp., 962 pta., 19 cm., mass-market paperback. Spanish translation by Pilar Giralt Gorina. ISBN 84-08-00073-X. * 2nd printing, March 1998. ISBN 84-08-00073-X.
kk. As: *Talismanen*. Copenhagen, Denmark: Artia, 1994, 692 pp., 348 KR, hard-

cover. Danish translation by Mogens Wenzel Andreasen. ISBN 87-89918-32-0.
ll. As: *El Talismán*. Barcelona, Spain: RBA, GRANDES ÉXITOS #92, 1994, 569 pp., 21 cm. Spanish translation by Pilar Giralt Gorina. ISBN 84-473-0727-1.
mm. As *Talismanen*. Stockholm, Sweden: Natur & Kultur/Norstedts, 1994, 798 pp., 77:00 SEK (Swedish Kronor), paperback. Swedish translation by Lennart Olofsson. ISBN 91-270-5183-8.
nn. As: *Talizman*. Budapest, Hungary: Europa Konyukiado, 1994, 857 pp., 598 ft, paperback. Hungarian translation by Zentai Eva. ISBN 963-07-5752-4.
oo. As: *Talizman*. Warszawa, Poland: Wydawnictwo Amber, 1994, 376 pp., paperback. Polish translation by Anna Kidawa and Sylwia Twardo. ISBN 83-7082-292-4.
pp. As: *El talismán*. Barcelona, Spain RBA: Coleccionables, January 1995, 576 pp., 966 pta, trade paperback [*cart.*]. Spanish translation by Pilar Giralt Gorina. ISBN 84-473-0727-1.
qq. As: *Der Talisman*. München, Germany: Wilhelm Heyne Verlag, 1995, 714 pp., DM 16,90; paperback. German translation by Christel Wiemken. ISBN 3-453-02523-7.
rr. As: *Il Talismano*. Bologna, Italy: Sperling & Kupfer, March 1996, 664 pp., L 32.900 [$15.92]. Italian translation. 2nd edition.
ss. London, England: New English Library, June 1996, 768 pp., £6.99, paperback. Cover art by Steve Crisp. ISBN 0-340-67445-8.
tt. Czech Republic: Perseus, 1996, 638 pp., 279 CZK. Czech translation by Ivo Reitmayer; cover art by Petr Bauer.
uu. As: *Le Talisman des Territoires* ['The Talisman of the Territories']. Paris, France: Éditions Robert Laffont, BEST SELLERS, June 1996, 654 pp., 149.00FF/ 22.71 Euro, trade paperback. French translation by Béatrice Gartenberg and Isabelle Delord. ISBN 2-221-08605-8.
vv. As: *De Talisman*. Amsterdam, Netherlands: Poema Pocket, 1996, 468 pp. Dutch translation by Margot Bakker. 8th printing. ISBN 90-245-2696-5.
ww. As: *Le Talisman*. Paris, France: Le Livre de Poche, 1997, 920 pp., 48 F., paperback. Illustrated by Philippe Bouchet. French translation by Béatrice Gartenberg and Isabelle Delord. ISBN 2-253-04181-5.
xx. As: *The Talisman*. Russia, 1997, 685 pp., hardcover. Russian translation by A. A. Kydpreuya. ISBN 5-15-000239-9.
yy. As: *Ty´lsy´m: Roman*. Istanbul, Turkey: Inky´âp Kitabevi/Anka Ofset, [1997?]. Turkish translation by Belky´s Çorakçy´.
zz. As: *Le talisman des territoires*. Paris, France: France Loisirs, 1998, 645 pp., 108 F, hardcover. French translation by by Béatrice Gartenberg and Isabelle Delord. ISBN 2-7441-1424-3.
aaa. As: *El talismán*. Barcelona, Spain: Planeta, BOOKET #238, GRANDES BEST-SELLERS, February 1998, 576 pp., 18 cm., paperback. Spanish translation by Pilar Giralt Gorina. ISBN 84-08-02430-2.
bbb. As: *El Talismán*. Barcelona, Spain: Planeta, BOLSILLO/LOS MEJORES BEST-SELLERS U.S.A., 1999, 569 pp., 20 cm. Spanish translation by Pilar Giralt

Gorina. ISBN 84-08-03132-5.
ccc. As: [Title unknown]. Korean translation.
ddd. As: [Title unknown]. Russia: Cadman, 19—. Russian translation.
eee. As: *A Talizmân*. Budapest, Hungary: Európa, 19—. Hungarian translation.
fff. As: *Talizman*. Slovenia: Ina, 19—. Slovenian translation.

ggg. As FILM: Film rights optioned by Steven Spielberg and Amblin Entertainment. Screen adaptation: Richard Lagravenese (22 May 1992). Film unproduced as of January 2001.

COMMENTS: The novel sold 880,207 hardcover copies in 1984. Its first printing of 600,000 hardcover copies was the largest of any King title to that date, buttressed by a $500,000 advertising campaign

A collaborative effort between two bestselling fantasists, *The Talisman* was eagerly anticipated before its publication and frequently excoriated afterward. In spite of the publicity hype, frequently emphasizing King and Straub as the "Titans of Terror," the narrative develops as more distinctively an epic quest than as straightforward horror, with concommitant generic shifts that seem to have puzzled a number of readers. The collaborative style reflects neither King's distinctive colloquialism nor Straub's controlled academic tone. Instead, a new, third voice emerges, one unexpected by either King's readership or Straub's—readers anticipating simply another *Pet Sematary* or *Floating Dragon* were inevitably disappointed. *The Talisman* may seem long, complex, convoluted, and at times oddly static; still, given the increasingly epic dimensions of the narrative, King and Straub remain true to their subject and treatment, producing a book that has retained its interest—if not increased it—over the years. In 2001, King and Straub published a sequel to the novel, *Black House*.

SELECTED ARTICLES AND REVIEWS:
"King Rejects Book Club Offer for *The Talisman*." *Science Fiction Chronicle* 6:4 (January, 1985): 4.
Adler, Constance. "Prince of Darkness: In His Reign of Best-selling Terror, Author Stephen King Remains Absolute Master of the Scary Story." *Philadelphia Magazine* Vol. 76 (August 1985): 85+. [3-page article]
Amantia, A. M. B. *Library Journal* Vol. 109 (1 November 1984): 2080.
Anders, Smiley. "Blockbuster of a Fantasy Tale Gets Guidance from Twain." *Morning Advocate* [Baton Rouge LA] 18 November 1984. As microfiche: *NewsBank: Literature* Vol. 11 (December 1984): Fiche 58, A8-A9.
Beagle, Peter. "King Plus Straub Equals Pure Cliché." *San Jose Mercury News* [CA] 28 October 1984. As microfiche: *NewsBank: Literature* Vol. 11 (November 1984): Fiche 45, G14-46, A1.
Blue, Tyson. "Collaboration of Two Masterful Authors Produces a Suspenseful 'The Talisman'." *Courier Herald* [Dublin GA] 10 November 1984.
Blue, Tyson. "Talisman Limited Review." *Castle Rock: The Stephen King Newsletter* Vol. 3, No. 1 (December 1986-January 1987): 6.
Book World Vol. 14 (14 October 1984): 1.

MICHAEL R. COLLINGS

Booklist Vol. 81 (15 January 1985): 686.

Bosky, Bernadette. "Stephen King and Peter Straub: Fear and Friendship." *Discovering Stephen King.* Edited by Darrell Schweitzer. STARMONT STUDIES IN LITERARY CRITICISM #8. Mercer Island, WA: Starmont House, 1985. 55-82.

Cheuse, Alan. "A Sci-Fi Quest Novel from King and Straub." *Los Angeles Herald Examiner* [CA] 18 November 1984. As microfiche: *NewsBank: Literature* Vol. 11 (December 1984): Fiche 57, G12-G14.

Clark, Theresa J. *Saturday Review* (November/December 1984): 85.

Collings, Michael R. *Hauntings: The Peter Straub Bibliography.* Woodstock GA: Overlook Connection Press, 2000.

Cortland, Will. "The King of Bump in the Night." *Dodge Adventurer* (Spring 1985): 17-18. As: "The Adventurer Looks at Stephen King." *Castle Rock: The Stephen King Newsletter* Vol. 1, No. 6 (June 1985): 11.

D'Angelo, John. "'Talisman' Tells of Modern-Day Huckleberry Finn." *Pittsburgh Press* [PA] 2 December 1984. As microfiche: *NewsBank*: Literature 11 (December, 1984): Fiche 58, A14.

Eaglen, Audrey. *Voice of Youth Advocates* (April 1985): 49.

English Journal Vol. 74 (December 1985): 57.

Esquire Vol. 102 (November 1984): 231.

Fazell, Daryl. "King and Straub Weave a Snug Yarn." *St. Petersburg Times* [FL] 28 October 1984. As microfiche: *NewsBank: Literature* 11 (November 1984): Fiche 46, A2.

Goldstein, William, interviewer. "A Coupl'a Authors Sittin' Around Talkin'." *Publishers Weekly* (11 May 1984). Reprinted: *The Stephen King Companion.* Edited by George Beahm. Kansas City MO: Andrews and McMeel, September 1989. 283-287.

Graham, Mark. "Masters of the Macabre." *Rocky Mountain News* [Denver CO] 7 October 1984: 34M.

Grooms, Roger. "'Talisman' Not Without Macabre Charm." *Cincinnati Enquirer* [OH] 21 October 1984. As microfiche: *NewsBank: Literature* Vol. 11 (November 1984): Fiche 46, A10.

Harvey, L. J. "Unlucky 'Talisman' Defeats Horror King." *Kansas City Star* [MO] 4 November 1984). As microfiche: *NewsBank*: Literature 11 (November, 1984): Fiche 46, A5.

Herbert, Frank. "When Parallel Worlds Collide." *Washington Post Book World* 14 (October 14, 1984): 1-2.

Kernan, Michael. "Kindred Spirits: Horror Pros Stephen King and Peter Straub Put Their Skills Together for a Best Seller." *Washington Post* [DC] Vol. 107, 27 November 1984: C1.

Kirk, Robin. "King and Straub, Masters of Horror, Team Up for Highly Derivative Yawner." *Tribune* [Oakland CA] 18 November 1984. As microfiche: *NewsBank: Literature* Vol. 11 (December 1984): Fiche 58, A1.

Kirkus Reviews Vol. 52 (15 August 1984): 771.

Kliatt Young Adult Paperback Book Guide Vol. 20 (Spring 1986): 22.

Leerhsen, Charles. "The Titans of Terror." *Newsweek* (24 December 1984): 61-62.
Lehmann-Haupt, Christopher. "Books of the Times" *The New York Times Daily* 8 November 1984: III, 27.
Lewis, Don. "'Talisman' Good, But No Supernovel." *Milwaukee Journal* [WI] 11 November 1984. As microfiche: *NewsBank: Literature* Vol. 11 (December 1984): Fiche 58, B4.
Liberatore, Karen. "Jack Sawyer in Fantasyland." *San Francisco Examiner* [CA] 7 October 1984. As microfiche: *NewsBank: Literature* Vol. 11 (November 1984): Fiche 45, G12-G13.
Lileks, James. "A Horror Novel That's a Splatter Version of 'The Wizard of Oz.'" *Minnesota Star and Tribune* 25 November 1984. As microfiche: *NewsBank: Literature* Vol. 11 (December 1984): Fiche 58, A10.
McC.Dresser, Sheila. "One Good Book by Two Masters of the Best-Seller List." *Sun* [Baltimore MD] 4 November 1984. As microfiche: *NewsBank: Literature* 11 (November 1984): Fiche 46, A3.
McLaurin, Preston. "Epic Tale from Masters of Macabre." *State* [Columbia SC] 11 November 1984. As microfiche: *NewsBank: Literature* Vol. 11 (December 1984): Fiche 58, B1.
Merritt, Robert. "Horrors! King, Straub Turn to Fantasy." *Richmond Times-Dispatch* [VA] 28 October 1984. As microfiche: *NewsBank: Literature* 11 (November 1984): Fiche 46, A11.
Miller, Faren. "*The Talisman:* Stephen King & Peter Straub." *Locus* Vol. 17, No. 10, #. 285 (October 1984).
Millhiser, Marlys. "When Nit Comes to Grit." *Denver Post* [CO] 18 November 1984. As microfiche: *NewsBank: Literature* Vol. 11 (December 1984): Fiche 58, A3.
Nathan, Paul S. "*The Talisman* and the Clubs." *Publishers Weekly* (November 23, 1984): 28.
Perry, Pamela M. "Lack of Structure Main Weakness of 'Talisman'." *Atlanta Journal-Constitution* [GA] 4 November 1984. As microfiche: *NewsBank: Literature* Vol. 11 (December 1984): Fiche 58, A6.
Pollack, Dale. "Fantasy Quest for the Reel Thing." *Los Angeles Times Book Review* [CA] 18 November 1984: 13.
Publishers Weekly Vol. 226 (7 September 1984): 73.
Publishers Weekly Vol. 228 (20 September 1985): 107.
Reuter, Madalynne. "502,000 Copies of *Talisman* Shipped in One Day." *Publishers Weekly* (26 October 1984): 25.
Richmond, Peter. "Striking Out With King (and Straub)." *Miami Herald* [FL] 25 November 1984. As microfiche: *NewsBank: Literature* Vol. 11 (December 1984): Fiche 58, A4-A5.
Rothenstein, Richard. "Two Terror Titans Team Up." *Daily News* [NY] 14 October 1984. As microfiche: *NewsBank: Literature* Vol. 11 (November 1984): Fiche 45, G10-G11.
Saidman, Anne. *Stephen King: Master of Horror.* Minneapolis MN: Lerner

Publications Company, THE ACHIEVERS, 1992, 56 pp., library-binding hardcover. 39-41. ISBN 0-8225-0545-2. Also issued in paperback, ISBN 0-8225-9623-7. Overview of *The Talisman* written for juvenile readers.
Sanders, Joe. "Vigorous, Messy, Untidy—And Compulsively Readable." *Fantasy Review* No. 76 (February 1985): 17-18.
Saturday Review Vol. 10 (November 1984): 85.
Schachtsiek-Freitag, Norbert. "Horror and Fantasy: Stephen Kings und Peter Straubs Der Talisman." *Frankfurter Rundschau* [Frankfurt, West Germany] 12 August 1986.
Schulte, Jean. "Two Grim Reapers Predictably Macabre in Modern Dark Ages." *Columbus Dispatch* [OH] 4 November 1984. As microfiche: *NewsBank: Literature* Vol. 11 (December 1984): Fiche 58, A12.
Schweitzer, Darrell. "Epic Fantasy in Modern Dress." *Philadelphia Inquirer* [PA] 11 November 1984. As microfiche: *NewsBank: Literature* Vol. 11 (December 1984): Fiche 58, A13.
Science Fiction Review No. 14 (February 1985): 41.
Shapiro, Anna. *New York Times Book Review* Vol. 89 (4 November 1984): 24. Excerpted: *Contemporary Literary Criticism*, Vol. 37. Edited by Daniel G. Marowski. Detroit MI: Gale Research, 1986. 205-206.
Sherman, David. "Nightmare Library." *Fangoria* No. 44 (1985): 39-40.
Shestak, George. "King/Straub Tale Overloads to a Point of Numbness." *Omaha World-Herald* [NB] 4 November 1984. As microfiche: *NewsBank: Literature* Vol. 11 (December 1984): Fiche 58, A11.
Skow, John. *Time* Vol. 124 (5 November 1984): 88.
Slay, Jack, Jr. "'The Road Laid Its Mark on You': Jack's Metamorphosis in *The Talisman* (or, Beyond Boy-Wonderdom)." *Castle Rock: The Stephen King Newsletter* Vol. 4, No. 7 (July 1988): 1, 4-5.
Small, Michael. "Peter Straub & Stephen King Team Up for Fear." *People Weekly* (28 January 1985): 50-52.
Smithers, Susan L. *School Library Journal* Vol. 31 (January 1985): 92.
Somerville, Richard. "Huck Meets Hobbit." *Des Moines Register* [IA] 4 November 1984. As microfiche: *NewsBank: Literature* Vol. 11 (December 1984): Fiche 58, A7.
Steinberg, Sylvia. "PW Forecasts: Fiction." *Publishers Weekly* 226 (September 7, 1984): 73. "This collaborative work by the two bestselling authors and close friends surpasses the expectations created by their separate past works.... Seamlessly written, *The Talisman* is a grand novel...."
Straub, Peter. "Straub Talks About Talisman." *Castle Rock: The Stephen King Newsletter* Vol. 1, No. 7 (July 1985): 1, 3.
Stuewe, Paul. *Quill and Quire* Vol. 50 (24 December 1984): 37.
The Magazine of Fantasy & Science Fiction Vol. 68 (March 1985): 16.
Toepfer, Susan. "'The Talisman': A Classic." *Daily News* [NY] 14 October 1984. As microfiche: *NewsBank: Literature* 11 (November 1984): Fiche 46, A6-A7.
Tucker, Ken. "Boo! Ha-Ha, You Sap!" *The Village Voice* Vol. 29, No. 43 (23

October 1984): 53. Excerpted: *Contemporary Literary Criticism*, Vol. 37. Edited by Daniel G. Marowski. Detroit MI: Gale Research, 1986. 205.

Turner, Billy. "King-Straub Combo Pleases, But Fails to Horrify." *Clarion-Ledger* [Jackson MS] 21 October 1984). As microfiche: *NewsBank: Literature* 11 (November 1984): Fiche 46, A4.

USA Today Vol. 3 (19 October 1984): 3D.

Village Voices Literary Supplement (May 1993): 25+.

Wallace, Gail Smith. "Happy Halloween Horrors to You!" *News and Observer* [Raleigh NC] 28 October 1984). As microfiche: *NewsBank: Literature* 11 (November 1984): Fiche 46, A8-A9.

West Coast Review of Books Vol. 11 (January 1985): 33.

Photo Credit: Andrew Unangst, 1984

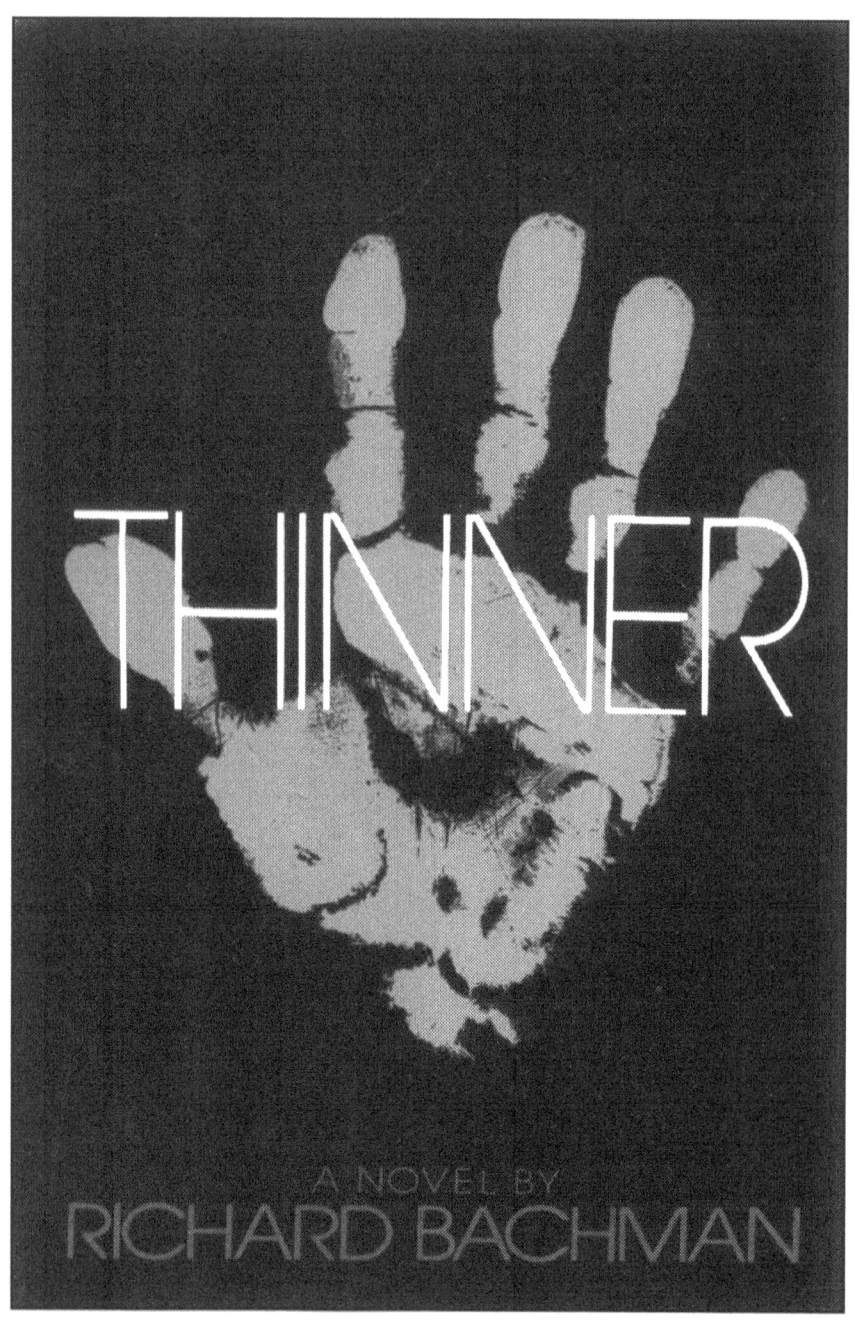

Thinner. New York, NY: New American Library, 1984. Hardcover.

A27.
THINNER
AS RICHARD BACHMAN
(1984)

A27. *Thinner*, by 'Richard Bachman.' New York: New American Library, 19 November 1984, 309 pp., hardcover. Horror novel. ISBN 0-453-00468-7.

PLOT SUMMARY: Billy Halleck, an overweight lawyer, accidentally kills an old gypsy woman. He is exonerated by a friendly court, but irremediably punished when the old woman's son touches his cheek and whispers, "Thinner." Halleck begins losing weight…rapidly, frighteningly, and inexorably. He can only save his life by having the curse removed—but how can he convince the outcast gypsy to do so?

REPRINTS AND ADAPTATIONS:
b. London, England: New English Library, August 1985, 310 pp., hardcover.
c. As: *Thinner*, by Stephen King. New York: Signet/New American Library, September 1985, 318 pp., mass-market paperback. ISBN 0-451-13796-5. * 29th printing, July 1992, $5.99, ISBN 0-451-15355-3.
d. Garden City NY: The Mystery Guild, [n.d.], hardcover.
e. Garden City NY: Science Fiction Book Club/New American Library, Doubleday Book Club, [n.d.], $7.98, hardcover. #138172.
f. London, England: New English Library, February 1986, 288 pp., paperback. * Reprint, August 1987, ISBN 0-450-05883-2. * 14th printing, August 1992.
g. As: *De Vervloeking* ['The curse'], by Richard Bachman. Utrecht, Belgium/Aartselaar: A. W. Bruna and Zoons, Summer 1985, 272 pp., 19.90fl, trade paper with plasticized cover. Dutch translation by Thomas Nicholaas. Includes a wrap-around band stating: "Stephen King writing as Richard Bachman." ISBN 9-022-98307-2.
h. As: *Der Fluch* ['The curse'], by Richard Bachman. Munich, Germany: Wilhelm Heyne, TB 6001, 1985, 346 pp., 7.80 DM, paperback. German translation by Nora Jensen. Note under the by-line indicates "Bachman est King— Stephen King is Bachman." ISBN 3-453-02195-9. * 15th printing, 1992. * 18th printing, 1993. * 20th printing, 1994.
i. Bath, England: Chivers Press, June 1986, 408 pp., hardcover. Large print edition.

j. As: *Maleficio* ['The curse'], by Stephen King "(con el nombre de Richard Bachman)." Buenos Aires, Argentina: Eméce, GRANDES NOVELISTAS V.8.621, September 1986, 301 pp., 20 cm., trade paperback. Spanish translation by Lorenzo Cortina. ISBN 950-04-0579-2. * Reprint, 1994.
k. As: *L'occhio del male* ['The eyes of evil']. Milan, Italy: Sonzogno, I ROMANZI, October 1986, 280 pp. Italian translation by Franco Brera.
l. As: *Thinner*, by Richard Bachman. Boston: G. K. Hall & Co., 1986, 397 pp., hardcover, trade paperback. Large print edition.
m. As: *Maleficio* ['The curse']. Esplugues de Llobregat, Barcelona, Spain: Plaza & Janés, ÉXITOS, 1986, 253 pp., 22 cm., paperback. Spanish translation by Lorenzo Cortina. ISBN 84-01-32181-6.
n. As: *Förbannelse* ['Curse'], by Stephen King. [Höganäs, Sweden]: Bra Spänning, 1986, 304 pp. Swedish translation by Love Kellberg.
o. As: *Förbannelse* ['Curse'], by Stephen King alias Richard Bachman. Stockholm, Sweden: Legenda, 1986, 304 pp., 22 cm., hardcover. Swedish translation by Love Kellberg. 91-582-0851-8. * Reprint, 1988.
p. As: *De Vervloeking* ['The curse']. Duerne, Belgium: A. W. Bruna and Zoons, 1987, 253 pp., 22 cm., 498 F. Dutch translation by Thomas Nicholaas. ISBN 90-229-7753-6.
q. As: *Förbannelse* ['Curse']. Höganäs, Sweden: Legenda, 1987, 304 pp. Swedish translation by Love Kellberg. 91-582-1133-0.
r. As: *L'occhio del male* ['The eyes of evil']. Milan, Italy: Bompiani, I GRANDI TASCABILI #84, April 1988, paperback. Italian translation by Franco Brera.
s. As: *Le peau sur les os* ['The skin on the bone.']. Paris, France: J'ai Lu, SUSPENSE #2435, 1988, 376 pp., 25 F, paperback. French translation by François Lasquin. ISBN 2-277-22435-9.
t. As: *Maleficio* ['The curse']. Barcelona, Spain: Plaza & Janés, JET 102, BIBLIOTECA DE STEPHEN KING #7, 1988, 332 pp., 18 cm., paperback. Spanish translation by Lorenzo Cortina. ISBN ISBN 84-01-49887-2
u. As: *Maleficio* ['The curse']. Barcelona, Spain: Círculo de Lectores, 1988, 293 pp., 22 cm.. Spanish translation by Lorenzo Cortina. ISBN ISBN 84-226-2553-9.
v. As: *Förbannelse* ['Curse']. Stockholm, Sweden: Legenda, 1988, 304 pp., mass-market paperback. Swedish translation by Love Kellberg.
w. As: *A Maldição do Cigano* ['The curse of the gypsy]. Rio de Janeiro, Brazil: Francisco Alves, MESTRES DO HORROR E DA FANTASIA, 1989, 309 pp., 21 cm., paperback. Portuguese translation by Louisa Ibanez. ISBN 85-265-0183-6. * 2nd printing, 1991.
x. As: *Maleficio* ['The curse']. Esplugues de Llobregat, Barcelona, Spain: Plaza & Janés Editores, BIBLIOTECA DE STEPHEN KING, VOL. 7. 1989, 256 pp., paper. Spanish translation by Lorenzo Cortina.
y. As: *Maleficio* ['The curse']. Barcelona, Spain: Círculo de Lectores, 1989, 296 pp., hardcover. Spanish translation by Lorenzo Cortina. ISBN 84-226-2553-9.
z. As: *De Vervloeking* ['The curse']. Utrecht, Belgium: Bruna, ZWARTE

BEERTJES #2360, [1990], 253 pp. Dutch translation by Thomas Nicholaas. ISBN 90-449-2360-9. * Reprint, 1998.
aa. As: *Hujsaj!* Ljubljana, Slovenia: Drzavna zalozba Slovenije, 1990, 257 pp., 20 cm. Croatian translation by Jure Potokar.
bb. New York: Book of the Month Club, October 1991, 309 pp., $17.95, hardcover. No ISBN assigned.
cc. As: *De Vervloeking* ['The curse']. Utrecht, Belgium: Bruna, 1992, 253 pp. Dutch translation by Thomas Nicholaas. ISBN 90-229-8070-7.
dd. As: *Manden der blev tyndere* ['The man who grew thinner']. Copenhagen, Denmark: Artia, 1992, 264 pp., 88 KR, paperback. Danish translation by Mogens Wenzel Andreasen. 1st Danish edition. ISBN 87-89918-19-3.
ee. As: *Maleficio* ['The curse']. Barcelona, Spain: Plaza & Janés, ÉXITOS, 1992, 253 pp., 23 cm. Spanish translation by Lorenzo Cortina. ISBN 84-01-32423-8.
ff. As: *Maleficio* ['The curse']. Barcelona, Spain: Plaza & Janés, JET 102, BIBLIOTECA DE STEPHEN KING #7, 1993, 358 pp., 18 cm., paperback. Spanish translation by Lorenzo Cortina. ISBN 84-01-49990-9. * Reprint, 1996, ISBN 84-01-49990-9. * Reprint, 1998, ISBN 84-01-49990-9.
gg. As: *Fluch/Menschenjagd/Sprengstoff: Drei Romane in einem Band* ['Curse/Manhunt/Explosive: three novels in one volume]. Munich, Germany: Wilhelm Heyne, #9116, September 1994, 346 pp., 15.00 DM, paperback. German translation by Nora Jensen. * 3rd printing, 1995. ISBN 3-453-07567-6.
hh. As: *Manden der blev tyndere* ['The man who became thinner']. Copenhagen, Denmark: Paperback Bogklubben, 1994, 263 pp. Danish translation by Mogens Wenzel Andreasen. ISBN 87-78035-20-1.
ii. As: *Le peau sur les os* ['The skin on the bone']. Paris, France: France Loisirs, 1994, 366 pp., 76 F, hardcover. French translation by François Lasquin. ISBN 2-7242-8190-X.
jj. As: *Misery/Maleficio.* Barcelona, Spain: Plaza & Janés, 1994, 346 + 332 pp., 19 cm. Spanish translations by María Mir and Lorenzo Cortina. ISBN 84-01-46107-3. Onmibus volume.
kk. New York: Signet, January 1995, 318 pp., $6.99, mass-market paperback. ISBN 0-451-16134-3
ll. New York: Signet, September 1996, 318 pp., $6.99, mass-market paperback. Movie tie-in edition. 30th printing. 0-451-19075-0.
mm. As: *L'occhio del male* ['The eyes of evil']. Milan, Italy: Sperling & Kupfer, NARRATIVA [#218], September 1996. Italian translation by Tullio Dobner. ISBN 88-200-2251-6.
nn. As: *Maleficio* ['The curse']. Barcelona, Spain: Plaza & Janés, 1996, 358 pp., 19 cm., paperback. Spanish translation by Lorenzo Cortina. ISBN 84-01-62029-5.
oo. As: *De Vervloeking* ['The curse']. Utrecht, Belgium: Bruna, 1997, 253 pp. Dutch translation by Thomas Nicholaas. ISBN 90-229-8307-2.
pp. As: *Kirous* ['Curse']. Helsinki, Finland: Tammi, 1997. Finnish translation.

qq. As: *Forbannelsen* ['Curse']. Oslo, Norway: Egmont Bøker Fredhøi, 1997, 318 pp., 59.50, paperback [*heftet*]. Norwegian translation. ISBN 82-04-04968-4.
rr. As: *Chudszy* '[Lean/gaunt']. Poznañ, Poland: Sysk i S-ka. Wydaw., 1997, 297 pp., 19 cm. Polish translation by Robert Lipski. ISBN 83-7150-304-0.
ss. As: *A Maldição do Cigano* ['The curse of the gypsy]. Rio de Janeiro, Brazil: Objetiva, 1998, 169 pp., 23 cm., paperback. Portuguese translation by Louisa Ibañez. ISBN 85-730-2186-1.
tt. As: *Maleficio* ['The curse']. Barcelona, Spain: Plaza & Janés, JET 102, BIBLIOTECA DE STEPHEN KING #7, 1998, 358 pp., 18 cm., paperback. Spanish translation by Lorenzo Cortina. ISBN 84-01-49990-9.
uu. As: [Title unknown]. Greek translation.
vv. As: [Title unknown]. Israel: Modan, 19—. Hebrew translation.
ww. As: [Title unknown]. Moscow, Russia: Cadman, 19—. Russian translation.

xx. AS AUDIOCASSETTE: *Thinner*. Downsview, Ontario, Canada: Listening for Pleasure, Ltd., 1985. 2 cassettes; 2 hours. Abridged by Sue Dawson. Read by Paul Sorvino.
SELECTED REVIEWS AND ARTICLES:
Beahm, George. "'Thinner' on Audiocassette." *The Stephen King Companion*. Edited by George Beahm. Kansas City MO: Andrews & McMeel, September 1989. 134-135.
Publishers Weekly (3 July 1987): 38.
Science Fiction Chronicle 7 (September 1986): 42.
Washington Post Book World 16 (26 October 1986): 10.

yy. AS AUDIOCASSETTE: *Thinner*. New York: Penguin Audiobooks, 1996. Read by Joe Mantagna. Abridged.

zz. AS FILM: *Stephen King's Thinner*. Republic/Spelling Films, 1996. Executive producer: Stephen F. Kester. Produced by Richard P. Rubinstein. Directed by Tom Holland. Screenplay by Michael McDowell and Tom Holland. Rated: R.
CAST: Robert John Burke, Michael Constantine, Joe Mantegna, Lucinda Jenney, Kari Wuhrer, John Horton, Sam Freed, Daniel van Bargen, Stephen King.
SELECTED ARTICLES, RESPONSES, AND REVIEWS:
Sight and Sound. Vol. 7, No. 8 (1997): 55.
Wood, Gary. "Upcoming Horrors, Thinner & Others." *Cinefantastique* Vol. 21. No. 4 (February 1991): 31.

aaa. AS VIDEOCASSETTE: Republic/Spelling Films, 1996. 92 minutes. Rated: R. VHS 6296.

HORROR PLUM'D

COMMENTS: The first printing was 26,000, with a total of 208,000 hardcover copies in the four printings. The book sold 28,000 copies before the Bachman pseudonym was revealed and almost immediately sold 280,000 more copies after King acknowledged his authorship. The book sold a total of some 300,000 hardcover copies in 1985.

The novel that finally revealed the 'Richard Bachman' pen-name, *Thinner* is demonstrably vintage King in tone, style, diction, plot structure, characterization, and atmosphere. The incursion of the supernatural is direct and fatal in this tale, and the concommitant deterioration of the central character both inexorable and externalized; we see overtly the consequences of guilt as in the lives of Halleck, Halleck's friends, his family, and the gypsies themselves.

SELECTED ARTICLES, RESPONSES, AND REVIEWS:

Adler, Constance. "Prince of Darkness: In His Reign of Best-selling Terror, Author Stephen King Remains Absolute Master of the Scary Story." *Philadelphia Magazine* Vol. 76 (August 1985): 85+. [3-page article]

Bangor Daily News [ME] 9 February 1985.

Barron, Neil. "'Bachman' Indeed Reads Like Stephen King." *Fantasy Review* No. 77 (March 1985): 15.

Blue, Tyson. "Richard Bachman's 'Thinner' is a Thriller of the First Magnitude." *Courier Herald* [Dublin GA] (February 1985).

Brown. Stephen P. "The Life and Death of Richard Bachman: Stephen King's Doppelgänger." *Kingdom of Fear: The World of Stephen King*. Edited by Tim Underwood and Chuck Miller. San Francisco CA: Underwood-Miller, 1986. 109-126.

Eidus, Janice. *The New York Times Book Review* 14 April 1985: 27. Excerpted: *Contemporary Literary Criticism*, Vol. 37. Edited by Daniel G. Marowski. Detroit MI: Gale Research, 1986. 206.

Fantasy Mongers Vol. 13 (Winter 1984/1985): 5.

Graham, Mark. "Fit for a King." *Rocky Mountain News* [Denver CO] 23 December 1984: 26M.

Kirkus Reviews Vol. 52 (15 September 1984): 864. Review of the novel by 'Richard Bachman'

Lehmann-Haupt, Christopher. "Books of the Times." *The New York Times* 11 July 1985: C21. Late edition.

Pepper, Michael. "The Growing Optimism of Stephen King: Bachman's Pessimism Gets Thinner." *Castle Rock: The Stephen King Newsletter* Vol. 3, No. 7 (July 1987): 1, 4.

Publishers Weekly Vol. 226 (28 September 1984): 99. Review of the novel by 'Richard Bachman'.

Publishers Weekly (22 March 1985): 43.

Rousch, Matt. "Bachman's Best Seller." *USA Today* Vol. 4 (18 October 1985).

Sallee, Wayne Allen. "*Thinner*: A Thinly Disguised King Novel." *Castle Rock: The Stephen King Newsletter* Vol 1, No. 5 (May 1985): 2.

Shestack, George. "You Win, Lose With a Pair of Kings." *Omaha World-Herald*

MICHAEL R. COLLINGS

[NE] 26 May 1985. As microfiche: *NewsBank: Literature* Vol. 11 (June 1985): Fiche 110, A3.
Timpone, Anthony. *Fangoria* No. 52 (1986): 55.
Washington Post Book World 9 April 1985: C1-C2.
"Weird Reviews." *Fan Plus* Vol. 2, No. 2 (1985).

Horror Plum'd

SKELETON CREW. New York, NY: G.P. Putnam & Sons, 1985. Hardcover.

A28.
SKELETON CREW
(1985)

A28. *SKELETON CREW*. New York: G. P. Putnam's Sons, 21 June 1985, 512 pp., $18.95, hardcover. Collection of short fiction and poetry. ISBN 0-399-13039-X.

CONTENTS: "Introduction," by King [see C132]; "The Mist" (1980; see B50); "Here There Be Tygers" (1968; see B5); "The Monkey" (1980; see B48); "Cain Rose Up" (1968; see B6); "Mrs. Todd's Shortcut" (1984; see B77); "The Jaunt" (1981; see B52); "The Wedding Gig" (1980; see B46); "Paranoid: A Chant" (poem; see D9); "The Raft" (1982; see B60); "Word Processor of the Gods" (1983; see B72); "The Man Who Would Not Shake Hands" (1982; see B58); "Beachworld" (1985; see B82); "The Reaper's Image" (1969; see B9); "Nona" (1978; see B42); "For Owen" (poem; see D8); "Survivor Type" (1982; see B71); "Uncle Otto's Truck" (1983; see B73); "Morning Deliveries (Milkman #1)" (1985; see B83); "Big Wheels: A Tale of the Laundry Game (Milkman #2)" (1980; see B47); "Gramma" (1984; see B76); "The Ballad of the Flexible Bullet" (1984; see B78); "The Reach" (As: "Do the Dead Sing?" 1981; see B56); "Notes," by King [see C133].

REPRINTS AND ADAPTATIONS:
b. As: *Stephen King's Skeleton Crew*. Santa Cruz, CA: Scream Press, 1985, xxiv+545 pp., hardcover. Illustrated by J. K. Potter. Includes "The Revelations of 'Becka Paulson" (excerpted from *The Tommyknockers* [1984; see B79]), in addition to the remaining stories and poems. * DELUXE LIMITED EDITION: 69 leather-bound and zippered copies, 17 presentation copies and 52 lettered copies. * LIMITED EDITION: 1,000 copies, numbered in silver ink and signed by author and artist Potter. $75.00. ISBN 0-910489-12-2.
c. London, England: Macdonald, June 1985, 700 pp., hardcover.
d. As: *Im Morgengrauen: Unheimlische Geschichten* ['In the grey of morning: uncanny stories']. Munich, Germany: Wilhelm Heyne TB 6553, 1985, 281 pp., 6.80 DM, paperback. German translation by Alexandra von Reinhardt. ISBN 3-453-02134-7. * 30th printing, 1996. CONTENTS: "Der Mann, der

Niemandem die Hand Geben Wollte" ["The Man Who Would Not Shake Hands"]; "Achtung—Tiger!" ["Here There Be Tygers"]; "Omi" ["Gramma"]; "Der Nebel" ["The Mist"].

e. Excerpted as: *Nona und die Ratten* ['Nona and the rats']. Munich, Germany: Wilhelm Heyne MINI-BÜCHER Mini-TB #2, 1985, 122 pp., 3.00 DM, paperback. German translation by Alexandra von Reinhardt. ISBN 3-453-35318-8.

f. New York: Signet/New American Library, June 1986, 573 pp., $4.95, mass-market paperback.; 3,000,000-copy 1st printing. ISBN 0-451-14293-4. * 12th printing by September, 1989. ISBN 0-451-16861-5

g. London, England: Futura, July 1986, 624 pp., £3.50, paperback. ISBN 0-7088-2916-3. 8th printing £4.99, May 1991.

h. As: *Nebel* ['Mist']. Linkenheim, Germany: Edition Phantasia, 1986, pp., hardcover. Illustrated by Herbert Brandmeier. Limited numbered edition of 500 numbered copies (I-XXX) and 30 presentation copies; most were seized by U.S. Customs Officers and only about 50 copies exist.

i. As: *Duistere Krachten: Verhalen van de Meester van de Horror* ['Dark forces: Stories by the master of horror']. Utrecht, Belgium, Netherlands: Luitingh/Veen, 1986, 413 pp., paperback. Dutch translation by Margot Bakker. ISBN 90-245-1731-1. * 2nd printing, 1988, 544 pp.
CONTENTS: 21 stories and poems, excluding "The Mist." "Vorwoord" ['Foreword'], by King; "Er zit dar een tijger" ["Here There Be Tigers"]; "De aap" ["The Monkey"]; "Kain stond tegen zijn broeder op" ['Cain stood up against his brother'="Cain Rose Up"]; "Mevrouw Todd gaat binnendoor" ["Mrs. Todd's Shortcut"]; "De Jaunt" ["The Jaunt"]; "De schnabbel" ["The Wedding Gig"]; "Paranoide: Een bezwering" ["Paranoid: A Chant"]; "Het vlot" ["The Raft"]; "Duistere kraften" ['Dark forces'="The Word Processor of the Gods"]; "De man die geen hand wilde geven" ["The Man Who Would Not Shake Hands"]; "Strandleven" ['Beach-life'="Beachworld"]; "Het spiegelbeeld van de maaier" ["The Reaper's Image"]; "Nona"; "Voor Owen" ["For Owen"]; "Overleven" ['Survival'="Survivor Type"]; "De vrachtauto van Oom Otto" ["Uncle Otto's Truck"]; "Vroege bestellingen (Melkman 1)" ["Early Deliveries'="Morning Deliveries: (Milkman 1)"]; "Zwaren wielen: Een vertelling rondom de wasserij (Melkman 2)" ['Heavy wheels'="Big Wheels: A Tale of the Laundry Game (Milkman 2)"]; "Grootma" ["Gramma"]; "De ballade van de flexible kogel" ["The Ballad of the Flexible Bullet"]; "Het rak" ["The Reach"].

j. As: *Dichte Mist* ['Heavy/thick mist']. Utrecht, Belgium, Netherlands: Luitingh, 1986, 160 pp., paperback. Dutch translation by Pauline Moody.
CONTENTS: "Dichte Miste" (pp. 5-150); "Stephen King," by Kim Foltz and Penelope Wang (pp. 151-156); plus four pages of black-and-white reproductions of King's books translated in Dutch.

k. Excerpted as: *La Niebla* ['The Mist']. Barcelona, Spain: Grijalbo, BESTSELLER ORO, 1986, 316 pp., 20 cm. Includes "La niebla," "El mono," "El atajo de al señora Todd." Spanish translation by Antonio Samons. ISBN 84-253-1859-9 [Spain]; 950-28-0115-6 [Argentina].

HORROR PLUM'D

l. As: *Den Förskräckliga Apan och Andra Berättelser* ['The fearful monkey and other stories']. Stockholm, Sweden: Legenda, 1986, 597 pp. Swedish translation by Karl G. Fredriksson and Lilian Fredriksson. ISBN 91-582-0832-1. * Reprint, 1987.

m. Excerpted as: *Der Fornit* (*Skeleton Crew*, part 3). Munich, Germany: Wilhelm Heyne, TB 6888, 1986, 251 pp., 6.80 DM, paperback. German translations by Monika Hahn, Joachim Körber, and Alexandra von Reinhardt. ISBN 3-453-00312-8. * 22nd printing, 1996.
CONTENTS: "Der Affe" ["The Monkey"]; "Paranoid: Ein Gesang" ["Paranoid: A Chant"]; "Der Textcomputer der Götter" ["The Word Processor of the Gods"]; "Für Owen" ["For Owen"]; "Überlebenstyp" ["Survivor Type"]; "Der Milchman Schlägt Wieder zu" ['The milkman leaves a bonus again'="Big Wheels: A Tale of the Laundry Game"]; "Der Fornit" ["The Ballad of the Flexible Bullet"]; "Der Dünenplanet" ["Beachworld"].

n. As: *Der Gesang der Toten* ['The Song of the dead'; Skeleton Crew, part 2]. Munich, Germany: Wilhelm Heyne TB 6705, 1986, paperback. German translations by Matrin Bliesse, Rolf Jurkeit, and Alexandra von Reinhardt. ISBN 3-453-02309-9.
CONTENTS: "Mrs. Todd's Abkürzung" ["Mrs. Todd's Shortcut"]; "Der Hochzeit Empfang" ["The Wedding Gig"]; "Travel" ["The Jaunt"]; "Kains Aufbegehren" ["Cain Rose Up"]; "Das Floß" ["The Raft"]; "Der Gesang der Toten" ["Do the Dead Sing?"]; "Der Sensenmann" ["The Reaper's Image"]; "Nona"; "Onkel Ottos Lastwagen" ["Uncle Otto's Truck"].

o. Excerpted as: *La Niebla* ['The Mist']. Barcelona, Spain: Grijalbo, EDIBOLSILLO, 1986, 320 pp., 18 cm., paperback. Spanish translation by Antonio Samons. ISBN 84-253-1928-5.

p. As: *Historias Fantásticas* ['Fantastic stories']. Esplugas de Llobregat, Barcelona, Spain: Plaza & Janés Editores, ÉXITOS, February 1987, 189 pp., 22 cm., trade paperback with folded cover flaps. Spanish translations by Rosa S. de Naveira. Thirteen stories and poems from *Skeleton Crew*, plus King's "Notes"; "The Mist" deleted. ISBN84-01-32195-6. * Reprint, 1989, ISBN 84-01-32195-6. * 2nd edition 1998, ISBN 84-01-32745-8.
CONTENTS: "Hay tigres" ['Here There Be Tygers']; "Apareció Caín" ['Cain appears'="Cain Rose Up]; "Zarabanda nupcial" ['The wedding sarabande/dance'="The Wedding Gig']; "Paranoia: un canto" ['Paranoid: A Song']; "El procesador de palabras de los dioses" ['The Word Processor of the Gods']; "El hombre que no quería estrechar manos" ['The Man Who Would Not Shake Hands']; "La playa" ['The beach'= "Beachworld']; "La imagen de la muerte" ['The image of Death'="The Reaper's Image']; "Para Owen" ['For Owen']; "El camión de Tío Otto" ['Uncle Otto's Truck']; "Reparto matutino (El lechero, 1)" ['Morning Deliveries (Milkman #1)"]; "RuedAs: un cuento de lavandería (El lechero, 2)" ['Wheels: a story of the launderette (milkman#2)'; "Big Wheels: A Story of the Laundry Trade (Milkman #2)']; "El brazo" ['The Arm'="The Reach"/"Do the Dead Sing?'].

MICHAEL R. COLLINGS

q. Excerpted as: *De Aap* ['The Monkey']. Utrecht, Belgium: Luitingh, 1987, 197 pp., paperback. Dutch translation by Margot Bakker. ISBN 90-245-1842-3. * 2nd printing, 1988
r. Excerpted as: *De Ballade van de Flexibele Kogel* ['The Ballad of the Flexible Bullet']. Utrecht, Belgium: Luitingh, 1987, 197 pp. Dutch translation by Margot Bakker. ISBN 90-245-1763-X.
s. As: *Tripulação de esqueletos* ['Crew of skeletons']. Rio de Janeiro, Brazil: Francisco Alves, MESTRES DO HORROR E DA FANTASIA, 1987, 487 pp., 21 cm. Portuguese translation by Louisa Ibanez. * 2nd printing, 1987, 487 pp., 21 cm., paperback. ISBN 85-265-0064-3.
t. As: *Brume: Nouvelles* ['Fog: Novellas']. Paris: Albin Michel, 1987, 643 pp., 140 F, 23 cm., paperback. French translation by Michèle Pressé and Serge Quadruppani. ISBN 2-226-03141-3.
u. As: *Brume: Nouvelles* ['Fog: Novellas']. [Paris, France]: le Grand livre du mois, 1987, 643 pp., 140 F, 23 cm., hardcover. French translation by Michèle Pressé and Gerge Quadruppani. Book Club edition.
v. Excerpted as: *Der Fornit*. Munich, Germany: Wilhelm Heyne, 1987. German translation
w. Excerpted as: *Het Spiegelbeeld van de Maaier* ["The mower's mirror-image'="The Reaper's Image"]. Utrecht, Belgium: Luitingh, 1987, 176 pp. Dutch translation by Margot Bakker. ISBN 90-245-1862-8. * 2nd printing, 1988
x. Excerpted as: *La Expedición* ['The expedition']. Barcelona, Spain, and Buenos Aires, Argentina: Grijalbo, BESTSELLER ORO, 1987, 206 pp. 20 cm. Spanish translation by Francisco Blanco. ISBN 84-253-1896-3 [Spain]; 950-28-0082-6 [Argentina].
CONTENTS: "La expedición" ('The Jaunt'); "Superviviente" ('Super-living'="Survivor Type"); "Abuela " ("Gramma") "La balada del proyectil flexible."
y. As: *Brume: Nouvelles* ['Fog: Novellas']. Paris: France Loisirs, 1988, 643 pp., 98 F, 24 cm., hardcover. French translation by Michèle Pressé and Serge Quadruppani. ISBN 2-7242-3942-3. * Reprint, 1994, ISBN 2-7242-7835-6.
z. Stockholm, Sweden: Legenda, 1988, 596 pp., pocket paperback. Swedish translation by Karl G. Fredrikkson and Lilian Fredriksson.
aa. As: *Scheletri* ['Skeleton']. Milan, Italy: Sperling & Kupfer, PANDORA [#423], January 1989. Italian translation by Tullio Dobner, Bruno Amato, Maria Barbara Piccioli, Olivia Crosio, Sofia Mohamed Hagi Hassan, and Maria Grazia Laviano.
CONTENTS: Introduzione; *La nebbia* [*The Mist*] pp. 9-136; "Tigri!" ["Here There Be Tygers"] pp. 137-141; "La Scimmia" ["The Monkey"] pp. 142-178; "Caino scatenato" ["Cain Rose Up"] pp. 179-184; "La scorciatoia della signora Todd" ["Mrs. Todd's Shortcut"] pp. 185-208; "Il Viaggio" ["The Jaunt"] pp. 209-233; "Marcia nuziale" ["The Wedding Gig"] pp. 234-249; "Ode del paranoide" pp. 250-252; "La zattera" ["The Raft"] pp. 254-281; "Il Word Processor degli dei" pp. 282-301; "L'uomo che non voleva stringere la mano"

["The Man Who Would Not Shake Hands"] pp. 302-320; "Sabbiature" ["Beachworld"] pp. 321-338; "L'immagine della Falciatrice" ["The Reaper's Image"] pp. 339-346; "Nona" pp. 347-382; "L'arte di sopravvivere" ["Survivor Type"] pp. 383-403; "Il camion dello zio Otto" ["Uncle Otto's Truck" pp. 404-421; "Consegne mattutine (Lattaio N. 1)" ["Big Wheels...No. 1"] pp. 422-426; "Quattroruote: la storia dei bei lavanderini (Lattaio N. 2" ["Big Wheels...No. 2"] pp. 427-441; "La nonna" ["Gramma"] pp. 442-472; "La ballata della pallottola flessibile" ["The Ballad of the Flexible Bullet"] pp. 473-521; "Il Braccio" ["The Reach"] pp. 521+.

bb. As: *Paranoïa—Brume 1* ['Paranoia—Fog 1']. Paris: J'ai Lu, EPOUVANTE #2578, 1989, 409 pp., 25 F, 17 cm., paperback. French translation by Michèle Pressé and Serge Quadruppani. ISBN 2-277-22578-9.

cc. As: *La faucheuse— Brume 2* ['The mower—Fog 2']. Paris: J'ai Lu, EPOUVANTE #2579, 1989, 409 pp., 25 F, paperback. French translation by Michèle Pressé and Serge Quadruppani. ISBN 2-277-22579-7.

dd. Excerpted as: *La Niebla* ['The Mist']. Barcelona, Spain: Ediciones Grijalbo, 1989, pp. Spanish translation

ee. As: *Historias Fantásticas* ['Fantastic stories']. Esplugues de Llobregat, Barcelona, Spain: Plaza & Janés, JET 102/10 , 1989, 186 pp., 18 cm. Spanish translation by Rosa S. de Naviera. ISBN 84-01-49890-2.

ff. As: *Historias Fantásticas* ['Fantastic stories']. Esplugues de Llobregat, Barcelona, Spain: Plaza Joven, HITS, 1989, 175 pp., 21 cm. Spanish translation by Rosa S. de Naviera. ISBN 84-7655-763-9.

gg. As: *The Monkey/Mrs. Todd's Shortcut/Short Stories.* Paris, France: Presses Pocket #3296, 1990, 222 pp., 35 F, paperback. French translation and notes by Michel Oriano. ISBN 2-266-02923-1. See A42.

hh. Excerpted as: *Le singe; suivi de Le chenal* ["The Monkey"; with 'The channel'="The Reach"]. Paris, France: J'ai Lu #4, 1990, 95 pp., 10 F, paperback. French translation by Michèle Pressé and Serge Quadruppani. ISBN 2-277-30004-7.

ii. As: *De schnabbel en andere verhalen* ['The Mist and other stories']. Utrecht, Belgium: Luitingh-Sijthoff, 1991, 373 pp., Dutch translation by Margot Bakker. 1st printing. ISBN 90-245-1538-6.

jj. As: *Het rak en andere verhalen* ['The Reach and other stories']. Utrecht, Belgium: Luitingh-Sijthoff, 1991, 345 pp. Dutch translation by Margot Bakker. 1st printing. ISBN 90-245-1548-3.

kk. As: *Jälkeen Keskiyön* ['After midnight'—*Skeleton Crew* 1]. Helsinki, Finland: Book Studio, 1991, 314 pp. Finnish translation by Tapio Tamminen. ISBN 951-611-380-X; 19 cm., ISBN 951-611-401-6.

ll. As: *Ennen Aamunkoittoa* ['Before dawn'—*Skeleton Crew* 2]. Helsinki, Finland: Book Studio, 1991. Finnish translation by Tapio Tamminen. ISBN 951-611-448-2.

mm. As: *Historias fantásticas* ['Fantastic stories']. [Barcelona], Spain: Círculo de Lectores, 1991, 191 pp., 23 cm. Spanish translation by Rosa S. de Naviera. ISBN 84-226-3247-0.

nn. As: *Im Morgengrauen: Unheimlische Geschichten* ['In the grey of morning: uncanny stories']. Gütersloh, Austria: Bertelsmann-Club, 1992, 284 pp., hardcover. German translation by Alexandra von Reinhardt. Book Club edition.

oo. As: *La Ballade de la balle elastique; suivi de L'homme qui refusait de serrer la main* ["The Ballad of the Flexible Bullet" with "The Man Would Not Shake Hands"]. Paris, France: J'ai Lu, 96 pp., 21 cm. French translation by Michele Presse and Serge Quadruppani. ISBN 2-277-30046-2.

pp. London, England: Warner Books, 1993, 612 pp. ISBN 0-7515-0438-6.

qq. As: *Der Gesang der Toten* ['The Song of the dead'; Skeleton Crew, part 2]. Gütersloh, Austria: Bertelsman Club, 1993, 255 pp., hardcover. German translations by Matrin Bliesse, Rolf Jurkeit, and Alexandra von Reinhardt. Book Club edition.

rr. As: *Den Förskräckliga Apan och Andra Berättelser* ['The fearful monkey and other stories']. Stockholm, Sweden: Legenda, NOK POCKET, 1993, 597 pp., 18 cm., paperback Swedish translation by Karl G. Fredriksson and Lilian Fredriksson. ISBN 91-27-0337302-2.

ss. As: *Scheletri* ['Skeleton']. Milan, Italy: Sperling Paperback, SUPERBESTSELLER #474, October 1995, 549 pp., 20 cm., paperback. Italian translation by Tullio Dobner, Bruno Amato, Maria Barbara Piccioli, Olivia Crosio, Sofia Mohamed Hagi Hassan, and Maria Grazia Laviano. ISBN 88-7824-573-9.

tt. As: *Stephen King #03-3 Vol. Boxed Set.* New York: Signet, mass-market paperback. ISBN 0-451-93138-6. Boxed set with *Different Seasons, Skeleton Crew,* and *Nightmares and Dreamscapes.*

uu. As: *Tågen og andre noveller.* Copenhagen, Denmark: Artia, 1995, 542 pp., 158 KR, paperback. Danish translation by Mogens Wenzel Andreasen. ISBN 87-89918-52-5.

vv. As: *Brume: Nouvelles* ['Fog: stories']. Volume I. Lyon, France: Chardon bleu, COLLECTION LARGEVISION, 1995, 180 pp., 140 F, 21 cm. paperback. French translation by Michèle Pressé and Serge Quadruppani. Large-print edition. ISBN 2-86833-101-7.

ww. As: *Brume: Nouvelles* ['Fog: stories']. Volume II. Lyon, France: Chardon bleu, COLLECTION LARGEVISION, 1995, 188 pp., 140 F, 21 cm., paperback. French translation by Michèle Pressé and Serge Quadruppani. Large-print edition. ISBN 2-86833-102-5.

xx. As: *Blut im Morgengrauen—Der Gesang der Toten—Der Fornit.* ['Blood in morning-grey'—'The song of the dead'—'The fornit']. Munich, Germany: Wilhelm Heyne #01-8900, May 1996, 18.90 dm., paperback. First complete German edition of *Skeleton Crew.* ISBN 3-453-09936-2.

yy. As: *Duistere Krachten: Verhalen van de Meester van de Horror* ['Dark forces: Stories by the master of horror']. Amsterdam, Netherlands: Poema Pocket, 1996, 585 pp., paperback. Dutch translation by Margot Bakker. ISBN 90-245-2473-3.

zz. As: *Historias Fantásticas* ['Fantastic stories']. Esplugas de Llobregat,

Barcelona, Spain: Plaza & Janés, JET 102/ BIBLIOTECA DE STEPHEN KING #10, 1996, 186 pp., 18 cm., paperback. Spanish translations by Rosa S. de Naveira. 8th printing. ISBN 84-01-47460-4. * Reprint, 1998, 246 pp., 18 cm., paperback, ISBN 84-01-49968-2.

aaa. As: *Der Fornit: unheimliche Geschichten* ['The fornit: uncanny stories']. [Marburg], Germany: Deutsche Blindenstudienanst., 19—. 65.00 DM.
bbb. As: [Title unknown] ['The Mist']. Greek translation.
ccc. As: [Title unknown] ['Skeleton Crew?]. Greek translation.
ddd. As: *Den Förskräckliga Apan*. Stockholm, Sweden. 19—.
eee. As: *Nightmares*. Thailand. Thai translation.

fff. As AUDIOCASSETTE: *Skeleton Crew, (Book One)*. Clinton MD: Recorded Books, 1985. Read by Frank Miller. 6 cassettes; 9 hours. Unabridged. #85210.
CONTENTS: "The Raft"; "The Reaper's Image"; "The Monkey"; "Cain Rose Up"; "The Jaunt"; "Beachworld"; "Survivor Type"; "Morning Deliveries"; "Big Wheels"; "For Owen"; "The Man Who Wouldn't Shake Hands"; "The Reach"; "Uncle Otto's Truck."
ggg. As AUDIOCASSETTE: *Skeleton Crew, (Book Two)*. Clinton MD: Recorded Books, 1985. Read by Frank Miller. 5 cassettes; 7 hours. Unabridged. #85220.
CONTENTS: "Mrs. Todd's Shortcut"; "The Wedding Gig"; "Nona"; "Paranoid: A Chant"; "Here There Be Tygers"; "The Ballad of the Flexible Bullet"; "Gramma."
hhh. As AUDIOCASSETTE: *Stories from Skeleton Crew*. New York: Warner Audio Publishing, Read by David Purdham and Gale Garnett. CONTENTS: "THE Monkey," "The Reaper's Image," "Gramma."

COMMENTS: *Skeleton Crew* provided the most comprehensive collection of King's short fiction to that date. More extensive than *Night Shift* or *Different Seasons*, with substantially greater breadth and depth than *The Dark Tower: The Gunslinger* or *The Dark Tower II: The Drawing of the Three*, it represents the range of King's career through 1985. His second professional sale is included ("The Reaper's Image"), as well as a story first published sixteen years later, "Beachworld." The collection opens with what some critics consider one of King's most sustained explorations of the terror of the unknown, "The Mist," itself almost a novel in length and complexity of characters and situations; and the volume concludes with "The Reach," an exquisitely crafted tale of ghosts and love, of death and life that may represent King at his finest—more frequently than any other title, this story is mentioned as evidence of King's prowess as a major American author and as among his finest individual works.

The book sold 600,000 copies in 1985, and was ranked #5 on the Bowker Annual hardcover fiction bestsellers list for 1985. Nominated as Best Anthology/Collection, World Fantasy Convention, 1986.

Michael R. Collings

SELECTED ARTICLES, RESPONSES, AND REVIEWS:

Adler, Constance. "Prince of Darkness: In His Reign of Best-selling Terror, Author Stephen King Remains Absolute Master of the Scary Story." *Philadelphia Magazine* [PA] Vol. 76 (August 1985): 85+. [3-page article]

Alley, Jerry. "Tasteless, Tame, Silly." *Virginian-Pilot* [Norfolk VA] 23 June 1985. As microfiche: *NewsBank: Literature* Vol. 12 (July 1985): Fiche 4, F7.

Bentkowski, Kent Daniel. "A Skeleton Crew Inside King's Closet." *Castle Rock: The Stephen King Newsletter* Vol. 1, No. 4 (April 1985): 2.

Bertin, Eddy C. *SF Gids* [Belgium] (1986): 20.

Bertin, Eddy C. "Stephen King in the Lowlands." *Castle Rock: The Stephen King Newsletter* Vol. 1, No. 11 (November 1985): 7-8.

Bertin, Eddy C. "Additions to 'Stephen King in the Lowlands.'" Letter.

Best Sellers Vol. 45 (August 1985): 168.

Blue, Tyson. "Stephen King's Short Stories Sure to Please His Many Fans." *Courier Herald* [Dublin GA] 22 June 1985.

Boesch, Barry. "Wide-Ranging 'Skeleton Crew' Looks at Internal, External Monsters." *Dallas Morning News* [TX] 4 August 1985. As microfiche: *NewsBank: Literature* Vol. 12 (September 1985): Fiche 23, G9-G10.

Bolotin, Susan. "Don't Turn Your Back on This Book." *The New York Times Book Review* Vol. 90 (9 June 1985): VII, 11.

Booklist Vol. 81 (15 December 1984): 538.

Brocale, Carla. "Stories in 'Skeleton Crew' Are Vintage King." *Kansas City Star* [MO] 14 July 1985. As microfiche: *NewsBank: Literature* Vol. 12 (August 1985): Fiche 12, D3.

Brown, Stephen. "Secretly Hidden Behind the Pen Name of Richard Bachman was Stephen King." *Daily News* [NY] 9 May 1985. As microfiche: *NewsBank: Literature* Vol. 11 (June 1985): Fiche 110, A1-A2.

Chute, David. "Chilling Horror from Stephen King." *Los Angeles Herald Examiner* [CA] 16 June 1985. As microfiche: *NewsBank: Literature* Vol. 12 (July 1985): Fiche 4, E11-E12.

Collings, Michael R. "King Collection Worth Waiting For." *Fantasy Review* Vol. 8, No. 6, Whole #80 (June 1985): 22.

Graham, Mark. "Stephen King Stories Never Seem to Die." *Rocky Mountain News* [Denver CO] 16 June 1985.

Halford, Celia C. "Boo! New Stephen King Anthology." *News and Courier* [Charleston SC] 28 July 1985. As microfiche: *NewsBank: Literature* Vol. 12 (August 1985): Fiche 12, D5.

Hartwell, David G. Headnote to "The Monkey." *The Dark Descent*. Edited by David G. Hartwell. New York: Tor, October 1988, hardcover. 382.

Hartwell, David G. Headnote to "The Reach." *The Dark Descent*. Edited by David G. Hartwell. New York: Tor, October 1988, hardcover. 15.

Hornbaker, Alice. "King Courts Royal Set of Scary Stories." *Cincinnati Enquirer* [OH] 2 June 1985. As microfiche: *NewsBank: Literature* Vol. 12 (July 1985): Fiche 4, F3.

Illustrated London News Vol. 273 (August 1985): 65.

Illustrated London News Vol. 273 (October 1985): 107.
Keller, Scott A. "Latest King Collection a Bit Disappointing." *Atlanta Journal-Constitution* [GA] 14 July 1985. As microfiche: *NewsBank: Literature* Vol. 12 (August 1985): Fiche 12, D1.
Kirkus Reviews Vol. 53 (1 May 1985): 386.
Kliatt Young Adult Paperback Book Guide Vol. 20 (Fall 1986): 38.
Kloer, Phil. "'Skeleton Crew': The Bare Bones of Stephen King." *Florida Times-Union* [Jacksonville FL] 30 June 1985. As microfiche: *NewsBank: Literature* Vol. 12 (July 1985): Fiche 4, E13-E14.
Lehmann-Haupt, Christopher. *New York Times* 11 July 1985: III, 21.
Library Journal Vol. 110 (1 May 1985): 78.
Los Angeles Times "Books" [CA] 25 August 1985: 4.
McCaffrey, Larry. "It's Time for King to Desert Treadmill." *San Diego Union* [CA] 4 August 1985. As microfiche: *NewsBank: Literature* Vol. 12 (September 1985): Fiche 23, G8.
The Magazine of Fantasy & Science Fiction Vol. 69 (November 1985): 12.
Merritt, Robert. "Collection Displays King's Childlike Mischief." *Richmond Times-Dispatch* [VA] 30 June 1985. As microfiche: *NewsBank: Literature* Vol. 12 (July 1985): Fiche 4, F8.
Moss, Chuck. "Multiple Shivers from a Champion of the Game." *The Detroit News* [MI] 16 June 1985: 2K. Excerpted: *Contemporary Literary Criticism*, Vol. 37. Edited by Daniel G. Marowski. Detroit MI: Gale Research, 1986. 207-208.
New Statesman Vol. 112 (12 September 1986): 30.
New York Times [Daily] Vol. 134 (11 June 1985): 17.
New York Times Book Review Vol. 91 (29 June 1986): 38.
Nicholls, Peter. "Beach Blanket Books: *Skeleton Crew*." *Washington Post Book World* Vol. 15 (16 June 1985): 1, 13. Excerpted: *Contemporary Literary Criticism*, Vol. 37. Edited by Daniel G. Marowski. Detroit MI: Gale Research, 1986. 206-207.
Nolan, William F. "The Good Fabric: Of Night Shifts and Skeleton Crews." *Kingdom of Fear: The World of Stephen King*. Edited by Tim Underwood and Chuck Miller. Columbia PA: Underwood-Miller, 1986. 99-106.
Potter, Chuck. "Out of 'The Mist' a Stephen King 'Skeleton Crew.'" *Wichita Eagle-Beacon* [KS] 23 June 1985. As microfiche: *NewsBank: Literature* Vol. 12 (August 1985): Fiche 12, D2.
Publishers Weekly Vol. 227 (19 April 1985): 72.
Publishers Weekly Vol. 229 (18 April 1986): 66.
Rickard, Dennis. "Horror Without Limits: Looking into *The Mist*." *Reign of Fear: Fiction and Film of Stephen King*. Edited by Don Herron. Los Angeles CA: Underwood-Miller, June 1988. 177-192.
Sallee, Wayne Allen. "No Bones About It." *Castle Rock: The Stephen King Newsletter* Vol. 1, No. 8 (August 1985): 2.
San Francisco Chronicle [CA] 24 June 1985: 55.
Schleier, Curt. "Stephen King's Stories Offer Evidence of Pact with the Devil."

Chicago Tribune [CA] 9 June 1985. As microfiche: *NewsBank: Literature* Vol. 12 (June 1985): Fiche 118, E8.

Science Fiction Chronicle (October 1985): 43.

Science Fiction Review No. 15 (February 1986): 24.

Shestak, George. "You Win, Lose With a Pair of Kings." *Omaha World-Herald* [NE] 26 May 1985. As microfiche: *NewsBank: Literature* Vol. 11 (June 1985): Fiche 110, A3.

Time Vol. 125 (1 July 1985): 59.

Turner, Billy. "Stephen King's Newest Is Recycled Old Stuff." *Clarion-Ledger* [Jackson MS] 16 June 1985. As microfiche: *NewsBank: Literature* Vol. 12 (July 1985): Fiche 4, F1.

Vicarel, Jo Ann. "Horror, Science Fiction Meet Horror-Story Mold." *Cleveland Plain Dealer* [OH] 13 July 1985. As microfiche: *NewsBank: Literature* Vol. 12 (August 1985): Fiche 12, D4.

Voice of Youth Advocates Vol. 10 (April 1987): 53.

West Coast Review of Books Vol. 11 (July 1985): 28.

Winter, Douglas E. "The King of Storytelling Is Back Again." *Philadelphia Inquirer* [PA] 30 June 1985. As microfiche: *NewsBank: Literature* Vol. 12 (July 1985): Fiche 4, F4-F6.

Winter, Douglas E. *Castle Rock: The Stephen King Newsletter* Vol. 1, No. 9 (September 1985): 1-2.

York, John. "King Collection Goes Back to the Beginning." *Charlotte Observer* [NC] 30 June 1985. As microfiche: *NewsBank: Literature* Vol. 12 (July 1985): Fiche 4, F2.

Horror Plum'd

Silver Bullet. New York, NY: Signet/New American Library, 1985. Trade paperback.

A29.
SILVER BULLET
(1985)

A29. *SILVER BULLET*. New York: Signet/New American Library, October 1985, 255 pp., $9.95, trade paperback. Illustrations by Berni Wrightson. Movie tie-in edition. Horror collection—fiction and screenplay. ISBN 0-451-82128-9.

CONTENTS: "Foreword," by King [see C142]; *Cycle of the Werewolf* (1983; see A21); *Silver Bullet* (screenplay).

REPRINTS AND ADAPTATIONS:
b. As: *Der Werewolf von Tarker Mills* ['The werewolf of Tarker Mills']. Bergisch Gladbach: Bastei-Lübbe TB28146, 1 October 1986, paperback. German translation by Helmut W. Pesch and Harro Christensen. "Deutsches erstausgabe."
c. As: *Silver Bullet*. Utrecht, Belgium: Luitingh, 1986. Dutch translation.
d. As: *Peur bleue* ['Blue fear']. Paris, France: J'ai Lu, ÉPOUVANTE #1999, 1986, 277 pp., 19 F. French translation. ISBN 2-277-21999-1.
e. As: [Title unknown]. Milan, Italy: Longanesi, 1986. Italian translation.
f. As: *Unico indizio: la luna piena* ['Single sign: full moon']. Milan, Italy: Editori Associati, TEADUE #12, January 1989. Italian translation by Carlo Brera. ISBN 88-7819-086-1.
g. As: *Ezüst Pisztolygolyoki* ['Silver bullet']. Budapest, Hungary: Ararát, 1990. Hungarian translation by Petrao Agnes.
h. As: *Der Werwolf von Tarker Mills* ['The Werewolf of Tarker Mills]. Bergisch Gladbach, Germany: Bastei-Lübbe, ALLGEMEINE REIHE, 1 March 1991, 382 pp., 9.80 DM, paperback. German translation by Harro Christensen and Helmut Pesch. ISBN 3-404-13299-8. * 3rd printing, 1992. * 9th printing, 1996.
    CONTENTS: "Vorwort" ("Foreword"); Das Jahr des Werwolfs ['The year of the werewolf,' *Cycle of the Werewolf*]; Der Werwolf von Tarker Mill ['The Werewolf of Tarker Mill,' *Silver Bullet*].
i. As: *Peur bleue* ['Blue fear']. Paris, France: France Loisirs, 1994, 299 pp., 76 F, hardcover. French translation by Michel Darroux, Bernadette Emerich, and François Lasquin. ISBN 2-7242-8194-2.

j. As AUDIOCASSETTE: *Der Werwolf von Tarker Mills*. Munich, Germany: Bastei-Lübbe Verlag/Lübbe Audio, 2 October 1997. 1 cassette, 111 minutes. 19.90 DM. Read by Joachim Kerzel. ISBN 3-7857-1023-2.

k. As FILM/VIDEOCASSETTE: *Stephen King's Silver Bullet*. Paramount Pictures, North Carolina Film Corporation (Dino de Laurentiis), October 1985. Produced by Martha Schumacher, with John M. Eckert. Directed by Daniel Attias. Screenplay by Stephen King. 95 minutes. Rating: R.
CAST: Gary Bussey, Everitt McGill, Corey Haim, Megan Follows.
SELECTED FILM REVIEWS AND ARTICLES.:
American Film Vol. 111 (October 1985): 86.
Blank, Ed. "King's 'Silver Bullet' Almost Hits the Mark." *Pittsburgh Press* [PA] 12 October 1985. As microfiche: *Newsbank: Film and Television* Vol. 12 (November 1985): Fiche 52, G13.
Blue, Tyson. "'Bullet' is SK's Best Screenplay." *Castle Rock: The Stephen King Newsletter* Vol. 2, No. 1 (January 1986): 6.
Blue, Tyson. "'Silver Bullet' a Werewolf Surprise." *Courier Herald* [Dublin GA] 12 October 1985.
Bunke, Joan. "Werewolf, Godzilla, and Ninja Flicks Rate Only as Halloween 'Nightmares.'" *Des Moines Register* [IA] 31 October 1985. As microfiche: *Newsbank: Film and Television* Vol. 12 (November 1985): Fiche 52, G10.
Cinefantastique Vol. 15, No. 1 (January 1985): 18.
Collings, Michael R. "Silver Bullet: Another Opinion." *Castle Rock: The Stephen King Newsletter* Vol. 1, No. 12 (December 1985): 3.
Cosford, Bill. "This 'Silver Bullet' Is a Blank." *Miami Herald* [FL] 14 October 1985. As microfiche: *Newsbank: Film and Television* Vol. 12 (November 1985): Fiche 52, G9.
Crumpler, David. "Stephen King's 'Silver Bullet' Takes Aim, Fires a Blank." *Florida Union-Times* [Jacksonville FL] 17 October 1985. As microfiche: *Newsbank: Film and Television* Vol. 12 (November 1985): Fiche 52, G8.
Dimeo, Steve. "Stephen King Script Little More Than Sheep in Wolf's Clothes." *Cinefantastique* Vol. 16, No. 11 (March 1986): 43, 54.
Ebert, Roger. *Roger Ebert's Movie Home Companion, 1988 Edition*. Kansas City MO: Andrews, McMeel & Parker, 1987. 552-553.
Everitt, David. "Stephen King's Silver Bullet." *Fangoria* No. 48 (1985): 30-32. Interview-article based on discussions with director Daniel Attias.
Freedman, Richard. "'Silver Bullet' Off Target in Teen's Werewolf Hunt." *Star-Ledger* [Newark NJ] 11 October 1985. As microfiche: *Newsbank: Film and Television* Vol. 12 (November 1985): Fiche 52, G11.
Grody, W. MD *Medical News Magazine* Vol. 29. No. 12 (December 1985): 108.

Hewitt, Tim. "*Silver Bullet*: Stephen King's Tale Pits Werewolf Against Wheelchair Hotrodder." *Cinefantastique* Vol. 15, No. 2 (May 1985): 12.

Kagan, Rick. "'Silver Bullet': A Sheep of a Movie in Wolf's Garb." *Chicago Tribune* [IL] 16 October 1985. As microfiche: *Newsbank: Film and Television* Vol. 12 (December 1985): Fiche 62, C5.

Maeder, Jay. "'Bullet' Should Be Shot." *Daily News* [NY] 11 October 1985. As microfiche: *Newsbank: Film and Television* Vol. 12 (October 1985): Fiche 44, A14.

Martin, Robert H. [Bob]. "Interview with a Werewolf." *Fangoria* No. 44 (1985): 41-44. Interview-article with Everett McGill, who played "Reverend Lowe" in *Silver Bullet*.

McGrady, Mike. "Stephen King Pounds Out Another One." *Newsday* [Long Island NY] 11 October 1985. As microfiche: *Newsbank: Film and Television* Vol. 12 (October 1985): Fiche 44, A14.

Newman, K. *Monthly Film Bulletin* Vol. 53, No. 629 (July 1986): 212.

Pettus, David. "Stephen King's Silver Bullet: A Review." *Castle Rock: The Stephen King Newsletter* Vol. 1, No. 11 (November 1985): 1, 4.

Reed, Rex. "King's Werewolf a Howler." *New York Post* 11 October 1985. As microfiche: *Newsbank: Film and Television* Vol. 12 (November 1985): Fiche 52, G12.

Spignesi, Stephen J. "The Unfinished King." *The Shape Under the Sheet: The Complete Stephen King Encyclopedia*. Ann Arbor MI: Popular Culture, Ink., May 1991. 778-780.

Stack, Peter. "Stephen King's Latest Werewolf." *San Francisco Chronicle* [CA] 12 October 1985. As microfiche: *Newsbank: Film and Television* Vol. 12 (November 1985): Fiche 52, G7.

Turner, N. *Film* 151 (December 1986): 3.

Variety Vol. 320, No. 12 (16 October 1985): 10.

Williams, Sharon. "Stephen King's *Cycle of the Werewolf* Becomes *Silver Bullet* for the Silver Screen." *Fantastic Films* (October 1985): 20-22.

Wuntch, Philip. "King Fires a Dud With 'Silver Bullet.'" *Dallas Morning News* [TX] 15 October 1985. As microfiche: *Newsbank: Film and Television* Vol. 12 (November 1985): Fiche 52, G14.

SELECTED ARTICLES, RESPONSES, AND REVIEWS:

Blue, Tyson. "*Silver Bullet*—Book Review." *Castle Rock: The Stephen King Newsletter* Vol. 2, No. 1 (January 1986): 5.

Booklist Vol. 82 (15 February 1986): 843.

THE BACHMAN BOOKS. New York, NY: New American Library, 1985. Hardcover.

A30.
THE BACHMAN BOOKS
(1985)

A30. THE BACHMAN BOOKS: FOUR EARLY NOVELS: RAGE, THE LONG WALK, ROADWORK, THE RUNNING MAN. New York: New American Library, October 1985, x+692 pp., $19.95, 24 cm., hardcover. Novel collection. ISBN 0-453-00507-1.

CONTENTS: Introduction, "Why I Was Bachman" [see C141]; *Rage* (1977; see A4); *The Long Walk* (1979; see A8); *Roadwork* (1981; see A10); *The Running Man* (1982; see A14).

REPRINTS AND ADAPTATIONS:
b. New York: Plume/New American Library, October 1985, x+692 pp., $9.95, trade paperback. ISBN 0-452-25774-3.
c. As: *I libri di Bachman* ['The books of Bachman']. Milan, Italy: Arnoldo Mondadori, PROPOSTE, August 1986. Italian translations by Beata Della Frattina (*La lunga marcia*=*The Long Walk*) and Delio Zinoni (*L'uomo in fuga*=*The Running Man*).
d. New York: Signet/New American Library, November 1986, xiii+923 pp., $5.95, mass market paperback. ISBN 0-451-14736-7. In stores by late August, 1986. * 10th printing by 1994.
e. London, England: Hodder & Stoughton/New English Library, May 1986, x+692 pp., £10.95, hardcover. ISBN 0-450-39552-9.
f. London/Dunton Green, England: New English Library, August 1987, xiii+865 pp., £4.95, paperback. ISBN 0-450-39249-X.
g. As: *4 X Stephen King*. Utrecht, Belgium: Luitingh, 1986, 605 pp., paperback. Includes: *Razernij* [*Rage*], translated by Margot Bakker; *De Marathon* [*The Long Walk*], translated by Mariella de Kuyper-Snel; *Werk in Uitvoering* [*Roadwork*], translated by Hugo Kuipers; *Vlucht Naar de Top* [*The Running Man*], translated by Frank de Groot. Dutch translation. ISBN 90-245-1611-0. * 13th printing, 1990. * 19th printing, 1994.
h. New York: Book of the Month Club, October 1991, 692 pp., $17.95, hardcover. No ISBN listed. Book Club edition.

i. As: *Os livros de Bachman* ['The books of Bachman']. Rio de Janeiro, Brazil: Francisco Alves, MESTRES DO HORROR E DA FANTASIA, 1992, 725 pp., 21 cm., paperback. Portuguese translation by Ruy Jungmann. ISBN 85-265-0292-1.
j. As: *Richard Bachman kirjat 1: Raivo & Pitkä Marssi* ['Richard Bachman books 1: Rage and The Long Walk']. Helsinki, Finland: Tammi, 1992. Finnish translation.
k. As: *Richard Bachman kirjat 2: Vumma & Juokse Tai* ['Richard Bachman books 2'] Helsinki, Finland: Tammi, 1993, 529 pp., 23 cm. Finnish translation by Leevi Lehto. ISBN 951-30-0100-2. * Reprint, 1994.
l. New York: New American Library, October 1996, 944 pp., mass-market paperback. ISBN 0-451-19193-5.

SELECTED ARTICLES, RESPONSES, AND REVIEWS: [see also reviews listed separately under each book in this collection]
Best Sellers Vol. 46 (April 1986): 6.
Blue, Tyson. "King Re-releases Novels Published by 'Bachman'." *Courier Herald* [Dublin GA] 28 September 1985. As: "Bachman Books are Interesting Trip." *Castle Rock: The Stephen King Newsletter* Vol. 1, No. 12 (December 1985): 5.
Booklist Vol. 82 (1 October 1985): 191.
Collings, Michael R. "New King, Vintage King." *Fantasy Review* No. 84 (October 1985): 18.
Costello, William J. "'Bachman Books' Is a Collection of Four King Novels." *Forum* [Fargo ND] (1986). As microfiche: *NewsBank: Literature* Vol. 12 (May 1986): Fiche 74, F3.
Field, Ben. "Bachman Isn't Vintage King." *Seattle Post-Intelligencer* [WA] 7 November 1985.
Kirkus Reviews Vol. 53 (15 September 1985): 968.
Lawson, John. *School Library Journal* Vol. 32 (April 1986): 105.
Publishers Weekly Vol. 228 (6 September 1985): 59.
Rousch, Matt. "King Can't Hide Behind Bachman." *USA Today* Vol. 4 (17 October 1985): 2D.
Science Fiction Chronicle Vol. 7 (February 1986): 34.
Smith, Gene. "King's Early Work." *Topeka Capital-Journal* [KS] 20 April 1986. As microfiche: *NewsBank: Literature* Vol. 12 (May 1986): Fiche 93, C12.
Voice of Youth Advocates 10 (June 1987): 103.

A31.
THE PLANT: PART 3
(1985)

A31. *THE PLANT* [PART 3]. Bangor ME: Philtrum Press, December (?) 1985, 56 pp., chapbook. Limited edition of 26 lettered copies signed by King plus 200 numbered copies. Horror-fiction pamphlet

COMMENTS: The third installment of a novel-in-progress [see A18 and A23], privately published by King as Christmas greetings. See the completion of Book One, Parts I-VI, as an internet publication [A71].

SELECTED ARTICLES, RESPONSES, AND REVIEWS:
Blue, Tyson. "The Plant: The Unseen King." *Castle Rock: The Stephen King Newsletter* 2:6 (June 1986): 1, 3.
Collings, Michael R., and David A. Engebretson. *The Shorter Works of Stephen King.* Starmont Studies in Literary Criticism, No. 9. Mercer Island WA: Starmont House, 1985. 173, 178.
Winter, Douglas E. Stephen King: *The Art of Darkness.* New York: New American Library, November 1984. 176.

It. New York, NY: Viking, 1986. Hardcover.

A32.
IT
(1986)

A32. *ES*. Linkenheim, West Germany: Edition Phantasia, [May] 1986, 859 pp., 148.00 DM, hardcover. German translation by Alexandra von Reinhardt. Limited edition of 280 numbered copies, bound in leather, red velvet slipcase; 30 copies numbered I-XXX, not offered for sale. This German-language edition is the true first appearance of the novel better known in the United States as *IT*. Horror novel. ISBN 3-924959-06-4.

PLOT SUMMARY: A richly interwoven tapestry of intricate plots and strong characters, *IT* focuses on the relationships among seven characters, following episodes in their lives as both children and adults; as they learn more about each other, about adult responsibility, and about life, they must also discover—and survive—the secrets of the horror that dwells beneath them in the sewers of Derry, Maine.

REPRINTS AND ADAPTATIONS:
b. As: *ES* ['It']. Munich, Germany: Wilhelm Heyne, JUMBO BÄNDE TB 6657, 1986, 859 pp., 24 cm., trade paperback. German translation by Alexandra von Reinhardt. * 18th printing, 1992.
c. As: *IT*. New York: Viking, 15 September 1986, x+1138 pp., $22.95 hardcover. ISBN 0-670-81302-8.
d. As: *IT*. London, England: Hodder & Stoughton, September 1986, 912 pp., £12.95, hardcover. ISBN 0-340-36477-7. Simuiltaneous with U.S. 1st edition. * Reprint, 1987, ISBN 0-450-41143-5.
e. As: *IT*. New York: Book-of-the-Month-Club], [n.d.], hardcover.
f. As: *Het* ['It']. Utrecht, Belgium: Luitingh, October 1986, 576 pp., paperback. Dutch translation by Margot Bakker. 1st Dutch printing 20,000 copies. ISBN 90-245-1613-7.
g. Excerpted: *Book-of-the-Month Club News* (October 1986): 4. Opening paragraphs of the novel.
h. As: *Es* ['It']. Gütersloh, Austria: Bertelsmann Lesering, 1986, 859 pp., hardcover (?).German translation by Alexandra von Reinhardt.

MICHAEL R. COLLINGS

i. As: *IT*. New York: Signet/New American Library, September 1987, 1093 pp., $4.95, mass-market paperback. ISBN 0-451-16951-3. * 13th printing, September 1989. * 20th printing, November 1990; tie-in edition with television mini-series. * Reprint, October 1999
j. As: *IT*. London/Dunton Green: New English Library, September 1987, 1116 pp., £4.50, paperback. 0-450-41143-5. Also issued as "Special Collector's edition," ISBN 0-450-42305-0.
k. As: *IT*. Milan, Italy: Sperling & Kupfer, SPERLING PAPERBACK #69; PANDORA #365, October 1987, 1238 pp., 20 cm. paperback. Italian translation by Tullio Dobner. ISBN 88-200-0705-3.
l. As: *Eso* ['It']. Buenos Aires, Argentina: Emecé, GRANDES NOVELISTAS, 1987, 956 pp., 22 cm. Spanish translation. ISBN 950-04697-7.
m. As: *A coisa* [The thing']. 2 vols. Rio de Janeiro, Brazil: Francisco Alves, 1987, 1265 pp., 21 cm. Portuguese translation by Luisa Ibanez. ISBN 85-265-0096-1.
n. As: *Det* ['It']. 2 vol. Höganäs and Stockholm, Sweden: Legenda/Bra Spänning, 1987, 564+624 pp., 24 cm., hardcover. Swedish translation by Roland Adlerberth. ISBN 91-582-1104-7
o. As: *IT = Eso*. Esplugues de Llobregat, Barcelona, Spain: Plaza & Janés, 1987, 1026 pp., 23 cm. Spanish translation by Edith Zilli. ISBN 84-01-32215-4.
p. As: *Ta*. Taipei, Taiwan: Huang Guan, 1987. Chinese translation by Wu An Lan.
q. As: *Se* ['It']. 2 vols. Helsinki, Finland: Tammi, 1988, 635+499 pp., 23 cm.. Finnish translation by Ilkka Rekiaro and Päivi Rekiao. ISBN 951-30-6879-X, 951-30-7046-8. 2nd printing 1991.
r. As: *Es* ['It']. Kornwesterheim, Austria: Europäische Bildungsgemeinschaft; Gütersloh, Austria: Bertelsmann Club; Vienna, Austria: Buchgemeinschaft Donauland; Zug, Switzerland: Buch-und-Schallplattenfreunde, December 1988, 859 pp., paperback. German translation. Book Club editions
s. Excerpted as: *Diamonds Are Forever: Writers and Artists on Baseball*. Washington: Smithsonian Institute.
t. As: *Ça* ['It']. 2 vols. Paris, France: Albin Michel, 1988 627+501 pp., 140+130 F, 24 cm., paperback. French translation by William Olivier Desmond. ISBN 2-226-03453-6, 2-226-03454-4. 7th best-selling French-language book.
u. As: *Eso* ['It']. Barcelona, Spain: Círculo de Lectores, 1988, 943 pp., 22 cm. Spanish translation by Edith Zilli. ISBN 84-226-2416-8.
v. As: *Ça* ['It']. Paris, France: France Loisirs, 1989, 1128 pp., 152 F, 25 cm., hardcover. French translation by William Olivier Desmond. ISGN 2-7242-4465-6.
w. Excerpted as: "Es" ['It'] *Die Jumbos von Heyne*. Munich, Germany: Wilhelm Heyne, JUMBO PAPERBACK, 1989, paperback. German translation by Alexandra von Reinhardt.
x. As: *IT [ESO]*. Esplugues de Llobregat, Barcelona, Spain: Plaza & Janés, JET

HORROR PLUM'D

102/13, BIBLIOTECA DE STEPHEN KING #13, 1989, 1215 pp., 18 cm., mass-market paperback. Spanish translation by Edith Zilli. ISBN 84-01-49893-7. * 2nd printing, 1989. * 6th edition, February 1992.

y. As: *IT.* Milan, Italy: Sperling Paperback, SUPERBESTSELLER #69, March 1990, paperback. Italian translation by Tullio Dobner. ISBN 88-7824-081-0.

z. As: *Det onde* ['The evil']. 3 vols. Copenhagen, Denmark: Artia, 1990, 391+402+239 pp., 198 KR each, 22 cm., paperback. Danish translation by Anders Westenholz. ISBN 87-89294-03-3 [complete], Vol. 1, 87-89294-07-6; Vol. 2, 87-89294-09-2; Vol. 3, 87-89294-11-4.

aa. As: *Ça* ['It']. 3 vols. Paris, France: J'ai Lu, EPOUVANTE #2892-2893-2894, 1990, 498+509+501 pp., 33 F [per volume], 17 cm., paperback. French translation by William Olivier Desmond. ISBN 2-277-22892-3, -22893-1, -22894-X.

bb. As: *Ça* ['It']. 2 vols. [Paris, France]: le grand livre du mois, 1992, 627+501 pp., 140 F+130 F, 25 cm., hardcover. French translation by William Olivier Desmond. Book Club edition.

cc. As: [Title unknown]. Israel: Modan, 1992, 991 pp. Hebrew translation.

dd. As: [Title unknown]. South Korea, 1992, 410+430+416 pp., 23 cm., Korean translation. ISBN 89-85259-01-6, 89-85259-03-2, 89-85259-04-0, 89-85259-05-9.

ee. As: *Det onde* ['The evil']. 3 vols. Copenhagen, Denmark: Asschenfeldt, 1993, 391+239+396 pp. Danish translation by Anders Westenholz. New edition. ISBN: Vol. 1, 87-597-1066-7; Vol. 2, 87-597-1067-5; Vol. 3, 87-597-1068-3.

ff. As: *Det onde* ['The evil']. 2 vols. Copenhagen, Denmark: Artia, [1993], 524+742 pp., 88 KR. each, paperback. Danish translation by Anders Westenholz. New edition. ISBN 87-89918-27-4 [complete]; Vol. 1 87-89918-28-2; Vol. 2, 87-89918-29-0.

gg. As: *Het* ['It']. Amsterdam, Netherlands: Luitingh-Sijthoff, [1993], 947 pp. Dutch translation by Theo Horsten. Revised edition; 18th Dutch printing. ISBN 90-245-1472-=X..

hh. As: *Ça* ['It']. Paris, France: France Loisirs, 1994, 1121 pp., 128 F, 25 cm., paperback. French translation by William Olivier Desmond. ISBN 2-7242-7839-9.

ii. As: *Es* ['It']. Munich, Germany: Wilhelm Heyne, #9903, 1996, 1214 pp., 19.90 dm, paperback. German translation by Alexandra von Reinhardt, with Joachim Körber. 2nd printing. ISBN 3-453-09994-X.

jj. As: *It: Eso.* Barcelona, Spain: Plaza & Janés, JET 102/13, BIBLIOTECA DE STEPHEN KING #13, 1996, 1502 pp., 18 cm., paperback. Spanish translation by Edith Zilli. ISBN 84-01-47463-9

kk. As: *It: Eso.* [Barcelona], Spain: Orbis, [1996], 1214 pp., 22 cm., paperback. Spanish translation. ISBN 84-402-2060-X.

ll. As: *To!* ['That/this']. Poznañ, Poland: Zysk i S-Ka Wydaw., KAMELEON, 1997, 1214 pp., 20 cm. Polish translation by Robert Lipski. ISBN 83-7150-253-2.

mm. As: *It: Eso*. Barcelona, Spain: Plaza & Janés, BIBLIOTECA DE STEPHEN KING, 1998, 1502 pp., 18 cm., paperback. Spanish translation by Edith Zilli. ISBN 84-01-49996-8.

nn. As: *Det*. Stockholm, Sweden: Legenda, LEGENDA POCKET, 1998, 1188 pp., 19 cm., paperback. Swedish translation by Roland Adlerberth. ISBN 91-582-1496-8.

oo. New York: New American Library, October 1999, $7.99, 1093 pp., mass-market paperback. ISBN 0-451-16951-4.

pp. As: *Es: Roman* ['It: novel']. Rheda-Wiedenbrück, Germany, and Gütersloh, Austria: RM-Buch-und-Medien Vertrieb, and others, 1999, 1214 pp. German translation by Alexandra von Reinhardt, with Joachim Körber. Book Club edition.

qq. As: *Az* ['It']. 2 vols. Budapest, Hungary: Európa, 19—. Hungarian tranlation.

rr. As: *It*. 4 vols. Russian translation.

ss. As: *It*. Norwegian translation

tt. As: *Oho*. 2 vols. Moscow, Russia: Cadman, 19—. Russian translation.

uu. As: *Oho*. 2 vols.Moscow, Russia: AST, 19__. Russian translation.

vv. As: *To Autó*. Greek translation.

ww. As TELEVISION MINI-SERIES: *It*. Konigsberg/Sanitsky Company In Association with Lorimar Television, 1990. ABC. Executive producers, Jim Green and Allen Epstein. Supervising producer, Matthew O'Connor. Directed by Tommy Lee Wallace. Teleplay by Lawrence D. Cohen, Tommy Lee Wallace [Part 2]. Four-hour mini-series. Sunday, November 18, 1990, 9:00-11:00 PM; Tuesday, November 20, 1990, 9:00-11:00 PM.

CAST: Harry Anderson, Tim Curry, Richard Masur, Annette O'Toole, Tim Reid, John Ritter, Richard Thomas, Dennis Christopher, Olivia Hussey, Jonathan Brandis, Brandon Crane, Adam Faraizi, Seth Green, Ben Heller, Emily Perkins, Marlon Taylor.

SELECTED FILM REVIEWS AND ARTICLES:

"At Least 'It' is Different." *Austin American-Statesman* [TX] 18 November 1990. As microfiche: *Newsbank: Film and Television* Vol. 17 (December 1990): Fiche 137, E11.

"The Best and Worst [of 1990-1991]." *TV Guide* Vol. 39, No. 27 #1997 (6 July 1991): 7. "Best horror thriller: 'Stephen King's It.' (ABC)."

Bianculli, David. "Bozo's Evil Twin." *New York Post* 15 November 1990. As microfiche: *Newsbank: Film and Television* Vol. 17 (December 1990): Fiche 137, E8.

"A Clown as Killer? 'It' Is a Horrible Film." *Washington Times* [D.C.] 16 November 1990. As microfiche: *Newsbank: Film and Television* Vol. 17 (December 1990): Fiche 137, E13.

Farrell, Peter. "Gripping 'It' a Pure Horror Story." *The Oregonian* [Portland OR] 18 November 1990. As microfiche: *Newsbank: Film and Television* Vol. 17 (December 1990): Fiche 137, E9-E10.

Gerber, Eric. "'It' Should Be Scarier." *Houston Post* [TX] 17 November 1990. As microfiche: *Newsbank: Film and Television* Vol. 17 (December 1990): Fiche 137, E12.

"Hazard Ye Not Unto the Depths of 'It'!" *Boston Globe* [MA] 17 November 1990. As microfiche: *Newsbank: Film and Television* Vol. 17 (December 1990): Fiche 137, E7.

Leonard, John. *New York* Vol. 23 (19 November 1990): 113.

Millman, Joyce. "Stephen King Lets Them Have 'IT,'" *San Francisco Examiner* [CA] 19 November 1990. As microfiche: *Newsbank: Film and Television* Vol. 17 (December 1990): Fiche 137, E5-E6.

"Play It Again, Steff." *Castle Rock: The Stephen King Newsletter* Vol. 2, No. 8 (August 1986): 6.

Richmond, Ray. "'It': 'Stand By Me' Meets 'Godzilla,'" *Orange County Register* [CA] 16 November 1990. Reprinted: *Register* [New Haven CT] 16 November 1990.

"Specials." *TV Guide* (9 September 1989): 6. Announcement of schedule for mini-series.

Spignesi, Stephen J. "The Art of Adaptation: A Synoptic Comparison of 'IT' and IT." *The Shape Under the Sheet: The Complete Stephen King Encyclopedia*. Ann Arbor MI: Popular Culture, Ink, May 1991, hardcover. 615-622.

Tucker, Ken. *Entertainment Weekly* (16 November 1990).

TV Guide (November 1990).

Wood, Gary. "IT: Burbank's Fantasy 2 Effects Met the Task of Enlivening the Novel's Horrors, Including Its Shape-shifting Giant Spider." *Cinefantastique* Vol. 21, No. 4 (February 1991): 48-49.

Wood, Gary. "Stephen King's IT." *Cinefantastique* (February 1990).

Zurawik, David. "ABC's 'It': This One Isn't for the Kiddies." *Sun* [Baltimore MD] 18 November 1990. As microfiche: *Newsbank: Film and Television* Vol. 18 (January 1991): Fiche 8, B2-B3.

xx. As videocassette: *It*. Warner Brothers, 1990/1998. VHS cassette (extended play recording); 192 minutes. Rated: Not rated.

COMMENTS: The Viking hardcover sold 1,206,200 copies in 1986; the novel ranked #1 on the Bowker Annual hardcover fiction bestsellers list for 1985. This novel was one of the few King books to receive an international award, receiving the British Fantasy Award for Best Novel.

King considered *IT* a culmination as well as a completion; certainly the novel represents the climax of over a decade of working with monsters (physical and psychological) and threatened children. The novel integrates the fears of childhood with the fears of adulthood and attempts a final resolution. Immediate responses to *IT* varied from acknowledgments of the book as King's masterwork, to scathing denunciations of the novel as overly long, pretentious, and numbingly pat in its final imagery and resolution.

MICHAEL R. COLLINGS

SELECTED ARTICLES, RESPONSES, AND REVIEWS:

Bennet, Ron. *Christian Science Monitor* Vol. 78 (19 September 1986): 21.

Bertin, Eddy C. "*IT* in the Netherlands, or: The Rape of Stephen King." *Castle Rock: The Stephen King Newsletter* Vol. 3, No. 9 (September 1987): 7.

Bleiler, E. F. "Books." *Twilight Zone Magazine* Vol. 6, No. 6 (February 1987): 8-9.

Blue, Tyson. "*IT*: A Journey into the Darkside." *Castle Rock: The Stephen King Newsletter* Vol. 2, No. 11 (November 1986): 1, 3.

Blue, Tyson. "*IT* Marks a Turning Point in King's Career." *Macon Telegraph & News* [Macon GA] 31 August 1986.

Blue, Tyson. "The Truth about *IT*." *Twilight Zone Magazine* Vol. 6, No. 5 (December 1986): 48-49.

Booklist Vol. 82 (15 June 1986): 1474.

Bryant, Edward. "Twilight Zone Review 1986." *Twilight Zone Magazine* Vol. 6, No. 6 (February 1987): 56.

Boston Globe [MA] 23 August 23, 1987.

Collings, Michael R. "*IT*: Stephen King's Comprehensive Masterpiece." *Castle Rock: The Stephen King Newsletter* Vol. 2, No. 7 (July 1986): 1, 4-6. Reprinted in: *The Stephen King Phenomenon*. Reprinted in: *Scaring Us to Death: The Impact of Stephen King on Popular Culture*..

Conner, John W., and Kathleen M. Tessmer. *English Journal* Vol. 77 (January 1988): 101.

Edwards, Thomas R. "Gulp!" *The New York Review of Books* 18 December 1986: 58-59.

Fangoria (March 1987).

Gates, David. "The Creature That Refused to Die." *Newsweek* (1 September 1986): 84.

Goldberg, Whoopi. *Los Angeles Times Book Review* 5 October 1986: B2.

Graham, Mark. "Awakening Childhood Nightmares." *Rocky Mountain News* [Denver CO] 12 October 1986: 34-M.

Grant, Charles L. "It Wasn't a Half Bad Year." *Amazing Stories* (September 1987).

Herron, Don. "Ravening Beast Meets Losers." *Newsday* [Long Island NY] 31 August 1986. As microfiche: *NewsBank: Literature* Vol. 13 (September 1986): Fiche 23, A10-A11.

Herron, Don. "Summation." *Reign of Fear: Fiction and Film of Stephen King*. Edited by Don Herron. Los Angeles CA: Underwood-Miller, June 1988. 209-240.

Hoffman, Barry. "*IT* an ABC Mini-Series: I Shudder at the Thought." *Castle Rock: The Stephen King Newsletter* Vol. 3, No. 11 (November 1987): 7-8.

Hoffman, Barry. "King's Kids...Less than Meets the Eye." *Castle Rock: The Stephen King Newsletter* Vol. 4, No. 7 (July 1988): 3.

Johnson, Eric W. *Library Journal* Vol. 111 (August 1986): 171.

Johnson, Kimball. "Letter." *Castle Rock: The Stephen King Newsletter* Vol. 3, No. 11 (December 1986/January 1987): 7.

Kanfer, Stefan. "King of Horror: The Master of Pop Dread Writes on...and on...and on...and on...." *Time* Vol. 128 (6 October 1986): 74-83.

Kaveney, Roz. *Times Literary Supplement* [London] 5 December 1986: 1368.

Kimberly, Judy. "Horror 'Wonderland.'" *Fantasy Review* No. 93 (July-August 1986): 28-29.

King, Stephen. "Stephen King Comments on It." *Castle Rock: The Stephen King Newsletter* Vol. 2, No. 7 (July 1986): 1, 5.

King, Stephen. "How *IT* Happened." *Book-of-the-Month-Club News* (October 1986).

"King's Latest Much More Than a Horror Novel." *Asbury Park Press* [Neptune NJ] 7 September 1986). As microfiche: *NewsBank: Literature* Vol. 13 (December 1986): Fiche 30, G11.

Kirkus Reviews Vol. 54 (1 June 1986): 811.

Kliatt Young Adults Paperback Book Guide Vol. 22 (January 1988): 11.

Koontz, Dean R. "The Specter of Death Shadows Stephen King's *IT*." *San Jose Mercury News* [CA] 31 August 1986. As microfiche: *NewsBank: Literature* Vol. 13 (December 1986): Fiche 30, G8.

Lai, Jill. "Stephen King's Newest is Creepingly Sinister." *Seattle Post-Intelligencer* [WA] 30 August 1986.

Lehmann-Haupt, Christopher. "Books of the Times." *The New York Times* 135 (21 August 1986): C21. Late edition.

Liberatore, Karen. "Another Ride on the Nightmare Roller Coaster." *San Francisco Examiner* [CA] 24 August 1986. As microfiche: *NewsBank: Literature* Vol. 13 (October 1986): Fiche 30, G6-G7.

Locus (August 1986).

The Magazine of Fantasy & Science Fiction Vol. 71 (November 1986): 18.

Moses, Michael. "Stanley Uris: World's Smallest Adult." *Castle Rock: The Stephen King Newsletter* Vol. 5, No. 7 (July 1989): 3, 10-11.

Moss, Chuck. "This is 'It,' a Scary Book with Real Merit." *Detroit News* [MI] 24 August 1986. As microfiche: *NewsBank: Literature* Vol. 13 (September 1986): Fiche 23, A7.

New Statesman Vol. 112 (12 December 1986): 31.

Norris, Gloria. "The October Selection: IT." *Book-of-the-Month Club News* (October 1986): 2, 4. Introduction to the novel.

Perry, Roy E. "King's 'It' the 'War and Peace' of Horror Stories." *Nashville Banner* [TN] 30 August 1986. As microfiche: *NewsBank: Literature* Vol. 13 (September 1986): Fiche 23, A12-A13.

Podhoretz, John. "An Encounter with the Horror King." *Washington Times* [DC] 25 August 1986. As microfiche: *NewsBank: Literature* Vol. 13 (September 1986): Fiche 23, A14-B1. As: "Stopping 'It' Before It's Too Late." *Insight* (25 August 1986): 68-69.

Publishers Weekly Vol. 229 (27 June 1986): 74.

Reese, Kathleen. "'It' Performs Feats of King-ly Magic." *Dallas Times Herald* [TX] 7 September 1986. As microfiche: *NewsBank: Literature* Vol. 13 (December 1986): Fiche 30, G12-G13.

Ringel, Faye. "Some Notes on It." *Castle Rock: The Stephen King Newsletter* Vol. 3, No. 9 (September 1987): 1, 4.
Rousch, Matt. *USA Today* (1986).
Rose, Lloyd. *Atlantic Monthly* 258 (September 1986): 102.
Sallee, Wayne Allen. "And So It Goes." *Castle Rock: The Stephen King Newsletter* Vol. 2, No. 11 (November 1986): 1, 5.
San Francisco Chronicle [CA] 23 August 1986.
Sarrantonio, Al. *Night Cry* Vol. 2, No. 3 (Spring 1987): 184-185.
Science Fiction Chronicle Vol. 8 (March 1987): 34.
Science Fiction Chronicle Vol. 8 (March 1987): 43.
Terrell, Carroll F. *Stephen King: Man and Artist.* Orono, ME: Northern Lights Publishing, 1990. 239-269.
Thompson, Don C. "This Is 'It,' The Real King: Long-Awaited Book Is Huge and Worth the Wait." *Denver Post* [CO] 7 September 1986. As microfiche: *NewsBank: Literature* Vol. 13 (December 1986): Fiche 30, G9-G10.
Tucker, Ken. "King of Macabre." *Louisville Globe-Democrat* [MO] 23 August 1986. As microfiche: *NewsBank: Literature* Vol. 13 (September 1986): Fiche 23, A8-A9.
Tucker, Ken. "Literature or Pop Fiction? What's the Difference, Eh?" *Birmingham News* [AL] 31 August 1986. As microfiche: *NewsBank: Literature* Vol. 13 (December 1986): Fiche 45, B2-B4.
Village Voice Vol. 32 (3 March 1987): 35.
Wager, Walter. "More Evil Than a 15-Foot Spider." *New York Times Book Review* Vol. 91 (24 August 1986): VII, 9.
Washington Post Book World Vol. 16 (24 August 1986): 1.
Washington Post Book World Vol. 17 (6 December 1987): 19.
West Coast Review of Books Vol. 12, No. 4 (1986): 35.
Wilson School Journal Vol. 208 (13 October 1986): 11.

HORROR PLUM'D

MISERY. New York, NY: Viking, 1987. Hardcover.

A33.
MISERY
(1987)

A33. *MISERY*. New York: Viking, 8 June 1987, 310 pp., $18.95, hardcover. ISBN 0-670-81364-8. Reprinted May 1990.

PLOT SUMMARY: Severely injured in a car accident, novelist Paul Sheldon finds himself at the mercy of his rescuer—a former nurse named Annie Wilkes, who is obsessed with Sheldon's fictional creation, Misery Chastain. Annie's insane determination to keep Sheldon to herself and to force him to resurrect Misery in one final story parallels Sheldon's equally desperate need to escape from Annie's control.

REPRINTS AND ADAPTATIONS:
b. London, England: Stodder & Houghton, September 1987, 320 pp., £11.95, hardcover. 0-340-39070-0.
c. Camp Hill PA: Quality Paperback Book Club, September 1987, 310 pp., $9.50, trade paperback. No ISBN assigned.
d. Utrecht, Belgium, Netherlands: Luitingh-Sijthoff, 1987, 352 pp. Dutch translation by Margot Bakker. ISBN 90-245-1633-1. * 7th printing, 1991. * 8th printing, ISBN 90-245-1918-7.
e. As: *Sie* ['She']. Munich, Germany: Wilhelm Heyne, JUMBO BÄNDE 7500, 41/2, 1987, 19.80 DM, paperback. German translation by Joachim Körber. ISBN 3-453-00289-X.
f. As: *Tsan pu gen tu* [or *Chan li yu hsi*]. Taipei, Taiwan: Kuang kuan chu pan she, 1987. Chinese translation by Wu An-Lan.
g. Milan, Italy: Sperling & Kupfer, PANDORA [#394], May 1988. Italian translation by Tullio Dobner. ISBN 88-200-0768-1.
h. As: *Sie* ['She']. Kornwesterheim, Austria: Europäische Bildungsgemeinschaft; Gütersloh, Austria: Bertelsmann Club; Vienna, Austria: Buchgemeinschaft Donauland; Zug, Switzerland: Buch-und-Schallplattenfreunde, May 1988, 400 pp., paperback. Translated by Joachim Körber. German translation. Book Club editions.
i. New York: Signet/New American Library, June 1988, 339 pp., $4.95, mass-

j. market paperback. ISBN 0-451-16952-2. * 16th printing, November 1990, $5.95. Movie tie-in edition. * 30th printing, 1994. * Reissue, December 1994, 352 pp., $7.99.

j. London/Sevenoaks, England: New English Library, June 1988, 370 pp., £3.50, paperback. Open Market edition not distributed in the U.K. ISBN 0-450-41739-5. * Reprint, November 1988. * Reprint, April 1990, £4.99. Movie tie-in edition. * 17th printing, August 1992, £4.99.

k. Bath, England: Windsor Selection Services/Chivers Press, September 1988, 504 pp., hardcover. Large print edition. ISBN 0-862-20253-1.

l. London, England: New English Library, November 1988, 384 pp., paperback.

m. Boston MA: G. K. Hall, LARGE PRINT CORE COLLECTION, 1988, 491 pp., hardcover and trade paperback. Large print edition.

n. As: *Misery: el riesgo de la fama* ['Misery: the risk/danger of fame']. Buenos Aires, Argentina: Emecé, GRANDES NOVELISTAS, 1988, 330 pp. 22/19 cm. Spanish translation. ISBN 950-04-0805-8. * Reprint, 1990. * Reprint, 1991. * Reprint, 1998.

o. As: *Angústia* ['Anguish/distress']. Rio de Janeiro, Brazil: Francisco Alves, MESTRES DO HORROR E DA FANTASIA, 1988, 345 pp., 22 cm.. Portuguese translation by Marisa Gomes. * 2nd printing, 1991.

p. Barcelona, Spain: Plaza & Janés, 1988, 320 pp., 22 cm. Spanish translation by Maria Mir. ISBN 84-01-32256-1. * 7th printing, 1995, ÉXITOS, ISBN 84-01-32256-1.

q. As: *Lida* ['Suffering']. Höganäs, Sweden: Bra Böcker, 1988, 352 pp. Swedish translation by Lennart Olofsson.

r. As: *Lida* ['Suffering']. Höganäs and Stockholm, Sweden: Legenda, Bra Spänning, 1988. 352 pp., 22 cm., hardcover. Swedish translation by Lennart Olofsson. ISBN 91-582-1178-0.

s. As: *Sie* ['She']. Stuttgart, West Germany: Deutscher Bücherbund, 1988, 400 pp. German translation by Joachim Körber. Book Club edition.

t. As: *Piina*. Helsinki, Finland: Tammi, 1989, 312 pp., 23 cm. Finnish translation by Ilkka Rekiaro. ISBN 951-30-8932-0. * 2nd printing, 1991.

u. Paris, France: Albin Michel, 1989, 391 pp., 98 F, paperback. French translation by William Olivier Desmond. ISBN 2-226-03673-3.

v. [Paris], France: [le Grande livre du mois], 1989, 391 pp., 98 F, hardcover. French translation by William Olivier Desmond. Book Club edition.

w. Barcelona, Spain: Círculo de Lectores, 1989, 333 pp., 23 cm. Spanish translation by María Ruiz. ISBN 84-226-3030-3.

x. Copenhagen, Denmark: Artia, 1990, 296 pp., 268 KR, paperback. Danish translation by Anders Westenholz. ISBN 87-89294-37-8.

y. Paris, France: France Loisirs, 1990, 391 pp., 78 F, hardcover. French translation by William Olivier Desmond. ISBN 2-7242-4749-3.

z. [Lisbon, Portugal]: Círculo de Leitores, 1990, 358 pp., 21 cm. Portuguese translation by Magda Viana. ISBN 972-42-0055-8.

aa. Barcelona, Spain: Plaza & Janés, JET 102, BIBLIOTECA DE STEPHEN KING #

14, 1990, 346 pp., 18 cm, paperback. Spanish translation by Maríia Mir. ISBN 84-01-49894-5.
bb. As: *Lida* ['Suffering']. [Stockholm, Sweden]: Legenda, 1990. 352 pp., 18 cm., paperback. Swedish translation by Lennart Olofsson. ISBN 91-582-1724-X.
cc. Milan, Italy: Sperling Paperback, SUPERBESTSELLER #114, January 1991, paperback. Italian translation by Tullio Dobner. ISBN 88-7824-132-6.
dd. Paris, France: J'ai Lu, ÉPOUVANTE #3112, 1991, 439 pp., 34 F, paperback. French translation by William Olivier Desmond. ISBN 2-277-23112-6.
ee. Warsaw, Poland: "Amber," HORROR, 1991, 333 pp., 21 cm. Polish translation by Robert P. Lipski. ISBN 83-8507-984-X.
ff. As: *Kidnappet* ['Kidnapped']. Oslo, Norway: Hjemmet, 1991, 311 pp. Norwegian translation by Jan Nergaard. ISBN 82-590-0715-0.
gg. As: [Title unknown]. South Korea, 1991, 342 pp., 23 cm. Korean translation.
hh. As: *The Shining/Carrie/Misery*: London, England: Chancellor Press, September 1992, 686 pp., £6.99, paperback. Omnibus edition. ISBN 1-85152-247-6.
ii. Copenhagen, Denmark: Bogklubben 12 Bøger, 1992, 296 pp. Danish translation by Anders Westenholz. ISBN 87-89327616. Book Club edition.
jj. As: *Kidnappet* ['Kidnapped']. Oslo, Norway: Hjemmets Bokforlag, EGMONT SPENNING #16, 1993, 310 pp., hardcover. Norwegian translation by Jan Nergaard. ISBN 82-04-03016-9.
kk. Barcelona, Spain: Àrea/Columna, EN EL LOMO #112, 1993, 283 pp., 24 cm. Spanish translation by Esteve Riambau I Saurí. ISBN 84-7783-037-1.
ll. Paris, France: France Loisirs, 1994, 391 pp., 96 F, hardcover. French translation by William Olivier Desmond. ISBN 2-7242-7845-3.
mm. Amsterdam, Netherlands: Poema Pocket, 1994, 352 pp., paperback. Dutch translation by Margot Bakker. 11th printing. ISBN 90-245-1279-4.
nn. Barcelona, Spain: Plaza & Janés, JET 224/14, BIBLIOTECA DE STEPHEN KING #14, 1994, 334 pp., 18 cm., paperback. Spanish translation by María Mir. ISBN 84-01-49997-6. * 8th printing, JET 102/14, BIBLIOTECA DE STEPHEN KING #14, ISBN 84-01-49997-6. * Reprint, 1998, 372 pp., ISBN 84 01 49997-6.
oo. As: *Misery/Maleficio*. Barcelona, Spain: Plaza & Janés, 1994, 346 + 332 pp., 19 cm. Spanish translations by María Mir and Lorenzo Cortina. ISBN 84-01-46107-3.
pp. Barcelona, Spain: Orbis, NOVELAS DE CINE, 1995, 320 pp., 21 cm. Spanish translation by María Mir. ISBN 84-402-1855-9.
qq. Milan, Italy: Arnoldo Mondadori, I MITI #54, August 1996. Italian translation by Tullio Dobner. ISBN 88-04-41344-1.
rr. As: *Sie* ['She']. Munich, Germany: Wilhelm Heyne, 1996, 413 pp. German translation.
ss. As: *Kidnappet* ['Kidnapped']. Oslo, Norway: Egmont Hjemmets, 1996, 311 pp., 179.00, hardcover [*innbundet*]. Norwegian translation by Jan Nergaard. ISBN 82-59-01655-9.

tt. Barcelona, Spain: Orbis, 1996, 320 pp., 22 cm. Spanish translation by María Mir. ISBN 84-402-2058-8.
uu. Barcelona, Spain: Plaza & Janès, 1996, 373 pp., 18 cm., paperback. Spanish translation by Mar ía Mir. ISBN 84-01-24219-3.
vv. [Valby], Denmark: Vinten/DBK, VINTENS PAPERBACKS, [1997], 282 pp., 88 KR, paperback. Danish translation by Anders Westenholz. ISBN 87-612-0162-6.
ww. Warsaw, Poland: "Amber," SREBRNA SERIA, 1997, 333 pp., 21 cm. Polish translation by Robert P. Lipski. ISBN 83-7169-278-1.
xx. Tartu, [Estonia?], and Tallinn, Estonia: Elmatar/Tallinna Raamatutrükikoda, 1998, 399 pp., 16 cm. Estonian translation by Jüri Kallas and Evelyn Mikenberg. ISBN 9985832817.
yy. Milan, Italy: Sperling Paperback, SUPERBESTSELLER, August 1999. Italian translation by Tullio Dobner. ISBN 88-7824-132-6.
zz. As: *Sie* ['She']. Munich, Germany: Wilhelm Heyne TB 13108, August 1999, 16.90 DM, paperback. German translation. ISBN 3-453-16293-5.
aaa. As: [Title unknown]. Israel: Modan, 19—. Hebrew translation.
bbb. As: [Title unknown]: Russia: Cadman, 19—. [2 separate editions].
ccc. As: *Tortúra*. Hungary: Árkádia. Hungarian translation.
ddd. As: *Tortúra*. Budapest, Hungary: Európa. Hungarian translation.

eee. As AUDIOCASSETTE: New York: Penguin Audiobooks, June 1995, $30.00. Read by Lindsay Crouse. 8 cassettes. ISBN 0-453-00927-1.
fff. As AUDIOCASSETTE: Los Angeles CA: Dove Entertainment, November 1995, $49.95. Spanish translation read by Jaime Ortiz Pino. ISBN 0-787-10604-6.

ggg. As FILM: Castle Rock Entertainment Association with Nelson Entertainment/Columbia. 30 November 1990. Produced by Andrew Scheinman, Rob Reiner. Directed by Rob Reiner. Screenplay by William Goldman. 105 minutes. Rated R.
CAST: James Caan, Cathy Bates, Richard Farnsworth, Frances Sternhagen, Lauren Bacall.
COMMENTS: The film earned an Academy Award for Best Supporting Actress for Cathy Bates. The film marks Reiner as the first filmmaker to direct two films from King's stories; both *Misery* and *Stand by Me* received wide-ranging and enduring popular and critical acclaim.
SELECTED ARTICLES, RESPONSES, AND REVIEWS:
Beahm, George. "It Is the Tale and He Who Tells It." *The Shape Under the Sheet: The Complete Stephen King Encyclopedia*. Ann Arbor MI: Popular Culture, Ink, May 1991. 612.
Bernard, Jami. "The Joys of 'Misery.'" *New York Post* 30 November 1990.
Caan, James. Interview. *Details Magazine* (December 1990).
Carroll, Kathleen. "'Misery' Checks in at Kathy Bates' Motel." *New York Daily News* 30 November 1990.

Clark, Mike. "Reiner's 'Misery' Makes Scary Company." *USA Today* 30 November 1990.
Ebert, Roger. "'Misery' Works, But King's Tale Holds Director Back." *Chicago Sun Times* [IL] 30 November 1990. As microfiche: *Newsbank: Film and Television* Vol. 18 (January 1991): Fiche 6, D1.
Falk, Sally. "Novelist Is Terrorized by Fan." *Indianapolis Star* [IN] 30 November 1990. As microfiche: *Newsbank: Film and Television* Vol. 17 (December 1990): Fiche 134, B14-C1.
Farber, Stephen. *Movieline* (December 1990).
Gleiberman, Owen. *Entertainment Weekly* 30 November 1990.
Graham, Mark. "Horror Writer Revisits State in 'Misery,'" *Rocky Mountain News* [Denver CO] 29 November 1990. As microfiche: *Newsbank: Film and Television* Vol. 18 (January 1991): Fiche 5, E5.
Johnson, Malcolm. "Makers Add Depth to 'Misery,'" *Hartford Courant* [CT] 30 November 1990. As microfiche: *Newsbank: Film and Television* Vol. 17 (December 1990): Fiche 134, B10-B11.
Johnson, Malcolm. "'Misery' Chilling Mix of Terror, Humor." *Hartford Courant* [CT] 30 November 1990. As microfiche: *Newsbank: Film and Television* Vol. 17 (December 1990): Fiche 134, B12.
"The Joys of 'Misery,'" *Detroit News* [MI] 30 November 1990. As microfiche: *Newsbank: Film and Television* Vol. 17 (December 1990): Fiche 134, C7.
Klinghoffer, David. "'Misery' Just Doesn't Get to Heart of Matters." *Washington Times* [DC] 30 November 1990. As microfiche: *Newsbank: Film and Television* Vol. 17 (December 1990): Fiche 134, C8.
Mahar, Ted. "This Love Isn't a Novel Idea." *The Oregonian* [Portland OR] 30 November 1990. As microfiche: *Newsbank: Film and Television* Vol. 18 (January 1991): Fiche 6, D2.
Movshowitz, Howie. "'Misery' Loves Erratic Fan's Company." *Denver Post* [CO] 30 November 1990. As microfiche: *Newsbank: Film and Television* Vol. 18 (January 1991): Fiche 6, C14.
Ringel, Eleanor. "Getting a Kick Out of 'Misery,'" *Atlanta Journal-Constitution* [GA] 30 November 1990. As microfiche: *Newsbank: Film and Television* Vol. 17 (December 1990): Fiche 134, B13.
Schickel, Richard. "Deadly Game of Nursing Care." *Time* (10 December 1990).
Sharkey, Betsy. "'Misery's' Company Loves a Good Time: Filming the Stephen King Thriller Is Serious Business with Time Out for a Laugh." *The New York Times* Vol. 139 (17 June 1990): H13.
Stark, Susan. "Tender, Loving Cruelty." *Detroit News* [MI] 30 November 1990. As microfiche: *Newsbank: Film and Television* Vol. 17 (December 1990): Fiche 134, C5-C6.

Strauss, Bob. "Going for the Scare Diminishes 'Misery,'" *Daily News* [Los Angeles CA] 30 November 1990. As microfiche: *Newsbank: Film and Television* Vol. 18 (January 1991): Fiche 6, C11.

Strauss, Bob. "What Scares Stephen King?" *Daily News* [Los Angeles CA] 29 November 1990. As microfiche: *Newsbank: Film and Television* Vol. 17 (December 1990): Fiche 134, B8-B9.

Sragow, Michael. "Not-So-Sweet Misery." *San Francisco Examiner* [CA] 30 November 1990. As microfiche: *Newsbank: Film and Television* Vol. 18 (January 1991): Fiche 6, C12-C13.

Verniere, James. "Menacing 'Misery,'" *Boston Herald* [MA] 30 November 1990. As microfiche: *Newsbank: Film and Television* Vol. 17 (December 1990): Fiche 134, C2-C4.

Wood, Gary. "Directing the Blood and Gore: 'Misery.'" *Cinefantastique* Vol. 21, No. 4 (February 1991).

Wood, Gary. "Hard Hitting Makeup Effects." *Cinefantastique* Vol. 21, No. 4 (February 1991): 23.

Wood, Gary. "Rob Reiner on Stephen King." *Cinefantastique* Vol. 21, No. 4 (February 1991): 21.

Wood, Gary. "Stephen King's Misery." *Cinefantastique* Vol. 21, No. 3 (February 1990).

Wood, Gary. "To Splatter or Not to Splatter: Rob Reiner Sounds as Tortured as Lady Macbeth." *Cinefantastique* Vol. 21, No. 4 (February 1991): 16-22.

Wuntsch, Philip. "Adding 'Misery' to Holiday Cheer." *Dallas Morning News* [TX] 30 November 1990. As mircofiche: *Newsbank: Film and Television* Vol. 18 (January 1991): Fiche 6, D3.

hhh. As VIDEOCASSETTE: Castle Rock Entertainment, with Nelson Entertainment, 1990. 107 minutes.
SELECTED ARTICLES, RESPONSES, AND REVIEWS:
Forer, Bruce. *Entertainment Weekly* No. 77 (2 August 1991): 64.
"Sun Screening." *Entertainment Weekly* No. 77 (2 August 1991): 67. Notes that Misery is no. 1 on the rental charts for the previous week, moving up from #3.

COMMENTS: 819,486 hardcover copies were sold in 1987; the novel ranked #4 on the *Bowker Annual* hardcover fiction bestseller list. King was represented on that list by *The Tommyknockers* (#1) and *The Eyes of the Dragon* (#10)—the three titles appearing simultaneously. The novel tied with Robert McCammon's *Swan Song* for the Bram Stoker Award [Horror Writers of America], June 1988, one of the few awards King has won. King has subsequently noted that *Misery* was originally intended to be published as a 'Richard Bachman' book.

A sparse, sharply defined treatment of the horrors implicit in being a public figure, and thereby considered public property, *Misery* is the stronger for its focus on two central and antithetical characters and its meticulous examination

HORROR PLUM'D

of the horrors of real life. The most frightening thing about the novel is the reader's subtle yet inevitable realization, supported by almost any evening news broadcast, that Annie Wilkes may be only a pale reflection of monsters who actually live among us.

SELECTED ARTICLES, RESPONSES, AND REVIEWS:
Allen, Jerry. "The Master of Disaster Hits Rock Bottom." *Virginian-Pilot* [Norfolk VA] 31 May 1987. As microfiche: *NewsBank: Literature* Vol. 13 (June 1987): Fiche 110, D9.
Amantia, A. M. B. *Library Journal* (1 May 1987): 83.
Booklist Vol. 83 (1 April 1987): 1153.
Beaulieu, Janet C. "A Book, and an Author to Be Taken Seriously." *Bangor Daily News* [ME] 9 June 1987. As microfiche: *NewsBank: Literature* Vol. 14 (July 1987): Fiche 7, B10.
Blue, Tyson. "Misery King's Most Horrifying Tale Yet." *Telegraph and News* "Books/The Arts" [Macon GA] 3 May 1987: 10E, 14E.
Books (September 1987): 11.
Book Report Vol. 6 (March 1988): 34.
Book World 14 June 1987: 1.
Brown, Jerry Earl. "Serious as Well as Scary." *Denver Post* [CO] 5 July 1987). As microfiche: *NewsBank: Literature* Vol. 14 (August 1987): Fiche 20, B11-B12.
Budrys, Algis. "Stephen King Bares His Soul (Maybe) in 'Misery.'" *Chicago Sun Times* [IL] 21 June 1987. As microfiche: *NewsBank: Literature* Vol. 14 (August 1987): Fiche 20, B13-B14.
Card, Orson Scott. "Books to Look for." *The Magazine of Fantasy & Science Fiction* (November 1987): 34-38.
Christian Science Monitor (3 July 1987): B4.
Craig, Paul. "Stephen King Does It Again." *Sacramento Bee* [CA] 21 June 1987. As microfiche: *NewsBank: Literature* Vol. 14 (August 1987): Fiche 20, B9-B10.
Dailey, Janet. "Book-Within-a-Book Lets Reader Get Inside Creative Writer's Mind." *Chicago Tribune* [IL] 17 May 1987: Section 14, 3. As microfiche: *NewsBank: Literature* Vol. 13 (June 1987): Fiche 110, D8.
de Lint, Charles. "Urban Thrills: Reviews of Short Horror and Contemporary Fantasy Fiction." *Short Form* [Greensboro NC] Vol. 1, Nos. 3/4 (1989): 56-70. Includes *Misery* on the "Best of the Year" list.
Duffy, Thom. "One Writer's 'Misery' Is Sure-Fire Horror." *Orlando Sentinel* [FL] 7 June 1987. As microfiche: *NewsBank: Literature* Vol. 14 (July 1987): Fiche 7, B8.
Flewelling, Lynn. "King Working on Book He Believes Could Be His Best." *Bangor Daily News* [ME] 11 September 1990. As Microfiche: *NewsBank: Names in the News* Vol. 12 (October 1990): Fiche 272, B9.

Geoghegan, Bill. "Stephen King's Latest Not for the Squeamish." *Washington Times* [DC] (6 July 1987. As microfiche: *NewsBank: Literature* Vol. 14 (July 1987): Fiche 7, C3-C4.

Graham, Mark. "King Shares 'Misery,' and Reader Grimaces." *Rocky Mountain News* [Denver CO] 21 June 1987. 28-M.

Harris, Ian. "Misery on Stage?" *Castle Rock: The Stephen King Newsletter* Vol. 3, No. 10 (October 1987): 3, 6.

Hogan, Patricia. "Misery...No Way!" *Castle Rock: The Stephen King Newsletter* Vol. 3, No. 4 (April/May 1987): 5.

Katzenbach, John. "Summer Reading: Sheldon Gets the Ax." *The New York Times Book Review* Vol. 92 (31 May 1987): VII, 20.

Keller, Scott A. "'Misery' Is Stephen King at His Terrifying Best." *Atlanta Journal-Constitution* 7 June 1987. As microfiche: *NewsBank: Literature* Vol. 14 (July 1987): Fiche 7, B9.

Kies, Cosette. *Voice of Youth Advocates* (10 February 1988): 281.

King, Tabitha. "Co-Miser-A-Ting with Stephen King." *Castle Rock: The Stephen King Newsletter* Vol. 3, No. 8 (August 1987): 1, 5.

Kirkus Reviews Vol. 55 (1 April 1987): 502.

Krim, Seymour. "Forced to Compose at Blowtorch-Point." *Newsday* [Long Island NY] 5 July 1987. As microfiche: *NewsBank: Literature* Vol. 14 (July 1987): Fiche 7, B12-13.

Lehmann-Haupt, Christopher. "Books of the Times." *The New York Times* Vol. 136 (8 June 1987): C 17.

Lehmann-Haupt, Christopher. "A King of Mystery Makes a Masterpiece of 'Misery.'" *Fairbanks Daily News-Miner* [AK] 21 June 1987. As microfiche: *NewsBank: Literature* Vol. 14 (July 1987): Fiche 7, B6-B7.

Liberatore, Karen. "King Whines and Oinks All the Way to the Bank." *San Francisco Examiner* [CA] 29 May 1987. As microfiche: *NewsBank: Literature* Vol. 13 (June 1987): Fiche 110, D5.

Listener Vol. 118 (24 September 1987): 22.

London Review of Books Vol. 10 (21 April 1988): 22.

Los Angeles Times Book Review 10 May 1987: 8.

Lowell, David M. "A KING-size Remedy That Worked!" *Castle Rock: The Stephen King Newsletter* Vol. 3, No. 9 (September 1987): 3.

Macknee, Salem. "King Serves Up His Own Nightmare." *The News and Observer* [Raleigh NC] 19 July 1987. As microfiche: *NewsBank: Literature* Vol. 14 (August 1987): Fiche 20, C1.

The Magazine of Fantasy & Science Fiction Vol. 73 (October 1987): 27.

The Magazine of Fantasy & Science Fiction Vol. 73 (October 1987): 36.

Miller, G. Wayne. "'Misery' Will Take Good Care of King's Horror Fans." *Journal* [Providence RI] 14 June 1987. As microfiche: *NewsBank: Literature* Vol. 14 (July 1987): Fiche 7, C2-C3.

Moore, J. R. T. "The Writer and His Shadow." *SFRA Newsletter* No. 182 (November 1990): 38-39.

Morrison, Michael A. "The Year in Horror, 1987." *Science Fiction & Fantasy*

Book Review Annual. Edited by Robert A. Collins and Robert Latham. Westport, CT: Meckler, 1988. 30-31.
Newman, Kim. *New Statesman* (11 September 1987): 30.
The New York Times Book Review Vol. 93 (12 June 1988): 38.
Paul, Steve. "A New Conquest for King Bibliophiles." *Kansas City Star* [MO] 7 June 1987. As microfiche: *NewsBank: Literature* Vol. 14 (July 1987): Fiche 7, B11.
Perry, Vern. "King's Latest Is Trip Down Thriller Lane." *Orange County Register* [Santa Ana CA] 24 May 1987. As microfiche: *NewsBank: Literature* Vol. 13 (June 1987): Fiche 110, D6-D7.
Pluto, Terry. "'Misery' Loves Company." *Akron Beacon Journal* [OH] 28 June 1987. As microfiche: *NewsBank: Literature* Vol. 14 (July 1987): Fiche 7, B14.
Publishers Weekly Vol. 231 (1 May 1987): 52.
Publishers Weekly Vol. 233 (25 March 1988): 63.
Sarrantonio, Al. "Horrors Red." *Mystery Scene* No. 10 (1987): 35-36.
Smith, Wendy. "King King of Popular Novelists." *Cleveland Plain Dealer* [OH] 24 May 1987. As microfiche: *NewsBank: Literature* Vol. 14 (July 1987): Fiche 7, C1.
Streitfield, David. "Stephen King's No. 1 Fans." *Washington Post* "Style" 8 May 1987.
Time Vol. 129 (8 June 1987): 82.
Washington Post Book World Vol. 17 (14 June 1987): 1.
Washington Post Book World Vol. 17 (6 December 1987): 19.
Wilson School Journal Vol. 209 (23 June 1987): 28.
Young, Elizabeth J. *New Statesman & Society* Vol. 3 (7 December 1990): 34.

The Dark Tower II: The Drawing of the Three. West Kingston, RI: Donald M. Grant, Publisher, 1987. Trade hardcover.

A34.
THE DARK TOWER II: THE DRAWING OF THE THREE
(1987)

A34. THE DARK TOWER II: THE DRAWING OF THE THREE. Illustrated by Phil Hale. West Kingston RI: Donald M. Grant, Publisher, May 1987, 400 pp., $35.00, hardcover. Illustrated by Phil Hale. ISBN 0-937986-91-7. Epic-Fantasy novel. * LETTERED STATE, 35 copies (A-Z, AA-II). * DELUXE LIMITED EDITION, $100.00, hardcover, 850 copies (800 offered for sale), numbered and signed by King and Hale, dust jacket and slipcase, ISBN 0-937986-90-9. * TRADE EDITION, $35.00, 30,000 copies, hardcover, ISBN 0-937-986-91-7. * 2nd edition, 1998, in boxed set with DTI and DTIII.

COMMENTS: The second volume in King's epic-quest-in-progress, The Dark Tower [see also A17, A43, and A61]

REPRINTS AND ADAPTATIONS:
b. Excerpted in: *Castle Rock: The Stephen King Newsletter* Vol. 3, No. 4 (April/May 1987): 1, 8-9, 11, 13.
c. London, England: Sphere, September 1988, 224 pp., paperback.
d. New York: Plume/New American Library, March 1989, 399 pp., $12.95, trade paperback. Illustrated by Phil Hale. ISBN 0-452-26214-3.
e. London, England: Sphere Overseas, May 1989, 400 pp., £6.99, trade paperback. ISBN 0-7474-0102-0. Open market edition, not distributed in the UK.
f. London, England: Sphere, September 1989, 400 pp., £6.99, trade paperback. Cover art by John Avon. ISVN 0-7474-0102-0. 1st edition in the UK.
g. As: *Drei: Der Dunkle Turm 2* ['Three: the dark tower 2']. Munich, Germany: Wilhelm Heyne, HEYNE-JUMBO-BÄNDE #41/14, 1989, 461 pp., paperback. German translation by Joachim Körber. ISBN 3-453-03271-3.
h. As: *Drei* ['Three']. Gütersloh, Austria: Bertelsmann Lesering, 1989, 461 pp., hardcover. German translation by Joachim Körber. Book Club Edition.

Michael R. Collings

i. As: *De donkere Toren II: Het Teken van de Drie* ['The dark tower 2: the token/sign of the three']. Utrecht, Belgium: Luitingh-Sijthoff, 1989, 413 pp. . Dutch translation by Hugo Timmerman. 1st Dutch edition. ISBN 90-245-1804-0. * 2nd printing, 1990, ISBN 90-245-1804-0.

j. New York: Signet/New American Library, January 1990, 463 pp., $5.95, mass-market paperback. No illustrations. ISBN 0-451-16352-4. * Reprint, June 1997. * 25th printing, November 1998.

k. Book-of-the-Month Club selection.

l. London, England: Sphere Overseas, May 1990, 400 pp., £3.99, trade paperback. Cover art by John Avon. ISBN 0-7474-0101-2. Open market edition not distributed in the UK.

m. As: *La chiamata dei tre* ['The call/summons of the three']. Milan, Italy: Sperling & Kupfer, PANDORA [#502], June 1990. Italian translation by Tullio Dobner. ISBN 88-200-1030-5.

n. London, England: Sphere, November 1990, 400 pp., £3.99, paperback. Cover art by John Avon; no illustrations. ISBN 0-7474-0101-2.

o. As: *La Invocación: La torre oscura 2* ['The invoking: the dark tower 2']. Barcelona, Spain: Ediciones B, ÉXITO INTERNACIONAL, 1990 (imp. 1994), 471 pp., 24 cm. Spanish translation by Cecilia Absatz. ISBN 84-406-1205-2. * 3rd printing, 1998, ISBN 84-406-1205-2.

p. As: *La Invocación: La torre oscura 2* ['The invoking: the dark tower 2']. Barcelona, Spain: Círculo de Lectores, 1990, 489 pp., 22 cm. Spanish translation. ISBN 84-226-3425-2.

q. As: *Det svarta tornet: Följeslagarna—2* [The dark tower: companions—2']. Stockholm, Sweden: Legenda 1990, 462 pp., 22 cm., hardcover. Swedish translation by Lennart Olofsson. ISBN 91-582-1511-5.

r. As: *Udvælgelsen: Det mørke tårn 2* ['Collection: The dark tower 2']. Copenhagen, Denmark: Artia, 1991, 483 pp., 298 KR, paperback. Danish translation by Mogens Wenzel Andreasen. ISBN 87-89294-42-4.

s. As: *Det svarta tornet: Följeslagarna—2* ['The dark tower: companions—2']. [Stockholm], Sweden: Legenda 1991, 462 pp., 22 cm., hardcover. Swedish translation by Lennart Olofsson. ISBN 91-582-1743-6.

t. As: *Les trois cartes* ['The three cards']. Paris, France: J'ai Lu, SCIENCE FICTION #3037, 1991, 498 pp., 37 F, paperback. French translation by Gérard Lebec. ISBN 2-277-23037-5.

u. As BOXED EDITION: *The Dark Tower: The Gunslinger, The Drawing of the Three, The Waste Lands.* New York: Plume, October 1992, trade paperback. ISBN 0-451-15346-8.

v. As: *La Invocación: La torre oscura 2* ['The invoking—the dark tower 2']. Barcelona, Spain: Ediciones B, VIB #13/2, 1992, 509 pp., 18 cm., paperback. Spanish translation by Cecilia Absatz. 1st edition in this format. ISBN 84-406-3014-X.

w. As: *Musta torni 2—Kolme korttia pakasta.* ['Black tower 2—pack the third card'(?)]']. Helsinki, Finland: Book Studio, 1993, 500 pp. Finnish translation by Kari Salminen. ISBN 951-611-545-4; 951-611-592-6.

x. As: *Les trois cartes* ['The three cards']. Paris, France: Éditions de la Seine, 1994, 498 pp., 79 F, hardcover. French translation by Gérard Lebec. ISBN 2-7382-0675-1.

y. As: *La tour sombrei* ['The dark tower']. Paris, France: France Loisirs, 1994, 1169 pp., 118 F, hardcover. French translations by Gérard Lebec, Jean-Daniel Brèque and Christiane Poulain. ISBN 2-7242-8191-8. Omnibus with *Le pistolero, Les troi cartes* and *Terres perdues.*

z. As: *Det svarta tornet: Följeslagarna—2.* ['The dark tower: Companions—2']. Stockholm, Sweden: Natur och Kultur, NOK POCKET, 1994, 462 pp., paperback. Swedish translation by Lennart Olofsson. ISBN 91-27-03921-8.

aa. As: *La chiamata dei tre* ['The call/summons of the three']. Milan, Italy: Sperling Paperback, SUPERBESTSELLER #436, May 1995, paperback. Italian translation by Tullio Dobner. ISBN 88-7824-414-7.

bb. As BOXED EDITION: *The Dark Tower: The Gunslinger, The Drawing of the Three, The Waste Lands.* New York: New American Library, September 1997, $23.97, mass-market paperback. ISBN 0-451-93554-3.

cc. New York: Plume, November 1997, $16.95, trade paperback. Reprint edition, 5th printing. ISBN 0-452-27961-5.

dd. As: *Drei: Der Dunkle Turm 2* ['Three: the dark tower 2']. Munich, Germany: Wilhelm Heyne #10429, November 1997, 16.90 DM, paperback. German translation by Joachim Körber. ISBN 3-453-12385-9.

ee. As BOXED EDITION: *The Dark Tower: The Gunslinger, The Drawing of the Three, The Waste Lands.* New York: New American Library, September 1997, $110.00, 3 slipcased hardcovers. Gift Set.

ff. London, England: New English Library, December 1997, 455 pp., £6.99, paperback. Cover art by Bob Warner. ISBN 0-340-70751-8.

gg. As: *Het Teken van de Drie: De donkere Toren II* ['The token/sign of the three']. Amsterdam, Netherlands: Poema Pocket, 1997, 413 pp., paperback. Dutch translation by Hugo Timmerman. 7th printing. ISBN 90-245-2738-4.

hh. As: *Drei* ['Three']. Rheda-Wiedenbrück, Germany: Bertelsmann-Club, 1998, 381 pp., hardcover. German translation by Joachim Körber. Book Club Edition.

ii. As: *Udvælgelsen: Det mørke tårn 2* ['Collection: the dark tower 2']. Copenhagen, Denmark: Vinten, VINTENS PAPERBACKS/VINTENS FANTASY, 1998, 371 pp., 98 KR, paperback. Danish translation by Mogens Wenzel Andreasen. ISBN 87-612-0167-7.

jj. As: *Musta torni 1-3.* ['Black tower 1-3']. Helsinki, Finland: Book Studio, 1998, 654 pp. Finnish translation . ISBN 951-611-901-8.

kk. As: *Les trois cartes* ['The three cards']. Paris, France: Éditions 84, 1998, 390 pp., 95 F, paperback. French translation by Gérard Lebec. ISBN 2-277-25033-3.

ll. As: *Het teken van drie* ['The sign/token of three']. Amsterdam, Netherlands: Luitingh-Sijthoff, 1998, 333 pp., Dutch translation by Claartje van Westerop. 9th printing. ISBN 90-245-1366-9.

mm. As: *The Dark Tower.* West Kingston RI: Donald M. Grant, February 1999,

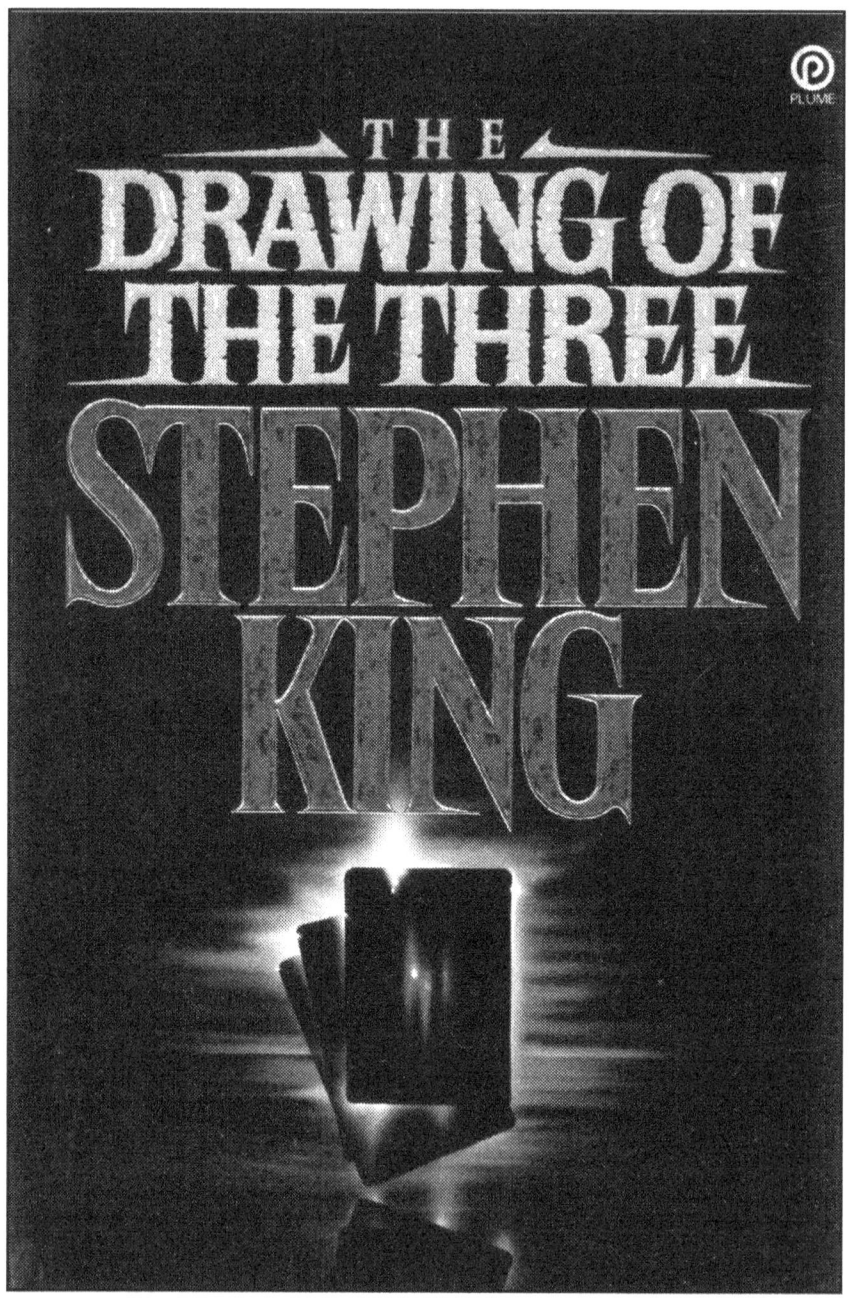

The Dark Tower II: The Drawing of the Three. New York, NY: Plume/New American Library, 1989. Trade paperback.

$117.00, boxed set containing *The Gunslinger*, 3rd printing; *The Drawing of the Three*, 2nd edition; and *The Waste Lands*. ISBN 1-880418-40-1.
nn. As: [Title unknown'].Moscow, Russia: AST, 19—. Russian translation
oo. As: *La Chiamata dei Tre* [The call/summons of the three']. Milan, Italy: Sperling & Kupfer. Italian translation.

pp. As AUDIOCASSETTE: *The Dark Tower II: The Drawing of the Three*. New Audio Library, 1988/1989. Read by Stephen King. 8 cassettes; 720 minutes. Unabridged. * LIMITED EDITION, 1988/1989, $125, 800 numbered sets, signed by King.
SELECTED ARTICLES, RESPONSES, AND REVIEWS:
AudioVideo Review Digest, 1989 Cumulation. Edited by Susan L. Stetler. Detroit MI: Gale Research, 1990. 619.
Blue, Tyson. "Dark Tower II Audio Tapes Released." *Castle Rock: The Stephen King Newsletter* Vol. 5, No. 3 (March 1989): 2, 6.
*Booklist.*Vol. 85 (15 June 1989): 1841.
Sweeting, Paul, and John Zinsser. *Publishers Weekly* Vol. 235 (3 March 1989): 76.
qq. As AUDIOCASSETTE: New York: Penguin Audiobooks, May 1998, $35.95. Unabridged. Read by Frank Muller. ISBN 0-140-86715-5.

SELECTED ARTICLES, RESPONSES, AND REVIEWS:
Beaulieu, Janet C. "Road to Dark Tower Powerful, Intense." *Bangor Daily News* [ME] 11 July 1989. As microfiche: *NewsBank: Literature* Vol. 16 (August 1989): Fiche 80, C14-D1.
Bertin, Eddy C. "DT Books Make Dutch Appearance." *Castle Rock: The Stephen King Newsletter* Vol. 5, No. 12 (December 1989).
Blue, Tyson. "Review: The Dark Tower II: The Drawing of the Three." *Castle Rock: The Stephen King Newsletter* Vol. 3, No. 7 (July 1987): 1, 7, 8.
Booklist Vol. 85 (15 December 1988): 666.
Condon, Garrett. "King's 'Other' Publisher Well-Kept Collector's Secret." *Hartford Courant* [CT] 28 August 1987. As microfiche: *NewsBank: Literature* Vol. 13 (October 1987): Fiche 41, E4-E5.
Coven, Laurence. "King Draws a Bead on New York City." *Daily News* [Los Angeles CA] 16 July 1989. As microfiche: *NewsBank: Literature Vol. 16 (August 1989)*: Fiche 80, C12-13.
de Lint, Charles. *Science Fiction & Fantasy Book Review Annual*. Edited by Robert A. Collins and Robert Latham. Westport, CT: Meckler, 1988, hardcover. 226-227.
Easton, Tom. *Analog Science Fiction-Science Fact* Vol. 109 (September 1989): 181+.
Fuller, Richard. *The New York Times* (8 January 1989): VII, 18.
Inside Books: The Bestseller Magazine (March 1989).
Kirkus Reviews Vol. 57 (1 January 1989): 8.
Locus Vol. 22 (May 1989): 48.

Miller, Faren. "*Dark Tower 2: The Drawing of the Three*, Stephen King." *Locus* Vol. 20, No. 8, #319 (August 1987).
Publishers Weekly Vol. 235 (13 January 1989): 86.
Ruiz, Estelle. "The King/Roland Quest." *Castle Rock: The Stephen King Newsletter* Vol. 3, No. 12/Vol. 4, No. 1 (December 1987-January 1988): 3, 13.
Science Fiction Chronicle Vol. 9 (October 1987): 39.
Voice of Youth Advocates Vol. 13 (June 1990): 138.
West Coast Review of Books Vol. 13, No. 3 (1987): 60.
West Coast Review of Books Vol. 14, No. 4 (1989): 25.

Horror Plum'd

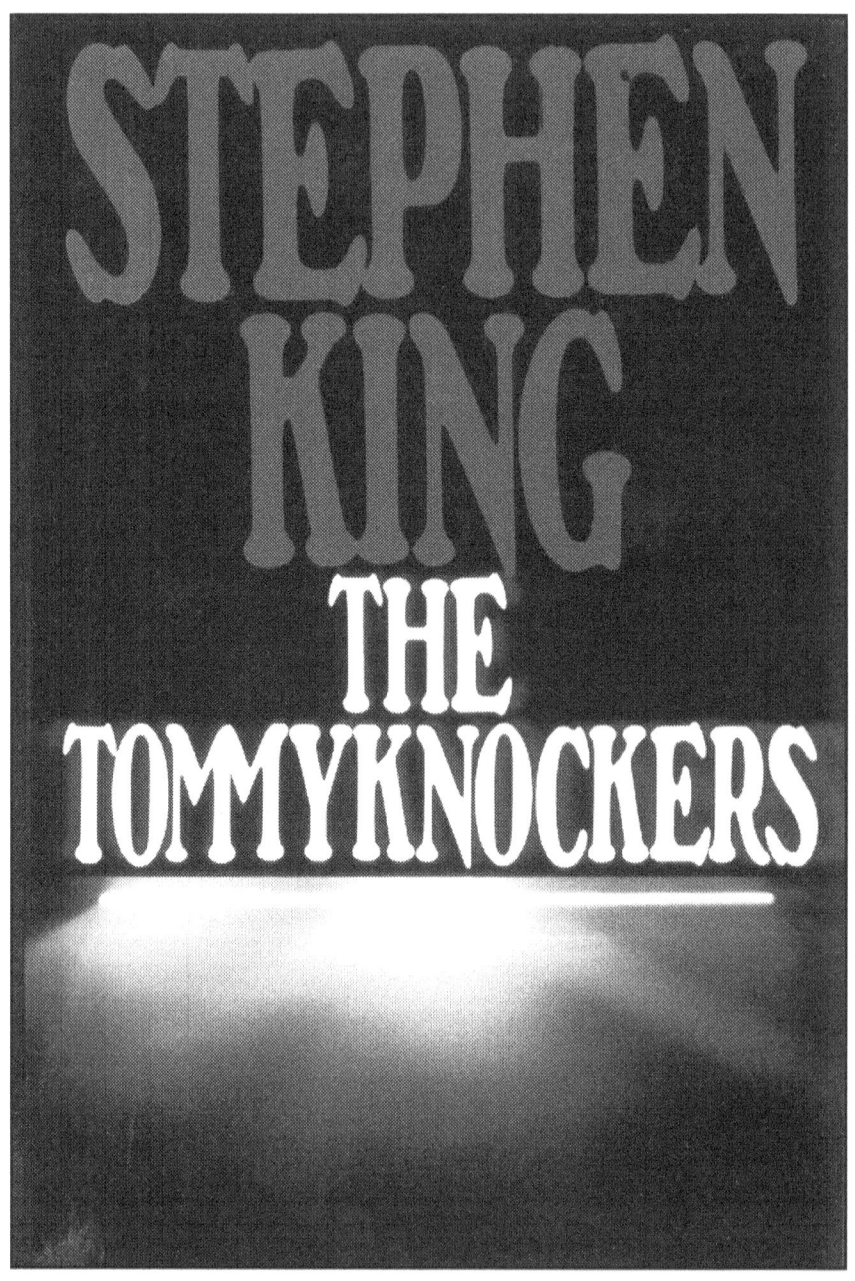

The Tommyknockers. New York, NY: G.P. Putnam & Sons, 1987. Hardcover.

A35.
THE TOMMYKNOCKERS
(1987)

A35. *THE TOMMYKNOCKERS.* New York: G. P. Putnam's Sons, 10 November 1987, 558 pp., $19.95, hardcover. Science-fiction/Horror novel. ISBN 0-399-13314-3.

PLOT SUMMARY: When an ancient alien spacecraft is unearthed near a small town, the inhabitants are gradually transformed physically and psychologically into something not quite human, something not quite alien.

REPRINTS AND ADAPTATIONS:
b. London, England: Hodder & Stoughton, February 1988, 563 pp., £12.95, hardcover. ISBN 0-340-39069-7.
c. London, England: New English Library, October 1988, 693 pp., £3.25, paperback. Open market edition, not distributed in U.K. ISBN 0-450-48835-7. * Reprint, October 1989.
d. New York: Signet/New American Library, November 1988, 747 pp., mass-market paperback. ISBN 0-451-15660-9. * 4th printing by September 1989.
e. Serialized in: *Australian Women's Day Magazine*. [Cited in *Castle Rock: The Stephen King Newsletter* Vol. 4, No. 7 (July 1988): 6].
f. As: *De Gloed* ['The glow']. Utrecht, Belgium, Netherlands: Luitingh, 1988, 560 pp. Dutch translation by Margot Bakker. ISBN 90-245-1923-3. * 2nd printing, 1988. * 5th printing, 1990. * 7th printing, 1993.
g. As: *Das Monstrum/Tommyknockers* ['The monstrous']. Hamburg, West Germany: Hoffman and Campe, 1988, 683 pp., 39.80 DM, hardcover. German translation by Joachim Körber. ISBN 3-455-01902-1. * 5th printing, 1988 (85,000 total). * 6th printing, 1991 (90,000 total).
h. As: *Le creature del buio* ['The creature of darkness']. Milan, Italy: Sperling & Kupfer, PANDORA [#445], June 1989. Italian translation by Tullio Dobner. ISBN 88-200-0903-X.
i. London, England: New English Library, 15 October 1989, [704] pp., paperback.
j. As: *Los Tommyknockers*. Buenos Aires, Argentina: Emecé, GRANDES NOVEL-

ISTAS, 1989, 614 pp., 22 cm. Spanish translation. ISBN 950-04-0849-X. * Reprint, February 1993.

k. As: *Les Tommuknockers*. Paris, France: Albin Michel, 1989, 604 pp., 140 F., paperback. French translation by Dominique Dill. ISBN 2-226-03926-0.

l. As: *Tommyknockers*. Barcelona, Spain: Plaza & Janés, ÉXITOS, 1989, 695 pp., 23 cm. Spanish translation by Edith Zilli. ISBN 84-01-32291-X.

m. As: *Los Tommyknockers*. Esplugues de Llobregat, Barcelona, Spain: Plaza & Janés, ÉXITOS, 1989, 695 pp., 23 cm. Spanish translation by Edith Zilli. 2nd edition. ISBN 84-01-32291-X.

n. As: *Knackarna* ['Creak/crack']. Stockholm, Sweden: Legenda, 1989, 838 pp., 22 cm., hardcover. Swedish translation by Roland Adlerbarth. ISBN 91-582-1341-4.

o. As: *Knackarna* ['Creak/crack']. [Höganäs, Sweden]: Bra Böcker, 1989, 839 pp., 23 cm., hardcover. Swedish translation by Roland Adlerbarth. ISBN not assigned.

p. As: *Os estranhos: os tommyknockers* ['The strange ones']. Rio de Janeiro, Brazil: Francisco Alves, 1990, 638 pp., 21 cm., paperback. Portuguese translation by Luisa Ibanez. ISBN 85-264-0217-4. * 2nd printing, 1991.

q. As: *Kolkuttajat* ['Knockers']. Helsinki, Finland: Tammi, 1990, 735 pp., 23 cm.. Finnish translation by Ilkka Rekiaro. ISBN 951-30-9342-5.

r. As: *Les Tommuknockers*. [Paris, France]: [le Grand livre du mois], 1990, 604 pp., 140 F, paperback. French translation by Dominique Dill. Book Club edition.

s. As: *Les Tommuknockers*. Paris, France: France Loisirs, 1990, 604 pp., 106 F., hardcover. French translation by Dominique Dill. ISBN 2-7242-6111-9.

t. As: *Das Monstrum.Tommyknockers* ['The monstrous']. Stuttgart and Munich, Germany: Deutsche Bücherbund, [1990], 683 pp. German translation by Joachim Körber. Book Club edition.

u. As: *Tommyknockers*. Esplugues de Llobregat, Barcelona, Spain: Plaza & Janés, JET 102/15, BIBLIOTECA DE STEPHEN KING #15, 1990, 695 pp., 18 cm., paperback Spanish translation by Edith Zilli. ISBN 84-01-49895-3. * Reprint, 1991, ISBN 84-01-19102-9 and 84-01-49895-3. * Reprint, 1992, ISBN 84-01-19102-9 and 84-01-49895-3. * Reprint, 1993, ISBN 84-01-19102-9 and 84-01-49895-3

v. As: *Tommyknockers—Le creature del buio* ['Tommyknockers—the creatures of darkness']. Milan, Italy: Sperling Paperback, SUPERBESTSELLER #256, January 1993, paperback. Italian translation by Tullio Dobner. ISBN 88-7824-262-4.

w. New York: Signet, 1993, mass-market paperback. Movie tie-in edition. ISBN 0-451-17842-4.

x. As: *Les Tommyknockers*. 3 vols. Paris, France: J'ai Lu, ÉPOUVANTE #3384-3385-3386, 1993, 314+314+318 pp., 30 F+30 F+30 F, paperback. French translation by Dominique Dill. ISBN 2-277-23384-6, -23385-4; -23386-2.

y. As: *Das Monstrum. Tommyknockers* ['The monstrous']. Munich, Germany: Wilhelm Heyne #7995, 1993, 675 pp., 14.90 DM, paperback. German trans-

z. As: *Carrie/Tommyknockers*. London, England: Hodder & Stoughton, July 1994, 791 pp., £6.99, hardcover. Omnibus volume. ISBN 0-340-62335-7.
aa. As: *Les Tommuknockers*. Paris, France: France Loisirs, 1994, 604 pp., 106 F., hardcover. French translation by Dominique Dill. ISBN 2-7242-7844-5.
bb. As: [Title unknown]. South Korea, 1994, 351+367+351 pp., 23 cm. Korean translation. ISBN 89-7720-043-1, 89-7720-042-3; 89-7720-044-X, 89-7720-045-8.
cc. As: *De Gloed* ['The glow']. Amsterdam, Netherlands: Poema Pocket, 1995, 560 pp., paperback. Dutch translation by Margot Bakker. 8th printing. ISBN 90-245-2379-6.
dd. As: *Tommyknocker*. Milan, Italy: Sperling & Kupfer, 1996. Italian translation.
ee. As; *Tommyknocker*. Barcelona, Spain: Plaza & Janés, JET 102/15, BIBLIOTECA DE STEPHEN KING #15, 1996, 962 pp., 18 cm., paperback. Spanish translation by Edith Zilli. ISBN 84-01-47465-5. * Reprint, 1998, ISBN 84-01-49998-4.
ff. As: [Title unknown]. Japan, 19—. 2 vols. Japanese translation.
gg. As: [Title unknown]. Moscow, Russia: Cadman, 19—. Russian translations. [2 separated editions].
hh. As: *A Remnoppantok (?)*. Hungary: Árkádia, 19—. Hungarian translation.
ii. As: *Das Monstrum—Tommyknockers*. Munich, Germany: Wilhelm Heyne. German translation [2 separate editions].

jj. As FILM: *The Tommyknockers*. ABC, 1993. Produced by Jayne Bieber and Jane Scott. Directed by John Power. Teleplay by Lawrence D. Cohen. Executive producers: Frank Konigsberg and Larry Sanitsky. Co-producer: Lawrence D. Cohen.
CAST: Jimmy Smits, Marg Helgenberger, John Ashton, Allyce Beasley, Robert Carradine, Joanna Cassidy, Annie Corley, Cliff DeYoung, Traci Lords, E. G. Marshall.
SELECTED ARTICLES, RESPONSES, AND REVIEWS:
Leonard, John. "Stephen King's The Tommyknockers." *New York* Vol. 26, No. 19 (10 May 1993): 64.
USA Today (22 July 1991).

kk. As VIDEOCASSETTE: Vidmark, 1993. 120 minutes. Rating: R.

COMMENT: Advance orders for the hardcover totaled 900,000 copies, with 1,405,000 hardcover copies sold in 1987, King's highest sales total to that date, placing King in the #1 spot on the hardcover fiction *BestSeller List* for the second consecutive year (the last time an author had appeared in consecutive years was 1973/1974). With *Misery* and *The Eyes of the Dragon* also on the list, King appeared a total of three times (for additional discussions of King on the lists, see

MICHAEL R. COLLINGS

Collings, *Scaring Us To Death.*)
An exercise in the controlled transition from science-fiction into horror, *The Tommyknockers* nicely illustrates King's strengths and illuminates his weaknesses. His self-referential treatment of earlier novels and characters can be seen either as summational (suggesting that *Tommyknockers*, like *IT*, represents a turning point for King), or as merely self-indulgent—although multiple additional examples in later novels more persuasively suggest an attempt at integrating the various landscapes of King's fictions a single imaginative whole, encapsulated, perhaps, in the on-going quest for the Dark Tower. References to topical issues have been similarly interpreted as King touching on his own times or as King indulging in lecturing for a captive audience—certainly his treatment of America's obsession with gadgetry is on a rather more subtle level than his more overt discussions of social problems in his novels of the late 1990's. Regardless of interpretations, however, the novel does tend to create oddly static portrayals, while simultaneously incorporating striking imagery, memorable characters, and effectively chilling episodes.

SELECTED ARTICLES, RESPONSES, AND REVIEWS:
Auerbach, Nina. "Not with a Bang but with an EEOOOOARRRHMM!" *The New York Times Book Review* Vol. 92 (5 December 1987): VII, 8.
Beaulieu, Janet C. "A Slow Start, But Rousing Finish." *Bangor Daily News* [ME] 8 December 1987. As microfiche: *NewsBank: Literature* Vol. 15 (January 1988): Fiche 8, C11.
Booklist Vol. 84 (1 October 1987): 170.
Books (February 1988): 18.
Card, Orson Scott. "Books to Look for." *The Magazine of Fantasy & Science Fiction* Vol. 75 (July 1988): 30+.
Cobb, Anne. "King's Latest Doesn't Raise Many Hairs." *Buffalo News* [NY] 6 December 1987. As microfiche: *NewsBank: Literature* Vol. 15 (January 1988): Fiche 8, C13.
Collings, Michael R. "The Revelations of 'Becka Paulson." *The Shorter Works of Stephen King*, by Michael R. Collings and David A. Engebretson. STARMONT STUDIES IN LITERARY CRITICISM, #9. Mercer Island WA: Starmont House, June 1985.173-181.
Collings, Michael R. "Stephen King, Sci-Fi, and The Tommyknockers." *Castle Rock: The Stephen King Newsletter* Vol. 3, No. 11 (November 1987): 1, 4-5. Reprinted in Collings, *The Stephen King Phenomenon*. Reprinted in Collings, *Scaring Us To Death: The Impact of Stephen King on Popular Culture*, 1997. 33-43.
Collings, Michael R. *SFRA Newsletter* [Science Fiction Research Association] No. 152 (October 1987): 34-35. Reprinted As: "The Tommyknockers." *Science Fiction & Fantasy Book Review Annual.* Edited by Robert A. Collins and Robert Latham. Westport, CT: Meckler, 1988, hardcover. 228-229.
Connolly, Sherryl. "You Scared? Well, I'm Not." *Daily News* [NY] 29

November 1987. As microfiche: *NewsBank: Literature* Vol. 14 (December 1987): Fiche 64, D8.
Donovan, Mark. *People Weekly* Vol. 29 (14 March 1988): 22+.
Dougherty, Marianne. "'Tommyknockers' Finds Stephen King as His Scary Best." *Pittsburgh Press* [PA] 13 December 1987. As microfiche: *NewsBank: Literature* Vol. 15 (January 1988): Fiche 8, D1.
Flick, Arend. "Stephen King as Nerd's Best Friend." *Los Angeles Times Book Review* [CA] 20 December 1987: B1, B12.
Frazell, Daryl. "Horror Turns to Disgust: Stephen King Lets Us Down When He Holds Human Spirit in Low Regard." *St. Petersburg Times* [FL] 6 December 1987. As microfiche: *NewsBank: Literature* Vol. 15 (January 1988): Fiche 8, C9.
Gorner, Peter. "King Foregoes Horror for Gore in 'The Tommyknockers.'" *Chicago Tribune* [IL] 22 November 1987: Section 14, 5. As microfiche: *NewsBank: Literature* Vol. 14 (December 1987): Fiche 64, D5-D6.
Graham, Mark. "King Epic Complex, Incongruous." *Rocky Mountain News* [Denver CO] 1 February 1988: 53.
Hauser, Jerald. "Stephen King's Latest Horror Lives Underground." *Milwaukee Journal* [WI] 13 December 1987. As microfiche: *NewsBank: Literature* Vol. 15 (January 1988): Fiche 8, D4.
Hemesath, James B. *Library Journal* Vol. 113, No. 1 (January 1988): 99.
Hermann, Spring. "New King Novel a Good Read Despite Structural Flaws." *Hartford Courant* [CT] 20 December 1987. As microfiche: *NewsBank: Literature* Vol. 15 (January 1988): Fiche 8, C7-C8.
Indick, Ben P. "H. P. Lovecraft and Those Tommyknockers." *Castle Rock: The Stephen King Newsletter* Vol. 4, No. 8 (August 1988): 4, 12.
Johnson, George. "New and Noteworthy." *New York Times Book Review* 13 November 1988: 66.
Kliatt Paperback Book Guide Vol. 23 (January 1989): 10.
Kloer, Phil. "King's Latest Has Mind-Warping Bogeymen from Space." *Atlanta Journal-Constitution* [GA] 6 December 1987. As microfiche: *NewsBank: Literature* Vol. 15 (January 1988): Fiche 8, C10.
Krolczyk, Gregory N. "'Tommyknockers': People Get Knocked Off, But Who Cares." *Sun* [Baltimore MD] 27 December 1987. As microfiche: *NewsBank: Literature* Vol. 15 (January 1988): Fiche 8, C12.
Larson, Susan. "Not Your Backyard, Garden-Variety UFO." *Houston Post* [TX] 29 November 1987. As microfiche: *NewsBank: Literature* Vol. 15 (January 1988): Fiche 8, D2-D3.
Lehmann-Haupt, Christopher. "Books of the Times." *The New York Times* Vol. 137 (5 November 1987): C 33. Late edition.
London Review of Books Vol. 10 (21 April 1988): 22.
Morrison, Michael A. "The Year in Horror, 1987." *Science Fiction & Fantasy Book Review Annual*. Edited by Robert A. Collins and Robert Latham. Westport, CT: Meckler, 1988, hardcover. 21-36.
New York Times Book Review Vol. 93 (13 November 1988: 66.

Publishers Weekly Vol. 232 (9 October 1987): 79.

Publishers Weekly Vol. 234 (26 August 1988): 83.

Reese, Kathleen. "Stephen King Mixes Movies and Monsters in 'The Tommyknockers.'" *Dallas Times Herald* [TX] 22 November 1987. As microfiche: *NewsBank: Literature* Vol. 14 (December 1987): Fiche 64, D9-D10.

Sarrantonio, Al. "Horrors Red." *Mystery Scene* No. 14 (1988): 48.

Schleier, Curt. "Newest King Thriller Isn't Up to His Previous Books." *Grand Rapids Press* [MI] 22 November 1987. As microfiche: *NewsBank: Literature* Vol. 14 (December 1987): Fiche 64, D7.

Schleier, Curt. "A Spaceship Gives 'Em Hell." *Newsday* [Long Island NY] 3 January 1988. As microfiche: *NewsBank: Literature* Vol. 15 (January 1988): Fiche 8, C14.

Schweitzer, Darrell. "Fear and the Future: King as a Science-Fiction Writer." *Castle Rock: The Stephen King Newsletter* Vol. 3, No. 11/Vol. 4, No. 1 (December 1987-January 1988): 1, 6-8. Reprinted: *Reign of Fear: Fiction and Film of Stephen King*. Edited by Don Herron. Los Angeles CA: Underwood-Miller, June 1988. 193-208.

Schweitzer, Darrell. "Schweitzer on TK, SK, and Science Fiction." *Castle Rock: The Stephen King Newsletter* Vol. 4, Nos. 5-6 (May-June 1988): 9.

Science Fiction Chronicle Vol. 9 (February 1988): 42.

Washington Post Book World Vol. 17 (November 29, 1987): 9.

West Coast Review of Books Vol. 13, No. 4 (1988): 28.

White, Sarah J. "Second Tommyknockers Quite Different." *Castle Rock: The Stephen King Newsletter* Vol. 4, Nos. 5-6 (May-June 1988): 5. [Comparative review of King's novel and *The Tommyknockers*, by Alan E. Leisk, 1987].

Williams, Mary A. *School Library Journal* Vol. 34 (February 1988): 95.

Horror Plum'd

MICHAEL R. COLLINGS

NIGHTMARES IN THE SKY. New York, NY & London, England: Viking, 1988. Hardcover.

A36.
NIGHTMARES IN THE SKY
(1988)

A36. *NIGHTMARES IN THE SKY: GARGOYLES AND GROTESQUES*. New York and London, England: Viking Studio Books, November 1988, 128 pp., hardcover. Text by Stephen King (35 pp.); photographs by f-Stop Fitzgerald. Photo-essay. ISBN 0-670-82307-4.

REPRINTS AND ADAPTATIONS:
Excerpted in: Penthouse (September 1988). [See C191.]
As: Nachtgesichter ['Night-faces']. Munich, Germany: Wilhelm Heyne, Gebundene Ausgabe, 1989, 124 pp. 48.00 dm, cloth-bound [gewebe]. German translation by Joachim Körber. ISBN 3-453-03221-7.
Germany: Droemer/Knaur Verlag, 1989, hardcover. German translation.

COMMENTS: This volume is a distinct oddity among King's publications—neither fish nor fowl, as it were, but enough of both/each to allow for argument. While it is included here as a book-length publication—even though King's text provides an extended introduction rather than a persistent commentary—there is simultaneously strong justification (as George Beahm points out in *Stephen King Collectibles*) for considering King's contribution as secondary to the artwork. King's name on the dust jacket, along with the identifying "text," may be read either as an assertion that this is indeed a significant King work; or, alternatively, as essentially a marketing device. Either way, the essay is of considerable interest and the photographs, particularly in the haunting tone they create, are both excellent and appropriate.

SELECTED ARTICLES, RESPONSES, AND REVIEWS:
Beahm, George. *Stephen King Collectibles*. Williamsburg VA: GB Books, 2000. 118.
Blue, Tyson. "Of New Frontiers and Gargoyles." *Castle Rock: The Stephen King Newsletter* Vol. 4, No. 11 (November 1988): 3.

MICHAEL R. COLLINGS

Booklist Vol. 85 (1 November 1988): 442.
Indick, Ben P. "Looking for Trouble: Nightmares in Daylight." *Castle Rock: The Stephen King Newsletter* Vol. 5, No. 1 (January 1989): 1, 7.
Washington Post Book World Vol. 18 (4 December 1988): 19.

Horror Plum'd

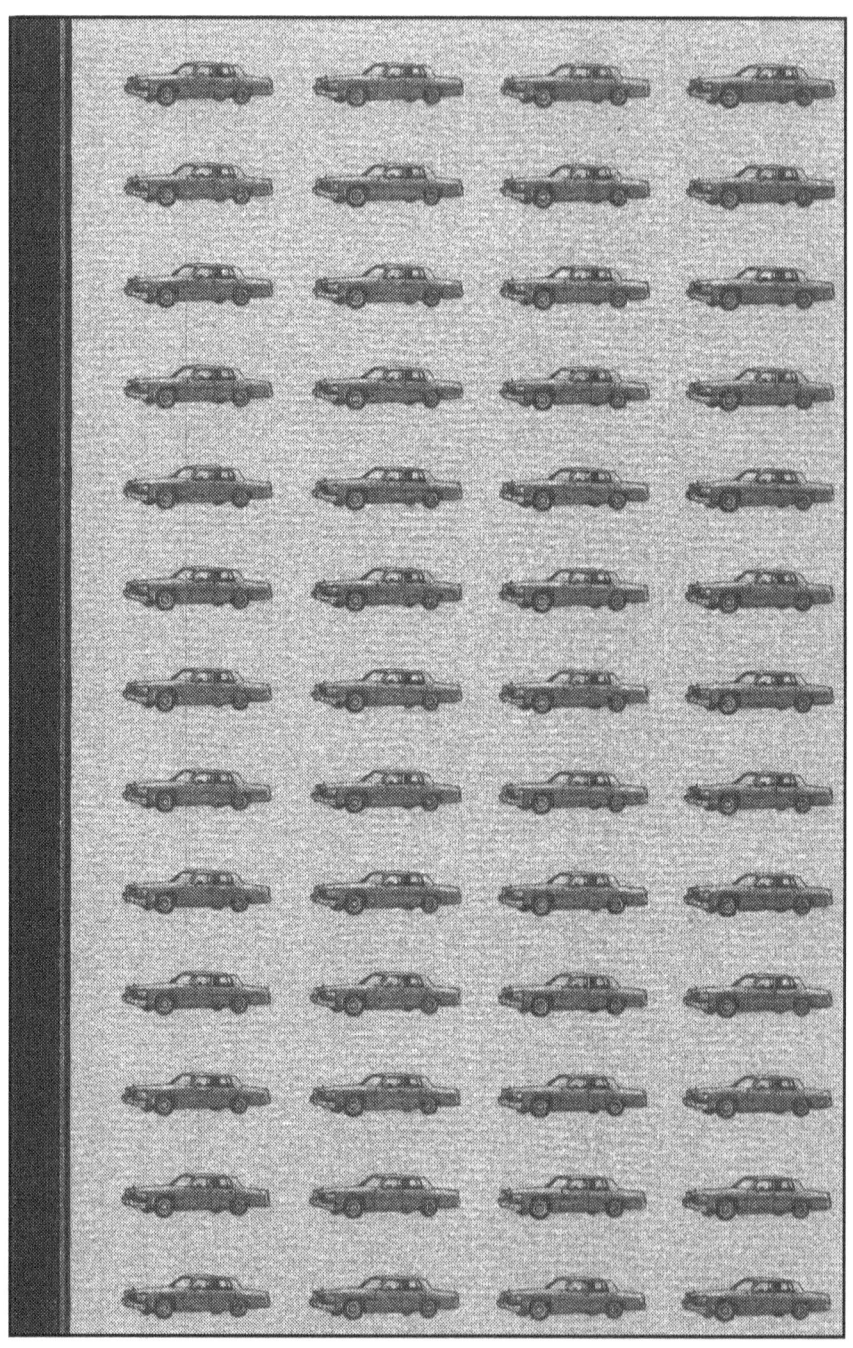

Dolan's Cadillac. Northridge, CA: Lord John Press, 1989. Hardcover.

A37.
DOLAN'S CADILLAC
(1989)

A37. *DOLAN'S CADILLAC*. Northridge, CA: Lord John Press, 1989, 64 pp., hardcover. See also B80. Horror novella. * LETTERED STATE: 26 copies (A-Z), half-bound in leather, in slipcase, signed by King. * DELUXE EDITION: 250 numbered copies, quarter-bound, signed by King. * LIMITED, SIGNED EDITION: 1000 numbered copies, signed by King, $100.00. ISBN 0-935716-46-7.

REPRINTS AND ADAPTATIONS:
b. Included in: *Nightmares & Dreamscapes*. New York: Viking, 1993, hardcover. 11-66. See A47.
c. As: *Dolan's Cadillac*. Utrecht, Belgium, Netherlands: Collectieve Propaganda van het Nederlandse Boek/Luitingh-Sitjhoff, 1992, 92 pp. Dutch translation by Thomas Wintner. ISBN 90-70066-97-1. Book Club special offer.

COMMENTS: The story originally appeared as a serial in *Castle Rock: The Stephen King Newsletter*, from February through June 1985 [See B80]. As did "The Blue Air Compressor" and "Crouch End," the story suggests the depths of King's debt to a previous writer—in this case Poe and "The Cask of Amontillado." King updates his story, amplifying his protagonist's motivation and suffering. Not among King's strongest works, it tends to lengthy explication that obscures the narrative movement. The story is currently (February 2001) in production as a film.

SELECTED ARTICLES, RESPONSES, AND REVIEWS:
Collings, Michael R., and David A. Engebretson. *The Shorter Works of Stephen King*. STARMONT STUDIES IN LITERARY CRITICISM, #9. Mercer Island WA: Starmont House, June 1985. 182-183.
Indick, Ben P. "A Cadillac for King's Used Car Lot." *Castle Rock: The Stephen King Newsletter* Vol. 5, No. 5 (May 1989): 8.
Indick, Ben P. "Dolan's Cadillac." *The Blood Review: The Journal of Horror Criticism* Vol. 1, No. 1 (October 1989): 68.

Michael R. Collings

My Pretty Pony. New York: Alfred A. Knopf, Random House, 1989. Oversized hardcover.

A38.
MY PRETTY PONY
(1989)

A38. *MY PRETTY PONY.* New York: Library Fellows of the Whitney Museum, Whitney Museum of Art, Artists and Writers series, September (or October) 1989, [64] pp., hardcover. Illustrated by Barbara Kruger (all illustrations in the limited edition are lithographed). Bound in stainless steel jacket with digital clock inset. Limited printing of 280 copies in several states; 150 offered for sale; list price, $2,200. See B104.

REPRINTS AND ADAPTATIONS:
b. New York: Alfred A. Knopf, Random House, September 1989, [64] pp., $50.00, oversized hardcover. Limited printing, 15,000 copies, red and white covers in slipcase. ISBN 0-394-58-37-0.
c. Included in: *Nightmares & Dreamscapes.* New York: Viking, 1993, hardcover. 437-466. [see A47].

SELECTED ARTICLES, RESPONSES, AND REVIEWS:
Blue, Tyson. "My Pretty Pony: A Treat for the Eye." *Castle Rock: The Stephen King Newsletter* Vol. 4, No. 12 (December 1988): 1, 8.
Blue, Tyson. "Affordable 'My Pretty Pony' Published by Whitney Museum." *Castle Rock: The Stephen King Newsletter* Vol. 5, No. 12 (December 1989).
Booklist Vol. 86 (1 December 1989): 724.
de la Ree, Gerry. Letter. *Castle Rock: The Stephen King Newsletter* Vol. 5, Nos. 9-10 (September-October 1989): 9.
de Lint, Charles. "Night Journeys—Reviews of Horror." *Mystery Scene* No. 26 (June 1990): 111.
Indick, Ben P. "My Pretty Pony: An Odd Couple Produces a Work of Art." *Castle Rock: The Stephen King Newsletter* Vol. 5, No. 4 (April 1989): 1, 9.
Keleher, Jean. *Library Journal* Vol. 114 (December 1989): 118+.
Locus Vol. 23 (November 1989): 56.
"*Mystery Scene* Horror Bestseller List." *Mystery Scene* No. 24 (January 1990): 96.
Streitfeld, David. "Long Live the King." *Washington Post Book World* [DC] 20 August 1989: 15.

Tallman, Susan. "Counting Pretty Ponies: Barbara Kruger and Stephen King Make a Book." *Arts Magazine* Vol. 63 (March 1989): 19-20.

Williams, Gene. "Short Story Is Something New for King." *Cleveland Plain Dealer* [OH] 22 April 1990. As microfiche: *NewsBank: Literature* (May 1990-August 1990): Fiche 48, A10.

West Coast Review of Books Vol. 15, no. 2 (1989): 50.

Winter, Douglas E. "Venturing a Bit into the Magical." *Washington Times* [DC] 29 November 1989. As microfiche: *NewsBank: Literature* 16 (December 1989): Fiche 126, A11.

HORROR PLUM'D

MICHAEL R. COLLINGS

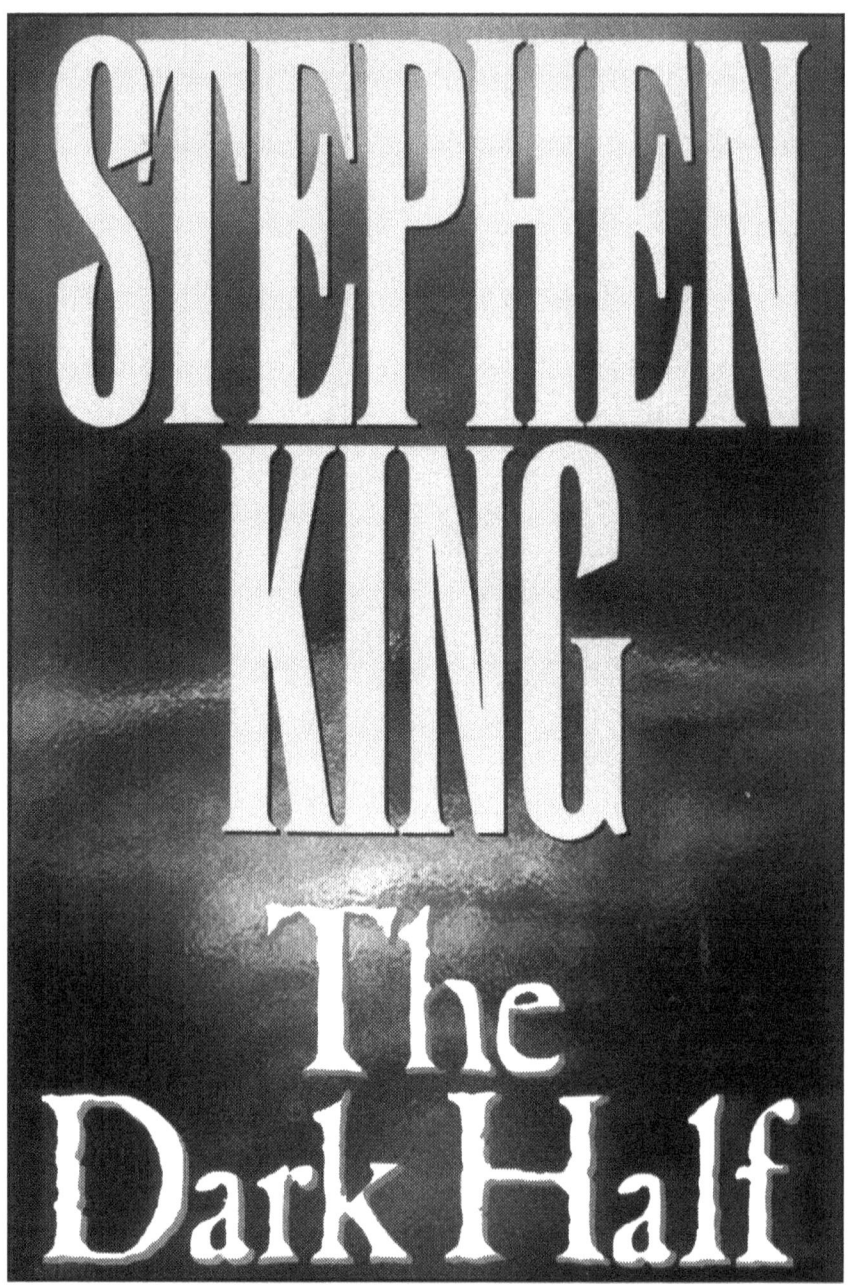

THE DARK HALF. New York, NY: Viking, 1989. Hardcover.

A39.
THE DARK HALF
(1989)

A39. *THE DARK HALF*. London, England: Hodder & Stoughton, 2 October 1989, 413 pp., £12.95, hardcover. Horror novel. ISBN 0-340-50911-2.

AUTHOR'S NOTE: "I'm indebted to the late Richard Bachman for his help and inspiration. This novel could not have been written without him."

PLOT SUMMARY: Novelist Thad Beaumont's vicious pseudonym, George Stark—who has been declared officially "dead and buried"—comes to life and demands that his character be resurrected. As a special 'Stark' touch, he begins the systematic destruction of every person involved in his "demise," including Beaumont and his family.

REPRINTS AND ADAPTATIONS:
b. New York: Viking, 20 October 1989, 431 pp., $21.95, 25 cm., hardcover. ISBN 0-670-82982-X. Intended as simultaneous with the Hodder & Stoughton edition but in fact some days later.
c. As: *De Duistere Kant* ['The dark side']. Utrecht, Belgium, Netherlands: Luitingh-Sitjhoff, 1989, 493 pp. Dutch translation by Frank de Groot. 1st Dutch edition. ISBN 90-245-1935-7.
d. As: *Stark: The Dark Half*. Hamburg, West Germany: Hoffmann und Campe, 1989, 475 pp., 39.80 DM, hardcover. German translation by Christel Wiemkin. ISBN 3-455-03738-0. * 4th printing, 1994 (85,000 total).
e. As: [Title unknown]. West Germany: Droemer/Knaur, 1989, 475 pp., hardcover. German translation.
f. New York: Book of the Month Club, July 1990, 413 pp., $18.95, hardcover. #77-7662. No ISBN issued.
g. As: *La Metá oscura* ['The dark side/half']. Milan, Italy: Sperling & Kupfer, PANDORA [#484], March 1990. Italian translation by Tullio Dobner. ISBN 88-200-0982-X.
h. New York: Signet, October 1990, 484 pp., $5.95, mass-market paperback. ISBN 0-451-16731-7.

Michael R. Collings

i. London, England: New English Library, October 1990, 469 pp., £4.99, paperback. ISBN 0-450-2468-X.
j. As: *Le Part des Ténèbres: Roman* ['The part of darkness']. Paris: Albin Michel, 1990, 464 pp., 140 F, paperback. French translation by William Olivier Desmond. ISBN 2-226-04902-9.
k. As: *La Mitad Siniestra* ['The sinister half']. México, D.F.: Editorial Grijalbo, 1990, 475 pp. Spanish translation by María Elisa Moreno Canaleja.
l. As: *La mitad oscura* ['The dark half]. Barcelona, Spain: Ediciones B, Éxitos internacional, 1990, 491 pp., 24 cm. Spanish translation by Hernán Sabaté. ISBN 84-406-1434-9. * 2nd printing, 1990. * 3rd printing, 1990. * Reprint, 1993, ISBN 84-406-1434-9.
m. As: *Stark*. Stockholm, Sweden: Legenda, 1990, 459 pp., 24 cm., hardcover. Swedish translation by Roland Adlerbarth. ISBN 91-582-1590-5.
n. As: *Stark*. Höganäs, Sweden: Bra Böcker, 1990, 460 pp., 23 cm., hardcover. Swedish translation by Roland Adlerbarth. No ISBN assigned.
o. Boston MA: G. K. Hall, 1991, xxiii + 608 pp., 25 cm. ISBN 0-8161-5109-1 [hardcover]; ISBN 0-8161-5123-7 [trade paperback].
p. As: *A metade negra* ['The black half']. Rio de Janeiro, Brazil: Francisco Alves, 1991, 358 pp., 21 cm., paperback. Portuguese translation by Luisa Ibanez. ISBN 85-265-0252-2.
q. As: *Mørkets halvdel* ['Dark's half']. Copenhagen, Denmark: Artia, 1991, 429 pp., 298 kr, paperback. Danish translation by Anders Westenholz. ISBN 87-89294-64-5.
r. As: *Pimeä puoli* ['The dark side/half']. Helsinki, Finland: Tammi, 1991, 475 pp., 23 cm. Finnish translation by Ilkka Rekiaro. ISBN 951-30-9439-0. * 2nd printing 1991.
s. As: *Le part des ténèbres* ['The part of darkness']. [Paris], France: [le Grande livre du mois], 1991, 461 pp., 140 F, hardcover. French translation by William Olivier Desmond. Book Club edition.
t. As: *Le part des ténèbres* ['The part of darkness']. Paris, France: France Loisirs, 1991, 461 pp., 106 F, hardcover. French translation by William Olivier Desmond. ISBN 2-7242-6467-3.
u. New York: Signet, July 1992, 484 pp., $5.99, mass-market paperback. 7th printing. ISBN 0-451-17181-0. * Movie tie-in edition, 15th printing, April 1983.
v. As: *Le part des ténèbres* ['The part of darkness']. Paris, France: Presses Pocket, Terreur #9072, 1992, 541 pp., 35 F, paperback. French translation by William Olivier Desmond. ISBN 2-266-04745-0.
w. As: *Stark—The Dark Half.* Munich, Germany: Wilhelm Heyne, #8269, 1992, 16.90 dm, 19 cm., paperback. German translation by Christel Wiemkin. * 5th printing, ISBN 3-453-04880-6.
x. As: *Den andre siden* ['The other side']. Oslo, Norway: Aschehoug, 1992, 426 pp., hardcover [*innbundet*]. Norwegian translation by Dag Heyerdahl Larsen. ISBN 82-03-16683-0, 82-598-0115-9. * Reprint, 1993, ISBN 82-03-17276-8. * Reprint as Maxibok, 1994, ISBN 82-03-20043-5.

y. As: *La mitad oscura* ['The dark half']. Barcelona, Spain: Ediciones B, VIB #13/3, 1992, 605 pp., 18 cm. Spanish translation by Hernán Sabaté. ISBN 84-406-3260-6.
z. As: *Mørkets halvdel* [Dark's half']. Copenhagen, Denmark: Bogsamleren, 1993, 341 pp., 72,50 KR, hardcover. Danish translation by Anders Westenholz. ISBN 87-7531-414-2. Book Club edition.
aa. As: *Mørkets halvdel* ['Dark's half']. Copenhagen, Denmark: Artia, EN ARTIA PAPERBACK, 1993, 342 pp., 69,50 KR, paperback. Danish translation by Anders Westenholz. ISBN 87-89918-20-7. * 2nd printing, 1995.
bb. As: [Title unknown]. Israel: Modan, 1993, 448 pp. Hebrew translation.
cc. As: *Mroczna polowa* ['The dark/dusky half']. Warsaw, Poland: "Mizar," "Amber," 1993, 403 pp., 21 cm. Polish translation by Pawel Korombel. ISBN 83-8530-937-3.
dd. As: [Title unknown.] South Korea, 1993, 335 pp., 23 cm. Korean translation. ISBN 89-7720-003-2
ee. As: [Title unknown.] South Korea, 1993, 343 pp., 23 cm. Korean translation. ISBN 89-7720-004-0.
ff. New York: Signet, December 1994, $7.99, mass-market paperback. ISBN 0-451-16731-7.
gg. As: *Le part des ténèbres* ['The part of darkness']. Paris, France: France Loisirs, 1994, 461 pp., hardcover. French translation by William Olivier Desmond. ISBN 2-7242-7884-4.
hh. As: *La Metá oscura* ['The dark side/half']. Milan, Italy: Sperling Paperback, SUPERBESTSELLER #482, November 1995, 467 pp., 20 cm., paperback. Italian translation by Tullio Dobner. ISBN 88-7824-585-2.
ii. As: *De Duistere Kant* ['The dark side']. Amsterdam, Netherlands: Poema Pocket, 1996, 493 pp., paperback. Dutch translation by Frank de Groot. 5th printing. ISBN 90-245-2646-9.
jj. As: *A metade sombria* ['The Dark Half']. [Lisbon, Portugal]: Círculo de Leitores, 1997, 545 pp., 21 cm. Portuguese translation by Catarina Horta Salgueiro. ISBN 972-42-1565-2.
kk. As: *Tamna polovica.* Zagreb, Croatia: Sara 93, BIBLIOTEKA DAKA, 1997, 525 pp., 20 cm. Croatian translation by Milica Luk´sic. ISBN 953-6187-25-6.
ll. As: *Den andre siden* ['The other side']. Oslo, Norway: Aschehoug, 1998, 426 pp., 62.00, [heftet]. Norwegian translation. By Dag Heyerdahl Larsen. ISBN 82-03-20360-4.
mm. As: *La Metá oscura* ['The dark side/half']. Milan, Italy: Sperling & Kupfer, 1998. Italian translation.
nn. As: *La mitad oscura* ['The dark side/half']. Barcelona, Spain: Ediciones B, BIBLIOTECA DE BOLSILLO #62, 1998, 603 pp., 19 cm., paperback. Spanish translation by Hernán Sabaté. ISBN 84-406-8032-5.
oo. Barcelona, Spain: RBA, [1998], 438 pp., 22 cm. Spanish translation by Hernán Sabaté. ISBN 84-473-1433-2.
pp. As: [Title unknown]. Russia: Cadman. Russian translation.
qq. As: *Halálos Árnyék*. Budapest, Hungary: Európa, 19—. Hungarian transla-

tions. [2 separate editions].
rr. As: *Hayati Emen Karanlik*. Turkish translation.

ss. As AUDIOCASSETTE: *The Dark Half*. London, England: Hodder & Stoughton, 19 October 1989. Read by Stephen King. 1 cassette; 60 minutes. Abridged.
tt. As FILM: *The Dark Half*. Orion Pictures, 1992. Produced by Declan Baldwin. Director, executive producer, and screenwriter George A. Romero. Associate producer, Christine Romero. 122 minutes. Rated: R.
   CAST: Timothy Hutton, Amy Madigan, Julie Harris, Michael Rooker.
   SELECTED ARTICLES, RESPONSES, AND REVIEWS:
   Porton, Richard. *Cineaste* Vol. 20, No. 1 (Winter 1993): 64.
   Travers, Peter. *Rolling Stone* No. 656 (13 May 1993): 113.
   Van Gelder, Lawrence. "A Writer's Dark Side." *The New York Times* Vol. 140 (30 November 1992): B5.
   Wood, Gary. "The Dark Half: George Romero Tries His Hand at Adapting a King Best-Seller." *Cinefantastique* Vol. 21, No. 4 (February 1991): 26.

uu. As VIDEOCASSETTE: *The Dark Half*. Orion Home Video, 1993. 122 minutes. Rating: R.
vv. As LASERDISC: Orion Pictures, 1993. 2 laserdiscs, 121 minutes.

COMMENTS: *The Dark Half* set a record of 1.5 million copies printed for the first hardcover edition. The Hodder & Stoughton publication packet announced *The Dark Half* as the first novel in a four-book sale. The book is the second in what has been called King's "Writer's Trilogy," comprised of *Misery*, *The Dark Half*, and "Secret Window, Secret Garden" (published separately and in *Four Past Midnight*), even though issues relating to writing and writers continue as a recurrent, if secondary, theme in many of his subsequent works, as in *Bag of Bones*.

SELECTED ARTICLES, RESPONSES, AND REVIEWS:
Alderman, John R. "Story of Two Novelists Is Not King at His Best." Richmond News Leader [VA] 14 February 1990. As microfiche: *NewsBank: Literature* Vol. 17 (March 1990): Fiche 27, D2.
Beaulieu, Janet C. "'The Dark Half' Brings Pseudonyms to Life." *Bangor Daily News* "Books in Review" [ME] 14 November 1989. As microfiche: *NewsBank: Literature* Vol. 16 (December 1989): Fiche 126, A7-A8.
Blue, Tyson. "The Misery of Pseudonyms." *The Blood Review: The Journal of Horror Criticism* Vol. 1, No. 1 (October 1989): 53-54.
Blue, Tyson. "New Novel Puts SK Back on Track." *Castle Rock: The Stephen King Newsletter* Vol. 5, No. 11 (November 1989).
Booklist Vol. 85 (August 1989): 1922.
Bryant, Edward. "*The Dark Half*, Stephen King." *Locus* Vol. 23, No. 3, #344 (September 1989).

Chandler, Randy. "The Story of King's Alter Ego Inspires Frightening 'Dark Half.'" *Atlanta Journal-Constitution* [GA] 15 October 1989. As microfiche: *NewsBank: Literature* Vol. 16 (November 1989): Fiche 112, F14.
Christian Science Monitor Vol. 82 (22 January 1990): 13.
Collings, Michael R. "Transforms Frankenstein Mythos." *The Blood Review: Journal of Horror Criticism* Vol. 1, No. 2 (January 1990): 53.
Coltrera, Francesca. "When An Evil Alter Ego Takes Over." *Boston Herald* [MA] 12 November 1989. As microfiche: *NewsBank: Literature* Vol. 16 (December 1989): Fiche 126, A9.
Connelly, Sherryl. "Stephen King is Back: Scared Yet?" *Daily News* [NY] 22 October 1989. As microfiche: *NewsBank: Literature* Vol. 16 (November 1989): Fiche 112, G2.
Costello, Matthew J. "Trying to Unlock the Secret." *The Blood Review: Journal of Horror Criticism* Vol. 1, No. 2 (January 1990): 52.
de Lint, Charles. "Night Journeys—Reviews of Horror: Installment #9." *Mystery Scene* No. 24 (January 1990): 87-88.
de Lint, Charles. "Night Journeys—Reviews of Horror." *Mystery Scene* No. 25 (March 1990): 78. *The Dark Half* listed as one of the top fifteen titles of 1989.
de Lint, Charles. "Night Journeys—Reviews of Horror." *Mystery Scene* No. 28 (January 1991): 96.
Donaldson, Stanley. "Doctors Find Man's Twin Inside His Head." *National Examiner* (20 August 1991): 9. While this article contains no reference to *The Dark Half*, the medical condition described is startlingly similar to Thad Beaumont's in the novel and thus provides an interesting sidelight to King's fiction.
Donovan, Mark. *People Weekly* Vol. 32 (18 December 1989): 44-45.
Duamant,Tasha. *MacLean's* Vol. 102 (18 December 1989): 57.
Foster, Prudence. "Suspenseful, Intriguing, Irritating." *The Blood Review: Journal of Horror Criticism* Vol. 1, No. 2 (January 1990): 52.
Gagliani, William D. "Danger Within: New King Novel Hits Close to Home." *Milwaukee Journal* [WI] 22 October 1989. As microfichc: *NewsBank: Literature* Vol. 16 (November 1989): Fiche 112, G4.
Hall, Melissa Mia. "An Experiment for King." *The Blood Review: Journal of Horror Criticism* Vol. 1, No. 2 (January 1990): 53.
Hautala, Rick. "Wrote from the Gut on This One." *The Blood Review: Journal of Horror Criticism* Vol. 1, No. 2 (January 1990): 53.
Kirkus Reviews Vol. 57 (15 July 1989): 1020.
Krolczyk, Gregory N. "End of Latest King Novel Doesn't Convince." *Sun* [Baltimore MD] 29 October 1989. As microfiche: *NewsBank: Literature* Vol. 16 (November 1989): Fiche 112, G1.
Lehmann-Haupt, Christopher. "Books of the Times: From Stephen King, a Writer's Demon." *The New York Times* "Word and Image" 23 October 1989: C20.Late edition.
Leonard, Stephanie. "Editor's Column." *Castle Rock: The Stephen King*

Newsletter Vol. 4, No. 11 (November 1988): 2. Notes that King has written a book under this title, "But at this time he has no plans to publish it."

Liberatore, Karen. "The 'Endsville' in the Horror Writer's Mind." *San Francisco Examiner* [CA] 19 October 1989. As microfiche: *NewsBank: Literature* Vol. 16 (November 1989): Fiche 112, F12-13.

Lileks, James. "The More You Think About It, The Scarier It Gets." *St. Paul Pioneer Press-Dispatch* [MN] 12 November 1989. As microfiche: *NewsBank: Literature* Vol. 16 (December 1989): Fiche 126, A10.

Locus Vol. 23 (September 1989): 17.

Locus Vol. 23 (September 1989): 25.

Los Angeles Times Book Review 30 September 1990: 14. Publication notice for paperback edition.

Massie, Elizabeth. "The Book Is a Success." *The Blood Review: Journal of Horror Criticism* Vol. 1, No. 2 (January 1990): 52.

Miller, G. Wayne. "The Pleasure/Pain of Being a Writer." *The Blood Review: Journal of Horror Criticism* Vol. 1, No. 2 (January 1990): 53.

Moore, J. R. T. "The Writer and His Shadow." *SFRA Newsletter* [Science Fiction Research Association] No. 182 (November 1990): 398.

New Statesman & Society Vol. 3 (7 December 1990): 34.

New York Times [late edition] Vol. 139 (23 October 1989): C20.

Publishers Weekly Vol. 237 (31 August 1990): 60.

Science Fiction Chronicle 11 (Fall 1990): 34.

Skow, John. *Time* Vol. 134 (20 November 1990): 105.

Stabiner, Karen. "Storytellers: New in November." *Los Angeles Times Book Review* [CA] 15 October 1989: 14.

Stade, George. "His Alter Ego is a Killer." *New York Times Book Review* 29 October 1989: VII 12. Half-page favorable review.

Steinberg, Sybil. *Publishers Weekly* Vol. 236 (1 September 1989): 76.

Streitfeld, David. "Long Live the King." *Washington Post Book World* [DC] 20 August 1989: 15.

Stumpf, Edna. "In Stephen King's Tale, a Writer's Alter Ego Is Out of Control." *Philadelphia Inquirer* [PA] 29 October 1989. As microfiche: *NewsBank: Literature* Vol. 16 (November 1989): Fiche 112, G3.

Vander Putten, Joan. "Another Masterpiece of Horror." *The Blood Review: Journal of Horror Criticism* Vol. 1, No. 2 (January 1990): 52.

Whitmore, Tom. "*The Dark Half,* Stephen King." *Locus* Vol. 23, No. 3, #344 (September 1989).

Will, George. "Odd, Isn't It, That History's Most Developed Society Has a Deep Craving for Gore." *Philadelphia Inquirer* [PA] 11 December 1989.

Winter, Douglas E. "Venturing a Bit into the Magical." *Washington Times* [DC] 29 November 1989. As microfiche: *NewsBank: Literature* 16 (December 1989): Fiche 126, A11.

Young, Elizabeth S. *New Statesman & Society* Vol. 3 (7 December 1990): 34.

Horror Plum'd

THE STAND: COMPLETE AND UNCUT. New York, NY: Doubleday, 1990. Hardcover.

A40.
THE STAND
THE COMPLETE & UNCUT EDITION
(1990)

A40. *THE STAND: THE COMPLETE & UNCUT EDITION.* New York: Doubleday, May 1990, xix+1153 pp., $24.95, hardcover. Cover art by John Cayea. Illustrated by Berni Wrightson. Novel [see A5]. ISBN 0-385-19957-0. * LIMITED EDITION: $325, 1250 copies, with 52 lettered copies not for sale; signed by King and Wrightson.

CONTENTS: "Author's Note" [see C204]; "A Preface in Two Parts"—"Part 1: To Be Read Before Purchase"; "Part 2: To Be Read After Purchase" [see C205]; *The Stand*.

REPRINTS AND ADAPTATIONS:
b. London, England: Hodder & Stoughton, May 1990, 1007 pp., £14.95, hardcover. Simultaneously with U.S. 1st edition. ISBN 0-340-35895-5.
c. New York: Book of the Month Club, June 1990, 1152 pp., $19.95, hardcover. Book club edition #90-1299.
d. As: *Apocalipsis* ['Calamity/apocalypse']. Esplugas de Llobregat, Barcelona, Spain: Plaza y Janés, ÉXITOS, November 1990, 1299 pp., 3495 pta., 23 cm., hardcover. Spanish translation by Lorenzo Cortina, Rosalía Vásquez, and Gloria Pons. ISBN 84-01-32351-7. Reprint 1992, 1354 pts., paperback. ISBN 80-01-49896-1. * 2nd edition, 1994, ISBN 84-01-49999-2.
e. As: *A danca da morte* ['Dance of death']. Rio de Janeiro, Brazil: Bertrand Brazil, 1990, 860 pp., 23 cm., paperback. Portuguese translation by Luisa Ibanez. ISBN 85-286-0098-X.
f. As: *Tukikohta* ['Base']. 2 vols. Helsinki, Finland: Book Studio, 1990, 675+670 pp., 18 cm. Finnish translation by Kari Nenonen. ISBN 951-611-370-2; 951-611-401-6.
g. New York: Book of the Month Club/Quality Paperback Book Club, [March 1991], 1152 pp., $12.95, trade paperback. No ISBN assigned.
h. As: *The Stand—Das letzte Gefecht* ['The Stand—the last battle']. Bergisch Gladbach, Germany: Bastei-Lübbe, 1990, 1082 pp., 46.00 DM, hardcover. German translation by Joachim Körber. ISBN 3-7857-0577-8.

i. New York: Signet, May 1991, xxv+1141 pp., $6.99, mass-market paperback. ISBN 0-451-16953-0.

j. London, England: New English Library, May 1991, 1423 pp., £6.99, paperback. ISBN 0-450-53737-4.

k. As: *L'Ombra dello Scorpione* ['The shadow of the scorpion']. Milan, Italy: Sonzogno, I ROMANZI, June 1991. Italian translation by Adriana Dell'Orto and Bruno Amato. Revised and enlarged edition. ISBN 88-454-0400-5.

l. As: *Le Fléau* ['The scourge/plague']. Éd. Intégrale. [Paris, France]: [le Grande livre du mois], 1991, 1183 pp., 199 F, hardcover. French translation by Jean-Pierre Quijano. Book Club edition.

m. As: *Le Fléau* ['The scourge/plague']. Éditions Intégrale. [Paris, France]: J.-C. Lattès, 1991, 1183 pp., 199 F, paperback. French translation by Jean-Pierre Quijano. ISBN 2-7096-1020-5. * Reprint, 1996, ISBN 2-7096-1281-X.

n. As: *Apocalipsis* ['Calamity/apocalypse']. Esplugas de Llobregat, Barcelona, Spain: Plaza y Janés, BIBLIOTECA DE STEPHEN KING #16; JET # 102/16, 1991, 1299 pp., 18 cm., paperback. Spanish translation by Lorenzo Cortina, Rosalía Vásquez, and Gloria Pons. ISBN 84-01-49896-1. * Reprint, 1994. ISBN 84-01-49999-2. * 3rd printing, 1997.

o. As: *De Beproevung—De Volledige Onverkorte Editie* ['The test/affliction—the complete unabridged edition']. Utrecht, Belgium, Netherlands: Luitingh-Sitjhoff, 1992, 1010 pp., hardcover [*geb.*]. Dutch translation by Theo Horsten. ISBN 90-245-1430-4.

p. As: *The Stand—Das Letzte Gefecht—erstmals vollständig* ['The last battle—for the first time complete']. Stuttgart, West Germany: Europäische Bildungsgemeinschaft; Gütersloh, Austria: Bertelsmann Club; Vienna, Austria: Buchgemeinschaft Donauland; Zug, Switzerland: Buch-und-Schallplattenfreunde, 1 May 1992, 1082 pp. German translation by Joachim Körber. Book Club edition.

q. As: *Le Fléau* ['The scourge/plague']. Éditions Intégrale. 3 vols. Paris, France: J'ai lu #3311-3312-3313, 1992, 509+505+509 pp., 36 F+36 F+36 F, paperback. French translation by Jean-Pierre Quijano. ISBN 2-277-23311-0; 2-277-23312-9; 2-277-23313-7.

r. As: *Le Fléau* ['The scourge/plague']. Éditions Intégrale. Paris, France: France Loisirs, 1992, xv+1183 pp., 138 F, 25 cm. hardcover. French translation by Jean-Pierre Quijano. ISBN 2-7242-6910-1. * Reprint, 1994, ISBN 2-7242-8034-2.

s. As: *The Stand—Das Letzte Gefecht—erstmals vollständig* ['The last battle—for the first time complete']. Bergisch Gladbach, Germany: Bastei-Lübbe, 1992, 1432 pp., 16.80 DM, paperback. German translation by Joachim Körber, with Wolfgang Neuhaus, based on the translation by Harro Christensen. ISBN 3-404-13411-7. * 9th printing, 1995, BASTEI-LÜBBA-TASCHENBUCH #25242, 1129 pp., paperback, ISBN 340-4252-42-X..

t. New York: Doubleday, October 1993, 1153 pp., $30.00, hardcover. Cover art by Thomas Holdorf. ISBN 0-385-19957-0.

u. New York: Signet, May 1994, 1142 pp., $6.99, mass-market paperback. Movie tie-in edition for the made-for-TV film. ISBN 0-451-17928-5.
v. As: *Opgøret* ['The Settlement/Decision']. Copenhagen, Denmark: Artia, 1994, 1125 pp., 498 KR, hardcover. Danish translation by Mogens Wenzel Andreasen. ISBN 87-89918-30-4.
w. As: *Opgøret* ['The Settlement/Decision']. Copenhagen, Denmark: Artia, 1995, 1125 pp. Danish translation by Mogens Wenzel Andreasen. ISBN 87-89918-43-6.
x. As: *De Beproeving* ['The test/ordeal']. Utrecht, Belgium: Luitingh-Sijthoff, 1996, 1010 pp. Dutch translation by Theo Horsten. ISBN 90-245-1897-0.
y. As: [title unknown]. 3 vols. South Korea, 1996, 372+364+360 pp., 23 cm. Korean translation. ISBN , 89-7158-011-9, 89-7158-012-7, 89-7158-014-3.
z. As: *Apocalipsis* ['Calamity/apocalypse']. Barcelona, Spain: Plaza y Janés, BIBLIOTECA DE STEPHEN KING #16; JET #102/16, 1997, 1584 pp., 18 cm. Spanish translation by Lorenzo Cortina, Rosalía Vásquez, and Gloria Pons. ISBN 84-01-47466-3. * Reprint, 1998.
aa. As: *The Stand—Das Letzte Gefecht.* Bergisch Gladbach, Germany: Bastei-Lübbe #25524, 1999, 1196 pp., 12.00 DM, paperback. German translation by Joachim Körber. ISBN 3-404-25524-0.

bb. As teleplay/miniseries: *Stephen King's The Stand.* ABC miniseries. Part I—The Plague: Sunday, 8 May 1994, 9:00-11:00pm. Part II: Monday, May 9, 1994, 9:00-11:00pm. Part III: Wednesday, May 11, 9:00-11:00pm. Part IV: Thursday, May 12, 1994, 9:00-11:00pm.
CAST: Gary Sinise, Adam Storke, Rob Lowe, Molly Ringwald, Corin Nemec, Ruby Dee, Jamey Sheridan, Miguel Ferrer, Ed Harris, Kathy Bates, Kareem Abdul-Jabbar, Laura San Giocomo, Matt Frewer, Ray Walston, Bill Fagerbakke, Shawnee Smith, Ossie Davis, Stephen King.
SELECTED ARTICLES AND REVIEWS:
Arrington, Carl Wayne. "Stephen King: The Making of 'The Stand.'" *TV Guide* Vol. 42, No. 19, #2145 (7 May 1994): 11-13.
Jarvis, Jeff. "The Couch Critic—*Stephen King's The Stand.*" *TV Guide* Vol. 42, No. 19, #2145 (7 May 1994): 7. "...*Stephen King's The Stand*...is the ultimate tale of the '90s—even if it was first written in '78—because it pierces our deepest fears."
Murphy, Mary. "Rob Lowe Saves Himself—and the World." *TV Guide* Vol. 42, No. 19, #2145 (7 May 1994): 14-16.
Schwed, Mark. "Playing the Devil's Advocate." *TV Guide* Vol. 42, No. 19, #2145 (7 May 1994): 17 [sidebar].

cc. As DVD SV-18: *Stephen King's The Stand.* 1999.

COMMENTS: More than merely an augmented edition, the 1991 *Stand* represents not only a restoration of materials deleted from the original edition (adding some 150,000 words and increasing the chapter count by ten), but an updating of the story as well, bringing it into the 1990s and confirming it as a core text in understanding American society in the latter years of the Twentieth Century.

SELECTED ARTICLES, RESPONSES, AND REVIEWS:
Beaulieu, Janet. "Uncut 'Stand' a Wonderful Read." *Bangor Daily News* [ME] 8 May 1990. As microfiche: *NewsBank: Literature* (May 1990): Fiche 48, A5-7.
Blue, Tyson. "Needful Kings." *The Blood Review: Journal of Horror Criticism* Vol. 1, No. 2 (January 1990): 11.
Book Watch Vol. 11 (August 1990): 3.
Booklist Vol. 86 (15 March 1990): 1394.
Collings, Michael R. *Mystery Scene* No. 27 (October 1990): 132.
Collings, Michael R. "Considering *The Stands*." *Gauntlet* No. 2 (April 1991): 179-188. Reprinted: *Gauntlet 2*. Edited by Barry Hoffman. Baltimore MD: Borderlands Press, May 1991. 129-134.
Castello, William. "King's Longer 'Stand' Is Better Saga." *Reno Gazette-Journal* [NV] 1 July 1990. As microfiche: *NewsBank: Literature* (May 1990-August 1990): Fiche 82, C1.
de Lint, Charles. *Mystery Scene* No. 27 (October 1990): 138.
Girard, James P. "King's 1978 Cult Classic Refurbished, Improved." *Wichita Eagle* [KS] 10 June 1990. As microfiche: *NewsBank: Literature* (May 1990): Fiche 71, D14-E1.
"It Appears This IS the End of the World—Death Can Only Come as a Kindness." *Dayton Daily News/Journal Herald* [OH] 24 June 1990. As microfiche: *NewsBank: Literature* (May 1990-August 1990): Fiche 71, E3.
Kiely, Robert. "Armageddon: Complete and Uncut." *The New York Times Book Review* 13 May 1990: VII 3. Full-page review-article: "Everything is processed through a gigantic American meat grinder."
Kirkus Reviews Vol. 58 (15 February 1990): 210.
Krolczyk, Gregory N. "King's Restoration Strengthens 'The Stand.'" *Sun* [Baltimore MD] 6 May 1990. As microfiche: *NewsBank: Literature* (May 1990-August 1990): Fiche 59, D9.
LaFaille, Gene. *Wilson Library Journal* Vol. 65 (October 1990): 111.
Locus Vol. 24 (June 1990): 19.
Martin, Sue. "'Stand' Corrected." *Los Angeles Times Book Review* 15 July 1990: 12.
McDowell, Edwin. "Reissuing a King Novel with 150,000 Words of Cuts Restored." *New York Times* [NY] Vol. 139 (31 January 1990): B2+.
Moss, Chuck. "The King's Last 'Stand' Is a Winner." *Detroit News* [MI] 9 May 1990. As microfiche: *NewsBank: Literature* (May 1990-August 1990): Fiche 59, D10.
Nash, Jesse. "King Fans Take a New 'Stand.'" *Times-Picayune* [New Orleans LA] 3 June 31990. As microfiche: *NewsBank: Literature* (May 1990): Fiche 71, E2.
Phillips, Rhonda. "Longer 'Stand' Still Rich Reading Experience." [Little Rock

AR] 1 July 1990. As microfiche: *NewsBank: Literature* (May 1990-August 1990): Fiche 71, E3.

Sanders, Joe. "The Stand in All Its Glory." *SFRA Newsletter* [Science Fiction Research Association] No. 181 (October 1990): 38-39.

Steinberg, Sybil. *Publishers Weekly* Vol. 237 (16 March 1990): 60.

Williams, Gene. "Best-Seller Reissued with Cuts Restored." *Cleveland Plain Dealer* [OH] 22 April 1990. As microfiche: *NewsBank: Literature* (May 1990): Fiche 48, A9.

FOUR PAST MIDNIGHT. London, England: Hodder & Stoughton, 1990. Hardcover.

A41.
Four Past Midnight
(1990)

A41. *Four Past Midnight.* New York: Viking, September 1990, xvi+763 pp., $22.95, hardcover. Cover art by Rob Wood-Stansbury. Novella collection. ISBN 0-670-83538-2.

CONTENTS: "Straight Up Midnight: An Introductory Note" [see C207]; "One Past Midnight: A Note on 'The Langoliers'" [see C208]; "The Langoliers" (1990; see B96); "Two Past Midnight: A Note on 'Secret Window, Secret Garden'" [see C209]; "Secret Window, Secret Garden" (1990; see B97); "Three Past Midnight: A Note on 'The Library Policeman'" [see C210]; "The Library Policeman" (1990; see B98); "Four Past Midnight: A Note on 'The Sun Dog'" [see C211]; "The Sun Dog" (1990; see B99).

REPRINTS AND ADAPTATIONS:
b. New York: Book of the Month, September 1990, 713 pp., $19.95, hardcover. Cover art by Rob Wood-Stansbury. No ISBN. Book Club edition.
c. London, England: Hodder & Stoughton, October 1990, 676 pp., £14.99, hardcover. Released in Australia prior to Viking's U.S. edition; however, the British edition was not released until October 1990. ISBN 0-340-53526-1.
d. "The Langoliers." Reprinted with *Get Shorty* by Elmore Leonard and *The Wings of Morning* by Thomas Tryon. *Book Digest*. Richmond VA: T-L Books, 1990, 511 pp., hardcover.
e. Boston MA: G. K. Hall, LARGE PRINT CORE COLLECTION, 2 vol., October 1991, hardcover and paperback. Large print edition. ISBN 0-8161-5135-0, -5136-9.
f. As: *Langoliers.* Munich, West Germany: Wilhelm Heyne, #41—DIE HEYNE-JUMBOS #26, 1990, 510 pp., 24.80 DM, paperback. German translation by Joachim Körber. ISBN 3-453-04674-9.
g. As: *Tweeduister/Schemerwereld* ['Two-darks/Shadow-world']. Utrecht, Belgium, Netherlands: Luitingh-Sijthoff, 1990, hardcover. 2 vols. Dutch translation by Frank de Groot. ISBN 90-245-1511-4.
CONTENTS: "De engelieren"; "Het geheime raam ['The secret window']; "Spookfotos" ['Ghost-photographs']; "De man met het litteken" ['The man with the scar']

h. As: *Quattro dopo mezzanotte* ['Four after midnight']. Milan, Italy: Sperling & Kupfer, PANDORA [#534], February 1991. Italian translation by Tullio Dobner. ISBN 88-200-1139-5.
i. New York: Signet, September 1991, xvi+744 pp., $6.99, mass-market paperback. ISBN 0-451-17038-5. * Reprint, New American Library, September 1991, 768 pp., $7.99.
j. London, England: New English Library, October 1991, 930 pp., £5.99, mass-market paperback. ISBN 0-450-54288-2.
k. New York: Book of the Month Club/Quality Paperback Book Club, November 1991, 800 pp., $11.95, trade paperback. Cover art by Rob Wood-Stansbury. No ISBN assigned.
l. London, England: Windsor, 1991. Large-print edition.
m. Excerpted as: *Langolinerne.* Copenhagen, Denmark: Artia, 1991, 276 pp., 198 KR, paperback. Danish translation of "The Langoliers" by Mogens Wenzel Andreasen. ISBN 87-89294-48-3.
n. As: *Sydänyö* ['Hearts']. Helsinki, Finland: Tammi, 1991, 887 pp., 23 cm. Finnish translations by Ilkka Rekiaro. ISBN 951-30-9435-9. * 2nd and 3rd printings, 1992.
o. As: *Minuit 2* ['Midnight 2']. Paris, France: Albin Michel, 1991, 448 pp., 140 F, paperback. French translation by William Olivier Desmond. ISBN 2-226-05398-0.
p. As: *Minuit 4* ['Midnight 4']. Paris, France: Albin Michel, 1991, 442 pp., 140 F, paperback. French translation by William Olivier Desmond. ISBN 2-226-05646-7.
q. As: *Minuit 2* ['Midnight 2']. [Paris, France]: [le Grande livre du mois], 1991, 448 pp., 140 F, hardcover. French translation by William Olivier Desmond. Book Club edition.
r. As: *Minuit 4* ['Midnight 4']. [Paris, France]: [le Grande livre cu mois], 1991, 442 pp., 140 F, hardcover. French translation by William Olivier Desmond. Book Club edition.
s. As: *Schemerwereld* ['Shadow-world']. Amsterdam, Netherlands: Poema Pocket, 1991, 394 pp., paperback. Dutch translation by Frank de Groot. ISBN 90-245-1939-X. * 4th printing, 1995, ISBN 90-245-2382-6.
t. As: *Etter Midnatt I-I: Langolierne; Hemmelig vindu, hemmelig hage* ['After midnight I-II: "The Langoliers"; "Secret Window, Secret Garden"]. Oslo, Norway: Aschehoug, 1991, 402 pp. Norwegian translation by Dag Heyerdahl Larsen. ISBN 82-03-16649-0; 82-598-0096-9. * Reprint, 1994, ISBN 82-04-20041-9. * Reprint, 1998, paperback, ISBN 82-03-20358-2.
u. As: *Etter Midnatt III-IV: Bibliotekpolitiet, Solhunden* ['After Midnight III-IV: "The Library Policemen," "The Sun Dog"]. Oslo, Norway: Aschehoug, 1991, 373 pp. Norwegian translation by Per Malde. ISBN 82-03-16729-2, 82-598-0097-7. * Reprint, 1994, ISBN 82-03-20042-7.
v. As: *Las dos después de medianoche* ['The two after midnight']. Barcelona, Spain: Ediciones B, ÉXITOS INTERNACIONAL, 1991, 441 pp., 24 cm. Spanish

translation of "The Langoliers" and "Secret Window, Secret Garden" by Susana Constante. ISBN 84-406-1969-3.
w. As: *Las dos después de medianoche* ['the two after midnight']. Barcelona, Spain: Círculo de Lectores, ÉXITOS INTERNACIONAL, 1991, 456 pp., 23 cm. Spanish translation of "The Langoliers" and "Secret Window, Secret Garden" by Susana Constante. ISBN 84-226-3767-7.
x. As: *Mardrömmar* ['Nightmare dreams']. Stockholm, Sweden: Legenda, 1991. Swedish translation.
y. As: *Nachts* ['Nights']. Munich, West Germany: Wilhelm Heyne, 1991. German translation.
z. As: *Mardrömmar* ['Nightmare dreams']. [Stockholm, Sweden]: Legenda, 1991, 836 pp., 24 cm., hardcover. Swedish translation by Ulf Gyllenhak. ISBN 91-582-1594-8.
aa. As: *Mardrömmar: Första Boken* ['Nightmare dreams: first book']. [Höganäs, Sweden]: Bra Böcker, [1991], 447 pp., 23 cm., hardcover. Swedish translation by Ulf Gyllenhak. ISBN 91-7133-058-5.
bb. As: *Depois da meia-noite* ['Then midnight']. Rio de Janeiro, Brazil: Francisco Alves, 1992, 667 pp., 21 cm., paperback. Portuguese translation by Luisa Ibanez. ISBN 85-265-0264-6.
cc. As: *Efter midnat* ['After midnight']. Copenhagen, Denmark: Artia, 1992, 585 pp., 298 KR, hardcover. Complete; Danish translation by Mogens Wenzel Andreasen. ISBN 87-89294-51-3.
dd. As: *Minuit 2* ['Midnight 2']. Paris, France: France Loisirs, 1992, 448 pp., 108 F, hardcover. French translation by William Olivier Desmond. ISBN 2-7242-6776-1. * Reprint, 1994, ISBN 2-7242- 7985-9.
ee. As: *Después de medianoche* ['After midnight']. Barcelona, Spain: Ediciones B, 1992, 856 pp., 23 cm. Spanish translation by Susan Constante. ISBN 84-406-2973-7.
ff. As: *Las cuatro después de medianoche* ['Four after midnight']. Barcelona, Spain: Ediciones B, ÉXITOS INTERNACIONAL, 1992, 432 pp., 2330 pta, 24 cm., hardcover. Spanish translation by Susana Constante. ISBN 84-406-2281-3.
gg. As: *Las cuatro después de medianoche* ['Four after midnight']. Barcelona, Spain: Círculo de Lectores, 1992, 432 pp., 1533 pta, 23 cm., hardcover. Spanish translation by Susana Constante. ISBN 84-226-4115-1
hh. As: *Ventana Secreta, Jardin Secreto*. Barcelona, Spain: Editorial Grijalbo, 1992. Spanish translation.
ii. As: *Mardrömmar: Andra Boken* ['Nightmare dreams: second book']. [Höganäs, Sweden]: Bra Böcker, [1992], 447-836 pp., 23 cm., hardcover. Swedish translation by Ulf Gyllenhak. ISBN 91-7133-059-3.
jj. As: *Minuit 2* ['Midnight 2']. Paris, France: J'ai Lu, #3529, 1993, 564 pp., 41 F, paperback. French translation by William Olivier Desmond. ISBN 2-277-23529-6. * Reprint, 1995.
kk. As: *Minuit 4* ['Midnight 4']. Paris, France: France Loisirs, 1993, 442 pp., 106 F, hardcover. French translation by William Olivier Desmond. ISBN 2-7242-7191-2. * Reprint, 1994, ISBN 2-7242-7986-7.

ll. As: [Title unknown]. South Korea, 1993, 635 pp., 23 cm. Korean translation. ISBN 89-12-11163-9, 89-12-11165-5.

mm. As: [Title unknown]. South Korea, 1993, 589 pp., 23 cm. Korean translation. ISBN 89-12-11164-7, 89-12-11165-5..

nn. As: *Las dos después de medianoche* ['Two after midnight']. Barcelona, Spain: Ediciones B, VIB #13/4, 1993, 605 pp., 18 cm. Spanish translation by Susana Constante. ISBN 84-406-3692-X.

oo. As: *Las cuatro después de medianoche* ['Two after midnight']. Barcelona, Spain: Ediciones B, VIB #13/5, 1993, 583 pp., 18 cm., paperback. Spanish translation by Susan Constante. ISBN 84-406-3691-1.

pp. As: *Czwarta po pólnocy* ['Four after midnight']. 2 vols. Warsaw, Poland: "Mizar," "Amber," 1994, 397+366 pp., 21 cm. Polish translation by PaweL Korombel. ISBN 83-7082-409-9 [complete].

qq. As: *Las dos después de medianoche* ['Two after midnight']. Barcelona, Spain: RBA, GRANDES ÉXITOS #50, 1994, 429 pp., 22 cm. Spanish translation by Susana Constante. ISBN 84-473-0433-7.

rr. As: *Las cuatro después de medianoche* ['Four after midnight']. Barcelona, Spain: RBA, GRANDES ÉXITOS #69, 1994, 415 pp., 966 pta., 22 cm., trade paperback. Spanish translation by Susana Constante. ISBN 84-473-0525-2.

ss. As: *Four Past Midnight: Featuring the Langoliers.* New York: Signet, May 1995, 744 pp., $6.99, mass-market paperback. Tie-in edition with television miniseries. ISBN 0-451-18597-8.

tt. As: *Ventana Secreta, Jardin Secreto.* New York: Penguin, October 1995, $4.99, 204 pp, mass-market paperback. Spanish translation, no translator given, published for distribution only in the United States and its possessions. ISBN 0-451-18657-5.

uu. As: *Raamatukogupolitseinik öudusromaan.* [Tallinn, Estonia]: Kupar, 1995, 189 pp., 20 cm. Translation by Teet Kallas and Tiito Himma. ISBN 9985610539.

vv. As: *Minuit 4* ['Midnight 4']. Paris, France: J'ai Lu #3670, 1995, paperback. French translation by William Olivier Desmond. ISBN 2-277-23670-5.

ww. As: *Tweeduister* ['Two darks']. Amsterdam, Netherlands: Poema Pocket, 1995, 433 pp. Dutch translation by Frank de Groot. 6th printing. ISBN 90-245-2491-1.

xx. As: *Quattro dopo mezzanotte. I volume* ['Four after midnight. Volume I']. Milan, Italy: Sperling Paperback, SUPERBESTSELLER #551, September 1996. Italian translation by Tullio Dobner. ISBN 88-7824-706-5.
CONTENTS: "I langolieri" pp. 11-280 ["The Langoliers"]; "Finestra segreta, giardino segreto" pp. 281+ ["Secret Window, Secret Garden"].

yy. As: *Quattro dopo mezzanotte. II volume* ['Four after midnight: Volume II']. Milan, Italy: Sperling Paperback, SUPERBESTSELLER #559, December 1996. Italian translation by Tullio Dobner. ISBN 88-7824-750-2.
CONTENTS: "Polizzioto della Biblioteca" pp. 7-232 ["The Library Policeman"]; "Il fotocane" pp. 2331+ ['The photo-dog'="The Sun Dog"].

zz. As: *Cetiri iza ponoci.* 2 vols. Zagreb, Croatia: Sara 93, BIBLIOTEKA DAKA, 1996, 508+477 pp., 21 cm. Croatian translation by Predrag Raos. ISBN 953-6187-19-1, 953-6187-20-5.
aaa. As: *Salaaken, salaaed: öudusromaan.* [Tallinn, Estonia]: Kupar, 1996, 195 pp., 20 cm. Translation by Teet Kallas and Tiito Himma. ISBN 9985611101.
bbb. As: *Meia-noite e dois* ['Midnight and two']. [Lisbon, Portugal]: Círculo de Leitores, 1997, 491 pp., 21 cm. Portuguese translation by Manuel Cordeiro. ISBN 972-42-1704-3.
ccc. As: *Las cuatro después de medianoche* ['Four after midnight']. Barcelona, Spain: Ediciones B., October 1998, 608 pp., 835 pta., paperback. ISBN 84-406-3691-1.
ddd. As: *Etter Midnatt I-II: Langolierne; Hemmelig vindu, hemmelig hage* ['After midnight I-II: "The Langoliers"; "Secret Window, Secret Garden"]. Oslo, Norway: Aschehoug, 1998, 402 pp., 62.00, paperback [*heftet*]. Norwegian translation by Dag Heyerdahl Larsen. ISBN 82-03-20358-2.
eee. As: *Etter Midnatt III-IV: Bibliotekpolitiet; Solhunden* ['After midnight III-IV: "The Library Policeman"; "The Sun Dog"]. Oslo, Norway: Aschehoug, 1998, 373 pp., 62.00, paperback [*heftet*]. Norwegian translation by Dag Heyerdahl Larsen. ISBN 82-03-20359-0.
fff. As: *Meia-noite e quatro* ['Midnight and four']. [Lisbon, Portugal]: Círculo de Leitores, 1998, 447 pp., 21 cm. Portuguese translation by Manuel Cordeiro. ISBN 972-42-1742-6.
ggg. As: *Nachts* ['Nights']. Munich, West Germany: Wilhelm Heyne, #9697, 1999, 509 pp., 16.90 DM, paperback. German translation by Joachim Körber. ISBN 3-453-09220-1.
hhh. As: *Las Dos Despues de Medianoche* ['Two after midnight']. Barcelona, Spain: Ediciones B, [1999], 383 pp., 22 cm. Spanish translation by Susana Constante. ISBN 84-473-1439-1.
iii. As: *Titkos ablak, Titkos hert.* Budapest, Hungary: Európa, 19—. Hungarian translation. Vol. 1. [2 separate editions]
jjj. As: *A Napkutya.* Budapest, Hungary: Európa, 19—. Hungarian translation. Vol. 2. [2 separate editions.]
kkk. Excerpted as: [Title unknown] ["The Library Policeman"]. Slovenia: Zalozby, 19—. Slovenian translation.
lll. As: *Bóka safris löggan.* Icelandic translation.
mmm. As: [Title unknown]. Russia, 19—. Russian translations [multiple].
nnn. As: [Title unknown] ["The Langoliers"]. Greece, 19—. Greek translation.
ooo. As: [Title unknown] ["The Library Policeman"]. Greece, 19—. Greek translation.
ppp. As: [Title unknown] ["Secret Window, Secret Garden"]. Greece, 19—. Greek translation.
qqq. As: [Title unknown] ["The sundog"]. Greece, 19—. Greek translation.
rrr. As: [Title unknown] ["The Langoliers"]. China, 19—. Chinese translation.
sss. As: [Title unknown] ["The Library Policeman"]. China, 19—. Chinese translation.

ttt. As: [Title unknown] ["Secret Window, Secret Garden"]. China, 19—. Chinese translation.
uuu. As: [Title unknown] ["The sundog"]. China, 19—. Chinese translation.
vvv. As: *Bóka safris löggan* ["The Library Policeman']. Iceland, Fródi, 2000(?). Icelandic translation.
www. As: *Sunov pas* ['The Sun Dog']. Serbia: Ridobradi Press, 2000 (?) Serbian translation.
xxx. As: [Title unknown] ['The Langoliers"]. Moscow, Russia: Cadman, 2000(?). Russian translation.

yyy. As AUDIOCASSETTE: See entries under individual stories.

zzz. As TELEVISION MINISERIES: See entries under individual stories.

aaaa. As VIDEOCASSETTE: See entries under individual stories.

SELECTED ARTICLES, RESPONSES, AND REVIEWS:
Belden, Elizabeth A., and Judith M. Beckman. *English Journal* Vol. 80, No. 4 (April 1991): 84.
Blue, Tyson. "Needful Kings." *The Blood Review: Journal of Horror Criticism* Vol. 1, No. 2 (January 1990): 11.
Bodart, Joni. Wilson *Library Journal* Vol. 69, No. 7 (March 1991): BT3.
Bookworld Vol. 20 (26 August 1990): 9.
Booklist Vol. 86 (15 June 1990): 1932.
Bryant, Edward. *Locus* Vol. 25, No. 4, #357 (October 1990).
Cameron, June. "'Four Past Midnight' More of the Unusual from King." *Pittsburgh Press* [PA] 7 October 1990. As microfiche: *NewsBank: Literature* (October 1990): Fiche 103, B9-B10.
Diehl, Digby. *Playboy.* Vol. 37 (October 1990): 30.
Donovan, Mark. *People Weekly* Vol. 34 (15 October 1990): 26+.
Flewelling, Lynn. "'Midnight' Eyes Supernatural." *Bangor Daily News* [ME] 11 September 1990. As microfiche: *NewsBank: Literature* (October 1990): Fiche 103, B2-3.
Gottlieb, Anne. "Three-Dimensional Characters Missing in King's Newest Thriller." *Denver Post* [CO] 2 September 1990. As microfiche: *NewsBank: Literature* (September 1990): Fiche 93, D10.
Hard, Annette. "Stephen King and the Monsters of the Mind: Four Horror Novellas." *Houston Chronicle* [TX] 14 October 1990. As microfiche: *NewsBank: Literature* (November 1990): Fiche 112, D11.
Hauser, Jerald. "King Serves Up a 4-Course Feast of Chilling Horror." *Milwaukee Journal* [WI] 26 August 1990. As microfiche: *NewsBank: Literature* (September 1990): Fiche 93, D14.
Johnson, Dean. "The King Is Back, Horror Fans." *Orlando Sentinel* [FL] 9 September 1990. As microfiche: *NewsBank: Literature* (October 1990): Fiche 103, A14.
Kirkus Reviews Vol. 58 (15 June 1990): 825.

Kloer, Phil. "King's Novella Collection." *Atlanta Journal-Constitution* [GA] 12 August 1990. As microfiche: *NewsBank: Literature* (September 1990): Fiche 93, D11.

Ladd, Susan. "Collection of Novellas Proves King Hasn't Lost His Touch." *Greensboro News and Record* [NC] 16 September 1990. As microfiche: *NewsBank: Literature* (October 1990): Fiche 103, B8.

Lawson, John. *School Library Journal* Vol. 37 (January 1991): 121.

Moore, J. R. T. "The Writer and His Shadow." *SFRA Newsletter* [Science Fiction Research Association] No. 182 (November 1990): 38-39. Brief review of *FPM* embedded in the last paragraph of a review of *The Dark Half*.

Moritz, Robert. *Seventeen* Vol. 49 (December 1990): 69.

Murphy, Ray. "Two Tales Stand Out in New King Quartet." *Boston Globe* [MA] 11 September 1990. As microfiche: *NewsBank: Literature* (October 1990): Fiche 103, B4-B5.

New Statesman & Society Vol. 3 (7 December 1990): 34.

Persico, Joyce J. "Time to Take a Whirlwind to Hell." *Times* [Trenton NJ] 28 October 1990. As microfiche: *NewsBank: Literature* (November 1990): Fiche 112, D9-D10.

Purvis, Kathleen. "King's a Writer, All Right, But He Worries." *Charleston Observer* [NC] 23 September 1990. As microfiche: *NewsBank: Literature* (October 1990): Fiche 103, B7.

Ray, Keith. "King's 'Midnight' May Disappoint Some Fans." *Arizona Daily Star* [Tucson AZ] 30 September 1990. As microfiche: *NewsBank: Literature* (November 1990): Fiche 112, D7.

Schrodt, Anita. "King Reveals How His Tales Started, But Not How They End." *Wichita Eagle* [KS] 23 September 1990. As microfiche: *NewsBank: Literature* (October 1990): Fiche 103, B1.

Schubert, Gail. "Stephen King Serves up New Tales of Terror." *Boston Globe* [MA] 30 September 1990. As microfiche: *NewsBank: Literature* (November 1990): Fiche 112, D8.

Skow, John. *Time* Vol. 136 (15 October 1990): 89.

Slater, Libby. "Sampler Is Vintage King." *Tulsa World* [OK] 26 August 1990). As microfiche: *NewsBank: Literature* (September 1990): Fiche 93, D12.

Solomon, Andy. "Scared But Safe." *New York Times Book Review* (2 September 1990): VII 21.

Stamm, Michael. "King's Title as Horror Fiction Master Remains Secure with Latest Release." *The Register Guard* [Eugene OR] 25 November 1990. As microfiche: *NewsBank: Literature* (1990): Fiche 4, C14.

Steinberg, Sybil. *Publishers Weekly* Vol. 237 (20 June 1990): 48.

Stumpf, Edna. "Four Novellas the Products of the King Horror Factory." *Philadelphia Inquirer* [PA] 26 August 1990. As microfiche: *NewsBank: Literature* (September 1990): Fiche 93, D13.

Tribune Books [Chicago IL] 15 June 1990: 4.

Tribune Books [Chicago IL] 26 August 1990: 3.

Wilson, Shirley. "Horror Returns in 4 King Tales." *The Detroit News and Free Press* [MI] 9 September 1990. As microfiche: *NewsBank: Literature*

(October 1990): Fiche 103, B6.
Young, Elizabeth J. *New Statesman and Society* Vol. 3 (7 December 1990): 34.

A42.
NOUVELLES
(1990)

A42. *NOUVELLES*. Paris: Presses Pocket, 1990, 223 pp., paperback. Bilingual edition of two King short stories intended for schools; French translations and other materials by Michael Oriano. Cover art by Marc Demoulin. ISBN 2-266-02923-1.

CONTENTS: "Comment utiliser ce livre," by Oriano; "Présentation," by Oriano; "The Monkey" (pp. 9-124); "Mrs. Todd's Shortcut" (pp. 125-202; "Enregistrement sonore," by Oriano; Index.

MICHAEL R. COLLINGS

THE DARK TOWER III: THE WASTELANDS. Hampton Falls, NH: Donald M. Grant Publisher, 1991. Limited edition hardcover.

A43.
THE DARK TOWER III
THE WASTE LANDS
(1991)

A43. *THE DARK TOWER III: THE WASTE LANDS*. Hampton Falls, NH: Donald M. Grant Publisher, August 1991, 509 pp., hardcover. Epic-Fantasy novel. * LIMITED EDITION, 1200 copies. Illustrated by Ned Dameron with 12 color illustrations. * TRADE HARDCOVER, $38.00, ISBN 0-937986-17-8.

PLOT SUMMARY: Having successfully "drawn" two others into his alternate world, Roland continues his quest for the Dark Tower. As the small company comes nearer to the center of an ancient Kingdom, they are joined by the boy Jake, likewise drawn by magic from his own world into Roland's. After safely negotiating the perils of a decaying city and its even more decadent inhabitants, the four set out across the waste lands in search of the Tower.

REPRINTS AND ADAPTATIONS:
b.   New York: Plume, January 1992, 422 pp., $15.00, trade paperback. Illustrated by Ned Dameron. Covers by Don Brautigam and Phil Heffernan. ISBN 0-452-26740-4.
c.   New York: Plume, January 1992, 422 pp., trade paperback. Boxed set with the first two books in the series.
d.   London, England: Sphere, January 1992, 512 pp., £8.99, trade paperback. 1st British edition. * Reprint, Avon. ISBN 0-7474-1188-3.
e.   London, England: Warner UK Overseas, August 1992, 512 pp., £3.99, mass-market paperback. Open market edition, not distributed in the UK. ISBN 0-7474-1187-5.
f.   As BOXED EDITION: *The Dark Tower: The Gunslinger, The Drawing of the Three, The Waste Lands.* New York: Plume, October 1992, trade paperback. ISBN 0-451-15346-8.
g.   As: *Terre Desolate* ['Desolate land']. Milan, Italy: Sperling & Kupfer, PANDORA [#625], November 1992. Italian translation by Tullio Dobner. ISBN 88-200-1442-4.
h.   As: *Terres perdues—La tour sombre 3* ['Ruined/wasted lands—the dark tower 3']. Paris, France: J'ai Lu #3243, 1992, 569 pp., 39 F, paperback.

French translation by Jean-Daniel Brèque and Christiane Poulain. ISBN 2-277-23243-2.

i. As: *Tot* ['Dead']. Munich, Germany: Wilhelm Heyne/Vorb, HEYNE-JUMBO-BÄNDE #41, 1992, 453 pp. German translation by Joachim Körber. 1st German edition. ISBN 3-453-05339-7.

j. As: *Tot* ['Dead']. Gütersloh, Austria: Bertelsmann Club, 1992, 453 pp., hardcover. German translation by Joachim Körber. Book Club edition.

k. As: *De Donkere Toren III: Het verloren Rijk* ['The dark tower III: the lost realm']. Utrecht, Belgium, Netherlands: Luitingh-Sijthoff, 1992, 534 pp. Dutch translation by Hugo Timmerman. ISBN 90-245-1628-5. 2nd printing 1993, ISBN 90-245-1628-5.

l. New York: Signet, January 1993 [December 1992], 590 pp., $6.99, mass-market paperback. ISBN 0-451-17331-7.

m. As BOXED EDITION: *The Dark Tower: The Gunslinger, The Drawing of the Three, The Waste Lands*. New York: Signet, January 1993, 590 pp., mass-market paperback.

n. As: *Ødemarken* ['Desert-fields/lands']. Copenhagen, Denmark: Artia, 1993, 442 pp., 298 KR, hardcover. Danish translation by Mogens Wenzel Andreasen. 1st Danish edition. ISBN 87-89918-13-4.

o. As: *Musta torni 3—Joutomaa*. ['"Dark tower 3: idle-land']. Helsinki, Finland: Book Studio, 1993, 654 pp. Finnish translation. ISBN 951-611-620-5; 951-611-620-4.

p. As: *La tour sombre*. Paris, France: France Loisirs, 1994, 1169 pp., 118 F, hardcover. French translations by Gérard Lebec, Jean-Daniel Brèque and Christiane Poulain. ISBN 2-7242-8191-8. Omnibus with *Le pistolero, Les troi cartes* and *Terres perdues*.

q. As: *Las Tierras Baldías—La Torre Oscura 3* ['The dark tower 3']. Barcelona, Spain: Ediciones B, ÉXITO INTERNACIONAL, 1994, 486 pp., 18 cm., paperback. Spanish translation by Jorge Luis Mustieles. ISBN 84-406-4430-2.

r. As: *Las Tierras Baldías—La Torre Oscura 3* ['The dark tower 3']. Barcelona, Spain: Círculo de Lectores, [1995], 633 pp., 22 cm. Spanish translation by Jorge LuisMustieles. ISBN 84-226-5577-2.

s. As: *Terre Desolate* ['Desolate land']. Milan, Italy: Sperling Paperback, SUPERBESTSELLER #519, June 1996. Italian translation by Tullio Dobner. ISBN 88-7824-655-7.

t. As BOXED EDITION: *The Dark Tower: The Gunslinger, The Drawing of the Three, The Waste Lands*. New York: New American Library, September 1997, $23.97, mass-market paperback. ISBN 0-451-93554-3.

u. New York: Penguin/Plume, November 1997, 422 pp., $17.95, trade paperback. Cover art by John Jude Palencar. 3rd printing.ISBN 0-452-27962-3.

v. London, England: New English Library, 584 pp., £6.99, paperback. Cover art by Bob Warner. ISBN 0-340-70752-6.

w. As: *Tot* ['Dead']. Munich, Germany: Wilhelm Heyne TB 10430, November 1997, 16.90 DM, paperback. German translation by Joachim Körber. ISBN 3-453-12386-7.

x. As: *Het verloren Rijk: De Donkere Toren III* ['The lost realm: the dark tower 3']. Amsterdam, Netherlands: Poema Pocket, 1997, 534 pp., paperback. Dutch translation by Hugo Timmerman. 3rd printing. ISBN 90-245-2718-X.
y. As: *Musta torni 1-3.* ['Black tower']. Helsinki, Finland: Book Studio, 1998, 654 pp. Finnish translation . ISBN 951-611-901-8.
z. As: *Terres perdues—La tour sombre 3* ['Wasted lands: the dark tower 3']. Paris, France: Éditions 84, 1998, 455 pp., 115 F, paperback. French translation by Jean-Daniel Brèque and Christiane Poulain. ISBN 2-277-25034-1.
aa. As: *Tot: Der Dunkle Turm 3* ['Dead; the dark tower 3']. Rheda-Wiedenbrück, Germany: Bertelsmann-Club, 1998, 509 pp., hardcover. New edition. German translation by joachim Körber. Book Club edition.
bb. As: *Ødemarken* ['Desert fields/land']. Copenhagen, Denmark: Vinten, VINTENS PAPERBACKS/VINTENS FANTASY, 1998, 463 pp., 98 KR, hardcover. Danish translation by Mogens Wenzel Andreasen. ISBN 87-612-0168-5.
cc. As: *De Donkere Toren III: Het verloren Rijk* ['The dark tower 3: the lost realm']. Amsterdam, Netherlands: Luitingh-Sijthoff, 1998, 455 pp. Dutch translation by Hugo Timmerman. 5th printing. ISBN 90-245-1090-2.
dd. As: *Las Tierras Baldías—La Torre Oscura 3.* Barcelona, Spain: Ediciones B, VIB #13/8, 1998, 684 pp., 18 cm., paperback. Spanish translation by Jordi Mustieles. ISBN 84-406-8799-0.
ee. As: *The Dark Tower.* West Kingston RI: Donald M. Grant, February 1999, $117.00, boxed set containing *The Gunslinger,* 3rd printing; *The Drawing of the Three,* 2nd edition; and *The Waste Lands.* ISBN 1-880418-40-1.
ff. As: [Title unknown]. Korean translation.
gg. As: [Title unknown]. Moscow, Russia: Cadman, 19—. Russian translation.
hh. As: [Title unknown]. Russian translation (additional to above).
ii. As AUDIOCASSETTE: *The Waste Lands: The Dark Tower III.* St. Paul, MN: Penguin-Highbridge Audio, 1991. Read by Stephen King. 12 cassettes; 18 hours.
   SELECTED REVIEWS:
   Smith, Kristen L. *Library Journal* Vol. 117, No. 3 (15 February 1991): 220.
jj. As AUDIOCASSETTE: New York: Penguin Audiobooks, May 1999, $45.95, unabridged. Read by Frank Muller. ISBN 0-140-86717-1.

COMMENTS: The third volume in The Dark Tower series, *The Waste Lands* is much less a collection of individual stories than the two previous books, and more a coherent segment of a novel-in-progress. Images and scenes from *The Waste Lands* recur in *Insomnia*, providing an important link between the two novels, a heightened sense of progression to the Dark Tower Tales, and the suggestion of 'ultimate' connections among a significant number of King's novels and stories.

SELECTED ARTICLES, RESPONSES, AND REVIEWS:
Analog Science Fiction/Science Fact Vol. 112 (June 1992): 162+.
Booklist Vol. 88 (15 October 1991): 382.
Booklist Vol. 88 (15 January 1992): 870.
Bloomsbury Review Vol. 11 (December 1991): 27.
Bookwatch Vol. 12 (October 1991): 3.
Kirkus Reviews Vol. 59 (15 September 1991): 1176.
Kliatt Young Adult Paperback Book Guide Vol. 26 (April 1992): 14+.
Locus Vol. 27 (November 1991): 21.
Locus Vol. 27 (November 1991): 56.
Locus Vol. 28 (January 1992): 57.
Nicholls, Richard E. *New York Times Book Review* Vol. 96 (29 September 1991): 14.
Publishers Weekly Vol. 238, No. 49 (8 November 1991): 60-61.
Rapport. *West Coast Review of Books*, "Art & Entertainment" Vol. 16 (5 May 1992): 21.
Science Fiction Chronicle Vol. 13 (October 1991): 42.
School Library Journal Vol. 38 (August 1992): 195.
Voice of Youth Advocates Vol. 15 (June 1992): 110.

Horror Plum'd

Needful Things. New York, NY: Viking, 1991. Hardcover.

A44.
NEEDFUL THINGS
(1991)

A44. *NEEDFUL THINGS: THE LAST CASTLE ROCK STORY.* New York: Viking, October 1991, 690 pp., $24.95, hardcover. Cover art by Rob Wood-Stansbury. Horror novel. ISBN 0-670-83953-1.

PLOT SUMMARY: The citizens of Castle Rock, Maine, are curious and excited when a new store opens; the proprietor, Leland Gaunt, seems to know just what each of them needs...or, at least, what each of them desperately *wants*. More remarkably, he also seems able to fill those needs for surprisingly little money and the promise of a small prank to be played on someone else. Only gradually does it become clear that Gaunt is orchestrating his pranks, manipulating individuals and events, and systematically playing one person's greed off against another's obsession, until the souls of Castle Rock's inhabitants are literally at stake.

REPRINTS AND ADAPTATIONS:
b. London, England: Hodder & Stoughton, October 1991, 698 pp., £15.99, hardcover. Simultaneous with U.S. 1st edition. ISBN 0-340-54673-5.
c. New York: Book of the Month Club, October 1991, 704 pp., $21.95, hardcover. No ISBN assigned.
d. As: *In Einer Kleinen Stadt—Needful Things* ['In a small town']. Hamburg, West Germany: Hoffman und Campe, 1991, 695 pp, 44.00 DM, hardcover. German translation by Christel Wiemkin. ISBN 3-455-03739-9. 2nd printing, 1992.
e. As: *De Noodzaak* ['The necessity']. Utrecht, Belgium, Netherlands: Luitingh-Sijthoff, 1991, 17.50fl. Dutch translation. ISBN 9-024-51599-8.
f. As: *Cose preziose* ['Precious things']. Milan, Italy: Sperling & Kupfer, PANDORA [#578], January 1992. Italian translation by Tullio Dobner. ISBN 88-200-1284-7.
g. New York: Signet/New American Library, July 1992, 736 pp., $6.99, mass-market paperback. Cover art by Rob Wood. ISBN 0-451-17281-7. * 10th printing, August 1993, movie tie-in edition, ISBN 0-451-17859-9.
h. New York: Book of the Month Club/Quality Paperback Club, August 1992,

690 pp., $13.95, trade paperback. Cover art by Rob Wood. No ISBN assigned.

i. London, England: New English Library, October 1992, 790 pp., £5.99, paperback. Open market edition not distributed in the U.K. ISBN 0-450-57458-X. * Reprint, October 1992 for U.K. distribution. * Reprint, May 1994, movie tie-in edition, ISBN 0-450-61361-5.

j. Boston: G. K. Hall & Co., 1992, hardcover and paperback. Large print edition.

k. Burnsville MN: Econo-Clad/Sagebrush, 1992, 731 pp., $15.70, library binding. #1030592.

l. As: *Tarpeelista tavaraa* ['Requisite articles']. Helsinki, Finland: Tammi, 1992, 734 pp., 23 cm. Finnish translation by Ilkka Rekiaro. ISBN 951-30-9436-7. * 2nd printing, 1992, ISBN 951-31-0135-5.

m. As: *Bazaar: Roman* ['Bazaar: Novel']. Paris, France: Albin Michel, 1992, 678 pp., 150 F, 24 cm., paperback. French translation by William Olivier Desmond. ISBN 2-226-05947-4.

n. As: *Bazaar: Roman* ['Bazaar: Novel']. [Paris, France]: le Grand livre du mois, 1992, 673 pp., 150 F, 25 cm., hardcover. French translation by William Olivier Desmond. Book Club edition.

o. As: *In einer kleinen Stadt* ['In a small town']. Gütersloh, Austria: Bertelsmann-Club; Vienna, Austria: Buchgemeinschaft Donauland Kremayr und Scheriau, and others, [1992], 695 pp., hardcover. German translation by Christel Wiemkin. Book Club editions.

p. As: *K'aesullok ui Pimil*. 3 vol. Seoul, South Korea: Toesong, 1992, 329+340+320 pp., 23 cm., paperback. Korean translation. ISBN 89-7177-018-X, 89-7177-019-8, 89-7177-020-1.

q. As: *De Noodzaak* ['The necessity']. Utrecht [later Amsterdam], Netherlands: Luitingh-Sijthoff, 1992, 616 pp. Dutch translation by Rein van Essen. ISBN 90-245-1988-8. * 8th printing, 1995.

r. As: *Trocas macabras* ['Macabre exchanges/trades']. Rio de Janeiro, Brazil: Francisco Alves, MESTRES DO HORROR E DA FANTASIA, 1992, 558 pp., 21 cm., paperback. Portuguese translation by Toni Thomson. ISBN 85-265-0283-2.

s. As: *Noe for enhver* ['Something for everyone']. Oslo, Norway: Aschehoug, 1992, 634 pp. Norwegian translation by Per Malde. ISBN 82-03-16981-6. Book club edition, ISBN 82-598-0129-9.

t. As: *La Tienda* ['The shop']. Barcelona, Spain: Ediciones B, ÉXITO INTERNACIONAL, 1992, 772 pp., 24 cm. Spanish translation by Hernán Sabaté. ISBN 84-406-2930-3.

u. As: *Köplust* ['Inclination to buy']. Höganäs, Sweden: Bra Böcker, 1992, 728 pp., 23 cm., hardcover. Swedish translation by Lennart Olafsson. 91-7133-060-7.

v. As: *Köplust* ['Inclination to buy']. Stockholm, Sweden: Legenda, 1992, 727 pp., 24 cm., hardcover. Swedish translation by Lennart Olafsson. 91-27-03213-2.

w. As: *Bazaar: Roman* ['Bazaar: novel']. Paris, France: France Loisirs, 1993,

678 pp., 114F, 25 cm., hardcover. French translation by William Olivier Desmond. ISBN 2-7242-7418-0.

x. As: *In Einer Kleinen Stadt—Needful Things* ['In a small town']. Munich, Germany: Wilhelm Heyne, #8653, 1993, 767 pp., 16.90 DM, paperback. German translation by Christel Wiemkin. ISBN 3-453-06131-4. * 5th printing, 1994. * 8th printing, 1995.

y. As: *La Tienda de los Deseps Malignos* ['The shop of malignant desires']. Miguel Hidalgo, Mexico: Grijalbo, BESTSELLER ORO, April 1993, 666 pp., trade paperback with jacket flaps. Spanish translation by Elisa Moreno. ISBN 970-05-0419-0.

z. As: *Köplust* ['Inclination to buy']. Stockholm, Sweden: Legenda, 1993, 727 pp., 24 cm., hardcover. Swedish translation by Lennart Olafsson. 91-27-03673-1.

aa. As: *Neobkhodimye Veshchi: Poslednaia Naibolee Polnaia Istoriia Kastl Roka*. L'vov: Khronos, 1993, 573 pp. Ukrainian translation by L. A. Gridin, O. V. Beimuk, and E. IU. Kharitonova.

bb. London, England: New English Library, 1994, 790 pp., mass-market paperback.

cc. As: *Begærets butik* ['Shop of desires']. Copenhagen, Denmark: Artia, 1994, 536 pp., 298 KR, hardcover. Danish translation by Anders Westenholz. 1st Danish edition. ISBN 87-89918-08-8.

dd. As: *Begærets butik* ['Shop of desires']. 2 vols. Copenhagen, Denmark: Paperback Bogklubben, 1994, 571 pp., 36 KR, paperback. Danish translation by Anders Westenholz. ISBN 87-7803-524-4, 87-7803-527-9.

ee. As: *Bazaar: Roman* ['Bazaar:novel']. 2 vols. Paris, France: J'ai Lu, #3817-3818, 1994, 382+446 pp., 41 F, 17 cm., paperback. French translation by William Olivier Desmond. ISBN 2-277-23817-1; 2-277-23818-X.

ff. As: *In Einer Kleinen Stadt—Needful Things* ['In a small town']. Munich, Germany: Wilhelm Heyne, #8999, 1994, 767 pp., 15.00 DM, paperback. German translation by Christel Wiemkin. 4th printing 1995. ISBN 3-453-07936-1.

gg. As: [Title unknown.]. Tel Aviv, Israel: Modan, 1994, 713 pp. Hebrew translation.

hh. As: *Noe for enhver* ['Something for everyone']. Oslo, Norway: Aschehoug, 1994, 634 pp. Norwegian translation by Per Malde. ISBN 82-03-20053-2.

ii. As: *La Tienda* ['The shop']. 2 vols. Barcelona, Spain: Ediciones B, GRANDES ÉXITOS #85-86, 1994, 22 cm. Spanish translation by Hernán Sabaté. ISBN 84-473-0691-7.

jj. As: *La Tienda* ['The shop']. Barcelona, Spain: Círculo de Lectores, [1994], 862 pp., 22 cm. Spanish translation by Hernán Sabaté. ISBN 84-226-4835-0.

kk. As: *Potrebne stvari*. 2 vols. Zagreb, Croatia: Sara 93, BIBLIOTEKA DAKA, 1996, 330+384 pp., 20 cm. Translation by Evelina Mi_cin. ISBN 953-6187-21-3.

ll. As: *Sklepik z marzeniami* ['Shop of drams/desires']. 2 vols. Warsaw, Poland: "Prima," 1996, 350+383 pp., 21 cm. Polisn translation by Krzysztof Sokolowski. ISBN 83-7152-028-X.

mm. As: *Begærets butik* ['Shop of desires']. Copenhagen, Denmark: Vinten, VINTENS PAPERBACKS, 1996, 571 pp., 98 KR, paperback. Danish translation by Anders Westenholz. ISBN 87-612-0152-9.

nn. As: *De Noodzaak* ['The necessity']. Amsterdam, Netherlands: Poema Pocket, 1997, 616 pp., paperback. Dutch translation by Rein van Essen. 11th printing. ISBN 90-245-1477-0.

oo. As: *Cose preziose* ['Precious things']. Milan, Italy: Sperling & Kupfer, 1998. Italian translation.

pp. As: *Cose preziose* ['Precious things']. Milan, Italy: Sperling Paperback, SUPERBESTSELLER #593, May 1997. Italian translation by Tullio Dobner. ISBN 88-7824-744-8.

qq. As: *Noe for enhver* ['Something for everyone']. Oslo, Norway: Aschehoug, 1998, 624 pp., 62.00, paperback [*heftet*]. Norwegian translation by Per Malde. ISBN 82-03-20363-9.

rr. As: *Sklepik z marzeniami*. 2 vols. Warsaw, Poland: Œwiat Ksiazki, 1998, 350+383 pp., 21 cm. Polisn translation by Krzysztof Sokolowski. ISBN 83-7129-642-8, 83-7129-643-6.

ss. As: *La Tienda* ['The shop']. Barcelona, Spain: Ediciones B, BIBLIOTECA DE BOLSILLO #58, 1998, 971 pp., 19 cm., paperback. Spanish translation by Hernán Sabaté. ISBN 84-406-8031-7.

tt. As: *La Tienda* ['The shop']. Barcelona, Spain: Ediciones B, 1998, 772 pp., 24 cm. Spanish translation by Hernán Sabaté. 4th printing. ISBN 84-473406-5013-2.

uu. As: *La Tienda* ['The shop']. Barcelona, Spain: Ediciones B, VIB #13/6, 2000, 965 pp., 18 cm., paperback. Spanish translation by Hernán Sabaté. ISBN 84-406-9568-3.

vv. As: [Title unknown]. Moscow, Russia: Cadman, 19—. Russian translation.

ww. As: *Hasznos Holmik* ['Useful things/belongings']. Budapest, Hungary: Európa, 19—. Hungarian translation.

xx. As: [Title unknown]. Greece: Bell, 19—. Greek translation.

yy. As: *La tienda* ['The Shop']. Barcelona, Spain: Ediciones B, GRUPO ZETA, February 2000, 974 pp., mass-market paperback. Spanish translation by Hernán Sabaté. 1st edition in this collection. ISBN 84-406-9568-3.

zz. As AUDIOCASSETTE: *Needful Things, Part I: Grand Opening Celebration*. New York: New American Library, 30 September 1991. Six cassettes, 9 hours, $29.95. Read by Stephen King. Re-released: St. Paul, MN: Penguin-Highbridge Audio, 1991.
    SELECTED ARTICLES, RESPONSES, AND REVIEWS:
    Cheuse, Alan. *Forbes* Vol. 149, No. 6 (16 March 1992): S24.

aaa. As AUDIOCASSETTE: *Needful Things, Part II: Sale of the Century*. New York: New American Library, September 30, 1991, $29.95. Six cassettes, 9 hours. Read by Stephen King. Re-released: St. Paul, MN: Penguin-Highbridge Audio, 1991.

bbb. As AUDIOCASSETTE: *Needful Things, Part III: Everything Must Go*. New

York: New American Library, 30 September 1991, $29.95. Six cassettes, 9 hours. Read by Stephen King. Re-released: St. Paul, MN: Penguin-Highbridge Audio, 1991.

ccc. As AUDIOCASSETTE: *Needful Things, Parts I, II, III*. New York: New American Library, 30 September 1991, $89.85. Eighteen cassettes, 27 hours. Read by Stephen King. Re-released: St. Paul, MN: Penguin-Highbridge Audio, 1991, $49.95.

ddd. As AUDIOCASSETTE: New York: Penguin Audiobooks, August 1993, $49.95, movie tie-in edition. Read by Stephen King. ISBN 0-453-00859-3.

EEE. As FILM: Columbia/Castle Rock Entertainment/New Line Cinema, 1993. Executive producer, Peter Yates. Produced by Jack Cummins. Directed by Fraser C. Heston. Screenplay by W. D. Richter. 121 minutes. Rated: R. CAST: Ed Harris, Max von Sydow, Bonnie Bedelia, J. T. Walsh, Valri Bromfield, Ray McKinnon, Amanda Plummer.

fff. As VIDEOCASSETTE: New Line Home Video/Columbia Tristar Home Video, 1994, #53223. 121 minutes. Rating: R.

COMMENTS: In what King has called the last Castle Rock story, he weaves his tapestry with an intricate number of strands (just as does Leland Gaunt), including multiple trademark references to past characters and stories; at the same time, he also creates his clearest, most successful direct confrontation between the White and the Dark, connecting this novel implicitly with such novels as *The Talisman,* the restored version of *The Stand,* and the on-going Dark Tower series.

SELECTED ARTICLES, RESPONSES, AND REVIEWS:
Blue, Tyson. "Needful Kings." *The Blood Review: Journal of Horror Criticism* Vol. 1, No. 2 (January 1990): 11.
Booklist Vol. 87 (15 June 1991): 1907.
Booklist Vol. 88 (15 March 1992): 1398.
Books (March 1994): 16.
Bookworld Vol. 21 (29 September 1991): 9.
Collings, Michael R. *Mystery Scene* No. 31 (October 1991): 51-52.
Kanfer, Stefan. *Time* Vol. 138, No. 19 (11 November 1991): GT12.
Kirkus Reviews Vol. 59 (1 July 1991): 813.
Kliatt Young Adult Paperback Book Guide Vol. 26 (November 1992): 9.
Lehmann-Haupt, Christopher. "Books of the Times: Turning Favors into Catastrophe." *New York Times* [late edition] Vol. 141 (3 October 1991): C23.
Locus Vol. 27 (July 1991): 23.
Locus Vol. 27 (August 1991): 29.
Locus Vol. 27 (December 1991): 53.
Locus Vol. 28 (August 1992): 53.
Los Angeles Times Book Review 20 October 1991: 6.

Magazine of Fantasy & Science Fiction Vol. 82 (January 1992): 45+.
Newsweek 118 (16 September 1991): 60.
Observer [London] (17 November 1991): 64.
Publishers Weekly Vol. 238, No. 32 (25 July 1991): 36.
Queenan, Joe. "And Us Without Our Spoons." *The New York Times Book Review* 29 September 1991: 13.
Schwartz, Gil. *Fortune* Vol. 124, No. 15 (30 December 1991): 137.
Science Fiction Chronicle Vol. 13 (March 1992): 20+.
Sutherland, John. *Times Literary Supplement* No. 4624 (15 November 1991): 6.
Voice of Youth Advocates Vol. 15 (December 1992): 293.
Voice of Youth Advocates Vol. 16 (April 1993): 16.

Horror Plum'd

Gerald's Game. New York, NY: Viking, 1992. Hardcover.

A45.
GERALD'S GAME
(1992)

A45. GERALD'S GAME. New York: Viking, May 1992, 332 pp., $23.50, hardcover. Cover art by Rob Wood. Illustrated by Bill Russell. ISBN 0-670-84650-3. Promotional limited advanced edition distributed at the ABA, September 1992.

PLOT SUMMARY: When Gerald Burlingame's marital bondage-game gets out of hand and his wife Jessie kicks him in the chest and groin, Gerald dies, leaving her handcuffed to the bed in their lakeside cabin. She struggles to free herself from the handcuffs and from emotional and psychological bondage she has endured for most of her life.

REPRINTS AND ADAPTATIONS:
b. London, England: Hodder and Stoughton, July 1992, 342 pp., £14.99, hardcover. ISBN 0-340-57493-3.
c. New York: Book of the Month Club, August 1992, $19.95, 332 pp., hardcover. Cover art by Rob Wood. No ISBN assigned.
d. London, England: BCA, 1992, 342 pp. Book Club edition.
e. Hingham, MA: Wheeler Publishing, 1992, 447 pp., Large print edition.
f. As: *De Spelbreker* ['The spoil-sport']. Utrecht, Belgium, Netherlands: Luitingh-Sijthoff, 1992, 314. Dutch translation by Lucien Duzee. 1st Dutch edition, ISBN 90-245-1239-5. * 3rd printing, 1993, ISBN 90-245-1239-5. * 5th printing, 1996, ISBN 90-245-2656-6.
g. As: *Das Spiel* ['The game']. Munich, Germany: Wilhelm Heyne, JUMBO-BÄNDE #42, 1992, 344 pp., paperback. German translation by Joachim Körber. ISBN 3-452-05703-1.
h. As: *Il gioco di Gerald* [Gerald's Game']. Milan, Italy: Sperling & Kupfer, PANDORA [#628], January 1993. Italian translation by Tullio Dobner. ISBN 88-200-1498-X.
i. London, England: New English Library, May 1993, 394 pp., £5.99, paperback. ISBN 0-450-58623-5.
j. New York: Signet, July 1993, 445 pp., $6.99, mass-market paperback. Cover art by Rob Wood. ISBN 0-451-17646-4. Reprinted July 1993.

MICHAEL R. COLLINGS

k. As: *Julma leikki* ['Cruel play']. Halsinki, Finland: Tammi, 1993, 367 pp., [*kartt.*]. Finnish translation by Heikki Karjalainen. ISBN 951-31-0128-2.
l. As: *Jessie: Roman*. Paris, France: Albin Michel, 1993, 389 pp., 130 F, paperback. French translation by Mimi Perrin and Isabelle Perrin. ISBN 2-226-06340-4.
m. As: *Jessie: Roman*. [Paris, France]: le Grande livre du mois, 1993, 389 pp., 130 F, hardcover. French translation by Mimi Perrin and Isabelle Perrin. Book Club edition.
n. As: *Jessie: Roman*. Paris, France: France Loisirs, 1993, 389 pp., 96 F, hardcover. French translation by Mimi Perrin and Isabelle Perrin. ISBN 2-7242-7673-6.
o. As: *Das Spiel* ['The game']. Gütersloh, Austria: Bertelsmann, 1993, 350 pp., hardcover. German translation by Joachim Körber. Book Club edition..
p. As: *El Juego de Gerald* ['Gerald's game']. Mexico, D.F.: Editorial Grijalbo, 1993, 452 pp. Spanish translation by María Vidal.
q. As: *El Juego de Gerald* ['Gerald's game']. Barcelona, Spain: Grijalbo, BESTSELLER ORO, 1993, 452 pp., 24 cm. Spanish translation by María Vidal. ISBN 84-253-2468-8.
r. As: *Geralds Lek* ['Gerald's game/play']. Oslo, Norway: Aschehoug, 1993, 279 pp. Norwegian translation by Steinar Moe. ISBN 82-03-20003-6. Book Club edition, 82-598-014108. * 2nd printing, 1994, ISBN 82-03-20052-4.
s. As: *El Juego de Gerald* ['Gerald's game']. Barcelona, Spain: Círculo de Lectores, [1993], 398 pp., 23 cm. Spanish translation by María Vidal. ISBN 84-226-4593-9.
t. As: *Geralds farlige leg* ['Gerald's dangerous game']. Copenhagen, Denmark: Artia, 1994, 346 pp., 228 KR, hardcover. Danish translation by Mogens Wenzel Andreasen. ISBN 87-89918-42-8.
u. As: *Geralds farlige leg* ['Gerald's dangerous game']. Copenhagen, Denmark: Bogklubben Egmont/DBK, 1994, 346 pp., 98 KR, hardcover. Danish translation by Mogens Wenzel Andreasen. ISBN 87-7803-122-2. Book Club edition.
v. As: *O jogo de Gerald* ['Gerald's game']. Venda Nova, Portugal: Bertrand, GRANDES ROMANCES #7, 1994, 330 pp., 23 cm. Portuguese translation by Luís Nazaré. ISBN 972-25-0857-1.
w. As: *Geralds Lek* ['Gerald's game/play']. Stockholm, Sweden: Natur och Kultur, 1994, 329 pp., 24 cm., hardcover. Swedish translation by Lennart Olofsson. ISBN 91-27-03979-X.
x. As: *Gra Geralda* ['Gerald's Game']. Warszawa, Poland: "Prima," 1994, 302 pp., 21 cm. Polish translation by Tomasz Wyzynski. ISBN 83-8585-533-5.
y. As: *Jogo perigoso* ['Dangerous game']. Rio de Janeiro, Brazil: Objetiva, [1995], viii+320 pp., 21 cm. Portuguese translation by Lia Wyler. ISBN 109876543.
z. As: *Jessie*. Paris, France: J'ai Lu #4027, 1995, 441 pp., 40 F, 18 cm., paperback. French translation by Mimi Perrin and Isabelle Perrin. ISBN 2-277-24027-3.

aa. As: *Das Spiel* ['The game']. Munich, Germany: Wilhelm Heyne, TB 9518, 1995, 411 pp., 14.90 DM, paperback. German translation. ISBN 3-453-08824-7.
bb. As: *Geralds farlige leg* ['Gerald's dangerous game']. Copenhagen, Denmark: Paperback Bogklubben, 1996, 319 pp., 39,50 KR, paperback. Danish translation by Mogens Wenzel Andreasen. ISBN 87-7803-523-6. Book Club edition.
cc. As: *El juego de Gerald* ['Gerald's game']. Barcelona, Spain: Grijalbo Mondadori, LIBRO DE MANO #50, 1996, 21 cm. Spanish translation by María Vidal. 1st edition in this collection. ISBN 84-253-2933-7.
dd. As: *Geralds farlige leg* ['Gerald's dangerous game']. Copenhagen, Denmark: Vinten/DBK, VINTENS PAPERBACKS, 1997, 319 pp., 88 KR, paperback. Danish translation by Mogens Wenzel Andreasen. ISBN 87-612-0151-0.
ee. As: *Igra Dzeralca*. Moscow, Russia: AST, 1997, 432 pp., 21 cm. Russian translation by V. Levitov (?). ISBN 5-03-003094-8.
ff. As: *Il gioco di Gerald* ['Gerald's Game']. Milan, Italy: Sperling Paperback, SUPERBESTSELLER #639, January 1998. Italian translation by Tullio Dobner. ISBN 88-7824-805-3.
gg. As: *O jogo de Gerald* ['The game of Gerald']. [Lisbon, Portugal]: Círculo de Leitores, GRANDES ROMANCES #7, 19—, 402 pp., 21 cm. Portuguese translation by Lídia Geer. ISBN 972-42-1666-7.
hh. As: *De Spelbreker* ['The spoil-sport']. Utrecht, Belgium: Luitingh-Sijthoff, 19—, paperback. Dutch translation.
ii. As: [Title unknown]. Greek translation.
jj. As: *D'jeraldo 'jaidimas*. Lithuanian translation.
kk. As: [Title unknown]. Tel Aviv, Israel: Modan, 19—. Hebrew translation.
ll. As: *Bilincsben*. Budapest, Hungary: Európa. Hungarian translation.

mm. As AUDIOCASSETTE: St Paul MN: Penguin-Highbridge Audio, July 1992. Twelve cassettes; unabridged, 13 hours. Read by Lindsay Crouse. ISBN 0-453 00800 3.
SELECTED ARTICLES, RESPONSES, AND REVIEWS:
Pober, Stanley. *Library Journal* Vol. 117, No. 16 (1 October 1992): 132.
nn. As AUDIOCASSETTE: *El juego de Gerald ['Gerald's Game']*. Los Angeles CA: Dove Books Audio. 1995. Spanish translation. Read by Marisa de Leon.

COMMENTS: There is little of the supernatural or of overt, external horror in *Gerald's Game*, and those few elements are either explained away or left largely undeveloped. More than most King works, this novel seems driven by a need to respond to a particular social agenda. The novel was, however, among the first to receive widespread positive responses from mainstream critics and reviewers, a number of whom celebrated the sense that with this novel Stephen King had finally left the 'monsters' behind and was finally prepared to tackle the real problems of the real world—an interesting interpretation, since at his finest King has consistently written about the 'real' world through the mediation of monsters/horrors-as-symbols.

SELECTED ARTICLES, RESPONSES, AND REVIEWS:
Booklist Vol. 88 (1 May 1992): 1563.
Books Vol. 7 (May 1993): 20.
Bryant, Edward. *Locus* Vol. 29, No. 3, #380 (September 1992): 21.
Doniger, Wendy. "Shackled to the Past." *New York Times Book Review* 16 August 1992): 3.
Entertainment Weekly (July 16, 1993): 53.
Gates, David. *Newsweek* Vol. 120, No. 1 (6 July 1992): 56.
Kirkus Reviews Vol. 60 (15 April 1992): 487.
Lehmann-Haupt, Christopher. "Books of the Times: To Be Read in Daylight, Away from Hungry Dogs." *New York Times* [late edition] Vol. 141 (29 June 1992): C13.
Locus Vol. 29 (August 1992): 53.
Locus Vol. 29 (July 1992): 50.
Locus Vol. 30 (August 1993): 46.
Magazine of Fantasy & Science Fiction Vol. 83 (December 1992): 31+.
New York Magazine Vol. 26 (2 August 1993): 21.
Publishers Weekly Vol. 239, No. 24 (25 May 1992): 38.
Schwartz, Gil. *Fortune* Vol. 126, No. 4 (24 August 1992): 148-149.
Science Fiction Chronicle Vol. 13 (August 1992): 49.
Time Vol. 140, No. 2 (13 July 1992): 81.
Washington Post Book World Vol. 22 (19 July 1992): 7.
West Coast Review of Books, "Art & Entertainment" Vol. 17 (January 1992): 26.

Horror Plum'd

MICHAEL R. COLLINGS

GERALD'S GAME. New York, NY: Viking, 1993. Hardcover.

A46.
DOLORES CLAIBORNE
(1993)

A46. *DOLORES CLAIBORNE.* New York: Viking, November 1993, 305 pp., $23.50, hardcover. Cover art by Rob Wood. Illustrated by Bill Russell. ISBN 0-670-84452-7. Novel.

PLOT SUMMARY: Dolores Claiborne appears late one evening at the Little Tall Island police station to clear herself of suspicion in one murder by admitting to another. To convince authorities that she did not kill her employer, she gives a detailed account of her relationship with Vera Donovan and of the circumstances surrounding the death of her husband, Joe St. George, years before.

REPRINTS AND ADAPTATIONS:
b. New York: Book of the Month Club, $19.95, 305 pp., hardcover. No ISBN listed.
c. London, England: BCA, 1992, 241 pp. Book Club edition of approximately 2,000 copies; possible the true first edition of the novel.
d. New York: Viking, 1993, 332 pp., paperback(?). Large print edition.
e. London, England: Hodder & Stoughton, February 1993, 241 pp., £14.99, hardcover. ISBN 0-340-54672-7.
f. London, England: New English Library, October 1993, 307 pp., £4.99, paperback. ISBN 0-450-58886-6.
g. New York: Signet, December 1993, 372 pp., mass-market paperback. Reissued May 1996, $7.99. ISBN 0-451-17709-6.
h. Sevenoaks, Kent: New English Library, 1993, 307 pp., mass-market paperback.
i. As: *Doloreksen Tunnustus* [Dolores' confession']. Helsinki, Finland: Tammi, 1993, 273 pp., paperback [*kart.*]. Finnish translation by Ilkka Rekiaro. ISBN 951-30-9437-5.
j. As: *Doloreksen Tunnustus* [Dolores' confession']. Helsinki, Finland: Suuri Suomalainen Kirjakerho, 1993, 273 pp., hardcover (?). Finnish translation by Ilkka Rekiaro. ISBN 651-643-427-4.
k. As: *Dolores Claiborne: Roman.* Paris, France: Albin Michel, 1993, 324 pp.,

120 F, paperback. French translation by Dominique Dill. ISBN 2-226-06604-7.

l. As: *Dolores Claiborne: Roman.*[Paris, France]: le Grande livre du mois, 1993, 324 pp., 120 F. hardcover. French translation by Dominique Dill. Book Club edition.

m. As: *Dolores.* Hamburg, Germany: Hoffman and Campe, 1993, 351 pp., 35.00 DM, hardcover. German translation by Christel Wiemkin. ISBN 3-455-03740-2. * 5th printing, 1993

n. Amsterdam, Netherlands: Luitingh-Sitjhoff, 1993. Dutch translation by Lucien Duzee. 1st Dutch edition.

o. México, D. F.: Editorial Grijalbo, 1993, 291 pp., paperback. Spanish translation by Irving Roffe.

p. Utrecht, Belgium, Netherlands: Luitingh-Sijthoff, 1993, 245 pp. Dutch translation by Lucien Duzee. ISBN 90-245-1069-4.

q. Barcelona, Spain: Ediciones B, ÉXITOS INTERNACIONAL, 1993, 307 pp., 24 cm. Spanish translation by Enrique de Hériz. 1st Spanish edition. ISBN 84-406-3775-6.

r. Stockholm, Sweden: Legenda, 1993, 284 pp., 24 cm., hardcover. Swedish translation by Lennart Olofsson. 91-27-03215-9.

s. Oslo, Norway: Aschehoug, 1993, 216 pp., 259.00, hardcover [*innbundet*]. Norwegian translation by Thor Dag Halvorsen. ISBN 82-032-0004-4. Bokklubben Dagens Bok, ISBN 82-7350-403-4.

t. As: *Dolores.* Gütersloh, Austria: Bertelsmann-Club; Vienna, Austria: Buchgemeinschaft Donauland Kremayr und Scheriau; Stuttgart, Germany: Deutsche Büucherband, and others, 1993, 351 pp., hardcover. German translation by Christel Wiemkin. Book Club editions.

u. Milan, Italy: Sperling & Kupfer, PANDORA [#683]; I LIBRI DI STEPHEN KING, January 1994, 266 pp., 22 cm. Italian translation by Tullio Dobner. ISBN 88-200-1668-0.

v. Thorndike, ME: G. K. Hall, LARGE PRINT CORE COLLECTION, April 1994, hardcover and paperback. Large print edition. ISBN 0-816-15641-7.

w. As: *Dolores.* Munich, Germany: Wilhelm Heyne #9047, May 1994, 351 pp., 14.90 DM, 18 cm., paperback. German translation by Christel Wiemkin. * 10th printing, 1996, ISBN 3-453-07497-1.

x. Copenhagen, Denmark: Artia, 1994, 211 pp., 198 KR, hardcover. Danish translation by Anders Westenholz. ISBN 87-89918-36-3.

y. Valby, Denmark: Bogsamleren, 1994, 253 pp., 79,50 KR, hardcover. Danish translation by Anders Westenholz. ISBN 87-7351-448-7. Book Club edition.

z. Budapest, Hungary: Európa, 1994, 260 pp., paperback? Hungarian translation by Endre Greskovits.

aa. Oslo, Norway: Aschehoug, MAXIBOK, 1994, 216 pp., trade paperback [*kartonn.*] Norwegian translation by Thor Dag Halvorsen. ISBN 82-03-20044-3.

bb. Warsaw, Poland: "Prima," 1994, 222 pp., 20 cm. Polish translation by tomasz Mirkowicz. ISBN 83-8585-532-7.

cc. [Lisbon], Portugal: Círculo de Leitores, 1994, 256 pp., 20 cm. Portuguese

translation by Maria Filomena Duarte. ISBN 972-42-0899-0.
dd. Barcelona, Spain: Círculo de Lectores, [1994], 229 pp., 22 cm. Spanish translation by Enrique de Hériz. ISBN 84-226-5014-2.
ee. As: *Dolores*. Istanbul, Turkey: ´Ynk´ylap Kitabevi, [1994]. Turkish translation by Mehmet Harmanc´y.
ff. New York: Signet, March 1995, 372 pp., $6.99, mass-market paperback. 11th printing; movie tie-in edition. ISBN 0-451-18411-4.
gg. London, England: New English Library, April 1995, 307 pp., £5.99, paperback. Cover art by Steve Crisp. ISBN 0-450-5886-6. 4th printing; movie tie-in edition.
hh. Copenhagen, Denmark: Vinten/DBK, Vintens paperbacks, 1995, 253 pp., 78 kr, paperback. Danish translation by Anders Westenholz. ISBN 87-414-2173-6, 87-414-2153-6.
ii. Copenhagen, Denmark: Paperback Bogklubben, 1995, 253 pp., 38 kr, paperback. Danish translation by Anders Westenholz. ISBN 87-608-0088-7.
jj. As: *Eclipse Total*. Rio de Janeiro, Brazil: Francisco Alves, 1995, 286 pp., 21 cm. Portuguese translation by Louisa Ibanez. ISBN 85-265-0347-2.
kk. [Ballerup], Denmark: Nyt Dansk Litteurselskab, MagnaPrintudgave, 1995, 245+249 pp, paperback. Danish translation by Anders Westenholz. ISBN 87-89988-15-9, 87-8988-15-9. Large print edition.
ll. Paris, France: Pocket #9070, 1995, 324 pp., 34 F, paperback. French translation by Dominique Dill. ISBN 2-266-04742-6.
mm. As: *Dolores*. Munich, Germany: Wilhelm Heyne #9631, December 1995, 351 pp., 14.90 dm, paperback. Movie tie-in; German premier 6 July 1995. German translation by Christel Wiemkin. 11th German printing. ISBN 3-453-09062-4.
nn. Amsterdam, Netherlands: Luitingh-Sitjhoff, 1995, 245 pp. Dutch translation by Lucien Duzee. 5th printing. ISBN 90-245-2417-2.
oo. Oslo, Norway: Aschehoug, Kaliber, 1995, 216 pp., paperback [*heftet*]. Norwegian translation. ISBN 82-03-20146-6. * Reprint, 1998, ISBN 82-03-20362-0.
pp. Warsaw, Poland: Œwiat Ksiazki, 1995, 222 pp., 21 cm. Polish translation by Tomasz Mirkowicz. ISBN 83-7129-094-2.
qq. As: *Dolores Kleiborn; Mizori*. Romany. L'vov: "Kameniar," 1995, 605 pp. Ukrainian translation by E. Kharitonova. Omnibus edition with *Misery*.
rr. As: *Stephen King: Three of the Latest and Greatest from Stephen King: Dolores Claiborne, Insomnia, Rose Madder*. New York: New American Library, September 1996, mass-market paperback. ISBN 0-451-93407-5. Omnibus edition.
ss. Skokie IL: Distribooks Intl., 1996. French translation. ISBN 2266047426.
tt. Zagreb, Croatia: Mozaik knjiga, 1997, 282 pp., 20 cm. Croatian translation by Divina Marion. ISBN 953-173-682-0.
uu. As: *Eclipse total*. Bacelona, Spain: Ediciones B, Genios de la narrativa actual, 1997, 307 pp., 21 cm. Spanish translation by Enrique de Hériz [Herz]. ISBN 84-406-7555-0.

MICHAEL R. COLLINGS

vv. As: *Eclipse total.* Bacelona, Spain: Ediciones B, GRANDES BEST SELLERS, 1997, 307 pp., 21 cm. Spanish translation by Enrique de Hériz. ISBN 84-406-7669-7
ww. Milan, Italy: Sperling Paperback, SUPERBESTSELLER #677, April 1998. Italian translation by Tullio Dobner. ISBN 88-7824-865-7.
xx. Amsterdam, Netherlands: Poema pocket, 1999, 245 pp., paperback. Dutch translation by Lucien Duzee. 8th printing. ISBN 90-245-3699-5.
yy. The Hague, Netherlands: Stichtint Uitgeverij XL #503, 1999, 366 pp., hardcover. Dutch translation by Lucien Duzee. ISBN 90-5542-503-6.
zz. As: *Eclipse total.* Bacelona, Spain: Ediciones B, VIB 13/7, 1999, 366 pp., 18 cm. Spanish translation by Enrique de Hériz. ISBN 84-406-5782-9.
aaa. As: *Dolores Claiborne.* Denmark: Vinten, 19—. Danish translation.
bbb. As [Title unknown]. Moscow, Russia: Cadman, 19—. Russian translation. Omnibus edition with *Gerald's Game.*

ccc. As AUDIOCASSETTE:. St. Paul MN: Penguin-Highbridge Audio, 1992. Read by Frances Sternhagen. 6 cassettes; 9 hours.
SELECTED REVIEWS:
Annichiarico, Mark. *Library Journal* Vol. 118, No. 1 (January 1993): 186.
Publishers Weekly Vol. 239, No. 53 (7 December 1992): 28.

ddd. As AUDIOCASSETTE: New York: Penguin Audiobooks, March 1995, $30.00. 9 cassettes. Read by Frances Sternhagen. ISBN 0-453-00957-3.
eee. As AUDIOCASSETTE: *Dolores Claiborne: Version Completa En La Voz de Elsa Gardenas.* Los Angeles CA: Dove Entertainment. Unabridged. Spanish translation read by by Elsa Gardenas. ISBN 0-787-10643-7.

fff. As FILM: *Dolores Claibourne.* Castle Rock Entertainment, 1994. Producers: Taylor Hackford and Charles Mulvehill. Director: Taylor Hackford. Screenwriter: Tony Gilmore. Rated: R.
CAST: Kathy Bates, Jennifer Jason Leigh, David Strathairn, Judy Parfitt, John C. Reilly, Eric Bogosian, Christopher Plummer.

ggg. As VIDEOCASSETTE: *Dolores Claibourne.* Castle Rock Entertainment/ Columbia Tristar Home Video, 1995. VHS #74753.

COMMENTS: While dealing with issues raised in *Gerald's Game*, particularly spouse and child abuse, *Dolores Claiborne* is remarkable for King's decision to tell the tale as a single block of uninterrupted, first-person narration—— monologue that reinforces the sense of emotional relief as the main character finally allows releases decades of pent-up anger, fear, and frustration. The strength of the novel relates directly to King's uncompromising portrait of Claiborne as wife, mother, and woman; he makes significant comments about social issues— spouse abuse, child abuse, alcholism, class and status relationships, marriage— without allowing them to interfere with the remarkable texture of his narrative.

SELECTED ARTICLES, RESPONSES, AND REVIEWS:

Blue, Tyson. "Needful Kings." *The Blood Review: Journal of Horror Criticism* Vol. 1, No. 2 (January 1990): 11. A brief mention of the then work-in-progress.

Booklist Vol. 89 (15 September 1992): 100.

Book Watch Vol. 14 (February 1993): 7.

Books Vol. 7 (January 1993): 15.

Bryant, Edward. "*Dolores Claiborne,* Stephen King." *Locus* Vol. 29, No. 5, #382, (November 1992): 19+

Johnson, Eric W. *Library Journal* Vol. 117, No. 18 (1 November 1992): 117.

Kent, Bill. *New York Times Book Review* (27 December 1992): 15.

Kirkus Reviews Vol. 60 (1 September 1992): 1081.

Lehmann-Haupt, Christopher. "Stephen King Peeks Beneath the Simple Horrors." *New York Times* [late edition] Vol. 142 (16 November 1992): C15.

Locus Vol. 30 (January 1993): 46.

Locus Vol. 30 (February 1993): 55.

Observer [London] 31 January 1993: 57.

Publishers Weekly Vol. 239 (12 October 1992): 64.

Skow, John. *Publishers Weekly* Vol. 239, No. 53 (7 December 1992): 28.

Steinhauer, Heidi M. *School Library Journal* Vol. 39, No. 4 (April 1993): 149.

Time Vol. 140 (7 December 1992): 81.

Washington Post Book World [DC] Vol. 22 (13 December 1992): 5.

West Coast Review of Books, "Art & Entertainment" Vol. 17 (March 1993): 20.

Wood, Michael. *The New York Review of Books.* Vol. 42, No. 16 (1995): 54.

NIGHTMARES & DREAMSCAPES. New York, NY: Viking, 1993. Hardcover.

A47.
NIGHTMARES & DREAMSCAPES
(1993)

A47. *NIGHTMARES & DREAMSCAPES*. New York: Viking, 1993, 816 pp., $27.50, hardcover. Cover art by Rob Wood. Horror story collection. ISBN 0-670-85108-6.

CONTENTS: "Introduction: Myth, Belief, Faith, and Ripley's Believe It or Not!" by King (see C230); "Dolan's Cadillac" (1985; see A37, B80); "The End of the Whole Mess" (1992; see B85); "Suffer the Little Children" (1972; see B15); "The Night Flier" (1988; see B89); "Popsy" (1987; see B88); "It Grows on You" (1973; see B22); "Chattery Teeth" (1992; see B103); "Dedication" (1988; see B92); "The Moving Finger" (1990; see B100); "Sneakers" (1988; see B91); "You Know They Got a Hell of a Band" (1992; see B102); "Home Delivery" (1989; see B95); "Rainy Season" (1989; see B93); "My Pretty Pony" (1989; see A38, B104); "Sorry, Right Number" (screenplay, 1987; see E4); "The Ten O'Clock People" (1993; see B105); "Crouch End" (1980; see B49); "The House on Maple Street" (1993; see B106); "The Fifth Quarter" (1972; see B16); "The Doctor's Case" (1987; see B87); "Umney's Last Case" (1993; see B107); "Head Down" (nonfiction, 1990; see C202); "Brooklyn August" (poem, 1971; see D6); "Notes," by Stephen King (see C231); "The Beggar and the Diamond" (1993; see B108).

REPRINTS AND ADAPTATIONS:
b. Issued with commemorative dust jacket, cover art by John Mercer, plus postcard set. Woodstock GA: Overlook Connection, 1994.
c. London, England: Hodder & Stoughton, September 1993, 593 pp., £35.00, hardcover. LIMITED EDITION: 2000 copies, slip-cased with facsimile signature. Simultaneously with the U. S. 1st edition. ISBN 0-340-60487-5.
d. London, England: Hodder & Stoughton, October 1993, 593 pp., £16.99, hardcover. ISBN 0-340-59282-6.
e. Utrecht, Belgium, Netherlands: Luitingh-Sijuhoff, 1993. Vol. 1,

Michael R. Collings

Nachtmerries ['Nightmares']; Vol. 2, *Droomlandschappen* [' 'Dream-landscapes']. Dutch translation by Mariette van Gelder and Frank de Groot.

f. As: *Alpträume* ['Alp-dreams' (?)]. Hamburg, Germany: Hoffman and Campe, 1993, 697 pp., hardcover. German translation by Joachim Körber. 1st German edition. ISBN 3-455-03741-0.

g. As: *Nachtmerries en Droomlandschappen* ['Nightmares and dream-landscapes']. Amsterdam, Netherlands: CPNB/Luitingh-Sijuhoff, 1993, 656 pp. Dutch translations by Frank de Groot. ISBN 90-245-1492-4.

CONTENTS: "Dolan's Cadillac"; "Weg met die rootzooi"; "Wees geduldig met kinderen"; "Die spookvlieger"; "Papsie"; "Het laat Je niet los"; "Klappertanden"; "Opdracht"; "De bewegende vinger"; "Sneakers"; "De sterren van de hemel"; "Thuisvevalling"; "Regendtijd"; "Mijn prachtige paard"; "Hallo met wie spreekt U"; "Het volk van tien uuhr's ochtends"; "Crouch End"; "Het huis aan Maple Street"; "Het vijfde kwart"; "De zaak van de doctor"; "Umney's laatste zaak"; "Kop omlaag!"; "Augustus in Brooklyn"; "De bedelaar en de diamant"

h. London, England: Hodder & Stoughton, January 1994, 593 pp., £9.99, paperback. ISBN 0-340-61355-6.

i. New York: Signet, September 1994, x+692 pp., $6.99, mass-market paperback. ISBN 0-451-18023-2.

j. As: *Incubi & Deliri* ['Nightmares and ravings']. Milan, Italy: Sperling & Kupfer, Narrativa [#163], September 1994. Italian translation by Tullio Dobner. ISBN 88-200-1871-3.

CONTENTS: Introduzione; "La Cadillac di Dolan" pp. 11-68; "La fine del gran casino: ["The End of the Whole Mess"] pp 69-97; "Bambinate" ["Suffer the Little Children"] pp. 98-112; "Il volatore notturno" ["The Night Flier"] pp. 113-152; "Ti prende poco a poco" ["It Grows on You"] pp. 153-185; "Denti Chiaccherini" ["Chattery Teeth"] pp. 186-221; "Dedica" pp. 222-269; "Il Dito" ["The Moving Finger"] pp. 270-307; "Scarpe da tennis" ["Sneakers"] pp. 308-337; "E hanno una band dell'altro mondo" ["You Know They Got a Hell of a Band"] pp. 338-384; "Parto in Casa" ["Home Delivery"] pp. 385-417; "La stagione delle piogge" ["Rainy Season"] pp. 418-441; "Il mio bel cavallino" ["My Pretty Pony"] pp. 442-469; "Spiacente, è il numero giusto" ["Sorry, Right Number"] pp. 470-507; "La Gente delle Dieci" ["The Ten O'Clock People"] pp. 508-564; "Crouch End" pp. 565-596; "La Casa di Maple Street" pp. 597-635; "Il quinto quarto" pp. 636-652; "Il caso del dottore" pp. 653-690; "L'ultimo caso di Umney" pp 691-745; "A testa bassa" ["Head Down"] pp; 746-802; "Agosto a Brooklyn" pp. 803-822; "Il Mendicante e il diamante" pp. 823+.

k. London, England: New English Library, October 1994, 836 pp., £5.99, paperback. ISBN 0-450-61009-8.

l. Thorndike, ME: G. K. Hall, G. K. Hall Large Print Core Collection, 1994, 1062 pp., hardcover and paperback. Large print edition. ISBN 0-8161-5881-9 [hardcover]; 0-8161-5882-7 [paperback].

m. As: *Alpträume* ['Alp-dreams']. Gütersloh, Austria: Bergelsmann Club, 1994,

697 pp., 199 DM, hardcover. German translation by Joachim Körber. Book Club edition.

n. As: *Rêves et Cauchemars* ['Day-dreams and Nightmares']. Paris, France: Albin Michel, 1994, 702 pp., 150 F, paperback. French translation by William Olivier Desmond. ISBN 2-226-07009-5.

o. As: *Rêves et Cauchemars* ['Day-dreams and nightmares']. [Paris, France]: le Grande livre du mois, 1994, 702 pp., 150 F, hardcover. French translation by William Olivier Desmond. Book Club edition.

p. As: *Pesadilias y Alucinaciones* ['Nightmares and hallucinations']. Barcelona, Spain: Grijalbo, 1994, 765 pp., 24 cm., paperback. Spanish translation by Bettina Blanch Tyroller. ISBN 84-253-2642-7.

q. As: *Pesadilias y Alucinaciones* ['Nightmares and hallucinations']. Barcelona, Spain: Círculo de Lectores, 1994, 862 pp., 22 cm., paperback. Spanish translation by Bettina Blanch Tyroller. ISBN 84-226-5267-6.

r. As: *Alpträume: Nightmares and Dreamscapes* ['Alp-dreams']. Munich, Germany: Wilhelm Heyne, #01-9369, March 1995, 16,90 DM., paperback. German translation. ISBN 3-453-50338-4.

s. As: *Abgrund: Nightmares and Dreamscape* ['Abyss/precipice': *Nightmares and Dreamscapes*, Volume 1]. Munich, Germany: Wilhelm Heyne. #01-9572, August 1995, 16,90 DM, paperback. ISBN 3-453-08888-3.

t. As: *Stephen King #03-3 Vol. Boxed Set.* New York: Signet, mass-market paperback. ISBN 0-451-93138-6. Boxed set with *Different Seasons, Skeleton Crew,* and *Nightmares and Dreamscapes.*

u. As: *Rêves et Cauchemars* ['Day-dreams and Nightmares']. Paris, France: France Loisirs, 1995, 702 pp., 118 F, hardcover. French translation by William Olivier Desmond. ISBN 2-7242-8467-4.

v. As: *Marzenia i koszmary* ['Dreams and nightmares']. 2 vols. Warsaw, Poland: "Prima," 1995/1996, 430+412 pp., 20/21 cm. Polish translation by Michal Wroczyñski and Witold Nowakowski [vol. 2]. ISBN 83-7152-009-3; 83-7152-027-1.

w. As: *Rêves et Cauchemar* ['Day-dreams and nightmares']. 2 vols. Paris, France: J'ai Lu #4305-4306, 1996, 506+504 pp., 43 Г, 18 cm., paperback. French translation by William Olivier Desmond. ISBN 2-290-04305.

x. As: *Droomlandschappen* ['Dream-landscapes']. Amsterdam, Netherlands: Poema Pocket, 1996, 400 pp., paperback. Dutch translation by Mariette van Gelder and Frank de Groot. 2nd printing. ISBN 90-245-2443-1.

y. As: *Nachtmerries* ['Nightmares']. Amsterdam, Netherlands: Poema Pocket, 1996, 415 pp., paperback. Dutch translations by Frank de Groot, Mariette van Gelder, and others. ISBN 90-245-2492-X. 2nd printing 1996.

z. As: *Marzenia i koszmary* ['Dreams and nightmares'. 2 vols. Warsaw, Poland: Œwiat Ksiazki, 1996, 430+412 pp., 20 cm. Polish translation by Michal Wroczyñski and Witold Nowakowski. ISBN 83-7129-201-5, 83-72\129-202-3.

aa. As: *El cadillac de Dolan y otros relatos: Pesadilias y Alucinaciones 1* ['Dolan's Cadillac and other stories: Nightmares and hallucinations, 1']. Barcelona, Spain: Grijalbo Mondadori, LIBRO DE MANO #65/1, [1996], 182 pp., 21 cm., paperback. Spanish translation by Bettina Blanch Tyroller. ISBN 84-253-2748-2.

bb. As: *La Boca Saltarina y otros delirios: Pesadilias y Alucinaciones 2* ['The skipping/jumping mouth and other deliriums: nightmares and hallucinations 2']. Barcelona, Spain: Grijalbo Mondadori, [1996], 181 pp., 21 cm. Spanish translation by Bettina Blanch Tyroller. ISBN 84-253-2976-0.

cc. As: *El dedo móvil y otras truculenciass: Pesadilias y Alucinaciones 3* ['The moving finger and other terrors/horrors: nightmares and hallucinations 3']. Barcelona, Spain: Grijalbo Mondadori, LIBRO DE MANO #65/3, [1996], 183 pp., 21 cm., paperback. Spanish translation by Bettina Blanch Tyroller. ISBN 84-253-2961-2.

dd. As: *La estación de las lluvias y otros desvariíos: Pesadilias y Alucinaciones 4* ['The rainy season and other ravings/deliriums: nightmares and hallucinations 4']. Barcelona, Spain: Grijalbo Mondadori, LIBRO DE MANO #65/4, [1996], 179 pp., 21 cm., paperback. Spanish translation by Bettina Blanch Tyroller. ISBN 84-253-2962-0.

ee. As: *La dedicatoria y otros despropósitos: Pesadilias y Alucinaciones 5* ['Dedication and other stupid remarks: nightmares and hallucinations 5']. Barcelona, Spain: Grijalbo Mondadori, LIBRO DE MANO #65/5, [1996], 184 pp., 21 cm., paperback. Spanish translation by Bettina Blanch Tyroller. ISBN 84-253-2982-5.

ff. As: *Pesadelos e paisagens noturnas* ['Nightmares and nocturtnal landscapes']. 2 vols. Rio de Janeiro, Brazil: Objetiva, 1997, 23 cm. Portuguese translation by M. H. C. Côrtes. ISBN 85-730-2131-4, 85-730-2133-0.

gg. As: *Incubi & Deliri* ['Nightmares and ravings']. Milan, Italy: Sperling Paperback, SUPERBESTSELLER #715, February 1999, paperback. Italian translation by Tullio Dobner. ISBN 88-7824-945-9.

hh. As: *Painajaisia ja unikuvia 1: Yksinäinen sormi* ['Nightmares and dream-patterns 1 (?): the moving finger']. Helsinki, Finland: Tammi, 1999, 435 pp., 23 cm. Finnish translations by Heikki Kaskimies and Heikki Karjalainen. ISBN 951-31-1177-6.

ii. As: *Painajaisia ja unikuvia 2: Anteeksi oikea numero* ['Nightmares and dream-patterns 2 (?): excuse me, right number']. Helsinki, Finland: Tammi, 1999. Finnish translation.

jj. As: *Nattmaror och Drömlandskap—Andra Bokeni* ['Nightmares and Dream-landscapes: book 2']. Viken, Sweden: Replik, 1999, 454 pp., 24 cm., hardcover. Swedish translation by Ylva Spångberg. ISBN 91-88818-24-1.

kk. As: [Title unknown]. Polish translation.

ll. As [Title unknown]. Russian translation.

mm. As: [Title unknown]. Hamburg, Germany: Hoffman und Campe, 19—, 48,- DM, hardcover. German translation. ISBN 3-455-03741-0.

nn. As: [Title unknown]. Greece: Bell, 19__. Greek translation.

oo. As: [Title unknown]. Bulgaria. 19—. Bulgarian translation.

pp. As: *Rémálmok es Lidercek*. Budapest, Hungary: Európa, 19—. Hungarian translation.

Horror Plum'd

qq. As AUDIOCASSETTE: *Nightmares & Dreamscapes*: I. St. Paul, MN: Penguin-Highbridge Audio, 1993. Read by Tim Curry, Whoopi Goldberg, Stephen J. Gould, Stephen King, Tabitha King, Rob Lowe, Robert B. Parker, Yardley Smith. 8 cassettes, 9 hours.
CONTENTS: "Suffer the Little Children," "Rainy Season," "The House on Maple Street."

rr. As AUDIOCASSETTE: *Nightmares & Dreamscapes*: II. St. Paul, MN: Penguin-Highbridge Audio, 1994. Read by Stephen King, Kathy Bates, Tim Curry, Matthew Broderick, David Cronenberg, Jerry Garcia, Eve Beglarian. 8 cassettes; 9 hours.
CONTENTS: "Chattery Teeth," "The Moving Finger," "Home Delivery," "Sneakers."
   SELECTED REVIEWS: *Publishers Weekly* Vol. 241, No. 14 (4 April 1994): 32.

ss. As AUDIOCASSETTE: *Nightmares & Dreamscapes*: III. St. Paul, MN: Penguin-Highbridge Audio, November 1994. Read by Stephen King, Gary Sinise, Frank Muller, Joe Morton, Dominic Cuskern, Grace Slick, Joe Mategna. 8 cassettes; 9 hours.
CONTENTS: "The Night Flier," "It Grows on You," "You Know They Got a Hell of a Band," "The Ten O'Clock People," "The Fifth Quarter," "The Beggar and the Diamond."

SELECTED ARTICLES, RESPONSES, AND REVIEWS:
Book Report Vol. 12 (March 1994): 40.
Booklist Vol. 89 (July 1993): 1918.
Books Vol. 7 (November 1993): 12.
Bookwatch Vol. 14 (December 1993): 6.
Entertainment Weekly (1 October 1993): 48+.
Kirkus Reviews Vol. 61 (1 July 1993): 807.
Locus Vol. 31 (October 1993): 29+.
Locus Vol. 31 (December 1993): 48.
Locus Vol. 32 (1994): 39.
Nicholls, Richard E. *New York Times Book Review* 24 October 1993: 22.
Publishers Weekly Vol. 240, No. 31 (2 August 1993): 62.
Publishers Weekly Vol. 241 (25 July 1994): 47+.
Science Fiction Chronicle Vol. 15 (March 1994): 33.
Chicago Tribune Books [IL] 7 November 1993: 9.
Washington Post Book World [DC] Vol. 23 (10 October 1993): 4.

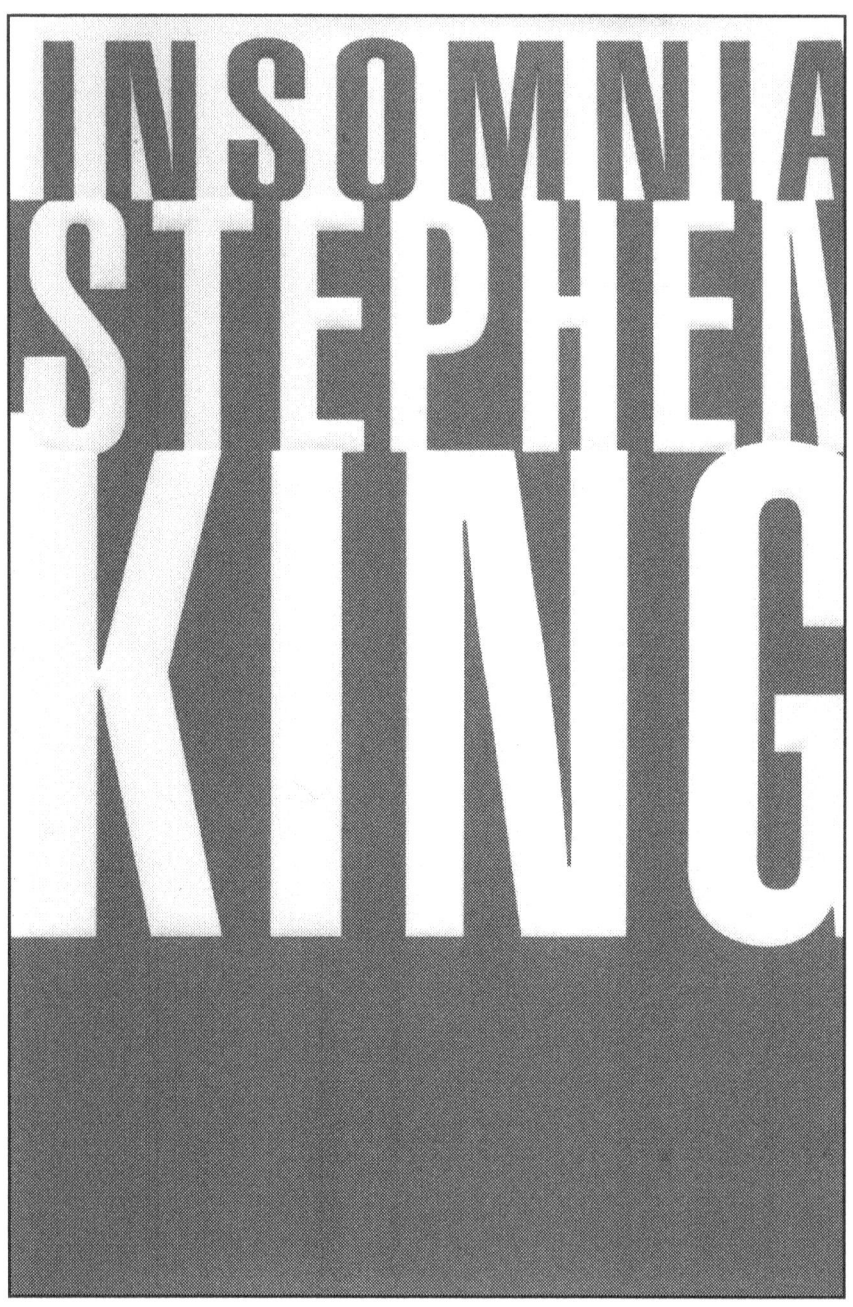

INSOMNIA. New York, NY: Viking, 1994. Hardcover.

A48.
INSOMNIA
(1994)

A48. *INSOMNIA: A NOVEL.* Shingletown, CA: Mark V. Ziesing Books, June 1994, 591 pp., hardcover. Illustrated by Phil Hale; cover art by Arnie Fenner. Horror novel. * SIGNED, LIMITED EDITION of 1250 copies, slipcased with jacket by Arnie Fenner $175.00; ISBN 0-929480-38-4. * GIFT EDITION of 3,750 copies, slipcased with jacket by Arnie Fenner, $75.00; ISBN 0-929480-37-6.

PLOT SUMMARY: Ralph Roberts' progressive insomnia intensifies until, able to sleep only an hour or so each night, haunted by fatigue and depression, he begins seeing things...including brilliant auras surrounding people and what he first believes to be aliens—little men in doctor's suits. But the truth, when it finally reveals itself, is even stranger: Ralph a handful of his closes acquaintances have become game-pieces in a cosmic confrontation.

REPRINTS AND ADAPTATIONS:
b. New York: Viking, October 1994, 787 pp., $27.95, hardcover. Illustrated by David Johnson. ISBN 0-670-85503-0.
c. New York: Book of the Month Club, October 1994, 787 pp., $21.95, hard cover. No ISBN.
d. London, England: Hodder & Stoughton, October 1994, 787 pp., £15.99, hardcover. Cover art by Steve Crisp. ISBN 0-340-60845-5. LIMITED EDITION: Boxed, signed, £100.00. LIMITED EDITION: 2000 copies, slipcased with facsimile signature, £35.00. ISBN 0-340-63269-0.
e. London, England: Quality Paperback Book Club UK, October 1994, 650 pp., £9.99, trade paperback. Cover art by Steve Crisp. ISBN 0-340-63338-7.
f. London, England: Hodder & Stoughton, November 1994, 650 pp., £8.99, trade paperback. ISBN 0-340-63791-9.
g. As: *Søvnløs* ['Sleepless']. Copenhagen, Denmark: Vinten, 1994, 539 pp., 99 KR, hardcover. Danish translation by Anne Vibeke Mortensen. ISBN 87-7531-437-1.
h. As: *Søvnløs* ['Sleepless']. [Valby], Denmark: Bogsamleren, 1994, 539 pp.,

INSOMNIA. Shingletown, CA: Mark V. Ziesing Books, 1994.
Limited edition hardcover.

248 KR, hardcover. Danish translation by Anne Vibeke Mortensen. ISBN 87-414-0084-4.
i. As: *Uneton Yö* ['Sleepless tonight']. Helsinki, Finland: Tammi, 1994, 713 pp., 23 cm. Finnish translation by Ilkka Rekiaro. ISBN 951-31-0414-01.
j. As: *Schlaflos: Roman* ['Sleepless: novel']. Munich, Germany: Wilhelm Heyne, 1994, 815 pp., hardcover. German translation by Joachim Körber. ISBN 3-453-08011-4.
k. Amsterdam, Netherlands: Luitingh-Sijthoff, 1994, 639 pp. Dutch translation by Eny van Gelder. 1st Dutch edition. ISBN 90-245-1099-6.
l. Oslo, Norway: Aschehoug, 1994, 628 pp., 247.00, hardbound [*innbundet*]. Norwegian translation by Steinar Moe. ISBN 82-03-20084-2.
m. Milan, Italy: Sperling & Kupfer, NARRATIVA [#177], January 1995. Italian translation by Tullio Dobner. ISBN 88-200-1941-8.
n. Thorndike, MA: G. K. Hall & Co., February 1995, paperback. Large print edition. ISBN 0-783-81183-7.
o. Barcelona, Spain: Grijalbo Mondadori, 28 February 1995, 610 pp., hardcover [*tela*], with dust jacket. Spanish translation by Bettina Blanch. 1st edition. ISBN 84-253-2790-3. * Reprint, paperback [*rústica*], ISBN 84-253-2790-3.
p. London, England: New English Library, July 1995, 760 pp., £5.99, paperback. Cover art by Steve Crisp. ISBN 0-450-60848-4.
q. New York: Signet, September 1995, 663 pp., $7.99, mass-market paperback. ISBN 0-451-18496-3.
r. London, England: New English Library, 1995, 760 pp., mass-market paperback.
s. As: *Nesanica*. Zagreb, Croatia: Algoritam, 1995, 686 pp., 24 cm. Croatian translation by Bo´zica Jakovlev. ISBN 953-6166-15-1.
t. As: *Insomnie: Roman* ['Insomnia: novel']. Paris, France: Albin Michel, 1995, 717 pp., 150 F, paperback. French translation by William Olivier Desmond. ISBN 2-226-07764-2.
u. As: *Insomnie: Roman* ['Insomnia: novel']. [Paris, France]: [le Grande livre du mois], 1995, 717 pp., 150 F, hardcover. French translation by William Olivier Desmond. Book Club edition.
v. As: *Schlaflos: Roman* ['Sleepless: novel']. Rheda-Wiedenbrück, Germany: Bertelsmann-Club; Vienna, Austria: Buchgemeinschaft Donauland Kremayr und Scheriau, and others, [1995], 765 pp., hardcover. German translation by Joachim Körber. Book Club editions.
w. As: [Title unknown]. 2 vols. South Korea, 1995, 377+361 pp., 23 cm. Korean translation. ISBN 89-12-11306-2, 89-12-11307-0
x. Oslo, Norway: Aschehoug, KALIBER, 1995, 628 pp, paperback [*heftet*]. Norwegian translation by Steinar Moe. ISBN 82-03-20147-4.
y. As: *Sömnlös* ['Sleepless']. Höganas, Sweden: Bra Böcker, 1995, 612 pp., 24 cm., hardcover. Swedish translation by John-Henri Holmberg. ISBN 91-7119-724-9.
z. As: *Stephen King: Three of the Latest and Greatest from Stephen King:*

Dolores Claiborne, Insomnia, Rose Madder. New York: New American Library, September 1996, mass-market paperback. ISBN 0-451-93407-5. Omnibus edition.

aa. As: *Søvnløs* ['Sleepless']. 2 vols. Copenhagen, Denmark: Vinten, VINTEN PAPERBACKS, 1996, 288+250 pp., paperback. Danish translation by Anne Vibeke Mortensen. ISBN 87-414-2486-7 [complete].

bb. As: *Søvnløs* ['Sleepless']. 2 vols. Copenhagen, Denmark: Paperback Bogklubben, 1996, 539 pp., 39,50 KR each, paperback. Danish translation by Anne Vibeke Mortensen. ISBN 87-7803-587-2, 87-7803-894-4. Book Club edition.

cc. As: *Insomnie* ['Insomnia']. Paris, France: France Loisirs, 1996, 717 pp., 120 F, hardcover. French translation by William Olivier Desmond. ISBN 2-7242-9264-2.

dd. As: *Schlaflos: Roman* ['Sleepless: novel']. Munich, Germany: Wilhelm Heyne, #9668, 1996, 815 pp., 16.00 DM, paperback. German translation by Joachim Körber. ISBN 3-453-09642-8.

ee. As: *Bezsennosc* ['Insomnia']. Warsaw, Poland: Prima, 1996, 654 pp., 21 cm. Polish translation by Srzysztof Sokowski. ISBN 8371520417.

ff. As: *Schlaflos: Roman* ['Sleepless: novel']. Munich, Germany: Wilhelm Heyne #10280, June 1997, 800 pp., 16.90 DM, paperback. German translation by Joachim Körber. ISBN 3-453-12449-9.

gg. As: *Insomnie* ['Insomnia']. 2 vols. Paris, France: J'ai Lu #4615-4616, 1997, 222+241 pp., 40 F per volume, paperback. French translation by William Olivier Desmond. ISBN 2-290-04615-9; 2-290-04616-7.

hh. Amsterdam, Netherlands: Poema Pocket, 1997, 639 pp., paperback. Dutch translation by Eny van Gelder. 4th printing. ISBN 90-245-1307-3.

ii. Oslo, Norway: Aschehoug, 1998, 628 pp., 62.00, paperback [*heftet*]. Norwegian translation by Steinar Moe. ISBN 82-03-20365-5.

jj. As: *Insónia* ['Insomnia']. [Lisbon, Portugal]: Círculo de Leitores, 1998, 743 pp., 21 cm. Portuguese translation by Manuel Cordeira. ISBN 972-42-1779-5.

kk. As: *Hem jön Szememre Alom.* Budapest, Hungary: Európa, 19—. Hungarian translation.

ll. As: [Title unknown]. Tel Aviv, Israel: Modan, 19—. Hebrew translation.

mm. As: [Title unknown]. Moscow, Russia: Cadman, 19—. Russian translation.

nn. As: *Insomnia.* Indonesia, 19—. Indonesian translation.

oo. As: *Insomnmie.* Greece, 19—. Greek translation.

pp. As AUDIOCASSETTE: New York: Penguin Audiobooks, December 1994, $79.95, unabridged. Read by Eli Wallach. 21 cassettes; 26 hours. ISBN 0-453-00910-7.

qq. As AUDIOCASSETTE:. London, England: Hodder Headline Audiobooks, 19—. Unabridged.

COMMENTS: Although *Insomnia* begins rather slowly, it gradually builds its own satisfying rhythms of plot, narrative, and image, until King abruptly reveals essential connections between this story and the cosmic/epic scope of his 'dark man' novels, including *The Stand, The Eyes of the Dragon,* and the Dark Tower series.

SELECTED ARTICLES, RESPONSES, AND REVIEWS:
Bohjalian, Chris. "The Ghouls Next Door."*The New York Times.* 30 October 1994: 24. Final edition.
Kirkus Reviews Vol. 62 (15 July 1994): 938.
Lehmann-Haupt, Christopher. "Lack of Sleep the Least of His Problems." *The New York Times* "Books of the Times" 6 October 1994. Late edition.
Publishers Weekly Vol. 241, No. 31 (1 August 1994): 69.

Rose Madder. New York, NY: Viking, 1995. Hardcover.

A49.
ROSE MADDER
(1995)

A49. *ROSE MADDER*. New York: Viking, July 1995, 420 pp., $25.95, hardcover. Dark-fantasy novel. ISBN 0-670-85869-2.

PLOT SUMMARY: After fourteen years of abuse by her husband, Norman, Rose Daniels walks out of her house and takes a bus to another town to rebuild her life. She buys a painting, *Rose Madder,* that shows a barbarian woman gazing over a ruined temple; gradually, the picture alters and Rose 'dreams' that she enters the painting into another world. When her policeman husband traces her to her new apartment and threatens her new life, Rose, Norman, and the woman in the painting must finally confront each other—and their deepest fears.

REPRINTS AND ADAPTATIONS:
b. London, England: Hodder & Stoughton, July 1995, 466 pp., £100.00, hardcover. Limited edition of 250 copies, slip-cased, with signed bookmarks. ISBN 0-340-65810-X. * Export edition, £8.99, trade paperback, ISBN 0-340-65365-5. * Open Market edition, £16.99, hardcover, ISBN 0-340-64013-8. * Reprint, September 1995.
c. New York: Book of the Month Club, August 1995, 420 pp., $20.75, hardcover. No ISBN assigned.
d. Boston: Compass Press, 1995, hardcover. Large print edition.
e. As: *Das Bild—Rose Madder* ['The Picture: Rose Madder']. Rheda-Wiedenbrück, Germany: Bertelsmann-Club, 1996, 597 pp., hardcover. German translation by Joachim Körber. Book Club edition.
f. Copenhagen, Denmark: Vinten, 1995, 446 pp., 248 KR, hardcover. Danish translation by Jette Røssell. ISBN 87-414-0086-0.
g. Copenhagen, Denmark: Bogklubben Egmont, 1995, 446 pp., 118 KR, hardcover. Danish translation by Jette Røssell. ISBN 87-608-0146-8.
h. As: *Naisen raivo* ['Female rage']. Finland: Tammi, 1995, 533 pp., 23 cm. Finnish translation by Heikki Karjalainen. ISBN 951-31-0516-4; 951-31-1460-0.
i. As: *Das Bild—Rose Madder* ['The picture: Rose Madder']. Munich,

ROSE MADDER. London, England: Hodder & Stoughton, 1995. Hardcover.

Germany: Wilhelm Heyne, 1995, 587 pp., 48.00 dm, hardcover. German translation by Joachim Körber. ISBN 3-453-09078-0.

j. As: *Rosie.* Amsterdam, Netherlands: Pandora/Poema Pockets, 1995, 459 pp., 15.00fl, paperback. Dutch translation by Lucien Duzee. ISBN 90-245-2350-8.

k. Oslo, Norway: Aschenhaug, 1995, 451 pp., 269.00 Nkr, hardcover [*innbundet*]. Norwegian translation by Steinar Moe. ISBN 82-03-20177-6. * Reprint, 1996, paperback, ISBN 82-03-20217.

l. Oslo, Norway: Bokkluben krim og spenning, 1995, 451 pp., hardcover. Norwegian translation by Steinar Moe. ISBN 82-598-0220-1. Book Club edition.

m. Milan, Italy: Sperling & Kupfer, NARRATIVA [#202], January 1996. Italian translation by Tullio dobner. ISBN 88-200-2134-X.

n. New York: Signet, June 1996, 479 pp., $7.50, mass-market paperback. ISBN 0-451-18636-2.

o. London, England: New English Library, June 1996, 595 pp., £5.99, paperback. Cover art by Bob Warner. ISBN 0-340-64014-6.

p. As: *Stephen King: Three of the Latest and Greatest from Stephen King: Dolores Claiborne, Insomnia, Rose Madder.* New York: New American Library, September 1996, mass-market paperback. ISBN 0-451-93407-5. Omnibus edition.

q. As: *Das Bild—Rose Madder* ['The picture: Rose Madder']. Munich, Germany: Wilhelm Heyne #10020, December 1996, 573 pp., 16.90 DM, paperback. German translation. ISBN 3-453-11614-3.

r. As: *Rosie.* Utrecht, Belgium, Netherlands: Luitingh-Sijthoff, 1995/6, hardcover. Dutch translation.

s. Rio de Janeiro, Brazil: Objetiva, 1996, 630 pp., 21 cm., paperback. Portuguese translation by Myrian Campello. 2nd printing. ISBN 85-730-2076-8.

t. Zagreb, Croatia: Algoritam, 1996, 508 pp., 24 cm. Croatian translation by Bo´zica Jakovlev. ISBN 953-6166-26-7.

u. Copenhagen, Denmark: Bogsamleren, 1996, 446 pp., 99,50 KR, hardcover. Danish translation by Jette Røssell. ISBN 87-7531-440-1.

v. Warsaw, Poland: "Prima," 1996, 461 pp., 20 cm. Polish translation by Zbigniew A. Królicki. ISBN 83-7152-036-0.

w. As: [Title unknown]. South Korea, 1996, 531 pp., 23 cm. Korean translation. ISBN 89-12-11241-4.

x. As: *El Retrato de Rose Madder* ['The portrait of Rose Madder']. Barcelona, Spain: Círculo de Lectores, [1996], 510 pp., 23 cm. Spanish translation by Bettina Blanch Tyroller. ISBN 84-226-5935-2.

y. As *Rasande Rose* ['Raging/frantic Rose']. Höganas, Sweden: Bra Böcker, 1996, 482 pp., 24 cm., hardcover. Swedish translation by John-Henri Holmberg. ISBN 91-7119-881-4.

z. Copenhagen, Denmark: Vinten, VINTENS PAPERBACKS, 1997, 448 pp., 98 KR, paperback. 2 vols. Danish translation by Jette Røssell. ISBN 87-612-0173-1, 87-612-0176-6.

aa. Copenhagen, Denmark: Paperback Bogklubben, 1997, 448 pp., 39,50 KR, paperback. 2 vols. Danish translation by Jette Røssell. ISBN 87-608-0697-4, 87-608-0698-2.
bb. Paris, France: Albin Michel, 1997, 543 pp., 140 F, paperback. French translation by William Olivier Desmond. ISBN 2-226-08463-0.
cc. Paris, France: le Grand livre du mois, 1997, 543 pp., 140 F, hardcover. French translation by William Olivier Desmond. Book Club edition.
dd. Paris, France: France Loisirs, 1998, 543 pp., 102 F, hardcover. French translation by William Olivier Desmond. ISBN 2-7441-1560-6.
ee. As: *Rosie*. Amsterdam, Netherlands: Poema Pocket, 1998, 453 pp., paperback. Dutch translation by Lucien Duzee. 6th printing. ISBN 90-245-0758-8.
ff. Oslo, Norway: Aschehoug, 1998, 451 pp., 62.00, paperback [*heftet*]. Norwegian translation by Steinar Moe. ISBN 82-03-20364-7.
gg. Warsaw, Poland: "Prima," BESTSELLERY ŒWIATOWEJ PROZY, 1998, 448 pp., 18 cm., paperback. Polish translation by Zbigniew A. Królicki. ISBN 83-7152-106-5.
hh. Warsaw, Poland: Œwiat Ksiazki, 1998, 461 pp., 21 cm. Polish translation by Zbigniew A. Królicki. ISBN 83-7129-776-9.
ii. As: [Title unknown]. Greece: Bell, 19—. Greek translation.
jj. As: *Ür álöqum* (?). Iceland: Fródi, 19—. Icelandic translation.
kk. As: *Rose Madder.* Denmark, 19—. Danish translation.
ll. As: *Akét Rose.* Budapest, Hungary: Európa, 19—. Hungarian translation.
mm. As: *Rose Madder.* Indonesia, 19—. Indonesian translation.

nn. As AUDIOCASSETTE: St. Paul, MN: Penguin-Highbridge Audio, 1995.
oo. As AUDIOCASSETTE: London, England: Hodder Headline Audiobooks, 19—. Unabridged.

COMMENTS: In one sense another entry in King's series of 'social issue novels'—beginning with *Gerald's Game*, including *Dolores Claiborne* and *Insomnia,* and continuing through *Bag of Bones—Rose Madder* demonstrates how adeptly King manages to incorporate trademark horror motifs with more clearly overt themes and concerns. A novel about abuse, it is also a multi-leveled narrative about art and reality, suggested almmost immediately by the complex puns on the two words of its title: 'Rose' and 'Madder', relating overtly to the main character, but also to rising physical action; to painting, art, and artifice; and to intense and intensifying emotional states. The novel seems more fully realized than *Gerald's Game* and indicates a significant direction for King's major fiction over the next half decade.

SELECTED ARTICLES, RESPONSES, AND REVIEWS:
Lehmann-Haupt, Christopher. "A Punch in the Nose, then a New Life Begins." *The New York Times Book Review* 26 June 1995. Late edition.
Michie, Jake. *Spectator.* Vol. 275, #8726 (1995): 48.
Wood, Michael. *The New York Review of Books* Vol. 42, No. 16 (1995): 54-57.

A51.
UMNEY'S LAST CASE
(1995)

A51. *UMNEY'S LAST CASE.* New York: Penguin, August 1995, 88 pp., $1.95, mass-market paperback. Penguin 60s Anniversary Edition. ISBN 0-14-600074-9. See also B107.

UMNEY'S LAST CASE. New York, NY: Penguin, August 1995. Mass-market paperback.

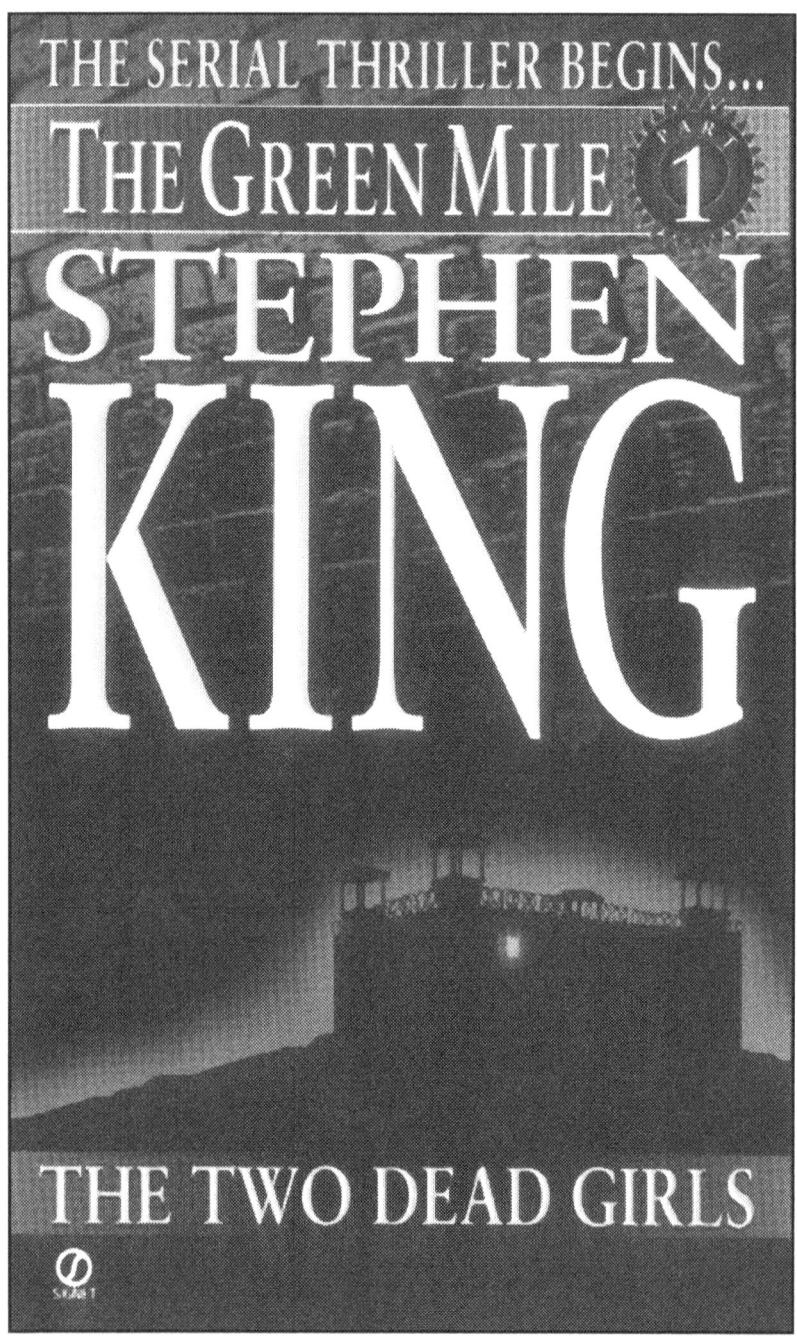

THE GREEN MILE PART 1: THE TWO DEAD GIRLS. New York, NY: Signet, March 1996. Mass-market paperback.

A52.
THE GREEN MILE
PART I–THE TWO DEAD GIRLS
(1996)

A52. THE GREEN MILE: PART I—THE TWO DEAD GIRLS. New York: Signet, March 1996, 92 pp., $2.99, mass-market paperback. ISBN 0-451-19049-1. [For six-volume boxed and single-volume omnibus editions of the complete novel, see A59]

REPRINTS AND ADAPTATIONS:
b. London, England: Penguin, March 1996, 92 pp., £1.99, paperback. ISBN 0-14-0258606. Simultaneous with the U.S. edition.
c. As: *The Green Mile: Teil 1—Der Tod der jungen Mädchen* [The death of the young girls']. Bergisch Gladbach, West Germany: Bastei-Lübbe, ALLGEMEINE REIHE, 1 April 1996, DM 5,00, paperback. German translation. ISBN 3-404-13950-X.
d. As: *Il Miglio Verde Parte prima. Le due bambine scomparse* ['The green mile part one: the two dead girls']. Milan, Italy: Sperling Serial, THE BEST ONE #1, April 1996. Italian translation by Tullio Dobner. ISBN 88-86845-01-4.
e. Burnsville MN: Econo-Clad/Sagebrush, 1996, 92 pp., $9.95, library binding.
f. As: *Zelena milja: Dio 1, Dvije mrtve djevojcice*. Zagreb, Croatia: Sysprint, 1996, 93 pp., 18 cm., paperback. Croatian translation by Predrag Raos.
g. As: *De to døde piger: Den grønne mil 1* ['the two dead girls: the green mile 1']. Copenhagen, Denmark: Vinten, VINTENS PAPERBACK, 1996, 92 pp., 48KR, paperback. Danish translation by Jette Røssell. ISBN 87-414-2432-8.
h. As: *De to døde piger: Den grønne mil 1* ['The two dead girls: the green mile 1']. Copenhagen, Denmark: Bogsamleren, 1996, 92 pp., 39,50 KR, paperback. Danish translation by Jette Røssell. ISBN 87-608-0249-9.
i. As: *Deux pettites filles mortes—La ligne verte 1* ['The two dead girls—the green line 1']. Paris, France: J'ai Lu #100, 1996, 88 pp., 10 F, paperback. French translation by Philippe Rouard. ISBN 2-277-30100-0.
j. As: *De groene mijl 1: De twee dode meisjes* ['The green mile 1: the two dead girls']. Amsterdam, Netherlands: Poema Pocket, 1996, 111 pp., paperback. Dutch translation by Hugo Kuipers. ISBN 90-245-2753-8.

k. As: *Dwie martwe dziewczynki: Zielona Mila 1* ['Two dead maidens: green mile 1']. Warsaw, Poland: "Prima," 1996, 94 pp., 20 cm. Polish translation by Andrzej Mila. ISBN 83-7152-061-1.

l. As: *Las gemelas asesinadas: El pasillo de la muerte, 1* ['Two murdered twins/girls: the corridor of death 1']. Barcelona, Spain: Plaza & Janés, 1996, 91 pp., 18 cm. Spanish translation by María Eugenia Ciocchini. ISBN 84-01-48500-2.

m. As: *Kuoleman Käytävä: Kaksi pientä tyttöä 1.* ['Death corridor: two little girls 1']. Helsinki, Finland: Tammi, 1997, 94 pp., 17 cm, paperback. Finnish translation by Heikki Kaskimies. ISBN 951-31-0796-5.

n. As: *Den grønne mil: de to døde pikel—1* ['The green mile: the two dead girls 1']. Oslo, Norway: Fredhøi, 1997, 91 pp., 305.00 K, [*heftet*]. Norwegian translation by Tor Rydningen. ISBN 82-04-04885-8.

o. As: *Den Gröna Milen: De två döda flickorna—1* ['The green mile: the two dead girls']. Höganäs, Sweden: Bra Böcker, 1997, 91 pp., 21 cm., bound [*inbunden*]. Swedish translation by John-Henri Holmberg. ISBN 91-7133-267-7.

p. As: [Title unknown]. Tel Aviv, Israel: Modan, 19—. Hebrew translation.

q. As: [Title unknown]. Moscow, Russia: AST, 19—. Russian translation.

r. As: *A Ket Hallott Lany*. Budapest, Hungary: Európa, 19—. Hungarian translation.

s. As:]Title unknown]. Japan, 19—. Japanese translation.

t. As AUDIOCASSETTE. New York: Penguin Audiobooks, March 1996, $7.95. Read by Frank Muller. ISBN 0-140-86377-X.

COMMENTS: The mass-market paperback publication of the first volume of *The Green Mile* constituted a publishing adventure for King, harkening back to the novels-by-installment traditions of the nineteenth-century. Fully as successful as his previous novels, with each of the six volumes finding a spot on national bestsellers lists, *The Green Mile* is simultaneously innovative in its setting, its first-person narrator, its careful modulation of past and present, its presentations of the corrupting influence of one sort of power and the redemptive effects of another, and its gradual but inevitable revelation of the supernatural, all set against a dual backdrop of death: a prison death-house and an equally bleak retirement home.

SELECTED ARTICLES, RESPONSES, AND REVIEWS:
Bryant, Edward. *Locus* Vol. 36, No. 3, #422 (March 1996).

Horror Plum'd

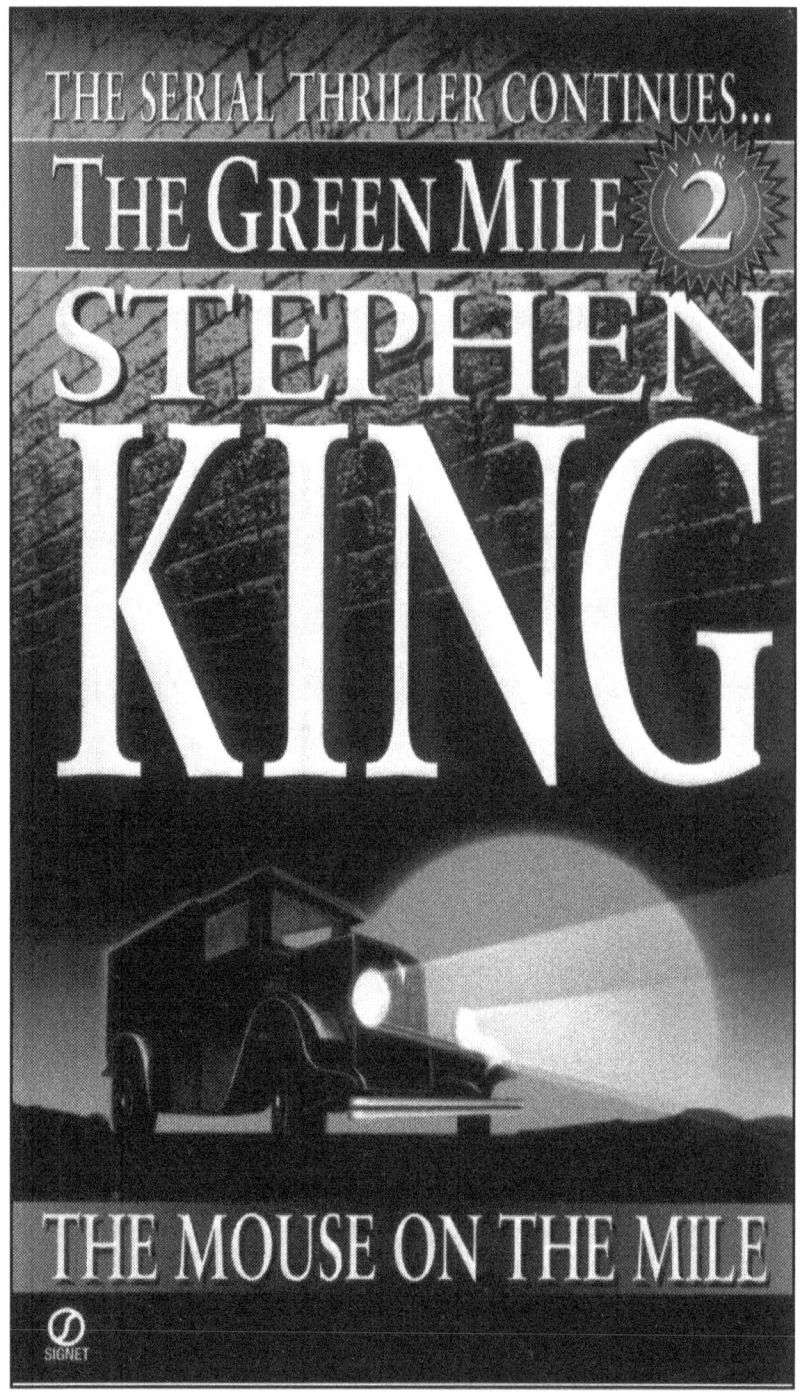

THE GREEN MILE PART 2: THE MOUSE ON THE MILE. New York, NY: Signet, April 1996. Mass-market paperback.

A53.
THE GREEN MILE
PART 2—THE MOUSE ON THE MILE
(1996)

A53. THE GREEN MILE: PART 2—THE MOUSE ON THE MILE. New York: New York: Signet, April 1996, 92 pp., $2.99, mass-market paperback. ISBN 0-451-19052-1. [For six-volume boxed and single-volume omnibus editions of the complete novel, see A59]

REPRINTS AND ADAPTATIONS:
b. London, England: Penguin, April 1996, 92 pp., £1.99, paperback. ISBN 0-14-02587-4.
c. As: *The Green Mile: Teil 2—Die Maus in Todesblock* ['The mouse in the death-house']. Bergisch Gladbach, West Germany: Bastei-Lübbe, ALLGEMEINE REIHE, 1 May 1996, 5.00 DM, paperback (*kartoniert*). German translation. ISBN 3-404-13951-8. "Deutsche Erstgausgabe."
d. As: *Il Miglio Verde Parte Seconda. La tana del topo* ['The green mile part two: the lair of the mouse']. Milan, Italy: Sperling Serial, THE BEST ONE #2, May 1996. Italian translation by Tullio Dobner. ISBN 88-86845-02-2.
e. Burnsville MN: Econo-Clad/Sagebrush, 1996, 92 pp., $9.95, library binding. #1030543.
f. As: *Zelena milja: Dio 2, Mi´z na milji*. Zagreb, Croatia: Sysprint, 1996, 91 pp., 18 cm., paperback. Croatian translation by Predrag Raos.
g. As: *Musen på milen: Den grønne mil 2* ['Mouse on the mile: the green mile 2']. Copenhagen, Denmark: Vinten, VINTENS PAPERBACK, 1996, 91 pp., 48 KR, paperback. Danish translation by Jette Røssell. ISBN 87-414-2433-6.
h. As: *Musen på milen: Den grønne mil 2* ['Mouse on the mile: the green mile 2']. Copenhagen, Denmark: Bogsamleren, 1996, 91 pp., 39,50 KR, paperback. Danish translation by Jette Røssell. ISBN 87-608-0250-2.
i. As: *Mister Jingles—La ligne verte 2* ['Mister Jungles—the green line 2']. Paris, France: J'ai Lu #101, 1996, 88 pp., 10 F, paperback. French translation by Philippe Rouard. ISBN 2-277-30101-9.
j. As: *De groene mijl 2: De muis* ['the green mile 2—the mouse']. Amsterdam, Netherlands: Poema Pocket, 1996, 94 pp., paperback. Dutch translation by Hugo Kuipers. ISBN 90-245-2654-X.

k. As: *Un ratón en el pasillo: El pasillo de la muerte 2* ['A mouse on the corridoe: the corridor of death 2']. Barcelona, Spain: Plaza & Janés, 1996, 100 pp., 18 cm., paperback. Spanish translation by María Eugenia Ciocchini. ISBN 84-01-48502-9.

l. As: *Kuoleman Käytävä: Hiiri käytävällä.* ['Death corridor: mouse on the corridor']. Helsinki, Finland: Tammi, 1997, 92 pp., 17 cm, paperback. Finnish translation by Heikki Kaskimies. ISBN 951-31-0881-3.

m. As: *Den grønne mil: Musen på milen—2* ['The green mile: mouse on the mile—2']. Oslo, Norway: Egmont Bøker Fredhøi, 1997, 91 pp., 395.00, paperback [*heftet*]. Norwegian translation by Tor Rydningen. ISBN 82-04-04886-6.

n. As: *Mysz Francuza: Zielona Mila 2* ['Mouse (?): green mile 2']. Warsaw, Poland: "Prima," 1997, 94 pp., 20 cm. Polish translation by Andrrzej Szulc. ISBN 83-7152-062-X.

o. As: *Den Gröna Milen: Musen på milen—2* ['The green mile: mouse on the mile']. Höganäs, Sweden: Bra Böcker, 1997, 96 pp., 21 cm., paperback [*heftet*]. Swedish translation by John-Henri Holmberg. ISBN 91-7133-281-2.

p. As: [Title unknown]. Moscow, Russia: AST, 19—. Russian translation.

q. As: *Egera a Halalsoron.* Hungary: Európa, 19—. Hungarian translation.

r. As: [Title unknown]. Japan, 19—. Japanese translation.

s. As AUDIOCASSETTE: *Green Mile, Part 2.* New York: Penguin, April 1996. Read by Frank Muller. ISBN 0-140-86378-8.

SELECTED ARTICLES, RESPONSES, AND REVIEWS:
Bryant, Edward. *Locus* Vol. 36, No. 5, #424 (May 1996).

HORROR PLUM'D

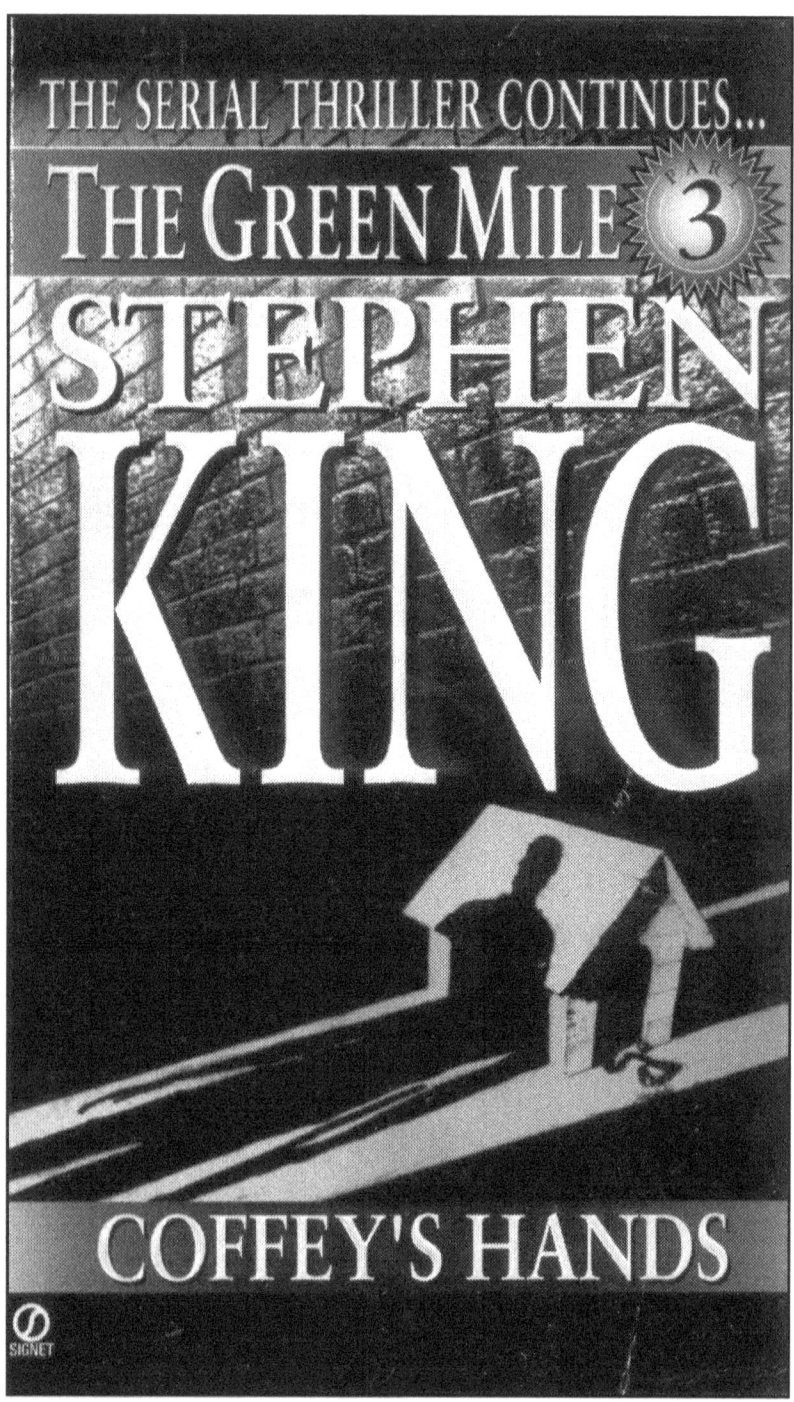

THE GREEN MILE PART 3: COFFEY'S HANDS. New York, NY: Signet, May 1996. Mass-market paperback.

A54.
THE GREEN MILE
PART 3–COFFEY'S HANDS
(1996)

A54. THE GREEN MILE: PART 3—COFFEY'S HANDS. New York: Signet, May 1996, 92 pp., $2.99, mass-market paperback. ISBN 0-451-19054-8. [For six-volume boxed and single-volume omnibus editions of the complete novel, see A59]

REPRINTS AND ADAPTATIONS:
a. London, England: Penguin, May 1996, 90 pp., £1.99, paperback. ISBN 0-14-025858-2.
B. As: *The Green Mile: Teil 3—Coffey's Hände* ['Coffey's hands']. Bergisch Gladbach, West Germany: Bastei-Lübbe, ALLGEMEINE REIHE, 1 June 1996, 5,00DM, paperback (*kartoniert*). German translation. ISBN 3-404-13952-6. "Deutsche Erstgausgabe".
c. As: *Il Miglio Verde Parte terza. Le mani di Coffey* ['The green mile part three: the hands of Coffey']. Milan, Italy: Sperling Serial, THE BEST ONE #3, June 1996. Italian translation by Tullio Dobner. ISBN 88-7824-673-5.
d. Burnsville MN: Econo-Clad/Sagebrush, 1996, 90pp., $9.95, library binding. #1030162.
e. As: *Zelena milja: Dio 3, Coffeyjeve ruke* ['Green mile: 3, Coffey's hands']. Zagreb, Croatia: Sysprint, 1996, 93 pp., 18 cm., paperback. Croatian translation by Predrag Raos.
f. As: *Coffeys Hænden: Den grønne mil 3* ['Coffey's hands: the green mile 3']. Copenhagen, Denmark: Vinten, VINTENS PAPERBACK, 1996, 92 pp., 48 KR, paperback. Danish translation by Jette Røssell. ISBN 87-414-2434-4.
g. As: *Coffeys Hænden: Den grønne mil 3* ['Coffey's hands: the green mile 3']. Copenhagen, Denmark: Bogsamleren, 1996, 92 pp., 39,50 KR, hardcover. Danish translation by Jette Røssell. ISBN 87-608-0251-0.
h. As: *Kuoleman Käytävä: Coffeyn kädet 3*. ['Death corridor: Coffey's hands']. Helsinki, Finland: Tammi, 1997, 92 pp., 17 cm, paperback. Finnish translation by Heikki Kaskimies. ISBN 951-31-0882-1.
i. As: *Les main de Caffey: La ligne verte 3* ['the hands of Coffey: the green line 3']. Paris, France: J'ai Lu #102, 1996, 10 F, paperback. French translation by Philippe Rouard. ISBN 2-277-30102-7.

j. As: *De groene mijl 3: Coffey's Handen* ['The green mile 3: Coffey's hands']. Amsterdam, Netherlands: Poema Pocket, 1996, 92 pp., paperback. Dutch translation by Hugo Kuipers. ISBN 90-245-2664-7.
k. As: *Las manos de Coffey* ['the hands of Coffey']. Barcelona, Spain: Plaza & Janés, BIBLIOTECA DE STEPHEN KING, 1996, 92 pp., 18 cm., paperback. Spanish translation by María Eugenia Ciocchini. ISBN 84-01-48502-9.
l. As: *Den grønne mil: Coffeys hender—3* ['The green mile: Coffey's hands—3']. Oslo, Norway: Egmont Bøker Fredhøi, 1997, 91 pp., 395.00 K, paperback [*heftet*]. Norwegian translation by Tor Rydningen. ISBN 82-04-04887-4.
m. As: *Dlonie Coffeya: Zielona Mila 3* ['Coffey's palms/hands: green mile 3']. Warsaw, Poland: "Prima," 1997, 94 pp., 20 cm. Polish translation by Andrzej Szulc. ISBN 83-7152-066-2.
n. As: *Den Gröna Milen: Coffeys händer—3* ['The green mile: Coffey's hands—3']. Höganäs, Sweden: Bra Böcker, 1997, 90 pp., 21 cm., bound [*inbunden*]. Swedish translation by John-Henri Holmberg. ISBN 91-7133-282-0.
o. As: [Title unknown]. Hungary: Európa, 19—. Hungarian translation.
p. As: [Title unknown]. Japan, 19—. Japanese translation.
q. As: [Title unknown]. Moscow, Russia: AST, 19—. Russian translation.

r. As AUDIOCASSETTE: *Green Mile, Part 3*. New york: Penguin Books, May 1996. Read by Frank Muller. ISBN 0-140-86379-6.

SELECTED ARTICLES, RESPONSES, AND REVIEWS:
Bryant, Edward. *Locus* Vol. 36, No. 6, #425 (June 1996).

Horror Plum'd

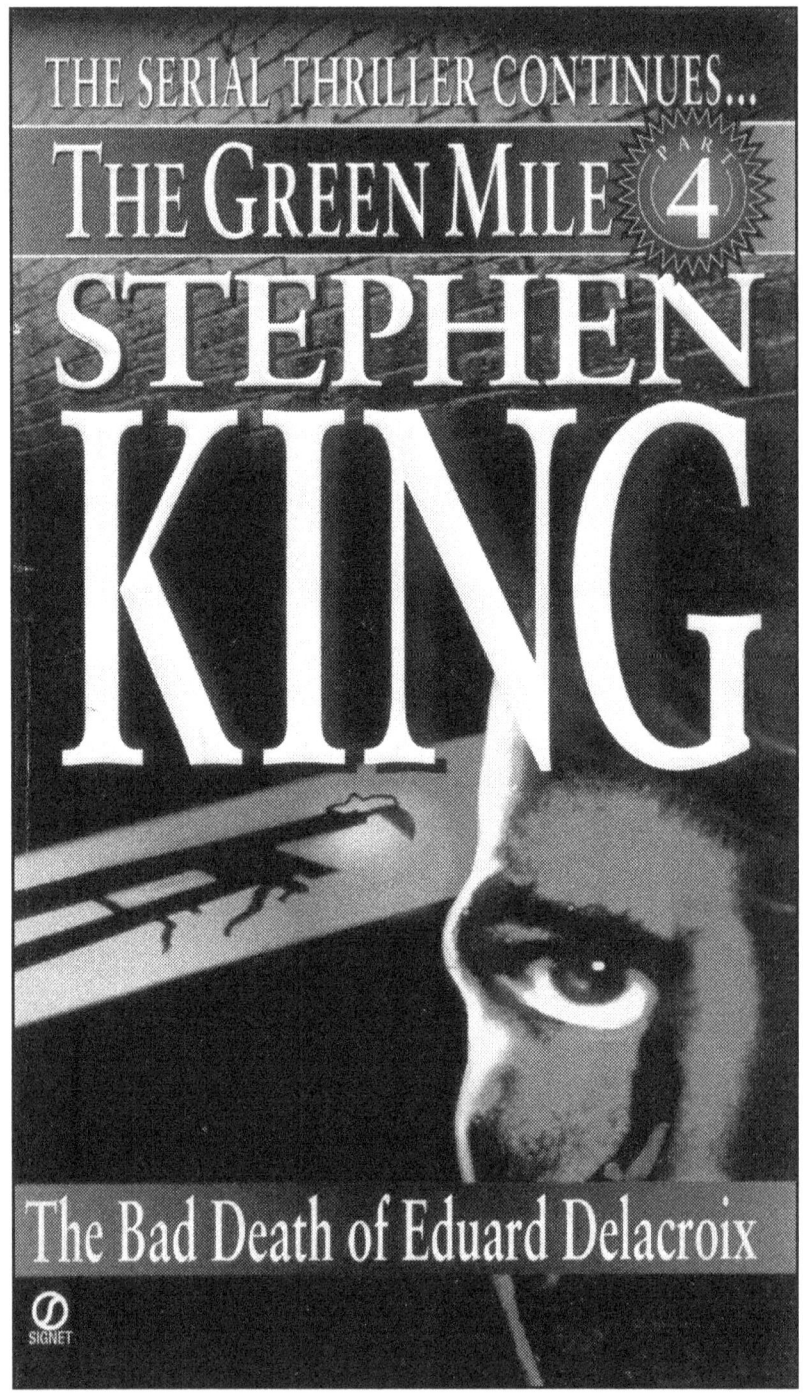

THE GREEN MILE PART 4: THE BAD DEATH OF EDUARD DELACROIX.
New York, NY: Signet, June 1996. Mass-market paperback.

A55.
THE GREEN MILE
PART 4-THE BAD DEATH OF EDUARD DELACROIX
(1996)

A55. THE GREEN MILE: PART 4—THE BAD DEATH OF EDUARD DELACROIX. New York: Signet, June 1996, 92 pp., $2.99, mass-market paperback. ISBN 0-451-19055-6. [For six-volume boxed and single-volume omnibus editions of the complete novel, see A59]

REPRINTS AND ADAPTATIONS:
b. London, England: Penguin, June 1996, 90 pp., £1.99, paperback. ISBN 0-14-025859-0.
c. As: *The Green Mile: Teil 4—Die qualvolle Tod* ['Part 4—the tortuous']. Bergisch Gladbach, West Germany: Bastei-Lübbe, ALLGEMEINE REIHE, 1 July 1996, 5.00 DM, paperback (*kartoniert*). German translation. ISBN 3-404-13953-4. "Deutsche Erstgausgabe."
d. As: *Il Miglio Verde Parte quarta. La strana morte di Eduard Delacroix* ['The green mile part four. The strange/odd death of Eduard Delacroix']. Milan, Italy: Sperling Serial, THE BEST ONE #4, July 1996. Italian translation by Tullio Dobner. ISBN 88-86845-04-9.
e. Burnsville MN: Econo-Clad/Sagebrush, 1996, 90 pp., $9.95, library binding. #1030022.
f. As: *En unhyggelig død: Den grønne mil 4* ['An uncomfortable death: the green mile 4']. Copenhagen, Denmark: Vinten, VINTENS PAPERBACKS, 1996, 94 pp., 48 KR, paperback. Danish translation by Jette Røssell. ISBN 87-414-2435-2.
g. As: *En unhyggelig død: Den grønne mil 4* ['An uncomfortable death: the green mile 4']. Copenhagen, Denmark: Bogsamleren, 1996, 94 pp., 39,50 KR, hardcover. Danish translation by Jette Røssell. ISBN 87-608-0252-9.
h. As: *La mort affreuse d'Edouard Delacroix—La ligne verte 4* ['The awful death of Eduard Delacroix']. Paris, France: Jai'Lu #103, 90 pp., 10 F, paperback. French translation by Philippe Rouard. ISBN 2-277-30103-5.
i. As: *De groene mijl 4: De vreslijke dood van Eduard Delacroix* ['The green

mile 4: the frightful death of Eduard Delacroix']. Amsterdam, Netherlands: Poema Pocket, 1996, 110 pp., paperback. Dutch translation by Hugo Kuipers. ISBN 90-245-2674-4.

j. As: *Una ejecución espeluznante: El pasillo de la muerte 4* ['A hair-raising execution: the corridor of death 4']. Barcelona, Spain: Plaza & Janés, 1996, 91 pp., 18 cm. Spanish translation by María Eugenia Ciocchini. ISBN 84-01-48504-5.

k. As: *Kuoleman Käytävä: Delacroisin kurja loppu 4.* ['Death corridor: Delacroix's miserable finish/ending']. Helsinki, Finland: Tammi, 1997, 93 pp., 17 cm, paperback. Finnish translation by Heikki Kaskimies. ISBN 951-31-0883-X.

l. As: *Zelena milja: Dio 4, Ru´zna smrt Eduarda.* Zagreb, Croatia: Sysprint, 1996, 93 pp., 18 cm., paperback. Croatian translation by Pregrad Raos.

m. As: *En uhyggelig død* ['A dismal/uncanny death']. Oslo, Norway: Egmont Bøker Fredhøi, 1997, 91 pp., 395.00, paperback [*heftet*]. Norwegian translation by Tor Rydningen. ISBN 82-04-04888-2.

n. As: *Zla œmierœ Eduarda Delacroix: Zielona Mila 4.* Warsaw, Poland: "Prima," 1997, 94 pp., 20 cm. Polish translation by Andrzej Szulc. ISBN 83-7152-069-7.

o. As: *Den Gröna Milen: Eduard Delacroix' onda död—4* ['The green mile: Eduard Delacroix's bad death']. Höganäs, Sweden: Bra Böcker, 1997, 91 pp., 21 cm., bound [*inbunden*]. Swedish translation by John-Henri Holmberg. ISBN 91-7133-283-9.

p. As: [Title unknown]. Hungary: Európa, 19—. Hungarian translation.

q. As: [Title unknown]. Japan, 19—. Japanese translation.

r. As: [Title unknown]. Moscow, Russia: AST, 19—. Russian translation.

s. As AUDIOCASSETTE: *The Green Mile, Part 4.* New York: Penguin Audiobooks, June 1996, $7.95. Read by Frank Muller. ISBN 0-140-86380-X.

SELECTED ARTICLES, RESPONSES, AND REVIEWS:
Bryant, Edward. *Locus* Vol. 37, No. 1, #426 (July 1996).

HORROR PLUM'D

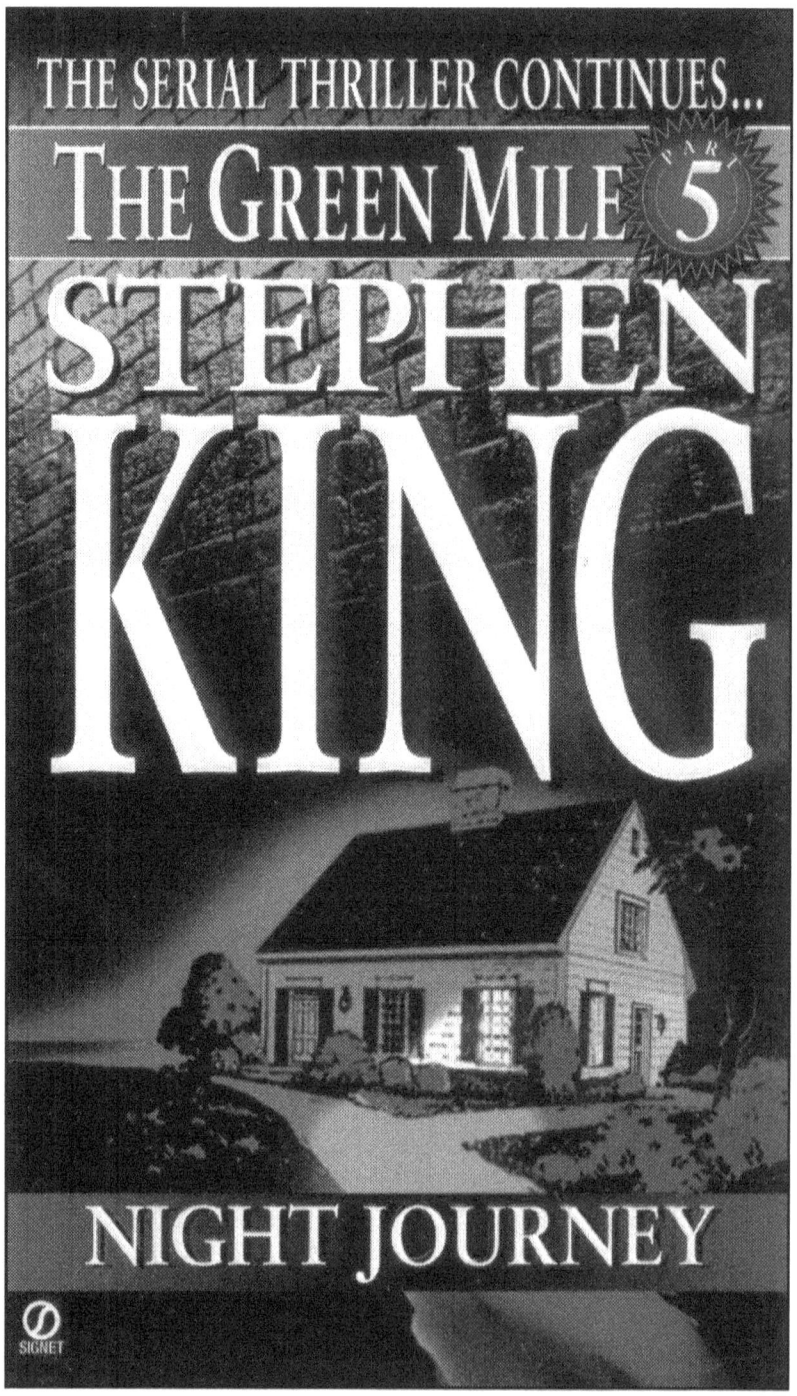

The Green Mile Part 5: Night Journey. New York, NY: Signet, July 1996. Mass-market paperback.

A56.
THE GREEN MILE
PART 5-NIGHT JOURNEY
(1996)

A56. *THE GREEN MILE: PART 5—NIGHT JOURNEY*. New York: Signet, July 1996, 92 pp., $2.99, mass-market paperback. ISBN 0-451-19056-4. [For six-volume boxed and single-volume omnibus editions of the complete novel, see A59]

REPRINTS AND ADAPTATIONS:
b. London, England: Penguin, July 1996, 90 pp., £1.99, paperback. ISBN 0-14-025860-4.
c. As: *The Green Mile: Teil 5—Reise in die Nacht* ['Part 5—journey in the night']. Bergisch Gladbach, West Germany: Bastei-Lübbe, ALLGEMEINE REIHE, 1 August 1996, 5,00DM, paperback (*kartoniert*). German translation. ISBN 3-404-13954-2. "Deutsche Erstgausgabe".
d. As: *Il Miglio Verde Parte quinta. Viaggio nella notte* ['The green mile part five. Journey through night']. Milan, Italy: Sperling Serial, THE BEST ONE #5, August 1996. Italian translation by Tullio Dobner. ISBN 88-86845-05-7.
e. Burnsville MN: Econo-Clad/Sagebrush, 1996, 90 pp., $9.95, library binding.
f. As: *Zelena milja: Dio 5, Nocno putovanje*. Zagreb, Croatia: Sysprint, 1996, 93 pp., 18 cm., paperback. Croatian translation by Pregrad Raos.
g. As: *En natlig udflugt: Den grønne mil 5* ['A nocturnal excursion/outing']. Copenhagen, Denmark: Vinten, VINTENS PAPERBACKS, 1996, 93 pp., 48 KR, paperback. Danish translation by Jette Røssell. ISBN 87-414-2436-0.
h. As: *En natlig udflugt: Den grønne mil 5* ['A nocturnal excursion/outing: the green mile 5']. Copenhagen, Denmark: Bogsamleren, 1996, 93 pp., 39,50 KR, hardcover. Danish translation by Jette Røssell. ISBN 87-608-0253-7.
i. As: *L'équipée nocturne—La ligne verte 5* ['The nocturnal escapade/prank']. Paris, France: J'ai Lu, 1996 #104, 1996, 88 pp., 10 F, paperback. French translation by Philippe Rouard. ISBN 2-277-30104-3.
j. As: *De groene mijl 5: Nachtreis* ['The green mile 5: night-journey']. Amsterdam, Netherlands: Poema Pocket, 1996, 112 pp., paperback. Dutch translation by Hugo Kuipers. ISBN 90-245-2684-1.

k. As; *Viaje nocturno—Pasilla de la muerte 5* ['Night journey: corridor of death 5']. Barcelona, Spain: Plaza & Janés, BIBLIOTECA DE STEPHEN KING, 1996, 93 pp., 18 cm., paperback. Spanish translation by María Eugenia Ciocchini. ISBN 84-01-48505-3.

l. As: *Kuoleman Käytävä: Öinen matka viides osa.* ['Death corridor: night journey fifth part']. Helsinki, Finland: Tammi, 1997, 99 pp., 17 cm, paperback. Finnish translation by Heikki Kaskimies. ISBN 951-31-0884-8.

m. As: *Den grønne mil: En nattlig utflukt—5* ['The green mile: A nocturnal excursion—5']. Oslo, Norway: Egmont Bøker Fredhøi., 1997, 91 pp., 395.00, paperback [*heftet*]. Norwegian translation by Tor Rydningen. ISBN 82-04-04889-0.

n. As: *Den Gröna Milen: Resa I natten—5* ['The green mile: journey at night']. Höganäs, Sweden: Bra Böcker, 1997, 98 pp., 21 cm., bound [*inbunden*]. Swedish translation by John-Henri Holmberg. ISBN 91-7133-284-7.

o. As: [Title unknown]. Hungary: Európa, 19—. Hungarian translation.

p. As: [Title unknown]. Japan, 19—. Japanese translation.

q. As: [Title unknown]. Moscow, Russia: AST, 19—. Russian translation.

r. As AUDIOCASSETTE: *The Green Mile, Part 5.* New York: Penguin Books, July 1996. Read by Frank Muller. ISBN 0-140-86381-8.

SELECTED ARTICLES, RESPONSES, AND REVIEWS:
Bryant, Edward. *Locus* Vol. 37, No. 2, #427 (August 1996).

Horror Plum'd

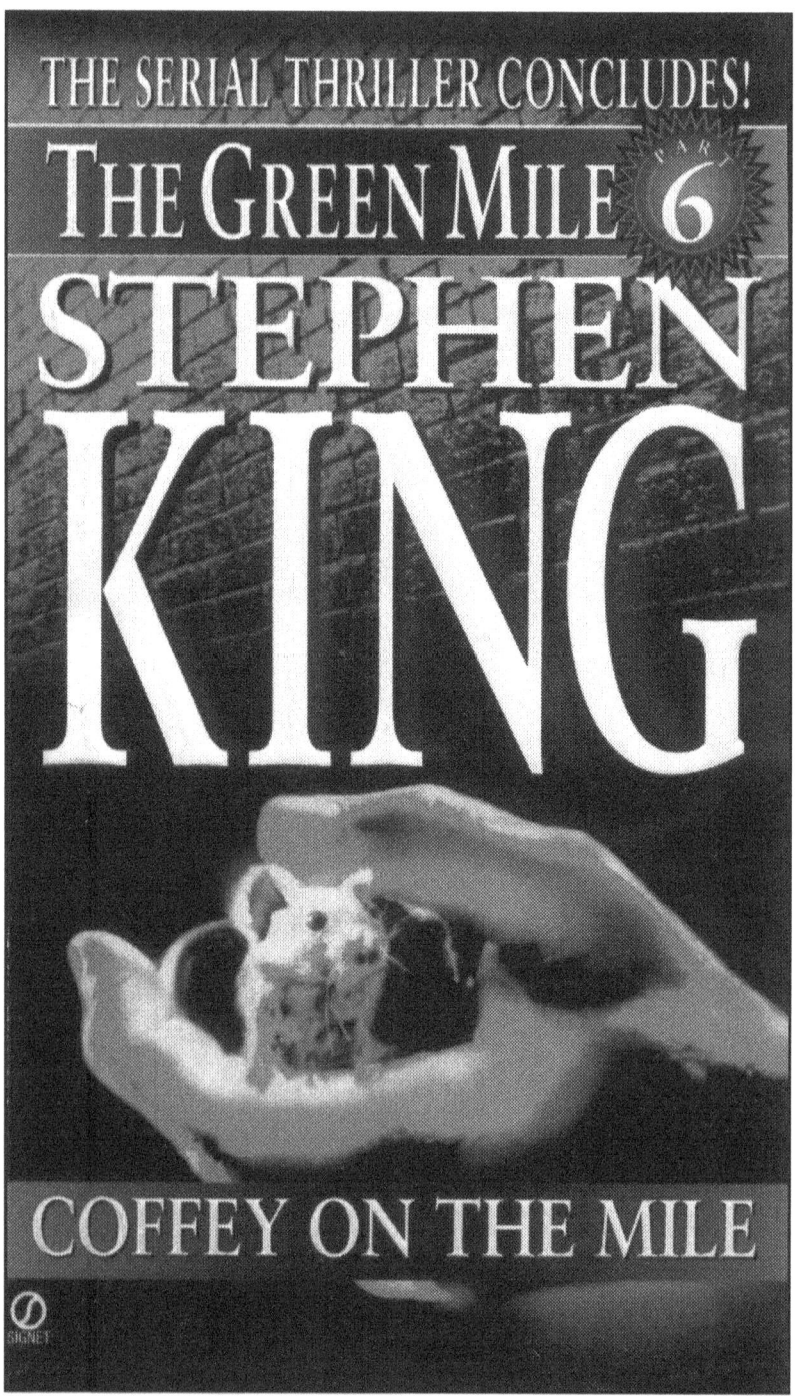

The Green Mile Part 6: Coffey on the Mile. New York, NY: Signet, August 1996. Mass-market paperback.

A57.
THE GREEN MILE
PART 6-COFFEY ON THE MILE
(1996)

A57. THE GREEN MILE: PART 6—COFFEY ON THE MILE. New York: Signet, august 1996, 138 pp., $3.99, mass-market paperback. ISBN 0-451-19057-1. [For six-volume boxed and single-volume omnibus editions of the complete novel, see A59]

REPRINTS AND ADAPTATIONS:
b. London, England: Penguin, August 1996, 138 pp., £1.99, paperback. ISBN 0-14-025761-2.
c. As: *The Green Mile: Teil 6—Coffey's Vermächtnis* ['Coffey's testament']. Bergisch Gladbach, West Germany: Bastei-Lübbe, ALLGEMEINE REIHE, 1 September 1996, 5,00DM, paperback (*kartoniert*). German translation. ISBN 3-404-13955-0. "Deutsche Erstgausgabe".
d. As: *Il Miglio Verde Parte sesta. L'ultimo viaggio di Coffey* ['The green mile part six: Coffey's last journey']. Milan, Italy: Sperling Serial, THE BEST ONE #6, September 1996. Italian translation by Tullio Dobner. ISBN 88-86845-06-5.
e. Burnsville MN: Econo-Clad/Sagebrush, 1996, 138 pp., $11.10, library binding. #1030154.
f. As: *Zelena milja: Dio 6, Coffey na milji.* Zagreb, Croatia: Sysprint, 1996, 127 pp., 18 cm., paperback. Croatian translation by Pregrad Raos.
g. As: *Coffey på milen: Den grønne mil 6* ['Coffey on the mile: the green mile 6']. Copenhagen, Denmark: Vinten, VINTENS PAPERBACKS, 1996, 93 pp., 48 KR, paperback. Danish translation by Jette Røssell. ISBN 87-414-2437-9.
h. As: *Coffey på milen: Den grønne mil 6* ['Coffey on the mile: the green mile 6']. Copenhagen, Denmark: Bogsamleren, 1996, 93 pp., 39,50 KR, hardcover. Danish translation by Jette Røssell. ISBN 87-608-0254-5.
i. As: *Caffey sur la ligne—La ligne verte 6* ['Coffey on the line: the green line 6']. Paris, France: J'ai Lu #105, 1996, 10 F, 21 cm., paperback. French translation by Philippe Rouard. ISGN 2-277-30105-1.
j. As: *De groene mijl 6: Coffey op de mijl* ['The green mile 6: Coffey on the mile']. Amsterdam, Netherlands: Poema Pocket, 1996, 128 pp., paperback. Dutch translation by Hugo Kuipers. ISBN 90-245-2694-9.

k. As: *La hora final de Coffey: El pasillo de la muerte 6* ['The last hour of Coffey: the corridor of death 6']. Barcelona, Spain: Plaza & Janés, BIBLIOTECA DE STEPHEN KING, 1996, 125 pp., 18 cm., paperback. Spanish translation by María Eugenia Ciocchini. 1st edition. ISBN 84-01-48506-1.
l. As: *Kuoleman Käytävä: Coffeyn viimeinen taival kuudes osa.* ['Death corridor: Coffey's last (?)']. Helsinki, Finland: Tammi, 1997, 128 pp., 17 cm, paperback. Finnish translation by Heikki Kaskimies. ISBN 951-31-0885-6.
m. As: *Den grønen mil: Coffee på milen—6* ['The green mile: Coffey on the mile—6']. Oslo, Norway: Egmont Bøker Fredhøi, 1997, 110 pp., 395.00, [*heftet*]. Norwegian translation by Tor Rydningen. ISBN 82-04-04890-4.
n. As: *Coffey na Mili: Zielona Mila 6* ['Coffey on the mile: green mile 6']. Warsaw, Poland: "Prima," 1997, 125 pp., 20 cm. Polish translation by Andrzej Szulc. ISBN 83-7152-101-4.
o. As: *Den Gröna Milen: Coffey på milen—6* ['The green mile: Coffey on the mile—6']. Höganäs, Sweden: Bra Böcker, 1997, 131 pp., 21 cm., bound. Swedish translation by John-Henri Holmberg. ISBN 91-7133-285-5.
p. As: [Title unknown]. Hungary: Európa, 19—. Hungarian translation.
q. As: [Title unknown]. Japan, 19—. Japanese translation.
r. As: [Title unknown]. Moscow, Russia: AST, 19—. Russian translation.

s. As AUDIOCASSETTE: *The Green Mile 6—Coffey on the Mile.* _New York: Penguin Audiobooks, August 1996. Read by Frank Muller. ISBN 0-140-86382-6.

SELECTED ARTICLES, RESPONSES, AND REVIEWS:
Bryant, Edward. *Locus* Vol. 37, No. 3, #428 (September 1996).

Horror Plum'd

Desperation. New York, NY: Viking, 1996. Hardcover.

A58.
DESPERATION
(1996)

A58. *Desperation*. Hampton Falls NH: Donald M. Grant, August 1996, 524 pp., hardcover. Cover art by Don Maitz. Horror novel. * Deluxe limited edition: 2,000 copies in tray-case, signed and numbered, $175.00. ISBN 1-880418-35-5. * Limited edition: 4,000 copies in slipcase, $75.00. ISBN 1-880418-36-3.

PLOT SUMMARY: Travellers approaching the isolated Nevada town of Desperation get to see more than just a dying mining concern; they get to die as well. Only a few intrepid journeyers into truth discover that the real dangers are as much to the soul as to the body, and that the monster they must confront is more than human.

REPRINTS AND ADAPTATIONS:
b. With *The Regulators:* London, England: Hodder & Stoughton, July 1996, 545 pp. + 334 pp., £125.00, hardcovers. Limited, signed edition, 200 copies, slipcased. Sold as a set only. ISBN 0-340-66575-0.
c. London, England: Hodder & Stoughton, September 1996, 545 pp., £16.99, hardcover. Cover art by Christ Moore. ISBN 0-340-65427-9.
d. New York: Viking, 24 September 1996, 690 pp., $27.95, hardcover. Cover art by Mark Ryden. ISBN 0-670-86836-1. Distributed in glassine slipcase with *The Regulators* and reading light; ISBN 0-670-77605-X. Subsequent sets packages with a paperback excerpt from *The Dark Tower IV: Wizard and Glass* [see A61]
e. Utrecht, Belgium, Netherlands: Luitingh-Sitjhoff, 1996. Dutch translation.
f. As: *Ocajavanje*. Zagreb, Croatia: Algoritam, 1996 [1997?], 512 pp., 25 cm. Croatian translation by Bo_ica Jakovlev. ISBN 953-6166-43-7.
g. Copenhagen, Denmark: Vinten/DBK, 1996, 502 pp., 248 kr, hardcover. Danish translation by Jette Røssell. ISBN 87-414-1054-8.
h. Copenhagen, Denmark: Bogklubben Egmont, 1996, 502 pp., 128 kr, hardcover. Danish translation by Jette Røssell. ISBN 87-608-0137-9. Book Club edition.

MICHAEL R. COLLINGS

i. As: *Epätoivon kaupunki* ['Desperate-town']. Helsinki, Finland: Tammi, 1996, 617 pp., hardcover. Finnish translation by Ilkka Rekiaro. ISBN 951-31-0698-5. * 2nd-3rd printings, 1997.

j. As: *Désolation*. Paris, France: Albin Michel, 1996, 571 pp., 140 F, paperback. French translation by Dominique Peters. ISBN 2-226-08817-2.

k. As: *Désolation*. [Paris, France]:[le Grand livre du mois], 1996, 571 pp., 140 F, hardcover. French translation by Dominique Peters. Book Club edition.

l. Munich, West Germany: Wilhelm Heyne, 1996, 671 pp., 48.00 DM, hardcover. German translation by Joachim Körber. ISBN 3-453-11498-1. * 3rd printing 1996.

m. Amsterdam, Netherlands: Luitingh-Sijthoff, 1996, 604 pp. Dutch translation by Robert Vernooy. 1st Dutch edition. ISBN 90-245-2596-9.

n. As: *Desperation, Nevada*. Oslo, Norway: Aschehoug, 1996, 502 pp., 269.00 hardcover [*innbundet*]. Norwegian translation by Steinar Moe. ISBN 82-03-20247-0. Reprinted 1997, ISBN 82-03-20274-8.

o. As: *Desperation, Nevada*. Oslo, Norway: Bokklubben krim og spenning, 1996, 502 pp., hardcover Norwegian translation by Steinar Moe. ISBN 82-598-0242-2.

p. As: *Desesperación*. Barcelona, Spain: Barcelona, Spain: Plaza & Janés, 1996, 611 pp., 23 cm.. Spanish translation by Carlos Milla Soler. New edition. ISBN 84-01-32684-2. * Reprint, 1998, ISBN 84-01-24266-5.

q. Milan, Italy: Sperling & Kupfer, NARRATIVA [#227], January 1997, 608 pp., 21 cm. Italian translation by Tullio Dobner. ISBN 88-200-2363-6.

r. Hingham MA: Wheeler, March 1997, $27.95, hardcover. ISBN 1568954204.

s. Boston MA; Melbourne, Australia; and England: Compass/Isis, March 1997, 761 pp., 24 cm. ISBN 1-5689-5420-4 [US]. Simultaneous large-print editions.

t. London, England: New English Library, July 1997, 720 pp., £6.99, paperback. Cover art by Christ Moore. ISBN 0-340-65428-7.

u. New York: Signet, August 1997, 547 pp., $7.99, mass-market paperback. Cover art by John Jude Palencar. ISBN 0-451-18846-2.

v. Munich, West Germany: Wilhelm Heyne TB 10446, December 1997, 638 pp., 16.90 DM, paperback. German translation by Joachim Körber. ISBN 3-453-12952-0.

w. As: *Desespero*. Rio de Janeiro, Brazil: Objetiva, 1997, 540 pp., 21 cm., paperback. Portuguese translation by Marcos Santarrita. ISBN 85-730-2123-3.

x. Copenhagen, Denmark: Bogsamleren, 1997, 502 pp., 98 KR, hardcover. Danish translation by Jette Røssell. ISBN 87-608-0136-0. Book Club edition.

y. As: *Désolation*. Paris, France: France Loisirs, 1997, 571 pp., 112 F, hardcover. French translation by Dominique Peters. ISBN 2-7441-0922-3.

z. As: *Desperation, Nevada*. Oslo, Norway: Aschehoug, 1997, 502 pp., 65.00, paperback [*heftet*]. Norwegian translation by Steinar Moe. ISBN 82-03-20274-8. Reprinted 1998, ISBN 82-03-20366-3.

aa. As: *Desperacja.* Warsaw, Poland: "Prima," 1997, 541 pp., 20 cm. Polish translation by Krysztof Sokolowski. ISBN 83-7186-012-9.
bb. As: *Desesperación.* Barcelona, Spain: Barcelona, Spain: Círculo de Loectores, 1997, 569 pp., 23 cm. Spanish translation by Carlos Milla Soler. New edition. ISBN 84-226-6475-5.
cc. Rheda-Wiedenbrück, Germany: Bertelsmann-Club; Zug, Switzerland: Bertelsmann-Medien; Vienna, Austria: Buch gemeinschaft Donauland Kremayr und Scheriau, and others, [1997], 671 pp. German translation by Joachim Körber. Book Club edition.
dd. Copenhagen, Denmark: Vinten/DBK, VINTENS PAPERBACKS, 1998, 502 pp., 98 KR, paperback. Danish translation by Jette Røssell. ISBN 87-414-2190-6.
ee. Copenhagen, Denmark: Paperback Bogklubben, 1998, 502 pp., 68 KR, paperback. Danish translation by Jette Røssell. ISBN 87-608-0137-9.
ff. As: *Desperacja.* Warsaw, Poland: Œwiat Ksiazki, 1998, 541 pp., 21 cm. Polish translation by Krysztof Sokolowski. ISBN 83-7227-047-3.
gg. Höganäs, Sweden: Bra Böcker, 1998, 565 pp., 24 cm., hardcover [*inbunden*]. Swedish translation by John-Henri Holmberg. ISBN 91-7133-275-8. Book Club edition.
hh. As: *Desesperación* Barcelona, Spain: Barcelona, Spain: Plaza & Janés, JET #102/21, BIBLIOTECA DE STEPHEN KING #21, 1998, 718 pp., 18 cm., paperback. spanish translation by Carlos Milla Soler. New edition. ISBN 84-01-47471-X.
ii. Amsterdam, Netherlands: Poema Pocket, 1999, 604 pp., paperback. Dutch translation by Robert Vernooy. 6th printing. ISBN 90-245-3602-2.
jj. As: *Desperacja.* Warsaw, Poland: "Prima," 1999, 541 pp., 18 cm. Polish translation by Krysztof Sokolowski. 2nd printing. ISBN 83-7186-066-8.
kk. As: *Desperation.* Denmark, 19—. Danish translation.
ll. As [Title unknown]. Budapest, Hungary: Európa, 19—. Hungarian translation.
mm. As: [Title unknown]. Israel, 1997, 555 pp. Hebrew translation
nn. As: [Title unknown].Japan, 19—. Japanese translation.
oo. As: [Title unknown]. Moscow, Russia: AST, 19—. Russian translation.
pp. As: NTESHERISON. Greece: Bell (?), 19—. Greek translation.

qq. As: AUDIOCASSETTE: *Desperation.* New York: Penguin, September 1996. Read by Kathy Bates. Abridged. ISBN 0-140-86318-4.

RR. As FILM: *Desperation/Stephen King's Desperation.* Scheduled: 2001. Director: Mick Garris. Screenplay by Stephen King.

COMMENTS: Part of a unique publishing event, Stephen King's *Desperation* links with 'Richard Bachman's posthumously published novel, *The Regulators,* giving readers intimate glimpses as to how the two imaginations, while beginning with essentially the same cast of characters (or at least the same *names* for characters) might create entirely different stories. *Desperation* does indeed reflect King as his best, with incremental horrors, children (and adults) in peril, monsters in human form, and a quintessential quasi-alien entity devoted to evil. It is significant that here King approaches making explicit the spiritual elements implicit in the conclusions to novels such as *Needful Things*; overt horror gives way to an understated sense of restitution and restoration.

SELECTED ARTICLES, RESPONSES, AND REVIEWS:
Bryant, Edward. "*Desperation,* Stephen King." *Locus* Vol. 37, No. 3, #428 (September 1996).
Polito, Robert. "Apocalypse Now." *The New York Times Book Review* 20 October 1996: 16. Late edition.

Horror Plum'd

The Regulators. New York, NY: Dutton, 1996. Hardcover.

A59.
THE REGULATORS
AS RICHARD BACHMAN
(1996)

A59. *THE REGULATORS*. New York: Dutton, 24 September 1996, 475 pp., $24.95, hardcover. Horror novel. ISBN 0-525-94190-8. * LIMITED EDITION: lettered state of 52 leather-bound copies in wooden case (the case is constructed such that the book rests on protruding Winchester cartridges). LIMITED EDITION: 500 numbered and signed copies, packaged in a replica toy box, with checks signed by 'Richard Bachman' tipped in. TRADE EDITION: distributed in glassine slipcase with *Desperation* and reading light. ISBN 0-670-77605-X. When the supply of sets with lights was exhausted, subsequent sets were distributed with a paperback excerpt from the upcoming *The Dark Tower IV: Wizard and Glass* [see A61].

PLOT SUMMARY: Without warning, the perfectly normal, normally placid neighborhood of Poplar Street, in Wentworth, Ohio, erupts in violence: invasion by gun-toting strangers, execution style murder of an innocent newsboy, and generalized mayhem. Only gradually do the surviving victims discover that more is at stake than first appears: they are caught in the middle of the Regulators' quest to destroy, and abruptly find the very fabric of their world—perhaps their universe—altering.

REPRINTS AND ADAPTATIONS:
b. With *Desperation:* London, England: Hodder & Stoughton, July 1996, 545 pp. + 334 pp., £125.00, hardcovers. Limited, signed edition, slipcased. Sold as a set only. ISBN 0-340-66575-0.
c. As: *De Regelaars* ['The governors/rulers']. Utrecht, Belgium, Netherlands: Luitingh-Sijthoff, 1996. Dutch translation.
d. As: *Regulatorerne*. Copenhagen, Denmark: Vinten/DBK, 1996, 363 pp., 198 KR, hardcover. Danish translation by Poul Buchwald Andersen. ISBN 87-414-1062-9.
e. As: *Regulatorerne*. Copenhagen, Denmark: Bogklubben Egmont, 1996, 363 pp., 128 KR, hardcover. Danish translation by Poul Buchwald Andersen. ISBN 87-608-0329-0. Book Club edition.

f. As: *Teloittajat* ['Executioners (?)']. Helsinki, Finland: Tammi, 1996. Finnish translation.
g. As: *Regulator.* Munich, Germany: Wilhelm Heyne, 1996, 519 pp., 44.00 DM, hardcover. German translation by Joachim Körber. ISBN 3-453-11499-X.
h. As: *Posesión* ['Possession']. Barcelona, Spain: Plaza & Janés, 1996, 411 pp., 23 cm. Spanish translation by María Eugenia Ciocchini. ISBN 84-01-32682-6.
i. As: *I Vendicatori* ['The avengers']. Milan, Italy: Sperling & Kupfer, NARRATIVA [#226], January 1997. Italian translation by Tullio Dobner. ISBN 88-200-2364-4.
j. New York: Signet, September 1997, 498 pp., $7.99, mass-market paperback. ISBN 0-451-19101-3.
k. London, England: New English Library, 1997. ISBN 0-340-67177-7.
l. As: *Os Justiceiros.* Rio de Janeiro, Brazil: Objetiva, 1997, 319 pp., 21 cm., paperback. Portuguese translation by Marcos Santarrita. ISBN 85-730-2153-5.
m. As: *Regulatorerne.* Copenhagen, Denmark: Bogsamleren, 1997, 363 pp., 98 KR, hardcover. Danish translation by Poul Buchwald Andersen. ISBN 87-608-0330-4. Book Club edition.
n. As: *Regulator.* Munich, Germany: Wilhelm Heyne, 1997, 447 pp., 16.90 DM, paperback. German translation by Joachim Körber. ISBN 3-453-12960-1.
o. As: *Regulator.* Rheda-Wiedenbrück, Germany: Bertelsmann-Club; Zug, Switzerland: Bertelsmann-Medien; Vienna, Austria: Buchgemeinschaft Donauland Mremayr und Scheriau, and others, [1997], 509 pp., hardcover. German translation by Joachim Körber. Book Club editions.
p. As: *Vokterne* ['Keepers'], by 'Richard Bachman.' Oslo, Norway: Aschehaug, 1997. Norwegian translation.
q. As: *Regulatorzy.* Warsaw, Poland: "Prima," 1997, 383 pp., 20 cm. Polish translation by Piotr Jankowski. ISBN 83-7186-011-0.
r. As: *Posesión* ['Possession']. Barcelona, Spain: Círculo de Lectores, [1997], 394 pp., 22 cm. Spanish translation by María Eugenia Ciocchini. ISBN 84-226-6472-3.
s. As: *Regulatorerne.* Copenhagen, Denmark: vinten/DBK, VINTENS PAPERBACKS, 1998, 363 pp., 88 KR, paperback. Danish translation by Poul Buchwald Andersen. ISBN 87-414-2460-3.
t. As: *Regulatorerne.* Copenhagen, Denmark: Paperback Bigklubben, 1998, 363 pp., 68 KR, paperback. Danish translation by Poul Buchwald Andersen. ISBN 87-608-0331-2.
u. As: *Regulatorzy.* Warsaw, Poland: "Prima," BESTSELLERY ŒWIATOWEJ PROZY, 1998, 383 pp., 18 cm., paperback. Polish translation by Piotr Jankowski. ISBN 83-7186-065-X.
v. As: *Posesión* ['Possession']. Barcelona, Spain: Plaza & Janés, JET 102/20, BIBLIOTECA DE STEPHEN KING #20, 1998, 485 pp., 18 cm, paperback. Spanish translation by María Eugenia Ciocchini. ISBN 84-01-47470-1.
w. As: *Les Regulateurs.* France, 19—. French translation.

x. As: *Väktarna* ['Keepers/watchers'] Sweden, 19—. Swedish translation.
y. As: *Arendesinálók.*
z. As: *Oi Pyqmistes.* Greece, 19—. Greek translation.

COMMENTS: The 'companion' volume to King's *Desperation,* the 'Richard Bachman' novel seems the less focused of the two, and simultaneously the most dependent on incursions of horror and supernatural characters and events into a commonplace landscape. The characters are more varied than those in *Desperation,* nor are they necessarily similar except in naming, with the result that it is more difficult to select a sympathetic protagonist through whose eyes to evaluate the uncanny events. Of the two, this is frequently considered the weaker.

SELECTED ARTICLES, RESPONSES, AND REVIEWS:
Polito, Robert. *The New York Times Book Review* 20 October 1996. Late edition.

THE GREEN MILE: THE COMPLETE SERIAL NOVEL. New York, NY: Scribner, 2000. Hardcover.

A60.
THE GREEN MILE
THE COMPLETE SIX-PART NOVEL
(1996)

A60. THE GREEN MILE: THE COMPLETE SIX-PART NOVEL. New York: New American Library, September 1996, $18.95, mass-market paperback. SIX-BOOK BOXED SET. ISBN 0-451-93302-8. * 20th printing, 1999.

REPRINTS AND ADAPTATIONS:
b. As: *The Green Mile, Teil 1-6* ['The green mile, parts 1-6']. Bergisch Gladbach, West Germany: Bastei-Lübbe, ALLGEMEINE REIHE, 1996, DM 30,00, paperback (*kartoniert*). German translation. ISBN 3-404-13865-1. Boxed set.
c. As: *O corredor da morte* ['The corridor of death']. 6 vols. Rio de Janeiro, Brazil: Objetiva, 1996, 17 cm. Portuguese translation by M. H. C. Côrtes. Vol. 1, *As duas meninas mortas;* Vol. 2, *Um rato no corredor*; Vol. 3, *As mãos de Coffey*; Vol. 4, *A morte horrenda de Eduard Delacroix*; Vol. 5, *Excursão noturna*; Vol. 6, *Coffey no corredor.*
d. As: *Den grønne mil* ['The green mile']. 6 vols. Copenhagen, Denmark: Vinten, 1996, 98 KR each, paperback. Danish translations by Jette Røssell. ISBN: Vol. 1, 87-414-2432-8; Vol. 2, 87-414-2433-6; Vol. 3, 87-414-2434-4; Vol. 4, 87-414-2435-2; Vol. 5, 87-414-2436-0; Vol. 6, 87-414-2437-9.
e. As: *La ligne verte* ['The green line']. Paris, France: J'ai Lu, 1996, 560 pp., paperback. French translation.
f. As: *De Groene Mijl: een verhaal in zes delen* ['The green mile: one story in six divisions']. Amsterdam, Netherlands: Luitingh-Sijthoff, 1996, 39.90fl, 394 pp., paperback. Dutch translation by Hugo Kuipers. ISBN 90-245-0278-0.
g. As: *The Green Mile: The Complete Serial Novel*. New York: Plume, New American Library, May 1997, 465 pp., $14.95, trade paperback. Cover art by Dave McKean; Introduction by Stephen King. ISBN 0-452-27890-2.
h. As: *La ligne verte* ['The green line']. Paris, France: France Loisirs, 1997, 546 pp., 70 F, hardcover. French translation by Philippe Rouard. ISBN 2-7441-0279-2.
i. As: *La ligne verte—roman feuilleton en six épisodes* ['The green line'].

- Paris, France: Éditions 84, 1997, 398 pp., 89 F, paperback. French translation by Philippe rouard. ISBN 2-277-25020-1.
- j. As: *Zeljonaja Mila* ['Green mile']. Moscow, Russia: AST, 1997, 496 pp. Russian translation by V. A. Vebera. ISBN 5-15-000766-8.
- k. As: *El pasillo de la muerte* ['The corridor of death']. Barcelona, Spain: Círculo de Lectores, [1997], 380 pp., 22 cm. Spanish translation by María Eugenia Ciocchini. Illustrations by Mark Geyer. ISBN 84-226-6766-5.
- l. As: *El pasillo de la muerte* ['The corridor of death']. Barcelona, Spain: Plaza & Janés, 1997, 379 pp., 22 cm. Spanish translation by María Eugenia Ciocchini. ISBN 84-01-32702-4.
- M. As: *The Green Mile: Der vollständige Roman* ['The green mile—the complete novel]. Bergisch Gladbach, West Germany: Bastei-Lübbe, ALLGEMEINE REIHE, 1 February 1998, paperback (*kartoniert*). German translation. ISBN 3-404-13958-5.
- n. As: *Il Miglio Verde*. Milan, Italy: Sperling Paperback, SUPERBESTSELLER #644, October 1998, paperback. Italian translation by Tullio Dobner. ISBN 88-7824-942-4. Omnibus with *Bag of Bones*.
- o. London, England: Orion, November 1998, xiv+465 pp., £10.99, trade paperback. Introduction and Foreword by King. ISBN 0-75282-146-6.
- p. As: *The Green Mile: der vollständige Roman* ['The green mile: the complete novel']. Rheda-Wiedenbrück, Germany: Bertelsmann-Club; Zug, Switaerland: Bertelsman-Medien; Vienna, Austria: Buchgemeinschaft Donauland Kremayr und Scheriau, and others, [1998]. German translation by Joachim Honnef. Book Club editions.
- q. As: *The Green Mile Roman*. Bergisch Gladbach, Germany: Bastei-Lübbe #13958, 1998, 572 pp., 18.90 DM, paperback. German translation by Joachim Honnef. ISBN 3-404-13958-5.
- r. As: *The Green Mile 1-6*. Rheda-Wiedenbrück, Germany: Bertelsmann-Club, 1998, 478 pp., hardcover. German translation by Joachim Honnef. Book Club edition.
- s. As: *El pasillo de la muerte* ['The corridor of death']. Barcelona, Spain: Plaza & Janés, 1998, 444 pp., 19 cm. Spanish translation by María Eugenia Ciocchini. ISBN 84-01-24258-4.
- t. New York: Pocket, March 1999, 536 pp., $7.99, mass-market paperback. Cover art by Tom Hallman. Movie tie-in edition. ISBN 0-671-03265-8.
- u. Burnsville MN: Econo-Clad/Sagebrush, October 1999, $15.70, library binding. #1078344. ISBN 0-613-17261-2.
- v. As: *Kuoleman Käytävä 1-6* ['Death corridor']. Helsinki, Finland: Tammi, 1999. Finnish translation by Heikki Kaskimies. * Reprint, 2000, ISBN 951-31-1815-0.
- w. As: *El pasillo de la muerte* ['The corridor of death']. Barcelona, Spain: Plaza & Janés, JET 102/23, BIBLIOTECA DE STEPHEN KING #23, 1999, 444 pp., 18 cm., paperback. Spanish translation by María Eugenia Ciocchini. ISBN 84-01-47473-6. * 2nd printing, 1999, ISBN 84-01-47473-6. * 3rd printing, 1999, ISBN 84-01-47473-6.

x. As: *Den Gröna Mile.* [Höganäs, Sweden]: Bra Böcker, 1999, 477 pp., 22 cm., hardcover. Swedish translation by John-Henri Holmberg.. ISBN 91-7133-522-6.

y. As AUDIOCASSETTE: New York: Penguin Audiobooks, September 1996, 18 cassettes. Read by frank Muller. ISBN 0-147-71135-5.

z. As AUDIOCASSETTE: New York: Simon & Schuster (Audio), December 1999, $39.95. Unabridged. Read by Frank Muller. ISBN 0-671-04721-3.

aa. As AUDIO CD: New York: Simon & Schuster (Audio), December 1999. $49.95. Unabridged. Read by Frank Muller. ISBN 0-671-04725-6.

bb. As FILM: *The Green Mile.* Warner Brothers/ Castle Rock, 1999. Produced by David Valdes. Directed by Frank Darabont. Screenplay by Frank Darabont and Stephen King. 188 minutes. Rated: R.
CAST: Tom Hanks, Michael Clarke Duncan, David Morse, James Cromwell, Bonnie Hunt, Graham Greene, Doug Hutchinson.
SELECTED FILM REVIEWS AND ARTICLES:
Schwartz, Charles. "CrankyCritic.com." Online review; archive 99.
"The Green Mile." 1999. Online at: thegreenmile.com.

cc. As SCREENPLAY: *The Green Mile.* New York: Scribner Paperback Fiction, 1999, trade paperback. Screenplay by Frank Darabont. Introduction by King.
REPRINTS AND ADAPTATIONS:
b. New York: Scribner, January 2000, 192 pp., $12.00, trade paperback. ISBN 0-684-87006-1.

dd. As VIDEOCASSETTE. *The Green Mile.* Warner Brothers/Castle Rock, 1999.

ee: New York: Scribner, 2000, 399 pp., $25.00, First US hard cover edition. Cover photograph by Raplh Nelson, courtesy of Castle Rock Entertainment. This is the first release of the complete novel in hard cover. Introduction by King's agent, Ralph Vicinanza. ISBN: 0-7432-1089-1.

SELECTED ARTICLES, RESPONSES, AND REVIEWS:
Delingpole, James. *Spectator* 21 November 1998: 50.
Polito, Robert. "Apocalypse Now." *The New York Times Book Review* 20 October 1996: 16-17. Late edition.
Sutherland. John. *The Times Literary Supplement* #4991 (1998): 21-22.

The Dark Tower IV: Wizard and Glass. Hampton Falls, NH: Donald M. Grant Publisher, 1997. Limited edition hardcover.

A61.
THE DARK TOWER IV:
WIZARD AND GLASS
(1997)

A61. *THE DARK TOWER IV: WIZARD AND GLASS.* Hampton Falls NH: Donald M. Grant, August 1997, 788 pp., $175.00, hardcover. Cover art by Dave McKean. * DELUXE LIMITED EDITION: 1,200 copies, boxed, signed. ISBN 1-880418-37-1. * TRADE EDITION, $45.00; ISBN 1-880418-38-X. Epic-fantasy novel [First complete book-length publication].

REPRINTS AND ADAPTATIONS:
b. Excerpted as: *The Dark Tower IV: An Excerpt from the Upcoming Wizard and Glass.* "A Gift from Stephen King." New York: Penguin, 1996, 60 pp., special paperback, not for separate sale; distributed with shrink-wrapped sets of *Desperation* and *The Regulators* as a substitute for earlier sets offered with reading lamps. CONTENTS: "Beneath the Demon Moon"; "The Falls of the Hounds." No ISBN listed.
c. Dutton/Plume, November 1997, 672 pp., $17.95, trade paperback. Cover art by John Jude Palencar. ISBN 0-452-27917-8.
d. London, England: Hodder and Stoughton, November 1997, xvi+672 pp., £14.99, hardcover. Cover art by Bob Warner. ISBN 0-340-69661-3.
e. As: *De Donkere Toren IV: Tovenaarsglas* ['The dark tower IV: magician's glass']. Amsterdam, Netherlands: Luitingh-Sijthoff, 1997, 666 pp. Dutch translation by Hugo Kuipers. ISBN 90-245-0936-X.
f. As: *Glas: Der Dunkle Turm 4* ['Glass: the dark tower 4']. Munich, Germany: Wilhelm Heyne, 1997, 847 pp.,48,-DM, hardcover. German translation. ISBN 3-453-13878-3.
g. Burnsville MN: Econo-Clad/Sagebrush, 1997, xv+699 pp., $15.70, library binding. #1026970.
h. London, England: New English Library, July 1998, 845 pp., £6.99, paperback. Cover art by Bob Warner. ISBN 0-340-69662-1.
i. New York: Signet, November 1998, 702 pp., $7.99, mass-market paperback. ISBN 0-451-19486-1.

THE DARK TOWER IV: WIZARD AND GLASS. New York, NY: Penguin, 1996. Special paperback.

j. As: *La sfers del buio* ['The circle of darkness']. Milan, Italy: Sperling & Kupfer, NARRATIVA [#245], January 1998. Italian translation by Tullio Dobner. ISBN 88-200-2603-1.
k. As: *Glas: Der Dunkle Turm 4* ['Glass: the dark tower 4']. Munich, Germany: Wilhelm Heyne, TB 10799, March 1998, 847 pp., 18.90 DM, hardcover and paperback (?). German translation by Joachim Körber. ISBN 3-453-13878-3, 3-453-14759-6.
l. As: *Troldmanden og glaskuglen: Det mørke tårn 4* ['Magician and glassball: the dark tower 4']. Copenhagen, Denmark: Vinten/DBK, VINTENS PAPERBACKS/VINTENS FANTASY, 1998, 692 pp., 249 KR, paperback. Danish translation by Mogens Wenzel Andreasen. ISBN 87-612-0282-7. * Reprint 1999, ISBN 87-612-0283-5.
m. As: *Musta torni 4—Velho* ['Black tower']. Helsinki, Finland: Book Studio, 1998. Finnish translation . ISBN 951-611-900-X.
n. As: *Magie et cristal La Tour sombre 4* ['Magician and crystal: the dark tower 4']. Paris, France: Éditions 84, 1998, 667 pp., 140 F, paperback. French translation by Yves Sards; illustrations by Dave McKean. ISBN 2-277-25035-X.
o. As: *Glas: Der Dunkle Turm 4.* Rheda-Wiedenbrück, Germany: Bertelsmann-Club, 1998, 847 pp., hardcover. German translation by Joachim Körber. Book Club edition.
p. As: *Magie et cristal La Tour sombre 4.* Paris, France: France Loisirs, 1999, 667 pp., 108 F, paperback. French translation by Yves Sards; illustrations by Dave McKean. ISBN 2-7441-2190-8.
q. As: *La bola de cristal: La torre oscura 4.* Bardelona, Spain: Editiones B, 1999, 731 pp., 24 cm., hardcover. Spanish translation by Maria Antonia Menini. ISBN 84-406-9013-4.

r. As AUDIOCASSETTE: New York: Penguin Audiobooks, November 1997, $49.95, unabridged. Read by Frank Muller. ISBN 0-140-86688-4.

SELECTED ARTICLES, RESPONSES, AND REVIEWS:
Bryant, Edward. "*Dark Tower IV: Wizard and Glass,* Stephen King." *Locus* Vol. 39, No. 4, #441 (October 1997).
Miller, Faren. "*Dark Tower IV: Wizard and Glass,* Stephen King." *Locus* Vol. 39, No. 4, #441 (October 1997).

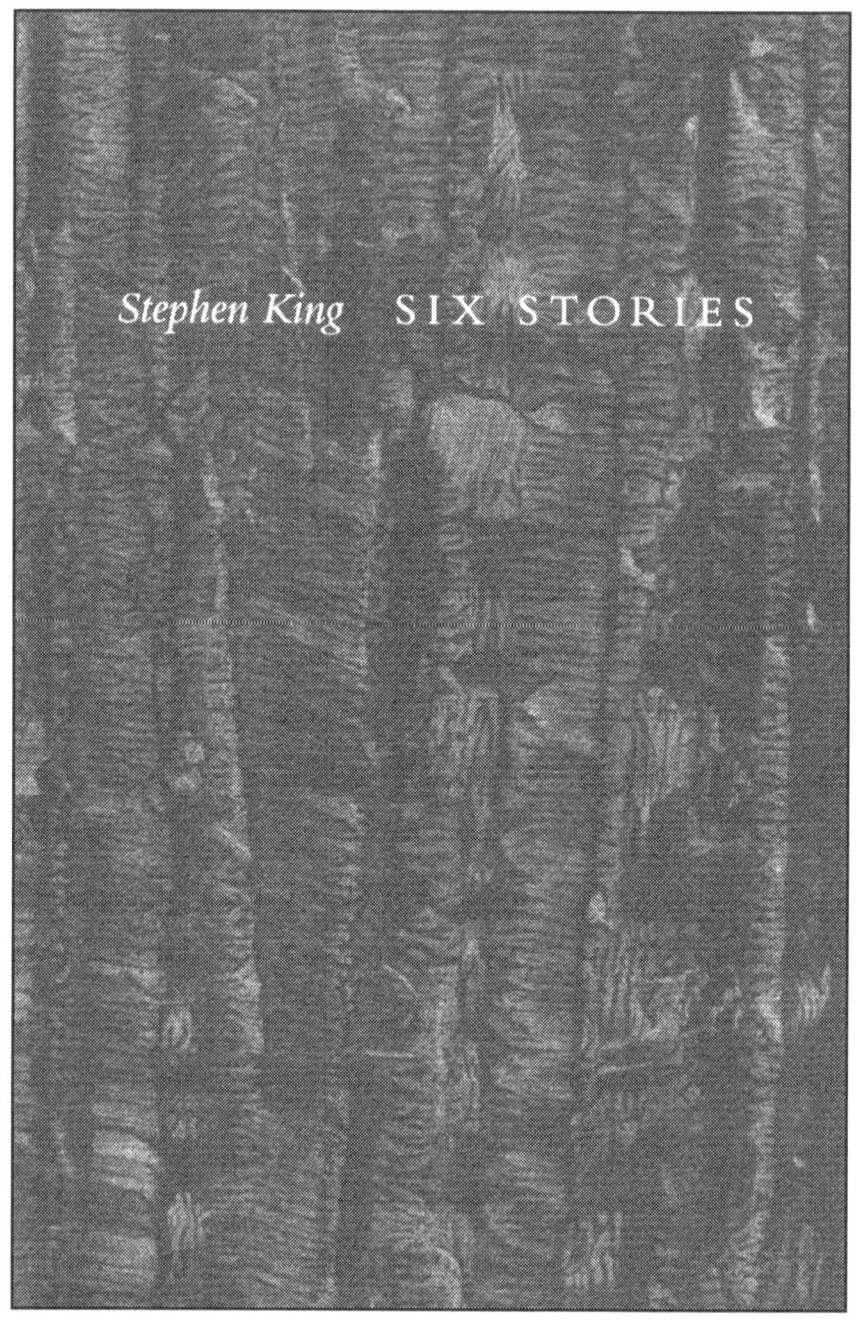

SIX STORIES. Bangor, ME: Philtrum Press, 1997.
Limited trade paperback.

A62.
SIX STORIES
(1997)

A62. *SIX STORIES*. Bangor ME: Philtrum Press, 1997, $80.00, trade paperback. Limited edition of 1100 signed and numbered copies, with 900 offered for sale.

CONTENTS: "Lunch at the Gotham Café" (B114); "L. T.'s Theory of Pets" (B115); "Luckey Quarter" (B113); "Autopsy Room Four" (B116); "Blind Willie" (B111); "The Man in the Black Suit" (B112)

BAG OF BONES. New York, NY: Scribner, 1998. Hardcover.

A63.
BAG OF BONES
(1998)

A63. BAG OF BONES. London, England: Hodder and Stoughton, August 1998, £16.99, 516 pp., hardcover. Cover art by Larry Rostant. Horror novel. ISBN 0-340-71819-6. 2000 copies released subsequently as a limited edition with signed bookplates. * TRADE PAPERBACK: 0-340-71873-0, £9.99. Hodder Australian edition ISBN 0-3407-1820-X.

PLOT SUMMARY: Novelist Mike Noonan retreats to his isolated summer home in Maine, in part to grieve for the death of his wife four years earlier, in part to struggle with his increasing writer's block. Instead of peace and restoration, however, Noonan discovers not only haunting secrets that force him to unravel the mystery of a long-past murder but also the possibility for present—perhaps even future—love.

REPRINTS AND ADAPTATIONS:
b. New York: Scribner, 1998, 532 pp., $28.00, 25 cm., hardcover. Cover art by Frank Onderan, John Fontana, and Brown Brothers. First U.S. edition. ISBN 0-684-85350-7.
c. England: BCA UK, October 1998, 516 pp., £9.99, hardcover. Reprint of Hodder and Stoughton edition.
d. As: *Muccio d'ossa* ['Pile of bones']. Milan, Italy: Sperling Paperback, SUPERBESTSELLER #644, October 1998. Italian translation by Tullio Dobner. ISBN 88-7824-942-4. Omnibus with *The Green Mile*.
e. As: *Skinn og bein* ['Bag of bones']. Oslo, Norway: Ascheoug, October 1998, 565 pp. 257.00K, hardcover [*innbundet*]. Norwegian translation
f. As: *Worek kosci* ['Bag of bones']. Warsaw, Poland: Proszynski i S-ka SA, POZA SERIA, 12 December 1998, 548 pp., paperback. Polish translation by Steinar Moe. ISBN 82-03-20409-0.
g. As: *Knogler* ['Bones']. Copenhagen, Denmark: Vinten/DBK, 1998, 486 pp., 249 KR, hardcover. Danish translation by Jette Røssell. ISBN 87-612-0288-6.
h. As: *Sara.* Munich, Germany: Wilhelm Heyne, 1998, 607 pp., DM 49,80, hardcover. German translation by Joachim Körber. ISBN 3-453-14297-7.

MICHAEL R. COLLINGS

i. As: *Vel over Been* ['Hide/bag of bones']. Amsterdam Netherlands: Luitingh-Sijthoff, 1998, 478 pp. Dutch translation by Hugo Kuipers. ISBN 90-245-0945-9.

j. As: *Kalpea Aavistus* ['Pale sense']. Helsinki, Finland: Tammi, 1998, 570 pp. Finnish translation. ISBN 951-31-1297-7.

k. As: *Skinn og bein* ['Bag of bones']. Oslo, Norway: Aschehoug, BOKKLUBBEN KRIM OG SPENNING, 1998, 565 pp., hardcover. Norwegian translation by Steinar Moe. ISBN 82-598-0276-7.

l. As: *Worek kosci* ['Bag of bones']. Warsaw, Poland: Prószyñski i S-ka SA, 1998, 547 pp., 19 cm., paperback. Polish translation by Arkadiusz Nakoniecznik. ISBN 83-7180-481-4

m. As: *Un Saco de Huesos* ['A bag of bones']. Barcelona, Spain: Plaza & Janés, 1998, 605 pp., 22 cm., trade paperback. Spanish translation by Margarita Cavándoli. 1st Spanish edition. ISBN 84-01-01194-9. * Reprint, 1998, 23 cm. ISBN 84-01-32743-1. * Reprint, 1999, 22 cm., ISBN 84-01-01194-9.

n. As: *Muccio d'ossa* ['Pile of bones']. Milan, Italy: Sperling & Kupfer, NARRATIVA [#271], January 1999. Italian translation by Tullio Dobner. ISBN 88-200-2792-5.

o. London, England: New English Library, March 1999, 660 pp., £6.99, paperback. Cover art by Larry Rostant. ISBN 0-340-71820-X. Reprinted June 1999, with "Blind Willie" included.

p. New York: Pocket Books, June 1999, 732 pp., $7.99, mass-market paperback. Cover art by Tom Hallman. ISBN 0-671-02423-X.

q. Burnsville MN: Econo-Clad/Sagebrush, 1999, 732 pp., $15.70, library binding. #1077148.

r. As: *Knogler* ['Bones']. Copenhagen, Denmark: Vinten/DBK, VINTENS PAPERBACKS, 1999, 486 pp., 99 KR, paperback. Danish translation by Jette Røssell. ISBN 87-612-0289-4.

s. As: *Knogler* ['Bones']. Copenhagen, Denmark: Paperback Bogklubben, 1999, 486 pp., 68 KR, paperback. Danish translation by Jette Røssell. ISBN 87-608-0867-5.

t. As: *Sara*. Munich, Germany: Wilhelm Heyne #13013, 1999, 637 pp., 16.90 DM, paperback. German translation by Joachim Körber. ISBN 3-453-16081-9.

u. As: *Sara*. Rheda-Wiedenbrück, Germany and Gütersloh, Austria: RM-Buch-und-Medien-Vertrieb, and others, [1999], 607 pp., hardcover. German translation by Joachim Körber. Book Club editions.

v. As: *Vel over been* ['Bag of bones']. The Hague, Netherlands: Stichting Uitgeverij XL #494, 1999, 424+440 pp., hardcover. Dutch translation by Hugo Kuipers. Large-print edition. ISBN 90-5542-494-3.

w. As: *Skinn og bein* ['Bag of bones']. Oslo, Norway: Aschehoug, 1999, 565 pp., paperback [*heftet*]. Norwegian translation by Steinar Moe. ISBN 82-03-20432-5.

x. As: *Un saco de huesos* ['A bag of bones']. Barcelona, Spain: Círculo de Lectores, [1999], 606 pp., 23 cm. Spanish translation by María Eugenia Ciocchini. ISBN 84-226-7609-5.

y. As: *Un Saco de Huesos* ['A bag of bones']. Barcelona, Spain: Plaza & Janés, 1999, 605 pp., 22 cm., trade paperback. Spanish translation by maría Eugenia Ciocchini. 2nd edition. ISBN 84-01-01194-9.
z. As: *Benrangel.* [Höganäs], Sweden: Bra Böker, 1999, 492 pp., 24 cm. Swedish translation by Thomas Preis. ISBN 91-7133-562-5.
aa. Thorndike, Maine: Thorndike, THORNDIKE LARGE PRINT BASIC SERIES, 1999, 901 pp., 23 cm. Large-print edition. ISBN 078621200 [hardcover]; 0786217219 [trade paperback].
bb. Excerpted: Internet. 1999. Opening chapter available at: http://www.dioxine.com/king/extraits/bagofbones.htm.

cc. As AUDIOCASSETTE: *Bag of Bones.* New York: Simon and Schuster, 1998. Read by Stephen King. 16 cassettes.

dd. As CD-ROM: *Bag of Bones.* New York: Simon & Schuster, 18998. Read by Stephen King.

COMMENTS: Winner of the Bram Stoker Award. *Bag of Bones* seems among King's stronger recent works, with a masterful blending of issues and narrative, of realist and surrealism, of landscape and dreamscape, and of life and imagination.

SELECTED ARTICLES, RESPONSES, AND REVIEWS:
Bryant, Edward. *Locus* Vol. 41, No. 3, #452 (September 1998).
Cavin, Pat. *SF Site Reviews.* 1998. At: www.sfsite.com/10b/bag43.htm .
Collings, Michael R. Review in *Stephen King from A to Z: An Encyclopedia of his Life and Work*, comp. by George Beahm. Kansas City MO: Andrews & McMeel, 1998, 12-14
Lehmann-Haupt, Christopher. "Death, Terror and Writer's Block." *The New York Times* 21 September 1998. Late edition.
Mendelsohn, Daniel. "Familiar Terrors." *The New York Times* 27 September 1998: 9. Late edition.

STORM OF THE CENTURY. New York, NY: Pocket, 1999.
Trade paperback.

A64.
STORM OF THE CENTURY
(1999)

A64. *STORM OF THE CENTURY*. New York: Pocket, 1 February 1999, 376 pp., $15.00, xix+376 pp., trade paperback. With introduction by King. Screenplay. ISBN 0-671-03264-X.

REPRINTS AND ADAPTATIONS:
b. New York: Pocket, 1999, hardcover. Book Club edition.
c. Burnsville MN: Econo-Clad/Sagebrush, October 1999, 377 pp., $23.75, library binding. ISBN 0-613-17533-6.
d. As: *Der Sturm des Jahrhunderts: Originaldrehbuch* ['The storm of the century: original-screenplay']. Munich, West Germany: Wilhelm Heyne, 1999, 477 pp., 32.00 DM, hardcover. German translation by Peter Robert. ISBN 3-453-15793-1.
e. As: *Der Sturm des Jahrhunderts* ['The storm of the century']. Rheda-Wiedenbrück, Germany, and Gütersloh, Austria: RM-Buch-und-Medien-Vertrieb, and others, 1999, 477 pp., hardcover. German translation by Peter Robert. Book Club edition.
f. As: *La tempête du Siècle* ['The storm of the century']. Paris, France: Albin Michel, 1999, 442 pp., 135 F., French translation by William Olivier Desmond. ISBN 2-226-10714-2.
g. As: *Der Sturm des Jahrhunderts* ['The storm of the century']. Munich, Germany: Wilhelm Heyne TB 13150, August 2000, 16.90 DM, paperback. German translation by Peter Robert. ISBN 3-453-17155-1.
h. As: *De Storm van de Eeuw* ['The storm of the century/age']. Amsterdam, Netherlands: Luitingh-Sijthoff, 1999, 425 pp. Dutch translation by Hugo Kuipers. ISBN 90-245-3623-5.
i. As: *La tormenta del siglo* ['The storm of the century']. Barcelona, Spain: Plaza & Janés, JET 102/25, BIBLIOTECA DE STEPHEN KING #25, 2000, 570 pp., 19 cm. Spanish translation by Patricia Antón. ISBN 84-01-47475-2.

j. As TELEPLAY: Executive producers, Mark Carliner and Stephen King. Produced by Thomas H. Brodek. Directed by Craig R. Baxley. Teleplay by Stephen King. 149 minutes.
CAST: Tim Daly, Colme Feore, Debrah Farentino, Casey Siemaszko, Jeffrey de Munn, Julianne Nicolson, Dyllan Chistopher.

HORROR PLUM'D

MICHAEL R. COLLINGS

THE GIRL WHO LOVED TOM GORDON. New York, NY: Scribner, 1999. Hardcover.

A65.
THE GIRL WHO LOVED TOM GORDON
(1999)

A65. *THE GIRL WHO LOVED TOM GORDON.* New York: Scribner, 1999, 224 pp., $16.95, hardcover. Novel. ISBN 0-684-86762-1.

PLOT SUMMARY: When nine-year-old Trisha McFarland becomes lost in the Maine wilderness, her survival becomes dependent upon the phantom figure of her idol, Tom Gordon.

REPRINTS AND ADAPTATIONS:
b. London, England: Hodder & Stoughton, April 1999, 216 pp., £12.99, hardcover. Cover art by Colin Thomas. ISBN 0-340-76558-5.
c. As: *La Bambina che amava Tom Gordon* ['The girl who loved Tom Gordon']. Milan: Sperling & Kupfer, NARRATIVA [#283], July 1999, 302 pp. Italian translation by Tullio Dobner. ISBN 88-200-2907-3.
d. As: *Piken som elsket Tom Gordon* ['Girl who loved Tom Gordon']. Oslo, Norway: Aschehaugs, November 1999, 221 pp., 248.00, hardcover [*innbundet*]. Norwegian translation by Kjell Ola Dahl. ISBN 82-03-20465-1.
e. London, England: Hodder & Stoughton, 1999, 216 pp., £8.99, trade paperback. ISBN 0-340-76560-7.
f. As: *Pigen der elskede Tom Gordon* ['Girl who loved Tom Gordon']. Copenhagen, Denmark: Vinten/DBK, 219 pp., 229 KR, hardcover. Danish translation by Jette Røssell. ISBN 87-612-0438-2.
g. As: *Eksyneiden jumala* ['God of the lost (?)']. Helsinki, Finland: Tammi, 1999, 299 pp., hardcover (?). Finnish translation by Ilkka Rekiaro. ISBN 951-31-1627-1.
h. As: *Het meisje dat hield van Tom Gordon*. Amsterdam, Netherlands: Luitingh-Sijthoff, 1999, 224 pp. Dutch translation by Cherie van Gelder. ISBN 90-245-3644-8.
i. As: *Piken som elsket Tom Gordon* ['Girl that loved Tom Gordon']. Oslo, Norway: Bokklubben krim og spenning, 1999, 221 pp., hardcover . Norwegian translation by Kjell Ola Dahl. ISBN 82-598-0310-0.
j. As: *Pokochala Toma Gordana* ['She loves Tom Gordon' (?)]. Warsaw,

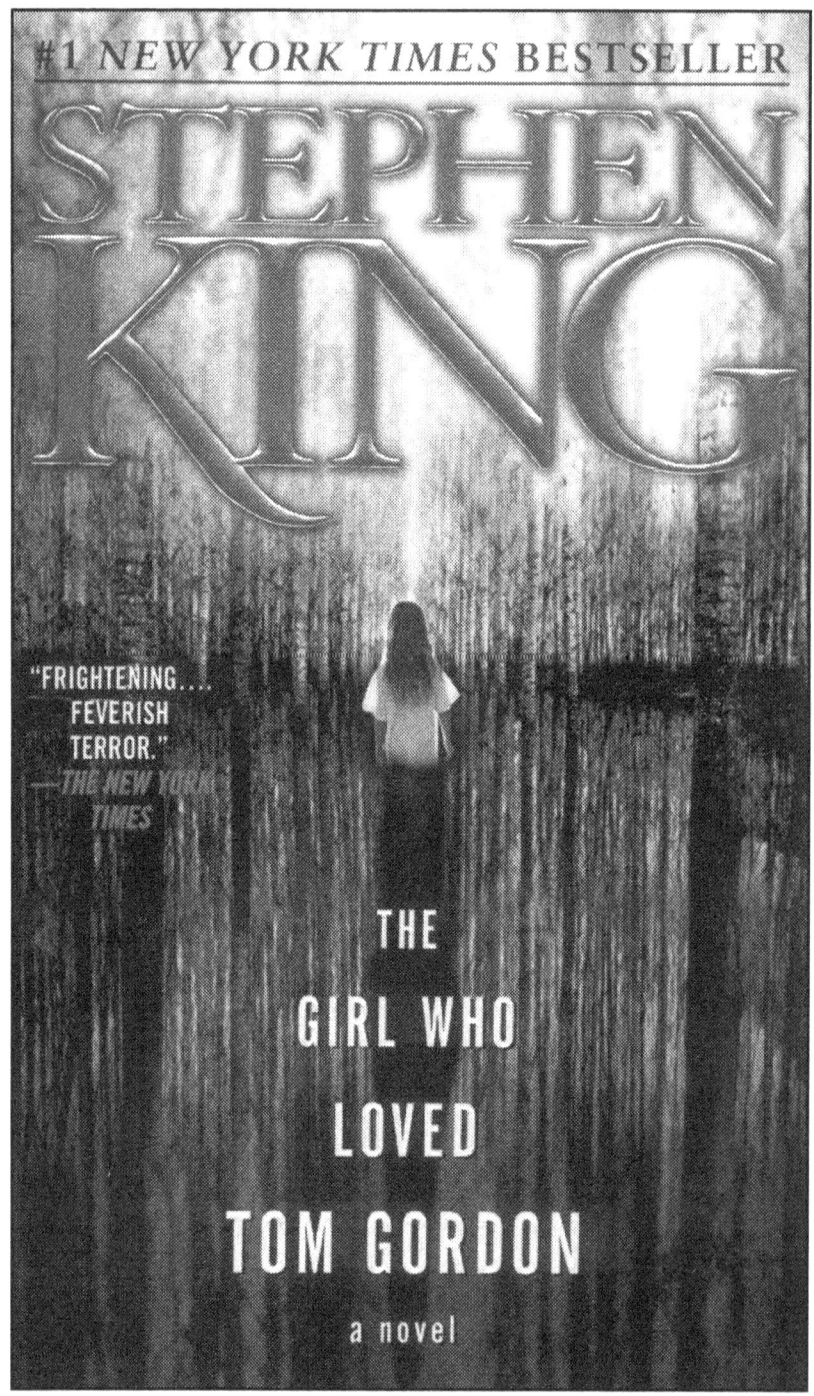

THE GIRL WHO LOVED TOM GORDON. New York, NY: Pocket Books, 2000. Mass-market paperback.

- k. As: *Devotska, Kotoraja Ljubila Toma Gordona.* Moscow, Russia: Izdatelstvo AST, 1999, 400 pp. Russian translation. ISBN 5-237-02949-3.
- l. New York: Pocket Books, February 2000, 264 pp., $6.99, mass-market paperback. ISBN 0-340-76559-3.
- m. As: *Das Mädchen der Tom Gordon Liebt* ['The girl who loved Tom Gordon']. Munich, Germany: Schneekluth, 2000, 38.00 DM, hardcover. German translation; available in black or white dust-jacket. ISBN 3-795-11749-6.
- n. As AUDIOCASSETTE and CD-ROM: *The Girl Who Loved Tom Gordon.* New York: Simon & Schuster, 1999. Read by Anne Heche. 6 cassettes.

SELECTED ARTICLES, RESPONSES, AND REVIEWS:

Bryant, Edward. *Locus* Vol. 42, No. 6, #461 (June 1999).

Der Spiegel [Germany] Vol. 53, No. 52 (1999): 20-25. Jan Philipp Reemtsma speaks about King and his new novel.

"King Pitches a tale about The Girl Who Loved Tom Gordon." *Library Journal* Vol. 124, No. 20 (1999): 205-206.

Poland, Prószyñski i S-ka, 1999, 175 pp., 19 cm. Polish translation by Krzysztof Sokolowski. ISBN 83-7255-342-4.

HEARTS IN ATLANTIS. New York, NY: Scribners, 1999. Hardcover.

A66.
HEARTS IN ATLANTIS
(1999)

A66. *HEARTS IN ATLANTIS*. New York: Scribners, 14 September 1999, 523 pp., $28.00, hardcover. ISBN 0-684-85351-5. Collection of five novellas.

CONTENTS: "Low Men in Yellow Coats" (B122); "Hearts in Atlantis" (B123); "Blind Willie" (B111); "Why We're in Vietnam" (B124); "Heavenly Shades of Night are Falling" (125).

REPRINTS AND ADAPTATIONS:
b. London, England: Hodder & Stoughton, 14 September 1999, 499 pp., £14.95, hardcover. ISBN 0-340-73890-1. Paperback: ISBN 0-340-75125-8.
c. As: *Atlantis*. Munich, Germany: Wilhelm Heyne, 1999, 591 pp., DM 44,00, hardcover. German translation. ISBN 3-453-15992-6.
d. [Australia]: Doubleday Book Club, 1999, 499 pp., 21 cm.
e. As: *Harten in Atlantis* ['Hearts in Atlantis']. Amsterdam, Netherlands: Luitingh-Sijthoff, 1999, 508 pp. Dutch translation by Hugo Kuipers. ISBN 90-245-1622-6.
f. As: *Corazones en la Atlantida* ['Hearts in Atlantis']. Spain, 1999. Spanish translation.
g. As: *Atlantis*. Copenhagen, Denmark: Vinten, 2000. Danish translation.
h. As: *Hears in Atlantins*. Höganäs, Sweden: Bra Böker, 2001 (?). Swedish translation.

SELECTED ARTICLES, RESPONSES, AND REVIEWS:
Crain, Caleb. "There but for Fortune." *The New York Times Book Review* 12 September 1999. "This time, instead of horror, King has written something with an emotional strategy much slower and much more diffuse. 'Hearts in Atlantis' is a book about survivor guilt."
Crowther, Peter. Review. *Cemetery Dance* Vol. 9, No. 2, #31 (1999): 73.
Appelo, Tim. Editorial Review. *Amazon.com*. 1999
Kirkus Reviews (1999).

MICHAEL R. COLLINGS

A67.
THE NEW LIEUTENANT'S RAP
(1999)

A67. *THE NEW LIEUTENANT'S RAP.* Bangor ME: Philtrum Press, [April 1999]. Limited edition of 500 copies; not offered for sale to the general public.

COMMENTS: The book was published by King's press as a memento to be given to guests at a celebration of his silver anniversary in publishing (April 1999). Along with *The New Lieutenant's Rap,* guests received a matching envelope and a specially designed piece of jewelry. The story is an extended version of "Why We're in Vietnam" from *Hearts in Atlantis* (A66, B124).

MICHAEL R. COLLINGS

RIDING THE BULLET. Bangor, ME: Philtrum Press/Simon & Schuster, 2000. Read-only downloadable E-book.

A68.
RIDING THE BULLET
(2000)

A68. *RIDING THE BULLET.* Bangor ME, and New York: Philtrum Press/Simon & Schuster, 12:01 pm, 14 March 2000, $2.50, read-only download. 16,000-word E-book.

REPRINTS AND ADAPTATIONS:
b. As: *Én På Katapulten*. Copenhagen, Denmark: Vinten, 2000, print version. Danish translation.

ON WRITING. New York, NY: Scribners, 2000. Hardcover.

A69.
ON WRITING
(2000)

A69. *ON WRITING: A MEMOIR OF THE CRAFT.* New York: Scribner, 2000, 290 pp., $25.00, hardcover. Non-fiction. ISBN 0-684-85352-3.

REPRINTS AND ADAPTATIONS:
- b. As: *Om At Skrive.* Copenhagen, Denmark: Vintent, 2000. Swedish translation.
- c. As: *Kirjoittamisesta.* Helsinki, Finland: Tammi, 2001. Finnish translation.
- d. As: *Att Skriva: En Hantverkares Memoarer.* Höganäs, Sweden: Bra Böker, 2001. Swedish translation.

MICHAEL R. COLLINGS

A70.
SECRET WINDOWS
ESSAYS AND FICTION ON THE CRAFT OF WRITING
(2000)

A70. *Secret Windows: Essays and Fiction on the Craft of Writing.* Bookspan/BOMC, 2000, $18.75, 433 pp., hardcover. Available only through the Book Club and STEPHEN KING LIBRARY.

CONTENTS: Introduction by Peter Straub; "Jumper" (see B129) and "Rush Call" (see B130) from *Dave's Rag*; "The Horror Market Writer and the Ten Bears: A True Story" (see C49); "Foreword to *Night Shift*" (see A6, C55); "On Becoming a Brand Name" (see C62); "Horror Fiction," from *Danse Macabre* (see A11); "An Evening at the Billerica [Massachusetts] Library" (see C255); "The Ballad of the Flexible Bullet" (see B78); "How It Happened" (see C161); "Banned Books and Other Concerns: The Virginia Beach Lecture" (see C256); "Turning the Thumbscrews on the Reader" (see C178); "'Ever Et Raw Meat?' and Other Weird Questions" (see C184); "A New Introduction to John Fowles's *The Collector*" (see C200); "What Stephen King Does for Love" (see C203); "Two Past Midnight: A Note on 'Secret Window, Secret Garden'" (see A41, C209); Introduction to Jack Ketchum's *The Girl Next Door*; "Great Hookers I Have Known" (see C258); "A Night at the Royal Festival Hall: Muriel Grey Interviews Stephen King" (see C259); "An Evening with Stephen King" (see C260); "In the Deathroom" (see B127, E8); Acknowledgements.

SELECTED ARTICLES AND REVIEWS:
"Book View." *Publishing Trends* (October 2000). Brief discussion as to how the book was developed. At: www.publishingtrends.com.

MICHAEL R. COLLINGS

A71.
THE PLANT, BOOK ONE
PARTS I-IV
(2000)

A71. *THE PLANT, BOOK ONE, PARTS I-VI.* Available for download, complete with formatted paging and title pages, online at StephenKing.com through 4 December, 2000.

MICHAEL R. COLLINGS

A72.
DREAMCATCHER
(2001)

A72. *Dreamcatcher.* New York: Scribner, 20 March 2001, 620 pp., $28.00, hardcover. ISBN 0-743-21138-3.

REPRINTS AND ADAPTATIONS:
b. New York: Simon & Schuster, March 2001, $28.00, hardcover. ISBN 0-743-21644-x. Large print edition.
c. As: AUDIOCASSETTE: New York: Simon & Schuster Audio. 20 March 2001. $49.95. Unabridged. ISBN 0-743-50444-5.
d. As AUDIO-CD: New York: Simon & Schuster Audio. 27 February 2001. $59.95. Unabridged. ISBN 0-743-50445-3.

MICHAEL R. COLLINGS

AB.
FORTHCOMING TITLES

The following titles are in production, or have been listed as future publications:

AB1. *The Dark Tower V.*
AB2. *Black House: The Talisman, Part II.* With Peter Straub.
AB3. *From a Buick 8*
AB4. *Rose Red*
AB5. *Everything's Eventual*
AB6. *Wolves of the Calla*
AB7. *Song of Susannah*
AB8. *The Dark Tower*

Section B.
Short Fiction:

INCLUDING PUBLISHED EXCERPTS FROM LONGER WORKS; SCREENPLAYS PUBLISHED IN ANTHOLOGIES; ETC.

NOTE: For additional reprint appearances of collected stories, see specific entries for King's short-fiction collections in Section A. In the interests of space, secondary studies, with the exception of significant articles and reviews of particular stories, are not repeated for each entry; general secondary resources about the short fiction includes—but is certainly not restricted to—the following book-length studies, collections, and internet sites:

Beahm, George, ed. *The Stephen King Companion.* Kansas City MO: Andrews and McMeel, 1989.
Beahm, George. *Stephen King Collectibles: An Illustrated Price Guide.* Williamsburg VA: GB Books, 2000.
Beahm, George. *Stephen King from A to Z: An Encyclopedia of His Life and Work.* Kansas City MO and Williamsburg VA: Andrews and McMeel, GB Books, 1998.
Blue, Tyson. *The Unseen King.* Mercer Island WA: Starmont House, 1989.
Collings, Michael R. "Acorns to Oaks: Explorations of Theme, Image, and Character in the Early Works of Stephen King, Part I." *Castle Rock: The Stephen King Newsletter* Vol. 5, No. 8 (August 1989): 1.

MICHAEL R. COLLINGS

Collings, Michael R. *Scaring Us to Death: The Impact of Stephen King on Popular Culture.* 2 ed., revised and expanded. San Bernardino CA: Borgo Press, 1997. [Expanded version of *The Stephen King Phenomenon*, Mercer Island WA: Starmont House, 1987]
Collings, Michael R. *The Annotated Guide to Stephen King: A Primary and Secondary Bibliography of the Works of America's Premier Horror Writer.* Mercer Island WA: Starmont House, October 1986.
Collings, Michael R. *The Many Facets of Stephen King.* Mercer Island WA: Starmont House, 1985.
Collings, Michael R. *The Work of Stephen King.* San Bernardino CA: Borgo Press, 1996.
Collings, Michael R., and David A. Engebretson. *The Shorter Works of Stephen King.* Mercer Island WA: Starmont House, June 1985.
Locus. Online listing at: http://www.sff.net/locus/s345.html#A9304
Magistrale, Tony. *Stephen King: The Second Decade,* Danse Macabre *to* The Dark Half. *Twayne's United States Authors Series* (TUSAS 599) New York: Twayne, 1992.
Quigley, Kevin, site-master. *Charnel House The Stephen King Site for the Discerning Reader.* Online at: http://members.tripod.com/~charnelhouse.
Reino, Joseph. *Stephen King: The First Decade,* Carrie *to* Pet Sematary. TWAYNE'S UNITED STATES AUTHORS SERIES (TUSAS 531). Boston: Twayne, February 1988.
Spignesi, Stephen J. *The Essential Stephen King: A Ranking of the 100 Greatest Novels, Short Stories, and Other Creations of the 20th Century's Reigning King of Horror.* Career Press, 2001 (announced).
Spignesi, Stephen J. *The Lost Work of Stephen King.* New York: Birch Lane Press, 1998. Marietta GA: Overlook Connection Press, 1998.
Spignesi, Stephen J. *The Shape Under the Sheet: The Complete Stephen King Encyclopedia.* Ann Arbor MI: Popular Culture, Ink, May 1991. * Reprint, Chicago IL: Contemporary Books.
Stephen King: A Reader's Guide and Reference Checklist. Middletown CT: CheckerBee, 1999.
The Official Stephen King Web Presence. Online at: www.stephenking.com.
Van Hise, James. *Enterprise Incidents Presents Stephen King.* Tampa, FL: New Media, 1984, 58 pp., paperback.
Van Hise, James. *Stephen King and Clive Barker: The Illustrated Guide to the Masters of the Macabre.* Las Vegas NV: Pioneer Books, 1990.
Winter, Douglas E. *The Art of Darkness.* New York: New American Library, November 1984, 252 pp., hardcover.

B1. "People, Places, Things," by Stephen King and Chris Chesley. Triad Publishing Company, 1960, 18 pp., typescript booklet. 2nd printing, 1963.

CONTENTS: "The Hotel at the End of the Road" (by King); "I've Got to Get Away" (by King); "The Dimension Warp" (by King); "The Thing at the Bottom of the Well" (by King); "The Stranger" (by King); "I'm Falling" (by King); "The Cursed Expedition" (by King); "The Other Side of the Fog" (by King); "Never Look Behind You" (by King and Chesley); "Genius" (by Chesley); "Top Forty, News, Weather and Sports" (by Chesley); seven other stories by Chesley.

COMMENTS: The booklet contained eighteen stories, eight by King, nine by Chesley, and one collaborative effort. All copies of the booklet were thought to have disappeared until one was discovered in a box of papers in King's home in 1985.

Along with "The Star Invaders" [see B2], these stories rank among King's fairly substantial list of uncollected juvenilia, in this case written when he was twelve or thirteen. In approach, content, theme, and treatment, however, they clearly suggest directions the mature King would explore in greater detail, and, since they were in fact published (even though by King himself), they represent his earliest extant attempts at reaching a specific readership. He has indicated that these stories, along with "The Star Invaders," "King's Garbage Truck," "Slade," "The Glass Floor," and others, are sufficiently flawed that he feels uncomfortable about allowing them to be reprinted.

B2. "The Star Invaders." Durham, ME: Triad, Inc. and Gaslight Books, 1964, 17 pp., paperback. Typed and stapled mimeographed half-sheets plus front matter.

COMMENTS: Among King's earliest extant short fiction, the story consists of seventeen typed, double-spaced half-sheets, stapled together, with a hand-drawn cover page complete with artistically arranged title and publisher's logo. The story is— as would be expected from a young author— superficial and derivative, concerning aliens who nearly conquer the Earth but are destroyed at the requisite last moment by Jed Pearce and his ray-gun. Although self-consciously science-fictional in content, the story has an odd sense of horror about it (primarily in the descriptions of the aliens), as well as hints of motifs King would incorporate into *Carrie* and subsequent stories over a decade later. Its primary value is biographical and historical, an early work on a par with C. S. Lewis's published Boxen stories. King has indicated that he does not intend to allow the story to be republished.

B3. "I Was a Teenage Grave Robber." *Comics Review* (1965).

REPRINTS AND ADAPTATIONS
b.   As: "In a Half-World of Terror." *Stories of Suspense* (1966): 1-12.

COMMENTS: In Marvin Wolfman's publication, the story covers twelve typed pages, poorly mimeographed and stapled together. Heralding King's first public appearance as a writer, the story concerns an unlikely hero, his improbable loss of a family fortune, and his subsequent involvement with a stereotypical mad scientist whose experiments with corpses result in gigantic maggots roaming the counterside.

B4. "The Glass Floor." *Startling Mystery Stories* 1 (Fall 1967): 23-29.

REPRINTS AND ADAPTATIONS
b. *Weird Tales* Vol. 52, No. 1, #98 (Fall 1990): 36-41.

COMMENTS: King's first professional sale. Until 1990 the story had never been reprinted, nor did King wish to permit it to be reprinted. Superior to his other early stories, it nonetheless promises more than it delivers. The story is static and lacks internal logic; settings and characters echo Poe much too closely for comfort. The final image, however, strengthens the story and demonstrates King's increasing command of genre and language.

B5. "Here There Be Tygers." *Ubris* [University of Maine, Orono] (Spring 1968): 8, 10.

REPRINTS AND ADAPTATIONS:
b. *Skeleton Crew*. New York: G. P. Putnam's Sons, 1985, hardcover. 135-139. See A28 for further editions.

B6. "Cain Rose Up." *Ubris* [University of Maine, Orono] (Spring 1968): 33-35.

REPRINTS AND ADAPTATIONS :
b. *Skeleton Crew*. New York: G. P. Putnam's Sons, June 1985, hardcover. 175-180. See A28.
c. *Horror Stories*. Edited by Susan Price. England: Kingfisher, September 1995, 255 pp., £4.99, paperback. 24-30. Anthology of 24 stories for young adult readers. ISBN 1-85697-187-2.

COMMENTS: Written during King's junior year at the University of Maine, Orono, and published in the university literary magazine, the story reflects the frustration endemic in student life. The story parallels *Rage, The Long Walk,* and *Roadwork* in its tense thematic development; the sense of entrapment by depression and frustration explodes into violence that parallels King's perceptions of Charles Whitman's shooting spree in Texas. King's revisions of the story for the *Skeleton Crew* reprint highlight Curt Garrish's sexual repression and obsession with death and amplify the graphic violence implicit in the original version.

B7. "Strawberry Spring." *Ubris* [University of Maine, Orono] (Fall 1968): 13-15.

REPRINTS AND ADAPTATIONS:
b. *Cavalier* (November 1975).
c. *Gent* (February 1977).
d. *Night Shift.* Garden City NY: Doubleday & Co., 1978, hardcover. 176-185. See A6 for further editions.
e. *An International Treasury of Mystery & Suspense.* Edited by Marie R. Reno. Garden City NY: Doubleday & Co., 1983, hardcover. 111-119.

COMMENTS: One of the central stories in *Night Shift,* this is a tight treatment of psychological terror overlaid with an eerie atmosphere perfectly reflecting the story's content. In spite of stereotypically dismembered corpses, the story works, primarily through implication and indirection, suggesting that true horror extends beyond surface terror. The *Night Shift* version represents an intensive re-working of the original; King adds flashbacks that give the later version an unnerving strength. What began as a moody atmosphere piece coalesces around King's altered purposes; his narrator emerges as an unknowing participant in the horrors he describes.

B8. "Night Surf." *Ubris* [University of Maine, Orono] (Spring, 1969): 6-10.

REPRINTS AND ADAPTATIONS:
b. *Cavalier* (August 1974).
c. *Cavalier Annual* (1976): 28-30.
d. *Night Shift.* Garden City NY: Doubleday & Co., 1978, hardcover. 54-62. See A6.

B9. "The Reaper's Image." *Startling Mystery Stories* 2 (Spring, 1969): 22-29.

REPRINTS AND ADAPTATIONS:
b. *The Seventeenth Fontana Book of Great Ghost Stories.* Edited by R. Chetwynd-Hayes. London, England: Fontana/Collins, 1981, paperback. 15-22.
c. *Skeleton Crew.* New York: G. P. Putnam's Sons, June 1985, hardcover. 321-338. See A28.
d. *Realms of Darkness.* Edited by Mary Danby. London, England: Octopus Books, 1985, 796 pp., $8.95, hardcover. 476-482. ISBN 0-86273-244-1. Reprinted: New York: Chartwell, 1988, hardcover. 476-482.

B10. "Stud City." *Ubris* [University of Maine, Orono] (Fall 1969).

REPRINTS AND ADAPTATIONS:
b. As: "'Stud City,' by Gordon Lachance. Originally published in *Greenspun*

Quarterly No. 45 (Fall, 1970). Used by Permission" [sic], as part of: "The Body: Fall from Innocence." *Different Seasons*. New York: Viking, 1982, hardcover. 322-334. See also A16, B63.

B11. "Slade." *The Maine Campus* [University of Maine, Orono] (June 11, 1970): 4; (June 18, 1970): 4; (June 25, 1970): 5; (July 2, 1970): 5, 7; (July 9, 1970): 5, 7; (July 23, 1970): 5; (July 30, 1970): 6; (August 6, 1970): 5.

COMMENTS: "Slade" is in some ways among the most revealing of King's uncollected early works, especially as it shows King reveling in the sheer joy of words, puns, and outrageous storytelling. It is an engaging explosion of off-the-wall humor, literary pastiche, and cultural criticism masquerading as a Western—the adventures of Slade (an early and distinctly comic adumbration of Roland) and his heart-wrenching quest for Miss Molly Peachtree of Paduka. The three final installments were published during the summer following King's graduation from UMO.

B12. "Graveyard Shift." *Cavalier* (October 1970).

REPRINTS AND ADAPTATIONS:
a. *Night Shift*. Garden City NY: Doubleday & Co., 1978. 36-53. See A6 for further editions.
b. *The 21st Pan Book of Horror Stories*. Edited by Herbert van Thal. London & Sydney: Pan Books, 1980, paperback. 104-121.
c. As FILM: *Stephen King's Graveyard Shift*. Paramount Pictures, 216 October 1990. Produced by William J. Dunn and Ralph S. Singleton. Executive producers, Bonnie and Larry Sugar. Directed by Ralph S. Singleton. Screenplay by John Esposito. 88 minutes. Rated: R.
   CAST: David Andrews, Kelly Wolf, Stephen Macht, Andrew Divoff, Vic Polizos, Brad Dourif, Robert Alan Beuth, Ilona Margolis, Jimmy Woodward, Jonathan Emerson
   SELECTED FILM REVIEWS AND ARTICLES:
   Burden, Martin. "Gross Graveyard." *New York Post* 27 October 1990). As microfiche: *Newsbank: Film and Television* Vol. 17 (December 1990): Fiche 131, E3.
   Dollar, Steve. "In 'Graveyard Shift,' Bare-bones King Rules." *Atlanta Journal-Constitution* [GA] 29 October 1990. As microfiche: *Newsbank: Film and Television* Vol. 17 (December 1990): Fiche 131, D13.
   Entertainment Weekly (7 June 1991): 67-68. The film received a "D+".
   Freedman, Richard. "'Graveyard Shift' a Yawn from Beginning to End." *Star-Ledger* [Newark NJ] 27 October 1990. As microfiche: *Newsbank: Film and Television* Vol. 17 (December 1990): Fiche 131, E2.
   Freedman, Richard. "Rats! 'Graveyard Shift' Is Monument to Movie

Cliches." *San Francisco Examiner* [CA] 29 October 1990. As microfiche: *Newsbank: Film and Television* Vol. 17 (December 1990): Fiche 131, D12.

"'Graveyard Shift' Digs Up a Lurking Menace." *Washington Post* [DC] 29 October 1990. As microfiche: *Newsbank: Film and Television* Vol. 17 (December 1990): Fiche 131, E5.

Leayman, Charles. "Graveyard Shift: With Numbing Mediocrity, Hollywood Makes Laborious and Incoherent What King Implied with a Few Well Chosen Words." *Cinefantastique* Vol. 21, No. 4 (February 1991): 50.

Leayman, Charles. "Shooting It in Maine: Bangor's Own Best-Selling Author Has Been a Boon to the State's Filmmaking Economy." *Cinefantastique* Vol. 21, No. 4 (February 1991): 45.

Mahar, Ted. "The Rat Patrol Stars in 'Graveyard Shift': Stephen King Tale Is Simplistic, Scary, and Slimy." *The Oregonian* [Portland OR] 31 October 1990. As microfiche: *Newsbank: Film and Television* Vol. 17 (December 1990): Fiche 131, E4.

McGarrigle, Dale. "Bangor-Area Filming of Stephen King Story Begins." *Bangor Daily News* [ME] 14 June 1990. As microfiche: *Newsbank: Film and Television* Vol. 17 (July 1990): Fiche 83, G9.

Sachs, Lloyd. "Rats! 'Stephen King's Graveyard Shift' Has No Bite." *Chicago Sun Times* [IL] 30 October 1990. As microfiche: *Newsbank: Film and Television* Vol. 17 (December 1990): Fiche 131, D14.

Sherman, Paul. "Headed for Early Grave: 'Graveyard Shift' Is Dead on Arrival." *Boston Herald* [MA] 27 October 1990. As microfiche: *Newsbank: Film and Television* Vol. 17 (December 1990): Fiche 131, E1.

Strauss, Bob. "You Can Always Smell a Rat in a King Movie." *Daily News* [Los Angeles CA] 27 October 1990. As microfiche: *Newsbank: Film and Television* Vol. 17 (December 1990): Fiche 131, D11.

Wood, Gary. "Stephen King's Graveyard Shift." *Cinefantastique* Vol. 21, No. 3 (February 1990).

d. As VIDEOCASSETTE: Paramount. June (?) 1991. 89 minutes

B13. "The Blue Air Compressor." *Onan* [University of Maine, Orono] (January 1971): 70-79.

REPRINTS AND ADAPTATIONS:
b. *Heavy Metal* (July 1981): 31-33. Revised.

COMMENTS: Written during King's student days at the University of Maine, Orono, the story reinforces indications of his early debt to Poe, as well as developing the twin (and recurring) themes of deadly machines and equally deadly "monstrous" women. The original version, in a UMO literary magazine, was heavily revised for its appearance a decade later (for a discussion of the revisions, see Collings and Engebretson. *The Shorter Works of Stephen King*, pp. 25).

B14. "I Am the Doorway." *Cavalier* (March 1971).

REPRINTS AND ADAPTATIONS:
b. *Night Shift.* Garden City NY: Doubleday & Co., 1978, hardcover. 63-75. See A6.
c. As: "Ich Bin das Tor" ['I am the door']. *Dämonengeschenk Gespensterbuch* ['Demon-gift ghost-book']. Edited by Michael Görden. Bergisch Gladbach: Bastei-Lübbe TB 72505, 1985, paperback, pp. German translation by Harro Christensen.
d. As: "Ich Bin das Tor" ['I am the door']. *Das Große Ferienbuch* ['The big holiday-book']. Edited by Ilse Walter. Gütersloh, Austria: Bertelsmann Lesering, 1989, pp. German translation by Harro Christensen.

B15. "Suffer the Little Children." *Cavalier* (February, 1972): 35-38, 90-94.

REPRINTS AND ADAPTATIONS:
b. *Nightmares.* Edited by Charles L. Grant. Chicago IL: Playboy Paperbacks, September 1979, 256 pp., paperback. 11-23. * 2nd printing, November 1979.
c. *The Evil Image: Two Centuries of Gothic Short Fiction and Poetry.* Edited by Patricia L. Skarda and Nora Crow Jaffe. New York: Meridian, New American Library, June 1981, trade paperback. 465-475.
d. *65 Great Spine Chillers.* Edited by Mary Danby. London, New York: Octopus Books, 1982, hardcover. 397-406. * 2nd edition, 1986, paperback. 397-406. ISBN 0-7064-1848-4.
e. As: "Laat de Kinderkens Tot Mÿ Komen" ['Let the little children come to me"]. *Duistere Machten* ['Dark powers']. Amsterdam: Loeb, 1983. Dutch translation
f. *Treasury of Great Short Stories.* New York: Exeter Books, 1986, hardcover.
g. *Nightmares & Dreamscapes.* New York: Viking, 1993. 95-108. See A47.

B16. "The Fifth Quarter," by 'John Swithen.' *Cavalier* (April 1972): 52-60, 90-94.

REPRINTS AND ADAPTATIONS:
b. As: "The Fifth Quarter," by Stephen King. *Twilight Zone Magazine* Vol. 5, No. 6 (February 1986): 24-28, 96.
c. *Nightmares & Dreamscapes.* New York: Viking, 1993, hardcover. 633-650. See A47.

COMMENTS: Other than the 'Bachman' novels, this is King's only pseudonymous work. It is more strictly crime fiction than horror, but King's recognizable overtones are present nonetheless. Characterization, plotting, and the puzzling title engage the reader's interest.

B17. "Battleground." *Cavalier* (September 1972).

REPRINTS AND ADAPTATIONS
b. *Cavalier Annual* (Fall, 1983): 58-60.
c. *Night Shift.* Garden City NY: Doubleday & Co., 1978, hardcover. 120-129. See A6.
d. *The Puffin Book of Horror Stories.* Edited by Anthony Horowitz. London, England: Viking UK, November 1994, 160 pp., £9.99, hardcover. 25-42. ISBN 0-670-85382-8.

COMMENTS: In the mode of *Maximum Overdrive, The Tommyknockers,* and *Trucks* (the film version), this story concentrates on the terrors of mechanization, on a society blindly enamored with gadgets that, in fine *Frankenstein* tradition, ultimately come to life and turn on their creators. The story explores the potentials for horror in normally neutral or positive objects, as well as defining the circularity (and ultimately the uselessness) of revenge, a theme that will recur in subsequent stories.

B18. "The Mangler." *Cavalier* (December 1972).

REPRINTS AND ADAPTATIONS:
b. *Night Shift.* Garden City NY: Doubleday & Co., 1978, hardcover. 76-95. See A6.
c. *The 21st Pan Book of Horror Stories.* Edited by Herbert van Thal. London & Sydney: Pan Books, 1980, paperback. 122-141.
d. *The Arbor House Celebrity Book of Horror Stories.* Edited by Martin H. Greenberg and Charles Waugh. New York: Arbor House, 1982, hardcover. 79-100. New York: Priam, 1982, paperback. 79-100.
e. *Tales of Dungeons and Dragons.* Edited by Peter Haining. London, England: Century, November 1986, 416 pp., £11.95, hardcover. 112-134. ISBN 0-7126-9542-7.
f. *Demons!* Edited by Jack Dann and Gardner R. Dozois. New York: Ace Books, July 1987, 283 pp., $3.50, mass-market paperback. 74-92.ISBN 0-441-14264-8.
g. *Dark Voices: The Best from the Pan Book of Horror Stories.* Edited by Stephen Jones and Clarence Paget. London & Sydney: Pan, April 1990, 348 pp., £3.99, paperback. 19-40. ISBN 0-330-31100-X. Hardcover, £13.95; ISBN 0-330-31565-X.
h. *Young Blood.* Edited by Mike Baker. New York: Zebra/Kensington., March 1994, 349 pp., $4.50, mass-market paperback. 99-120. ISBN 0-8217-4498-4. Anthology of stories written when their authors were under thirty.

i. As FILM: *The Mangler.* New line Cinema, 1995. Director: Tobe Hooper. Adapted for screen by Tobe Hooper, Stephen David Brooks, and Peter Welbeck. 104 minutes.
   CAST: Robert Englund, Ted Levine, Daniel Matmor, Jeremy Crutchley, Vanessa Pike.
   COMMENTS: With *Graveyard Shift,* and *Children of the Corn* (and its seemingly endless non-King-affiliated sequels), the film stands out as a weak transformation of King's original.

j. As VIDEOCASSETTE: *The Mangler.* August 1995. VHS, VHS unrated version, laserdisc director's cut.

B19. "The Boogeyman." *Cavalier* (March 1973).

REPRINTS AND ADAPTATIONS:
b. *Gent* (December, 1975).
c. *Night Shift.* Garden City NY: Doubleday & Co., 1978, hardcover. 96-107. See A6.
d. *The 25th Pan Book of Horror Stories.* Edited by Herbert van Thal. London & Sydney: Pan Books, 1984, 157 pp., £1.50, paperback. 107-118. ISBN 0-330-28206-9.
e. As: "Das Schreckgespenst" ['The horror-ghost']. *Mal Gänsehaut* ['Sometimes goose-flesh']. Edited by Jason Dark. Bergisch Gladbach: Bastei-Lübbe, TB13052, 1986, paperback, pp. German translation by Harro Christensen.
f. *House Shudders.* Edited by Martin Harry Greenberg and Charles G. Waugh. New York: DAW Books, September 1987, 332 pp., $3.50, paperback. 220-232. Anthology of stories about haunted houses. ISBN 0-88677-223-0.
g. *Horrorscape.* Edited by Gary Goshgarian. Dubuque IA: Kendall/Hunt, 1993, 252 pp., trade paperback. 119-130. ISBN 0-8403-8181-6.
h. As: "L'uomo Nero" ["The dark man']. *Le case del brivido* [The house of shudders'/*House Shudders*']. Rome, Italy: Newton & Compton, I NUOVI BEST-SELLER #11, June 1995. 215+. Italian translation by Gianni Pilo. ISBN 88-452-3553-X.

i. As FILM: *The Boogeyman.* Tantalus, 1982, 1984.. Produced, directed, written, and edited by Jeffrey C. Schiro. 30 minutes.
   CAST: Michael Reid, Bert Linder, Terence Brady, Mindy Silverman, Jerome Bynder, Bobby Persicheth, Michael Dagostino.
   SELECTED ARTICLES, RESPONSES, AND REVIEWS:
       Collings, Michael R. *Castle Rock: The Stephen King Newsletter* Vol. 1, No. 9 (September 1985): 4. A letter-review.
       Frank, Janrae. "*Stephen King's Night Shift*: Student Shorts of Stephen King Tales Headed for Videocassette Release." *Cinefantastique* Vol. 15, No. 3 (July 1985): 12.

Sallee, Wayne Allen. "It's Really Only a Game." *Castle Rock: The Stephen King Newsletter* Vol. 2, No. 4 (April 1986): 2.

j. As VIDEOCASSETTE: *The Night Shift Collection: The Boogeyman*. Tantalus, 1982, 1984. VHS

B20. "**Trucks.**" *Cavalier* (June 1973).

REPRINTS AND ADAPTATIONS:
b. *Night Shift*. Garden City NY: Doubleday & Co., 1978, hardcover. 130-146. See A6 for further editions.
c. *Mysterious Motoring Stories*. Edited by William Pattrick [pseudonym for Peter Haining]. London, England: W. H. Allen & Co., February 1987, 244 pp., £10.95, hardcover. 193-210. ISBN 0-491-03643-4.
d. *Duel and Other Horror Stories of the Road*. Edited by William Pattrick [pseudonym for Peter Haining]. London, England: Star, W. H. Allen & Co., 1987, paperback. 193-210. Reprint of prvious entry.

e. As AUDIOCASSETTE: *Trucks*. Bergish Gladbach, Germany: Lübbe Audio, 1998. 1 CD. Read by Joachim Kerzel. 29.90 DM. ISBN 3-7857-1045-3.

f. As FILM: *Maximum Overdrive*. De Laurentiis Entertainment Group, 18 July 1986. Produced by Martha Schumacher. Directed by Stephen King. Screenplay by Stephen King. 95 minutes. Rating: R.
 CAST: Emilio Estevez, Pat Hingle, Laura Harrington, Yeardley Smith, John Short, Ellen McElduff; cameo role by King.
 SELECTED ARTICLES, RESPONSES, AND REVIEWS:
 Ahlgren, Calvin. "King of Horror Finds Directing Unnerving." *San Francisco Chronicle* [CA] July 1986. As microfiche: *Newsbank: Film and Television* Vol. 13 (August 1986): Fiche 14, D8-D9.
 Blue, Tyson. "King Goes into Overdrive." *Twilight Zone Magazine* 5 (February 1986): 30-31.
 Blue, Tyson. "Overdrive Movie Set Relaxed." *Castle Rock: The Stephen King Newsletter* Vol. 1, No. 11 (November 1985): 3.
 Blue, Tyson. "Maximum Overdrive Video Reviewer." *Castle Rock: The Stephen King Newsletter* Vol. 3, No. 2 (February 1987): 5, 7.
 Blue, Tyson. "Stephen King's Debut as Director Is a Maximum Thriller." *Courier Herald* [Dublin GA] 26 July 1986.
 Blue, Tyson. "Stephen King's First Film, *Maximum Overdrive*, as Intense as His Books." *Macon Telegraph and News* [Macon GA] 25 July 1986.
 "Castle Rock Readers Comment on *Maximum Overdrive*." *Castle Rock: The Stephen King Newsletter* Vol. 2, No. 9 (September 1986): 6-7.
 "Castle Rock Readers Comment on *Maximum Overdrive*." *Castle Rock: The Stephen King Newsletter* Vol. 2, No. 10 (October 1986): 6.

Cosford, Bill. "'Overdrive': A Good Idea Badly Done." *Miami Herald* [FL] 26 July 1986. As microfiche: *Newsbank: Film and Television* Vol. 13 (August 1986): Fiche 14, E1.
Crist, Judith. *Coming Attractions* (January 1987). One-page review.
Daily News "L.A. Life" [Los Angeles CA] 26 July 1986.
Denerstein, Robert. "Minimum 'Max.'" *Rocky Mountain News* [Denver CO] 26 July 1986. As microfiche: *Newsbank: Film and Television* Vol. 13 (August 1986): Fiche 14, D13.
"Dress Rehearsal for Death." *New York Daily News* 17 April 1986.
Ewing, Darrell, and Dennis Myers. "King of the Road." *American Film* Vol. 11, No. 8 (June 1986): 44-47.
Fangoria No. 54 (1986). Article with photographs.
Fangoria No. 56 (August 1986). King Interview.
Garrett, Robert. "'Overdrive': Bodies by King." *Boston Globe* [MA] 26 July 1986.
Goodman, Walter. *New York Times* 3 August 1986: II, 17.
Harris, Judith P. "*Maximum Overdrive*: Sneak Preview of Rampaging Truck Shocker Shows Stephen King Knows How to Direct." *Cinefantastique* Vol., 16, No. 3 (July 1986).
Hellman, I. *People Weekly* (8 August 1986): 10.
Hewitt, Tim. "Overdrive." *Cinefantastique* Vol. 16, No. 1 (March 1986): 9.
Hewitt, Tim. "*Maximum Overdrive*: Stephen King Rises from the Ashes of His Latest Adaptation in the Driver's Seat." *Cinefantastique* Vol. 16, Nos. 4/5 (October 1987): 96.
Johnson, Malcolm. "King Is in High Gear in 'Maximum Overdrive.'" *Hartford Courant* [CT] 26 July 1986. As microfiche: *Newsbank: Film and Television* Vol. 13 (August 1986): Fiche 14, D14.
Jones, A. *Cinefantastique* Vol. 16, Nos. 4/5 (October 1987): 101.
"King's Movie Is a Humbling Affair." *Toronto Globe and Mail* [Ontario, Canada] 28 July 1986.
Kogan, Rick. "King's a Horror at Directing." *Chicago Tribune* [IL] 26 July 1986. As microfiche: *Newsbank: Film and Television* Vol. 13 (August 1986): Fiche 14, E2.
Lovell, Glen. "King's at Helm of 'Overdrive.'" *San Jose Mercury News* [CA] 23 July 1986. As microfiche: *Newsbank: Film and Television* Vol. 13 (August 1986): Fiche 13, G13-G14.
Martin, Robert H. [Bob]. "George
Pet Sematary." *Fangoria* No. 48 (October 1985): 43-47.
"Maximum Overdrive." *Magill's Cinema Annual, 1987: A Survey of the Films of 1986*. Edited by Frank N. Magill. Englewood Cliffs, NJ: Salem Press, 1987. 497.
Miller, G. Wayne. "King of Horror." *Journal* [Providence RI] 3 August 1986. As microfiche: *Newsbank: Film and Television* Vol. 13 (August 1986): Fiche 14, A1-A4.

Miller, G. Wayne. "Machines Are King's, Violence Reigns in 'Maximum Overdrive.'" *Journal* [Providence RI] 26 July 1986. As microfiche: *Newsbank: Film and Television* Vol. 13 (August 1986): Fiche 14, E6.

Mueller, Roxanne T. "Horror King's Film Is Horrible." *Cleveland Plain Dealer* [OH] 29 July 1986. As microfiche: *Newsbank: Film and Television* Vol. 13 (August 1986): Fiche 14, E5.

New York Post (22 April 1989).

O'Grady, F. *Cinema Papers* 61 (January 1987): 51.

Pareles, Jon. "Film: By Stephen King, *Maximum Overdrive*." *New York Times* 25 July 1986: III, 17.

Ratliff, Larry. "Stephen King's *Maximum Overdrive* Spins its Wheels." __ [San Antonio TX].

Rhetts, Jo Ann. "The Titan of Terror." *Escondido Times-Advocate*, "North County Magazine" [CA] 3 October 1985: 30-31.

Ross, Peter. "Gore Is Still Gore, Even If It's Done by Machines." *Detroit News* [MI] 28 July 1986. As microfiche: *Newsbank: Film and Television* Vol. 13 (August 1986): Fiche 14, E3.

Schaefer, Stephen. "The King Is Director." *Film Comment* Vol. 22, No. 3 (May/June 1986): 6-7.

Shapiro, Susin. "One Picture Is Worth a Million Words." *Daily News* [NY] 13 July 1986: 8-13. As microfiche: *Newsbank: Film and Television* Vol. 13 (August 1986): Fiche 14, D10-D12. Also as microfiche: *NewsBank: Names in the News* Vol. 9 (August 1986): Fiche 5, E12-E14.

Star-Ledger [Newark NJ] 22 April 1989.

Treadway, Joseph. "King on Directing Maximum Overdrive for Dino De Laurentiis." *Cinefantastique* Vol. 17, No. 2 (March 1987): 49.

Trussell, Robert C. "King Authors a Bad Film." *Kansas City Star* [MO] 27 July 1986. As microfiche: *Newsbank: Film and Television* Vol. 13 (August 1986): Fiche 14, E4.

Variety Vol. 324, No. 1 (30 July 1986): 18.

Vincent, Mal. "'Overdrive' Offers Minimal Entertainment." *Virginian-Pilot* [Norfolk VA] 2 August 1986. As microfiche: *Newsbank: Film and Television* Vol. 13 (August 1986): Fiche 14, E7-E8.

Weldon, M. J. *Video Review* Vol. 7, No. 12 (March 1987): 70.

Wiater, Stanley. "Stephen King Shifts into High Gear on the Highway to Hell-Driving Horror." *Mediascene Prevue* (May/July 1986): 52-55, 71.

Wood, Gary. "Stephen King: To Direct or Not to Direct." *Cinefantastique* Vol. 21, No. 4 (February 1991): 47.

Wuntch, Phillip. "Reviews of 'Maximum Overdrive' Don't Faze Author-Turned-Director." *Dallas Morning News* [TX] 28 July 1986. As microfiche: *Newsbank: Film and Television* Vol. 13 (August 1986): Fiche 14, A5-A6.

g. As FILM: *Trucks.* Tristar, 1997. Executive producers: Mark Amin, Derek Mazur. Co-producers: Michael Scott, Bruce David Eisen, Jonathan Komack Martin. Producers: Jerry Leder and Richard S. Reisberg. Director: Brian Taggert. Screenplay, based on Stephen King's story, by Christ Thomson. 99 minutes. Rated: R.

CAST: Timothy Busfield, Brenda Bakke, Aiden Devine, Jay Brazeau, Brendan Fletcher, Amy Stewart.

COMMENTS: This version of the story interweaves King's symbolically cautionary tale with the modern mythologies surrounding "Area 51" and its overt suggestions of alien possession, and with the equally symbolic patterns of urbanite flight to the putative safety of the country.

h. As VIDEOCASSETTE: *Maximum Overdrive.* Karl-Lorimer Home Video, December 1986.
i. As VIDEOCASSETTE: *Trucks.* TristarHome Video, 1998. VHS.

B21. "Gray Matter." *Cavalier* (October 1973).

REPRINTS AND ADAPTATIONS:
b. *Cavalier* Annual (1975): 4-6.
c. *Night Shift.* Garden City NY: Doubleday & Co., 1978, hardcover. 108-120. See A6.
d. *The Arbor House Necropolis: Voodoo! A Chrestomathy of Necromany; Mummy! A Chrestomathy of Cryptoology; Ghoul! A Chrestomathy of Ogrery.* Edited by Bill Pronzini. New York: Arbor House, 1981, paperback. 702-716.
e. *Tales of the Dead.* Edited by Bill Pronzini. New York: Crown/Bonanza Books, October 1986, 711 pp., $11.95, hardcover. 689-702. ISBN 0-517-61818-4.
f. *The 28th Pan Book of Horror Stories.* Edited by Clarence Paget. London & Sydney: Pan Books, 1987, paperback. 70-81.

B22. "It Grows on You." *Marshroots* (Fall 1973): 63-72.

REPRINTS AND ADAPTATIONS:
b. *Whispers* (August 1982): 59-65.
c. *Death.* Edited by Stuart David Schiff. New York: Playboy Paperbacks, 1982, paperback. 215-225.
d. *Weird Tales* Vol. 52, No. 4, #301 (Summer 1991): 65-71. Special Ramsey Campbell issue.
e. *Nightmares & Dreamscapes.* New York: Viking, 1993, hardcover. 161-178. See A47.

B23. "Sometimes They Come Back." *Cavalier* (March 1974).

REPRINTS AND ADAPTATIONS:
b. *Night Shift.* Garden City NY: Doubleday & Co., 1978, hardcover. 147-175. See A6.
c. As: "Manchmal Kommen Sie Wieder" ['Sometimes they come again']. *Nachtspuk: Gespensterbuch 1* ['Night-phantom: ghost-book 1']. Edited by Michael Görden. Bergisch Gladbach: Bastei-Lübbe, TB72501, 1984, paperback, pp. German translation by Barbara Heidkamp.
d. As: *Cours, Jimmy, cours: et autre nouvelles* [Heart, Jimmy, heart—and other stories']. Paris, France: J'ai Lu #214, 1998, 91 pp., 10 F, paperback. French translation by Lorris Murail and Natalie Zimmermann. ISBN 2-277-30214-7.

e. As TELEPLAY: *Stephen King's "Sometimes They Come Back."* Paradise Films, 1991. Executive producer: Dino De Laurentiis. Producer: Michael S. Murphey. Co-producer: Milton Subotsky. Director: Tom McLoughlin. Teleplay by Lawrence Konner and Mark Rosenthal. CBS. 2 hours.
   CAST: Tim Matheson, Brooke Adams, Robert Rusler, Chris Demetral, Robert Hy Corman, William Sanderson, Nicholas Sadler, Bentley Mitchum.
   COMMENTS: The story was altered radically to meet the time requirements for the film. King's use of the occult and his originally pessimistic conclusion were abandoned; the film generated a 1999 non-King-affiliated sequel, *Sometimes They Come Back...for More.*
   SELECTED FILM REVIEWS AND ARTICLES:
   "The Best and Worst [of 1990-1991]." *TV Guide* Vol. 39, No. 27 #1997 (6 July 1991): 7.
   "Worst horror thriller: 'Stephen King's Sometimes They Come Back.' (ABC). Sometimes they shouldn't bother."

B24. "The Lawnmower Man." *Cavalier* (May 1975).

REPRINTS AND ADAPTATIONS:
b. *Night Shift.* Garden City NY: Doubleday & Co., 1978, hardcover. 203-212. See A6.
c. *Bizarre Adventures* 29 (October 1981): 21. A comic-book adaptation.
d. *The 30th Pan Book of Horror Stories*. Edited by Clarence Paget. London & Sydney: Pan Books, September 1989, 208 pp., £2.99, paperback. 7-16. ISBN 0-330-31099-2.
e. *Space Movies*: *Classic Science Fiction Films*. Edited by Peter Haining. England: Severn House, June 1995, 266 pp., £15.99, hardcover. 201-213. ISBN 0-7278-4790-2.
f. *Vintage Science Fiction.* Edited by Peter Haining. New York: Carroll & Graf, August 1999, 513 pp., $11.95, trade paperback. 201-213. ISBN 0-7867-0647-3.

g. AS FILM: *The Lawnmower Man.* Allied Vision Lane Pringle Productions/Fuji Eight Co., 1993. Producer: Gimel Everett. Executive producers: Edward Simons, Steve Lane, Clive Turner, Robert Pringle. Associate producers: Peter McRae, Masao Takiyama. Co-producer: Milton Subotsky. Director: Brett Leonard. Screenplay by Brett Leonard and Gimel Everett. "Based on a story by Stephen King." Rated: R..

   CAST: Pierce Brosnan, Jeff Fahey, Geoffrey Lewis, Jenny Wright, Mark Bringleson, Jeremy Slate.

   COMMENTS: While many film adaptations of King's works diverge markedly from the original print source, often to the demonstrable detriment of the resulting film, the sole connections between this film and King's story seem to be the title and the fact that in the film someone uses a lawnmower. This tale of virtual reality and a blindly stereotypic mad scientist bears no resemblance to King's blend of horror, fantasy, and oddly resonant myth—nor does the tale as continued in a sequel film. King successfully insisted that his name be removed from the film credits.

   SELECTED ARTICLES, RESPONSES, AND REVIEWS:

   Cox, Dan. "New Line Raked over 'Lawn'." *Variety* Vol. 352, No. 9 (4 April 1994): 15.

   O'Steen, Kathleen. "King Wants Name Off 'Lawnmower.'" *Variety* Vol. 347, No. 8 (8 June 1992): 18.

h. AS VIDEOCASSETTE: *The Lawnmower Man.* June 1987. New York University Student film production. Produced by Jim Gonis. Directed by Jim Gonis. Script by Mike DeLuca. 12 minutes.

   CAST: E. D. Phillips, Andy Parks, Helen Hanft, Tony Di Sante, Robert Tossberg, Neil Schimmel.

   SELECTED ARTICLES, RESPONSES, AND REVIEWS:

   Blue, Tyson. "SK Flicks Not Found at a Theatre Near You." *Castle Rock: The Stephen King Newsletter* Vol. 5, No. 1 (January 1989): 1, 8.

   Spignesi, Stephen J. "Student Cinema Focuses on Stephen King: 'The Last Rung on the Ladder' and 'The Lawnmower Man,'" *The Complete Stephen King Encyclopedia.* Ann Arbor MI: Popular Culture, Ink, May 1991. 602-605.

i. AS VIDEOCASSETTE: *The Lawnmower Man.* New Line Cinema, 1992. Director's cut; unrated.

B25. "The Revenge of Lardass Hogan." *The Maine Review* (July 1975 [?]): 37-51.

REPRINTS AND ADAPTATIONS:
b. As: "From 'The Revenge of Lardass Hogan,' by Gordon Lachance. Origi-

nally published in *Cavalier* magazine, March, 1975. Used by permission" [sic], incorporated into "The Body: Fall From Innocence." *Different Seasons.* New York: Viking, 1982, hardcover. 380-388. See also A16, B63.

B26. "'Salem's Lot." *Cosmopolitan* (March 1976). 20-page excerpt from the novel. See A2.

B27. "Weeds." *Cavalier* (May 1976).

REPRINTS AND ADAPTATIONS:
b. *Nugget* (April 1979).
c. As: "The Lonesome Death of Jordy Verrill." *Creepshow.* New York: Plume/New American Library, July 1982, trade paper, unpaginated. A comic-book adaptation. See A15, B66.

d. As FILM: "The Lonesome Death of Jordy Verrill," an episode in George Romero's, *Creepshow*, with King portraying the title role.

B28. "The Ledge." *Penthouse* (July 1976): 146-148, 166, 172-182.

REPRINTS AND ADAPTATIONS:
b. *Night Shift.* Garden City NY: Doubleday & Co., 1978, hardcover. 186-202. See A6.
c. As: "Wer im Penthouse Sitzt Sollte Nicht um Liebe Spielen" ['One who sits in a penthouse should not Play around with love"]. *Lui* No. 5 (May 1981). German translation
d. *The 29th Pan Book of Horror Stories.* Edited by Clarence Paget. London & Sydney: Pan Books, December 1988, 238 pp., £2.50, paperback. 72-88. ISBN 0-330-30481-X.

e. As FILM: *Cat's Eye.* 1985, one of three episodes. See entry under *Night Shift* [A6].

B29. "I Know What You Need." *Cosmopolitan* (September 1976).

REPRINTS AND ADAPTATIONS:
b. *Night Shift.* Garden City NY: Doubleday & Co., 1978, hardcover. 234-256. See A6.
c. *Spells: Isaac Asimov's Magical Worlds of Fantasy #4.* Edited by Isaac Asimov, Martin H. Greenberg, and Charles G. Waugh. New York: Signet/New American Library, May 1985, 350 pp., $3.95, mass-market paperback. 259-281. ISBN 0-451-13578-4.
d. As: "Ich Weiß, Was Du Brauchst" ['I know what you (familiar/intimate term) need']. *Schattenhochzeit: Gespensterbuch 7* ['Shadow-marriage: ghost-book 7']. Edited by Michael Görden. Bergisch Gladbach: Bastei-

Lübbe, TB72507, 1985, paperback, pp. German translation by Ingrid Herrmann.
e. *The 27th Pan Book of Horror Stories*. Edited by Clarence Paget. London & Sydney: Pan Books, October 1986, 187 pp., £1.95, paperback. 101-122. ISBN 0-330-29219-6.
f. As: "Ich Weiß, Was Du Brauchst" ['I know what you (familiar/intimate term] need']. *Märschenwelt der Fantasy* ['Fairy-tale-world of fantasy']. Edited by Isaac Asimov, Martin H. Greenberg, and Charles G. Waugh. Bergisch Gladbach: Bastei-Lübbe, TB28152, 1987, paperback, pp. German translation by Ingrid Herrmann.

B30. "The Cat from Hell." *Cavalier* (March 1977). Partial publication of the first 500 words.

REPRINTS AND ADAPTATIONS:
b. *Cavalier* (June 1977). The complete story (see below).
c. *Second Book of Unknown Tales of Horror*. Edited by Peter Haining. London, England: Sidgwick & Jackson, 1978. 132-143.
d. *Tales of Unknown Horror*. Edited by Peter Haining. London, England: New English Library, 1978, paperback, pp.132-143.
e. *Tales of Unknown Horror*. Edited by Peter Haining. New York: Signet/New American Library, 1978, paperback.
f. *Year's Finest Fantasy*. Edited by Terry Carr. New York: Berkley, 1978, hardcover. 55-69.
g. *Year's Finest Fantasy*. Edited by Terry Carr. New York: Berkley, July 1979, $1.95, paperback. 55-69. 425-03808-4.
h. *New Bern Magazine* (March-April 1984).
i. *Magicats!* Edited by Jack Dann and Gardner Dozois. New York: Ace, June 1984,267 pp., $2.95, mass-market paperback. 33-49. ISBN 0-441-51530-4.
j. *Top Horror: de Beste Griezelverhalen* ['Top horror: the best horror stories']. Edited by Josh Pachter. Amsterdam, Netherlands: Loeb, 1985, 366 pp. Dutch translation by W. H. M. van den Hout. ISBN 90-6213-584-6.
k. *Top Horror*. Edited by Josh Pachter. Munich, West Germany: Heyne, DIE UNHEIMLICHE BÜCHER #20, 1986, paperback. German translation.
l. *Katsf: 13 katten beleven geheimzinnige en spannende avonturen in 10 verhalen....* Edited by Jack Dann and Gardner Dozois. Amsterdam, Netherlands: Meulenhoff, 1987, 171 pp., paperback. Dutch translation by Jaime Martijn. ISBN 90-290-2026-1.
m. As: "Il gatto infernale." *Artigli e fusa* [*Magicats!*]. Edited by Jack Dann and Gardner Dozois. Florence [Firenze], Italy: Salani, September 1993. 57+. Italian translation by Christina Res. ISBN 88-7782-272-4.
n. *Kat uit de hel: horrorverhalen* ['Cat out of hell: horror stories']. Amsterdam, Netherlands: In den Toren, TOREN POCKETS, 366 pp., paperback. Dutch translation of *Top Horror*. 2nd printing. ISBN 90-6074-882-4.
o. *Twists of the Tale*. Edited by Ellen Datlow. New York: Dell, November

1996., 366 pp., $5.50, mass-market paperback. 216-233. 0-440-21771-7.

p. As: "Il gatto che viene dall'inferno." *Gatti da brivido* [*Twists of the Tale*]. Edited by Ellen Datlow. Rome, Italy: Fanucci Editore, ECONOMICA TASCABILE #87, June 1998. 247+. Italian translation by Ornella Ranieri Davide. ISBN 88-347-0617-X.

q. In: *Kat uit de hel: horrorverhalen.* Amsterdam, Netherlands: HMP, 1999, 159 pp., hardcover. Dutch translation of *Top Horror.* ISBN 90-5795-032-4.

r. In: *Katmagie: 13 katten beleven geheimzinnige en magische avonturen in 10 verhalen....* Amsterdam, Netherlands: eXperience Meuelenhoff-M, 1999, 171 pp. Dutch translation by Jaime Martijn. Selections from *Magicats!*, 4th printing. ISBN 90-290-6551-6.

s. As FILM: *Tales from the Darkside—The Movie.* Paramount Pictures, May 1990. Produced by Richard P. Rubinstein. Directed by John Harrison. Screenplay for "The Cat from Hell," by George A. Romero. 93 minutes. Rated: R.
   EPISODES: "The Wraparound Story"; "Lot 249"; "The Cat From Hell"; "Lover's Vow."
   CAST for "The Cat From Hell": David Johansen, Paul Greeno, William Hickey, Alice Drummond, Delores Sutton, Mark Margolis.
   SELECTED FILM REVIEWS AND ARTICLES:
   Bernard, Jami. *New York Post* 5 May 1990.
   Boonstra, John. *Advocate* [New Haven CT] 14 May 1990.
   New York Daily News 15 May 1990.

t. As VIDEOCASSETTE: *Tales from the Darkside: The Movie.* Paramount, 1990. VHS. 93 minutes.
   SELECTED ARTICLES, RESPONSES, AND REVIEWS:
   Collins, Max Allan. "Mystery Seen." *Mystery Scene* No. 26 (June 1990): 50.

COMMENTS: Originally published as part of a competition sponsored by *Cavalier*, the story was begun by King, who invited the magazine's readers to complete it. The winning story was published along with King's version. George Beahm's *The Stephen King Companion* discusses the genesis of the story.

B31. "Children of the Corn." *Penthouse* (March 1977): 65-68, 124-126, 141-148.

REPRINTS AND ADAPTATIONS:
a. *Night Shift.* Garden City NY: Doubleday & Co., 1978, hardcover. 257-286. See A6 for further editions..
b. *The Year's Best Horror Stories: Series VI.* Edited by Gerald W. Page. New York: DAW Books, 1978, paperback. 131-159. ISBN 0-87997-387-0.
c. As: "I figli del granturco." *Horroriana.* Milan, Italy: Arnoldo Mondadori,

BIBLIOTECA DI FANTASY E HORROR 2., October 1979. 257+. Italian translation by Silvia Sereni.
d. As: "De Maiskindern." *Griezel-Omnibus: Het Verschrikkelijke Geheim (E. A. Verhalen)* ['The corn-children—The horror-omnibus: The terrible secret and other stories']. Amsterdam/Brussels: Elsevier, APOLLO SERIES, 1982. Dutch translation. Book Club edition.
e. *Cults!: An Anthology of Secret Societies, Sects, and the Supernatural*. Edited by Martin H. Greenberg and Charles C. Waugh. New York: Beaufort Books, 1983, hardcover. 227-254.
f. As: "Kinder des Zorns" ['Children of wrath"]. *Totentanz: Gespensterbuch 3* ['Death-dance: ghost-book 3']. Edited by Michael Görden. Bergisch Gladbach: Bastei-Lübbe TB72503, 1984, paperback. German translation by Wolfgang Holbein.
g. *A Treasury of American Horror Stories*. Edited by Charles Waugh, Martin H. Greenberg, and Frank D. McSherry Jr. New York: Crown/Bonanza Books, 1985, 670 pp., $10.00, hardcover. 345-368. ISBN 0-517-48075-1.
h. As: [Title unknown]. *Las Mejores Historias del Terror V* ['Great tales of terror V']. Edited by Gerald Page (?). Barcelona, Spain: Ediciones Martinez Roca, [1986?], paperback, pp. Spanish translation.
i. As: "I figli del grano." *I mille volti del terror.* Edited by Gerald W. Page. Rome, Italy: Newton & Compton, I NUOVI BEST-SELLER #9, November 1994. 139+. Italian translation by Gianni Pilo. ISBN 88-7983-705-2.
j. As: *Maissilapset*. Helsinki, Finland: Book Studio, 1995. Finnish translation.

k. As AUDIOCASSETTE: *Stephen King: Kinder des Zorns*. Munich, Germany: Lübbe Audio, 7 April 1997, 1 cassette, 92 minutes. 19,90DM. Read by Joachim Kerzel.

l. As FILM: *Children of the Corn*. New World Pictures, Hal Roach Studios, Gatlin Productions, June 1984. In association with Angeles Entertainment Group, Inverness Productions, Inc. Produced by Donald Borchers and Terence Kirby. Directed by Fritz Kiersch. Screenplay by George Goldsmith. 93 minutes. Rating: R.
   CAST: Peter Horton, Linda Hamilton, R. G. Anthony, John Franklin, Courtenay Gains.
   SELECTED FILM REVIEWS AND ARTICLES:
   Adams, Jan. "'Children of the Corn' Designed to Be Shocking, Yet Entertaining." *Manchester Union Leader* [NH] 5 May 1984. As microfiche: *Newsbank: Film and Television* Vol. 10 (June 1984): Fiche 115, A12-A13.
   Advokat, Stephen. "Shucks, 'Corn' Is a Disappointment." *Detroit Free Press* [MI] 29 April 1984. As microfiche: *Newsbank: Film and Television* Vol. 10 (May 1984): Fiche 104, E6.
   Briggs, Joe Bob [pseud. for John Bloom]. "Gary Hart Is Strange and So Is This Movie About Cornflake Kids." *Joe Bob Goes to the Drive-*

In. New York: Delacorte Press, 1987. Reprinted: *The Stephen King Companion*, by George Beahm. Kansas City MO: Andrews and McMeel, September 1989. 254-246.

Butler, Richard W. "'Corn' Has Less Than a Kernel of Quality." *Kansas City Star* [MO] 27 April 1984. As microfiche: *Newsbank: Film and Television* Vol. 10 (May 1984): Fiche 104, E7.

Cain, Scott. "A Brisk Chiller Is Harvested from Nebraska's Cornfields." *Atlanta Journal-Constitution* [GA] 3 April 1984. As microfiche: *Newsbank: Film and Television* Vol. 10 (May 1984): Fiche 104, E4.

"'Children of the Corn' Short on Vulgar Thrills." *Sun* [Baltimore MD] 13 March 1984. As microfiche: *Newsbank: Film and Television* Vol. 10 (April 1984): Fiche 96, A3.

Cosford, Bill. "Kids Get the Upper Hand in King's 'Corn.'" *Miami Herald* [FL] 19 March 1984. As microfiche: *Newsbank: Film and Television* Vol. 10 (April 1984): Fiche 95, G14.

Counts, Kyle. *Cinefantastique* Vol. 14, Nos. 4/5 (September 1984): 102.

Counts, Kyle. *Cinefantastique* Vol. 14, Nos. 4/5 (September 1984): 108.

Drake, Kerry. "'Children' Capitalizes on King's Fame." *Wyoming State Tribune* [Cheyenne WY] 1 April 1984. As microfiche: *Newsbank: Film and Television* Vol. 10 (May 1984): Fiche 104, E10-E11.

Edelstein, D. *The Village Voice* Vol. 29, No. 13 (27 March 1984): 52.

"Eerie in Parts, But Stretched Out." *Grand Rapids Press* [MI] 1 May 1984. As microfiche: *Newsbank: Film and Television* Vol. 10 (June 1984): Fiche 115, A10.

Ehrenstein, David. "Harvest of Schlock in 'Children of the Corn.'" *Los Angeles Herald Examiner* [CA] 9 March 1984. As microfiche: *Newsbank: Film and Television* Vol. 10 (April 1984): Fiche 95, G10.

Everitt, David. "Stephen King's Children of the Corn." *Fangoria* No. 35 (1984): 42-45.

Fiely, Dennis. "Movie Makers Creamed 'Corn.'" *Columbus Dispatch* [OH] 1 May 1984. As microfiche: *Newsbank: Film and Television* Vol. 10 (June 1984): Fiche 115, A14.

Fox, Thomas. "Mix in 'Corn' Caters to Taste for the Gory." *Commercial Appeal* [Memphis TN] 28 April 1984. As microfiche: *Newsbank: Film and Television* Vol. 10 (May 1984): Fiche 104, E9.

Gagne, Paul R. *Cinefantastique* Vol. 14, No. 3 (May 1984): 18.

Hassor, Alan. "'Corn' Slashflick—Plow It Under." *Idaho Statesman* [Boise ID] 30 March 1984. As microfiche: *Newsbank: Film and Television* Vol. 10 (May 1984): Fiche 104, E5.

Haun, Harry. "Children of the Corn." *Daily News* [NY] 16 March 1984. As microfiche: *Newsbank: Film and Television* Vol. 10 (April 1984): Fiche 96, A4.

Johnson, Malcolm. "'Children of the Corn' Silly, Not Chilling." *Hartford Courant* [CT] 2 May 1984. As microfiche: *Newsbank:*

Film and Television Vol. 10 (June 1984): Fiche 115, A9.

"King's Reign Deserves a Boo in Bloody 'Corn.'" *Virginian-Pilot* [Norfolk VA] 21 March 1984. As microfiche: *Newsbank: Film and Television* Vol. 10 (April 1984): Fiche 96, A6.

Kloer, Phil. "Children Are King in This Horror Movie." *Florida Times-Union* [Jacksonville FL] 22 March 1984. As microfiche: *Newsbank: Film and Television* Vol. 10 (April 1984): Fiche 95, G13.

Loderhose, Willy. "Kinder des Zorns—Bemerkungen zur Entstehung des Films" ['Children of anger: comments on the film']. *Katzenauge* ['Cat's Eye']. Bergisch Gladbach, West Germany: Bastei-Lübbe, 1986.

Lyman, Rick. "Film: Cult Worship in Midwest Cornfield." *Philadelphia Inquirer* [PA] 10 March 1984. As microfiche: *Newsbank: Film and Television* Vol. 10 (April 1984): Fiche 96, A5.

Mahar, Ted. "Corny, Over-Long 'Children of the Corn' Has Mere Kernel of Plot." *The Oregonian* [Portland OR] 2 May 1984. As microfiche: *Newsbank: Film and Television* Vol. 10 (June 1984): Fiche 115, B1.

Matheny, Dave. "'Children of the Corn' Fails to Reap Horror." *Minneapolis Star and Tribune* [MN] 11 May 1984. As microfiche: *Newsbank: Film and Television* Vol. 10 (June 1984): Fiche 115, A11.

Minton, L. *McCalls* Vol. 111, No. 9 (May 1984): 46.

Mueller, Roxanne. "Agri-Flick of Stephen King Short Story Scary But Corny." *Cleveland Plain Dealer* [OH] 30 April 1984. As microfiche: *Newsbank: Film and Television* Vol. 10 (May 1984): Fiche 104, E8.

Murphy, R. *Monthly Film Bulletin* Vol. 512, No. 106 (August 1984): 238.

Sabulis, Tom. "'Children of the Corn': Cheap Production Makes Decent Thriller." *St. Petersburg Times* [FL] 20 March 1984. As microfiche: *Newsbank: Film and Television* Vol. 10 (April 1984): Fiche 96, A1.

Schulman, M. *Punch* [England] Vol. 287, No. 7496 (1 August 1984): 57.

Siskel, Gene. "Too Much Gore Overpowers Suspense in 'Children of the Corn.'" *Chicago Tribune* [IL] 13 March 1984. As microfiche: *Newsbank: Film and Television* Vol. 10 (April 1984): Fiche 96, A2.

Stanley, John. "Aw Shucks, Not a Kernel of Gore." *San Francisco Chronicle* [CA] 11 March 1984. As microfiche: *Newsbank: Film and Television* Vol. 10 (April 1984): Fiche 95, G12.

Variety Vol. 314, No. 7 (14 March 1984): 22.

Wheen, F. *New Statesman* Vol. 108, No. 2784 (27 July 1984): 32.

Wiater, Stanley. "Stephen King and George Romero: Collaboration in Terror." *Bloody Best of Fangoria* (1982): 28-29. On *Creepshow* and *Children of the Corn*, with backgrounds for both films.

Williams, George. "Cornball Story Not Stephen King's Best." *Sacramento Bee* [CA] 3 March 1984. As microfiche: *Newsbank: Film and Television* Vol. 10 (April 1984): Fiche 95, G11.
Williamson, B. *Playboy* Vol. 31, No. 6 (June 1984): 29.

m. As VIDEOCASSETTE: New World Pictures, 1984. Beta, VHS, Laser, CED. 93 minutes

COMMENTS: This concise tale of religion, fanaticism, and inexplicable horror has generated a number of interpretations, including Anthony Magistrale's reading of the story as paralleling America's distress during the Vietnam period (see Collings and Engebretson, *The Shorter Works of Stephen King,* 71-72). The story is enigmatic, concise, taut, fast-paced, and oppressively pessimistic, unlike the subsequent movie version, *Children of the Corn* (almost unanimously accepted as among the worst transformations of King stories to film to date). It has been followed by a series of sequels (five to 1999) that have raised the original film to a quasi-eminence among 'schlock' horror films.

SELECTED ARTICLES, RESPONSES, AND REVIEWS:
Magistrale, Anthony S. "Stephen King's Vietnam Allegory: An Interpretation of 'Children of the Corn.'" *Cuyahoga Review* (Spring-Summer 1984): 61-66. * Reprint, *Footsteps* V (April 1985): 61-65.

B32. "One for the Road." *Maine* (March/April 1977).

REPRINTS AND ADAPTATIONS:
b. *Night Shift.* Garden City NY: Doubleday & Co., 1978, hardcover. 306-322. See A6.
c. *Young Monsters.* Edited by Isaac Asimov, Martin H. Greenberg, and Charles G. Waugh. New York: Harper & Row, April 1985, 213 pp., $11.95, hardcover. 190-215. Library binding for younger readers. ISBN 0-06-020170-3.
d. *Asimov's Monsters.* Edited by Isaac Asimov, Martin H. Greenberg, and Charles G. Waugh. London, England: Dragon Books, 1986, paperback, pp.
e. *Strange Maine.* Edited by Charles Waugh, Martin Greenberg, and Frank D. McSherry Jr. Augusta ME: Lance Tapley, October 1986, 295 pp., $9.95, trade paperback. 77-92. Anthology of horror stories with Maine locales. ISBN 0-912769-10-6.
f. *Vamps: An Anthology of Female Vampire Stories.* Edited by Martin Greenberg and Charles Waugh. New York: DAW Books, March 1987, 365 pp., $3.50, mass-market paperback. 12-30. ISBN 0-88677-190-0.
g. As: "Eines auf den Weg" ['One on the way'] *Vampire!* Edited by Martin H. Greenberg and Charles G. Waugh. Bergisch Gladback: Bastei-Lübbe BLTB, 1988, paperback. German translation by Stefan Sturm.
h. *Asimov's Ghosts & Monsters.* Edited by Isaac Asimov, Martin H. Greenberg, and Charles G. Waugh. London, England: Armada, June 1988, 413 pp.,

£2.50, mass-market paperback .383-407. Omnibus issue of *Young Monsters* and *Young Ghosts*. ISBN 0-00-693176-6.
i. As: "Alla salute della strade" [A salute for the road'] *Vampire* [*Vamps*]. Edited by Martin H. Greenberg and Charles Waugh. Milan: Arnoldo Mondadori, OSCAR HORROR #16, June 1991. 7+. Italian translation by Anna Guerzoni. ISBN 88-04-34799-6.
j. In: *Vamps, las chupadoras de sangre* ['Vampires, the suckers of blood']. Edited by Martin H. Greenberg and Charles G. Waugh. Madrid, Spain: Valdemar, ANTOLOGÍAS, 1991, 285 pp., 24 cm. Spanish translation by Albert Solé. ISBN 84-7702-038-8.
k. As: "Return to 'Salem's Lot." *The Vampire Omnibus*. Edited by Peter Haining. England: Orion, July 1995, 497 pp., £8.99, trade paperback. 324-339. ISBN 1-85797-684-3.
l. In: *Legacies*. Abington MD: Cemetery Dance, May 1999 [announced; publication delayed until late 2000 (?)]. Hardcover, limited edition of 500 copies. Also announced as: paperback; audiocassette; E-book.

B33. "**The Shining.**" *Ramada Reflections* (June 1977). Excerpt from *The Shining*. See A3 for further editions.

B34. "**The Man Who Loved Flowers.**" *Gallery* (August 1977): 68-70, 82.

REPRINTS AND ADAPTATIONS:
b. *Night Shift*. Garden City NY: Doubleday & Co., 1978, hardcover. 299-305. See A6.
c. As: "Der Mann, der Blumen Liebte" ['The man who loved flowers'] *Phantastische Literatur* 84. Edited by Michael Görden. Bergisch Gladbach: Bastei-Lübbe, TB 72033, 1983, paperback, pp. German translation by Bernd Seligmann.

B35. "**The Night of the Tiger.**" *The Magazine of Fantasy & Science Fiction* 54 (February 1978): 82-93.

REPRINTS AND ADAPTATIONS:
b. *More Tales of Unknown Horror*. Edited by Peter Haining. London, England: New English Library, 1979, paperback. 127-140.
c. *The Year's Best Horror Stories, Series VII*. Edited by Gerald W. Page. New York: DAW Books, 1979, $1.95, mass-market paperback. 20-33. ISBN 0-87997-476-1.
d. As: "La noche del tigre." *Ciencia ficción: selección 37* ['Science fiction: selection 37']. Barcelona, Spain: Bruguera, LIBRO AMIGO #667, 1979 (?), 218 pp., 17 cm., paperback. Spanish translation by Juan Carlos Silvi. ISBN 84-02-06512-0.
e. *The Third Book of Unknown Tales of Horror*. Edited by Peter Haining. London, England: Sidgwick & Jackson, 1980, hardcover. 161-175.

Horror Plum'd

f. *Chamber of Horrors*. Anonymously edited by Emma Blackley. London, England: Octopus Books, 1984, 352 pp., hardcover. 179-189. ISBN 0-7064-2053-5.
g. *The Best Horror Stories from The Magazine of Fantasy & Science Fiction*. Edited by Edward L. Ferman and Anne Jordan. New York: St. Martin's Press, July 1988, 403 pp., $22.95, hardcover. 81-93. ISBN 0-312-10894-0.
h. *The Best Horror Stories from The Magazine of Fantasy & Science Fiction*, Vol. 1. Edited by Edward L. Ferman and Anne Jordan. New York: St. Martin's Press, April 1989, 260 pp., $3.95, mass-market paperback. 104-119. ISBN 0-312-91499-7.
i. As: "Die Nacht des Tigers." *Die Besten Horrorstories* ['The best horror-stories'] Edited by Edward L. Ferman. Munich, Germany: Droemer Knaur, PAPERBACK 1835, 1989, paperback, pp. German translation
j. *The Best of Modern Horror*. Edited by Edward L. Ferman and Anne Jordan. London, England: Viking, 1989, hardcover. 81-93.
k. *Horror 5: Lo mejor del terror contemporáneo* ['Horror 5: the best of contemporary terror']. Edited by Edward L. Ferman and Anne Jordan. Barcelona, Spain: Martínez Roca, GRAN SUPER TERROR, 1989, 431 pp., 22 cm. Spanish translations by Albert Solé and Jordi Fibla. ISBN 84-270-1303-5.
l. As: "La notte della tigre." *La finestra e altre storie dell'orrore dal "Magazine of Fantasy & SF.* Edited by Edward L. Ferman and Anne Jordan. Milan, Italy: Arnoldo Modadori, OSCAR HORROR #13, October 1991. 127 +. Italian translation by Marina Cornara. ISBN 88-04-34115-7.
m. As: "La notte della tigre." *Inverno Horror 1991. I romanzo e 14 racconti* ['Winter horror 1991: a novel and 14 tales']. Milan, Arnoldo Mondadori, HORROR [#1], October 1991. 133+. Italian translation by Maria Teresa Marenco.
n. *Horrorstory, Volume Three: The Year's Best Horror Stories VII; The Year's Best Horror Stories VIII; The Year's Best Horror Stories IX*. Edited by Karl Edward Wagner and Gerald W. Page. Novato CA, Lancaster PA: Underwood-Miller, January 1992, 541 pp., $39.95, hardcover. 11-22. ISBN 0-88733-107-6. LIMITED EDITION: March 1992, $150.00; ISBN 0-88733-108-4.
o. As: "La notte della tigre." *Orrori e incubi* ['Horror and nightmares': *The Years Best Horror Stories: Series* VII]. Edited by Gerald W. Page. Rome, Italy: Newton & Compton, I NUOVI BEST-SELLER #43, March 1998. 25+. Italian translation by Gianni Pilo. ISBN 88-8183-940-7.

B36. "The Gunslinger." *The Magazine of Fantasy & Science Fiction* Vol. 55 (October 1978).

REPRINTS AND ADAPTATIONS
b. *The Year's Finest Fantasy*, Vol. 2. Edited by Terry Carr. New York: Berkley Publishing Corp., July 1979, hardcover. 91-140.

c. *The Year's Finest Fantasy*, Vol. 2. Edited by Terry Carr. New York: Berkley Publishing Corp., 1979, $1.95, paperback. ISBN 425-04155-7.
d. *The Dark Tower: The Gunslinger.* West Kingston RI: Donald M. Grant, 1984, hardcover. 11-66. See A17.
e. As: "Der Revolvermann." *Sterbliche Götter* (*Die Besten Geschichten aus The Magazine of Fantasy & Science Fiction*, 55. Folge) ['Mortal gods: the best stories from *The Magazine*....]. Edited by Manfred Kluge. Munich, Germany: Wilhelm Heyne, TB3718, 1980, paperback. German translation by Marvel Bieger.

B37. "Man with a Belly." *Cavalier* (December 1978): 35, 77-81.

REPRINTS AND ADAPTATIONS:
b. *Gent* (November/December 1979).

B38. "Jerusalem's Lot." *Night Shift.* Garden City NY: Doubleday & Co., 1978, hardcover. 1-35. See A6; for a related narrative, see also A2.

REPRINTS AND ADAPTATIONS:
b. *World Fantasy Awards*, Volume Two. Edited by Stuart David Schiff and Fritz Leiber. Garden City NY: Doubleday & Co., 1980, hardcover. 20-56.
c. As: "Briefe aus Jerusalem" ['Letters from Jerusalem"]. *Phantastische Literatur* 84. Bergisch Gladbach, West Germany: Bastei-Lübbe TB 72033, 1983, paperback. German translation by Barbara Heidkamp.
d. *Baker's Dozen: 13 Short Horror Novels.* Edited by Martin H. Greenberg and Charles G. Waugh. New York: Crown/Bonanza Books, December 1987, 758 pp., $8.98, hardcover. 1-38. ISBN 0-517-63171-7.
e. *Tales of the Cthulhu Mythos.* [Edited anonymously by August Derleth and James Turner]. Sauk City WI: Arkham House, November 1989, 529 pp., $23.95, hardcover. 468-502. ISBN 0-87054-159-5.
f. As: *Celui qui garde le ver: et autres nouvelles* ['The one who guards/keeps the worm; and other stories']. Paris, France: J'ai Lu #193, 1997, 123 pp., 10 F, paperback. French translation by Lorris Murail and Natalie Zimmerman. ISBN 2-277-30193-0.
g. As: AUDIOCASSETTE: *Joachim Kerzel liest Stephen King, Briefe aud Jerusalem* ['Joachim Kerzel reads Stephen King, letter from Jerusalem']. Bergisch Gladbach: Lübbe Audio, 1999. 2 CDs. 39.90 DM. ISBN 3-7857-1042-9.

B39. "The Last Rung on the Ladder." *Night Shift.* Garden City NY: Doubleday & Co., 1978, hardcover. 287-298. See A6 and GE18.

REPRINTS AND ADAPTATIONS:
b. AS FILM: *The Last Rung on the Ladder.* Talisman Productions, 1987.

Produced by James Cole. Directed by James Cole and Dan Thron. Screenplay by James Cole and Dan Thron. 12.5 minutes.
> CAST: Adam Houhoulis, Melissa Whelden, Nat Wordell, Agam Howes. Student film.
> SELECTED FILM REVIEWS AND ARTICLES:
> Blue, Tyson. "SK Flicks Not Found at a Theatre Near You." *Castle Rock: The Stephen King Newsletter* Vol. 5, No. 1 (January 1989): 1, 8.
> Cole, James. "The Good and Bad of Film Adaptation." *Castle Rock: The Stephen King Newsletter* Vol. 4, No. 9 (September 1988): 1, 6.
> Spignesi, Stephen J. "Student Cinema Focuses on Stephen King: 'The Last Rung on the Ladder' and 'The Lawnmower Man,'" *The Complete Stephen King Encyclopedia*. Ann Arbor MI: Popular Culture, Ink, May 1991. 602-605.

B40. "Quitters, Inc." *Night Shift*. Garden City NY: Doubleday & Co., 1978, hardcover. 213-233. See A6 and G9.

REPRINTS AND ADAPTATIONS:
b. *Best Detective Stories of the Year.* Edited by Edward D. Hoch. New York: Dutton, 1979, hardcover. .
c. *The Science Fiction Weight-Loss Book*. Edited by Isaac Asimov, George R. R. Martin, and Martin H. Greenberg. New York: Crown Publishers, 1983, hardcover. 231-249.

d. As FILM: The print original for an episode in King's film, *Cat's Eye* [see entries under *Night Shift*, A6].

B41. "The Woman in the Room." *Night Shift*. Garden City NY: Doubleday & Co., 1978, hardcover. 323-336. See A6.

b. *The 25th Pan Book of Horror Stories*. Edited by Herbert van Thal. London & Sydney: Pan Books, 1984, paperback. 139-152.
c. *The Complete Masters of Darkness*. Edited by Dennis Etchison. Novato CA, Lancaster PA: Underwood-Miller, February 1991, 766 pp., $39.95, hardcover. 727-740. ISBN 0-88733-116-5.
d. *Masters of Darkness III*. Edited by Dennis Etchison. New York: Tor, May 1991, 322 pp., $3.95, mass-market paperback. 303-319. ISBN 0-812-51766-0.

e. As FILM/VIDEOCASSETTE: *The Woman in the Room*. Darkwoods, 1983. Granite Entertainment, Canoga Park, CA. Produced by Gregory Melton. Directed by Frank Darabont. Screenplay by Frank Darabont. VHS, Beta. 30 minutes.
> CAST: Michael Cornelison, Dee Croxton, Brian Libby, Bob Brunson, George Russell

COMMENTS: Darabont's sensitive re-creation of the tone, the brooding atmosphere, and the stark characterization of King's print original foreshadows his equally remarkable screenplay treatments of subsequent King texts, including "Rita Hayworth and Shawshank Redemption" [*The Shawshank Redemption*] and *The Green Mile*.

SELECTED ARTICLES, RESPONSES, AND REVIEWS:
Collings, Michael R. *Castle Rock: The Stephen King Newsletter* Vol. 1, No. 9 (September 1985): 4. Letter-review.
Frank, Janrae. "*Stephen King's Night Shift*: Student Shorts of Stephen King Tales Headed for Videocassette Release." *Cinefantastique* Vol. 15, No. 3 (July 1985): 12.
Sallee, Wayne Allen. "It's Really Only a Game." *Castle Rock: The Stephen King Newsletter* Vol. 2, No. 4 (April 1986): 2.

COMMENTS: "The Woman in the Room" is a rarity among the stories in *Night Shift* for its autobiographical undercurrents, its raw emotional intensity, and its carefully realized, frighteningly mundane realism. Lacking in supernatural elements, the story concentrates on a painful decision—whether or not to assist in a terminally ill mother's suicide.

B42. "**Nona.**" *Shadows*. Edited by Charles L. Grant. Garden City NY: Doubleday & Co., 1978, hardcover. 151-182.

REPRINTS AND ADAPTATIONS:
b. *Shadows*. Edited by Charles L. Grant. New York: Playboy Paperbacks, October 1980, mass-market paperback. 187-223. * 2nd printing: New York: Berkley, September 1982, 223 pp., $2.50, mass-market paperback. 187-223. ISBN 0-425-05955-3. Identical to the Playboy publication.
c. *The Dodd, Mead Gallery of Horror*. Edited by Charles L. Grant. New York: Dodd, Mead, 1983, hardcover. 333-365.
d. *A Gallery of Horror*. Edited by Charles L. Grant. London, England: Robson, 1983, hardcover. 333-365.
e. As: "Nona." *Das Große Gruselkabinett* ['The great chamber of horrors']. Edited by Charles L. Grant. Munich, Germany: Wilhelm Heyne DIE UNHEIMLICHE BÜCHER #16, 1984, paperback. German translation by Rolf Jurkeit.
f. *Skeleton Crew*. New York: G. P. Putnam's Sons, June 1985, hardcover. 329-358. See A28 for further editions.
g. *Horror: lo mejor del terror contemporaneo* ['Horror: the best of contemporary terror']. Edited by Charles L. Grant. Barcelona, Spain: Matrinez Roca, 1986. Spanish translation of *The Dodd, Mead Gallery of Horror.*
h. *Shadows* II. Edited by Charles L. Grant. London, England: Headline, 1987, hardcover.
i. As: "Nona." *Ombre* [*Shadows*]. Edited by Charles L. Grant. Milan, Italy:

HORROR PLUM'D

Arnoldo Mondadori, OSCAR HORROR #7, January 1990. 235+. Italian translation by Maria Benedetta de Castiglione. ISBN 88-04-32704-9.

j. *Gallery of Horror: 20 Chilling Tales by the Modern Masters of the Dread.* Edited by Charles L. Grant. New York: New American Library, February 1996, $21.95, hardcover. ISBN 0-451-45461-8. Reprint of 1983 edition.

k. *Gallery of Horror.* Edited by Charles L. Grant. New York: New American Library, June 1997, 416 pp., $6.99, mass-market paperback. ISBN 0-451-45515-0.

B43. "The Crate." *Gallery* (July 1979).

REPRINTS AND ADAPTATIONS:

b. *Fantasy Annual III.* Edited by Terry Carr. New York: Timescape, Pocket Books, May 1981, $2.95, mass-market paperback. 1-32. ISBN 0-671-41272-8.

c. *The Arbor House Treasury of Horror and the Supernatural.* Edited by Bill Pronzini, Barry N. Malzberg, and Martin H. Greenberg. New York: Arbor House, 1981, hardcover. 570-599.

d. *The Arbor House Treasury of Horror and the Supernatural.* Edited by Bill Pronzini, Barry N. Malzberg, and Martin H. Greenberg. New York: Priam Books/Arbor House, 1981, trade paperback. 570-599.

e. *Great Tales of Horror and the Supernatural.* Edited by Bill Pronzini, Barry N. Malzberg, and Martin H. Greenberg. New York: A&W, Galahad Books, 1985, 597 pp., $8.98, hardcover. 568-597. ISBN 0-88365-699-X.

f. *Creepshow.* New York: Plume/New American Library, July 1982, trade paper, [no pagination]. Comic book format; illustrated by Berni Wrightson. [see A15].

g. As: "Die Kiste." *Unheimliches* ['Sinister']. Edited by Bill Pronzini, Barry N. Malzberg, and Martin H. Greenberg. Munich, Germany: Wilhelm Heyne, JUBILÄUMSBAND #9, 1985, paperback. German translation by Sonja Hauser and Bernd Lenz.

h. As FILM/VIDEOCASSETTE/DVD: see entries under *Creepshow* [A15].

COMMENTS: The early prose version of the story succeeds without requiring the visual overlay of E.C. comics in the published *Creepshow* version or the serio-comic performances by Adrienne Barbeau and Hal Holbrook in the film adaptation. The narrative begins in the middle of crisis, with flashbacks and explication to set the stage. The monster is fleetingly compared to the Tasmanian Devil (appropriate for the comic-book ancestry of the story), but only generally described; King's text relies on evocation of the unknown for its primary impact.

B44. "The Way Station." *The Magazine of Fantasy & Science Fiction* 58 (April 1980).

REPRINTS AND ADAPTATIONS:
b. *The Dark Tower: The Gunslinger.* West Kingston RI: Donald M. Grant, 1984, hardcover. 71-113. See A17.
c. As: "Das Rasthaus." *Grenzstreifzüge (Die Besten Geschichten aus The Magazine of Fantasy & Science Fiction, 58. Folge)* ['"Rest-house" Border-strife-moves (the best stories from *The Magazine...*)']. Edited by Manfred Kluge. Munich, Germany: Wilhelm Heyne, TB3792, 1981, paperback, pp. German translation by Wolfgang Schrader.

B45. "Firestarter." *Omni* Vol. 2 (July 1980). Excerpt from the novel. See A9.

B46. "The Wedding Gig." *Ellery Queen's Mystery Magazine* (1 December 1980): 127-139.

REPRINTS AND ADAPTATIONS:
b. *Skeleton Crew.* New York: G. P. Putnam's Sons, June 1985, hardcover. 227-240. See A28.
c. As: "Der Hochzeitempfang" ['The wedding-reception']. *Jubiläumsbuch* ['Jubilee-book']. Edited by Günther Fetzer. Munich, Germany: Wilhelm Heyne TB6700, 1988, paperback, pp. German translation by Alexandra von Reinhardt.
d. *Great Tales of Madness & the Macabre.* Edited by Charles Ardai. New York: Galahad Books, May 1990, 518 pp., $9.98, hardcover. 269-281. ISBN 0-88365-750-3.

B47. "Big Wheels: A Tale of the Laundry Game." *New Terrors* 2. Edited by Ramsey Campbell. London & Sydney: Pan Books, 1980, paperback. 177-188.

REPRINTS AND ADAPTATIONS:
b. *New Terrors.* Edited by Ramsey Campbell. New York: Pocket Books, October 1982, paperback. 250-262.
c. As: "Big Wheels: A Tale of the Laundry Game (Milkman #2)." *Skeleton Crew.* New York: G. P. Putnam's Sons, June 1985, hardcover. 401-414. See A28.
d. *Omnibus of New Terrors.* Edited by Ramsey Campbell. London, England: Pan, 1985, xii+649 pp., £7.99, paperback. 493-504. ISBN 0-330-28854-7.
e. As: "Der Milchmann Schlägt Wieder Zu" ['The Milkman Gives a Bonus Again']. *Das Ferien-lesebuch* ['The holiday-reader']. Edited by Günther Fetzer. Munich, Germany: Wilhelm Heyne, TB7834, 1989, paperback. German translation by Alexandra von Reinhardt.

Horror Plum'd

COMMENTS: In "Beach Blanket Books" Peter Nicholls refers to the story as "Something out of the way for King: a piece of true-blue surrealism, beautifully judged and paced.... The horror in this one bubbles up through the beer cans that are central to its imagery, and the reader discovers more about the soft white underbelly of blue-collar life than he could conceivably want to know" (p. 13); in *The Dark Descent*, David G. Hartwell similarly points to the surrealistic nature of the story, noting that this story, "Mrs. Todd's Shortcut," and "Crouch End" represent King's most intensive "concern with alterations in base or consensus reality" (p. 690). Douglas Winter describes both "Big Wheels" and "Morning Deliveries" as part of an unfinished novel, "Milkman" (*Art of Darkness*, pp.161).

B48. "The Monkey." *Gallery* (November 1980).

REPRINTS AND ADAPTATIONS:
b. *Modern Masters of Horror*. Edited by Frank Coffey. New York: Coward, McCann & Geoghegan, 1981, hardcover. 13-56.
c. *The Year's Best Horror Stories, Series IX*. Edited by Karl Edward Wagner. New York: DAW Books, August 1981, paperback. 15-53. ISBN 0-87997-647-0.
d. *Horrors*. Edited by Charles L. Grant. New York: Berkley, August 1981, 223 pp., $2.95, mass-market paperback. 186-223. ISBN 0-425-07692-X. Identical to the Playboy edition.
e. *Horrors*. Edited by Charles L. Grant. New York: Playboy Paperbacks, October 1981, $2.25, mass-market paperback. 186-223. ISBN 0-872-16905-7. * 2nd printing, November 1981.
f. *Fantasy Annual IV*. Edited by Terry Carr. New York: Timescape, Pocket Books, November 1981, $3.50, paperback. 1-40. ISBN 0-671-41273-6.* Reprint as: Book Club edition.
g. *Modern Masters of Horror*. Edited by Frank Coffey. New York: Ace Books, 1982, paperback.
h. *Skeleton Crew*. New York: G. P. Putnam's Sons, June 1985, hardcover. 141-174. See A28.
i. *Heyne Jahresband 1986* ['Heyne yearbook 1986']. Munich, Germany: Wilhelm Heyne, TB 6600, 1986, paperback. German translation by Alexandra von Reinhardt.
j. *Horrors!* Barcelona, Spain: Martinéz Roca, 1986, paperback, pp. Spanish translation
k. *The Dark Descent*. Edited by David G. Hartwell. New York: Tor, October 1987, 1011 pp., $29.95, hardcover. 382-409. ISBN 0-312-93035-6.
l. *Modern Masters of Horror*. Edited by Frank Coffey. New York: Berkley Books, July 1988, $3.50, mass-market paperback; ISBN 0-425-10952-6.
m. *The Mammoth Book of Short Horror Novels*. Edited by Mike Ashley. London, England: Robinson, 1988, trade paperback. 1-34. ISBN 0-948164-82-4. * Reprint, 1994. * Reprint, New York: Carroll & Graf, 1988, paperback, 1-34.

n. *The Mammoth Book of Short Horror Novels*. Edited by Mike Ashley. New York: Carroll & Graf, 1988, $8.95, trade paperback, 1-34. ISBN 0-88184-429-2. * Reprint, 1994, $9.95, trade paperback. ISBN 0-7867-0091-2.

o. As: "La scimmia" ['The Monkey']. *Il colore del male* ['The color of evil'=*The Dark Descent*]. Edited by David G. Hartwell. Milan, Italy: Armenia Editore, November 1989. 350+. Italian translation by Nicoletta Spagnol. ISBN 88-344-0406-8.

p. *The Dark Descent 2: The Medusa in the Shield.* Edited by David G. Hartwell. London, England: Grafton, November 1990, 368 pp., £7.99, trade paperback. 109-138. ISBN 0-246-13751-7.

q. *Nouvelles* [Stories']. Paris, France: Presses Pocket, 1990, 223 pp., paperback. 9-124. Bi-lingual edition with introduction and discussions by Michael Oriano. See A42.

r. *The Medusa in the Shield: The Dark Descent, Vol. 3*. Edited by David G. Hartwell. New York: Tor Horror, November 1991, 498 pp., $4.99, mass-market paperback. 146-185. ISBN 0-812-50966-8.

s. *Gestalten in de Nacht* [*Horrors*] ['Shapes/patterns in the night'], edited by Charles L. Grant. Amsterdam, Netherlands: Loeb, HORRORS & CRIME 9, [1991], 185 pp. Dutch translation by Anita C. ven de Ven. ISBN 90-379-0208-1.

t. As: "La scimmia" ['The monkey']. *La Scimmia* (The Year's Best Horror Series IX, 1981). Edited by Karl A Wagner. Rome, Italy: Fanucci Editore, ECONOMICA TASCABILE #15, February 1994, 239 pp., 19 cm. 7+. Italian translation by Rosa Russo. ISBN 88-452-2167-9.

u. As: "El Mono" ['The monkey']. *El gran libro del terror* ['The great book of terror']. Compiled by David G. Hartwell. Buenos Aires, Argentina: Martínez Roca/Planeta, 1994, 474 pp., 24 cm. Spanish translation. ISBN 950-870-039-4.

v. *Horrorstory, Vol. Three: The Year's Best Horror Stories VII; The Year's Best Horror Stories VIII; The Year's Best Horror Stories IX.* Edited by Karl Edward Wagner and Gerald W. Page. Novato CA, Lancaster PA: Underwood-Miller, January 1992, 541 pp., $39.95, hardcover. 369-400. ISBN 0-88733-107-6. * LIMITED EDITION: March 1992, $150.00; ISBN 0-88733-108-4.

w. As AUDIOCASSETTE: "The Monkey." New York: Warner Audio, Summer 1986, 1988. 1 cassette. Read by David Purdham. Unabridged.
    SELECTED REVIEWS:
    Publishers Weekly (3 July 1987): 36-37.

x. As RADIO ADAPTATION: "The Monkey." 31 October 1985, Halloween Night. UNICEF. By Dennis Etchison.
    COMMENTS: Special segment that included Etchison's "The Night Man," Richard Matheson's "The Children of Noah," William F. Nolan's "The Party," and the King story.

SELECTED ARTICLES AND REVIEWS
Sanders, Joe. " 'Monsters from the Id!' in Stephen King's 'The Monkey.'" *Extrapolation* [Kent State University] Vol. 41, No. 3 (October 2000): 257+.

B49. "Crouch End." *New Tales of the Cthulhu Mythos.* Edited by Ramsey Campbell. Sauk City, WI: Arkham House, 1980, hardcover. 3-32.

REPRINTS AND ADAPTATIONS:
b. *The Dark Descent.* Edited by David G. Hartwell. New York: Tor, October 1987, 1101 pp., $29.95, hardcover. 690-711. ISBN 0-312-93035-6.
c. As: "Crouch End." *Il colore del male* [['The color of evil'=*The Dark Descent*]. Edited by David G. Hartwell. Milan, Italy: Armenia Editore, November 1989. 626+. Italian translation by Nicoletta Spagnol. ISBN 88-344-0406-8.
d. In: *Orrore a Crouch End* ['Horror at Crouch End']. Edited by Ramsey Campbell. Rome, Italy: Fanucci Editore, I MAESTRI DEL FANTASTICO [#9], June 1990, 9+. Italian translation by Gianni Pilo and Roberto Russo. ISBN 88-347-0079-1. Reprinted March 1992.
e. *The Dark Descent 3: A Fabulous, Formless Darkness.* Edited by David G. Hartwell. London, England: HarperCollins UK, September 1991, 422 pp., hardcover and trade paperback. 78-100. ISBN 0-246-13753-3, 0-246-13752-5.
f. *A Fabulous, Formless Darkness: The Dark Descent, Vol. 3.* Edited by David G. Hartwell. New York: Tor, 1992, paperback. 107-138.
g. *Nightmares & Dreamscapes.* New York: Viking, 1993, hardcover. 559-592. See A47.
h. *El gran libro del terror* ['The great book of terror']. Compiled by David G. Hartwell. Buenos Aires, Argentina: Martínez Roca/Planeta, 1994, 474 pp., 24 cm. Spanish translation. ISBN 950-870-039-4.
i. *Eternal Love: The Persistence of H. P. Lovecraft in Popular Culture.* Edited by Jim Turner. Collinsville IL: Golden Gryphon Press, October 1998, 411 pp., $25.95, hardcover. 169-193. ISBN 0-9655901-7-8.

COMMENTS: The story demonstrates King's awareness of and debt to Lovecraft's unique vision and world view; it is also unique in King's canon for its exclusively English atmosphere and milieu.

B50. "The Mist." *Dark Forces: New Stories of Suspense and Supernatural Horror.* Edited by Kirby McCauley. New York: Viking Press, August 1980, hardcover. 419-550.

REPRINTS AND ADAPTATIONS:
b. *Dark Forces: New Stories of Suspense and Supernatural Horror.* Edited by Kirby McCauley. New York: Viking Press, November 1980, hardcover. 374-492. Science Fiction Book Club edition.

c. *Dark Forces: New Stories of Suspense and Supernatural Horr*or. Edited by Kirby McCauley. Toronto, New York: Bantam Books, December 1981, paperback. 1-130.

d. As: "De Mist." *Macaber Carnaval* ['Macabre Carnival']. Amsterdam: Loeb, 1983. Dutch translation.

e. *Skeleton Crew*. New York: G. P. Putnam's Sons, June 1985, hardcover. 21-134. See A28 for additional editions.

f. As: *Nebel* ['Fog']. Linkenheim, Germany: Edition Phantasia, 1986, cloth. German translation.

g. As: *Dichte Mist* ['Thick Mist']. Utrecht, Belgium: Luitingh, 1986, 156 pp., paperback. Dutch translation by Pauline Moody. Includes an article on King. ISBN 90-245-1741-9.

h. As: "Der Nebel" ['The fog']. *Horror*. Munich, Germany: Wilhelm Heyne JUBILÄUMSBAND #21, 1987, paperback. German translation by Alexandra von Reinhardt.

i. In: *Brume* ['Mist/Haze']. France, 19—, 656 pp. French translation.

j. As AUDIOCASSETTE: *The Mist*. Clinton MD: Recorded Books, 1985. Read by Frank Muller. #85230. 3 cassettes; running time, 4 hours. Unabridged recording.

k. As AUDIOCASSETTE: *The Mist*. Fort Edward NY: ZBS Productions, 1984. Directed by Bill Raymond. Adapted by M. Fulton. Musical score by Tim Clark. One cassette; reading time, 90 minutes. 3-D sound.

l. As AUDIOCASSETTE: *The Mist in 3D Sound*. New York: Simon & Schuster (Audio), May 1986, $12.00, 90 minutes. ISBN 0-671-62138-6.
    SELECTED AUDIO REVIEWS AND ARTICLES:
    Barron, Neil. "King Between Your Ears." *Fantasy Review* No. 76 (February 1985): 16-17.
    Beahm, George. "'The Mist' on Audiocassette: A Sound Idea." *The Stephen King Companion*. Edited by George Beahm. Kansas City MO: Andrews & McMeel, September 1989. 131-133.
    Blue, Tyson. "Review: 'The Mist' in 3-D Sound." *Castle Rock: The Stephen King Newsletter* Vol. 2, No. 7 (July 1986): 5.
    Publishers Weekly (4 April 1986): 41-42.
    Publishers Weekly (3 July 1987): 38.
    Quill & Quire Vol. 52 (September 1986): 78.
    Time 128 (July 21, 1986): 71.
    Washington Post Book World 17 (22 February 1987): 11.

m. As AUDIO CD: *The Mist in 3-D Sound*. New York: Simon & Schuster (Audio), September 1993, $15.00. Digitally remastered from audiocassette. ISBN 0-671-87475-6.

n. As COMPUTER GAME: *The Mist*. Northridge IL: Mindscape Software.

B51. "The Oracle and the Mountain." *The Magazine of Fantasy & Science Fiction* 60 (February 1981).

REPRINTS AND ADAPTATIONS:
b. *The Dark Tower: The Gunslinger.* West Kingston RI: Donald M. Grant, 1984, hardcover. 117-144. See A17.
c. As: "Das Orakel und die Berge" ['The oracle and the mountain'] *Cyrion in Bronze (Die Besten Geschichten aus The Magazine of Fantasy & Science Fiction, 65. Folge)* ['Cyrion in bronze (the best stories from *The Magazine of...*)']. Edited by Ronald M. Hahn. Munich, Germany: Wilhelm Heyne, TB3965, 1983, paperback, pp. German translation by Wolfgang Schrader.

B52. "The Jaunt." *The Twilight Zone Magazine* Vol. 1 (June 1981).

REPRINTS AND ADAPTATIONS:
b. *Gallery* (December 1981).
c. *Great Stories from Rod Serling's* The Twilight Zone Magazine, *1983 Annual*. Edited by T. E. D. Klein. New York: TZ Publications, 1982, paperback. 22-34.
d. As: "Travel." *Schattenlicht* ['Shadowlight']. Edited by Rolf Jurkeit. Munich, Germany: Wilhelm Heyne, TB6428, 1984, paperback, pp. German translation by Rolf Jurkeit.
e. *Skeleton Crew*. New York: G. P. Putnam's Sons, June 1985, hardcover. 203-225. See A28.

B53. "The Slow Mutants." *The Magazine of Fantasy & Science Fiction* Vol. 61 (July 1981).

REPRINTS AND ADAPTATIONS:
b. *The Dark Tower: The Gunslinger.* West Kingston RI: Donald M. Grant, 1984, hardcover. 149-192. See A17.
c. As: "Die Geistermutanten" ['The Spirit-Mutants"]. *Im Fünften Jahr der Reise: Die Besten Geschichten aus The Magazine of Fantasy & Science Fiction, 66. Folge* ['In the fifth year of the journey: the best stories from *The Magazine of...*)']. Edited by Ronald M. Hahn. Munich, Germany: Wilhelm Heyne, TB4005, 1983, paperback, pp. German translation by Jürgen Langowski.

B54. "The Monster in the Closet." *Ladies' Home Journal* (October 1981). Excerpt from the novel. See A12 for further editions.

B55. "The Bird and the Album." *A Fantasy Reader: The Seventh World Fantasy Convention Program Book*. Edited by Jeff Frane and Jack Rems. Berkeley CA: The Seventh World Fantasy Convention, 30 October 1981, 79-85. Excerpt from chapter 13 of the manuscript IT. 1,000 copies printed.

REPRINTS AND ADAPTATIONS:
b. Incorporated into: *IT*. New York: Viking, 1986, hardcover. 701-707. See A32.

COMMENTS: "The Bird and the Album" constitutes an early version of "Part 4: July of 1958" and "Chapter 14: The Album"—Parts 1 and 2 [partial]. The passage has been substantially revised, including a shift of verb tense from past to present.

B56. "Do the Dead Sing?" *Yankee* (November 1981): 139-143, 238-264.

REPRINTS AND ADAPTATIONS:
b. *The Best of Yankee*, 1935-1985. Edited by Jud Hale. 1985.
c. As: "The Reach." *Skeleton Crew*. New York: G. P. Putnam's Sons, June 1985, hardcover. 487-505. See A28.
d. As: "Der Gesang der Toten" ['The Song of the Dead']. *Das Winterlesebuch* ['The winter-reader']. Edited by Manfred Kluge. Munich, Germany: Wilhelm Heyne, TB6759, 1986, paperback. German translation by Alexandra von Reinhardt.
e. As: "The Reach." *The Dark Descent*. Edited by David G. Hartwell. New York: Tor, October 1987, 1101 pp., $29.95, hardcover. 15-30. ISBN 0-312-93035-6.
f. As: "Lo Stretto" ['The narrow'] *Il colore del male* ['The color of evil'=*The Dark Descent*]. Edited by David G. Hartwell. Milan, Italy: Armenia Editore, November 1989. 23+. Italian translation by Nicoletta Spagnol. ISBN 88-344-0406-8.
g. As: "The Reach." *The Dark Descent 1: The Colour of Evil*. Edited by David G. Hartwell. London, England: Grafton, June 1990, 292 pp., £7.99, trade paperback. 13-28. ISBN 0-246-13668-5..
h. As: "The Reach." *The Color of Evil: The Dark Descent, Vol. 1*. Edited by David G. Hartwell. New York: Tor, September 1991, 438 pp., $4.99, mass-market paperback.15-30. ISBN 0-812-51898-5.
i. As: "The Reach." *The Horror Hall of Fame*. Edited by Robert Silverberg and Martin H. Greenberg. New York: Carroll & Graf, July 1991, 416 pp., $21.95, hardcover. 380-401. ISBN 0-88184-692-9.
j. As: "El Brazo" ['The arm']. *El gran libro del terror* ['The great book of terror']. Compiled by David G. Hartwell. Buenos Aires, Argentina: Martínez Roca/Planeta, 1994, 474 pp., 24 cm. Spanish translation. ISBN 950-870-039-4.
k. As: "The Reach." *American Gothic Tales*. Edited by Joyce Carol Oates. New York: Plume, December 1996, 547 pp., $14.95, trade paperback. 378-397. ISBN 0-452-27489-3.

COMMENTS: Winner of the World Fantasy Award, 1981, this story appeared in *Skeleton Crew* with King's original title. "Do the Dead Sing?" is a gentle story that, as David G. Hartwell notes, carefully distances the horrific to concentrate on the human; the result is "a work of unusual subtlety and sentiment, a ghost story of love and death, a virtuoso performance..." (*The Dark Descent* 15). The story of Stella Flanders and her ninety-six years of life on Goat Island, and of her journey across the frozen Reach, modulates from stark realism into a meditation on life and death, fear and love. Justly applauded by most readers, it concludes *Skeleton Crew* and continues to claim a place among King's best stories. (On a personal note: this story remains among my selections for King's most effective writing—MRC.)

B57. "The Gunslinger and the Dark Man." *The Magazine of Fantasy & Science Fiction* Vol. 61 (November 1981).

REPRINTS AND ADAPTATIONS:
b. *The Dark Tower: The Gunslinger.* West Kingston RI: Donald M. Grant, 1984, hardcover. 197-216. See A17.
c. As: "Der Revolvermann und der Mann in Schwarz" ['The gunman and the man in black']. *Mythen der Nahen Zukunft (Die Besten Geschichten aus The Magazine of Fantasy & Science Fiction, 68. Folge)* ['Myths of the near future: the best stories from *The Magazine…*']. Edited by Ronald M. Hahn. Munich, Germany: Wilhelm Heyne, TB4062, 1984, paperback, pp. German translation by Andreas Decker.

B58. "The Man Who Would Not Shake Hands." *Shadows 4*. Edited by Charles L. Grant. Garden City NY: Doubleday & Co., 1981, hardcover. 1-17.

REPRINTS AND ADAPTATIONS:
b. *Shadows 4*. Edited by Charles L. Grant. New York: Berkley Books, 1985, paperback. 1-20.
c. *Shadows*. Edited by Charles L. Grant. London, England: Headline, 1987, hardcover.
d. *Skeleton Crew*. New York: G. P. Putnam's Sons, June 1985, hardcover. 289 304. See A28.
e. As: "Der Mann, der Niemandem die Hand Geben Wollte" ['the man who would not give anyone his hand']. *Mordslust, Band 2* ['Murder-lust/blood-thirst, Vol. 2]. Edited by Viragilio Iafrate. Munich, Germany: Westarp Verlag, 1987. German translation by Alexandra von Reinhardt.
f. *The Best of Shadows*. Edited by Charles L. Grant. New York, London, England: A Foundation Book, Doubleday, October 1988, hardcover. 63-82.
g. As: *La ballade de la balle èlastique; suivi de L'homme qui refusait de serrer la main* ['The ballad of the flexible bullet; with the man who refused to shake hands']. Paris, France: J'ai Lu, 1994, 95 pp., 10F, 21 cm., paperback. Two excerpted stories from *Skeleton Crew*. French translations by Michèle Pressé and Serge Quadruppani. ISBN 2-277-30046-2.

B59. "Cujo." *Science Fiction Digest* 1 (January/February 1982). Excerpt from the novel. See A12 for further editions.

B60. "The Raft." *Gallery* (November 1982).

REPRINTS AND ADAPTATIONS:
b. *Twilight Zone Magazine* Vol. 3 (May/June 1983): 32-46.
c. *Skeleton Crew.* New York: G. P. Putnam's Sons, June 1985, hardcover. 245-270. See A28.
d. As: "Das Floß" ['The raft']. *Dämmerlight* ['Twilight']. Edited by Rolf Jurkheit. Munich, Germany: Wilhelm Heyne, TB7498, 1985, paperback. German translation by Rolf Jurkeit.
e. Unauthorized reprint in a college publication in Arkansas.
f. *Horrorscape.* Edited by Gary Goshgarian. Dubuque IA: Kendall/Hunt, 1993, 252 pp., trade paperback. 165-188. ISBN 0-8403-8181-6.

g. As: FILM: Print original for episode in George Romero's *Creepshow* II. See E1.

SELECTED ARTICLES, RESPONSES, AND REVIEWS:
Rhodes, Wayne. "Cut Adrift in a Plagiarized Raft." *Castle Rock: The Stephen King Newsletter* Vol. 5, No. 12 (December 1989).

B61. "Rita Hayworth and Shawshank Redemption." *Different Seasons.* New York: Viking Press, 1982, hardcover. 1-101. See A16 for further editions.

REPRINTS AND ADAPTATIONS:
b. *Rita Hayworth and Shawshank Redemption.* Thorndike, ME: Thorndike Press, 1983, 181 pp., hardcover. Large print edition. Short novel.
c. COMMENTS: *Castle Rock: The Stephen King Newsletter* (May 1986) reported this title as *Hope Springs Eternal*; a representative of Thorndike Press, however, indicated that the book was issued as noted above. Originally published as part of the collection, *Different Seasons* [see A16].
d. As: [Title unknown]. South Korea, 1995, 361 pp., 23 cm. Korean translation.
e. As: *The Shawshank Redemption: The Shooting Script,* by Frank Darabont. London, England: Nick Hern Books, 1996, xvii+188. ISBN 1854593609.

f. As AUDIOCASSETTE: "Rita Hayworth & Shawshank Redemption." Clinton MD: Recorded Books, 1984. Read by Frank Muller. 3 cassettes; 4 hours. Unabridged. 84063.
g. As AUDIOCASSETTE: *The Shawshank Redemption.* New York: Penguin Audiobooks, September 1995, 3 cassettes. Read by Frank Muller. Movie tie-in. ISBN 0-140-86213-7.

h. As FILM: *The Shawshank Redemption.* October 1994. Directed and screenplay by Frank Darabont. CAST: Tim Robbins, Morgan Freeman. By November 1994 the film had reached 10th place in box office earnings; its gross to that date exceeded $10 million.

i. As screenplay: *Shawshank Redemption: The Shooting Script,* by Frank Darabont. New York: Newmarket Press, March 1996. Introduction by King.
REPRINTS AND ADAPTATIONS:
New York: Newmarket Press, 1998, 208 pp., mass-market paperback. Movie tie-in edition. ISBN 1557042462.

j. As VIDEOCASSETTE: *The Shawshank Redemption.* 1994.

B62. "Apt Pupil: Summer of Corruption." *Different Seasons.* New York: Viking Press, 1982, hardcover. 103-296. See A16 for further editions.

REPRINTS AND ADAPTATIONS:
b. As AUDIOCASSETTE: New York: Penguin, November 1998. $24.95, unabridged. Read by Frank Muller. ISBN 0-140-86935-2.
c. As AUDIOCASSETTE: "Apt Pupil." Clinton MD: Recorded Books, 1984. Read by Frank Muller. #84065. 5 cassettes; 7 hours. Unabridged.
SELECTED ARTICLES AND REVIEWS:
"Stephen King Becomes Teacher in His Tale of the Apt Pupil." *Library Journal* Vol. 124, No. 10 (1999): 204-208.

d. As FILM: *Apt Pupil.* Producers: Richard Kobritz and William Frye. Director: Alan Bridges. Screenplay by Jim Wheat and Ken Wheat (an earlier, unused screenplay had been completed by B. J. Nelson). Filming abandoned in 1988, after about ten weeks of shooting, reportedly only eleven days from completion. See B62.
CAST: Ricky Schroeder, Nicol Williamson, Richard Masur.
COMMENTS: According to Kobritz, the film "may very well have been the definitive translation of Stephen King into film" (Wood, 36). Reviving work on the film was discussed in January 1988 and January 1989; Kobritz, however, ultimately rejected the possibility of completing the film.
SELECTED ARTICLES, RESPONSES, AND REVIEWS:
Twilight Zone (October 1988).
Wood, Gary. "Apt Pupil: The Story Behind the Filming of King's Novella from 'Different Seasons,' Never to be Seen." *Cinefantastique* Vol. 21, No. 4 (February 1991): 36-37.

e. As FILM: *Apt Pupil.* Tri-Star and Phoenix Pictures, 1998. Producer: Tim Habert. Director: Bryan Singer. Screenplay by Brandon Boyce. 111 minutes. Rated: R.
CAST: Ian McKellen, Brad Renfro, David Schwimmer.

f. As VIDEOCASSETTE: Columbia Tristar Home Video, 1998. VHS. ISBN 0-8001-4189-X.

COMMENTS: "Apt Pupil" is one of King's most intense psychological explorations of horror within the bounds of consensus reality; without recourse to monsters or denizens of the dark, King's straightforward narrative of corruption and disillusionment compels in its starkness and simplicity. The increasingly (and reciprocally) deadly relationship between an archetypal clean-cut American boy and a Nazi war criminal in hiding illuminates several of King's persistent themes, most remarkably intergenerational conflict, lack of family unity, and the failure of the American educational system.

B63. **"The Body: Fall From Innocence."** *Different Seasons.* New York: Viking Press, 1982, hardcover. 299-451. See A16 for further editions. Incorporates "Stud City" and "The Revenge of Lardass Hogan."

REPRINTS AND ADAPTATIONS:
b. As: *Het Lijk* ['The body']. Utrecht, Belgium: Luitingh-Sijthoff, 1991, 301 pp., paperback. Dutch translation by Pauline Moody. ISBN 90-245-1528-9.
c. As: *The Body: Fall from Innocence.* [Copenhagen, Denmark]: Gyldendal, 1991, 232 pp., with notes, 94 KR, paperback. Norwegian translation by Jørgen Riber Christensen. ISBN 87-00-0344-6.
d. As: *Fall from Innocence: The Body.* Retold by Robin Waterfield. Harlow, England: Addison Wesley Longman, 1998. ISBN 058240259X.

e. As AUDIOCASSETTE: "The Body." Clinton MD: Recorded Books, 1984. Read by Frank Muller. 4 cassettes; 6 hours. Unabridged. #84064.
f. As AUDIOCASSETTE: New York: Penguin Audiobooks, January 2000, #24.95. Unabridged. Read by Frank Muller. ISBN 0-141-80012-7

g. As FILM: *Stand by Me.* Columbia Pictures, August 8, 1986. Producers: Andrew Scheinman, Bruce A. Evans, and Raynold Gideon. Director: Rob Reiner. Screenplay by Raynold Gideon and Bruce A. Evans. 110 minutes. Rating: R.
    CAST: Wil Wheaton, Richard Dreyfuss, River Phoenix, Corey Feldman, Jerry O'Connell, Kiefer Sutherland
    SELECTED ARTICLES, RESPONSES, AND REVIEWS:
    American Film Vol. 12, No. 6 (April 1987): 57.
    Ansen, David. "Growing Up in the '50s." *Newsweek* Vol. 108, No. 8 (25 August 1986): 63.
    Blue, Tyson. "*Stand By Me* Is a King-ly Rendition." *Courier Herald* [Dublin GA] 8 August 1986.
    Blue, Tyson. "'Stand By Me': The Best King Film Ever." *Castle Rock: The Stephen King Newsletter* Vol. 2, No. 10 (October 1986): 1, 4.
    Brooks, David. "What Is Death, What Is Goofy?" *Insight* (1 September 1986): 57.

Carroll, Kathleen. "And Along the Way, They All Grow Up." *Daily News* [NY] 8 August 1986: 3.
Carson, Norman. "*Stand By Me*." *Magill's Cinema Annual, 1987: A Survey of the Films of 1986*. Edited by Frank N. Magill. Englewood Cliffs, NJ: Salem Press, 1987, hardcover. 413-417.
Clark, Mike. "*Stand by Me* Is a Summer Standout." *USA Today* 8 August 1986.
Corliss, Richard. "No Slumming in Summertime." *Time* Vol. 128, No. 8 (25 August 1986): 62.
Cunleff, Tom. "*Stand By Me*." *People Weekly* "Picks & Pans" (1 September 1986): 12.
Denby, D. *New York Magazine* Vol. 19, no. 32 (18 August 1986): 58.
Denby, D. *New York Magazine* Vol. 19, No. 50 (22-29 December 1986): 141.
Edelstein, D. *The Village Voice* Vol. 31, No. 33 (19 August 1986): 54.
Fangoria No. 57 (September 1986). Four-page article with photographs.
Films in Review 37 (November 1986): 550.
Flatley, G. *Cosmopolitan* Vol. 201, No. 4 (October 1986): 62.
Floyd, N. *Monthly Film Bulletin* Vol. 54, No. 638 (March 1987): 88.
Forshey, G. E. *Christian Century* Vol. 103, No. 31 (22 October 1986): 920.
Freedman, Richard. "Boys Will Be Boys in Refreshing *Stand By Me*." *The Star-Ledger* [Newark NJ] 8 August 1986): 49.
Goodman, Walter. "Film: Rob Reiner's *Stand by Me*." *New York Times* 135 (8 August 1986): C10.
Harmetz, A. *New York Times* 16 September 1987: C17.
Holden, Stephen. "At the Movies: Rob Reiner Films Unusual Teen Drama." *New York Times* 135 (8 August 1986): C8.
Holdship, B. *Creem* Vol. 18, No. 4 (December 1986): 62.
Kael, Pauline. *The New Yorker* Vol. 62, no. 29 (8 September 1986): 110.
Lally, Kevin. "Here's a Movie to Stand By: Stephen King Adaptation Is a Sleeper." *The Courier-News* [Bridgewater NJ] 8 August 1986: C-1.
Levy, M. Z. *Video Review* Vol. 8, No. 11 (April 1987): 88.
Los Angeles Times 8 August 1986: VI, 1.
Maginot, M. *American Cinematographer* Vol. 68, No. 3 (March 1987): 95.
McCalls Vol. 114, No. 2 (November 1986): 162.
Newsweek Vol. 108 (25 August 1986: 63.
Quart, A. *Cineaste* Vol. 15, No. 3 (1987): 48.
Rebello, S. *Cinefantastique* 17:1 (January 1987): 52.
Reed, Rex. "*Stand by Me*—A Corny Kids' Caper." *New York Post* 8 August 1986: 22.
Reed, Susan, and James Grant. "The Child of Flower Children, Actor

River Phoenix Rises from a Strange Past to Bloom in *Stand By Me*." *People* Vol. 26, No. 13 (26 September 1986): 73-74.
Rothstein, M. *New York Times* Vol. 136, No. 47 (19 July 1987): H24.
Simon, J. *National Review* Vol. 38, No. 19 (10 October 1986): 59.
Smith, L. *Classical Images* 136 (October 1986): 14.
Somtow, S. P. "Stand by Stephen King: A Certain Slant of 'I'" *Fantasy Review* No. 95 (October 1986): 11,16.
"Stand By Me." *Los Angeles Times* "Calendar" 31 August 1986: 27.
Variety Vol. 324, No. 1 (30 July 1986): 16.
The Wall Street Journal 208 (7 August 1986): 16.
The Washington Post (22 August 1986): D1.

h. As VIDEOCASSETTE: *Stand by Me*. RCS/Columbia Pictures Home Video, March 1987. VHS, Beta. 87 minutes. Rated: R.

COMMENTS: As the print original for Rob Reiner's superlative film, *Stand by Me*, "The Body" has established itself as one of King's finest—and also most autobiographical-seeming—short stories. His re-creation of the frustrations of childhood-verging-on-adulthood is accurate, penetrating, and moving. The story is important symbolically and thematically for its variations on the theme of the sacrificial child, as represented in different ways by each of the four central characters, coupled with the quest and the search for meaning in death. The narrative is heavily autobiographical as well; one of King's childhood friends was killed while playing on railroad tracks, and the short stories credited to Gordon Lachance were early works of King's own. King recognizes the centrality of the story when he states that *IT*, arguably his most extensive exploration of childhood and adulthood and the rites of transition between the two states, is "The Body" extended and transformed into myth (Letter, 3 March 1986). With its sharp evocation of time and place, largely accomplished through King's (and Reiner's) deft inclusion of cultural icons from the early sixties, "The Body" resonates whether experienced as short fiction or as film. See also B10.

SELECTED ARTICLES, RESPONSES, AND REVIEWS:
1. Terrell, Carroll F. "The Body." *Stephen King: Man and Artist*. Orono, ME: Northern Lights Publishing, 1990, hardcover. 191-217.

B64. "The Breathing Method: A Winter's Tale." *Different Seasons*. New York: Viking Press, 1982, hardcover. 453-518. See A16 for further editions.

REPRINTS AND ADAPTATIONS:
b. As: *The Breathing Method*. Bath, England: Chivers Press, LYTHWAY SUPERNATURAL, September 1984, 106 pp., hardcover. Large print edition.
c. As: *De Ademhalingsmethode* ['The Breathing-method']. Utrecht, Belgium: Luitingh, 1987, 214 pp. Dutch translation by Pauline Moody. ISBN 90-245-1852-0. 2nd printing 1988.

d. As: *A Winter's Tale: The Breathing Method.* Retold by John Escott. Harlow, England: Addison Wesley Longman, 1998.

e. As AUDIOCASSETTE: "The Breathing Method." Clinton MD: Recorded Books, 1984. Read by Frank Muller. 3 cassettes; 4 hours. Unabridged. #85230.

f. As AUDIOCASSETTE: New York: Viking Penguin Audio, January 2000, $18.95. Read by Frank Muller. ISBN 0-140-86944-1.

COMMENTS: King creates an eerie atmosphere in this climax story to the *Different Seasons* collection by combining the disparate traditions of the winter's tale, at least as old as Shakespeare; the men's club tale, including the inscrutable and mysteriously knowledgeable butler [see also King's "The Man Who Would Not Shake Hands" and Peter Straub's *Ghost Story*); and the ghost story proper.

B65. "Father's Day." *Creepshow.* New York: Plume/New American Library, July 1982, paper, unpaginated. See A15 for further editions.

B66. "The Lonesome Death of Jordy Verrill." *Creepshow.* New York: Plume/New American Library, July 1982, paper, unpaginated. See A15 for further editions.

B67. "Something to Tide You Over." *Creepshow.* New York: Plume/New American Library, July 1982, paper, unpaginated. See A15 for further editions.

B68. "They're Creeping Up on You." *Creepshow.* New York: Plume/New American Library, July 1982, paper, unpaginated. See A15 for further editions.

B69. "Before the Play." *Whispers* 17/18 (August 1982): 19-47. * DELUXE LIMITED EDITION: 6 lettered copies, hardcover. * LIMITED EDITION: 350 numbered hardcover copies, signed by King. * Trade paperback edition.

REPRINTS AND ADAPTATIONS:
b. *TV Guide* Vol. 45, No. 17, Issue 2300 (26 April–2 May 1997): 22+. Illustrations by Berni Wrightson. Abridged.

COMMENTS: Deleted from the final version of *The Shining* [see A3], these episodes reinforce the original five-act dramatic/tragic structure King envisioned for the novel. While not critical to a fully satisfactory reading of the novel, the passages provide interesting insights into key characters, including Jack Torrance, and into the history of the Overlook itself.

The segment was originally slated to be included in Stephen Spignesi's *The Shape Under the Sheet: The Complete Stephen King Encyclopedia* (May 1991), but King later reconsidered and withdrew it from further publication.

B70. "Skybar." *The Do-It-Yourself Bestseller.* Edited by Tom Silberkleit and Jerry Biederman. Garden City NY: Doubleday & Co., 1982, hardcover.

REPRINTS AND ADAPTATIONS:
b. New York: Dolphin, 1982, paperback, pp.15-16, 20.

COMMENTS: King wrote the first four paragraphs and the conclusion of this partial tale, leaving the body for aspiring writers to complete. The piece suggests *IT*, as well as demonstrating traditional King stylistics and techniques: brand names and a painfully precise realism as backdrop for fear.

B71. "Survivor Type." *Terrors.* Edited by Charles L. Grant. New York: Playboy Paperbacks, July 1982, $2.50, mass-market paperback. 203-222. ISBN 0-867-21138-5.

REPRINTS AND ADAPTATIONS:
b. As: "Das Überlebenstyp" ['Survivor type']. *Das Weißbuch des Schwarzen Humors* ['The white book of black humor']. Edited by Hans Gamber. Munich, Germany: Wilhelm Heyne, TB6351, 1984, paperback. German translation by Monika Hahn.
c. *Skeleton Crew.* New York: G. P. Putnam's Sons, June 1985, hardcover. 361-378. See A28.
d. *De duistere engel* ['The dark angel'], edited by Charles L. Grant and Stephen King. Amsterdam, Netherlands: Loeb, HORROR & CRIME 6, 1991, 183 pp. Dutch translation by Anita C. van de Ven. ISBN 90-379-0190-5.

B72. "The Word Processor." *Playboy* (January 1983): 173, 217-226.

REPRINTS AND ADAPTATIONS:
b. As: "Taste des Todes" ['Touch of death']. *Playboy* No. 11 (November 1984). German translation; translator unknown.
c. As: "De Tekstverwerker" ['The word-processor'] *Playboy* (June 1985). Dutch translation
d. As: "The Word Processor of the Gods." *Skeleton Crew.* New York: G. P. Putnam's Sons, June 1985, hardcover. 271-288. Restores King's original title. See A28.
e. As: "Der Textcomputer der Götter" ['The work-processor/text-computer of the gods']. *Das Ferien-lesebuch* ['The vacation reader']. Edited by Günther Fetzer. Munich, Germany: Wilhelm Heyne, TB6678, 1986, paperback. German translation by Alexandra von Reinhardt.
f. As: "Cudesni procesor." *Najduze putovanje.* Edited by Poul Anderson. Zagreb, Croatia: Vjesnik, 1986, 128 pp., 20 cm. Translation by Sonja Lovasic.
g. As: "The Word Processor of the Gods." *Tales from the Darkside, Vol. One.* Edited by Mitchell Galin and Tom Allen. New York: Berkley Books, October 1988, 248 pp., $3.50, mass-market paperback. 17-36. ISBN 0-425-11095-8.

HORROR PLUM'D

h. As: "The Word Processor." *The Playboy Book of Science Fiction.* Edited by Alice K. Turner. New York: HarperPrism, May 1998, 469 pp., $23.00, hardcover. 287-308. ISBN 0-06-105288-4.

i. As TELEPLAY: "The Word Processor of the Gods." *Tales from the Darkside.* Laurel Entertainment. 19 November 1985. Executive Producer: David E. Vogel. Producer: William Teitler. Director: Michael Gornick. Teleplay by Michael McDowell. 30 minutes.
   CAST: Bruce Davidson, Karen Schallo, Bill Cain, Jonathan Matthews, Patrick Piccininni, Miranda Beeson, Paul Sparer.
   EPISODES: "The Word Processor of the Gods," from a story by Stephen King; "Slippage," by David Patrick Kelly; "D'Jinn, No Chaser," by Charles Levin.
   SELECTED ARTICLES, RESPONSES, AND REVIEWS:
   "Episode Guide: *Tales from the Darkside.*" *Starburst* 80 (1984): 19-22. References to "The Word Processor of the Gods," listing scriptwriter, director, and cast.
   Harris, Judith P. "Timid, One-Note Stories Need Padding to Fill Even 30 Minutes." *Cinefantastique* (July 1985).
   Scapperotti, Dan. "Tales from the Darkside." *Cinefantastique* (January 1985): 15, 52.

j. As VIDEOCASSETTE: *Tales from the Darkside.* Laurel, 1985 (?). VHS, 70 minutes.

COMMENTS: With "The Word Processor" and "The Reach," King explores the possibility of order and justice in an unjust, disordered universe. Stella Flanders discovers truth at the end of her long life; Richard Hagstrom does not have to wait so long to find self-fulfillment and happiness. Although based partially on W. W. Jacobs's "The Monkey's Paw," "The Word Processor of the Gods" avoids the darkness of *Pet Sematary*, bringing the traditional three wishes to a satisfying conclusion. Read in the context of *IT*, both "The Reach" and "The Word Processor of the Gods" prefigure the mythic order King creates at the conclusion of that novel.

B73. "Uncle Otto's Truck." *Yankee* (October 1983).

REPRINTS AND ADAPTATIONS:
b. *The Year's Best Horror Stories, Series XII.* Edited by Karl Edward Wagner. New York: DAW Books, November 1984, 239 pp., $2.95, paperback. 17-35. ISBN 0-87997-975-5.
c. As: "Onkel Ottos Lastwagen" ['Uncle Otto's truck'] *Die Gruselgeschichten des Jahres* ['The horror-stories of the year']. Edited by Karl Edward Wagner. Munich, Germany: Wilhelm Heyne, TB6614, 1986, paperback. German translation by Martin Bliesse.

d. *Skeleton Crew.* New York: G. P. Putnam's Sons, June 1985, hardcover. 379-394. See A28.
e. As: "Onkel Ottos Lastwagen" ['Uncle Otto's truck'] *Phantastische Weltliteratur 1986* ['Fantastic world-literature']. Edited by Michael Görden. Bergisch Gladbach: Bastei-Lübbe, TB72044, 1986, paperback. German translation.
f. *Horrorstory, Vol. Four: The Year's Best Horror Stories X; The Year's Best Horror Stories XI; The Year's Best Horror Stories XII*, edited by Karl Edward Wagner. Novato CA, Lancaster PA: Underwood-Miller, October 1990, 641 pp., $39.95, hardcover. 447-462. ISBN 0-88733-094-0. LIMITED EDITION: signed, ISBN 0-88733-095-9.
g. As: "Il camion dello zio Otto" ['The lorry/truck of Uncle Otto'] *Ai confini dell'orrore* ['At the boundaries of horror'=*The Year's Best Horror Stories: Series XII*]. Edited by Karl Edward Wagner. Rome, Italy: Newton & Compton, I BIG NEWTON #5, February 1999. 19+. Italian translation by Bianni Pilo. ISBN 88-8289-152-6.

B74. "Cycle of the Werewolf." *Heavy Metal* (December 1983). Excerpt from *Cycle of the Werewolf.* See A21.

B75. "The Return of Timmy Baterman." *Satyricon II Program Book*. Edited by Rusty Burke. Knoxville TN: Satyricon II/DeepSouthCon XXI, 1983, paperback. Excerpt from *Pet Sematary.* See A22.

B76. "Gramma." *Weirdbook* No. 19 (Spring 1984): 3-16.

REPRINTS AND ADAPTATIONS:
b. *Skeleton Crew.* New York: G. P. Putnam's Sons, June 1985, hardcover. 415-441. See A28.
c. As: "Omi" ['Grandma']. *Hexengeschichten* ['Witch-stories']. Edited by Ernst M. Frank. Munich, Germany: Wilhelm Heyne, TB7701, 1988, paperback. German translation by Alexandra von Reinhardt.
d. *Tales of Witchcraft.* Edited by Richard Dalby. London, England: Michael O'Mara Books, October 1991, 243 pp., £13.99, hardcover. 137-164. Anthology of stories about witchcraft. ISBN 1-85479-039-0.
e. *The Television Late Night Horror Omnibus.* Edited by Peter Haining. London, England: Orion, September 1993, 578 pp., £8.99, trade paperback. 502-530. Anthology of 32 stories. ISBN 1-85797-092-6. Hardcover, £14.99, ISBN 1-85797-091-8.

f. As AUDIOCASSETTE: "Gramma." New York: Audio Books/Random House, 1986, 1988. 1 cassette; 100 minutes. Read by Gale Garnett. Unabridged.
    SELECTED REVIEWS AND ARTICLES:
    Publishers Weekly (3 July 1987): 36.

g. As TELEPLAY: "Gramma." *The New Twilight Zone.* CBS. 14 February 1986. Produced by Harvey Fraud. Directed by Bradford May. Teleplay by Harlan Ellison. 30 minutes.
   CAST: Barrett Oliver, Darl Anne Fluegel, Frederick Long.
   SELECTED ARTICLES, RESPONSES, AND REVIEWS:
   Bentkowski, Kent Daniel. "King's 'Gramma' Makes Her Small Screen Debut." *Castle Rock: The Stephen King Newsletter* Vol. 2, No. 4 (April 1986): 5, 8.
   Blue, Tyson. "Gramma Update." *Castle Rock: The Stephen King Newsletter* Vol. 2, No. 3 (March 1986): 4.
   Blue, Tyson. "Praise for Ellison's 'Gramma'." *Castle Rock: The Stephen King Newsletter* Vol. 2, No. 4 (April 1986): 1, 5.
   Goldberg, Lee. "Now Re-Entering 'The Twilight Zone.'" *Starlog* 99 (October 1985): 38-40. King's stories being used as bases for scripts on the television series, specifically "Gramma."
   Herndon, Ben. "Real Tube Terror: The Secretaries Were Afraid to Type 'Gramma'." *Twilight Zone Magazine* (December 1985): 10A-11A. Article based on Ellison's comments about writing the teleplay.
   Rebeaux, Max. "Twilight Zone." *Cinefantastique* Vol. 15, No. 4 (October 1985): 13, 53. References to the teleplay "Gramma."

COMMENTS: The story combines third-person narrative with interior monologue approaching stream-of-consciousness to evoke incremental, Lovecraftian horror. Gramma is one of King's most obsessive and oppressive "monstrous women," and Georgie one of his most intensive sacrificial children. The story integrates the Lovecraftian elements more subtly than did Harlan Ellison's otherwise fine screenplay for *Twilight Zone.*

B77. "Mrs. Todd's Shortcut." *Redbook* (May 1984): 56, 58, 178-188.

REPRINTS AND ADAPTATIONS:
b. *Skeleton Crew.* New York: G. P. Putnam's Sons, June 1985, hardcover. 181 202. See A28.
c. *The Year's Best Horror Stories, Series XIII.* Edited by Karl Edward Wagner. New York: DAW Books, October 1985, 251 pp., $2.95, mass-market paperback. 13-40. ISBN 0-88677-086-6.
d. As: "Mrs. Todds Abkürzung" ['Mrs. Todd's abbreviation/short cut']. *Die Gruselgeschichten des Jahres 2* ['Horror-stories of the year, 2']. Edited by Karl Edward Wagner. Munich, Germany: Wilhelm Heyne, TB6793, 1987, paperback. German translation by Alexandra von Reinhardt.
e. *Horrorstory, Volume Five: The Year's Best Horror Stories XIII; The Year's Best Horror Stories XIV; The Year's Best Horror Stories XV.* Novato CA, Lancaster PA: Underwood-Miller, November 1989, 704 pp., $40.00, hardcover. 5-28. ISBN 0-88733-078-9. * LIMITED EDITION: leatherbound, $150.00, ISBN 0-88733-077-0.

f. *Nouvelles* ['Stories']. Paris, France: Presses Pocket, 1990, 223 pp., paperback. 125-202. Bi-lingual edition with introduction and discussions by Michael Oriano. See A42.
g. As: "La scorciatoia della signora Todd" ['The shortcut of Mrs. Todd']. *L'orrore del buico* ['Horror of darkness (?)'=*The Year's Best Horror Stories, Series XIII*]. Rome, Italy: Newton & Compton, I NUOVI BEST-SELLER #16, 8 February 1996. 15+. Italian translation by Gianni Pilo. ISBN 88-8183-198-8.

h. AS AUDIOCASSETTE: "Mrs. Todd's Shortcut." New York: Warner Audio, Summer 1986. 1 cassette. Read by David Purdham. Unabridged.
i. AS AUDIOCASSETTE: *THE Author Talks: Stephen King*. Clinton MD: Recorded Books. 1 cassette; 1 hour. Profile, interview, and reading of "Mrs. Todd's Shortcut." #87380.

B78. "The Ballad of the Flexible Bullet." *The Magazine of Fantasy & Science Fiction* Vol. 67, No. 1 (June 1984): 6-48.

REPRINTS AND ADAPTATIONS:
b. *Skeleton Crew*. New York: G. P. Putnam's Sons, June 1985, hardcover. 443-486. See A28.
c. As: "I Fornit." *Tre storie del soprannaturale* ['Three stories of the supernatural']. Milan, Italy: Arnoldo Modadori, URANIA #1003, 18 August 1985. Italian translation by Marco and Dida Paggi. Three stories by King, Frederick Forsyth, and Edith Wharton.
d. *The Best Fantasy Stories from The Magazine of Fantasy & Science Fiction*. Edited by Ed Ferman. London, England: Octopus Books, 1985, $9.98, 792 pp., hardcover. 459-503. ISBN 0-7064-2568-5.
e. As: "La Ballata della pallottola fessibile" ['The ballad of the flexible bullet']. *Racconti fantasici del '900. Vol. 2* ['Fantastic stories of '900. Vol. 2']. Edited by Giuseppe Lippi. Milan, Italy: Arnoldo Mondadori, OSCAR #1985, October 1987. 671+. Italian translation by Marco and Dida Paggi. ISBN 88-04-30333-6.
f. As: *La ballade de la balle èlastique; suivi de L'homme qui refusait de serrer la main* ['The ballad of the flexible bullet/elastic ball'; with the man who refused to shake hands']. Paris, France: EJL, 1994, 95 pp., 10F, paperback. Two excerpted stories from *Skeleton Crew*. French translations by Michèle Pressé and Serge Quadruppani. ISBN 2-277-30046-2.
g. *Secret Windows: Essays and Fiction on the Craft of Writing*. Bookspan/BOMC, 2000, $18.75, 433 pp., hardcover. 261-320. A70.

h. AS AUDIOCASSETTE: *The Ballad of the Flexible Bullet*. Clinton MD: Recorded Books. Unabridged reading by Frank Muller. 2 cassettes; 3 hours. #85330.

B79. "The Revelations of 'Becka Paulson." *Rolling Stone* (July 19-August 2,

1984): 82-85, 110. An early version of portions of *The Tommyknockers*. See A35.

REPRINTS AND ADAPTATIONS:
b. *Skeleton Crew*. Santa Barbara, CA: Scream/Press, 1985, hardcover. Included in the limited edition only. See A28.
c. *I Shudder at Your Touch*. Edited by Michele Slung. New York: Roc, Penguin, June 1991, 379 pp., $19.95, hardcover. 1-21. ISBN 0-451-45079-5.
d. As: "Le rivelazioni di 'Becka Paulson." *Se mi tocchi ho un brivido* ["I shudder at your touch"]. Edited by Michele Slung. Milan, Italy: Longanesi, LA GAJA SCIENZA #380, July 1992. 15+. Italian translation by Luigi Spangol. ISBN 88-304-1088-8.
e. In: *Ik griezel van genot: mieuwe verhalen vol erotiek en horror* ['I bristle/shudder with joy/delight: stories full of eroticism and horror']. Edited by Michele Slung. Houten, Netherlands: Van Holkema & Warendorf, 1992, 208 pp., Dutch translation by Mariette van Gelder. ISBN 90-269-7187-7.
f. As: "La revelación de Becka Paulson." *Caricias de horror* ['Caresses of horror']. Compiled by Michele Slung. Buenos Aires, Argentina: Emecé, GRANDES NOVELISTAS, 1993, 404 pp., 22 cm. Spanish translation. ISBN 950-04-1292-6. Reprint 1994.
g. As: "Le rivelazioni di 'Becka Paulson." *Se mi tocchi ho un brivido* ["I shudder at your touch']. Edited by Michele Slung. Milan, Italy: Leditori Associatii, TEADUE #258, July 1994. 15+. Italian translation by Luigi Spangol. ISBN 88-7819-633-9.
h. As AUDIOCASSETTE: "The Revelations of 'Becka Paulson." *I Shudder at Your Touch*. 1992.
   SELECTED REVIEWS:
   Annichiarico, Mark. *Library Journal* Vol. 117, No. 19 (15 November 1992): 124.

SELECTED ARTICLES, RESPONSES, AND REVIEWS:
LaFaille, Gene. Wilson *Library Journal* Vol. 66, No. 2 (October 1991): 111.
Schwartz, Gil. *Fortune* Vol. 124, No. 5 (1991?).

B80. "Dolan's Cadillac." *Castle Rock: The Stephen King Newsletter* 1:2 (February 1985): 2-6; and 1:3 (March 1985): 2-6; and Vol. 1, No. 4 (April 1985): 2-9; and Vol 1, No. 5 (May 1985): 1, 4; and Vol. 1, No. 6 (June 1985): 1-2, 5.

REPRINTS AND ADAPTATIONS:
b. As: *Dolan's Cadillac*. Northridge, CA: Lord John Press, 1989, 64 pp., hardcover. See A37.

c. As FILM: "Dolan's Cadillac." In production, 2001 (?)

B81. "Heroes for Hope: Starring the X-Men." *Marvel Comics* (1985): 10-12. Comic book.

COMMENTS: As part of a campaign for famine relief and recovery in Africa, King joined over a dozen other writers—including Harlan Ellison, George Martin, and Stan Lee—to create an adventure based on hunger, guilt, and human responsibility. Each writer contributed from one to three pages of text, each segment drawn, inked, lettered, and colored by different artists. King's contribution includes the ghoulishly skeletal figure of Hunger and the image of food melting into a putrescent slush. All proceeds from the magazine were donated to famine relief.

B82. "Beachworld." *Weird Tales* Vol. 49, No. 1 (Fall 1984): 16-24.

REPRINTS AND ADAPTATIONS:
b. *Skeleton Crew*. New York: G. P. Putnam's Sons, June 1985, hardcover. 305-320. See A28.

COMMENTS: One of King's closest approximations to strict, conventional science fiction, "Beach-world" uses a traditional SF motif of human explorers stranded on an alien world—this one composed of sand dunes. The world is controlled by a planetary sentience, on the order of the world-ocean of Stanislaw Lem's *Solaris*, that is ultimately unknowable, inimical to humanity, and, on its own terms, horrific.

B83. "Morning Deliveries (Milkman #1)." *Skeleton Crew*. New York: G. P. Putnam's Sons, June 1985, hardcover. 395-400. See A28.

COMMENTS: A companion piece to "Big Wheels: a Tale of the Laundry Game (Milkman #1)." Both are excerpts from a longer manuscript, both share a surrealistic quality, and both deal with an abrupt intrusion of the irrational into the rational. "Morning Deliveries" is more immediately accessible, but paradoxically more disturbing in its suggestion of mindless, purposeless death set against a pastoral setting.

B84. "For the Birds." *Bred Any Good Rooks Lately?* Edited by James Charlton. Garden City NY: Doubleday & Co., October (?) 1986, 117 pp., $4.95, trade paperback. 15. ISBN 0-385-23477-5.

B85. "The End of the Whole Mess." *Omni* Vol. 9 (October 1986).

REPRINTS AND ADAPTATIONS:
b. *Nightmares & Dreamscapes*. New York: Viking, 1993, hardcover. 67-94. See A47.

B86. "**The Dark Tower: The Drawing of the Three.**" Excerpted in *Castle Rock: The Stephen King Newsletter* Vol. 3, No. 4 (April/May 1987): 1, 8-9, 11, 13. See A34.

B87. "**The Doctor's Case.**" *The New Adventures of Sherlock Holmes: Original Stories by Eminent Mystery Writers.* Edited by Martin Harry Greenberg and Carol-Lynn Rössel Waugh. New York: Carroll & Graf, 1987, hardcover. 303-334.

REPRINTS AND ADAPTATIONS:
b. As: "Der Fall des Doktors" ['The case/instance of the doctor']. *Heyne Krimi Jahresband zum Jubiläums-Jahr 1988* ['Heyne Crime Year-book for the Jubilee-Year 1988']. Munich, Germany: Wilhelm Heyne, 1988, paperback. German translation by Joachim Körber (given incorrectly in text as Körleer).
c. As: "Der Fall des Doktors" ['The case/instance of the doctor']. *Die Neuen Abenteur des Sherlock Holmes* ['The new adventures of Sherlock Holmes']. Edited by Martin H. Greenberg and Carol-Lynn Rössel-Waugh. Bergisch Gladbach: Bastei-Lübbe, PAPERBACK 28179, 1988, paperback. German translation by Joachim Körber.
d. *Nieuwe avonturen van Sherlock Holmes* ['New adventures of Sherlock Holmes']. Edited by Martin Harry Greenberg and Carol-Lynn Rossel Waugh. Amsterdam, Netherlands: Loeb, 324 pp. Dutch translations by August Hans den Boef and Mariella de Kuyper. ISBN 90-6213-845-4.
e. *Nieuwe avonturen van Sherlock Holmes* ['New adventures of Sherlock Holmes']. Edited by Martin Harry Greenberg and Carol-Lynn Rossel Waugh. Baarn, Netherlands: In den Tores, TOREN POCKETS, 1992, 324 pp., paperback. Dutch translations by August Hans den Boef and Mariella de Kuyper. 2nd printing. ISBN 90-6074-794-1.
f. *Las neuvas aventuras de Sherlock Holmes* ['The new adventures of Sherlock Holmes']. Edited by Martin Harry Greenberg and Carol Lynn Rössel. Madrid, Spain: Valdemar, LOS ARCHIVOS DE BAKER STREET #7, 1992, 290 pp., 25 cm. Spanish translations by Lorenzo Díaz. ISBN 84-7702-062-0.
g. *Nightmares & Dreamscapes.* New York: Viking, 1993, hardcover. 651-686. See A47.

B88. "**Popsy.**" *Masques II: All-New Stories of Horror and the Supernatural.* Edited by J. N. Williamson. Baltimore MD: Maclay & Associates, June 1987, 221 pp., $19.95, hardcover. 13-24. ISBN 0-940776-24-3. * LIMITED EDITION, 300 copies. * TRADE EDITION: 1987, hardcover. 13-24.

REPRINTS AND ADAPTATIONS:
b. *The Best of Masques.* Edited by J. N. Williamson. New York: Berkley Books, June 1988, 228 pp., $3.50, mass-market paperback. 209-220. ISBN 0-425-10693-4.
c. *Karl Edward Wagner Presents The Year's Best Horror Stories XVI.* Edited by

Karl Edward Wagner. New York: DAW Books, October 1988, 303 pp., $3.50, mass-market paperback. 15-30. ISBN 0-88677-300-8.

d. *Popsy und 25 Weitere Geschichten nach Mitternacht* ['Popsy and 25 more stories past/about midnight']. Edited by J. N. Williamson. Bergisch Gladbach: Bastei-Lübbe, TB13150, 1 June 1988, paperback (*kartoniert*). German translations by Ingrid Herrmann. Includes short fiction by King, James Herbert, Robert Bloch, Richard Christian Matheson, and others; this is probably adapted from one of Williamson's *Masque* anthologies. "Deutsche Erstausgabe" ISBN 3-404-13150-9.

e. As: "Popsy." [*Masques II*]. Milan, Italy: Garden Editoriale, HORROR STORY #1, July 1988. 11+. Italian translation by Alda Carrer. Reprinted April 1994.

f. *Nightmares & Dreamscapes*. New York: Viking, 1993, hardcover. 147-160. See A47.

g. *Popsy e altri racconti* ['Popsy and other stories'=*Masques II*]. Rome, Italy: Fanucci Editore, ECONOMICA TASCABILE #23, January 1995, paperback. 5+. Italian translation by Alda Carrer. ISBN 88-347-04380-X.

h. *L'ora della paura* ['The hour/time of fear'=*The Year's Best horror XVI*]. Rome, Italy: Newton & Compton, I NUOVI BEST-SELLER #32, January 1997. Italian translation by Gianni Pilo. ISBN 88-8183-572-X.

B89. "The Night Flier." *Prime Evil: New Stories by the Masters of Modern Horror*. Edited by Douglas E. Winter. West Kingston RI: Donald M. Grant, Publisher, April 1988, hardcover. 13-47. Limited to 1000 copies.

REPRINTS AND ADAPTATIONS:

b. In: *Prime Evil*. Edited by Douglas E. Winter. New York: NAL Books, New American Library, June 1988, 322 pp., $18.95, hardcover. 13-47. ISBN 0-453-00572-1.

c. In: *Prime Evil*. Edited by Douglas E. Winter. New York: Signet/New American Library, April 1989, paperback. 25-63.

d. In: *Prime Evil*. Edited by Douglas E. Winter. New York: New American Library, [n.d.]. 3-33. Science Fiction Book Club edition.

e. As: "Der Nachtflieger." *Horror vom Feinsten* ['Horror from the finest']. Edited by Douglas E. Winter. Munich, Germany: Wilhelm Heyne, JUMBO PAPERBACK 41/17, Fall 1989, paperback. German translation by Joachim Körber.

f. As: "El Aviador Nocturno" ['The night aviator']. *Escalofríos* ['Shivers']. Compiled by Douglas E. Winter. Buyenos Aires, Argentina: Grijalbo, 1989, 246 pp., 20 cm. Spanish translation by Eduardo G. Murillo. ISBN 950-28-0143-1.

g. In: *Ondskans väsen: Nya Skräckberättelser* ['Malevolent beings: New horror-stories']. Stockholm, Sweden: Legenda, 1989, 364 pp., 22 cm., hardcover. Swedish translations by Jimmy Hofsö. ISBN 91-582-1408-9.

h. As: "Il succhiatore volante" ['The flying sucker']. *In principio era il male* [*Prime Evil*]. Edited by Douglas E. Winter. Milan, Italy: Arnoldo Modadori,

MYSTBOOKS, October 1990. 21+. Italian translation by Maria Teresa Marenco. ISBN 88-04-34175-0. Reprinted: BESTSELLERS OSCAR #446,October 1994. ISBN 88-04-38873-).

i. In: *Kauhujen Kirja 2* ['Horror book 2']. Helsinki, Finland: Book Studio, 1992, 341 pp. Finnish translation by Jorma-Veikko Sappinen. ISBN 951-611-469-5.

j. In: *Nightmares & Dreamscapes*. New York: Viking, 1993, hardcover. 109-146. See A47.

k. As AUDIOCASSETTE: *Prime Evil: A Taste of Blood.* Selections from *Prime Evil.* Edited by Douglas E. Winter. New York: Simon and Schuster Audio Works, 1988, 1989. 2 cassettes; 150 minutes. Read by Ed Begley. Unabridged. Includes "The Night Flier" and two other stories. First of a series of audiocassettes based on Winter's collections.

SECONDARY SOURCES AND COMMENTS:
AudioVideo Review Digest, 1989 Cumulation. Edited by Susan L. Stetler. Detroit MI: Gale Research, 1990, hardcover. 619.
Audio Video Review Digest Vol. 2, No. 3 (December 1990): 155, 255.
Diehl, Digby. *Playboy* Vol. 36 (March 1989): 33.
Locus Vol. 22 (April 1989): 13.
Washington Post Book World Vol. 20 (11 February 1990): 11.

l. As FILM: *Stephen King's The Night Flier.* New Line Cinema/New Amsterdam Entertainment, 1997. Executive producer: David Keppes. Producers: Richard P. Rubenstein and Mitchell Galin. Co-producer: Alfredo Cuomo. Director: Mark Pava. Screenwriter: Mark Pavia and Jack O'Connell. Rated: R.
   CAST: Miguel Ferrer, Julie Entwisle, Dan Monahan, Michael H. Moss.
   SELECTED FILM REVIEWS AND ARTICLES:
   Wood, Gary, "Upcoming Horrors, Thinner & Others."
   Cinefantastique Vol. 21, No. 4 (February 1991): 31.

m. As VIDEOCASSETTE: *Stephen King's The Night Flier.* New Amsterdam Entertainment/HBO Home Video, 1997. 97 minutes. #91466. ISBN 0-7831-1257-2.

COMMENTS: The story represents King's continuing exploration of the vampire motif, this time as translated into a uniquely American, late-1980s' idiom. The story not only remains true to vampire lore, but expands it to include many levels of American society as well. Psychologically at least, King's vampire ("Dwight Renfield") shares much with the story's protagonist and by extension with the millions of Americans who satisfy their sublimated bloodlust by following the most recent horrific headlines in tabloid newspapers. The vampire literally consumes blood; the rest do so figuratively, but just as obsessively.

SELECTED ARTICLES, RESPONSES, AND REVIEWS:
Enfantino, Peter. "Quick Chills." *The Scream Factory* No. 3 (Summer 1989): 29-32. This review of *Prime Evil* argues that, except for King's story and Dennis Etchison's "The Blood Kiss," the anthology was lackluster and unoriginal. Its success was "100% due to the name Stephen King on the cover" (29).
Holman, Curt. "Horrors: New Books Fall Short of Mark." *Nashville Banner* [TN] (August 1988). As microfiche: *NewsBank: Literature* Vol. 15 (September 1988): Fiche 102, D5.
Schweitzer, Darrell. "Anthology of New Horror Tales: Interviews with Stephen King." *Philadelphia Inquirer* [PA] 24 July 1988. As microfiche: *NewsBank: Literature* Vol. 15 (September 1988): Fiche 102, D4.

B90. "The Reploids." *Night Visions 5*. Edited by Douglas E. Winter. Arlington Heights IL: Dark Harvest, May 1988, 274 pp., $75.00, hardcover. 35-58. Original stories by King, Dan Simmons, and George R. R. Martin. ISBN 0-913165-31-X. ISBN 0-913165-31-X. * LIMITED EDITION: illustrated by Ron Lindahm.* TRADE EDITION: 1988.

REPRINTS AND ADAPTATIONS:
b. As: "I reploidi." *Visioni della Notte* ['Visions of the night']. Edited by Douglas E. Winter. Florence [Firenze], Italy: Salani, July 1989. 15+. Italian translation by Ferdinando Giorgieri. ISBN 88-7782-128-0.
c. In: *Dark Visions: All Original Stories*. Edited by Douglas E. Winter. London, England: Gollancz, 1989, £3.99, 272 pp., paperback. ISBN 0-575-04711-9.
d. In: *The Skin Trade*. Edited by Douglas E. Winter. New York: Berkley Books, March 1990, 330 pp., $4.95, mass-market paperback. 11-29. ISBN 0-425-12003-1.
e. In: *Kauhujen Kirja* ['Horror book']. Helsinki, Finland: Book Studio, 1991, 320 pp. Finnish translation by Kari Salminen. ISBN 951-611-394-X.
f. As: "Dubbelgångarna" ['Doppelganger']. *Svarta Syner—Amerikanska Skräckvisioner* ['Black sins (?)—American Horror-visions']. [Stockholm, Sweden]: B. Wahlström, 1991, 308 pp., 23 cm., hardcover. Swedish translation by Jan Winter and Lillemor Idling. ISBN 91-32-31591-0.
g. In: *Nachtvisionen* ['Night-visions']. Munich, Germany: Wilhelm Heyne TB #8098, 19—,12.90 DM, paperback. ISBN 3-453-04218-2.

B91. "Sneakers." *Night Visions 5*. Edited by Douglas E. Winter. Arlington Heights, IL: Dark Harvest, May 1988, 274 pp., $75.00, hardcover. 35-58. Original stories by King, Dan Simmons, and George R. R. Martin. ISBN 0-913165-31-X. * LIMITED EDITION: illustrated by Ron Lindahm. * TRADE EDITION: 1988.

REPRINTS AND ADAPTATIONS:
b. As: "Scarpe da tennis" ['Shoes for tennis']. *Visioni della Notte* ['Visions of the night']. Edited by Douglas E. Winter. Florence [Firenze], Italy: Salani,

July 1989. 29+. Italian translation by Ferdinando Giorgieri. ISBN 88-7782-128-0

c. In: *Dark Visions: All Original Stories.* Edited by Douglas E. Winter. London, England: Gollancz, 1989, £3.99, 272 pp., paperback. ISBN 0-575-04711-9.

d. *The Skin Trade.* Edited by Douglas E. Winter. New York: Berkley Books, March 1990, 330 pp., $4.95, mass-market paperback. 31-57. ISBN 0-425-12003-1.

e. In: *Kauhujen Kirja* ['Horror book']. Helsinki, Finland: Book Studio, 1991, 320 pp. Finnish translation by Kari Salminen. ISBN 951-611-394-X.

f. As: "Dojan." *Svarta Syner—Amerikanska Skräckvisioner* ['Black sins (?)—American horror-visions']. [Stockholm, Sweden]: B. Wahlström, 1991, 308 pp., 23 cm., hardcover. Swedish translation by Jan Winter and Lillemor Idling. ISBN 91-32-31591-0.

g. *Nightmares & Dreamscapes.* New York: Viking, 1993, hardcover. 303-332. See A47.

h. In: *Nachtvisionen* ['Night-visions']. Munich, Germany: Wilhelm Heyne TB #8098, 19—, 12.90 DM, paperback. ISBN 3-453-04218-2.

B92. "Dedication." *Night Visions 5.* Edited by Douglas E. Winter. Arlington Heights, IL: Dark Harvest, May 1988, 274 pp., $75.00, hardcover. 35-58. Original stories by King, Dan Simmons, and George R. R. Martin. ISBN 0-913165-31-X. * LIMITED EDITION: illustrated by Ron Lindahm. * TRADE EDITION: 1988.

REPRINTS AND ADAPTATIONS:

b. As: "Dedica." *Visioni della Notte* ['Visions of the night']. Edited by Douglas E. Winter. Florence [Firenze], Italy: Salani, July 1989. 50+. Italian translation by Ferdinando Giorgieri. ISBN 88-7782-128-0

c. In: *Dark Visions: All Original Stories.* Edited by Douglas E. Winter. London, England: Gollancz, 1989, £3.99, 272 pp., paperback. ISBN 0-575-04711-9.

d. *The Skin Trade.* Edited by Douglas E. Winter. New York: Berkley Books, March 1990, 330 pp., $4.95, mass-market paperback. 59-110. ISBN 0-425-12003-1.

e. In: *Kauhujen Kirja* ['Horror book']. Helsinki, Finland: Book Studio, 1991, 320 pp. Finnish translation by Kari Salminen. ISBN 951-611-394-X.

f. As: "Hängiven Tillägnan" ['Devoted dedication']. *Svarta Syner—Amerikanska Skräckvisioner* ['Blaci sins (?)—American horror-visions']. [Stockholm, Sweden]: B. Wahlström, 1991, 308 pp., 23 cm., hardcover. Swedish translation by Jan Winter and Lillemor Idling. ISBN 91-32-31591-0.

g. *Nightmares & Dreamscapes.* New York: Viking, 1993, hardcover. 215-262. See A47.

h. In: *Nachtvisionen* ['Night-visions']. Munich, Germany: Wilhelm Heyne TB #8098, 19—, 12.90 DM, paperback. ISBN 3-453-04218-2.

B93. "**Rainy Season.**" *Midnight Graffiti* No. 3 (Spring 1989): 14-24.

REPRINTS AND ADAPTATIONS:
b. *Midnight Graffiti*. Edited by Jessica Horsting and James Van Hise. New York: Warner Books, October 1992, 365 pp., $5.99, 18 cm., mass-market paperback. 5-29. ISBN 0-446-36307-3.
c. *Nightmares & Dreamscapes*. New York: Viking, 1993, hardcover. 413-436. See A47.

B94. "**The Dark Half.**" *Fear: Fantasy and Science Fiction* [England] No. 10 (October 1989): 36-39. Excerpt from the novel [see A39], with Stephen King cover illustration.

B95. "**Home Delivery.**" *Book of the Dead*. Edited by John Skipp and Craig Spector. Willimantic CT: Mark V. Ziesing, 1989, hardcover. 33-58. Limited edition; trade edition. Anthology of zombie stories set in the fictional universe of George A. Romero's *Night of the Living Dead*.

REPRINTS AND ADAPTATIONS:
b. *Book of the Dead*. Edited by John Skipp and Craig Spector. New York: Bantam Books, July 1989, 390 pp., $4.50, mass-market paperback. 51-79. ISBN 0-553-27998-X.
c. Excerpted in: *Midnight Graffiti* No. 2 (Fall, 1988).
d. *Nightmares & Dreamscapes*. New York: Viking, 1993, hardcover. 381-412. See A47.
e. *Il libro dei morti viventi* ['Book of the living dead'=*Book of the Dead*]. Milan, Italy: Bompiani, GLI SQUALI #4, April 1995. 66+. Italian translation by Gianni Montanari. ISBN 88-452-2440-6.

SELECTED ARTICLES, RESPONSES, AND REVIEWS:
Cupp, Scott A. "Penny Dreadfuls." *Mystery Scene* No. 23 (October 1989): 75-76.
Graham, Mark. "Skipp & Spector's Book of the Dead: Gross, Shocking, Darkly Humorous." *The Blood Review: The Journal of Horror Criticism* Vol. 1, No. 1 (October 1989): 18.

B96. "**The Langoliers.**" *Four Past Midnight*. New York: Viking, 1990. 3-246. See A41 for further editions; see A50 for Spanish-language publication.

DEDICATION: "This is for Joe, Another White-Knuckle Flier."

REPRINTS AND ADAPTATIONS:
B. As: *Los Langoloides/The Langoliers*. New York: Signet/New American Library, May 1995, 317 pp., $4.99, paperback. Spanish-language edition of the short novel. ISBN 0-451-18656-7.
c. As: *Langoliers*. Munich, Germany: Wilhelm Heyne #01.10472, August

1998, 18,90 DM, paperback. German translation. ISBN 3-453-13053-7.

d. As AUDIOCASSETTE: *One Past Midnight*: The Langoliers." New York: Penguin/High Bridge Audio, November 1990. Read by Willem Dafoe.
SELECTED ARTICLES, RESPONSES, AND REVIEWS:
Bauers, Sandy. Wilson *Library Journal* Vol. 65, No. 8 (April 1991): 71-72.
Publishers Weekly Vol. 238, No. 6 (1 February 1991): 45.

e. As TELEPLAY: *Stephen King's The Langoliers.* ABC/Laurel Entertainment. Two-part miniseries beginning 25 February 1995. Executive producers: Richard P. Rubenstein and Mitchell Galin. Producer: David Kappes. Director: Tom Holland. Teleplay by Tom Holland.
CAST: Patricia Wettig, David Morse, Dean Stockwell, Bronson Ponchot, Mark Lindsay Chapman, Frankie Faison, Baxter Harris, Kimber Riddle, Christopher Collet, Kate Maberly.

f. As VIDEOCASSETTE: *Stephen King's The Langoliers.* Republic Entertainment, VHS #6190, 1995. 2 cassettes. Rated: PG "for violence and some sci-fi terror.' ISBN 0-7820-0465-2.

B97. "Secret Window, Secret Garden." *Four Past Midnight.* New York: Viking, 1990, pp. 253-399. See A41 for other editions.

DEDICATION: "This is for Chuck Verrill."

REPRINTS AND ADAPTATIONS:
b. As AUDIOCASSETTE: *Two Past Midnight: "Secret Window, Secret Garden."* St. Paul MN: Penguin/High Bridge Audio. Read by James Wood.
SELECTED REVIEWS:
Publishers Weekly Vol. 238, No. 25 (7 June 1991): 44.

c. As AUDIOCASSETTE: *Cuatro Despues de la Medianoche: Ventana Secreta, Jardin Secreto.* Los Angeles CA: Dove Audio, November 1995, $29.95. Spanish translation read by Eduardo Monsalvo. ISBN 0-787-10605-4.

B98. "The Library Policeman." *Four Past Midnight.* New York: Viking, 1990. 407-604. See A41 for further editions.

DEDICATION: "This is for the staff and patrons of the Pasadena Public Library."

REPRINTS AND ADAPTATIONS:
b. As AUDIOCASSETTE: *Three Past Midnight: "The Library Policeman."* St Paul MN: Penguin/High Bridge Audio, May 1991. Read by Ken Howard.
SELECTED REVIEWS:
Cheuse, Alan. *Forbes* Vol. 148, No. 12 (25 November 1991): F44.
Hiett, John. *Library Journal* Vol. 116, No. 12 (July 1991): 154.

B99. "The Sun Dog." *Four Past Midnight.* New York: Viking, 1990, 613-763. See A41.

DEDICATION: "This is in memory of John D. MacDonald. I miss you, old friend—and you were right about the tigers."

REPRINTS AND ADAPTATIONS:
b. As: *Perro de la Sol.* New York: Signet, December 2001 (scheduled), $5.99, paperback. Spanish translation. ISBN 0-451-18661-3.

c. As AUDIOCASSETTE: *Four Past Midnight: The Sun Dog.* New York: Penguin Audiobooks, September 1991, 6 cassettes, $23.95. Read by Tim Sample. ISBN 0-453-00757-0.
   SELECTED REVIEWS:
   Annichiario, Mark. *Library Journal* Vol. 116, No. 14 (1 September 1991): 250
d. As AUDIOCASSETTE: *Cuatro Despues de la Medianoche: El Perro Sun—Versión Completa.* Los Angeles: Dove Audio, November 1995, $22.95. Spanish translation read by Jaime Ortiz Pino. ISBN 0-787-10606-2.

COMMENTS: King notes that this story provides a narrative link between *The Dark Half* and *Needful Things,* his "final" Castle Rock novel.

B100. "The Moving Finger." *The Magazine of Fantasy & Science Fiction* Vol. 79, No. 6 #475 (December 1990): 8-43. A Special Stephen King issue. * LIMITED EDITION, printed with linen cover stock, signed by King.

b. *Nightmares & Dreamscapes.* New York: Viking, 1993, hardcover. 263-302. See A47 for further editions.

B101. "The Bear." *The Magazine of Fantasy & Science Fiction* Vol. 79, No. 6, #475 (December 1990): 61-88. An excerpt from *The Dark Tower III: The Waste Lands* [see A43]. A Special Stephen King issue. * LIMITED EDITION, printed with linen cover stock, signed by King.

B102. "You Know They Got a Hell of a Band." *Shock Rock.* Edited by Jeff Gelb. New York: Pocket Books, January 1992, 270 pp., $4.99, mass-market paperback. 1-45. ISBN 0-671-70150-9.

REPRINTS AND ADAPTATIONS:
b. *Kingpins.* Edited by Cynthia Manson and Charles Ardai. New York: Carroll & Graf, 1992, hardcover.
c. *Nightmares & Dreamscapes.* New York: Viking, 1993, hardcover. 330-380. See A47.

B103. "Chattery Teeth." *Cemetery Dance* Vol. 4, No. 4 (Fall 1992): 4-22.

REPRINTS AND ADAPTATIONS:
b. *Nightmares & Dreamscapes.* New York: Viking, 1993, hardcover. 179-214. See A47.

c. In: *the Best of Cemetery Dance.* Edited by Richard Chizmar. Abington MD: Cemetery Dance, 1998, hardcover in three states. Lettered state of 52 copies, signed, in traycase. Limited edition of 400 numbered copies, signed. Trade hardcover.

d. As FILM: *Quicksilver Highway.* National Studios, Inc./20th Century Fox, 1997. Executive producers: John McTiernan, Donna Dubrow, Sandra Rush. Co-executive producers: Tarquin Gotch, Bob Lemchen. Director and screenwriter: Mick Garris.
   CAST: Christopher Lloyd, Matt Frewer, Raphael Sbarge, Missy Crider, Veronica Cartwright.
   COMMENTS: The film adapts two short stories into a single framed narrative: King's "Chattery Teeth" and Clive Barker's "The Body Politic."

e. As VIDEOCASSETTE: *Quicksilver Highway.* 20th Century Fox, 1998, VHS #4808. Not rated.

B104. "My Pretty Pony." *Nightmares & Dreamscapes.* New York: Viking, 1993, hardcover. 437-466. See also A38 and A47.

B105. "The Ten O'Clock People." *Nightmares & Dreamscapes.* New York: Viking, 1993, hardcover. 501-558. See also A47.

B106. "The House on Maple Street." *Nightmares & Dreamscapes.* New York: Viking, 1993, hardcover. 593-632. See also A47.

B107. "Umney's Last Case." *Nightmares & Dreamscapes.* New York: Viking, 1993, hardcover. 687-741. See also A47, A51.

SELECTED ARTICLES, RESPONSES, AND REVIEWS:
"King Work to Be Offered Only on Internet Network." *Wall Street Journal* [NY] 17 September 1993: B3 (W), B6 (E).

B108. "The Beggar and the Diamond." *Nightmares & Dreamscapes.* New York: Viking, 1993, hardcover. 813-816. See also A47.

B109. "Jhonathan and the Witches." *First Words: Earliest Writing from Favorite Contemporary Authors.* Edited and compiled by Paul Mandelbaum. Chapel Hill NC: Algonquin Books of Chapel Hill, 1993, 502 pp., hardcover. 286-288. ISBN 0-945575-71-8.

COMMENTS: The first publication of the earliest extant story King wrote (at age nine), in an anthology featuring early works by authors such as Isaac Asimov and Joyce Carol Oates. The section includes a transcription of the story, annotations, facsimile of a manuscript page, and photographs of King as a child and as an adult.

B110. "Killer." *Famous Monsters of Filmland* (1994).

COMMENTS: The story was sent to Forrest J Ackerman in the mid-1960s, but not published until now.

B111. "Blind Willie." *Antaeus: Final Issue.* Ecco Press, 1993.

REPRINTS AND ADAPTATIONS.
b. *Six Stories.* Bangor ME: Philtrum Press, 1997, $80.00, trade paperback. See A62.
c. *Hearts in Atlantis.* New York: Scribners, 14 September 1999, 523 pp., $28.00, hardcover. 411-457. ISBN 0-684-85351-5. See A66 for further editions.

B112. "The Man in the Black Suit." *The New Yorker* (31 October 1994).

REPRINTS AND ADAPTATIONS
j. *Six Stories.* Bangor ME: Philtrum Press, 1997, $80.00, trade paperback. See A62.
k. *The Year's Best Fantasy and Horror, Eighth Annual Collection.* Edited by Ellen Datlow and Terri Winding. New York: St. Martin's, 1995, $27.95, hardcover. ISBN 0-312-13220-4.

COMMENTS: The story received the O.Henry fiction award for 1996.

B113. "Luckey Quarter." *USA Weekend* 30 June-2 July 1995: 4-7. Distributed in newspapers throughout the United States as a Sunday supplement.

REPRINTS AND ADAPTATIONS:
b. *Six Stories.* Bangor ME: Philtrum Press, 1997, $80.00, trade paperback. See A62.

B114. "Lunch at the Gotham Café." *Dark Love.* Edited by Nancy A. Collins, Edward E. Kramer, and Martin Harry Greenberg. New York: Penguin/Roc, November 1995, 414 pp., $22.95, hardcover. 17-54. Anthology of original horror fiction. ISBN 0-451-45472-3.

REPRINTS AND ADAPTATIONS:
b. *The Year's Best Fantasy and Horror, Ninth Annual Collection.* Edited by

Ellen Datlow and Terri Winding. New York: St. Martin's, 1996, $26.95, hardcover. ISBN 0-312-14449-0.
c. *The Year's Best Fantasy and Horror, Ninth Annual Collection.* Edited by Ellen Datlow and Terri Winding. New York: St. Martin's, 1996, $17.95, trade paperback. ISBN 0-312-14450-4.
d. *Six Stories.* Bangor ME: Philtrum Press, 1997, $80.00, trade paperback. See A62.
e. As: "Colazione al Gotham Café." *Dark Love.* Milan, Italy: Sperling & Kupfer, I LIBRI DELLA MEZZANOTTE [#1], October 1997. 1+. Italian translation by Tullio Dobner and others. ISBN 88-200-2507-8.
f. In: *Macabere liefde* ['Macabre love']. Amsterdam, Netherlands: Luitingh-Sijthoff, 1997, 397 pp. Dutch translation by Anton Steenhouwer. ISBN 90-245-2086-X.
g. In: *Malignos y macabros* ['Malignant and macabre']. Barcelona, Spain: Plaza & Janés, JET # 344/1, 1997, 535 pp., 18 cm., paperback. Spanish translation by Daniel Aguirre Oteiza. ISBN 84-01-47971-1.
h. As: AUDIOCASSETTE: *Blood and Smoke.* New York: Simon & Schuster Audio, 22 November 1999, $23./50, audiocassette and simultaneous CD-Rom. Read by Stephen King. ISBN 0671046160. Collection of three stories.

B115. "L.T.'s Theory of Pets." *Six Stories.* Bangor ME: Philtrum Press, 1997, $80.00, trade paperback. See A62.

REPRINTS AND ADAPTATIONS
b. *The Best of the Best.* Edited by Elaine Koster and Joseph Pittman. New York: Penguin/Signet, January 1998, $22.95, 35 pp., hardcover. 191-212. ISBN 0-451-19390-3.

COMMENTS: The anthology included short fiction by Lawrence Block, E. L. Doctorow, Stephen Frey, Erika Jong, Tabitha King, Ed McBain, Sharyn McCrumb, Joyce Carol Oates, and others, in addition to King's story. Special volume commemorating Signet's 50th anniversary

B116. "Autopsy Room 4." *Six Stories.* Bangor ME: Philtrum Press, 1997, $80.00, trade paperback. See A62.

REPRINTS AND ADAPTATIONS:
b. *Robert Bloch's Psychos.* Edited by Robert Bloch. Abingdon MD: CD Productions/Horror Writers Association, November 1997, 341 pp., $30.00, hardcover. 1-26.
c. As: "Autopsia 4." *Psychos.* Edited by Robert Bloch. Milan, Italy: I LIBRI DELLA MEZZANOTTE [#2], October 1998. 1+. Italian translation by Tullio Dobner and others. ISBN 88-200-2738-0.

B117. "General." *Screamplays*. Edited by Richard Chizmar and Martin H. Greenberg. New York: Ballantine/Del Rey, September 1997, 545 pp., $14.50, trade paperback. 1-40. Anthology of previously unpublished screenplays by Harlan Ellison, Richard Matheson, Joe R. Lansdale, Ed Gorman, Richard Laymon, and King. ISBN 0-345-39429-1.

B118. "Everything's Eventual." *Magazine of Fantasy & Science Fiction.* Vol. 93, Nos. 4/5, #556 (October/November 1997): 193-239. Novella.

B119. "That Feeling, You Can Only Say What It Is in French." *The New Yorker* (22-29 June, 1998). Short story.

B120. "Little Sisters of Eluria." *Legends: Short Novels by the Masters of Modern Fantasy* Edited by Robert Silverberg. New York: Tor, October 1998, 715 pp., hardcover. 5-58. LIMITED EDITION: 200 leather, boxed, signed copies, $250.00, ISBN 0-312-86863-4. TRADE EDITION: $29.95, ISBN 0-312-86787-5.

REPRINTS AND ADAPTATIONS.
b. London, England: HarperCollins, 1998, 591 pp., £17.99, hardcover. Cover art by Josh Kirby, Geoff Taylor. Distributed in the Netherlands by Nillson & Lamm.
c. London, England: Voyager, 1998, xiii+591 pp. ISBN 0002256665.
d. London, England: Voyager, 1999, xiv+352 pp., paperback. Special overseas edition.
e. In: *Legendy*. Poznañ, Poland: Dom Wydawniczy Rebis, 1999, 739 pp., 24 cm. Polish translation by Piotr W. Cholewa and others. ISBN 83-7120-822-7.
f. In: *Legends Volume I: Short Novels by the Masters of Modern Fantasy*. Edited by Robert Silverberg. New York: TOR, September 1999, 380 pp., $6.99, mass-market paperback. 1-122. ISBN 0-812-56663-7. Reprints stories by King, Silverberg, Card, and Feist from the original hardcover anthology.

g. As audiocassette: *Legends: Stories by the Masters of Fantasy* (Vol. I). Harper Audio, May 1999, $34.95, unabridged story. Read by Frank Muller. ISBN 0-694-52113-2.

COMMENTS: Other contributors to the hardcover anthology include Ursula K. Le Guin, Robert Jordan, Raymond E. Feist, Tad Williams, Terry Pratchett, Terry Goodking, Stephen King, Anne McCaffrey, and George R. R. Martin.

SELECTED ARTICLES AND REVIEWS:
1. Henrikksen, Karl. At: http://www.hoh.se/fantasyfinder/legends.html.
2. Orie, Marcel. 2 June 1999. At: http://www.simplex.nl/~vdputte /ncsf/hsf/hsf199901/recencies_gb.htm. Dutch-language review.

B121. "**Leaf-Peepers.**" *The New Yorker* (28 December 1998). Short-short.

B122. "**Low Men in Yellow Coats.**" *Hearts in Atlantis.* New York: Scribners, 14 September 1999, $28.00, hardcover. 11-254. ISBN 0-684-85351-5. See A66 for further printings.

B123. "**Hearts in Atlantis.**" *Hearts in Atlantis.* New York: Scribners, 14 September 1999, $28.00, hardcover. 255-407. ISBN 0-684-85351-5. See A66 for further printings.

B124. "**Why We're in Vietnam.**" *Hearts in Atlantis.* New York: Scribners, 14 September 1999, $28.00, hardcover. 461-505. ISBN 0-684-85351-5. See A66 for further printings; see also A67.

B125. "**Heavenly Shades of Night are Falling.**" *Hearts in Atlantis.* New York: Scribners, 14 September 1999, $28.00, hardcover. 509-522. ISBN 0-684-85351-5. See A66 for further printings.

B126. "**The Road Virus Heads North.**" *999: New Stories of Horror and Suspense.* Edited by Al Sarrantonio. Abington MD: Cemetery Dance/Hill House, 1999, hardcover. * LIMITED EDITION of 52 copies, signed and lettered, $350. * LIMITED EDITION of 500 copies, leather in presentation case, $125.00.

REPRINTS AND ADAPTATIONS:
b. New York: Avon, September 1999, trade hardcover.
c. As: "Il Virus della strada va a Nord." *999.* Edited by Al Sarrantonio. Milan, Italy: Sperling & Kupfer, I LIBRI DELLA MEZZANOTTE [#5], November 1999. 91+. Italian translation byTullio Dobner. ISBN 88-200-2904-9.
d. New York: Science Fiction Book Club/Doubleday Direct, 1999, $13.75. #033787. Book club edition.

B127. "**1408.**" As audio-story: *Blood and Smoke.* New York: Simon & Schuster Audio, 22 November 1999, $23.50, audiocassette and simultaneous CD-Rom. Read by Stephen King. ISBN 0-671-04616-0. (See E8).

B128. "**In the Deathroom.**" As audio-story. *Blood and Smoke.* New York: Simon & Schuster Audio, 22 November 1999, $23.50, audiocassette and simultaneous CD-Rom. Read by Stephen King. ISBN 0-671-04616-0. (See E8).

REPRINTS AND ADAPTATIONS:
b. *Secret Windows: Essays and Fiction on the Craft of Writing.* Bookspan/BOMC, 2000, $18.75, 433 pp., hardcover. 403-432. A70

B129. "Jumper." *Secret Windows: Essays and Fiction on the Craft of Writing.* Bookspan/BOMC, 2000, $18.75, 433 pp., hardcover. A70.

B130. "Rush Call." *Secret Windows: Essays and Fiction on the Craft of Writing.* Bookspan/BOMC, 2000, $18.75, 433 pp., hardcover. A70.

B131. "All That You Love Will Be Carried Away." *The New Yorker* (29 January 2001).

SELECTED ARTICLES AND REVIEWS:
Quigley, Kevin. Review. *Charnelhouse* [on-line Stephen King newssite]. 24 January 20001. "This is the type of tale that proves that King is the best writer of our time."

Section C.
Short Non-Fiction

King's nonfiction ranges from formal criticism to fan appreciation and political statements, from serious cultural appraisals to semicomic statements on a variety of subjects. His voice is unique, whether speaking through criticism or narrative—everything he writes is tinged with a sense of the novelist, even when he defines current trends in culture, society, politics, baseball, or rock and roll music.

The following list identifies King's published utterances in many circumstances: introductions and afterwords to his own works, introductions to works by other writers, and speculations on the nature of American society. Yet each illuminates his own fiction through comments made in other contexts.

For a brief listing of secondary book-length studies including discussions of King's non-fiction, see the introduction to section B.

C1. "King's Garbage Truck," by "Steve King." *The Maine Campus* 20 February 1969: 9.

COMMENTS: The first issue of King's weekly column for the student publication at the University of Maine, Orono. The columns are uneven but fascinating, giving at times unusual insight into the young King. For detailed discussions of each column, see Collings's *The Stephen King Phenomenon* and the expanded second edition, *Scaring Us To Death*.

C2. "King's Garbage Truck," by "Steve King." *The Maine Campus* (27 February 1969): 7.

C3. "King's Garbage Truck," by "Steve King." *The Maine Campus* (6 March 1969): 9.

C4. "King's Garbage Truck," by "Steve King." *The Maine Campus* (13 March 1969): 7.

C5. "King's Garbage Truck," by "Steve King." *The Maine Campus* (20 March 1969): 7.

C6. "King's Garbage Truck," by "Steve King." *The Maine Campus* (27 March 1969): 7.

C7. "King's Garbage Truck," by "Steve King." *The Maine Campus* (10 April 1969): 6.

C8. "King's Garbage Truck," by "Steve King." *The Maine Campus* (17 April 1969): 7, 13.

C9. "King's Garbage Truck," by "Steve King." *The Maine Campus* (24 April 1969): 11.

C10. "King's Garbage Truck," by "Steve King." *The Maine Campus* (1 May 1969): 7.

C11. "King's Garbage Truck," by "Steve King." *The Maine Campus* (8 May 1969): 6.

C12. "King's Garbage Truck," by "Steve King." *The Maine Campus* (15 May 1969): 7.

C13. "King's Garbage Truck," by "Steve King." *The Maine Campus* (22 May 1969): 7.

C14. **"King's Garbage Truck,"** by **"Steve King."** *The Maine Campus* (12 June 1969): 4.

C15. **"King's Garbage Truck,"** by **"Steve King."** *The Maine Campus* (20 June 1969): 6.

C16. **"King's Garbage Truck,"** by **"Steve King."** *The Maine Campus* (27 June 1969): 5, 6.

C17. **"King's Garbage Truck,"** by **"Steve King."** *The Maine Campus* (4 July 1979): 4.

C18. **"King's Garbage Truck,"** by **"Steve King."** *The Maine Campus* (11 July 1969): 5.

C19. **"King's Garbage Truck,"** by **"Steve King."** *The Maine Campus* (18 July 1969): 7.

C20. **"King's Garbage Truck,"** by **"Steve King."** *The Maine Campus* (27 July 1969): 5, 6.

C21. **"King's Garbage Truck,"** by **"Steve King."** *The Maine Campus* (1 August 1969): 4, 7.

C22. **"King's Garbage Truck,"** by **"Steve King."** *The Maine Campus* (8 August 1969): 4.

C23. **"King's Garbage Truck,"** by **"Steve King."** *The Maine Campus* (18 September 1969): 7.

C24. **"King's Garbage Truck,"** by **"Steve King."** *The Maine Campus* (25 September 1969): 5.

C25. **"King's Garbage Truck,"** by **"Steve King."** *The Maine Campus* (3 October 1969): 5.

C26. **"King's Garbage Truck,"** by **"Steve King."** *The Maine Campus* (9 October 1969): 5.

C27. **"King's Garbage Truck,"** by **"Steve King."** *The Maine Campus* (16 October 1969): 4, 6.

C28. **"King's Garbage Truck,"** by **"Steve King."** *The Maine Campus* (23 October 1969): 6.

C29. "King's Garbage Truck," by "Steve King." *The Maine Campus* (30 October 1969): 5.

C30. "King's Garbage Truck," by "Steve King." *The Maine Campus* (6 November 1969): 5.

C31. "King's Garbage Truck," by "Steve King." *The Maine Campus* (13 November 1969): 5.

C32. "King's Garbage Truck," by "Steve King." *The Maine Campus* (4 December 1969): 5.

C33. "King's Garbage Truck," by "Steve King." *The Maine Campus* (11 December 1969): 5.

C34. "King's Garbage Truck," by "Steve King." *The Maine Campus* (18 December 1969): 6.

C35. "King's Garbage Truck," by "Steve King." *The Maine Campus* (8 January 1970): 5.

C36. "King's Garbage Truck," by "Steve King." *The Maine Campus* (15 January 1970): 5.

C37. "King's Garbage Truck," by "Steve King." *The Maine Campus* (5 February 1970): 10.

C38. "King's Garbage Truck," by "Steve King." *The Maine Campus* (12 February 1970): 5.

C39. "King's Garbage Truck," by "Steve King." *The Maine Campus* (19 February 1970): 8.

C40. "King's Garbage Truck," by "Steve King." *The Maine Campus* (26 February 1970): 5.

C41. "King's Garbage Truck," by "Steve King." *The Maine Campus* (19 March 1970): 5.

C42. "King's Garbage Truck," by "Steve King." *The Maine Campus* (26 March 1970): 5.

C43. "King's Garbage Truck," by "Steve King." *The Maine Campus* (4 April 1970): 5.

C44. "King's Garbage Truck," by "Steve King." *The Maine Campus* (16 April 1970): 5.

C45. "King's Garbage Truck," by "Steve King." *The Maine Campus* (30 April 1970): 5.

C46. "King's Garbage Truck," by "Steve King." *The Maine Campus* (7 May 1970): 5.

C47. "A Possible Fairy Tale." *The Paper* (8 May 1970): 5. Account of a fictional anti-war demonstration by American students against the continuing war in Cambodia, beginning with a UMO (University of Maine, Orono) student strike on May 8 and ending with Nixon withdrawing US troops from Cambodia on May 18.

C48. "King's Garbage Truck," by "Steve King." *The Maine Campus* (21 May 1970): 5.

REPRINTS AND ADAPTATIONS:
b. *Maine* [Alumni Magazine, University of Maine, Orono] (1989).

C49. "The Horror Market Writer and the Ten Bears." *Writer's Digest* (November, 1973): 10-13.

REPRINTS AND ADAPTATIONS:
b. As: "Horror Stories and the Ten Bears." *Fiction Writers Market*. Edited by John Brady and Jean M. Fredette. Cininnati OH: Writer's Digest books, 1981 622 pp., $15.95. 273-277. ISBN 0-89879-048-4.
c. As: "The Horror Writer and the Ten Bears: Foreword." *Kingdom of Fear: The World of Stephen King*. Edited by Tim Underwood and Chuck Miller. San Francisco CA, Columbia PA: Underwood-Miller, 1986, hardcover. 11-19.
d. *Secret Windows: Essays and Fiction on the Craft of Writing*. Bookspan/BOMC, 2000, $18.75, 433 pp., hardcover. 11-22. A70.

COMMENTS: A discussion of the ten fears that readers respond most readily to. The 1986 reprint is presented essentially unchanged from the 1973 version, resulting in a number of out-of-date or by then inaccurate items.

C50. "Writing a First Novel." *The Writer* Vol. 88, No. 6 (June 1975): 25-27. The fourth and final segment in a series by new novelists.

REPRINTS AND ADAPTATIONS:
b. Excerpted in: *The Writer* Vol. 100, No. 4 (April 1987): 15.

C51. "Not Guilty." *The New York Times Book Review* (24 October 1976): 55.

COMMENTS: In this response to criticism, King comments on *'Salem's Lot* as an "accessible" novel, written with the author's intention of doing the best job he could. King compares his advance for the book with the $15,000 received by David Madden for *Bijou*; although not assertively great literature, *'Salem's Lot*, says King, justly earned what it received.

C52. [Title unknown]. *Coda: Poets and Writers Newsletter* Vol. 4, No. 2 (November/ December 1976): 20. Discussion of the impact movies have on reading audiences.

C53. "The Fright Report." *Oui* (January 1978): 76-78, 107-108. Critical and autobiographical essay discussing horror films from the 1930s through the 1970s.

REPRINTS AND ADAPTATIONS:
b. As: "An Annoying Autobiographical Pause, Part 4." *Stephen King's Danse Macabre*. New York: Everest House, 1981. 103-110. See A11.

C54. "The Doll Who Ate His Mother." *Whispers* No. 11/12 (October 1978): 63. Review of Ramsey Campbell as horror writer.

REPRINTS AND ADAPTATIONS:
b. In: *Stephen King's Danse Macabre*. New York: Everest House, 1981. See A11.

C55. "Foreword." *Night Shift*. Garden City NY: Doubleday & Co., 1978. xi-xxii. See A6, A70.

REPRINTS AND ADAPTATIONS:
b. Excerpted as: "Warum Lesen Wir Phantastische Geschichten?" ['Why do we read fantasy stories']. *Phantastische Literatur* 83. Edited by Michael Görden. Bergisch Gladbach: Bastei-Lübbe, TB72022, 1983, paperback. German translation by Michael Görden.
c. In: *Secret Windows: Essays and Fiction on the Craft of Writing*. Bookspan/BOMC, 2000. See A70.

COMMENTS: Early attempt at defining the nature of horror, beginning with the memorable lines, "Let's talk you and I. Let's talk about fear." King discusses his belief in horror fiction as therapeutic, adaptive, and spellbinding, as well as the literary and cultural influences on his early works.

C56. "How to Scare a Woman to Death." *Murderess Ink: The Better Half of the Mystery*. Edited by Dilys Winn. New York: Bell, 1979, hardcover. 173-175.

Simultaneously in trade paperback. Tips on "throwing a jolt into what some of us still refer to as the fairer sex" (p. 173).

C57. "Introduction." *Frankenstein, Dracula, Dr. Jekyll and Mr. Hyde*, by Mary Shelley, Bram Stoker, and Robert Louis Stevenson. New York: Signet/New American Library, December 1978, $3.95, mass-market paperback. v-viii. ISBN 0-451-51781-4. Extensive discussion of strengths and weaknesses in three classic horror tales.

REPRINTS AND ADAPTATIONS:
b. *Frankenstein; Dracula; Dr. Jekyll and Mr. Hyde.* London, England: Penguin, November 1988, 660 pp., £3.99, paperback. ISBN 0-14-011666-4. 1st U.K. edition.
c. As: "Inleidung" ['Introduction"]. *Die Grote Horror-Omnibus* ['The big horror omnibus']. Amsterdam: Loeb, 1983, paperback (?). 5-14. Dutch translation.
d. *Three Classics of Horror: Frankenstein, Dracula, Dr. Jekyll and Mr. Hyde.* London, England: Penguin, December 1994, 664 pp., £5.99, trade paperback. v+. ISBN 0-14-023994-4.

SELECTED ARTICLES, RESPONSES, AND REVIEWS:
Zagorski, Edward J. *The Novels of Stephen King.* New York: New American Library, 1981, paperback.

C58. "Introduction" to "The Cat from Hell." *Top Horror.* Edited by Josh Pachter. Munich, Germany: Wilhelm Heyne, DIE UNHEIMLICHE BÜCHER #20, 1986, paperback. German translation by Rolf Jurkeit. Short introduction commissioned specifically for this volume—has appeared only in the German translation. See B30.

C59. "The Writing Life: An Interview with Myself." *Writer's Digest* (January 1979): 16-17. King answers questions about writing in general and horror writing in particular.

C60. "The Horrors of '79." *Rolling Stone* (27 December 1979-10 January 1980): 17-21. Discussion of the strongest films of 1979, including *Breaking Away, Rocky II, The Deer Hunter, Apocalypse Now, Phantasm, Nightwing, Prophecy, Alien, Lord of the Rings, Watership Down,* and *Dawn of the Dead* ("the finest horror film of the year, perhaps of the decade").

C61. "A Pilgrim's Progress." *American Bookseller* (January 1980).

C62. "On Becoming a Brand Name." *Adelina* (February 1980): 40-45, 82-83. King's career as novelist to 1980, with intentional inaccuracies to protect the "Bachman" pseudonym.

REPRINTS AND ADAPTATIONS:
b. As: "Foreword—On Becoming a Brand Name." *Fear Itself: The Horror Fiction of Stephen King*. Edited by Tim Underwood and Chuck Miller. San Francisco CA: Underwood-Miller, 1982. 15-44.
c. *Secret Windows: Essays and Fiction on the Craft of Writing*. Bookspan/BOMC, 2000, $18.75, 433 pp., hardcover. 39-70. A70.

C63. "Books: The Sixties Zone." *Adelina* (June 1980): 12. Review of Leslie Waller's *The Brave and the Free*, with mention of Robert Marasco's *Burnt Offerings*; the review defends "another BIG NOVEL OF THE SIXTIES," and critiques reviewers who miss the power of long novels.

C64. "Books: Critic Critique." *Adelina* (July 1980): 9. Continuation of the Waller review [see C63] and critique of contemporary reviewers who insist on separating popular literature from "great literature," an approach King views as dangerous.

C65. "Books: Two for Terror." *Adelina* (August 1980): 12. Review of Thomas H. Block's *Mayday* and Michael McDowell's *The Amulet*, one of "the best paperback original horror fiction[s] to be found over the last four or five years."

C66. "Imagery and the Third Eye." *The Writer* (October 1980): 11-14, 44.

REPRINTS AND ADAPTATIONS:
b. *Maine Alumnus* (December 1981).
c. *The Writer's Handbook*. Edited by Sylvia Burack. Boston: The Writer Inc., 1984, hardcover.
d. In: *Stephen King's Danse Macabre*. New York: Everest House, 1981. See A11.

C67. "Some Notes on Tales of the Vampyre." *Opera New England of Northern Maine* (Fall 1980): [n.p.]. Two-page program notes to a production of *Tales of the Vampyre*; text by Wohlbrück, music by Marschner.

C68. "Introduction." *The Shapes of Midnight: Horror by Joseph Payne Brennan*, by Joseph Payne Brennan. New York: Berkley Books, October 1980, 176 pp, mass-market paperback. ix-xvi. ISBN 0-435-04567-6.

C69. "Books: Love Those Long Novels." *Adelina* (November 1980): 12. Discussion of negative reactions to long novels, including *The Dead Zone* and *The Stand*. Contemporary critics tend to judge such novels negatively on their length, not their merit.

C70. **"Why We Crave Horror Movies."** *Playboy* (January 1981): 150-154, 237-246. Excerpts from *Danse Macabre*, 131-175. See A11.

REPRINTS AND ADAPTATIONS:
b. *The St. Martin's Guide to Student Writing.* Edited by Rise B. Axelrod and Charles R. Cooper. Short 2nd ed. New York: St. Martin's Press, 1988, paperback. 294-96.
c. *Literature: The Human Experience, Shorter Fifth Edition with Essays.* Edited by Richard Abcarian and Marvin Klotz. New York: St. Martin's Press, November 1991, paperback.

C71. **"Scare Movies."** *Cosmopolitan* (April 1981).

C72. **"Guilty Pleasures."** *Film Comment* (May-June 1981).

C73. **"Notes on Horror."** *Quest* (June 1981): 28-31, 87. Excerpts from *Danse Macabre* [see A11], concluding that horror is not a dance of death at all, but a "dance of dreams that arouses the child inside" (p. 87).

C74. **"When Is TV Too Scary for Children?"** *TV Guide* (13-19 June 1981).

C75. **[Untitled**—opening line: "I don't have many dreams"]. *Dreamworks* (Summer 1981). Repeating dream/nightmare described by King.

C76. **"Danse Macabre."** *Book Digest* (September 1981). 24-page extract from *Danse Macabre*. See A11.

C77. **"The Healthy Power of a Good Scream."** *Self* (September 1981). Excerpt from *Danse Macabre*. See A11.

C78. **"The Cannibal and the Cop."** *Washington Post Book World* 1 November 1981: 1-3.

REPRINTS AND ADAPTATIONS:
b. *Shadowings.* Edited by Douglas E. Winter. Mercer Island WA: Starmont House, 1983. 27-29.

COMMENTS: Review of Thomas Harris's *Red Dragon*, "probably the best popular novel to be published in America since *The Godfather*." King criticizes critics ignoring the novel merely because of its huge sales potentials.

C79. **"The Sorry State of TV Shows: You Gotta Put on the Gruesome Mask and Go Booga-Booga."** *TV Guide* (5-11 December 1981): 65-68. Excerpts from *Danse Macabre*, "The Glass Teat" (especially 216-238). See A11.

C80. "Forenote." *Danse Macabre.* New York: Everest House, 1981. 9-12. See A11. Outlines the genesis of *Danse Macabre*, from King's teaching a course in supernatural literature at the University of Maine, Orono, through discussions with Bill Thompson about publishing the study. Autobiographical emphasis.

C81. "Afterword." *Danse Macabre.* New York: Everest House, 1981. 381-382. See A11.

C82. "Foreword." *Tales from the Nightside.* Edited by Charles L. Grant. Sauk City, WI: Arkham House, 1981, hardcover. vii-xii. An appreciation of Grant as writer: "The man is a pro."

REPRINTS AND ADAPTATIONS:
b. London, England: Futura, April 1988, 228 pp., £2.95, hardcover. vii+. ISBN 0-7088-3713-1.

C83. "Introduction." *The Arbor House Treasury of Horror and the Supernatural.* Compiled by Bill Pronzini, Barry Malzberg, and Martin H. Greenberg. New York: Arbor House, 1981, hardcover and trade paperback. 11-19.

REPRINTS AND ADAPTATIONS:
b. Reprinted as: *Tales of Horror and the Supernatural.* New York: A&W, Galahad Books, 1985, 597 pp., $8.98, hardcover. 11-19. Anthology, slightly abridged. ISBN 0-88365-699-X.
c. "Einführung." *Unheimliches.* Edited by Bill Pronzini, Barry N. Malzberg, and Martin H. Greenberg. Munich, Germany: Wilhelm Heyne, JUBILÄUMSBAND #9, 1985. German translation by Sonja Hauser and Bernd Lenz.

COMMENTS: Discussion of horror as not only an outward escape "into a kind of never-never-land," but an escape "inward, toward the very center of our perceived humanity."

C84. "Introduction." *When Michael Calls*, by John Farris. New York: Pocket Books, 1981, paperback. i-iv.

C85. "Between Rock and a Hard Place." *Playboy* (January 1982): 120-122, 238-242.

C86. "Visit with an Endangered Species." *Playboy* (January 1982): 122, 244. Tribute to hard-rock Disc jockey "Mighty John" Marshall of station WAZC, Bangor, Maine.

C87. "The Ludlum Attraction." *Washington Post Book World* 7 March 1982: 1, 10.

Michael R. Collings

COMMENTS: Review of Ludlum's *The Parsifal Mosaic* in the form of a letter from Reed Smalley (of Smalley, Hally, and Polly) to Theodore Smoot (of Smoot, Hoot, Doot, and Foot); the review analyzes Ludlum's audience and techniques, as well as the book's ability to "keep you occupied without engaging you or troubling you or removing your mind for more than one second after the bookmark has been placed and the book closed" (10).

C88. "**Mentors.**" *Rolling Stone College Papers* 15 April 1982. Tribute to Burton Hatlen, one of King's college professors at the University of Maine, Orono, and among his earliest and most astute commentators and interpreters.

C89. "**Favorite Films.**" *Washington Post* 24 June 1982.

C90. "**Digging The Boogens.**" *Twilight Zone Magazine* (July 1982): 9-10.

COMMENTS: Extensive essay-review of James L. Conway's film, *The Boogens*. The piece develops more as a definition of horror as genre than as analysis or criticism of a specific film.

C91. "**On *The Shining* and Other Perpetrations.**" *Whispers* No. 17/18 (August 1982): 11-16.

COMMENTS: Discussion of the genesis of *The Shining* in its original conception as based on five-act Shakespearean tragedy. Many points discussed are demonstrated in "Before the Play" [see B69].

C92. "**Peter Straub: An Informal Appreciation.**" *World Fantasy Convention '82*. Edited by Kennedy Poyser. New Haven CT: The Eighth World Fantasy Convention, 1982, paperback.

C93. "**Horrors!**" *TV Guide* (30 October-5 November 1982): 54-58. Annotated list of the ten best videocassettes for Halloween, 1982: *Night of the Living Dead, An American Werewolf in London, Invasion of the Body Snatchers, The Thing, The Shining, Rabid, Wolfen, Dead of Night, The Fog,* and *The Toolbox Murders*.

C94. "***The Evil Dead*: Why You Haven't Seen It Yet...And Why You Ought To.**" *Twilight Zone Magazine* 2 (November 1982): 20-22.

COMMENTS: Assesses Steve Raini's film as the "most ferociously original horror film of 1982"; it has the "simple stupid power of a good campfire story," yet is a "black rainbow" of horror that defines the genre.

C95. **[Title unknown].** *Playboy Guide: Electronic Entertainment* (Fall/Winter 1982). King discusses films that should be preserved on videocassette.

C96. "Afterword." *Different Seasons.* New York: G. P. Putnam's Sons, 1982. 519-527. See A16.

C97. "Afterword." *Firestarter.* New York: Signet/New American Library, 1982, paperback. 402-403. Unique to this edition. See A9.

C98. "Foreword." *Stalking the Nightmare*, by Harlan Ellison. Huntington Woods MI: Phantasia Press, 1982, hardcover. Limited edition. Reprinted: New York, Berkley, 1984. Paperback.

COMMENTS: King rates Ellison as a "ferociously talented writer, ferociously in love with the job of writing stories and essays, ferociously dedicated to the craft of it as well as its art."

C99. "Introduction" to Ramsey Campbell's "The Companion." *The Arbor House Celebrity Book of Horror Stories.* Edited by Charles G. Waugh and Martin H. Greenberg. New York: Arbor House, 1982, hardcover. 131-132.

COMMENTS: King identifies stories that influenced him as a writer: H. P. Lovecraft's "Pickman's Model," "The Rats in the Walls," and "The Colour Out of Space"; Robert Bloch's "Sweets to the Sweet"; and Ramsey Campbell's "The Companion."

C100. "My High School Horrors." *Sourcebook: The Magazine for Seniors* (1982): 30-33.

REPRINTS AND ADAPTATIONS:
b. As: "High School Horrors." *Castle Rock: The Stephen King Newsletter* Vol. 2, No. 2 (February 1986): 8.

COMMENTS: Semi-comic treatment of classroom "horrors" based on King's experience as a high-school teacher. The list includes "the thing that wouldn't shut up," "the classroom of the living dead," and "the smell from hell."

C101. "Introduction: The Importance of Being Forry." *Mr. Monster's Movie Gold*, by Forrest J Ackerman. Virginia Beach, Norfolk VA: Donning, 1982, trade paperback. 8-12.

COMMENTS: Autobiographical account of King discovering Ackerman's Famous Monsters of Filmland. Ackerman "stood up for a generation of kids who understood that if [horror] was junk, it was magic junk" (12).

C102. "Special Make-Up Effects and the Writer." *Grande Illusions: A Learn-by-Example Guide to the Art and Technique of Special Make-Up Effects*, by Tom Savini. Pittsburgh PA: Imagine Inc., January 1983, trade paperback. 6-7. Appreciation of Savini's work and reminiscences of filming *Creepshow*

REPRINTS AND ADAPTATIONS:
b. *Bizarro*, by Tom Savini. New York: Crown/Harmony, 1983, 135 pp., paperback. ISBN 0-517-55319-8.

C103. "Don't Be Cruel." *TV Guide* (30 April-6 May 1983): A-1.

COMMENTS: Letter commenting favorably on Dave Marsh's article on Elvis Presley (*TV Guide*, 9 April 1983), and clarifying King's interest in and responses to rock 'n' roll.

C104. "Dear Walden People." *Waldenbooks Book Notes* (August 1983).

REPRINTS AND ADAPTATIONS:
b. *Bare Bones: Conversations on Terror With Stephen King*. Edited by Tim Underwood and Chuck Miller. San Francisco, CA: Underwood-Miller, 1988; New York: McGraw-Hill, 1988. 123-124. See F20.
c. *The Stephen King Companion*, by George Beahm. Kansas City MO: Andrews and McMeel, 1989. 207-208. See F24.
d. As: *King over Stephen King: de meester van de horror aan het woord*. Utrecht, Belgium, Netherlands: Luitingh-Sijthoff, 1990, 278 pp. Dutch translation by Annette Zeelenberg. ISBN 90-245-1800-8.
e. As: *Paljut luut* ['bare bones']. Helsinki, Finland: Mabuse, 1991, 256 pp., 21 cm. Finnish translation by Inkeri Lahtinen. ISBN 952-9502-03-6.

C105. "Horrors!" *Games* (October 1983). Crossword puzzle; clues by King, grid by Mike Shenk.

REPRINTS AND ADAPTATIONS:
b. *Castle Rock: The Stephen King Newsletter* Vol 1, No. 5 (May 1985): 6.

C106. "A Profile of Robert Bloch." *World Fantasy Convention 1983*. Edited by Robert Weinberg. Oak Forest IL: Weird Tales Ltd., 1983, paperback. 11-14.

C107. "Ross Thomas Stirs the Pot." *Washington Post Book World* 16 October 1983: 1-2. Review of Thomas's *Missionary Stew*.

C108. "Berni Wrightson: An Appreciation." *Cycle of the Werewolf*. Westland MI: Land of Enchantment, 1983, portfolio. Signed and limited edition of 300 copies.

C109. "Black Magic and Music: A Novelist's Perspective on Bangor." Bangor ME: Bangor Historical Society, 1983, paperback.

REPRINTS AND ADAPTATIONS:
b. Later reprint without advertisements.

C110. "Introduction." *Tales by Moonlight*. Edited by Jessica Amanda Salmonson. Chicago: Robert T. Garcia, 1983, hardcover.

REPRINTS AND ADAPTATIONS:
b. New York: Tor, 1985, 286 pp., $2.95, mass-market paperback. xii-xviii. ISBN 0-812-52552-3.

COMMENTS: King gives an overview of the fiction of the 1980s, decrying the dangerous position of the short story and poetry (the latter now the "sole property of college eggheads and groaning, discontented high school students" (xii), the disappearance of the pulps and slicks, and the current threat to the novel from "junky *romans á clef*" and nonfiction books on Rubik's cubes and faddish dressing. Popular literature is "withdrawing in a long and melancholy roar," but *Tales by Moonlight* and other anthologies are valuable markets for short fiction. Horror fiction comes from the jungle; parents don't want children in that jungle, and "serious critics acknowledge that jungle only reluctantly, but it is there, in all its ripe-rotten mystery" (xviii).

C111. "Introduction." *Frankenstein; or, The Modern Prometheus*, by Mary Shelley, illustrated by Berni Wrightson. New York: Dodd, Mead, 1983, Limited edition hardcover and trade paperback. 6-9.

REPRINTS AND ADAPTATIONS:
b. As: "A Marvel Illustrated Novel." Marvel Comics Group, 1983.
c. In: *Frankenstein.* Underwood-Miller, 1994. Limited edition of 26 lettered copies signed by Wrightson; limited edition of 300 copies signed by Wrightson; trade hardcover; trade paperback.

C112. "Last Waltz: Horror and Morality, Horror and Magic." *1983/1984 Fiction Writer's Market*. Edited by Jean M. Fredette. Cincinnati OH: Writer's Digest, 1983, hardcover. 172-195.

C113. "Stephen King." *A Gift From Maine, by Maine's Foremost Artists and Writers and James Plummer's Sixth Grade Class.* Portland ME: Gannet, 1983, trade paperback. 91. Autobiographical sketch mentioning King's education and family, and the fact that he has written novels and short stories.

C114. "Stephen King's 10 Favorite Horror Books or Short Stories." *The Book of Lists #3*. Compiled by Amy Wallace, David Wallechinsky, and Irving Wallace. New York: William Morrow, 1983, hardcover. 237-238.

COMMENTS: Includes Peter Straub's *Ghost Story*, Bram Stoker's *Dracula*, Shirley Jackson's *The Haunting of Hill House*, Robert Louis Stevenson's *Dr. Jekyll and Mr. Hyde*, Robert Marasco's *Burnt Offerings*, M. R. James's "Casting the Runes," Lord Dunsany's "Two Bottles of Relish," Arthur Machen's "The Great God Pan," H. P. Lovecraft's "The Colour Out of Space," and Marion Crawford's "The Upper Berth."

C115. "Letter." *Fantasy Review* (January 1984): 45. Brief discussion of anthologies and reprint publishing.

C116. "The Irish King." *New York Daily News* 16 March 1984. Discussion of King's Irish family roots.

C117. "1984: A Bad Year If You Fear Friday the 13th." *New York Times* 12 April 1984. Overview of lore surrounding Friday the 13th and fear of the number thirteen—*triskadekaphobia*.

REPRINTS AND ADAPTATIONS:
b. As: "The Triple Whammy." *Castle Rock: The Stephen King Newsletter* Vol. 3, No. 11 (November 1987): 1, 8.

C118. "Dr. Seuss and the Two Faces of Fantasy." *Fantasy Review* No. 68 (June 1984): 10-12.

COMMENTS: Guest-of-Honor Address to the International Conference on the Fantastic in the Arts, 24 March 1984, Boca Raton FL, featuring King's reminiscences on fantasy. King discusses sources and forms of horror, childhood influences, relationships between children's fiction and his adult-oriented tales.

C119. "Why I Am for Gary Hart." *The New Republic* (4 June 1984): 14-16. Comments on King's support for Hart's 1984 Presidential campaign.

C120. "My First Car." *Gentleman's Quarterly* (July 1984): 147.

COMMENTS: King describes his 1964 Ford Galaxie, with mention of *Cujo* and photograph of King with his second car, a 1956 Plymouth that resembles Christine.

C121. [Title unknown]. *Twilight Zone Magazine* Vol. 4 (August 1984). King discusses filming of *Firestarter*.

C122. [Title unknown]. *Money!* (September 1984). Discusses word processors.

C123. "Childress Debut with 'World' Shows Uncanny Style and Eye for Detail." *Atlanta Journal-Constitution* [GA] 21 October 1984 [or 5 November 1984]. Reviews *A World Made of Fire*, by Mark Childress.

C124. "Afterword." *The Dark Tower: The Gunslinger.* West Kingston RI: Donald M. Grant, Publisher, 1984, hardcover. 219-224. See A17.

C125. "Introduction." *The Blackboard Jungle*, by Evan Hunter. New York: Arbor House, Library of Contemporary Americana, 1984, paperback. v-x.

COMMENTS: Discussion of the novel as exemplifying "American naturalism," with its author a "brave voice speaking out suddenly and with surprising vigor from the literary horse latitudes of the mid-fifties" (x).

C126. "Basic Bread/Lunchtime Gloop/Egg Puff." *The Famous New Englanders Cookbook.* Dublin NH: 1984, paperback. Recipe.

REPRINTS AND ADAPTATIONS:
b. As: "Lunchtime Gloop." *Riverdriver's Cookbook.* Bangor ME: Bangor Convention and Visitor's Center, 1997.

C127. "What Went Down When the Magyk Went Up." *New York Times Book Review* 10 February 1985: 7. Review of Elmore Leonard's Glitz, perhaps "the best crime novel of the year."

C128. [Letter]. *Fangoria* No. 45 (1985).

C129. "Theodore Sturgeon—1918-1985." *Washington Post Book World* 26 May 1985: 11.

REPRINTS AND ADAPTATIONS:
b. *Locus* (1985).
c. *SFWA Bulletin* Vol. 19, No. 2 (Summer 1985): 14-15.
d. As: "Viewpoint: Theodore Sturgeon—1918-1985." *Isaac Asimov's Science Fiction Magazine* Vol. 10, No. 1 (January 1986): 33-35.

C130. "King Testifies." *Fantasy Review* (May 1985): 11.

COMMENTS: Repudiation of a hoax-review by 'Helen Purcell' of an erotic novel, *Love Lessons*, by 'John Wilson' but credited to King in the April *Fantasy Review* column. King denies authorship of that or any other erotic novel and warns would-be collectors against buying copies.

C131. "Cat From Hell." *Castle Rock: The Stephen King Newsletter* Vol. 1, No. 6 (June 1985): 9. Discussion of how King wrote the story. See B30.

C132. "Introduction." *Skeleton Crew*. New York: G. P. Putnam's Sons, June 1985, hardcover. 13-18. Anecdotal essay with backgrounds to several stories and introducing the critical thematic motif, "Do you love?" See A28.

C133. "Notes." *Skeleton Crew*. New York: G. P. Putnam's Sons, June 1985, hardcover. 507-512. Annotations for several stories, particularly "The Mist" and "The Raft." See A28.

C134. "The Politics of Limited Editions." *Castle Rock: The Stephen King Newsletter* Vol. 1, No. 6 (June 1985): 3-4, 6; and Vol. 1, No. 7 (July 1985): 1-2, 5. King's response to readers frustrated by limited printings of *The Dark Tower, The Eyes of the Dragon*, and *Cycle of the Werewolf*, with a justification of allowing limited printings of certain works.

C135. "His Creepiest Movies." *USA Today* 27 August 1985. One of King's "lists that matter."

C136. "Lists That Matter (Number 7)." *Castle Rock: The Stephen King Newsletter* Vol. 1, No. 8 (August 1985): 6. Lists King's best-of-all-time films: *Casablanca, E.T., The Godfather Part II, West Side Story, The Haunting, Psycho, Stagecoach, Sorcerer, Cool Hand Luke,* and *The Wizard of Oz*.

C137. "Lists That Matter (Number 8)." *Castle Rock: The Stephen King Newsletter* Vol. 1, No. 9 (September 1985): 7. Lists the ten worst movies of all time: *Blood Feast, Plan Nine from Outer Space, Teenage Monster, Old Yeller, Missing in Action, Children of the Corn, Bring Me the Head of Alfredo Garcia, Love Story, The Gauntlet,* and *Oceans Eleven*.

C138. "Lists That Matter (Number 14)." *Castle Rock: The Stephen King Newsletter* Vol. 1, No. 10 (October 1985): 7. King's ten worst fears, including reaching the point of no return on a transatlantic flight and knowing you're doomed if something happens; checking the circuit breakers in a dark cellar; taking a shower in a strange motel; driving on a deserted street late at night and hearing breathing in the back seat; and being in a tall building on a windy day and wondering "if skyscrapers ever tip over." Number ten is left blank, for the reader to fill in.

C139. "Ghostmaster General." *Castle Rock: The Stephen King Newsletter* Vol. 1, No. 10 (October 1985): 1, 7. Halloween article, telling how to enjoy safe Trick-or-Treating.

C140. "The King Speaks." *Twilight Zone Magazine* Vol. 5, No. 4 (October 1985): 8. Response to the *Fantasy Review* hoax review.

C141. "Why I Was Bachman." *The Bachman Books: Four Early Novels by Stephen King.* New York: New American Library, October 1985. v-x. Discussion of the reasons why King assumed the "Richard Bachman" pseudonym. See A30.

REPRINTS AND ADAPTATIONS:
b. As: "Warum Ich Richard Bachman War" ['Why I was Richard Bachman']. *Phantistiche Zeiten* ['Fantastic times'] Vol. 5, No. 4 (1988). German translation by Nora Jensen.

C142. "Foreword" and "Afterword." *Silver Bullet.* New York: Plume/New American Library, October 1985, trade paperback. 7-16. See A29. Backgrounds to King's relationship with Christopher Zavisa, the publisher responsible for *Cycle of the Werewolf*, and Dino De Laurentiis, who helped transform the book into a film.

C143. "What Ails the U.S. Male: Fire and Ice Cream." *Mademoiselle* 91 (November 1985): 137. Men feel vulnerable because there are "certain things we don't want to admit to women."

C144. "My Say: Stephen King." *Publishers Weekly* 226 (20 December 1985): 60. Discusses the declining paperback market.

REPRINTS AND ADAPTATIONS:
b. *The Stephen King Companion*. Edited by George Beahm. Kansas City MO: Andrews & McMeel, September 1989. 103-105.

C145. "Regis Reprimandum." *Fantasy Review* (December 1985): 40. Reply to Jack L. Chalker's article on specialty presses and to the errors that have plagued references to King in *Fantasy Review*, with special focus on *The Eyes of the Dragon* and Philtrum Press

REPRINTS AND ADAPTATIONS:
b. As: "Fie on Fantasy." *Castle Rock: The Stephen King Newsletter* Vol. 2, No. 1 (January 1986): 2.

C146. "Lists That Matter." *Castle Rock: The Stephen King Newsletter* Vol. 2, No. 1 (January 1986): 7. Chronological list of the ten "Best Things in Life," ranging from an ice-cream cone" (age 7) to "being alive, healthy, and fully functional" (age 70).

C147. [Title unknown]. *Twilight Zone Magazine* (February 1986). Article on *Firestarter* the film.

C148. "You Are here Because You Want the Real Thing." *Albacon III Program Book*. Glasgow, Scotland, 28-31 March 1986. Appreciation of horror writer Clive Barker.

REPRINTS AND ADAPTATIONS:
b. As: "Introduction." *The Inhuman Condition*, by Clive Barker. New York: Poseidon Press, August 1986, hardcover.
c. Issued as a promotional booklet to booksellers.
d. *Clive Barker's Shadows in Eden*. Edited by Stephen Jones. ____: Underwood-Miller, October 1991, 466 pp., $39.95. xiii-xviii. ISBN 0-88733-073-8.

C149. "Hello Mary Lou, Goodbye Rick." *Spin* (April 1986). On the death of Ricky Nelson.

C150. "Let's Scare Dick and Jane." *Washington Post Book World* 11 May 1986: 1, 18.

REPRINTS AND ADAPTATIONS:
b. Revised in: *The Creative Child and Adult Quarterly* Vol. 13, Vol. 2 (1988).

COMMENTS: Response to *The Day After* as "a sanitized and fairly unrealistic television film"; also a discussion of children's adaptability to horror and dependence upon storytelling, noting that *Bambi* was "one of the scariest movies ever made."

C151. "Red Sox Fan Crows About Team, But May Have to Eat Chicken." *Bangor Daily News* [ME] 17 May 1986: 17.

COMMENTS: King's response to Bob Haskell's column criticizing the Boston Red Sox during the 1986 season; the article ends with a bet on the team's standings by July 1, the loser to eat a chicken dinner on the lawn of the *Bangor Daily News* office in his underwear. King won.

C152. "Tough Talk and Tootsies, Just 25 Cents." *USA Today* 23 May 1986: 4D. Original title: "Escape for a Quarter." Discusses paperback originals of the 1950s—John D. MacDonald's *The Executioners* and works by Elmore Leonard, Kate Wilhelm, Evan Hunter, Richard Matheson, and Louis L'Amour.

C153. "**King vs. Chalker: One Last Round.**" *Fantasy Review* (May 1986): 6, 40.

COMMENTS: In this final installment of King's exchange with Jack L. Chalker over publication of *The Eyes of the Dragon*, King refutes nine charges made by Chalker.

C154. "**Say 'No' to the Enforcers.**" *Maine Sunday Telegram* [Portland ME] 6 June 1986. Argument against proposed anti-pornography law before the Maine electorate; the proposal was later defeated.

REPRINTS AND ADAPTATIONS:
b. *Castle Rock: The Stephen King Newsletter* Vol. 2, No. 8 (August 1986): 7.

C155. "**King Awaits His Chicken and Haskell Should Shop for Shorts.**" *Bangor Daily News* [ME] June 1986. Guest-columnist follow-up to the Boston Red Sox bet. See C151.

C156. "**Everything You Need to Know About Writing Successfully—In Ten Minutes.**" *The Writer* Vol. 99, No. 7 (July 1986): 7-10, 46.

REPRINTS AND ADAPTATIONS:
b. *The Writer's Handbook*. Edited by Sylvia K. Burrack. Boston: The Writer, 1989, hardcover. 15-21.
c. *Fractal* No. 1 (Fall 1993): 66+.

C157. "**All American Love Story.**" *Washington Post Book World* 6 June 1986. Review of Thomas Williams's novel.

C158. "**Stephen King Comments on IT.**" *Castle Rock: The Stephen King Newsletter* Vol. 2, No. 7 (July 1986): 1, 5. Letter-response to article by Michael R. Collings.

C159. "**Red Sox Stretch Out to the World Series.**" *Bangor Daily News* [ME] 12 September 1986.

C160. "**On the Far Side,**" Foreword to *The Far Side Gallery 2*, by Gary Larson. Kansas City MO: Andrews and McMeel, September 1986, trade paperback. 5-6.

C161. "**How IT Happened.**" Book-of-the-Month Club News (October 1986): 3, 5.

REPRINTS AND ADAPTATIONS:
b. As: "Writing the #1 Bestseller...How *IT* Happened." *The Writer* Vol. 100,

No. 4 (April 1987): 14-15.
c. *Secret Windows: Essays and Fiction on the Craft of Writing.* Bookspan/BOMC, 2000, $18.75, 433 pp., hardcover. A70.

C162. [Title unknown]. *Bangor Daily News* [ME] (1986). Halloween advertisement.

C163. "86 Is Just the Ticket." *Boston Globe* [MA] 6 October 1986.

REPRINTS AND ADAPTATIONS:
b. *The Red Sox Reader: 30 Years of Musings on Baseball's Most Amusing Team.* Edited by Dan Riley. Thousand Oaks CA: Ventura Arts, March 1987, trade paperback. 200-202.

C164. "The Opera Ain't Over...." *Bangor Daily News* [ME] 14 October 1986.

C165. "Why I Chose Batman," Introduction in *Batman Comics* #400 (October 1986).

C166. "Write-in." *Writing!* (October 1986 [?]).

C167. "How Much am I Hurting?" *Bangor Daily News* "Maine Weekend" [ME] 1-2 November 1986: 12. Article on the Boston Red Sox.

C168. "Big Jim Thompson: An Appreciation." *Now and On Earth*, by Jim Thompson. Belem, NM: Dennis Macmillan Publications, 1986, hardcover. Four-page introduction to limited edition of 400 copies.

REPRINTS AND ADAPTATIONS:
b. In: *Ici et maintenant,* by Jim Thompson. Preface by Stephen King. Paris, France: Rivages, 1992, 294 pp., 139 F, paperback. French translation by Michèle Valencia. ISBN 2-86930-548-6.
c. In: *Ici et maintenant,* by Jim Thompson. Preface by Stephen King. Paris, France: Rivages, RIVAGES NOIR #229, 1995, 293 pp., paperback. French translation by Michèle Valencia. ISBN 2-86930-987-2.

C169. "The Dreaded X." *Castle Rock: The Stephen King Newsletter* Vol. 3, No. 1 (December 1986/January 1987): 1, 4-5, 9, 10.

REPRINTS AND ADAPTATIONS:
b. *Gauntlet: Exploring the Limits of Free Expression* No. 2 (April 1991): 69-84.
c. *Gauntlet 2.* Edited by Barry Hoffman. Baltimore MD: Borderlands Press, May 1991. 45-59.

COMMENTS: A fervent discussion of the rating system for films, with special attention to *Maximum Overdrive* and the threat of an "X" rating because of several scenes in King's screenplay.

C170. **"Postscript to 'Overdrive.'"** *Castle Rock: The Stephen King Newsletter* Vol. 3, No. 2 (February 1987): 1, 5. Additional thoughts on the film industry's rating system.

C171. **"Why I Wrote The Eyes of the Dragon."** *Castle Rock: The Stephen King Newsletter* Vol. 3, No. 2 (February 1987): 1, 6. Discusses the genesis of the novel as a bedtime story for King's daughter Naomi. See A24.

C172. **"What's Scaring Stephen King?"** *Omni* Vol. 9 (February 1987): 16. Article on censorship, with photograph.

C173. **"A Look at the Red Sox on the Edge of '87."** *Bangor Daily News* [ME] 28-29 March 1987.

REPRINTS AND ADAPTATIONS:
b. *Castle Rock: The Stephen King Newsletter* Vol. 3, No. 7 (July 1987): 5.

C174. **"Whining About the Movies in Bangor: Take That 'Top Gun.'"** *Bangor Daily News* [ME] 9 April 1987.

C175. **"Argument."** *The Dark Tower II: The Drawing of the Three.* 11-12. See A34.

C176. **"Afterword."** *The Dark Tower II: The Drawing of the Three.* 400+. See A34.

C178. **"Turning the Thumbscrews on the Reader."** *Book-of-the-Month Club News* (June 1987): 5. Article on writing *Misery*. See A33.

REPRINTS AND ADAPTATIONS:
b. In: *Secret Windows: Essays and Fiction on the Craft of Writing.* Bookspan/BOMC, 2000. See A70.

C179. **"On John D. MacDonald."** *The Mystery Scene Reader: A Special Tribute to John D. MacDonald.* Edited by Ed Gorman. Cedar Rapids IA: Fedora, August 1987, trade paperback. 26-29.

COMMENTS: King's tribute to MacDonald as a writer and as a person, with backgrounds on why MacDonald agreed to write the introduction to *Night Shift* and how that affected King's career.

C180. "Foreword." *Scars and Other Distinguishing Marks*, by Richard Christian Matheson. Los Angeles CA: Scream Press, August [December] 1987, 168 pp., $20.00, hardcover. i–iv. ISBN 0-910489-15-7.

REPRINTS AND ADAPTATIONS:
b. *Scars & Other Distinguishing Mark*, by Richard Christian Matheson. New York: Tor, July 1988, 262 pp., $3.95, mass-market paperback. xi-xiv. ISBN 0-812-52254-0.

C181. "Entering the Rock Zone; or, How I Happened to Marry a Rock Station from Outer Space." *Castle Rock: The Stephen King Newsletter* Vol. 3, No. 10 (October 1987): 1, 5. King's involvement with WZON, rock station in Bangor ME.

C182. "Introduction." *Transylvania Station: A Mohonk Mystery*, by Donald and Abby Westlake. Mohonk Mystery Series. Miami Beach FL: Dennis McMillan Publications, October 1987, paperback. Includes participation by King, Peter Straub, Gahan Wilson, and others.

SELECTED ARTICLES, RESPONSES, AND REVIEWS:
b. King, Naomi. "Mystery Weekend Is Novelized." *Castle Rock: The Stephen King Newsletter* Vol. 4, No. 3 (March 1988): 8.

C183. "The Ideal, Genuine Writer: A Forenote." *The Ideal, Genuine Man*, by Don Robertson. Bangor ME: Philtrum Press, October 1987, hardcover. LIMITED EDITION, 500 numbered copies, signed by King and Robertson. Trade hardcover. Introduction to the second full-length book produced by King's press.

SELECTED ARTICLES, RESPONSES, AND REVIEWS:
b. Blue, Tyson. "The Ideal, Genuine Novel." Castle Rock Vol. 3, No. 10 (October 1987): 3, 6.

C184. "'Ever Et Raw Meat?' and Other Weird Questions." *New York Times Book Review* 6 December 1987.

REPRINTS AND ADAPTATIONS:
b. As: "Who Ever Et Raw Meat." *Twilight Zone Magazine* Vol. 8, No. 2 (June 1988): 26-27.
c. *The Writer* Vol. 101 (July 1988): 7-8.
d. As: "Letters From Hell." Northridge CA: Lord John Press, September 1988, 18" x 24" broadsheet, printed in three colors. Limited edition of 500 copies signed by King. Discussion of fan's letters and questions.
e. Reprint of the Lord John Press broadsheet in reduced format. *Castle Rock: The Stephen King Newsletter* Vol. 4, No. 12 (December 1988): 11. Ad-

vertisement for the broadsheet, reproducing the original text.
i. *Book Talk* (Winter 1989).
j. *Secret Windows: Essays and Fiction on the Craft of Writing*. Bookspan/BOMC, 2000, $18.75, 433 pp., hardcover. 333-338. A70.

C185. "**This Guy is Really Scary.**" *Joe Bob Goes to the Drive-in*, by Joe Bob Briggs [pseudonym for John Bloom]. New York: Delacorte Press, 1987, trade paperback.

C186. "**Afterword.**" *The Dark Tower II: The Drawing of the Three*. West Kingston RI: Donald M. Grant, 1987, hardcover. 400. See also A34.

C187. "**SK Criticized for References to Blacks: Stephen King Replies.**" *Castle Rock: The Stephen King Newsletter* Vol. 4, No. 3 (March 1988): 1, 5.

C188. "**Quinn's Book.**" *Times Union* [Albany NY] 24 April 1988. Review of the book by William Kennedy.

C189. [Title unknown]. *The Register* [Bangor ME] 11 May 1988. Discusses drunk driving.

C190. [Title unknown]. *The Register* [Bangor ME] 18 May 1988. Discusses tabloids.

C191. [Title unknown]. *The Register* [Bangor ME] 25 May 1988. Discusses cocaine.

C192. "**SK Clarifies Gardner Reference.**" *Castle Rock: The Stephen King Newsletter* Vol. 4, No. 5-6 (May-June 1988): 3. Discusses literary and personal sources for the 'Sunshine' Gardner character in *The Talisman*. See A26.

C193. [Title unknown]. *The Register* [Bangor ME] 1 June 1988. Discusses Elvis Presley.

C194. "**The Ultimate Catalogue.**" *Bangor Daily News* [ME] June 1988.

REPRINTS AND ADAPTATIONS:
b. *Castle Rock: The Stephen King* Newsletter Vol. 5, No. 6 (June 1989): 3.

C195. [Title unknown]. *Penthouse* (September 1988). Excerpt from *Nightmares in the Sky*. See A36.

C196. "**Why Red Sox Fans Believe....**" *USA Today* 4 October 1988.

C197. "Introduction" to *The Killer Inside Me*, by Jim Thompson. Los Angeles CA: Blood & Guts Press, October 1988, hardcover. Lettered edition, 26 copies, signed by King. Limited edition, 350 copies, signed by King.

C198. "Robert Marasco: Burnt Offerings." *Horror: 100 Best Books*. Edited by Stephen Jones and Kim Newman. London, England: Xanadu, 1988, hardcover. 156-161. Limited edition of 300 copies.

REPRINTS AND ADAPTATIONS:
b. London, England: Xanadu, 1988, hardcover. 156-161. Trade edition.
c. New York: Carroll & Graf, 1988, hardcover. 156-161.

C199. "Remembering John." *Bangor Daily News* [ME] (1988).

C200. "Introduction" to *The Collector*, by John Fowles. New York: Book-of-the-Month Club, [1988], trade hardcover.

REPRINTS AND ADAPTATIONS:
b. Paperback reprint of King's introduction, issued separately.
c. *Secret Windows: Essays and Fiction on the Craft of Writing*. Bookspan/BOMC, 2000, $18.75, 433 pp., hardcover. 339-352. A70.

SELECTED ARTICLES, RESPONSES, AND REVIEWS:
Indick, Ben P. "Here's An Unusual King Collectible." *Castle Rock: The Stephen King Newsletter* Vol. 5, No. 11 (November 1989).

C201. "From Stephen King." *Richard Matheson: Collected Stories*, by Richard Matheson. ____: Scream Press, October 1989, 899 pp., trade paperback. 899. 350 copies for distribution as the 1989 World Fantasy Convention. Appreciation.

C202. "Head Down: The Sporting Scene [Little League]." *The New Yorker* Vol. 66 (16 April 1990): 68+.

REPRINTS AND ADAPTATIONS:
b. In: *The Best American Sports Writing: 1991*. Edited by David Halberstrom. Series editor, Glenn Stout. Boston MA: Houghton Mifflin, 1991.
c. *Nightmares & Dreamscapes*. New York: Viking, 1993. 741-794. See A47.

C203. "What Stephen King Does for Love." *Seventeen* Vol. 49, No. 4 (April 1990): 240+.

REPRINTS AND ADAPTATIONS:
b. *Secret Windows: Essays and Fiction on the Craft of Writing*. Bookspan/BOMC, 2000, $18.75, 433 pp., hardcover. 353-360. A70.

C204. "Author's Note." *The Stand: The Complete & Uncut Edition.* New York: Doubleday, May 1990, hardcover. [vii]. See A40.

C205. "A Preface in Two Parts—Part I: To Be Read Before Purchase; Part 2: To Be Read After Purchase." *The Stand: The Complete & Uncut Edition.* New York: Doubleday, May 1990, hardcover. ix-xii. See A40.

C206. "Stephen King's Desert Island." *Condé Nast Traveler* (July, 1990).

C207. "Straight Up Midnight: An Introductory Note." *Four Past Midnight.* New York: Viking, 1990. xi-xvi. See A41.

C208. "One Past Midnight: A Note on 'The Langoliers.'" *Four Past Midnight.* New York: Viking, 1990. 3-5. See A41.

C209. "Two Past Midnight: A Note on 'Secret Window, Secret Garden.'" *Four Past Midnight.* New York: Viking, 1990. 249-251. See A41.

REPRINTS AND ADAPTATIONS:
b. *Secret Windows: Essays and Fiction on the Craft of Writing.* Bookspan/BOMC, 2000, $18.75, 433 pp., hardcover. 361-364. A70.

C210. "Three Past Midnight: A Note on 'The Library Policeman.'" *Four Past Midnight.* New York: Viking, 1990. 403-405. See A41.

C211. "Four Past Midnight: A Note on 'The Sun Dog.'" *Four Past Midnight.* New York: Viking, 1990. 607-611. See A41. Refers to the story as the "connective tissue" between *The Dark Half* and *Needful Things*.

C212. "Introduction" to "The Glass Floor." *Weird Tales* No. 298 (Fall 1990).

C213. "Scare Tactics." *Reader's Digest* 137:832 (November 1990): 20. Brief excerpt from *Bare Bones*.

C214. "My New Year's Resolution (or, Look What Dave's Got Us Doing Now)." *The Overlook Connection* (Winter 1990): 22. Three-paragraph New Year's Resolution with accompanying photo of King on a motorcycle.

C215. "King on *Firestarter*: Who's to Blame." *Cinefantastique* Vol. 21, No. 4 (February 1991): 35. Letter response to Mark Lester's comments about King's published criticisms of the film.

C216. "The Importance of Being Archie." *Archie Americana Series: Best of the Forties.* Edited by Scott D. Fulop. New York: Archie Comic Publications, 1 March 1991, $10.95, 128 pp., trade paperback, omnibus volume of comic books; introduction by King. 1879794004.

C217. **"Author's Note"** to "The Woman in the Room." *Masters of Darkness III.* Edited by Dennis Etchison. New York: Tor, May 1991, paperback. 319-320.

C218. **"From Stephen King."** *Mystery Scene* No. 30 (July-August 1991): iv.

COMMENTS: Open letter to Barry R. Levin, in which King criticizes the bookdealer for offering the pirated German edition of The Mist, which was "produced in arrant violation" of King's copyright. King urges Levin to "pass on any future acquisitions not covered by an original copyright."

C219. **"How I Created Golden Years...and Spooked Dozens of TV Executives."** *Entertainment Weekly* No. 77 (2 August 1991): 28-32. Overview of the genesis of the TV series, with photos.

C220. **"A Warning from Stephen King."** *Disney Adventures* (October 1991): 118. One-page introduction to King's choice as the winning entry in a children's "scary stories" contest: Aaron M. Carmichael's "Mr. Tilmore" (printed on pp. 119-121).

C221. **[Title Unknown].** *Bangor Daily News* [ME] 29 March 1992. Guest editorial discussing censorship.

C222. **"A World without Fritz."** *Locus* (October 1992).

REPRINTS AND ADAPTATIONS:
b. *Nebula Awards 28.* Edited by James Morrow. New York: Harcourt Brace, April 1994, 328 pp., $12.95, trade paperback. ISBN 0-15-600039-3. Hardcover, $24.95, ISBN 0-15-100082-4.

C223. **"James Herbert: Introduction."** *James Herbert: By Horror Haunted. Edited by Stephen Jones.* London, England: New English Library, 1992, 322 pp., £17.99, hardcover. 9-18. ISBN 0-450-53810-9.

C224. **"Introduction."** *Graven Images: The Best of Horror, Fantasy, and Science Fiction Film Art from the Collection of Ronald V. Borst and Margaret A. Borst.* Edited by Ronald V. Borst, Keith Burns, and Leith Adams. New York: Grove/Atlantic, 1992, hardcover. Includes reminiscences by Clive Barker, Harlan Ellison, Peter Straub, and Forrest J Ackerman.

SELECTED ARTICLES, RESPONSES, AND REVIEWS:
Letofsky, Irv. *The Los Angeles Times Book Review* 20 December 1992: 11.

C225. **"Son of Best Seller Stalks the Moors."** *The New York Times Book Review* 6 June 1993: 59. Includes a list of ten rules for packaging blockbuster best-sellers.

C226. **"A Guy to Have in Your Corner."** *Time* Vol. 142, No. 13 (27 September 1993): 95. Defends Scott Smith's first novel, *A Simple Plan*.

C227. **"A Satiric Punch."** *Time* Vol. 142, No. 15 (11 October 1993): 12.

C228. **Introduction.** *Horripilations: The Art of J. K. Potter.* Artwork by Potter; text by Nigel Suckling. England: Dragon's World/Paper Tiger, November 1993, 128 pp., £12.95, trade paperback. ISBN 1-85028-255-2.

REPRINTS AND ADAPTATIONS:
b. Overlook Press, October 1995, 128 pp., $24.95, trade paperback. ISBN 0-87951-613-5.

C229. **"Stephen King on Censorship."** *War of Worlds: The Censorship Debate.* Edited by George Beahm. Kansas City MO: Andrews & McMeel, 1993, trade paperback. 31.

COMMENTS: Excerpted from a videotaped interview conducted by New American Library for its sales personnel in 1989. King argues that censorship has no place in "public institutions and libraries," and urges people to support books that have been censored.

C230. **"Introduction: Myth, Belief, Faith, and Ripley's Believe It or Not!"** *Nightmares & Dreamscapes.* New York: Viking, 1993, hardcover. 1-9. See A47.

C231. **"Notes."** *Nightmares & Dreamscapes.* New York: Viking, 1993, hardcover. 797-812. See A47.

C232. **"Fritz Leiber."** *Gummitch & Friends,* by Fritz Leiber. Hampton Falls NH: Donald M. Grant, February 1993, 222 pp., $30.00, hardcover. 27-29. ISBN 1-880418-18-5.

C233. **"On J. K. Potter: The Art of the Morph."** *Interzone* [Brighton, England], #77 (November 1993): 23-24. Article.

C234. **"Introduction."** *Fugitive Recaptured: The Thirtieth Anniversary Companion to a Television Classic,* by Ed Robertson. Foreword by Barry Morse. Pomegranate Press, September 1993, $17.95, 208 pp., trade paperback. ISBN 0-938817-34-5. Online: http://www.pompress.com.

REPRINTS AND ADAPTATIONS:
b. As: AUDIOCASSETTE: *The Fugitive Recaptured.* Narrated by Barry Morse, Jacquiline Scott, and Roy Huggins. 2 audiocassettes; 90 minutes. $16.95. ISBN 0-92\38817-37-X.

C235. "The Neighborhood of the Beast." *Mid-life Confidential: The Rock Bottom Remainders Tour America with Three Chords and an Attitude,* edited by Dave Marsh; photographs by Tabitha King. New York: Viking, August 1994, 222 pp., $20.95, hardcover. ISBN 0-670-85234-1. Also video: ASIN 0-452-27459-1

C236. "Stephen King on the Internet." 6 October 1994.

COMMENTS: An internet posting by King (?) in conjunction with his appearance at Cornell University. The memo, with King's name on it, discusses some points about *Rose Madder* and the next Dark Tower novel. See A49.

C237. Foreword. *Steve Lyons: Psychoanalysis,* by Steve Lyons. Sports Publishing, 1 May 1995, $19.95, 224 pp., hardcover. ISBN 1-57167-010-6. Book on baseball. Online information: www.sportspublishinginc.com

C238. "Robert Bloch: An Appreciation." *Robert Bloch: Appreciations of the Master.* Edited by Richard Matheson and Ricia Mainhardt. New York: Tor, October 1995, 382 pp., $24.95, hardcover. 299-300. ISBN 0-312-85976-7.

C239. Introduction. *Headed Home: Growing Up in Baseball,* photographs by Harry Connelly. New York: Rizzoli, 1995. Collection of Little League Baseball photographs.

C240. "Rita Hayworth and the Darabont Redemption." *Shawshank Redemption: The Shooting Script,* by Frank Darabont. Newmarket Press, March 1996, 208 pp., $16.95, trade paperback. ISBN 1557042462.

C241. Photograph and explanatory text. In *The Writer's Desk,* by Jill Kementz. New York: Random House, 1996, p. 4.

C242. "Foreword." *Edgeworks 2: Spider Kiss* and *Stalking the Nightmare,* by Harlan Ellison. THE COLLECTED ELLISON, Vol. 2, ___: White Wolf, November 1996, 471 pp., $21.99, hardcover. ix-xix. ISBN 1-56504-961-6. For further information: www.white-wolf.com.

REPRINTS AND ADAPTATIONS
a. White Wolf, September 1999, $16.99, trade paperback. ISBN 1-56504-830-X.

C243. [Extracts from King interview]. *Dark Thoughts: On Writing, Advice and Commentary From Fifty Masters of Fear and Suspense.* Edited by Stanley Wiater. Grass Valley CA: Underwood Books, 1997, 206 pp., $13.00, trade paperback. ISBN 1-887424-30-X.

REPRINTS AND ADAPTATIONS:
b. Limited edition announced for 1999.

C244. "Introduction." *The Green Mile.* New York: Plume, 1997. London, England: Orion, November 1998, xiv+465 pp., £10.99, trade paperback. v-x. See also A60.

C245. "Afterword." *The Green Mile.* New York: Plume, 1997. London, England: Orion, November 1998, xiv+465 pp., £10.99, trade paperback. v-x.

C246. "Foreword: A Letter." *The Green Mile.* London, England: Orion, November 1998, xiv+465 pp., £10.99, trade paperback. ix-xiv. ISBN 0-75282-146-6. New introduction with this edition. See also A60.

C247. "Afterword." *The Dark Tower IV: Wizard and Glass.* Hampton Falls NH: Donald M. Grant, August 1997. See A61 for subsequent printings.

C248. "Author's Note." *Bag of Bones.* New York: Scribner, 1998, [not paginated]. See A63 for subsequent printings. Single-page note following copyright page.

C249. "Lunch-time Ghoul-ash." *Eating Between the Lines: A Maine Writer's Cookbook.* Brunswick ME: MWPA, 1998, $16.00. Recipe.

C250. "Basic Bread." *Eating Between the Lines: A Maine Writer's Cookbook.* Brunswick ME: MWPA, 1998, $16.00. Recipe.

C251. "Introduction." *The Green Mile,* screenplay by Frank Darabont. New York: Scribner Paperback Fiction, 1999, trade paperback.

C252. "Introduction." *Storm of the Century.* New York: Pocket, 1999. See A64 for subsequent printings.

C253. "Author's Postscript." *The Girl Who Loved Tom Gordon.* New York: Scribner, 1999. See A65 for subsequent printings.

C254. "Author's Note." *Hearts in Atlantis.* New York: Scribners, 1999, p. 523. See A66 for subsequent printings.

C255. "An Evening at the Billerica [Massachusetts] Library." *Secret Windows: Essays and Fiction on the Craft of Writing.* Bookspan/BOMC, 2000. 231-260. See A70.

C256. "Banned Books and Other Concerns: The Virginia Beach Lecture." *Secret Windows: Essays and Fiction on the Craft of Writing.* Bookspan, BOMC, 2000. 325-330. See A70.

FIRST APPEARANCE:
The Stephen King Companion, edited by George Beahm. Kansas City MO and New York: Andrews and McMeel, 1989, $10.95, 364 pp., trade paperback. 51-61. ISBN 0-8362-7978-6 [My apologies to George Beahm—this reference was inadvertently deleted from an early draft of this book; the error was not noted until just prior to publication—MRC]

C257. "Turning the Thumbscrews on the Reader." *Secret Windows: Essays and Fiction on the Craft of Writing.* Bookspan/BOMC, 2000. 331-332. See A70.

C258. "Great Hookers I Have Known." *Secret Windows: Essays and Fiction on the Craft of Writing.* Bookspan/BOMC, 2000. 373-380. See A70.

C259. "A Night at the Royal Festival Hall: Muriel Grey Interviews Stephen King." *Secret Windows: Essays and Fiction on the Craft of Writing.* Bookspan/BOMC, 2000. 381-386. See A70.

C260. "An Evening with Stephen King." *Secret Windows: Essays and Fiction on the Craft of Writing.* Bookspan/BOMC, 2000. 387-402. See A70.

C261. "Advice for Writers." *USA Today* "Bookstreet" (22 September 2000).

C262. "On Ed McBain." *Mystery Scene* No. 70 (March 2001): 25-26.

COMMENTS: One segment in "A Tribute to Evan Hunter/Ed McBain," with contributors including Pete Hamill, John Jakes, Donald Westlake, Lawrence Block, Stuart Kaminsky, and others.

Section D.
Poetry

Since King has published only a handful of poems—most of those relatively early in his career; because they are nearly completely overshadowed by the enormous popularity of his fiction and non-fiction, there is an equivalent dearth of substantive criticism or analysis of it. The poems are, however, treated specifically in the following, additional in other works listed in the introduction to Section B:

Blue, Tyson. *The Unseen King*. STARMONT STUDIES IN LITERARY CRITICISM, #26. Mercer Island WA: Starmont House, 1989. Includes the first authorized reprint of "Brooklyn August."

Collings, Michael R. "Acorns to Oaks: Explorations of Theme, Image, and Character in the Early Works of Stephen King, Part I." *Castle Rock: The Stephen King Newsletter* Vol. 5, No. 8 (August 1989): 1, 8.

Collings, Michael R. "The Radiating Pencils of His Bones: The Poetry of Stephen King." *The Shape Under the Sheet: The Complete Stephen King Encyclopedia*. Edited by Stephen Spignesi. Ann Arbor MI: Popular Culture, Ink., May 1991.

Collings, Michael R., and David A. Engebretson. *The Shorter Works of Stephen King*. STARMONT STUDIES IN LITERARY CRITICISM, #8. Mercer Island WA: Starmont House, 1985.

Spignesi, Stephen J. *The Lost Work of Stephen King*. New York: Birch Lane Press, 1998. Marietta GA: Overlook Connection Press, 1998.

Spignesi, Stephen J. *The Shape Under the Sheet: The Complete Stephen King Encyclopedia*. Ann Arbor MI: Popular Culture, Ink, May 1991. * Reprint, Chicago IL: Contemporary Books.

Michael R. Collings

D1. "Harrison State Park '68." *Ubris* [University of Maine, Orono] (Fall 1968): 25-26.

COMMENTS: The earliest extant published poem to date; the free verse stanzas, theme (a murder victim found in a nearby park), characterization, and vocabulary all foreshadow directions King would follow in subsequent poems and in his more substantive body of prose.

D2. "The Dark Man." *Ubris* [University of Maine, Orono] (Spring 1969): [n.p.].

REPRINTS AND ADAPTATIONS:
Moth (1970): [n.p.]. Published as by Steve King

COMMENTS: This is one of three poems attributed to "Steve King" in the 1970 issue of *Moth*. It suggests the powerful and threatening Dark-Man motif that recurs throughout King's fiction, particularly in *The Stand*, *The Eyes of the Dragon*, and the Dark Tower novels; to that extent it represents a possible beginning date for King's interest defining the nature—and frequently the embodiment—of evil, of manifestations of the Dark as it contends with the Light for human souls.

D3. "Donovan's Brain," by Steve King. *Moth* (1970): [n.p.].

COMMENTS: Based on Curt Siodmak's novel and the subsequent film of the same name, the poem focuses on Shratt, the victim of a pseudo-science that transmutes into horror.

D4. "Silence," by Steve King. *Moth* [University of Maine, Orono] (1970): [n.p.].

COMMENTS: Only twelve lines long, this poem appeared with "The Dark Man" and "Donovan's Brain" in Moth, all under the name of Steve King. It is a non-narrative evocation of feeling, with everyday objects creating the "feary silence of fury."

D5. [Untitled poem], "In the Key-Chords of Dawn." *Onan* (1971).

COMMENTS: Using the imagery of fishing, the 24-line poem defines a metaphor for love, and concludes that when one sees fishing as a "loom of complexity," as responsibility rather than pleasure, it is time to "put away our poles."

D6. "Brooklyn August." *Io* No. 10 (1971): 147. King's paean to baseball in Ebbetts Field, with few touches of his characteristic horror or style.

REPRINTS AND ADAPTATIONS:
The Unseen King, by Tyson Blue. Mercer Island WA: Starmont House, 1989. 107-108.
Nightmares & Dreamscapes. New York: Viking, 1993. 795-796. See A47.

D7. "The Hardcase Speaks," by Stephan King [sic]. *Contraband 2*. Arranged and edited by Bruce Holsapple and Michael Barriault. Portland ME: Contraband, 1 December 1971, unpaginated, paper.

COMMENTS: Given the date and place of publication, the other contributors (including Jim Bishop, Burton Hatlen, Tabitha King, James Lewissohn, Herb Coursen, David Impfield, and Karl T. Kelley—the first four at least publicly associated with King), the format of publication, and the internal evidence, it seems a strong likelihood that this poem (located by Lee Finley) is by King in spite of the anomalous spelling of the first name.

The poem consists of block paragraphs in irregular free verse, couched in a harsh vocabulary consistent with the title and with King's poetic personae in other poems. Theme and image are also familiar—the image of a woman dismembered, her blood used to scrawl the killer's message on the wall: "PLEASE STOP ME BEFORE I KILL AGAIN...." The poem touches on the role of art and the artist; evokes a crucial element from *IT* in the image of "virgins pedaling bikes with playing cards affixed" to the spokes "with clothes pins"; and is sufficiently "brand-name" oriented to suggest King's authorship. Within two typewritten pages, he refers to Chuck Berry, Charles Starkwether, Budweiser beer, Diamond matches, Red Man tobacco, Baby Ruth candy bars, and assorted localities: Redcliff, Small Falls, Mestalinas, Harlow, Dover-Foxcroft, Dukane, Grand Rapids, and Cedar Falls.

D8. "For Owen." *Skeleton Crew*. New York: G. P. Putnam's Sons, June 1985. 359-360. See A28.

COMMENTS: Part surrealism, part symbolist poetry, the piece is less graphic than is usual with King; horror is implicit rather than explicit in either content or language.

D9. "Paranoid: A Chant." *Skeleton Crew*. New York: G. P. Putnam's Sons, June 1985. 241-244. See A28.

COMMENTS: The poem recreates an extended moment of madness, using erratic free-verse lines, elliptical punctuation, and colloquial language. The internal monologue, reminiscent of Robert Browning's in such poems as "Porphyria's Lover," invites the reader to define an external, objective reality that is entirely different from the internal reality the speaker perceives.

D10. "Leighton Street" [fragment by 'James Eric Gardner']. *The Tommyknockers*. New York: Putnam's, 1987, hardcover. 66-67. See also A35.

COMMENTS: While it may seem odd to incorporate fragments of verse putatively written by characters in novels, it is nevertheless appropriate here, since

King consistently uses his poetry to explore additional possibilities of tone, atmosphere, linguistic texture, and rhythm, beyond what is available to him in prose—particularly in a prose as consciously non-rhetorical(-seeming) and unadorned as his own. In the instances cited here and below, the lines cited aptly provide either a counterpoise or a parallel go the characters' emotional states, to the contexts in which they find themselves, and, perhaps more significantly, to the themes King is developing at that moment in his storytelling.

D11. "My Vase" [fragment by 'Mary Jackson']. *Desperation.* New York: Viking, 1996, hardcover. 579. See also A58.

Section E.
Audio and/or Video Adaptations or Original King Materials

NOTE: This section does not include specific novels or short fiction adapted for film or television—see entries under individual titles.

E1. *The Shotgunners* [announced and partially completed]. Directed by Sam Peckinpah from an original script by Stephen King. Peckinpah died during pre-production in 1984.

SELECTED ARTICLES, RESPONSES, AND REVIEWS:
Wood, Gary. "Shotgunners: King & Peckinpah." *Cinefantastique* Vol. 21, No. 4 (February 1991): 43.

E2. *Creepshow* 2. Laurel Entertainment, New World Pictures, 2 May 1987. Executive producer: Richard P. Rubinstein. Producer: David Ball. Director: Michael Gornick. Screenplay by George A. Romero. 89 minutes. Rating: R.
 CAST: Lois Chiles, George Kennedy, Dorothy Lamour, Daniel Beer, Jeremy Green, Page Hannah, Don Harvey, David Holbrook, Holt Mc-Callany, Frank S. Salsedo, Paul Satterfield, Tom Wright; cameos by Stephen King, Tom Savini.
 EPISODES: Wraparound #1 [5 minutes]; "Old Chief Wood'nhead" [28 minutes]; "Wraparound #2" [1 minute]; "The Raft" [21 minutes; see B60]; Wraparound #3 [2 minutes]; "The Hitchhiker" [24 minutes]; Wraparound #4 [6 minutes].

SELECTED ARTICLES, RESPONSES, AND REVIEWS:
"About the Filmmakers: Some *Creepshow* II Notes." *Castle Rock: The Stephen King Newsletter* Vol. 3, No. 6 (June 1987): 1, 6.
Blank, Ed. "Tepid '*Creepshow* 2' Trades on Names of Romero, King." *Pittsburgh Press* [PA] 29 May 1987. As microfiche: *Newsbank: Film and Television* Vol. 14 (July 1987): Fiche 3, F8.
Butler, Robert W. "This Show Is Worse Than Creepy." *Kansas City Star* [MO] (May 31, 1987). As microfiche: *Newsbank: Film and Television* Vol. 14 (July 1987): Fiche 3, F6.
Cinefantastique Vol. 17, No. 1 (January 1987): 8.
Cotton, Tim. "*Creepshow* 2: Somewhere Between a 5 and a 9." *Castle Rock: The Stephen King Newsletter* Vol. 3, No. 6 (June 1987): 1, 6.
"*Creepshow* II." *Castle Rock: The Stephen King Newsletter* 3:1 (December 1986/January,1987): 11-12.
"*Creepshow* 2." *Magill's Cinema Annual, 1988: A Survey of the Films of 1987*. Edited by Frank N. Magill. Englewood Cliffs, NJ: Salem Press, 1988. 398.
Fangoria No. 64 (1987). Four-page article with photographs.
Forrest, W. *Cinefantastique* Vol. 17, Nos. 3/4 (June 1987): 12.
Harris, J. P. *Cinefantastique* Vol. 17, No. 5 (September 1987): 50.
Harti, John. "'*Creepshow* 2': You've Seen It Before." *Seattle Times* [WA] 30 May 1987. As microfiche: *Newsbank: Film and Television* Vol. 14 (July 1987): Fiche 3, F10.
Hemming, R., and G. P. Fagan. *Video Review* Vol. 8, No. 6 (September 1987): 102.
Hicks, Christopher. "'*Creepshow* 2' Is Worse Than the First Time Out." *Deseret*

News [Salt Lake City UT] 22 May 1987. As microfiche: *Newsbank: Film and Television* Vol. 14 (July 1987): Fiche 3, F9.
Marquee (May 1987). One-page article with photographs.
Maslin, J. *New York Times* Vol. 136, No. 47 (4 May 1987): C17.
Pally, Marcia. "Creepy, Crawly Things Haunt '*Creepshow* II,'" *Boston Herald* [MA] 22 May 1987. As microfiche: *Newsbank: Film and Television* Vol. 14 (July 1987): Fiche 3, F4-F5.
People Weekly (13 December 1982). On George Romero and King.
Pitts, M. *The Village Voice* Vol. 32, No. 20 (19 May 1987): 64.
Premiere Vol. 1, No. 1 (July/August 1987): 83.
Smith, L. *Classical Images* 145 (July 1987): 33.
Smith, Patricia. "'*Creepshow* 2' Beats Formula to a Pulp." *Chicago Sun Times* [IL] 4 May 1987. As microfiche: *Newsbank: Film and Television* Vol. 14 (July 1987): Fiche 3, F3.
"A Stephen King Kind of Creep Show." *Newsday* [Long Island NY] 2 May 1987. As microfiche: *Newsbank: Film and Television* Vol. 14 (July 1987): Fiche 3, F7.
Strissel, Jodi. "Another Look at *Creepshow* 2." *Castle Rock: The Stephen King Newsletter* Vol. 3, No. 8 (August 1987): 2.
Variety Vol. 327, No. 3 (13 May 1987): 19.

As VIDEOCASSETTE: *Creepshow* 2. New World Pictures, 1989. VHS. 92 minutes. Rated R.

E3. Stephen King's Sleepwalkers. Columbia Pictures, 1992. Executive producers: Dimitri Logothetis and Joseph Medawar. Producers: Mark Victor, Michael Grais, and Nabeel Zahid. Co-producer: Richard Stenta Director: Mick Garris. Screenplay by Stephen King. 89 minutes. Rated: R.
CAST: Brian Krause, Mädchen Amick, Alice Krige, Stephen King.

SELECTED ARTICLES, RESPONSES, AND REVIEWS:
Cohn, Lawrence. *Variety* Vol. 347, No. 1 (29 April 1992): 47.
Floyd, Nigel. *Sight and Sound* Vol. 2, No. 4 (August 1992): 62.

As: VIDEOCASSETTE: *Stephen King's Sleepwalkers*. Columbia Tristar Home Video, 89 minutes, 1992. Rating: R

E4. "Sorry, Right Number." Original episode for *Tales from the Darkside*. 20 November 1987. Executive producers: Richard P. Rubinstein, George A. Romero, Jerry Golod. Producer: Anthony Santa Croce. Director: John Sutherland. Teleplay by Stephen King. 30 minutes.
CAST: Arthur Taxier, Deborah Harmon, Rhonda Dotson, Katherine Britton, Brandon Stewart, Nichold Huntington, Catherine Battistone, Paul Sparer.

REPRINTS AND ADAPTATIONS:
Nightmares & Dreamscapes. New York: Viking, 1993. See A47.

SELECTED REVIEWS:
Blue, Tyson. "Sorry, Right Number." *Castle Rock: The Stephen King Newsletter* Vol. 3, No. 10 (October 1987): 5.

E5. *Stephen King's Golden Years*. CBS. Director: Ken Fink. Teleplay by Stephen King. Episode 1—16 July 1991, 9:00-11:00, 2 hours; Episode 2—18 July 1991, 10:00-11:00, 1 hour; Episode 3—25 July 1991, 10:00-11:00, 1 hour.
> CAST: Keith Szarabajka, Frances Sternhagen, Felicity Huffman, Bill Raymond, Ed Lauter, R. D. Call, Stephen Root, J. R. Horne, Graham Paul, Phil Lenkjowsky, Kathleen Piche, Tim Guinee, Brad Greenquist, Mert Hatfield.

As: VIDEOCASSETTE: ***Stephen King's Golden Years***. Produced in two formats: SP, 2-hour speed, two tapes, $29.95; EP, 6-hour speed, one tape, $19.95. Both include a conclusion never broadcast.

SELECTED REVIEWS:
Beck, Marilyn. "Insider Grapevine: Glad About Being Golden." *TV Guide* Vol. 39, No. 29, #1999 (20 July 1991): 18-19.
Droesch, Paul. "This Week on TV: Stephen King, New '50s Sitcom, Working Women." *TV Guide* Vol. 39, No. 28 #1998 (13-19 July 1991).
King, Stephen. "How I Created Golden Years…and Spooked Dozens of TV Executives." *Entertainment Weekly* No. 77 (2 August 1991): 28-32.
Sharbutt, Jay. "Fountain of Youth Stephen King Style." *News Chronicle* [Thousand Oaks CA] 16 July 1991: C6.
"Stephen King 'Golden Years' Drama to Debut July 16 on CBS." *News Chronicle* [Thousand Oaks CA] 19 June 1991: C8.
"Stephen King's 'Golden Years'." *Variety* Vol. 344, No. 1 (15 July 1991): 42.
Zoglin, Richard. *Time* Vol. 138, No. 3 (22 July 1991): 56.

E6. *Ghosts*. 25-31 October 1996. Executive producer: Carolyn Baron. Producers: Michael Jackson, Stan Winston, and David Nicksay. Director: Stan Winston. Based on an original idea by Michael Jackson, and King. Screenplay by Stan Winston and Mick Garris. 38 minutes.
> CAST: Michael Jackson (portraying five roles), Pat Dade, Amy Smallman, Edwina Moore, Danta Bezi.

ADAPTATIONS:
As: Limited edition boxed set
As: Video/DVD
As: Home Movie.

SELECTED ARTICLES AND REVIEWS.
Copeland, Jeff B. "Michael Jackson Stars in Stephen King Film." *Eonline! News.* 25 October 1996. At: eonline.com/News.

COMMENTS: The music video screened just before the film adaptation of King's *Thinner,* showing in selected theaters in eleven cities. King's original script was completed in 1993 but the project remained in abeyance for several years. Following its limited release in the U.S., *Ghosts* screened in May 1997 at the 50th Cannes Film Festival,

E7. "Chinga." *X-files.* Twentieth Television/Fox Broadcasting Company. 8 February 1998, 9:00-10:00 PM. Executive producer and series creator: Chris Carter. Director: Kim Manners. Teleplay by Chris Carter and King.

    CAST: David Duchovny, Gillian Anderson, Susannah Hoffman, Jenny Lynn Hutcheson, Carolyn Tweedle.

E8. *Blood and Smoke*. New York: Simon & Schuster Audio, 22 November 1999, $23.50, audiocassette and simultaneous CD-Rom. Read by Stephen King. ISBN 0-671-04616-0. Collection of three stories.

    CONTENTS: "Lunch at the Gotham Café" (1995; see B113); "1408" (see B127); "In the Deathroom" (see A70).

ADAPTATIONS:
As AUDIO-CD: New York: Simon and Schuster Audio, 22 November 1999, $27.50. Read by Stephen King. ISBN 0671046179.
As BOOK: Release date, January 2000.

COMMENTS: The last two stories in the collection were written directly for the audiocassette; all three are connected by recurring images of smokers and smoking.

SELECTED ARTICLES, RESPONSES AND REVIEWS:
Appelo, Tim. Editorial review. *Amazon.com.* 1999.
"Stephen King's Newest Available Only on Audio." *Publishers Weekly* Vol. 246, No. 44 (1999): 38-41.

Index To Titles

Note: All titles are by King unless otherwise indicated. Non-print materials, including films and television mini-series and episodes, are identified in brackets.

Novels;
Book-Length Non-Fiction and Other Studies;
Screenplays and Teleplays

Apt Pupil [film]: see "Apt Pupil"
Bachman Books, The: A30; see also A4, A8, A10, A14, C141
Bad Death of Eduard Delacroix, The: see *Green Mile, The: Part 4*
Bag of Bones: A63
Blood and Smoke [original audiocassette]: E8; see also B113, B127
Blood Thirst: 100 Years of Vampire Fiction, edited by Leonard Wolf: A2
Carrie: A1; see also A2, A3, A6, A13, A35
Castle Rock: The Stephen King Newsletter: A37
Cat's Eye [film]: A6, B28, B40
Children of the Corn [film]: see "Children of the Corn"
Christine: A19
Coffey on the Mile: see *Green Mile, The: Part 6*
Coffey's Hands: see *Green Mile, The: Part 3*
Creepshow 2 [screenplay episodes]: E2; see also B60
Creepshow II [film]: E2
Creepshow: see *Stephen King's Creepshow*
Cujo: A12, B54, B59; see also A9
Cycle of the Werewolf: A21. See also *Silver Bullet*
Danse Macabre: see *Stephen King's Danse Macabre*
Dark Half, The: A39, B94
Dark Tower II, The: see *Drawing of the Three, The*

Dark Tower III, The: see *Waste Lands, The*
Dark Tower IV, The: Wizard and Glass: see *Wizard and Glass*
Dark Tower V, The: AB1
Dark Tower, The: The Gunslinger: see *Gunslinger, The*
Dead Zone, The: A7
Desperation: A58, A59; see also A61
Different Seasons: A16
Dolan's Cadillac [film]: B80
Dolan's Cadillac: A37. See also "Dolan's Cadillac"
Dolores Claiborne: A46, A48, A49
Drawing of the Three, The: The Dark Tower II: A24, B86; see also A17, A34, A43, C175, C176
Dreamcatcher: A72
Eyes of the Dragon, The: A24
Firestarter: A9, B45, C97; see also A12
Four Past Midnight: A41; see also B96, B97, B98, B99, C207, C208, C209, C210, C211
From a Buick 8: AB3
Gerald's Game: A45; see also A46
Ghosts [music video concept and original script]: E6
Girl who Loved Tom Gordon, The: A65
Golden Years [teleplay script]: see *Stephen King's Golden Years*
Gramma [teleplay]: B76
Green Mile, The: Part 2—The Mouse on the Mile: A53, A60
Green Mile, The: Part 3—Coffey's Hands: A54, 60
Green Mile, The: Part 4—The Bad Death of Eduard Delacroix: A55, A60
Green Mile, The: Part 5—Night Journey: A56, A60
Green Mile, The: Part 6—Coffey on the Mile: A57, A60
Green Mile, The—Part I, The Two Dead Girls: A52, A60
Green Mile, The—The Complete Novel: A60.
Gunslinger, The: The Dark Tower I: A17; see also A24, A34, A43, A60, B36, B44, B51, B53, B57, C124
Hearts in Atlantis: A66, B111, B122, B123, B124, B125
Insomnia: A48; see also A46
It: A32, B55
Langoliers, The [teleplay]: see *Stephen King's The Langoliers*
Last Rung on the Ladder, The [film]: see "Last Rung on the Ladder, The"
Lawnmower Man, The [film]: see B24
Long Walk, The, by 'Richard Bachman': A8; see also A4, A30
Maximum Overdrive [film]: B20
Mid-life Confidential: The Rock Bottom Remainders Tour America with

Three Chords and an Attitude, edited by Dave Marsh; photographs by Tabitha King: C235
Misery: A33; see also A1, A27, A46, C178
Mouse on the Mile, The: see *Green Mile, the: Part 2*
My Pretty Pony: A38
Needful Things: A44
New Lieutenant's Rap, The: A67
Night Flier, The [film]: see *Stephen King's The Night Flier*
Night Journey: see *Green Mile, The: Part 5*
Night Shift: A6, B7, B8, B12, B14, B17, B18, B19, B21, B23, B24, B28, B29, B31, B32, B34, B38, B39, B40, B41, C55; see also A1, A2, A3, A13
Nightmares & Dreamscapes: A47, C230, B15, B16, B22, B49, B80, B85, B87, B88, B89, B91, B92, B93, B95, B100, B102, B103, B104, B105, B106, B107, B108, C202, C231, D6, E4; see also A37, A38
Nightmares in the Sky: Gargoyles and Grotesques, photographs by f-Stop Fitzgerald: A36
Nouvelles [French translations]: A42, B48, B77
On Writing: A Memoir of the Craft: A69
One Headlight: AB5
Pet Sematary: A22, B75
Plant, The, parts 1-6: A18, A23, A31, A71
Plant, The—Book One, Parts I-VI: A71
Quicksilver Highway [film]: B103. See "Chattery Teeth"
Raft, The [film]: see B60, E2
Rage, by 'Richard Bachman': A4; see also A8, A30
Regulators, The, by 'Richard Bachman': A59; see also A58, A61
Riding the Bullet: A68
Roadwork, by 'Richard Bachman': A10; see also A14, A27, A30
Rose Madder: A49; see also A46, A48
Rose Red: AB4
Running Man, The, by 'Richard Bachman': A14; see also A8, A10, A27, A30
Salem's Lot: A2; see also A1, A3, A6, A11, A13
Secret Windows: Essays and Fiction on the Craft of Writing: A70; see also A11, B78, B127, B128, B129, C49, C55, C62, C161, C184, C200, C203, C209, C255, C256, C257, C258, C259, C260
Shawshank Redemption [film]: see A16, B61
Shawshank Redemption: The Shooting Script, by Frank Darabont: C240
Shining, The: A3; see also A1, A2, A6, A11, A13, B33, B69, C91
Shotgunners, The [screenplay]: E1

Silver Bullet: A29. See also *Cycle of the Werewolf*
Six Stories: A62, B111, B112, B113, B114, B115, B116,
Skeleton Crew: A28, B5, B6, B9, B42, B46, B47, B48, B50, B52, B56, B58, B60, B71, B72, B73, B76, B77, B78, B82, B83, C132, C133, D8, D9
Sleepwalkers [film]: see *Stephen King's Sleepwalkers*
Sometimes They Come Back [film]: see B23
Stand by Me [film]: see "Body, The"
Stand, The (1990—unexpurgated version): A40; see also C204, C205
Stand, The (original edition): A5; see also A1, A2
Stephen King's "Sometimes They Come Back" [film]: see B23
Stephen King's Creepshow: A15, B43
Stephen King's Danse Macabre: A11, C53, C54, C66, C70, C73, C76, C77, C79, C80, C81; see also A2, A3
Stephen King's Golden Years: E5
Stephen King's Silver Bullet: see *Silver Bullet*
Stephen King's Sleepwalkers [screenplay]: E3
Stephen King's The Langoliers [teleplay]: B96
Stephen King's The Night Flier [film]: B89
Stephen King's The Stand, mini-series: see entries under *The Stand*
Storm of the Century: A64.
Tales from the Darkside [television series]: B72
Tales from the Darkside—The Movie: see "Cat from Hell, The"
Talisman, Part II—Black House: AB2
Talisman, The, with Peter Straub: A26
Thinner, by 'Richard Bachman': A27; see also A10, A14, A30, A33
Tommyknockers: A35; see also A1, A28, B79
Trucks [film]: B20
Two Dead Girls, The: see *Green Mile, The—Part 1*
Umney's Last Case: A51. See also short fiction, "Umney's Last Case"
Waste Lands, The: The Dark Tower III: A43, B101; see also A17, A34
Wizard and Glass: The Dark Tower IV: A61
Woman in the Room, The [film]: see "Woman in the Room, The"
Word Processor of the Gods [teleplay]: B72

Short Fiction; Non-Fiction Articles and Reviews; Poetry and Other Short Work

[Extracts from King interview] in *Dark Thoughts: On Writing, Advice and Commentary From Fifty Masters of Fear and Suspense.* Edited by Stanley Wiater: C243

[Photograph and explanatory text] in *The Writer's Desk,* by Jill Kementz: C241

[Title unknown] in *Bangor Daily News* [ME]: C161, C221

[Title unknown] in *Money!*: C122

[Title unknown] in *Penthouse*: C195

[Title unknown] in *Playboy Guide: Electronic Entertainment*: C95

[Title unknown] in *The Register* [Bangor ME]: C189, C190, C191, C193

[Title unknown] in *Twilight Zone Magazine*: C121, C147

[Untitled poem—first line: "In the Key-Chords of Dawn"]: D5

[Untitled—opening line: "I don't have many dreams"]: C75

"1984: A Bad Year If You Fear Friday the 13th": C117

"86 Is Just the Ticket": C163

"A Look at the Red Sox on the Edge of '87": C173

"A World without Fritz": C222

"Afterword." *The Dark Tower II: The Drawing of the Three*: C176; see also A34.

"Afterword" to *Danse Macabre*: A11, C81

"Afterword" to *Different Seasons*: A16, C96

"Afterword" to *Firestarter* (1982 edition): C97
"Afterword" to *Silver Bullet*: C142
"Afterword" to *The Dark Tower II: The Drawing of the Three*: A34, C186
"Afterword" to *The Dark Tower IV: Wizard and Glass*: A61, C247
"Afterword" to *The Dark Tower: The Gunslinger*: A17, C124
"Afterword" to *The Green Mile*: A60, C245
"All American Love Story": C157
"All That You Love Will Be Carried Away": B131
"Apt Pupil": A16, B62
"Argument" to *The Dark Tower II: The Drawing of the Three*: C175; see also A34
"Author's Note" to "The Woman in the Room": C217
"Author's Note" to *Bag of Bones*: C248
"Author's Note" to *Hearts in Atlantis*: A66, C255
"Author's Postscript" to *The Girl Who Loved Tom Gordon*: A65, C253
"Authors Note" to *The Stand* (1990): A40, C204
"Autopsy Room Four": A62, B116
"Ballad of the Flexible Bullet, The": A28, A70, B78
"Banned Books and Other Concerns: The Virginia Beach Lecture": A70, C256
"Basic Bread/Lunchtime Gloop/Egg Puff": C126, C250
"Basic Bread" [recipe]: C250
"Battleground": A6, B17
"Beachworld": A28, B82
"Bear, The": A43, B101
"Before the Play": A3, B69
"Beggar and the Diamond, The": A47, B108
"Berni Wrightson: An Appreciation": C108
"Between Rock and a Hard Place": C85
"Big Jim Thompson: An Appreciation": C168
"Big Wheels: A Tale of the Laundry Game (Milkman #2)": A28, B47
"Bird and the Album, The": A32, B55
"Black Magic and Music: A Novelist's Perspective on Bangor": C109
"Blind Willie": A62, A66, B111
"Blue Air Compressor, The": B13
"Body, The": A16, B63
"Boogeyman, The": A6, B19
"Books: Critic Critique": C64
"Books: Love Those Long Novels": C69
"Books: The Sixties Zone": C63
"Books: Two for Terror": C65

"Breathing Method, The": A16, B64
"Brooklyn August": A47, D6
"Cain Rose Up": A28, B6
"Cannibal and the Cop, The": C78
"Cat from Hell, The": B30, C131
"Chattery Teeth": A47, B103
"Children of the Corn": A6, B31
"Childress Debut with 'World' Shows Uncanny Style and Eye for Detail": C123
"Chinga" [teleplay script for *X-files*]: E7
"Crate, The": A15, B43
"Crouch End": A47, B49
"Cujo": A12, B59
"Cursed Expedition, The": B1
"Cycle of the Werewolf ": A21, B74
"Danse Macabre": A11, C76
"Dark Half, The" [excerpt]: A39, B94
"Dark Man, The": D2
"Dark Tower, The: The Drawing of the Three" [excerpt]: B86
"Dear Walden People": C104
"Dedication": A47, B92
"Dedication": A47, B92
"Digging The Boogens": C90
"Dimension Warp, The": B1
"Do the Dead Sing?": A28, B56
"Doctor's Case, The": A47, B87
"Dolan's Cadillac": A37, A47, B80. See also *Dolan's Cadillac*
"Doll Who Ate His Mother, The": A11, C54
"Don't Be Cruel": C103
"Donovan's Brain": D3
"Dr. Seuss and the Two Faces of Fantasy": C118
"Dreaded X, The": C169. See also *Maximum Overdrive*
"End of the Whole Mess, The": A47, B85
"Entering the Rock Zone; or, How I Happened to Marry a Rock Station from Outer Space": C181
"Evening at the Billerica [Massachusetts] Library, An": A70, B255
"Evening with Stephen King, An": A70
"'Ever Et Raw Meat?' and Other Weird Questions": A70, C184
"Everything You Need to Know About Writing Successfully—In Ten Minutes'" C156
"Everything's Eventual": B118

"Fall from Innocence": see "The Body"
"Father's Day": A15, B65
"Favorite Films": C89
"Fie on Fantasy": C145; see "Regis Reprimandum"
"Fifth Quarter, The": A47, B16
"Firestarter" [excerpt]: A9, B45
"For Owen": A28, D8
"For the Birds": B84
"Forenote" to *Danse Macabre*: A11, C80
"Foreword." *Edgeworks 2: Spider Kiss* and *Stalking the Nightmare*, by Harlan Ellison: C242
"Foreword." *Scars and Other Distinguishing Marks,* by Richard Christian Matheson: C180
"Foreword: A Letter" in *The Green Mile* [London edition]: A60, C246
"Foreword" to *Night Shift*: A70, A6, C55
"Foreword" to *Silver Bullet*: C142
"Foreword" to *Stalking the Nightmare*, by Harlan Ellison: C98
"Foreword" to *Steve Lyons: Psychoanalysis,* by Steve Lyons: C237
"Foreword" to *Tales from the Nightside*, edited by Charles L. Grant: C82
"Four Past Midnight: A Note on 'The Sun Dog'": C211
"Fright Report, The": C53. See also A11
"Fritz Leiber": C232
"From Stephen King": C201
"From Stephen King": C218
"General" [screenplay]: B 117
"Ghostmaster General": C139
"Glass Floor, The": B4
"Gramma": A28, B76
"Graveyard Shift": A6, B12
"Gray Matter": A6, B21
"Great Hookers I Have Known": A70, C258
"Guilty Pleasures": C72
"Gunslinger and the Dark Man, The": A17, B57
"Gunslinger, The": A17, B36
"Guy to Have in Your Corner, A": C226
"Hardcase Speaks, The": D7
"Harrison State Park '68": D1
"Head Down": A47, C202
"Healthy Power of a Good Scream, The"; A11, C77
"Hearts in Atlantis": A66, B123
"Heavenly Shades of Night are Falling": A66, 125

"Hello Mary Lou, Goodbye Rick": C149
"Here There Be Tygers": A28, B5
"Heroes for Hope: Starring the X-Men": B81
"His Creepiest Movies": C135
"Home Delivery": A47, B95
"Hope Springs Eternal": see "Rita Hayworth and Shawshank Redemption"
"Horror Fiction" from *Danse Macabre*: A11
"Horror Market Writer and the Ten Bears, The: A True Story": A70, C49
"Horrors of '79, The": C60
"Horrors!" [crossword puzzle]: C105
"Horrors!": C93
"Hotel at the End of the Road": B1
"House on Maple Street, The": A47, B106
"How I Created Golden Years…and Spooked Dozens of TV Executives'": C219
"How It Happened": A70, C161
"How Much am I Hurting?": C167
"How to Scare a Woman to Death": C56
"I Am the Doorway": A6, B14
"I Know What You Need": A6, B29
"I Was a Teenage Grave Robber": B3
"I'm Falling": B1
"I've Got to Get Away": B1
"Ideal, Genuine Writer, The: A Forenote": C183
"Imagery and the Third Eye": A11, C66
"Importance of Being Archie, The" C216
"In the Deathroom": A70, B127, E8
"Introduction: Myth, Belief, Faith, and Ripley's Believe It or Not!" in *Nightmares & Dreamscapes*: A47, C230
"Introduction: The Importance of Being Forry" in *Mr. Monster's Movie Gold*, by Forrest J Ackerman: C101
"Introduction" to "The Cat from Hell": C58. See also B30
"Introduction" to "The Glass Floor": C212
"Introduction" to *Frankenstein, Dracula, Dr. Jekyll and Mr. Hyde*, by Mary Shelley, Bram Stoker, and Robert Louis Stevenson: C57
"Introduction" to *Frankenstein; or, The Modern Prometheus*, by Mary Shelley, illustrated by Berni Wrightson: C111
"Introduction" to *Fugitive Recaptured: The Thirtieth Anniversary Companion to a Television Classic,* by Ed Robertson": C234
"Introduction" to *Graven Images: The Best of Horror, Fantasy, and Science Fiction Film Art from the Collection of Ronald V. Borst and Mar-*

garet A. Borst, edited by Ronald V. Borst, Keith Burns, and Leith Adams: C224

"Introduction" to *Headed Home: Growing Up in Baseball,* photographs by Harry Connelly: C239

"Introduction" to *Horripilations: The Art of J. K. Potter,* artwork by Potter, text by Nigel Suckling: C228

"Introduction" to Jack Ketchum's *The Girl Next Door*: A70

"Introduction" to John Fowles's *The Collector*: A70, C200

"Introduction" to Ramsey Campbell's "The Companion": C99

"Introduction" to *Skeleton Crew*: A28, C132

"Introduction" to *Storm of the Century*: A64, C255

"Introduction" to *Tales by Moonlight,* edited by Jessica Amanda Salmonson: C110

"Introduction" to *The Arbor House Treasury of Horror and the Supernatural,* compiled by Bill Pronzini, Barry Malzberg, and Martin H. Greenberg: C83

"Introduction" to *The Blackboard Jungle,* by Evan Hunter: C125

"Introduction" to *The Collector,* by John Fowles: A70, C200

"Introduction" to *The Green Mile,* screenplay by Frank Darabont: C251

"Introduction" to *The Green Mile*: A60, C244

"Introduction" to *The Killer Inside Me,* by Jim Thompson": C197

"Introduction" to *The Shapes of Midnight: Horror by Joseph Payne Brennan,* by Joseph Payne : C68

"Introduction" to *Transylvania Station: A Mohonk Mystery,* by Donald and Abby Westlake: C182

"Introduction" to *When Michael Calls,* by John Farris: C84

"Irish King, The": C116

"It Grows on You": A47, B22

"James Herbert: Introduction": C223

"Jaunt, The": A28, B52

"Jerusalem's Lot": A6, B38

"Jhonathan and the Witches": B109

"Jumper": B129

"Killer": B110

"King Awaits His Chicken and Haskell Should Shop for Shorts": C155; see also C141

"King Family and the Wicked Witch, The": BA1

"King on *Firestarter*: Who's to Blame": C215

"King Speaks, The": C140

"King Testifies": C130

"King vs. Chalker: One Last Round": C153

"King's Garbage Truck": C1, C2, C3, C4, C5, C6, C7, C8, C9, C10, C11, C12, C13, C13, C14, C15, C16, C17, C18, C19, C20, C21, C22, C23, C24, C25, C26, C27, C28, C29, C30, C31, C32, C33, C34, C35, C36, C37, C38, C39, C40, C41, C42, C43, C44, C45, C46, C48
"L. T.'s Theory of Pets": A62, B115
"Langoliers, The": A41, B96
"Last Rung on the Ladder, The": A6, B39
"Last Waltz: Horror and Morality, Horror and Magic": C112
"Lawnmower Man, The": A6, B24
"Leaf-Peepers": B121
"Ledge, The": A6, B28
"Leighton Street" [poem-fragment by 'James Eric Gardner']: A35, D10
"Let's Scare Dick and Jane": C150
"Letter" in *Fangoria*: C128
"Letter" in *Fantasy Review*: C115
  "Letters From Hell": see "'Ever Et Raw Meat?' and Other Weird Questions
"Library Policeman, The": A41, B98
"Lists That Matter (Number 14): C138
"Lists That Matter (Number 7)": C136
"Lists That Matter (Number 8)": C137
"Lists That Matter": C146
"Little Sisters of Eluria": B120
"Lonesome Death of Jordy Verrill, The": A15, B66
"Low Men in Yellow Coats": A66, B122
"Luckey Quarter": A62, B113
"Ludlum Attraction, The": C87
"Lunch at the Gotham Café": A62, B114
"Lunch-time Ghoul-ash" [recipe]: C249
"Lunchtime Gloop": C126
"Man in the Black Suit, The": A62, B112
"Man Who Loved Flowers, The": A6, B34
"Man Who Would Not Shake Hands, The": A28, B58
"Man with a Belly": B37
"Mangler, The": A6, B18
"Mentors": C88
"Milkman #1": see "Morning Deliveries"
"Milkman #2": see "Big Wheels"
"Mist, The": A28, B50
"Monkey, The": A28, A42, B48
"Monster in the Closet, The": A12, B54

"Morning Deliveries (Milkman #1)": A28, B83
"Moving Finger, The": A47, B100
"Mrs. Todd's Shortcut": A28, A42, B77
"My First Car": C120
"My High School Horrors": C100
"My New Year's Resolution (or, Look What Dave's Got Us Doing Now)": C214
"My Pretty Pony": A38, A47, B104
"My Say: Stephen King": C144
"My Vase" [fragment by 'Mary Jackson']: A58, D11
"Never Look Behind You" by King and Chris Chesley: B1
"Night at the Royal Festival Hall, A: Muriel Grey Interviews Stephen King": A70, C260
"Night Flier, The": A47, B89
"Night of the Tiger, The": B35
"Night Surf": A6, B8
"Nona": A28, B42
"Not Guilty": C51
"Notes on Horror": A11, C73
"Notes," to *Nightmares & Dreamscapes*: A47, C231
"Notes" to *Skeleton Crew*: A28, C133.
"On Becoming a Brand Name": C62
"On Ed McBain": C261
"On J. K. Potter: The Art of the Morph": C233
"On John D. MacDonald": C179
"On the Far Side," Foreword to *The Far Side Gallery 2*, by Gary Larson: C160
"On *The Shining* and Other Perpetrations": C91
"One for the Road": A6, B32
"One Past Midnight: A Note on 'The Langoliers'": A41, C208
"Opera Ain't Over…, The": C164
"Oracle and the Mountain, The": A17, B51
"Other Side of the Fog, The": B1
"Paranoid: A Chant": A28, D9
"People, Places, Things," by King and Chris Chesley: B1
"Peter Straub: An Informal Appreciation": C92
"Pilgrim's Progress, A": C61
"Politics of Limited Editions, The": C134
"Popsy": A47, B88
"Possible Fairy Tale, A": C47
"Postscript to 'Overdrive'": C170

"Preface in Two Parts, A" for *The Stand* (1990): C205
"Profile of Robert Bloch, A": C106
"Quinn's Book": C188
"Quitters, Inc": A6, B40
"Raft, The": A28, B60
"Rainy Season": A47, B93
"Reach, The": see "Do the Dead Sing?"
"Reaper's , The": A28, B9
"Reaper's Image, The": A28, B9
"Red Sox Fan Crows About Team, But May Have to Eat Chicken": C151; see also C155
"Red Sox Stretch Out to the World Series": C159
"Regis Reprimandum": C145
"Remembering John": C199
"Reploids, The": B90
"Return of Timmy Baterman, The": A22, B75
"Revelations of 'Becka Paulson": A28, B79
"Revenge of Lardass Hogan, The": A16, B25, B63
"Rita Hayworth and Shawshank Redemption": A16, B61
"Rita Hayworth and the Darabont Redemption": C240
"Road Virus Heads North, The": B126
"Robert Bloch: An Appreciation": C238
"Robert Marasco: Burnt Offerings": C198
"Ross Thomas Stirs the Pot": C107
"Rush Call": B130
"Salem's Lot": A2, B26
"Satiric Punch, A": C227
"Say 'No' to the Enforcers": C154
"Scare Movies": C71
"Scare Tactics": C213
"Secret Window, Secret Garden": A41, B97
"Shining, The": A3, B33
"Silence": D4
"SK Clarifies Gardner Reference": C192
"SK Criticized for References to Blacks: Stephen King Replies": C187
"Skybar": B70
"Slade": B11
"Slow Mutants, The": A17, B53
"Sneakers": A47, B91
"Sneakers": A47, B91
"Some Notes on Tales of the Vampyre": C67

"Something to Tide You Over": A15, B67
"Sometimes They Come Back": A6, B23
"Son of Best Seller Stalks the Moors": C225
"Sorry State of TV Shows, The: You Gotta Put on the Gruesome Mask and Go Booga-Booga": A11, C79.
"Sorry, Right Number" [teleplay script]: A47, E4
"Sorry, Right Number": A47
"Special Make-Up Effects and the Writer": C102
"Star Invaders, The": B2
"Stephen King Comments on IT": C158
"Stephen King on Censorship": C229
"Stephen King on the Internet": C236
"Stephen King's 10 Favorite Horror Books or Short Stories": C114
"Stephen King's Desert Island": C206
"Stephen King" in *A Gift From Maine, by Maine's Foremost Artists and Writers and James Plummer's Sixth Grade Class:* C113
"Straight up Midnight: An Introductory Note" to *Four Past Midnight*: A41, C207
"Stranger, The": B1
"Strawberry Spring": A28, B7.
"Stud City": A16, B10, B63
"Suffer the Little Children": A47, B15
"Summer of Corruption": see "Apt Pupil"
"Sun Dog, The": A41, B99
"Survivor Type": A28, B71
"Ten O'Clock People, The": A47, B105
"That Feeling, You Can Only Say What It Is in French": B119
"*The Evil Dead*: Why You Haven't Seen It Yet…And Why You Ought To": C94
"The Neighborhood of the Beast": C235
"Theodore Sturgeon—1918-1985": C129
"They're Creeping Up on You": A15, B68
"Thing at the Bottom of the Well, The": B1
"This Guy is Really Scary": C185
"Three Past Midnight: A Note on 'The Library Policeman'": C210
"Tough Talk and Tootsies, Just 25 Cents": C152
"Trucks": A6, B20
"Turning the Thumbscrews on the Reader": A70, C178
"Two Past Midnight: A Note on 'Secret Window, Secret Garden'": A41, C209
"Two Past Midnight: A Note on 'Secret Window, Secret Garden'": A41,

A70, C209
"Ultimate Catalogue, The": C194
"Umney's Last Case": A47, A51, B107
"Uncle Otto's Truck": A28, B73
"Visit with an Endangered Species": C86
"Warning from Stephen King, A": C220
"Way Station, The": A17, B44
"Wedding Gig, The": A28, B46
"Weeds": A15, B27, B66.
"Weeds": A15, B27, B66
"What Ails the U.S. Male: Fire and Ice Cream": C143
"What Stephen King Does for Love": A70, C203
"What Stephen King Does for Love": C203
"What Went Down When the Magyk Went Up": C127
"What's Scaring Stephen King?": C172
"When Is TV Too Scary for Children?": C74
"Whining About the Movies in Bangor: Take That 'Top Gun'": C174
"Who Ever Et Raw Meat": see "'Ever Et Raw Meat?' and Other Weird Questions
"Why I Am for Gary Hart": C119
"Why I Chose Batman": C165
"Why I Was Bachman": A30, C141
"Why I Wrote The Eyes of the Dragon": C171; see also A24
"Why Red Sox Fans Believe....": C196
"Why We Crave Horror Movies": A11, C70
"Why We're in Vietnam": A66, B124
"Winter's Tale, A": see "Breathing Method, The"
"Woman in the Room, The": A6, B41, C217
"Word Processor of the Gods, The": A28, B72
"Word Processor, The": B72
"Write-in": C166
"Writing a First Novel": C50
"Writing Life, The: An Interview with Myself":C59
"Writing the #1 Bestseller...How *IT* Happened": C161
"You Are here Because You Want the Real Thing": C148
"You Know They Got a Hell of a Band": A47, B102

Publishers of Original Signed Limited Editions, Hard Covers, and Trade Paperbacks.

- STEPHEN KING
- YVONNE NAVARRO
- PETER STRAUB
- JACK KETCHUM
- RICHARD LAYMON
- GARY RAISOR
- LUCY TAYLOR
- ORSON SCOTT CARD
- EDWARD LEE
- HARLAN ELLISON
- MICHAEL MARSHALL SMITH
- KEVIN J. ANDERSON
- WILLIAM RELLING JR.
- MICHAEL R. COLLINGS
- CHRISTOPHER FAHY...

all these authors and more have been published by OCP.

JOIN Our Mail List!
Sign up for our e-mail updates for current and future information on all our titles.

Discounts available for Bookstores and Libraries.

OVERLOOK CONNECTION PRESS
PO Box 1934 • HIRAM, GA • 30141
PHONE: 678-567-9777 • FAX: 770-222-6192
EMAIL: overlookcn@aol.com
www.overlookconnection.com

Hauntings:
The Official Peter Straub Bibliography

MICHAEL R. COLLINGS

- Trade Paperback   ISBN: 1-892950-15-4 $29.95
- Hard Cover   ISBN: 1-892950-16-2 $49.95

ORIGINAL COVER ART BY ERIK WILSON

An Exclusive interview with Peter Straub by Stan Wiater

The first volume documenting and collecting Peter Straub's work for the last thirty years. Peter Straub, has won the British Fantasy Award, Two Bram Stoker Awards, and two World Fantasy Awards. His novels include *Koko, Mystery, The Throat* (these three comprising the "Blue Rose" trilogy), *The Talisman* (co-authored with Stephen King), *Ghost Story, Shadowland, Mister X*, and *The Hellfire Club*. The Overlook Connection Press realized that there was a lot more of Mr. Straub's work that was out there, but not documented in one volume. We're here to bring you every novel, story, poem—every word that has been published—and then some in the

Peter Straub Bibliography by Michael R. Collings. This is a must for any reader, fan, or library who wants to learn everything about this wonderful author's work.

CHAPTERS FEATURED IN THE BIBLIOGRAPHY:
- Book-Length Publications: Fiction, Poetry
- Short Fictions: Short Stories, Novella
- Non-Fiction: Introductions, Essays, Reviews, Afterwords
- Poetry
- Liner Notes: Jazz Records and CDs
- Selected Secondary Sources: Interviews, Reviews, Articles, Biographical sketches, etc.
- ALSO: Cover art of most novels and collections, rare chapbooks, reproduced here

OVERLOOK CONNECTION PRESS
PO BOX 1934 • HIRAM, GA • 30141
PHONE: 678-567-9777 • FAX: 770-222-6192
EMAIL: overlookcn@aol.com
www.overlookconnection.com

STORYTELLER

THE OFFICIAL BIBLIOGRAPHY & GUIDE TO THE WORKS OF
Orson Scott Card

MICHAEL R. COLLINGS

- Hard Cover   ISBN: 1-892950-26-X $59.95
- Sterling 1/200 Signed $99.95

ORIGINAL COVER ART BY ERIK WILSON

- "Fantasy and the Believing Reader" an Afterword by Orson Scott Card
- Over 500 pages of text and over 80 cover reproductions of novels, rare publications, collections

CHAPTERS FEATURED IN THE BIBLIOGRAPHY:
- Bibliography: Book-Length Publications: Fiction, Poetry, Plays
- Short Fictions: Short Stories, Novellas
- Unpublished manuscripts
- Non-Fiction: Science Fiction Criticism, Theoretical Essays, and Reviews.
- Video and Audio Tape Dramatic Presentations
- Selected Secondary Sources: Interviews, Reviews, Articles, Biographical sketches
- This bibliography is Indexed

The first volume documenting and collecting Orson Scott Card's work for the last thirty years. Orson Scott Card has won the Hugo, Nebula, World Fantasy, Japanese Science Fiction, and John Campbell Awards among many other awards and honors. His novels include *Ender's Game, Tales of Alvin Maker Saga, The Worthing Saga, Xenocide, Speaker For the Dead, Folk of the Fringe, The Abyss, The Homecoming Saga, Maps In the Mirror, Lost Boys* and many other novels and short story collections. The Overlook Connection Press is proud to bring you every novel, story, poem—every word that has been published—and then some in the *Orson Scott Card Bibliography* by Michael R. Collings. This is a must for any reader, fan, or library who wants to learn everything about this authors extensive work and career.

 **OVERLOOK CONNECTION PRESS**
PO Box 1934 • HIRAM, GA • 30141
PHONE: 678-567-9777 • FAX: 770-222-6192
EMAIL: overlookcn@aol.com
www.overlookconnection.com

This Is A Girl You'll Never Forget. NEVER.

The Girl Next Door
BY JACK KETCHUM

- Trade Paperback   ISBN: 1-892950-61-8 $25.95
- Hard Cover   ISBN: 0-9633397-4-5 $39.95

INTRODUCTION BY STEPHEN KING
ORIGINAL COVER ART BY NEAL McPHEETERS

"The Girl Next Door is alive...in a way most works of poplular fiction never attain; it does not just promise terror but actually delievers it. But it's a page-turner, all right; no doubt about that."
    —From the Introduction to *The Girl Next Door* by Stephen King

Suburbia in the 1950s. A nice quiet simpler time to grow up—unless you count the McCarthy trials and red-scares and the cold Cold War, unless you could see the dark side emerging. And on a quiet, tree lined dead-end street, in the dark damp basement of the Chandler house, it's emerging big-time for teenage Meg and her crippled little sister Susan—whose parents are dead now, who are now left captive to the savage whims and rages of a distant Aunt, who is rapidly descending into madness. It is a madness that infects all three of her sons—and finally, an entire neighborhood. Only one troubled boy stands hesitantly between Meg and Susan and their lingering, cruel, tortuous death. One boy with a very adult decision to make. Between love and compassion, and lust and evil.

    And thus begins the descent into real terror that Jack Ketchum takes you. A novel so intense that you will never forget it.

OVERLOOK CONNECTION PRESS
PO Box 1934 • HIRAM, GA • 30141
PHONE: 678-567-9777 • FAX: 770-222-6192
EMAIL: overlookcn@aol.com
www.overlookconnection.com

AfterAge

YVONNE NAVARRO

- Hard Cover — ISBN: 1-892950-23-5 — $45.00
- Sterling 1/100 — ISBN: 1-892950-24-3 — $85.00
- Lettered/Leather 1/26 — ISBN: 1-892950-25-1 — $300.00

INTRODUCTION BY BRIAN HODGE

ORIGINAL COVER ART BY ROB BAZYLEWICZ

• • SPECIAL FEATURES • •
- *Red City*—First chapter to the sequel of *Afterage*
- "Victory's Ode"—Original short story that inspired *Afterage*
- Afterword by Yvonne Navarro

"*...a classic vampire novel that deserves to be ranked equally with McCammon's* They Thirst *and John Skipp and Craig Spector's* The Light at the End... AfterAge *is incredible and soul-shattering good.*"
—*The Buzz Review*

"*Navarro has skillfully constructed an epic tale which embraces all the proven elements of the great saga... manipulating and motivating her characters believably through a world that is almost too horrific to imagine...*"
—Peter Crowther, *Interzone*

"*To paraphrase an old vampire maxim, you can have your blood and drink it too.*"
—Edward Bryant, *Locus* Special Features

A plague of vampirism has swept across the world. Once-thriving cities are ghost towns, entire countries reduced to handfuls of terrified survivors. In Chicago, a few of those survivors hide behind the fortified walls of office buildings and museums, raiding deserted stores for dwindling supplies of clothing and food and fighting to stay alive...and unnoticed.

Meanwhile, a hungry vampire population also struggles for continued existence as their prey grows scarce, forcing them to capture alive the last remaining humans as breeding stock to ensure their future.

Now a small band of humans makes a dangerous last stand against their vampire conquerors, desperate to find a weapon that will kill the dead...

 **OVERLOOK CONNECTION PRESS**
PO BOX 1934 • HIRAM, GA • 30141
PHONE: 678-567-9777 • FAX: 770-222-6192
EMAIL: overlookcn@aol.com
www.overlookconnection.com

www.ingramcontent.com/pod-product-compliance
Lightning Source LLC
Chambersburg PA
CBHW020117240426
43673CB00038B/513